Global Tourism

Second edition

Edited by William F. Theobald

BUTTERWORTH
HEINEMANN

OXFORD AUCKLAND BOSTON JOHANNESBURG MELBOURNE NEW DELHI

Butterworth-Heinemann
Linacre House, Jordan Hill, Oxford OX2 8DP
225 Wildwood Avenue, Woburn, MA 01801-2041
A division of Reed Educational and Professional Publishing Ltd

 A member of the Reed Elsevier plc group

First published 1994
Reprinted 1994
Paperback edition 1995
Reprinted 1996
Second edition 1998
Reprinted 1999, 2001

British Library Cataloguing in Publication Data
Global tourism – 2nd ed.
  1. Tourist trade
  I. Theobald, William F.
  338.4′7′91

ISBN 0 7506 4022 7

Printed and bound in Great Britain by Biddles Ltd
www.biddles.co.uk

Contents

Foreword

Tourism is one of the most remarkable success stories of modern times. The industry, which only began on a massive scale in the 1960s, has grown rapidly and steadily for the past 30 years in terms of the income it generates and number of people who travel abroad. It has proved to be resilient in times of economic crisis and will continue to grow at a rapid pace of almost 4 per cent a year in the next century.

According to our World Tourism Organization (WTO) forecasts, more than 700 million people will be travelling internationally by the year 2000, generating more than US$620 billion in earnings. The outlook for the first decades of the next century is even more astounding. Our forecasts predict 1.6 billion international tourists by the year 2020, spending more than US$2 trillion annually – or US$5 billion every day.

As more and more governments recognize the important role that tourism can play in generating badly needed foreign exchange earnings, creating jobs and contributing to tax revenues, the competition for tourist spending is becoming ever more intense. Pressure on national and local governments to rapidly develop their tourism potential to meet demand and produce benefits, makes it more essential than ever to plan carefully and consider the human and environmental impacts of tourism development. That is why, as Secretary-General of the World Tourism Organization, I am pleased to see the serious analysis of the problems and prospects of the tourism sector as presented in this second edition of this book, *Global Tourism*.

Tourism is an extremely complex endeavour. Not only are huge amounts of money at stake; we are, in addition, providing economic incentives for protecting the natural environment, restoring cultural monuments, and preserving native cultures. We are, in a small but important way, contributing to understanding among peoples of very different backgrounds. But, above all, we are in the business of providing a break from the stress of everyday routine and fulfilling the dreams of leisure travellers.

This book goes a long way towards increasing our understanding about those dreams and complexities that make up the tourism industry.

Francesco Frangialli
Secretary-General
World Tourism Organization

Preface

This book was the result of a need for such a collection which the editor personally experienced when attempting to teach a seminar in tourism where no traditional source books were available. It is intended for anyone who is or will be engaged in the tourism industry, regardless of their particular field of interest . The work is planned on original lines because the editor has found in his experience as teacher and author that the needs of students and practitioners, whether in university or graduate school, in government or in the private sector are not met by the usual 'Introduction to Tourism' book. Rather, the need is for a new view of the subject which ordinary textbooks tend to separate.

This volume draws together the insights of thirty-three observers commonly concerned with the effects of tourism on contemporary society. The chapters represent various viewpoints from leading educators and practitioners from such disciplines as anthropology, economics, environmental science, geography, marketing, political science, psychology, public administration, sociology and urban planning.

The purpose of this book is to present critical issues, problems and opportunities facing the tourism industry. Tourism problems are complex and interrelated and they suggest a myriad of crises such as overcrowding of tourist attractions, overuse and destruction of natural resources; resident–host conflicts; loss of cultural heritage, increased crime and prostitution; inflation and escalating land costs, and a host of other political, socio-cultural, economic and environmental problems that may be brought about or exacerbated by tourism development.

The approach taken by this book does not focus on a particular subject, but rather the exploration of issues facing those involved in the tourism domain. The scope of the book provides each chapter as a mini-treatise on tourism, from an *international* perspective. Individual chapters scrutinize, reflect upon and question the changes and transformations needed. Each chapter provides an exploration of concerns, issues, assumptions, values and perceptions, and the reasoning for a view taken by individual authors. The issues raised in the book will hopefully bring about much needed thought, discussion, reflection, argumentation and, perhaps, debate.

It would be patently absurd to claim that this book encapsulates all that might or should be said about tourism. It should be discerned however, that an attempt has been made to present the viewpoints of both those who look with optimism at tourism and those who scrutinize it with some scepticism. It has not been a goal to prove any individual point of view as the 'right' one, but rather to examine the phenomena of tourism as fully as possible.

The impetus for this second edition came in large measure from the extremely helpful and highly positive reviews of the first book from the following individuals and publications: Derek Hall, *Tourism Management*; Paul F. Wilkinson, *Annals of Tourism Research*; Jonathan Goodrich, *Journal of Travel Research*; J.R. McDonald, *Choice Magazine*; John Joseph Courtney, *Journal of Vacation Marketing*; and, reviewer unknown, *Future Survey*. Now, let me turn to those special individuals whom I sincerely wish to recognize and thank.

It would not be possible to have undertaken this project without the love, support and total commitment of my wife, Sharon. Thank you for being by my side through the years. To my children, Gregg and Amanda, may your lives be filled with as much happiness as you have given me over the years.

As editor I wish to acknowledge the contribution of Brian Archer, who not only provided encouragement to undertake this project, but also recommended it to the publisher, Butterworth-Heinemann. Thanks are also extended to my colleagues at the Universities of Surrey (UK) and Waterloo (Canada) for the many opportunities they provided which helped expand my view of tourism as an international phenomenon.

Acknowledgement is made of both the World Tourism Organization (WTO) and the Travel and Tourism Research Association (TTRA) who granted permission to reproduce selected portions of previously published materials. The editor is indebted to Francesco Frangialli, Secretary-General of the WTO, who generously agreed to write the Foreword to the book and to Deborah Luhrman, WTO Press and Communications, for her kindness and logistical assistance.

I wish to thank Professor Kazuhiko Tamamura of Doshisha University in Koyoto for his excellent translation in the Japanese edition of the book. Appreciation is also extended to Suzy Nierste and Kim Lehnan for their direction of the voluminous facsimile and postal communications between the editor and contributing authors.

The editor wishes to thank Kathryn Grant, Publishing Director (Business Books), and Jonathan Glasspool, Commissioning Editor, at Butterworth-Heinemann for their enthusiastic support of the idea underlying this book and their cogent suggestions throughout its compilation. In addition, the publisher's editorial staff are acknowledged for their help with the completed manuscript.

The editor wishes to acknowledge the contribution of those individuals who, having adopted the book for their classes, so generously provided constructive criticism of the text in order to strengthen the second edition: George Taylor, University of Central Lancashire; Richard Taylor,

Swansea Institute of Higher Education; Andrew Holden, University of North London; P.R. Fridgeon, Thames Valley University; and Julia Fallon, Cardiff Institute of Higher Education.

Finally, a specific note of appreciation is extended to the contributors to this volume for their wholehearted efforts in bringing their knowledge, ability, experience and expertise to the task at hand. It was an exhilarating experience working with them. I am indebted to them, and I am also quite proud to count them as colleagues.

William F. Theobald
Purdue University
West Lafayette, Indiana

List of Contributors

John Ap is an Associate Professor in Tourism Management at the Hong Kong Polytechnic University. Formerly, he was a certified town planner with the Wollongong City Council (Australia) and also served as a project manager with the Tourism Commission of New South Wales (Australia). A native of Australia, he has an bachelors degree from the University of New South Wales, a masters degree from the Wollongong University and a PhD from Texas A&M University. Dr Ap's research interests include tourism impacts, service quality in the hospitality industry, amusement parks, and tourism/recreation planning. His work has been published in journals including the *Annals of Tourism Research, Journal of Travel Research,* and *Tourism Management.*

Brian Archer is Professor Emeritus and former Pro-Vice-Chancellor at the University of Surrey (UK), where previously he was Head of the Department of Management Studies for Tourism and Hotel Industries. Prior to joining the University of Surrey in 1978 he was Director of the Institute of Economic Research at the University College of North Wales, Bangor. He has degrees in Economics (University of London), Geography (University of Cambridge) and a PhD (University of Wales), and is a Fellow of the Tourism Society and of the Hotel, Catering and Institutional Management Association. His principal research interest is the economics of tourism and he has conducted research and consultancy assignments in over forty countries and spoken at conferences in over thirty. He is the author of several monographs, a large number of reports and over a hundred articles. Much of his early work was concerned with the development of models to measure the economic impact of tourism.

Bill Bramwell is Reader in Tourism Management at the Centre for Tourism at Sheffield Hallam University (UK). He has a masters degree in Geography from Cambridge University and a PhD from the University of London. He was formerly Tourism Development Manager with the English Tourist Board, where he worked on a series of local tourism development and marketing programmes around England and was responsible for the Board's rural tourism policies. He has conducted consultancy projects for several government organizations and the European Union. Dr Bramwell is the author of many articles in academic tourism journals, is co-founder and co-editor of the *Journal of Sustainable Tourism,* and is co-editor of the book *Rural Tourism and Sustainable Rural Development* (1994). His research interests include urban tourism development, tourism planning, tourism place marketing, sustainable tourism and cultural tourism.

Chris Cooper is Professor and Director of Research at the International Centre for Tourism and Hospitality Research, Bournemouth University (UK). He holds the PhD in Geography from the University of London. Before rejoining academic life, he worked in market planning for a major tour operator and major retailer in the UK. His principal research interests lie in destination management and in tourism education and training. He is the author of many articles, books and conference papers in tourism and serves as editor of *Progress in Tourism and Hospitality Research*, a quarterly refereed research journal.

Graham M.S. Dann is Professor in Tourism at the University of Luton (UK). A native of Edinburgh, he obtained his doctorate from the University of Surrey (UK) and lectured in sociology at the University of the West Indies (Barbados). Professor Dann is the author of seven books and over seventy refereed articles. He is an associate editor of *Annals of Tourism Research*, a founding member of the International Academy for the Study of Tourism, and President of the Research Committee on International Tourism of the International Sociological Association. His research interests in tourism focus principally on motivation and the semiotics of promotion, brought together in his latest book, *The Language of Tourism* (1996).

Thomas Lea Davidson was, until his death, Principal and CEO of Davidson-Peterson Associates, Inc., a company he founded with Karen Ida Peterson. A full-service marketing research and strategic planning consulting company based in York, Maine (USA), they specialize in the travel, tourism, accommodations, meetings and conventions, entertainment and recreation marketplace. Formerly, he was Executive VP of Davidson-Lasco, and Oxtoby-Smith, Inc. He was an adjunct faculty member at several universities including Northwestern and Connecticut (USA) where he was also Associate Director of Graduate Studies in Business. Mr Davidson was a member of the editorial board of the *Journal of Travel Research*, and the US Department of Commerce Task Force on Assessment Research Methods (Performance Accountability). A past national chairperson, board member and committee chair of the Council of American Survey Research Organizations (CASRO), he also chaired the Certification Committee of the Association of Travel Marketing Executives.

Sara Dolnicar is Assistant Professor at the Institute for Tourism and Leisure Studies at the University of Economics and Business Administration (Austria), where she received her doctorate. She lectures in marketing, business administration and tourism. Her research interests are centred on issues of tourism market segmentation and the use of neural network techniques in tourism data analysis. Dr Dolnicar is Secretary General of the Austrian Society for Applied Research in Tourism located in Vienna, Austria.

Bill (H.W.) Faulkner is the Director of the Centre for Tourism and Hotel Management Research at Griffith University, Gold Coast (Australia). Former positions held included: founding Director of the Australian Bureau of Tourism Research; senior policy research positions in the Australian Government's tourism and transport administrations, and an academic position at Wollongong University. Dr Faulkner is on the editorial boards of several international tourism research journals, including *Tourism Management, Journal of Tourism Studies, Pacific Tourism Review, Turizam* and *Anatalia*. His doctoral research was conducted in the Research School of Pacific Studies at the Australian National University, while undergraduate studies were completed at the University of New England.

Donald Getz is Professor of Tourism and Hospitality Management at the University of Calgary (Canada). Formerly he was in the Department of Recreation and Leisure Studies at University of Waterloo, and he also served as an urban and regional planner. His interest in festivals and event tourism stems from research in the Spey Valley of Scotland where both traditional and new events acted both as tourist attractions and community focal points. He is active as a festival volunteer organizer and strategic planner, he conducts seminars and consults on managing and marketing events. Dr Getz is the co-founder and co-editor of *Festival Management and Event Tourism: An International Journal*. His books include *Event Management and Event Tourism* (1997), *Festivals, Special Events and Tourism* (1991), and he co-editor of *The Business of Rural Tourism* (1997).

Alison Gill is an Associate Professor at Simon Fraser University and Director of the Department of Geography. Dr Gill teaches graduate level courses in community tourism development and tourism systems in the School of Resource and Environmental Management. She also delivers tourism courses in the University's Geography programme. Her research interests are closely aligned to the study of single industry and small community development processes and issues. Dr Gill currently is specializing in research related to planning and development processes in resort communities.

Frank M. Go is the Bewetoer Professor of Tourism Management and Chairman of the Centre for Tourism Management at the Rotterdam School of Management, Erasmus University, Rotterdam (the Netherlands). He was formerly professor and head of the Department of Hotel and Tourism Management at Hong Kong Polytechnic University and served on the Faculty of Management at the University of Calgary (Canada). Dr Go is the co-author of *Competitive Strategies in the International Hotel Industry*, and co-editor of the *World Travel and Tourism Review, Volumes I and II*. His present teaching and research interests are in the areas of entrepreneurship and innovation in tourism, and management education and professionalization in tourism.

David Harrison studied sociology at Goldsmiths' College, London, and anthropology at University College London and is primarily interested in the social and cultural implications of tourism. He lectured for twenty years in sociology at the University of Sussex, England, and in 1996 became Coordinator of Tourism Studies at the University of the South Pacific (Fiji). Author of *The Sociology of Modernization and Development* (1988), he has written articles on tourism in the Caribbean, Swaziland and Bulgaria, and edited *Tourism and the Less Developed Countries* (1992). With Briguglio et al., he edited *Sustainable Tourism in Islands and Small States: Case Studies* (1996) and also contributed a chapter to Briguglio et al., *Sustainable Tourism in Islands and Small States: Theoretical Issues* (1996). In addition, he collaborated with Martin Price on the Introduction to Price, M. (ed), *People and Tourism in Fragile Environments* (1996).

Donald E. Hawkins has served as Professor of Tourism Studies since 1971 at The George Washington University (USA). He was appointed as the Dwight D. Eisenhower Professor of Tourism Policy in 1994. He is the Director of the International Institute of Tourism Studies, which was initiated in 1988, and is jointly sponsored by the World Tourism Organization and the GWU School of Business and Public Management.

Myriam Jansen-Verbeke is Professor of Social and Economic Geography at the Catholic University of Leuven (Belgium). Formerly, she was an endowed Professor in Tourism Management at the Erasmus University Rotterdam (Netherlands) and Senior Lecturer in Urban and Regional Planning at the Catholic University of Nijmegen (Netherlands). She is a member of the International Academy for the Study of Tourism, a Resource Editor *for Annals of Tourism Research*, the *Journal of Sustainable Tourism*, and the *Journal of Festival Management and Event Tourism*. Her research is focused on urban and cultural tourism, shopping and tourism, and in particular on planning issues in tourism. She has published in several books and articles on urban tourism.

Maryam M. Khan has recently completed her doctoral research at Virginia Polytechnic Institute and State University (USA), in the area of ecotourism and service quality. She is a recipient of 1995 National Tour Foundation's Graduate Research Award. She has served as an Instructor in the Department of Hospitality and Tourism Management and Graduate Administrative Assistant at Virginia Tech (USA). Currently she is a Research Consultant for Hospitality Management Services, Inc.

Donald Macleod was Visiting Professor in Cultural Anthropology at Macalester College (USA) from 1995 to 1996. For the two years preceding he had tutored Social Anthropology at both Oxford and London Universities (UK). This teaching followed his graduation from Oxford University in 1993 with a DPhil in Social Anthropology. It was during research for his doctorate that he developed an interest in tourism whilst working in the Canary Islands. Dr Macleod has co-edited *Tourists and Tourism: Identifying With People and Places,* and is negotiating publication of his ethnography, *Globalizing La Gomera: Changing Livelihoods and Complex Identities on a Canary Island.* He has published a number of review articles in academic journals, and is currently a Visiting Scholar at Oxford University, researching the Huilliche of Chile, reviewing issues involving tourism, anthropology and the natural environment.

Josef A. Mazanec is Professor at the Vienna University of Economics and Business Administration (Austria), where he received his doctorate, and Director of the Institute for Tourism and Leisure Studies. He has been a member of the Austrian delegation to the European Association of Advertising Agencies and a Visiting Scholar at the Sloan School of Management, MIT (USA). Dr Mazanec's main research interests include models of consumer/tourist behaviour, strategic planning, tourism and hospitality marketing, mutivariate methods and decision support systems. A member of the International Academy for the Study of Tourism, he is a resource editor for the *Annals of Tourism Research.*

David Mercer is Associate Professor in the Department of Geography and Environmental Science at Monash University (Australia) where he has been teaching since 1967. He holds degrees in Geography from Cambridge and Monash Universities. Dr Mercer's principal research interests are environmental policy, tourism impacts, recreation planning and indigenous land and sea rights. He has published over 100 academic papers and eleven books. His most recent book is *A Question of Balance: Natural Resource Conflict Issues in Australia* (2nd edition, 1995). Dr Mercer has also been an advisor to local, state and the Australian Commonwealth governments on a wide range of environmental and tourism-related issues.

Michael Morgan is a Senior Lecturer in Tourism Marketing at Bournemouth University (UK), where he is Course Tutor of the MA in European Tourism Management. He joined the college in 1987 after fifteen years in marketing and operations management for Sealink, the cross-channel ferry operator. His interest in beach resorts began during his time with Sealink at Weymouth which claims to be the original sea bathing resort from the time of George III. As well as his teaching duties, he has worked as consultant to the Southern Tourist Board, analysing the effectiveness of the board's tourism brochures. His work on the changing market for Mediterranean beach resorts has been published in *Tourism Management*. He is also the author of *Marketing for Leisure and Tourism* (1996).

Peter E. Murphy is Rino Grollo Chair in Tourism and Hospitality and Head of the Centre for Tourism and Hospitality Studies at La Trobe University in Melbourne (Australia). He was formerly Professor and Head of the Tourism Management Program, School of Business at the University of Victoria (Canada). His best known work is in community tourism, with his books, *Tourism: A Community Approach* and *Tourism in Canada: Selected Issues and Options.* He has recently edited a volume on urban tourism titled *Quality Management in Urban Tourism* published by John Wiley. He is planning to combine the findings of sustainable development research with business management principles in order to enhance the adoption of sustainable tourism practices.

Philip L. Pearce is Foundation Professor of Tourism at James Cook University of North Queensland (Australia). With degrees in Psychology and Education from the University of Adelaide (Australia), he received his doctorate from Oxford, examining the social and environmental perceptions of overseas tourists. Dr Pearce has authored three books on tourism, and over sixty academic articles on visitor and community studies of tourism. He is also editor of the *Journal of Tourism Studies*, and is a founding member of the International Academy for the Study of Tourism.

Stanley C. Plog is founder and Chairman/CEO of Plog Research (USA). He earned a doctorate in Social Science research from Harvard University. Prior to forming his first company, he was academic director of the training programme in social psychiatry at UCLA. Plog Research, Inc. – now a subsidiary of NFO Research, Inc. of Greenwich, Connecticut – opened its doors in 1974 and quickly came to dominate the field of travel research and consulting. Each year it conducts more studies for more clients in the travel industry than any other organization. The company also collects and maintains the largest number of databases used by the industry. Dr Plog has written six books, two of which are on travel. The first is *Leisure Travel. Making it a Growth Market . . . Again!* (1991)

and the second, *Vacation Places Rated* (1995) is now in its second printing. Dr Plog's clients include most major airlines, many hotel chains and cruise lines, and resorts and destinations worldwide.

Linda K. Richter is Professor of Political Science at Kansas State University (USA) where she teaches in the areas of public administration, public policy, gender politics and developing areas. She has lectured and conducted field research on tourism policies in twenty nations throughout Asia and the Pacific. Dr Richter has published over forty articles and book chapters on tourism issues and is the author of *Land Reform and Tourism Development: Policy Making in the Philippines*, (1982) *The Politics of Tourism in Asia*, (1989), and is co-author of *Tourism Environment* (1991). She is a resource editor of *Annals of Tourism Research*, a former member of the US Travel and Tourism Advisory Board, and a member of the International Academy for the Study of Tourism. She is currently an associate editor of the forthcoming *Encyclopedia of Tourism*.

Regina G. Schlüter is Professor, co-founder and Director of the Center for Tourism Studies and Research at the John F. Kennedy University in Buenos Aires (Argentina). She graduated in Demography and Tourism, and received her doctorate in Social Psychology. She serves as Editor of the social science journal, *Estudios Y Perspectivas en Turismo*, and is the author of several articles in various journals in Argentina, Brazil, the UK, USA and Canada. Dr Schlüter has written several books: *Turismo y Sexo: Una Aproximación al Estudio de la Prostitución y el Turismo en Argentina* (1985); *Turismo y Parques Nacionales: Una Perspectiva* (1987); *Social and Cultural Impact of Tourism Plans and Programs in Latin America* (1991); *Mundo Turístico* (1995); and *El Fenómeno Turístico* (1997).

Valene L. Smith is Professor of Anthropology at California State University, Chico (USA). She is the editor of *Hosts and Guests: The Anthropology of Tourism* (1977, 1989), and senior editor of *Tourism Alternatives: Potentials and Problems for the Development of Tourism* (1992). Dr Smith serves on the editorial board of the *Annals of Tourism Research* for which she has edited four Special Issues: 'Tourism and Development: Anthropological Perspectives'; 'Domestic Tourism'; 'Pilgrimage and Tourism: The Quest in Guest'; and 'Antarctic Tourism'. She is senior editor for a multi-volume book series, *Tourism Dynamics*, appearing initially in 1997.

Edmund Swinglehurst is an author, an archivist and an artist who retired from Thomas Cook and Son, London (UK) where he served as Public Relations Manager and established the company's travel archive and library. He has worked and travelled throughout South America and Europe for over forty years. He joined the Cook organization in 1953 after studying painting in Paris with Fernand Léger and André L'Hôte and at the Beaux Arts. Mr Swinglehurst is the author of *The Romantic Journey: The Story of Thomas Cook and Victorian Travel* (1974); *The Victorian and Edwardian Seaside* (1978) with his wife Janice Anderson; *Cooks Tours* (1982); *The Midi* (1986); *Italy* (1987), and; *Viva Espana* (1989). He has written a number of other travel-related volumes including: *Wonders of the World; Beautiful Britain; Venice Guide; Britain – Land of Contrasts; The Lake District: A Celebration of Cumbria; Britain, Then and Now,* and; *Robert Burns Country.* His books on fine art include: *Salvador Dali; Florentine Drawings; Seascapes; Botticelli; Monet; Landscapes; Post-Impressionists;* and *Pre-Raphaelites.* Two new books are awaiting publication, *Monet's Garden* and *Renoir.* Currently, Mr Swinglehurst is compiling a definitive book providing a comprehensive account of twentieth-century travel and tourism.

Gordon D. Taylor has been a tourist consultant since his retirement in 1988 from Tourism Canada where he was Manager, Special Research Projects. Formerly he was Director, Research and Planning, Manitoba Department of Tourism, Recreation and Cultural Affairs and a research officer with both the National Parks Service and British Columbia Provincial Parks. He served as an Adjunct Professor of Geography at Carleton University for fifteen years prior to his retirement. Mr Taylor was the president of the Travel and Tourism Research Association in 1976, and served on the Board of Directors of the Canada Chapter, TTRA, from 1988 to 1994. He has published articles have appeared in *Tourism Management, Journal of Travel Research, Journal of Travel and Tourism Marketing, Turismo y Sociedad,* and *Tourism Reports.* Mr Taylor is currently President of the British Isles Family History Society of Greater Ottawa.

William F. Theobald is Professor and Chairman of both the Interdisciplinary Graduate Program in Travel and Tourism, and the Leisure Studies Division at Purdue University (USA) where he teaches tourism and recreation management. Formerly, Professor and Head of the Recreation and Leisure Studies Department at the University of Waterloo (Canada), he has also served as Visiting Professor at The George Washington University (USA) and the University of Surrey (UK). Dr Theobald's research interests are tourism planning and development. He has contributed to a variety of social science and professional journals, and is editor of *Global Tourism: The Next Decade* (1994); author of *The Evaluation of Human Service Programs* (1985); *Evaluation of Recreation and Park Programs* (1979); and *The Female in Public Recreation* (1976). He has served as an associate editor or reviewer for *Tourism Economics,* the *Journal of Leisure Research* and *Leisure Sciences,* and has conducted numerous studies and reports on tourism planning and development for private corporations and various branches of government.

Turgut Var is Professor, Department of Recreation, Park and Tourism Sciences at Texas A&M University (USA). He has taught at Simon Fraser University (Canada), the Universities of Kansas and Hawaii (USA), the University of Houston (USA) and Northern Territory University (Australia). He holds degrees in Business Administration from Claremont Men's College (USA), a MBA in Finance from the University of Chicago (USA), and a doctorate in Accounting from the University of Ankara (Turkey). Dr Var is a Fellow of the Academy of Hospitality Research, a Certified Hotel Administrator of the American Hotel/Motel Association and a member of the International Academy for the Study of Tourism. He is author of over eighty articles and fifteen books including *Managerial Accounting, Financial Accounting* and the *VNR Hospitality and Tourism Encyclopedia.* He is editor of the *Journal of Academy of Hospitality Research,* associate editor of *Annals of Tourism Research,* and serves on the editorial boards of *Journal of Travel Research, Tourism Economics, International Journal of Quantitative Management, Journal of Tourism and Hospitality* and *Tourism Analysis.*

Stephen Wanhill is Travelbag Professor of Tourism in the School of Service Industries at Bournemouth University in the UK and Director of Tourism Research at Bornholms Forskningscenter in Denmark. His post at Bournemouth receives sponsorship from Travelbag, a leading direct sell tour operator in the UK, with whom the School of Service Industries has a close association. His work in tourism goes back more than twenty-five years, with his involvement in airport planning. His main research interests lie in destination development and project planning. He has previously held professorships at the University of Surrey and the University of Wales, Cardiff. He has also been a Tourism Advisor to the UK House of Commons and a Board Member of the Wales Tourist Board. He also serves as editor of the international journal, *Tourism Economics.*

Peter W. Williams is Director of Simon Fraser University's Centre for Tourism Policy and Research, as well as the School of Resource and Environmental Management. He teaches graduate level tourism policy, planning and development courses in the School of Resource and Environmental Management. His research interests are centred on issues related to growth management strategies in tourism settings and behavioural dimensions of tourism product development. Dr Williams is particularly involved with research addressing issues of sustainability in tourism development.

Stephen F. Witt holds the Chair of Tourism Forecasting at the School of Management Studies for the Service Sector, University of Surrey (UK). He is also Visiting Researcher at the Research Centre of Bornholm,

Denmark. Formerly he held the Lewis Chair of Tourism Studies in the European Business Management School at the University of Wales Swansea (UK). His major research interests are tourism demand modelling and forecasting. Professor Witt has published over 100 journal papers/book chapters. His books include: *Practical Business Forecasting* (1987); *Practical Financial Management* (1988); *Modelling and Forecasting Demand in Tourism* (1992); *Portfolio Theory and Investment Management* (2nd edition, 1994); *Tourism Marketing and Management Handbook* (2nd edition, 1994, student edition, 1995); and *The Management of International Tourism* (2nd edition, 1995). He is on the editorial boards of the *Journal of Travel Research, Tourism Management* and *Tourism Economics.*

Andreas H. Zins is Associate Professor at the Institute for Tourism and Leisure Studies at the Vienna University of Economics and Business Administration (Austria) where he received his doctorate. He lectures in international marketing, business administration, tourism marketing planning, consumer and travel behaviour models. Dr Zins is active in research in the fields of tourist behaviour, marketing research, cost-benefit analyses, social impacts, computer assisted interviewing, theme parks and related leisure attractions. He has served as Project Manager of the National Austrian Guest Survey since 1988. German language books on leisure attractions (1991), strategic management for tourism organizations (1993) and tourism expenditures (1996) have been published in Austria. Articles on behavioural and psychographic issues of tourism are published in the *Journal of Marketing Management, Journal of Travel and Tourism Marketing, Journal of Business Research* and *Journal of Travel Research.*

Part One

Clarification and Meaning: Issues of Understanding

Introduction

Tourism has grown significantly since the creation of the commercial airline industry and the advent of the jet airplane in the 1950s. By 1992, it had become the largest industry and largest employer in the world. Together with this growth there have emerged a number of extremely critical issues facing the industry in terms of the impacts it has already had on destination areas and their residents, and the future prospects for people and places into the twenty-first century.

One of the major issues in gauging tourism's total economic impact is the diversity and fragmentation of the industry itself. **Theobald** (Chapter 1) suggests that this problem is compounded by the lack of comparable tourism data since there has been no valid or reliable means of gathering comparable statistics. He proposes that the varying definitions of tourism terms internationally, and the complex and amorphous nature of tourism itself have led to difficulty in developing a valid, reliable and credible information system or database about tourism and its contribution to local, regional, national and global economies.

The author provides an introduction to the context, meaning and scope of tourism beginning not simply with basic definitions, but also a discussion on the derivation of those definitions. This leads to sections on how tourism data is gathered, measures of tourism, basic tourism units, and classification of both tourism supply and demand. Finally, he chronicles the major international developments that have occurred between 1936 and 1994 whose objectives were to reduce or eliminate the incomparability of gathering and utilizing tourism statistics.

Davidson (Chapter 2) links the question of whether tourism is really an industry to the misunderstanding, resistance and hostility that often plague proponents of travel and tourism as worthy economic forces in a modern economy. He questions the common practice, especially as suggested in the literature of referring to tourism as an industry. He contends that such a designation may not be correct, and that tourism is not an industry at all. He states that much of the current misunderstanding, resistance and even hostility plaguing proponents of tourism may be due to its mistakenly being called an industry. Three arguments for tourism's designation as an industry are: it needs to gain the respect it now lacks among other competing economic sectors; it needs sound, accurate and meaningful data in order to assess its economic contribution, and; it needs to provide a sense of self-identity to its practitioners.

Similar to the previous chapter, the author decries the difficulty in defining the terms 'tourist' and 'tourism' among others. He contends that tourism is not an industry at all and suggests that rather than a production activity or product, tourism should be viewed as a social phenomenon, an experience or a process. Therefore, defining tourism as an industry is incorrect and demeaning to what it really is. While the editor agrees with the author that tourism is largely a social phenomenon and experience, and the tourism industry is complex and difficult to define precisely, nevertheless, he believes the preponderance of evidence supports the position that tourism can be industrially classified and measured, and therefore, can indeed be counted as an industry. The debate continues.

For many people, much time and effort is expended by looking back to a earlier time in their lives, perhaps in an attempt to recapture a past that for them was happier or more rewarding than what the future might hold. The past has always been more orderly, more memorable, and most of all, safer.

A provocative insight on the meaning and substance of tourism is provided by **Dann** (Chapter 3), striking at the heart of the motivation for so much travel: nostalgia. The Western drive of escapism to the numerous outlets of yesteryear is enhanced by the 'evocation of the past as a promise to the future'. The author states that tourism is the nostalgia industry of the future. He suggests that tourism has employed nostalgia for its own financial advantage. A strong connection between nostalgia and tourism is explored, especially tourist resources such as hotels and museums. In addition, it is pointed out that tourists often have a strange fascination for tragic, macabre or other equally unappealing historical sites.

Nostalgia is grounded in dissatisfaction with social arrangements, both currently and the likelihood of their continuing into the future. Natives in Third World countries living for generations in one village could not comprehend the concept of nostalgia. On the other hand, today's dislocated Western tourist often travels in order to experience nostalgia. Tourism collateral literature and publicity which is based upon nostalgic images of the past promote glamour and happiness, provide something to be envied, and return love of self to the reader. Nostalgia is big business, and when it is associated with the world's leading industry, tourism, it offers unlimited financial possibilities.

The notion that tourism is actually regarded as a pursuit for peaceful relations is challenged by **Var** and **Ap** (Chapter 4) who examine the relationship between tourism and world peace from two perspectives, political and socio-cultural. The results of a cross-national study of the relationship between tourism and world peace revealed that tourism was viewed as positively contributing to both economic development and peace, but the strength of that relationship was tenuous. This finding suggests that the role of tourism as a contributor to world peace is uncertain and may not be perceived by respondents to be as critical as most tourism proponents believe. While some individuals associated with tourism education or the tourism industry (as well as speakers of a second language) have linked tourism with peace, much more research must be undertaken in order to substantiate the connection.

1 The meaning, scope and measurement of travel and tourism

William F. Theobald

Background

Travel has existed since the beginning of time when primitive man set out, often traversing great distances, in search of game which provided the food and clothing necessary for his survival. Throughout the course of history, people have travelled for purposes of trade, religious conviction, economic gain, war, migration and other equally compelling motivations. In the Roman era, wealthy aristocrats and high government officials also travelled for pleasure. Seaside resorts located at Pompeii and Herculaneum afforded citizens the opportunity to escape to their vacation villas in order to avoid the summer heat of Rome. Travel, except during the Dark Ages has continued to grow, and throughout recorded history, has played a vital role in the development of civilizations.

Tourism as we know it today is distinctly a twentieth century phenomenon. Historians suggest that the advent of mass tourism began in England during the industrial revolution with the rise of the middle class and relatively inexpensive transportation. The creation of the commercial airline industry following the Second World War and the subsequent development of the jet aircraft in the 1950s signalled the rapid growth and expansion of international travel. This growth led to the development of a major new industry, tourism. In turn, international tourism became the concern of a number of world governments since it not only provided new employment opportunities, but it also produced a means of earning foreign exchange.

Tourism today has grown significantly in both economic and social importance. Services has been the fastest growing economic sector of most industrialized countries over the past several years. One of the largest segments of the service industry, although largely unrecognized

Table 1.1 WTTC research projections for economic and employment growth

(world estimates 1996–2006)

	1996	2006	Real growth
Jobs	255 million	385 million	50.1%
Jobs (%)	10.7%	11.1%	–
Output	US$3.6 trillion	US$7.1 trillion	48.7%
Gross domestic product	10.7%	11.5%	49.6%
Investment	US$766 billion	US$1.6 trillion	57.3%
Exports	US$761 billion	US$1.5 trillion	51.2%
Total taxes	US$653 billion	US$1.3 trillion	49.6%

Source: World Travel and Tourism Council, Research and Statistical Data, Worldwide Web page, 22 January 1997, http://www.wttc.org/

as an entity in some of these countries, is travel and tourism. According to the World Travel and Tourism Council (1996), 'Travel and tourism is the largest industry in the world on virtually any economic measure including: gross output, value added, capital investment, employment, and tax contributions'. In 1996, the industry's gross output was estimated to be US$3.6 trillion, 10.7 per cent of all consumer spending. The travel and tourism industry is the world's largest employer, with 255 million jobs, or almost 11 per cent of all employees. This industry is the world's leading industrial contributor, producing over 10 per cent of the world gross domestic product, and accounting for capital investment in excess of US$766 billion in new facilities and equipment. In addition, it contributes over US$650 billion in direct, indirect and personal taxes each year. In addition, as indicated by Table 1.1, research conducted for the World Travel and Tourism Council (WTTC) suggests that there will continue to be significant increases in tourism during the next decade.

However, one of the major problems of the travel and tourism industry that has hidden or obscured its economic impact is the diversity and fragmentation of the industry itself. The travel industry includes hotels, motels and other types of accommodation; restaurants and other food services; transportation services and facilities; amusements, attractions and other leisure facilities; gift shops and a large number of other enterprises. Since many of these businesses also serve local residents, the impact of spending by visitors can easily be overlooked or underestimated. In addition, Meis (1992) points out that the tourism industry involves concepts that have remained amorphous to both analysts and decision-makers. Moreover, in all nations, this problem has made it difficult for the industry to develop any type of reliable or credible tourism information base in order to estimate the contribution it makes to regional, national and global economies. However, the nature of this very diversity makes travel and tourism an ideal vehicle for economic development in a wide variety of countries, regions or communities.

Once the exclusive province of the wealthy, travel and tourism have become an institutionalized way of life for most of the world's middle-class population. In fact, McIntosh, Goeldner and Ritchie (1995) suggest that tourism has become the largest commodity in international trade for many world nations, and for a significant number of other countries it ranks second or third. For example, tourism is the major source of income in Bermuda, Greece, Italy, Spain, Switzerland and most Caribbean countries.

In addition, Hawkins and Ritchie (1991), quoting from data published by the American Express Company, suggest that the travel and tourism industry is the number one ranked employer in Australia, the Bahamas, Brazil, Canada, France, (the former) West Germany, Hong Kong, Italy, Jamaica, Japan, Singapore, the UK and the USA. Because of problems of definition which directly affect statistical measurement, it is not possible with any degree of certainty to provide precise, valid or reliable data about the extent of world-wide tourism participation or its economic impact. In many cases, similar difficulties arise when attempts are made to measure domestic tourism.

The problem of definition

It is extremely difficult to define precisely the words *tourist* and *tourism* since these terms have different meanings to different people, and no universal definition has yet been adopted. For example, *Webster's New University Dictionary* (Soukhanov and Ellis, 1984) defines tourism as 'traveling for pleasure; the business of providing tours and services for tourists', and a tourist as 'one who travels for pleasure'. These terms are inadequate synonyms for travel, and their use as such adds further confusion when the field of travel is variously referred to as the *travel industry*, the *tourism industry*, the *hospitality industry* and most recently, the *visitor industry* (see the following chapter for a different view of whether or not they should be so named).

Why is so much attention given to these definitions? According to Gee, Makens and Choy (1989), the concern is both from an academic and a practical perspective. 'First, travel research requires a standard definition in order to establish parameters for research content, and second, without standard definitions, there can be no agreement on the measurement of tourism as an economic activity or its impact on the local, state, national or world economy.' Therefore, comparable data are necessary requisites, and identical criteria must be utilized in order to obtain such data. For example, in North America, the US Census Bureau and the US Travel Data Center's annual travel statistics consider only those trips taken that are 100 miles or more (one-way) away from home. However, Waters (1987) argued that this criteria is unreasonably high, and proposed instead in his annual compendium on travel that similar to the US National Tourism Resources Review Commission's guidelines (1973), distances of fifty miles or more are a more realistic criteria. On the other hand, the Canadian government specifies that a tourist is one who travels at least twenty-five miles outside his community. Therefore, each of these four annual data sets are quite different, and which (if any) contains the most accurate measurement of tourism activity?

The United Nations was so concerned about the impossible task of compiling comparative data on international tourism that they convened a Conference on Trade and Development which issued guidelines for tourism statistics (UNCTAD Secretariat, 1971). The ensuing report suggested that the functions of a comprehensive system of national tourism statistics could serve:

(a) To measure from the demand side the volume and pattern of foreign (and domestic) tourism in the country (as well as outgoing tourism) . . .
(b) To provide information about the supply of accommodation and other facilities used by tourists . . .
(c) To permit an assessment to be made of the impact of tourism on the balance of payments and on the economy in general . . .

Therefore, accurate statistical measurement of travel and tourism is important in order to assess its direct, indirect and induced economic impacts; to assist in the planning and development of new tourist facilities and resources; to determine current visitor patterns and help formulate marketing and promotional strategies; and to identify changes in tourist flows, patterns and preferences.

The derivation of definitions

Etymologically, the word *tour* is derived from the Latin, 'tornare' and the Greek, 'tornos', meaning 'a lathe or circle; the movement around a central point or axis'. This meaning changed in modern English to represent 'one's turn'. The suffix *-ism* is defined as 'an action or process; typical behaviour or quality', while the suffix, *-ist* denotes 'one that performs a given action'. When the word *tour* and the suffixes *-ism* and *-ist* are combined, they suggest the action of movement around a circle. One can argue that a circle represents a starting point, which ultimately returns back to its beginning. Therefore, like a circle, a tour represents a journey in that it is a round-trip, i.e., the act of leaving and then returning to the original starting point, and therefore, one who takes such a journey can be called a tourist.

There is some disagreement as when the word *tourist* first appeared in print. Smith (1989) suggests that 'Samuel Pegge reported the use of "tourist" as a new word for traveller c. 1800; England's *Sporting Magazine* introduced the word "tourism" in 1911'. Feifer (1985) proposes that the word tourist 'was coined by Stendhal in the early nineteenth century [1838]'. Mieczkowski (1990) states that 'The first definition of tourists appears in the *Dictionnare universel du XIX siecle* in 1876', defining tourists as 'persons who travel out of curiosity and idleness'. Kaul (1985) argues that even though the word *tourist* is of comparatively recent origin, nevertheless invaders were commonly referred to as tourists in the hope that one day they would leave. In addition, Kaul points out that:

> In the 17th and early 18th centuries, the English, the Germans, and others, traveling on a grand tour of the continent, came to be known as 'tourists.' . . . In 1824, Scott, in *San Roman's* stated thus, 'it provoked the pencil of every passing tourist.'

Leiper (1979) relates that the word *tourism* appears to have first been used in England to describe young male British aristocrats who were being educated for careers in politics, government and diplomatic service. In order to round-out their studies, they embarked upon a customary three year grand tour of the European continent, returning home only after their cultural education was indeed completed. According to Inskeep (1991), the first guide book for this type of travel was Thomas Nugent's *The Grand Tour*, published in 1778. Far from the traveller of 1778, today's tourist tends to connote a singularly negative image, one who is a bargain hunter, who travels en masse, and according to Eliot (1974), is one who is sought out for his cash, but despised for his ignorance of culture.

In addition, tourism has been variously defined (or refined) by governments and academics to relate to such fields as economics, sociology, cultural anthropology and geography. Economists are concerned with tourism's contributions to the economy and economic development of a destination area, and focus on supply/demand, foreign exchange and balance of payments, employment and other monetary factors. Sociologists and cultural anthropologists study the travel behaviour of individuals and groups of people, and focus on the customs, habits, traditions and life-styles of both hosts and guests. Geographers are concerned with the spatial aspects of tourism, and study travel flows and locations, development dispersion, land use and changes in the physical environment.

It is generally recognized that there are two different types of tourism definitions, each with its own rationale and intended usage. Burkart and Medlick (1981) suggest that there are *conceptual* definitions which attempt to provide a theoretical framework in order to identify the essential characteristics of tourism, and what distinguishes it from similar, sometimes related, but different activity.

Examples of such a conceptual definition would include that proposed by Jafari (1977) who states that 'tourism is a study of man away from his usual habitat, of the industry which responds to his needs, and of the impacts that both he and the industry have on the host socio-cultural, economic, and physical environments'. In addition, Mathieson and Wall (1982) conclude that 'Tourism is the temporary movement of people to destinations outside their normal places of work and residence, the activities undertaken during their stay in those destinations, and the facilities created to cater to their needs.'

There are also *technical* definitions which provide tourism information for statistical or legislative purposes. The various technical definitions of tourism provide meaning or clarification that can be applied in both international and domestic settings. This later approach, technical definitions, can be seen in the actions taken to help standardize comparative international tourism data collection.

Finally, Leiper (1979) postulated that there are three approaches in defining tourism: economic, technical and holistic. Economic definitions view tourism as both a business and an industry. Technical definitions identify the tourist in order to provide a common basis by which to collect data. Holistic definitions attempt to include the entire essence of the subject.

Dimensions of travel

Although technical definitions such as suggested previously should be applicable to both international and domestic tourism, such definitions are not necessarily utilized by all countries with respect to domestic tourism. However, most have adopted the three elements of the international definition: (1) purpose of trip; (2) distance travelled; and (3) duration of trip. In addition, two other dimensions or elements are sometimes used to define travellers. One that is frequently used is: (4) residence of traveller; and one that is used less often is (5) mode of transportation.

1 *Purpose of trip*: The notion behind this tourism dimension was to include the major components of most travel today. However, there are a number of destination areas that only include non-obligated

or discretionary travel in defining tourists. They only view leisure travellers as tourists, and purposely excluded travel *solely* for business purposes. However, one might well argue that business travel is often combined with some amount of pleasure travel. In addition, business travel to attend meetings or conferences should be included since it is considered to be discretionary travel rather part of the normal, daily business routine.

2 *Distance travelled*: For statistical purposes, when measuring travel away from home (non-local travel), a number of national, regional and local agencies use total round-trip distance between place of residence and destination as the distinguishing statistical measurement factor. As indicated earlier, these distances can and do vary from zero to 100 miles (0–160 kilometers). Therefore, attractions that are less than the minimum prescribed distance(s) travelled are not counted in official estimates of tourism, thereby creating both artificial and arbitrary standards.

3 *Duration of trip*: In order to meet the written criteria for defining travellers, most definitions of tourists and/or visitors include at least one overnight stay at the destination area. However, this overnight restriction then excludes many leisure-related one-day trips which often generate substantial business for attractions, restaurants and other recreation resources.

4 *Residence of traveller*: When businesses attempt to identify travel markets and associated marketing strategies, it is often more important for their business to identify where people live than to determine other demographic factors such as their nationality or citizenship.

5 *Mode of transportation*: Used primarily for planning purposes, a number of destination areas collect information on visitor travel patterns by collecting information on their mode of transportation: air, train, ship, coach, auto or other means.

Finally, according to Williams and Shaw (1991):

Each national tourist organization may record different types of information. For example, duration of stay, mode of travel, expenditure, age, socio-economic group, and number of accompanying persons are all important aspects of tourism but these are not recorded in all tourist enumerations.

Major definition developments

The growth of world receipts from international tourism that occurred between the two World Wars led to the need for a more precise statistical definition of tourism. An international forum held in 1936, The Committee of Statistical Experts of the League of Nations, first proposed a that a 'foreign tourist' is one who 'visits a country other than that in which he habitually lives for a period of at least twenty-four hours'. In 1945, the United Nations (which had replaced the League of Nations) endorsed this definition, but added to it a maximum duration of stay of less than six months. Other international bodies have chosen to extend this to one year or less.

A United Nations (UN) Conference on International Travel and Tourism held in Rome in 1963 and sponsored by IUOTO, the International Union of Official Travel Organizations (now the WTO, World Tourism Organization), recommended that a new word, 'visitor' be adopted which would define tourists as 'any person visiting a country other than that in which he has his usual place of residence, for any reason other than following an occupation remunerated from within the country visited'. Visitors included two distinct categories of travellers: (1) tourists – temporary visitors staying at least twenty-four hours in the country visited, and whose purpose was for leisure, business, family, mission or meeting; and (2) excursionists – temporary visitors staying *less* than twenty-four hours in the destination visited and not staying overnight (including cruise ship travellers). Since 1963, most world nations have accepted the definitions of *visitor, tourist* and *excursionist* that were proposed by the UN Conference and many of the revisions made subsequently.

At their 1967 meeting in Geneva, the United Nations Statistical Commission recommended that a separate class of visitor be established. Tourists stay at least twenty-four hours, but since some visitors take excursions then return back to their place of residence the same day, they were to be called, 'excursionists'. This group included daily visitors with purposes other than employment, cruise passengers and visitors in transit. Excursionists could be easily distinguished from other visitors since there was no overnight stay involved.

The definition of the term *visitor* refined in 1963 refers only to international tourism. However, although it is more difficult to measure, it is quite obvious that it is also applicable to national (domestic) tourism as well. For example, in 1980, the WTO's Manila Declaration implicitly extended the definition to all tourism. According to Bar-On (1989), the Working Party on Tourism Statistics of the WTO Commission for Europe agreed that recommendations on domestic tourism, although narrower than international tourism, were nevertheless compatible. These definitions have undergone subsequent refinements, and it would appear that the WTO/UN definition of tourism should have created a uniform basis for collection of standardized tourism data. Although the majority of countries utilize these definitions, unfortunately, not all adhere to them.

Incomparability of tourism statistics

The principal difficulty in measuring the extent of tourism demand is the basic incomparability of tourism statistics. Such incomparability exists not only when attempting to compare data from various nations but also creates problems when regions, provinces, states or cities within a country attempt to compare with one another data on tourism demand. At the international level, there are a number of reasons for this incomparability.

The definitions of a *tourist* and a *visitor* vary, especially at frontiers where statistics are collected. Not all countries have adopted the United Nations Statistical Commission's definitions, while others use their own definitions. Even when the UN definitions are utilized, data collection methods vary widely so that some countries may not gather information on the purpose of a visit or whether or not the visitor will be (or has been) remunerated. In addition, although most countries gather statistical data at their frontiers, others rely on information provided by hotel registrations. In this case, even though the same definitions may be used, the two data sets are not comparable.

Some countries do not even count the arrivals of foreign nationals from bordering countries, especially if there is a unique or special relationship between the countries. Often, in some world nations visitors who are travelling for business or other similar purposes are not regarded as tourists, and therefore they are not recorded as such. In addition, students who spend most of the academic year studying abroad in foreign countries are also often overlooked when compiling statistical data.

Excursionists and other day visitors are included in the statistical data of some countries, but are excluded in others. Special situation visitors such as cruise ship passengers are often not counted in some countries since they are considered to be transients. Flight crews and other visitors in transit are often treated likewise.

Frechtling (1992) suggests that of the 184 nations in the world, 166 report tourism data to the World Tourism Organization each year, and

Of these 166 countries, four do not have a measure of international visitors or tourists. Thirteen countries have no recent measure of international tourism receipts, and 46 do not estimate international travel expenditures. More than one-half (84) have no measure of international departures, and two-thirds (113) do not count visitor nights in all accommodation establishments.

At the sub-national level, similar situations also exist. For example, in the United States, there is no standard definition valid throughout the country. As a result, definitions of tourism vary from state to state. Gee,

Makens and Choy (1989) suggest that in Florida, 'a tourist is an out-of-state resident who stays at least one night in the state for reasons other than necessary layover for transportation connections or for strictly business transactions'. In Alaska, 'a tourist is a nonresident travelling to Alaska for pleasure or culture and for no other purpose'. Massachusetts defines a tourist as 'a person, not on business, who stays away from home overnight'. For Arizona, 'a tourist is a nonresident traveller in the state, while a traveller is used to identify Arizona residents travelling within the state'. In Utah, 'a tourist will participate in some activity while in the state, while a traveller simply passes through on their way to another state'. Finally, in Nevada, 'tourists are residents of states other than Nevada who visit the state or stop somewhere in the state while en route through and without regard for trip purpose'.

The confusion in terminology is by no means limited to the United States. A review of any of the statistics published by the UN/WTO points up the innumerable footnotes to the data indicating national variations, differences in data collection methodology, and significant diversity in terminology standards. Indeed, one of the important tasks of the WTO is to work systematically to improve and help develop definitions and classifications of tourism that are of world-wide application and that emphasize both clarity and simplicity in their application.

Common measures of tourism

In June 1991, 250 individuals representing ninety countries participated in a landmark meeting co-sponsored by the World Tourism Organization and Tourism Canada held at Ottawa, Canada. The International Conference on Travel and Tourism Statistics had three primary aims:

1 Development of a uniform and integrated definition and classification system of tourism statistics.
2 Implementation of a strict methodology for determining the economic impact of tourism and the performance of various sectors of the industry.
3 Establishment of both a means of dialogue between governments and the tourism industry and a coherent work program for collecting tourism statistics and information.

The conference was successful in agreeing on approaches to standardize tourism terminology and industrial classifications, as well as indicators of market growth, economic impact and overall industry development.

All delegates to the conference endorsed the concepts, measures and definitions that were proposed in the resolutions that came out of the meetings. In 1993, the United Nations accepted the report of the WTO and adopted the recommendations of the UN Secretariat's Statistical Division pertaining to tourism statistics.

One of the principal findings that came out of the conference resolutions (World Tourism Organization, 1991) recommended that tourism be defined as:

> the activities of a person travelling to a place outside his or her usual environment for less than a specified period of time and whose main purpose of travel is other than the exercise of an activity remunerated from within the place visited . . .

In addition, tourism was further defined as the activities of people travelling for leisure, business and other purposes to places outside their usual environment and staying for no more than one consecutive year. Bar-On (1996) has compiled a helpful list of those UN-WTO adopted definitions as shown in Table 1.2.

The Ottawa Conference further recommended the development and implementation of a system of performance measures and indicators which could help measure trends and provide forecasts for the industry as a whole, thereby maximizing tourism's economic contribution to national benefits. They recommended that the concept of satellite accounting systems which derive their principle aggregates and basic concepts from the United Nations System of National Accounts be supported, and that all countries introduce such accounting systems into their analytic base for tourism data on an incremental basis.

In an effort to measure modern service sectors such as travel and tourism in this system of national accounts, the UN and WTO (1994) approved the delineation of the Standard International Classification of Tourism Activities (SICTA). The purpose of this system was to classify all elements of tourism economic activity in a consistent and comprehensive manner. In order to be useful, such a classification system for tourism that was based on supply-side economic activity had at some level to be consistent with, and allow the identification of the primary activities or products of tourism as traditionally identified from the demand-side. Therefore, if the travel and tourism sector were evaluated as economists measure other industries, its total economic impact would be substantially larger than the traditional estimates of visitor arrivals and tourist expenditures. It would appear that past comparative statistical instability within the tourism industry may end due to the adoption and implementation of two key elements, the WTO/UN tourism definitions and the SICTA classification system.

Table 1.2 Travel and tourism definitions

(1) *Visitor* (V): Any person travelling to a place *other than that of his/her usual environment for up to 12 months* and whose main *purpose of trip is* leisure, business, pilgrimage, health, etc, other than the exercise of an activity remunerated from within the place visited or migration.

Transport Crew and Commercial Travellers (even those travelling to different destinations over the year) may be regarded as travelling in their usual environment and excluded from visitors (Transport Crew are usually excluded from Frontier Control), also those travelling year-round (or most of the year) between two places of residence (eg weekend homes, residential study).

(2) *Tourist* (T, stay-over/overnight): A visitor staying at least one night in the place visited (not necessarily in paid accommodation).

(3) *Same-day visitor* (SDV, Excursionist, Day-visitor): A visitor who does not stay overnight in the place visited, eg:
   (a) *Cruise Visitor* (CV), who may tour for one or more days, staying overnight on the ship (includes foreign naval personnel off duty).
   (b) *Border Shopper* (BS), who may have high expenditures on purchases of food, drink, tobacco, petrol etc; excluding border workers.

(4) *Travellers*: Visitors and
   (a) *Direct Transit Travellers* (DT, eg at an airport, between two nearby ports);
   (b) *Commuters*, routine travel for work, study, shopping etc;
   (c) *Other Non-commuting Travel* (ONT), eg occasional local travel, transport crew or commercial traveller (to various destinations), migrants (including temporary work), diplomats (to/from their duty station).

(5) *Passengers* (PAX, Revenue): Travellers excluding crew, non-revenue (or low-revenue) travellers eg infants, free or travelling on a discount of up to 25%.

(6) *Tourism*: The activities of visitors, persons travelling to and staying in places outside their usual environment for up to 12 months for leisure, business, pilgrimage, etc.
   (a) *International*: (i) Inbound, (ii) Outbound: may include overnight stay(s) in country of residence,
   (b) *Domestic* (in country of residence).

(7) *Tourism industry*: Establishments providing services and goods to visitors, including:
   (a) *Hospitality* (hotels, restaurants, etc),
   (b) *Transport*,
   (c) *Tour Operators* and *Travel agents*, *Attractions*,
   (d) Other branches of the economy supplying visitors (some of these may also provide a significant volume of services and goods to non-visitors, and the proportion of revenue, etc due to visitors is important in estimating receipts from tourism).

(8) *The Travel and Tourism Industry* (TTI): The tourism industry (and receipts from tourism, etc) together with the provision of goods and services by establishments to other non-commuting travellers, occasional local travellers etc.[a]

---

[a] WTTC, *Travel and Tourism's Economic Perspective 1995, 2005*, WTTC, Brussels, 1995.
Source: Based on UNSTAT, *Recommendations on Tourism Statistics, op cit*, Ref 1.

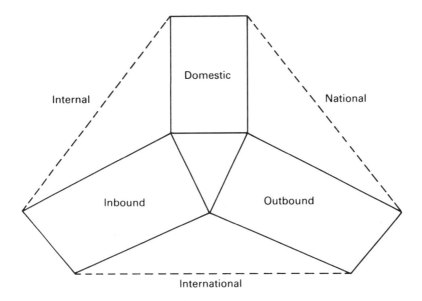

Figure 1.1 Forms of tourism

Source: World Tourism Organization

Basic tourism units

As indicated by Figure 1.1, for a given country, three basic forms of tourism were first identified, then defined as: (1) *domestic tourism* – comprised of residents visiting their own country; (2) *inbound tourism* – comprised of non-residents travelling in a given country; and (3) *outbound tourism* – comprised of residents travelling in another country. These forms can be combined in a number of ways in order to derive the following categories of tourism: (a) *internal tourism* – involves both domestic and inbound tourism; (b) *national tourism* – involves both domestic and outbound tourism; and (c) *international tourism* – involves both inbound and outbound tourism. It should be noted that although this figure refers to a country, it could be applied to any other geographic area(s).

Basic tourism units refer to individuals/households that are the subject of tourism activities and therefore can be considered as statistical units in surveys. 'Travellers' refer to all individuals making a trip between two or more geographic locations, either in their country of residence (domestic travellers) or between countries (international travellers). However, as can be seen in Figure 1.2, there is a distinction made between two types of travellers: *visitors* and *other travellers*.

All travellers who are engaged in the activity of tourism are considered to be 'visitors'. The term 'visitor' then becomes the core concept around

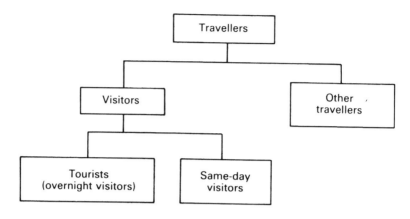

Figue 1.2 Traveller typology

Source: Travel and Tourism Research Association

which the entire system of tourism statistics is based. A secondary division of the term 'visitor' is made into two categories:

1 'Tourists (overnight visitors)'.
2 'Same-day visitors' (formerly called 'excursionists').

Therefore, the term 'visitor' can be described for statistical purposes as 'any person travelling to a place other than that of his/her usual environment for less than twelve months and whose main purpose of trip is other than the exercise of an activity remunerated from within the place visited'.

Classification of tourism demand

An extended classification system of tourism demand delineating the main purpose(s) of visits or trips by major groups was developed (see Figure 1.3), based upon that first proposed by the United Nations (1979). This system was designed to help measure the major segments of tourism demand for planning and marketing purposes. The major groups include:

1 Leisure, recreation and holidays.
2 Visiting friends and relatives.
3 Business and professional.
4 Health treatment.
5 Religion/pilgrimages.
6 Other (crews on public carriers, transit and other or unknown activities).

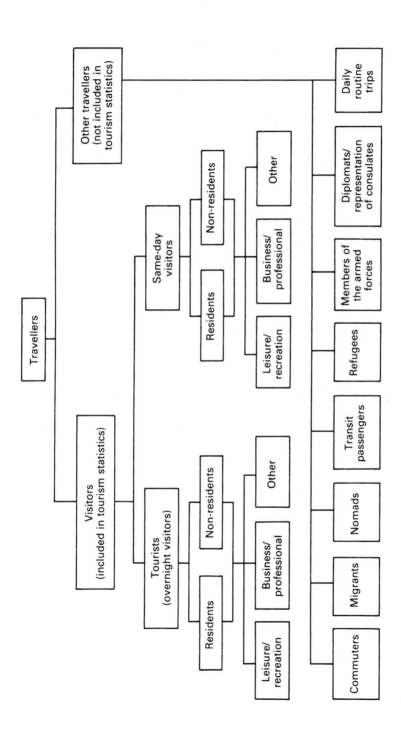

Figure 1.3 Classification of travellers

Sources: World Tourism Organization and the Travel and Tourism Research Organization

Other measures of tourism demand enumerated were:

(a)   duration of stay or trip;
(b)   origin and destination of trip;
(c)   area of residence or destination within countries;
(d)   means of transportation;
(e)   tourism accommodation.

Each of these demand measures were first defined, then where possible, specific examples of each were indicated.

Paci (1992) argued however, that not only tourism demand be considered, but more importantly, tourism 'must seek to more clearly delineate a supply-based conceptual structure for its activities because that is the source of most national economic statistics'. When incorporated into supply-based statistics, the relationship and relative importance of tourism to other economic sectors can be more easily recognized. In addition, Paci pointed out that such a system would not only foster and provide for greater comparability among national tourism statistics, but would also 'provide statistical linkage between the supply side of tourism and the demand side'.

Classification of tourism supply

Tourism expenditure data are one of the most significant indicators used to monitor and evaluate the impact of tourism on an economy and on the various representative tourism industry segments. The conference has defined *tourism expenditure* as 'the total consumption expenditure made by a visitor or on behalf of a visitor for and during his/her trip and stay at destination'.

It has been proposed that tourist expenditures be divided into three broad categories, depending upon the specific periods of time the visitor makes those expenditures. The first, advanced spending that is necessary to prepare for the trip (trip purpose); second, expenses while travelling to, and those at the travel destination (trip location) and; third, travel related spending made at home after returning from the trip (trip conclusion).

It has been recommended that tourism consumption expenditures should be identified by a system of main categories, and should include:

1   Packaged travel (holidays and prepaid tour arrangements).
2   Accommodations (hotels, motels, resorts, campgrounds, etc.).
3   Eating and drinking establishments (restaurants, cafes, taverns, etc.).

4 Transport (airplane, rail, ship, bus, auto, taxi, etc.).
5 Recreation, culture and sporting activities.
6 Shopping.
7 Other.

Summary

For too long, the tourism industry, both international and domestic, has had great difficulty making statistical comparisons with other sectors of the economy. In all nations, this has led to difficulty in developing valid, reliable and credible information or data bases about tourism and its contribution to local, regional, national and global economies.

A number of individuals throughout the world who are involved in the travel and tourism industry have long recognized the interdependent nature of travel and tourism statistical systems at all levels of government. Further, they realized the need for ongoing reviews and revisions of both concepts and working definitions of travel and tourism that are used internationally. The Ottawa Conference recommendations which were adopted by the United Nations Statistical Commission laid the foundation for new, expanded and modified international definitions and standards for travel and tourism. Those principles and guidelines provide for the harmonious and uniform measurement of tourism among world nations.

Now that an such an international definition/classification system for the tourism sector does exist, there is finally a universal basis for the collection of standardized data on tourism activity. However, although there has been significant progress in reaching consensus on what constitutes *international* tourism, there is no such consensus in *domestic* tourism terminology. Therefore, caution must be exercised since a clear distinction must be made between basic definitions of tourism and those elements which describe tourists themselves, and their demographic and behavioural characteristics. Since the tourist is the principal component of tourism, it is therefore unrealistic to develop uniform tourism data without first deciding the types of variables and the range of phenomena that should be included in data collection efforts.

The World Tourism Organization will be largely responsible for reviewing and revising the definitions, classifications, methodologies, data collection and analysis of international tourism proposed by the Ottawa Conference. However, the ultimate success or failure of gathering and utilizing comparable tourism statistical data lies with their acceptance and implementation by the entire world community.

References

Australian Bureau of Statistics (1996) *Framework for the Collection and Publication of Tourist Statistics,* Australian Bureau of Statistics, Canberra, p. 78

Bar-On, Raymond (1989) *Travel and Tourism Data: A Comprehensive Research Handbook on the World Travel Industry,* Euromonitor Publications, London, p. 19

Bar-On, Raymond (1996) Databank: definitions and classifications, *Tourism Economics*, **2**(4), December, p. 370

Burkart, A.J. and Medlik, S. (1981) *Tourism: Past, Present and Future*, London, Heinemann, p. 39

Eliot, E. (1974) Travel, *CMA Journal*, 2 February, p. 271

Feifer, Maxine (1985) *Tourism in History: From Imperial Rome to the Present,* Stein and Day, New York, p. 2

Frechtling, Douglas C. (1992) International Issues Forum: World Marketing and Economic Research Priorities for Tourism, *Tourism Partnerships and Strategies: Merging Vision With New Realities*. Proceedings of the 23rd Travel and Tourism Research Association Conference. Minneapolis, 14–17 June, p. 20

Gee, Chuck Y., Makens, James C. and Choy, Dexter J.L. (1989) *The Travel Industry,* 2nd edn, Van Nostrand Reinhold, New York, pp. 10–11

Hawkins, Donald E. and Ritchie, J.R. Brent (eds) (1991) *World Travel and Tourism Review: Indicators, Trends and Forecasts*, Vol. 1. CAB International, Wallingford, UK, pp. 72–73

Inskeep, Edward (1991) *Tourism Planning: An Integrated and Sustainable Development Approach*, Van Nostrand Reinhold, New York, p. 6

Jafari, Jafar (1977) Editor's Page, *Annals of Tourism Research*, **V**, Special Number, October/December, p. 8

Kaul, R.N. (1985) *The Dynamics of Tourism, Volume 1: The Phenomenon*, Sterling Publishers Private Limited, New Delhi, India, p. 2

Leiper, Neil (1979) The Framework of Tourism: Towards a Definition of Tourism, Tourist, and the Tourist Industry, *Annals of Tourism Research*, **6**(4), October/December, pp. 391, 394

Mathieson, Alister and Wall, Geoffrey (1982) *Tourism: Economic, Physical and Social Impacts*, Longman, London, p. 1

McIntosh, Robert W., Charles R. Goeldner and J.R. Brent Ritchie. (1995) *Tourism Principles, Practices, Philosophies*, 7th edn, John Wiley & Sons, New York, p. 4

Meis, Scott (1992) International Issues Forum: Response, *Tourism Partnerships and Strategies: Merging Vision With New Realities*, Proceedings of the 23rd Travel and Tourism Research Association Conference, Minneapolis, 14–17 June, p. 17

Mieczkowski, Zbigniew (1990) *World Trends in Tourism and Recreation*, Peter Lang, New York, p. 20

Paci, Enzo (1992) International Issues Forum: Common Measures of Tourism, *Tourism Partnershpis and Strategies: Merging Vision with New Realities*, Proceedings of the 23rd Travel and Tourism Research Association Conference, Minneapolis, 14–17 June, p. 10

Smith, Stephen L.J. (1989) *Tourism Analysis: A Handbook*, London, Longman Scientific & Technical, p. 17

Soukhanov, Anne H. and Ellis, Kaethe (eds) (1984) *Websters II New Riverside University Dictionary*, Houghton Mifflin, Boston, p. 1221

UNCTAD Secretariat (1971) Conference on Trade and Development, *Guidelines for Tourism Statistics*, United Nations, New York, p. 6

United Nations (1979) Statistical Division, *Provisional Guidelines on Statistics of International Tourism*, Statistical Papers, Series M, No. 62, United Nations, New York

United Nations and World Tourism Organization (1994) *Recommendations on Tourism Statistics*, Department for Economic and Social Information and Policy Analysis, Statistical Division, Series M, No. 83, United Nations, New York, p. 77

Waters, Somerset (1987) *Travel Industry World Yearbook: The Big Picture* (annual), Child and Waters, New York, p. 21

Williams, Allan M. and Shaw, Gareth (eds) (1991) *Tourism and Economic Development: Western European Experiences*. 2nd edn, Belhaven Press, London, p. 11

World Tourism Organization (1983) General Assembly, Definitions Concerning Tourism Statistics, *Report of the Secretary-General On The Execution Of The General Programme Of Work For The Period 1982–1983: Addendum (C.3.5)*, New Delhi, 3–14 October, pp. 7–9

World Tourism Organization (1991) *International Conference on Travel and Tourism Statistics: Ottawa (Canada), 24–28 June 1991 Resolutions*, Madrid, World Tourism Organization, p. 4

World Travel and Tourism Council (1996) *The WTTC 1996/7 Travel & Tourism Research Report*. 6th edn, World Travel and Tourism Council, London

World Travel and Tourism Council (1997) Research & Statistical Data, Research Projections for Economic and Employment Growth, Worldwide Web page, 22 January, *<http://www.wttc. org/>*

2 What are travel and tourism: are they really an industry?

Thomas Lea Davidson

Introduction

Common practice, at least among those who are involved in the development and marketing of tourism, is to refer to (travel and) tourism as an industry. In fact, considerable effort has been devoted to creating the impression that tourism is a legitimate industry worthy of being compared to other industries such as health services, energy or agriculture. The importance of tourism is underscored by referring to it as 'one of the top three industries in most states', 'largest or next to largest retail industry', or 'largest employer (industry) in the world'.

The intent of this chapter is to suggest that this designation may not be correct. In fact, I will contend that tourism is not an industry at all. At best, it is a collection of industries. Furthermore, I will suggest that referring to tourism as an industry may be a major contributor to the misunderstanding, resistance and even the hostility that often plague proponents of travel and tourism as worthy economic forces in a modern economy.

Background

By way of preface, let us consider why so much effort has been devoted toward making tourism an industry. Historically, tourism has not been taken seriously by economists, economic developers, even government. Tourism is seen as fun and games, recreation, leisure, unproductive. Under this view tourism is just the opposite of the traditional work ethic. Residents see tourists as crowds, enemies of the environment, undesirable – the 'ugly visitor' from wherever he or she may have come. Too bad that tourists spend money or there would be no redeeming virtue to hosting tourists in one's community.

This negativism culminated in the early 1970s when petrol sales were banned on Sunday as a way to address the fuel crisis. Although this ban crippled tourism, it was not viewed as critical – except by the businesses whose customers could not, or would not, come.

In response, those in the business of tourism undertook to gain respect by defining tourism as an industry and then by measuring the economic impact of the tourism industry in terms that were comparable to those used for other industries. 'Industry' was a positive term connoting work, productivity, employment, income, economic health – all attributes that tourism wanted but did not have.

Tourism as an industry

Under this 'industry' view, the tourism industry is composed of a clearly defined grouping of firms that are perceived to be primarily in the business of selling to or serving tourists. Hotels, restaurants, transportation and amusements are examples of the types of firms that comprise the tourism industry. The United Nations identifies seven industrial areas while the US Travel Data Center includes some fourteen types of businesses as defined by the Standard Industrial Classification (SIC) system.

What are the advantages of designating tourism as an industry? Let me suggest three.

1 First is the **need to gain respect**, respect based on understanding the contribution that tourism makes to economic health. Tourism has an image problem. It is not really perceived as a legitimate part of economic development. For some, tourism is not even a legitimate part of government and in today's budget crises, not worthy of funding. If tourism can argue that it really *is* an industry worthy of being considered on the same terms as other recognized industries, then the image of and the support for tourism will improve.
2 Second is the **need for a sound framework to tabulate, analyse and publish data about tourism** – data that are accurate, meaningful and believable. Historically, economists have used the 'industry' as the basis for measurement and study. If tourism wants to be measured and studied seriously, it follows then that tourism must be an industry. Only by treating tourism as an industry can tourism be compared to other industries in the world economy.
3 Third, there is a **need among some in 'tourism' for a format for self-identity**. Being part of an industry is a clear and easy way to achieve identity and the self-esteem that goes with identity.

Tourism is beset by many outside pressures: world events; budget problems and mounting deficits; recession; the staggering need for funds to support education, health care, social needs and crime prevention; and the maturing, competitive tourism marketplace. In this environment, a great effort has been devoted to legitimizing tourism as a key industry in today's service economy. In great measure, these efforts have been successful. But, is this 'success' really positive? Or has the 'industry' label actually hurt the cause that this designation is supposed to champion. To answer this question we need to define what an industry is, use this definition as a framework to look at tourism, and then consider the ramifications of the difference.

What is an industry?

We can look to two sources for an answer:

1   Economics defines an industry as being a group of independent firms all turning out the same product. Whether or not two products are 'the same' is defined in terms of their substitutability expressed as the cross-elasticity of demand. In lay terms, the more that the purchase of Product A replaces (can be substituted for) the purchase of Product B, the more A and B are the same and hence in the same industry.
2   The second source for definitions are the Standard Industrial Classification (SIC) manuals. Such publications suggest that the SIC system was developed to classify establishments by the type of activity in which they are engaged. To be recognized as an industry, a group of establishments must share a *common primary activity* and be *statistically significant in size.*

It is clear that the focus of 'industry' is:

• Individual business establishments grouped together.
• The revenue *received* by these economic units.
• Producing and selling a common product, i.e., the product of one firm is a substitute for the product of any other firm in the same industry.

And it is equally clear that the 'manufacturing' sector provides the framework for this focus. Thus, to the extent that tourism is an industry, economists and others will position tourism in terms of these factors – individual businesses, revenues of those businesses, and a common product.

But just what is tourism?

But what is travel and tourism? Do they fit this industry mould? To answer these questions we need to define a tourist and tourism and then relate this phenomenon to an industry as defined above.

Clearly, there is confusion and controversy surrounding the definitions of travel and tourism. Are they the same or are tourists only seeking pleasure while travellers may also be on business? How far must one travel from home to be a tourist/traveller? Does paying for a room make one a tourist? . . . And so forth.

From the viewpoint of economic development and/or economic impact, a visitor – nominally called a tourist – is someone who comes to an area, spends money and leaves. We employ an economic framework to be comparable with the concept of 'industry' which is an economic term. The reasons for the visit, length of stay, length of trip, or distances from home are immaterial.

Thus, we define a tourist as *a person travelling outside of his/her normal routine – either normal living or normal working routine – who spends money.* This definition of visitor/tourist includes:

- People who stay in hotels, motels, resorts or campgrounds.
- People who visit friends or relatives.
- People who visit while just passing through going somewhere else.
- People who are on a day trip (do not stay overnight).
- An 'all other' category of people on boats, who sleep in a vehicle of some sort, or who otherwise do not fit the above.

For purposes of this definition a resident (or someone who is not a tourist) is defined as a person staying more than thirty days.

Note that visitors/tourists can:

- Be attending a meeting or convention.
- Be business travellers outside of their home office area.
- Be on a group tour.
- Be on an individual leisure/vacation trip – including recreational shopping.
- Be travelling for personal or family-related reasons.

In today's world there are three problems with this definition:

1 Some people travel considerable distances to shop, especially at factory outlets. They may do so many times a year. They are difficult to measure. Technically they are not tourists; their shopping has become routine.

2   Some people maintain two residences – a winter home and a summer home. The stay in either one usually exceeds one month and these people are *not* classified as tourists. Again, their travel is routine. However, short-stay visitors to their homes whether renting or not *are* tourists.

3   When people live in an area just outside of a destination and have friends or relatives visit them, how are these visitors classified when they visit the destination? Actually, the problem here is not whether they are tourists – those visiting friends or relatives clearly are. Rather, the question is which area gets the credit? Or, how should the people they are visiting be classified? Again, while measurement is difficult, the destination area should be credited for money spent therein.

Tourism, then can be viewed as:

*   A social phenomenon, *not* a production activity.
*   The sum of the expenditures of all travellers or visitors for all purposes, *not* the receipt of a select group of similar establishments.
*   An experience or process, *not* a product – an extremely varied experience at that.

To underscore this view of tourism, let us focus on the economic impact of tourism on the economic health of a community. The best measure of this economic impact is not the receipts of a few types of business. Rather, the economic impact of tourism begins with the *sum total of all expenditures by all tourists*. Yes, this impact includes some of the receipts of accommodations, restaurants, attractions, petrol (gas) stations – the traditional tourism-orientated businesses. (We might note that these are vastly dissimilar businesses.) However, it also includes retail purchases that often amount to more than the money spent for lodging. These include services (haircuts, car repairs), highway tolls in some countries, church contributions, and so forth. In fact, visitors spend money on just about everything that residents do. Thus, any and every 'industry' that sells to consumers is in receipt of cash from tourism. Clearly, the criteria of similar activity or common product or production process are *not* met in tourism!

Further, the requirement of substitution is not met either. More often than not, most of these expenditures go together as complementary or supplementary purchases. Thus, food is not competitive with lodging. A visitor buys both.

Seen this way, travel and tourism – the movement of people outside their normal routine for business, pleasure or personal reasons – is much, much more than an 'industry' in the traditional sense. As an economic force, it is the impact of everything the visitor/tourist spends. Thus, we really have an expenditure-driven phenomenon, not a receipts-driven one.

So what? Why raise the issue at all?

With so much effort to sell tourism as an industry, specifically an 'export industry', what is the purpose of questioning this designation? Are not many of these people just going to fight for their viewpoint? Won't this conflict be a problem?

These are legitimate questions. However, I believe that there are several important – and negative – ramifications in attempting to make tourism an industry when, in fact, it is not an industry in the traditional sense. Let me comment on three such negative ramifications.

The first negative ramification comes from the disbelief that is created. Somehow, whether it is conscious or subconscious, people know that tourism does not fit the traditional definition of an industry. This disbelief tends to discredit the arguments supporting the importance of tourism and the level of support that tourism and tourism growth deserve. How often do we hear economic development proponents say that tourism is not an industry and therefore, not economic development?

In essence, this ramification says that when people recognize – correctly – that tourism does not fit the classic definition of an industry, then they discredit the argument that tourism deserves the benefits that accrue to a legitimate industry.

The second negative ramification is more subtle. It says that the attempt to define tourism as an industry has led to attempts to employ traditional methods of measurement and analysis to the study of tourism. But traditional methods just do not work well. One result has been inaccurate results that often understate the size, impact or benefits to a community of the tourism phenomenon. Let me offer two examples:

1 The issue of business receipts *vs.* total tourism expenditures. Receipts of specific businesses are the traditional method for measuring an industry. Usually, the total receipts of all of the relevant business units are summed. Yet few businesses receive all of their receipts from tourists and few consumer businesses receive no money at all from tourists. Thus, tourist expenditure is the better measure of the size, scope, and impact of tourism.
2 The issue of substitute/competitive goods *vs.* supplementary or complementary goods. Traditionally, members of an industry compete on some level for the same money. If a visitor stays tonight in Hotel

A, he or she does not spend tonight in Hotel B, and hotels are an industry. However, many expenditures of tourists are complementary. When spending the night in Hotel A, the tourist travels, eats, pays for entertainment and may buy a gift to take home. Taking one action does not necessarily exclude taking another action. It is more probable that all are done during the course of the stay.

The third negative ramification relates directly to the disadvantage tourism faces for public funding. When tourism – an industry composed of individual business firms seeking their own benefit – comes up against education, public health, crime prevention, infrastructure repair or development etc. (all seen as serving society as a whole), the problem before the appropriations committee is clear. Why should government use limited funds to support one industry – and a 'frivolous' one at that – when there are so many social ills that demand attention? As an industry, tourism is often seen as self-serving when, in fact, it is a key ingredient in the economic health of the community. Thriving tourism can be key to attending to these other issues.

Thus, the question raised by this issue is, 'Does the "industry" designation make it harder to argue – and win – the broader implication?' Frankly, as one who has been intimately involved in these confrontations, I believe that it does. The net of this argument is that to truly understand, measure, analyse and sell tourism we need to go beyond traditional thinking. We need to 'think outside of the box'.

- If we are to study tourism to expand it or to control it, is it not better to have an accurate understanding and definition?
- If we are to communicate the value of tourism, is it not more effective to reflect the totality of tourism and not just champion a few industries?

In sum, I believe that *defining tourism as an industry is incorrect*; and further, *this definition demeans what tourism really is*. Tourism is a social/economic phenomenon that acts both as an engine of economic progress and as a social force. Tourism is much more than an industry. Tourism is more like a 'sector' that impacts a wide range of industries. Tourism is not just businesses or governments – it is people. Supporting rational tourism growth and development needs to be viewed in this broader context.

Given today's economic conditions, environmental concerns, evil, turmoil and strife, positioning tourism properly takes on added importance. Maybe now is the time to rethink the 'industry' classification and find a way to communicate more clearly just how important tourism's health is to our economy.

3 'There's no business like old business': tourism, the nostalgia industry of the future

Graham M.S. Dann

Introduction

Today a great deal of time and energy is devoted to looking backwards. Our quest is the capture of a past which, in every conceivable manner, is portrayed by the media as far superior to the chaotic present and dreaded future. This soft-focus world of yesteryear, with its swing bands, honky tonks, golden oldies, vintage prints, and former comedy shows featuring the likes of Jack Benny, *Yes Minister* and *Fawlty Towers*, is above all a safe haven, an orderly and comforting environment (Lowenthal, 1993: 4). The way we were is projected as an improvement on the way we are, or are ever likely to be. How else can one explain the success of Nostalgia TV or Radio Yesteryear, publications such as *This England*, and the rapid growth of the ubiquitous retail outlet *Past Times*?

In Britain, which is now officially advertised a 'World Capital of Tradition' (British Tourist Authority, 1993), there has been a massive revival in preserving the past, one that has reached almost epidemic proportions. Not only is the countryside romantically promoted as a return to nature and childhood (Dann, 1996a; 1997), but industrial centres previously associated with coal mining, cotton spinning and steam engines have been appropriated and marketed by the 'heritage industry' (Urry, 1990). Whether one's taste is rural or urban now one can visit Dickens' or Shakespeare's London, undertake the Macbeth experience, follow in the steps of Captain Cook, participate in the Linlithgow Story, tread the Pendle Way, explore Beatrix Potter's Hill Top Farm, or (with a map in Latin provided by Ordnance Survey), march across Roman Britain. Indeed, it is even possible to gaze upon the burial site of Alice in Wonderland, the House that Jack Built, the birthplace of Dick Whittington, and the precise spot where George slew the dragon (Coutts Heritage Print and Design, 1981). In the words of William Davis (1992: 21), former chairman of the British Tourist Authority and English Tourist Board, 'many people tend to see Britain as some kind of medieval Disneyland. This is good for the tourist trade.'

But Britain is not alone in promoting itself through its past. In the United States there is, for example, Colonial Williamsburg, Baltimore's Harbor Place, Olde Illinois, Plymouth Plantation and New Salem. Australia has Sydney's Darling Harbour, Israel has the Museum of the Jewish Diaspora, and Poland the renovated town square in Warsaw; the list goes on and on. Anywhere and everywhere, it would seem, the one thing that unites this ever increasing bricolage of yearning is the realization that 'there's no business like old business' (Morley, 1972 in Lowenthal, 1993: 4). Moreover, when the nostalgia industry is linked to the world's number one enterprise – that of tourism – such an alliance has limitless pecuniary possibilities.

It is the purpose of this exploratory essay to examine some of this nostalgia tourism connection with reference to:

1   Hotels ('the tourist in his castle, the rich man at his gate').
2   Museums and other emporia ('sales of the centuries').
3   Infamous sites ('milking the macabre').
4   Dirty dumps ('where there's muck there's brass').

Finally, there is a brief discussion on the mechanics of promoting the past by projecting it into the future. The complementary counterparts to this presentation can be found in several of the author's other works (Dann, 1994a; 1994b; 1994c; 1996a; 1997).

1   The tourist in his castle, the rich man at his gate

This distorted line from an otherwise well-known hymn has been irreverently changed to depict the inversion that takes place when tourism offers its proteges the luxury of being a King or a Queen for a day (Gottlieb, 1982), where

> To live for a short time surrounded by gracious deferring servants may have powerful appeal among those seeking escape from 'egalitarian affirmative action norms' as well as those middle class, do-it-yourself capitalists who are ready to pay for a week or two of being treated as visiting potentates. Sleeping in a castle or chateau and surrounded by a covey of fawning attendants, are, for more than we may appreciate, a dream realized. (Buck, 1978: 110)

But how can this transformation take place in a contemporary era which obliterates divisions based on class, gender and race? Only by imaginatively reverting to a period where the distinctions between lord and serf were most pronounced, and then by drawing them into the present and future. In such a manner the de-differentiation of post-modern society becomes suspended or bracketed and one begins to live 'as if' it did not exist.

In the case of some Indian hotels (e.g. the Lake Palace at Udaipur, Rambagh Palace at Jaipur and Umaid Bhawan Palace at Jodhpur; cf. Sigman, 1991), such romanticization becomes possible because the establishments either were, or still are, abodes of the maharajahs. In this way these Mogul style pavilions, with their vast marble bathrooms and banqueting halls, can be retained along with the sculptured grounds and retinue of turbaned waiters. All the tourist has to do is to pay the going room rate and then sink into palatial luxury.

More often than not, however, the tourism industry assumes the corporate responsibility for renovating a hotel in the style of its erstwhile glory. Thus the restored Manila Hotel, originally opened in 1912, harks back to the former era by having a 258-page history book and an archives room with memorabilia depicting illustrious guests. At the same time it retains its marble floors, mahogany doors and old fashioned service (Deans, 1990).

The Ritz Carlton (Naples, Florida), on the other hand, emphazises its links with the past by spending $2 million on art and antiques, along with its displayed collection of 200 oil paintings, Persian carpets and nineteenth-century crystal chandeliers. The public rooms are done out like the interiors of London clubs, the lounges have butlers, and tea and scones are offered from a silver service. Reportedly, one guest was so taken in by the gracious old worldliness of the place that he recalled his grandparents' wedding on the premises. Yet the hotel was not opened until 1985 (List, 1990)!

Then there is the case of the legendary Raffles Hotel in Singapore which recently spent more than $100 million on renovations in order to restore as closely as possible the atmosphere and decor of 1915. Today, each of the 104 suites, with oriental throw rugs, wicker furniture and silver ice buckets, is reached through open air courtyards and attended by three bellhops apiece. This former haunt of Somerset Maugham Rudyard Kipling and Noel Coward manages to capture something of its heyday with its turn-of-the century theatre and memento-stuffed museum. Only the prices are different (McArthur, 1992). Interestingly, Raffles, in its promotions, relies almost entirely on its nostalgic links with the past (Dann, 1996a: 200, 225). So too does Disney, whether one is talking about indulging in the romance of the Hotel Queen Mary's first-class staterooms and dancing in a lounge once frequented by celebrities of yore, or, more recently, patronizing its latest resort – The BoardWalk. Promotion of the latter receives the full nostalgia treatment, complete with a sepia-toned photograph of a well-heeled family of days gone by. The headline announces, 'There was a time when the finest of families summered along the boardwalk', followed in bold by, 'At Walt Disney World, that time begins July 1996'. The body copy suitably reinforces the message:

> They flocked to the seaside in crisp summer linens. To soak up the excitement and romance. They came to stroll along the boardwalk. And dream sweet dreams in villas by the water. Now you can experience the charm of that bygone era, combined with the modern day indulgences of a luxury resort. At Disney's BoardWalk. It's as charming as a seaside village. As exciting as those boardwalks of yesteryear. And as magical as the whole Disney experience. With elegant dining and a lively brew pub. Big band dancing and shoreside shopping. Cozy nightclubs and a boisterous sports bar. Side by side in an architectural setting that recalls the romance of a summer at the shore – all year round . . . Come relive the enchantment of yesteryear. Call 1–407-W-DISNEY or your travel agent. And make the dream come true. (Walt Disney, Inc., 1996)

Over in the UK, the Savoy Group of hotels parallels this treatment in a recent double page advertisement. On one side are four icons: the Faience dove at Claridge's (evoking the first visit by Queen Victoria in 1856), a doorhandle from the Berkeley (where Edward courted Mrs Simpson), a chair at the Lygon Arms (in which Cromwell slept on the eve of the Battle of Worcester) and Kaspar the Cat (from the Pinafore Room at the Savoy, where Winston Churchill used to dine regularly). On the other side, a message proclaims:

> The Savoy Group's hotels in London and the countryside have all played an important role in England's history. Generations of famous people have stayed in them. And still do today. We would like you to join us. So as well as the usual sightseeing tour, try ours. WHEN YOU VISIT ENGLAND, DON'T JUST SEE THE SIGHTS, STAY IN THEM.

However in the UK, the epitome of nostalgia is located not so much in an hotel, as in the British manor house set amid such dreamlike places as Bowston-on-the-Water and Stow-on-the-Wold. In one of these stately homes in a nearby county, a Canadian travel writer thus describes his luxurious stay:

> I supped my champagne (G.H. Mumm, Cuvee Rene Lalou, 1982), leaned back in my chaise longue . . . and contemplated the scene. Elegant, but casually elegant, people nibbling at their raspberries and cream – by the side of the outdoor pool . . . Ah yes, that pool. It has a little niche in history.

Narrow your eyes a little and you imagine you see a beautiful auburn-haired girl emerge from it, naked, cavort happily around the deck and run smack into a tall, balding gent in a tuxedo. The girl was Christine Keeler, a sometime model, and the man was John Profumo. And that first meeting at Cliveden in Berkshire . . . set in motion an affair that turned into a scandal that finally toppled the Tory government of Harold Macmillan. But that's a story from the 1960s. This is 1990 and Cliveden is no longer the home of Profumo's friend Lord Astor. Now it's a hotel. But what a Hotel! (Smyth, 1990)

The author then goes on to describe the sixty bedroom, 324-year-old mansion situated in 376 acres, where guests pay £310 a night. For this small sum they are met by a liveried chauffeur in a Rolls-Royce, they enjoy the comforts of a king size bed, an emperor size bathroom and a dictator size drawing room, while all the time surrounded by oil paintings, sculptures and other *objets d'art*. No wonder that at Cliveden one has a butler, whereas in 'a lesser establishment you would call him the hotel manager'.

Here the journey back into the past occurs in two stages. First there is a brief stop at the naughty 1960s, a reflection on the lifestyle of the aristocracy, and how this in turn was embroiled at the highest level of British politics. Afterwards there is the deep plunge into the gracious seventeenth century of the stately home where power and affluence were still as synonymous as they are supposedly rejected at present. The upmarket tourist is permitted to enter this world of the past continuous, while never, of course being able to appropriate it.

2 Sales of the centuries

Safely ensconced in his Berkshire castle, Smyth (1990) is further able to meditate on the temporal transformation of the British countryside; on

> weavers cottages [that] are now weekend retreats for London stockbrokers and doctors, barns and stables [that] are now self-catering apartments, the mill that's now a museum, the jail that's an art gallery.

In this connection, MacCannell observes that

> In modern society 'symbols' of the past are collected in museums when they are small enough and when they are too large they are left outside in parks and called 'monuments'. Some, as in the case of the paddle boat, San Francisco's cable cars and large old homes, are restored and kept functioning as 'living reminders' of the past. (1976: 88)

Just as 'almost everywhere and everything from the past may be conserved' (Urry, 1990: 105) so too can it be retained by making it a spectacle, a commodity or a service. Part of this process is museumization, the freezing of heritage and the selling of the frozen product.

In some instances, the content of the package is simply a romantic gaze at a slice of history, whether remote or proximate, as for example in Frannies Teddy Bear Museum, with its sentimental $2 million collection of 1600 furry pieces so evocative of childhood (MacDonald, 1990).

There is also San Antonio's Alamo shrine with relics from the days of Davy Crockett, Jim Bowie and William B. Travis. Nearby, in Ripley's 'Believe it or Not' Museum, sightseers can behold the stuffed remains of the first monkey in space, or even a pair of fleas dressed as bride and groom (*Toronto Star*, 1990).

Sometimes the museum is dedicated to a famous, or better still, infamous person, whose legendary, exploits (exploitation?) permit voyeurs to engage nostalgically in a reactionary political discourse which would otherwise be quite unacceptable if voiced among their liberal peers. The Malacanang Presidential Palace Museum in Manila, for instance, would seem to cater to such a mindset, for here are displayed 1700 pairs of shoes belonging to Imelda Marcos, along with her bullet-proof bra. Yet, in spite of, or even because of, her intimate association with the late dictator of the Philippines, this representative (though arguably inadequate) sample of footwear (symbolizing the downtreader?) manages to attract 500 visitors a week (Bragg, 1991).

On other occasions, the museum becomes an emporium actually retailing nostalgia, thereby allowing the tourist to purchase trophies from the past as 'souvenirs' or memories. The Cumberland General Store in Homestead, Tennessee, for example, has an exclusive collection of artefacts including spittoons, harps, bowler hats, goose quill pens, along with such books as 'Be Your Own Chimney Sweep' or 'Learning to Play the Community Fiddle'. What is so attractive about these memorabilia is that they 'all evoke images of a simpler lifestyle, of the days when people were self-sufficient' (Kroll and Kroll, 1990).

However, perhaps the biggest 'sale of the century' is the Presley business where 'you can't travel 50 miles on any interstate, it seems, without passing an Elvis car museum, an Elvis memorabilia shop, or an "Elvis pelvised here" plaque' (Cohn, 1991). According to CBI TV, the late King's annual worth is $210 million, and, if present trends continue, by 2001 this figure should easily top the one billion dollar mark. At Graceland alone, the family home and grave of the nostalgia monarch (purchased in 1957 for $100,000), there are on average as many an 4000 visitors a day (almost 1.5 million a year) who are fed through the mansion in groups of twenty on a conveyor belt (Cohn, 1991). Certainly, Elvis is financially much better dead than ever he was alive.

By way of partial summary and explanation, Urry observes:

> We have seen a spectacular growth in the number of museums in western
> countries. This is clearly part of the process by which the past has come to
> be much more highly valued in comparison with both the present and the
> future. And the attraction of museums increases as people get older – thus
> the 'greying' of the population in the west is also adding to the number
> and range of museums. (1990: 128)

3 Milking the macabre

It was previously noted that tourists have a particular fascination with
notorious characters, whether these be drawn from the distant or close
past (Dann, 1994c). Nostalgia, it would seem, knows no limits, to the
virtual extent that the worse the experience the more appealing the attraction (cf. Urry, 1990). Hence the success of the Gestapo Prison Museum in Berlin, the Japanese Prisoner of War Museum in Singapore, the
Auschwz visitor centre in Poland, the Inquisition Museum in Lima, Peru,
the sea wall prison in Panama City, Los Angeles' cemetery tour, Palermo's
skeleton filled catacombs and the Bloody Tower in London.

Such celebration of atrocity may, of course, be simply explained in
terms of morbid curiosity, in a similar fashion to the gathering of contemporary ghouls to witness a car crash, a fire, or some other disaster –
the 'thank God it's not me syndrome'. Yet, however valid this interpretation for present day events, it does not appear to account fully for a
fascination with an ignominious past. More likely in this connection is
nostalgia's ability to filter out unpleasant experiences by first of all concentrating upon them, recognizing them as safe and dead (Urry, 1990:
109), and then going on to hanker after what is left. Thus the good old
days of the 1930s somehow manage to omit the depression, the 1940s
war and the 1950s McCarthyism (Davis, 1979: 109, quoting M. Marty),
once the symbols of those eras, along with their monuments and shrines,
have been acknowledged, visited and deleted. At the same time, one
should recognize that the sources of nostalgia are most evident at those
points in the past which pose the greatest threats to continuity and identity (Davis, 1979: 107).

Seen in this light we can begin to appreciate that:

> Every country in the world has its macabre tourist attractions – Madame
> Tussaud's Chamber of Horrors in London, Lizzie Borden of Fall River,
> Mass., who gave her mother forty whacks with an axe, or Salem, also in
> Massachusetts, where witches were burned at the stake. (MacDonald, 1991)

One example, provided by MacDonald (1991), is Jamaica's (in)famous Rose Hall, which manages to attract 100,000 tourists annually. According to Gray (1991), this haunted property has recently been restored to its original grandeur at a cost of $2.5 million. It was the home of one Annie Palmer, an English woman who allegedly murdered her three husbands (successively imprisoning them in their own bedrooms), and thereafter taking countless slave lovers before eventually being slain herself by one of them. After visiting the place and listening to various accounts, Gray reckoned 'it was easy to believe the story that the white witch of Rose Hall, as her neighbours called her, was still on the premises.' Thus, even though he would also have been exposed to the version which found Mrs Palmer to be an upright and respectable lady (MacDonald, 1991), he preferred to go along with the more sensational variant even to the point where he could almost sense her presence. Otherwise, of course Rose Hall would simply have been another Great House, another instance of 'dog does not bite man'.

A second example of touring the terrible can be found in the KGB's infamous Lubyanka headquarters in the heart of Moscow. Here '*post-glasnost*' visitors may now, on twice-weekly three-hour tours, view the windowless cells where prisoners were once tortured, the office of former KGB and Soviet chief Yuri Andropov, suitable references to Kim Philby and George Blake, and all sorts of captured spy paraphernalia, ranging from poison pellets hidden inside eyeglasses to drop boxes disguised as sticks and stones, cameras concealed inside pens and watches, and a stun gun masquerading as a flashlight. When tour guide KGB Lieutenant Valery Vozdvizhinsky is asked about his former colleagues' participation in Stalinist purges, he simply states that they were acting under orders, and when quizzed about Soviet spy hardware, he replies 'I believe such devices are in the museums of our counterparts around the world.' The 300 interrogation chambers have been closed since 1962, but six unused cells remain 'just in case' (McKinsey, 1992).

A third illustration of milking the macabre can be found in Bodie, the remains of a late nineteenth century California gold mining town. According to the publicity pamphlet, Bodie

was second to none for wickedness, badmen and the worst climate out of doors. One little girl whose family was taking her to the remote and infamous town, wrote in her diary, 'Goodbye God, I'm going to Bodie.' The phrase came to be known throughout the west. Killings occurred with monotonous regularity, sometimes becoming almost daily events. The fire bell, which tolled the ages of the deceased when they were buried, rang often and long. Robberies, stage hold-ups, and street fights provided variety, and the town's 65 saloons offered many opportunities for relaxation after hard days of work in the mines. The Reverend F.M. Warrington saw

it in 1881 as a 'sea of sin, lashed by the tempests of lust and passion'.
(California Department of Parks and Recreation, 1988: 3)

Today, thousands of visitors drive on unpaved roads to this remote ghost town. They can walk along Bonanza Street, Maiden Lane and Virgin Alley, and other haunts of the ladies of the night, view the town jail from which a vigilante group extricated and hanged Joseph de Roche, enter the only Protestant church which was heavily vandalized and from which a painting of the ten commandments ('thou shalt not steal') was purloined, and see the remains of the schoolhouse which was burned down by one of its pupils.

But what is so attractive about Bodie and its badmen, which now has a Friends of Bodie Society to ensure its preservation? Perhaps it is nostalgia for the pioneering days of the goldrush era where everyone theoretically had the possibility of getting rich, and for the myth of equality of opportunity which treezes out the seedier side of reality by making a spectacle of it (in much the same way as the nostalgic movies *Bonnie and Clyde* and *Butch Cassidy and the Sundance Kid* had done so successfully before). Seen in this perspective, 'tourism becomes the new gold mine'. As Cernetig (1991) goes on to observe a propos the goldrush of 1896.

There isn't much easy gold in the Klondike field. Today the real pay dirt is the tourists who roll into Lawson. It's the past, not gold or grubstaked miners, that has become the no. 1 industry in Dawson City. 'Nowadays we sell nostalgia,' Dawson Mayor Peter Jenkins says.

4   Where there's muck there's brass

This old Yorkshire saying (with its early nostalgic counterparts in the song 'My Old Man's a Dustman' and the once popular TV show *Steptoe and Son*), suggests that money can be made from junk, discarded refuse, the unclean and unwholesome, something which the tourism industry has realized for decades. Thus, MacCannell (1976: 57) remarks that 'In Paris at the turn of the century, sightseers were given tours of the sewers, the morgue, a slaughterhouse, tobacco factory . . .' all of which could be somehow viewed as 'muck' bringing forth 'brass'. For him functioning establishments, occupations, transportation networks and public works figure prominently as tourist attractions because they represent alienated leisure (MacCannell, 1976: 51–7). Hence the significance of the morgue, where 'This final display of working class stiffs illustrates, as well as any other example, how the display of even a horrible object normalizes it' (MacCannell, 1976: 72).

In Britain, Urry (1990) points to several other instances where money can be made from the industrial past. As examples he gives the Wigan Pier Heritage Centre in Lancashire, Quarry Bank Mill in Cheshire, Black Country World near Dudley, the Birmingham Canal, the Gloucester Docks, the Salford Quays, the Chemical Museum in Widnes, the Living Dock-yard in Chatham, the Pencil Museum in Keswick and the Big Pit in South Wales. Just one of these, the Albert Dock in Liverpool, welcomes as many as 3 million visitors a year. On the drawing board are planned the Rhondda Heritage Park (which will include the Lewis Merthyr Coal-mine), and the Roman Centre (Diva) in Chester, complete with Roman coins and Roman food. According to Urry (1990: 104–7), there are now 464 UK museums displaying industrial material, and matters have even reached the stage where locations such as Bradford, which formerly sent its holidaymakers to Morecombe, have now become major tourist attrac-tions in their own right. Furthermore, such is the business potential of these projects, that now the private sector has taken over in exploiting the various ways of representing history and of commodifying the past. Interestingly also, the proportion of the service class patronizing these centres is about three times that of manual workers (from whom the majority of these ventures originated).

As an explanation for this fascination with the often heroic and back-breaking work of *others*, Urry reckons that it is closely bound up with the postmodern breaking down of boundaries, particularly between the front and backstage of people's lives, or what he terms 'a postmodern museum culture' in which almost anything can become an object of curi-osity for visitors. Coterminously, the process is facilitated by a parallel rapid de-industrialization (especially in the North of England, South Wales and Central Scotland), and hence a sense of loss of 'certain types of technology (steam engines, blast furnaces, pit workings) and of the social life that had developed around those technologies' (Urry, 1990: 107). Clearly, a rosy future lies ahead for 'factory tourism', and plants produc-ing cars, planes, processed food, submarines, etc., can all be opened up for public gaze. At present, the English Tourist Board calculates that up to 6 million people visit a factory each year, and this figure will soon reach 10 million. In becoming an object of sightseeing, the factory has been museumized (Urry, 1990: 131–2).

Finally, it should be noted that the French equivalent connecting 'muck' with 'brass' is termed 'nostalgie de la boue'. Literally, this 'nostalgia for mud' is a broader concept than the English expression since it is said to reside in an ambivalent attraction for all that is vulgar (i.e. American). Thus Monaco's casinos and real estate surrender to the crowd pullers of glamour, glitz and gossip, initially imported by Princess Grace (Theobald, 1992: 76).

Discussion

> As the end of a century and, perhaps even more important, a millennium, approach, academic interest as well as popular curiosity appear to be increasingly preoccupied with rediscovery and reassessment of the past. (Buck, 1979: 2)

This brief overview has highlighted four areas where the tourism industry has successfully employed nostalgia to its own financial advantage. Now is the time to examine the mechanics of the operation. In the first place, it should be noted that nostalgia is not simply an antiquarian feeling, or mindless yearning. Rather it is 'a positively toned evocation of a lived past in the context of some negative feeling toward present or impending circumstance' (Davis, 1979: 18). In other words, nostalgia relates to and is rounded in dissatisfaction with current social arrangements and concern over their continuation into the future. It is therefore to be expected, rather than anomalous, that tourism's largest shrines to nostalgia, Disney World and Disneyland, are located in two of the most future-oriented states of the union (Davis, 1979: 119–21) and that EuroDisney has recently opened close to one of that continent's most progressive capitals. As Urry observes:

> Indeed the way in which all sorts of places have become centres of spectacle and display and the nostalgic attraction of 'heritage' can both be seen an elements of the postmodern. (1991: 93–4)

Alternatively stated, remote Third World villagers living for generations in one place would be baffled by nostalgia. It is the dislocated Western traveller of today who experiences nostalgia to its fullest, and who, incidentally, travels precisely on account of such disorientation (cf. Davis, 1979: 50). Thus 'a daily allowance of nostalgia can be a tonic to the ills of the here and now' (Schoemer 1992: 59).

The second point to note is that the way the past is promoted by tourism, like the discourse of all other form of advertising:

> knows no present, and only speaks of the future with reference to the past. This allows viewers and readers to project themselves into new situations which often permit the carrying of personality equipment and nostalgia rewarding experiences into the future. (Dann, 1996b: 69)

Hence, tourism publicity which is based on nostalgic images has to sell the past to the future (Berger, 1983: 139). In so doing, it promotes glamour and happiness (rather than pleasure); it provides something enviable; it steals love of self and offers it back to the client to be consumed (Berger, 1983: 132).

Third, the evocation of the past as a promise to the future, contains elements which lead to that future. They are drawn out of time into an eternal moment where both time and space become incorporated into the structure of myth. The promotion therefore takes the present out of real time and replaces it with the metaphysical time of the advertisement, and history becomes appropriated by memory or projection, in order that consumers can fill the void by identifying themselves with the product (Williamson, 1983: 152–5). Thus the hazy nostalgic picture of the brochure creates an aura of the collective past which we are called upon to remember, and to which by future action we can become transported in one magical moment (Williamson, 1983: 156–60). McLuhan was therefore surely correct when he relatedly observed that in this way the media can travel into the future with one eye cocked on the rearview mirror (Davis, 1979: 135).

Fourth, it should be remembered that nostalgia is a selective recall of the past (cf. Davis, 1979; Lowenthal, 1993). In recalling the 'nice times' we conveniently overlook negative situations. The tourism industry follows a similar pattern when it promotes locations and experiences and events of yesteryear as attractions of today and tomorrow. Thus plantation houses, for instance, once horrific scenes of the disease, lack of hygiene, squalor and torture associated with slavery, are portrayed instead as symbols of genteel living associated with the colonial plantocracy, and then projected as part of a Third World nation's glorious patrimony to be enjoyed by tourists. Similarly, in developed countries, images of aristocratic raffishness (as in Brighton, England, for example), can be translated by the tourism industry into townscapes and landscapes decked out with the accoutrements of an *imagined* bygone era for postmodern consumption. Hence, Brighton, with its Royal Pavilion retailing Victorian jewellery and Regency preserves, its maypole dancing, its medieval mystery plays, and its lanes replete with antique shops and cast iron black and gold furnishings, is now projected as an international centre once patronized by royalty, but enjoyable today via conspicuous middle class consumption. Yet behind the facade, the reality of the situation is that Brighton is still a place of rock, dodgem cars, candy floss, naughty postcards and dirty weekends. In fact, it is one of the most depressed areas in the whole of Britain, and is highly dependent on an urban aid programme (Meethan, 1996).

Fifth, the main reason why nostalgia operates so successfully in tourism is that it manages the unfamiliarity of a strange environment by giving us the impression that we have been there before. Novelist Stephen King (1986: 434–5) captures the phenomenon when he writes:

The force of memory almost dizzied him for a moment when he stepped into the mild light of the hanging glass globes. The force was not physical – not like a shot to the jaw or a slap. It was more akin to that queer feeling of time doubling back on itself that people call, for want of a better term, *deja vu*. Ben had had the feeling before but it had never struck him with such disorienting power; for a moment or two he stood inside the door, he felt literally lost in time, not really sure how old he was. Was he thirty-eight or eleven?

Seen in the light of the foregoing points, the ancient and glamorous hotel of yesterday becomes the 'old green grass of home' of tomorrow. The associated lifestyles of the rich and famous become envied and enviable, only satiated (we are led to believe) when we become those regal occupants disdainfully looking out of the picture at our longing and hopeless admirers. Museums and emporia are now no longer viewed simply as showcases containing trophies of a bygone era. They are to be entered and possessed and their booty is to be paraded as a symbol of the good life ahead. Even the macabre world of Robbie Burns' 'ghoulies and ghosties and long-ledgedy beasties' becomes attractive to the extent that it replaces the monotony and alienation of the present with an exciting future agenda drawn from the past. Murder and mayhem, the wildness of the wicked west, hangmen and other horrors, become forthcoming heroes whose exploits symbolically reverse present day justice towards favouring the mythical underdog. Finally, the lure of the beachcomber, the satanic mills and the grease and grime of yesteryear point us in a counter direction to the clinical clean and green of today. After all, and in spite of the rhetoric of ecotourism, the natural after which we hanker is often warm and earthy.

Through the calligraphy and iconography of tourism promotional literature, the holiday is thus transformed into its original meaning (a holy day in which we venerate the past), a vacation becomes a rest from and a suspension of the present, and a trip – well, a trip is a trip down memory lane and a voyage into the well-charted waters of the future.

References

Berger, J. (1983) *Ways of Seeing*, British Broadcasting Corporation and Penguin, London and Harmondsworth

Bragg, R. (1991) Strange encounters and weird stories around the world. *Toronto Star*, 9 November

British Tourist Authority (1993) Advertisement, *Gourmet*, 10–11 May

Buck, R. (1978) Toward a synthesis in tourism theory, *Annals of Tourism Research*, **5**, 110–11

Buck, R. (1979) Bloodless theatre: images of the old order Amish in tourism literature, *Pennsylvania Mennonite Heritage*, **2**(3), 2–11

California Department of Parks and Recreation (1988) *Bodie State Historic Park*

Cernetig, M. (1991) Tourism becomes a new gold mine, *Globe and Mail*, 3 July

Cohn, N. (1991) Two for the show, *Sunday Times*, 24 March

Coutts Heritage Print and Design (1981) *England and Wales Heritage Colour Pictorial Map*, L.J. Young, Blarney

Dann, G. (1994a) Tourism and nostalgia: looking forward to going back, *Vrijetijd en Samenleving*, **12**(1/2), 75–94

Dann, G. (1994b) Travel by train: keeping nostalgia on track. In *Tourism. The State of the Art*, (ed. A. Seaton, *et al.*) Wiley, Chichester, pp. 775–82

Dann, G. (1994c) Hyping the destination image through the rich and (in)famous: the boundaries of name dropping, *Cahiers du Tourisme*, serie C, no. 187

Dann, G. (1996a) *The Language of Tourism. A Sociolinguistic Perspective*, CAB International, Wallingford

Dann, G. (1996b) The people of tourist brochures. In *The Tourist Image. Myths and Myth Making in Tourism* (ed. T. Selwyn), Wiley, Chichester, pp. 61–81

Dann, G. (1997) The green green grass of home: nature and nurture in rural England. In *Tourism Sustainability and Growth* (ed. J. Pigram and S. Wahab), Routledge, London

Davis, F. (1979) *Yearning for Yesterday. A Sociology of Nostalgia*, Free Press, New York

Davis, W. (1992) History at work, *High Life*, May, 20–9

Deans, B. (1990) Manila Hotel a 'mirror to passing generations', *Globe and Mail*, 20 October

Gottlieb, A. (1982) Americans' vacations, *Annals of Tourism Research*, **9**, 165–87

Gray, B. (1991) Jamaica: for mature audiences. *Globe and Mail*, 9 November

King, S. (1986) *It*. Hodder and Stoughton, London

Kroll, B. and Kroll, R. (1990) Tennessee store practical fun, *Toronto Star*, 3 November

List, W. (1990) Putting on the Ritz, *Globe and Mail*, 24 November

Lowenthal, D. (1993) *The Past is a Foreign Country*, Cambridge University Press Cambridge, p. 4

McArthur, D. (1992) Raffles Hotel reborn, *Globe and Mail*, 18 January

MacCannell, D. (1976) *The Tourist. A New Theory of the Leisure Class*, Macmillan, London

MacDonald, J. (1990) Travel trends, *Toronto Star*, 17 November

MacDonald, J. (1991) Jamaica's white witch certainly was no lady, *Toronto Star*, 2 November

McKinsey, K. (1992) KGB open to tourists in the 'new' Moscow, *Toronto Star*, 8 February

Meethan, K. (1996) Place, image and power: Brighton as a resort. In *The Tourist Image. Myths and Myth Making in Tourism* (ed. T. Selwyn), Wiley, Chichester, pp. l79–96

Morley, S. (1972) There's no business like old business, *Punch*, 29 November, p. 777

Savoy Group (1996) Advertisement, *Conde Nast Traveler*, April, 14–15

Schoemer, K. (1992) Thoroughly modern madrigals, *Mademoiselle*, February, 59–60

Sigman, D. (1991) Exploring the splendour of the Rajahs, *Globe and Mail*, 16 November

Smyth, M. (1990) Away from it all, *Toronto Star*, 27 October

Theobald, S. (1992) Fractured fairy tale – the real lives of Princesses Caroline and Stephanie, *Mademoiseile*, October, 68–76

Toronto Star (1990) San Antonio offers a multi-faceted experience, Discover USA Winter Sun, advertising feature section, 22 November

Urry, J. (1990) *The Tourist Gaze*, Sage, London

Walt Disney Inc. (1991) Hotel Queen Mary, *San Francisco Examiner*, 14 July

Walt Disney Inc. (1996) Advertisement, *Conde Nast Traveler*, April, p. 99

Williamson, J. (1983) *Decoding Advertisements. Ideology and Meaning in Advertising*, Marion Boyars, London

Acknowledgement

Gratitude is expressed to Paul and Doh Wilkinson of Toronto, whose conscientious clippings from the Canadian press supplied much of the material on which this chapter in based.

4 Tourism and world peace

Turgut Var and John Ap

I have watched the cultures of all lands blow around my house and other
winds have blown the seeds of peace, for travel is the language of peace.

Mahatma Gandhi

Introduction

Among the positive benefits attributed to the social and cultural impacts
of tourism are the promotion of goodwill, understanding and peace between people of different nations (Gartner, 1996; McIntosh, Goeldner,
and Ritchie, 1995; Pearce, 1991; D'Amore, 1988; D'Amore and Jafari, 1988;
International Union of Tourist Organizations, 1974; World Tourist Organization, 1980). The role of tourism as an ambassador and a vehicle of
international understanding and peace has been recognized by international bodies such as the United Nations. In 1980, the World Tourism
Conference in Manila declared that 'world tourism can be a vital force
for world peace'. Recognition of the role and importance of the development of world peace through tourism was declared through the 'Columbia Charter', which was prepared at the First Global Conference: Tourism
– A Vital Force for Peace, held at Vancouver in 1988. The conference
provided a forum for examining tourism and its many dimensions as
a force of peace. According to McIntosh, Goeldner and Ritchie (1995),
the conference brought recognition that tourism has the potential to be
the largest peace-time movement in the history of humankind because
tourism involves people: their culture, economy, traditions, heritage, and
religion. Tourism provides the contacts that makes understanding possible among peoples and cultures.

Many world leaders and statesmen have also recognized this benefit
and attribute of tourism. Famous Christian theologian and philosopher
St Augustine of Hippo (AD 354–430) mentioned that the world was a
great book, of which they who never stir from home read only a page
(McIntosh, Goeldner, and Ritchie 1995). Similarly, the late US President

John F. Kennedy (1963) called attention to the world significance of tourism and stated that:

> Travel has become one of the great forces for peace and understanding in our time. As people move throughout the world and learn to know each other, to understand each other's customs and to appreciate the qualities of the individuals of each nation, we are building a level of international understanding which can sharply improve the atmosphere for world peace.

While there is general recognition of the contribution of tourism towards world peace, there has been very little research on this subject. In the limited studies that have been conducted, researchers have suggested that tourism helps promote mutual understanding and therefore, peace (Rovelstad, 1988). In another study it was found that one of the primary motivations for overseas travel by Americans was to learn more about the people and culture in foreign countries (Skidmore and Pyszka, 1988). Such motivation provides a conducive setting to developing harmonious relations and peace. However, the real question – Does tourism enhance peace? – has not yet been answered nor demonstrated through empirical research. World peace is an intangible attribute, and its impact resulting from tourism is a difficult concept to measure. While it is generally recognized that peace is a pre-condition for tourism, some have suggested that the relationship between tourism and peace is tenuous. For example, it has been stated that:

> The universal desire for peace and the desire to see tourism as an avenue for cross-cultural understanding which is a prerequisite to such goals, have long been expressed. Unfortunately, such expressions of desire and hope have never been actually pursued beyond ritual occasions . . . Thus, at this stage, 'Tourism as a vital force for peace', remains at best a futuristic statement. (Din, 1988)

A similar sentiment was expressed by Barlow (1988), who stated that 'tourism has a long way to go before it is universally accepted as a force that helps mankind reach a state of peace and harmony'. However, if the tourism industry and its supporters are to maintain its credibility and continue to espouse world peace as a positive attribute of tourism, attempts to measure its impact and verify the relationship between tourism and peace are necessary. This raises a serious question – is the promotion of world peace a realistic attribute of tourism, or is it a mere platitude?

The purpose of this chapter is: (1) to examine the relationship between tourism and world peace, and (2) to discuss the findings and implications of a cross-national study on this issue.

Defining and measuring peace in the tourism context

According to the Webster's dictionary, peace is defined as:

> 1. a state of tranquillity or quiet: as (a) freedom from disturbance (b) a state of security or order within a community provided for by the law and customs. 2. freedom from disquieting or oppressive thoughts or emotions. 3. harmony in personal relations. 4. a pact or agreement to end hostilities between those who have been at war or in a state of enmity.

This definition highlights the diverse nature and concept of peace. Within the context of tourism, peace applies to the concept of harmonious relations. Despite existence of this definitional concept of peace, the majority of research and literature on peace has focused upon its concept as the absence of war (Boulding, 1978; Newcombe, 1984). Peace is more than the absence of war, and consideration of peace as a positive concept within the context of tourism, it is believed, will lead to a better understanding of the meaning of peace.

This role of tourism and peace can be viewed from two perspectives, namely, socio-cultural and political. A typical socio-cultural perspective is embodied in comments such as:

> ... tourism has been recognized to be an instrument of social and cultural understanding by the opportunity offered to bring different people in contact and to provide facilities for acquisition and exchange of information about the way of life, cultures, language and other social and economic endowments of the people as well as a chance for making friendships and achieving goodwill. (Kaul, 1985)

The socio-cultural perspective is the predominant viewpoint which has been advocated. It focuses upon tourism as a cultural ambassador and the fact that tourism provides an opportunity for people to understand each other's customs and to exchange information and ideas. The oft-cited increase in worldwide understanding resulting from international tourism, according to Pearce (1991), is perhaps exaggerated, given the nature and duration of tourist–host contact, but what information there is available suggests that tourism has a positive effect in this domain (Giourgas, 1985). Survey research in the European Community, for instance, indicates that attitudes towards the unification of Europe are stronger amongst those who have travelled, especially those visiting several countries (Pearce, 1991). However, an absence of research on this aspect of tourism was acknowledged by one author who commented that:

Empirical description and insightful analyses of various combinations of these situational pressures and cultural norms are greatly needed to increase our knowledge of social relationships and to determine what steps could be taken to increase the likelihood that touring will, indeed, contribute to understanding and comity among nations. (Sutton, 1967)

Even after three decades, this call for 'empirical descriptions and insightful analysis . . . that touring will indeed contribute to understanding and comity among nations' has virtually gone unheeded. The fact that there has been very little research is no doubt attributed to the intangibility and subjective nature of peace.

The political perspective on tourism and world peace focuses upon tourism as a promoter of national integration and international understanding, goodwill and peace (Kaul, 1985; Matthews, 1979). This perspective acknowledges the importance of tourism as a means of establishing and improving political relations with other countries. An example that illustrates this point well was evidenced by the manner in which the People's Republic of China opened its doors to the Western world in the 1970s. Tourism has been an important avenue by which the People's Republic of China has established links with other countries. Furthermore, it has been pointed out that, 'Political stability, improved relations between nations and international peace accelerate travel and tourism. World travel is a fundamental expression of international cooperation' (Kaul, 1985).

Three levels of international relations that are generated by world tourism have been identified (Matthews, 1979). First, at the non-governmental level private citizens of different nations come into contact with and experience cultures different from their own: 'A kind of private international relations develop: [which] can, of course, be altered by government action' (Matthews, 1979: 91). Second, there is a public level of international relations which relates to government-to-government dealings on matters essential to the industry; for example, agreements on air transport, immigration and custom procedures and double taxation treaties. Finally, there is a corporate sector–government level of international relations where tourism is found in the interaction of national government with private foreign investment. Examples of these relations include airlines, banks, hotels and tour operators.

When examining the perceptions of individuals towards tourism and world peace it is the first level – 'private' international relations – that is suggested as the appropriate means for examining this relationship. Critics may argue that it is incongruous to seek individual perceptions of a 'group' concept such as peace. In other words, peace is viewed as a condition that applies to groups, not individuals. Hence, it is not practical to attempt to measure accurately individual responses to a group condition. However, this argument is based upon the concept of peace as the absence of war or hostilities in which group action is generally involved. Consideration of the individual's perception on tourism and peace is based upon the positive concept of peace as a harmonious relationship. This may occur at an individual-to-individual or group level, or at any of the other two levels of international relations which have been identified. There has been very little research conducted on the positive social, cultural and political impacts of tourism and its role in contributing to world peace. Research conducted by Mings (1988) in Barbados is quite interesting since he found little evidence that international tourism obstructed international understanding in that Caribbean country. Fears that 'ugly American' tourists may be spreading ill will and generating international misunderstanding everywhere were not consistent with the findings of his study.

Dann (1988) describes some of the classic arguments against tourism as a form new imperialism and capitalist exploitation, and as promoter of master/servant relationships. He countered each argument against tourism with equally compelling evidence supporting tourism as a means of promoting understanding and social as well as economic exchange. Although no substantial evidence exists to support the statement that tourism is a force for peace, it is clear that peace is not attainable without tourism (Gartner, 1996).

More research does, however, exist on the negative social and cultural aspects of tourism (Chesney-Lind and Lind, 1986; Farrell, 1982; Mathieson and Wall, 1982; O'Grady, 1982) which challenged the validity of the time-honoured belief that tourism promotes understanding between people of different nationalities. Despite this attention on the negative impacts of tourism it has been suggested that tourism can bring understanding and prosperity if it is properly planned, organized and managed (Bloomstrom et al., 1978; deKadt, 1979). People-to-people interaction is necessary for understanding and discovery of common ground, and tourism provides the stage for such social exchange to occur (Gartner, 1996).

The literature on the perceived impacts of tourism forms a basis upon which to develop measures to identify the relationship between tourism and world peace. Knowledge of people's perceptions must be investigated in order to ascertain whether there are any variables that may enable a better description of this relationship. In support of such an approach, some researchers have indicated that cross-national comparisons appear to be useful in identifying common parameters and establishing norms in terms of perceptual differences in the attitudes of people (Liu et al., 1987; Korzay et al., 1997).

One of the positive social impacts perceived by host populations which relates to world peace is that tourism promotes understanding of different people through cultural exchanges. Two studies provided empirical data which indicated that 50 per cent or more of those interviewed agreed that tourism brought positive benefits through cultural exchange (Belisle and Hoy, 1980; Liu et al., 1987). Through cultural exchange an understanding and appreciation of people from different cultures may be obtained, and, in so doing, may remove misconceptions or prejudices between residents and tourists. In a study of American international travellers it was found that the principal motivation for international travel was to be exposed to another culture and thus learn about other people and other cultures (Skidmore and Pyszka, 1988). But, in another study on mass tourists from Japan visiting Singapore, it was found that stereotypic images may in fact be reinforced rather than reduced (Hassan, 1975). Nevertheless, findings from most studies offer support as to the role of tourism in breaking down cultural barriers.

In the development of measures to quantify the contribution of tourism toward world peace, it has been advocated that: '[we] think in terms of a positive definition of peace' (D'Amore, 1988). In following this line of thought two related aspects of tourism come to mind. One is the promotion of cultural exchange as a means of breaking down the barriers between peoples of different nations. The other is the development of greater understanding between individuals or people of different nations resulting form this exchange. It is suggested that these two aspects of tourism are necessary conditions that enable peace to exist and flourish. Thus, they can be used as variables to quantify the relationship between tourism and peace.

Findings of a cross-national study on tourism and world peace

In an exploratory attempt to examine the relationship between tourism and world peace, a cross-national study was conducted in six countries (Australia, Canada, England, Korea, Turkey and United States of America). Details of the study will not be reported here and can be found elsewhere (Var et al., 1988). Rather, attention is primarily focused upon the main findings and their implications.

Background

A college/university student sample was used in this study because students are at a stage of life where there is a greater propensity for travel and convenience for administration of the survey. A total of 1064 responses were obtained and the demographic characteristics of this sample appear representative of a student population (that is, predominantly in the 20–24 years age group and of single marital status). Moreover, within the past five years nearly 60 per cent had travelled to a foreign country with an average of 2.6 countries being visited.

A two-part questionnaire was devised for the study. The first part consisted of fifteen statements, each representing a variable relating to an impact of tourism, including peace. The three statements used to measure the peace variables were, 'I believe that tourism promotes cultural exchange', 'I believe that tourism brings greater understanding of people from different cultures' and 'I believe that tourism promotes world peace'. Respondents were asked to check their response to each statement on a scale that ranged from one (strongly agree) to five (strongly disagree).

The second part of the questionnaire sought classification information from the respondent. Classification of respondents was made with respect to six variables: (1) formal training or education in the tourist industry; (2) work experience in the tourist industry; (3) ethnic background; (4) bilingualism; (5) existence of relatives in a foreign country; and (6) have visited a foreign country. Differences in perceptions were postulated between those who possessed an attribute and those who did not. For the first two variables it was expected that the greater the knowledge of work experience, the greater the appreciation and awareness of the role of tourism in promoting world peace. Thus, it was suggested respectively that those with formal training in the tourist industry had a more positive perception of tourism and world peace than those who do not.

Differences in perceptions were also postulated on the basis of ethnicity and related attributes. The ethnic background of the respondent, their ability to speak a second language and existence of relatives in a foreign country were independent variables which were also included for measurement. Generally speaking those who were ethnically different from the dominant racial group of the country they live in, were likely to have some close affinity and relationship to their ethnic origins. This affinity was often maintained through use of the respondent's native tongue in the home situation and close contact with relatives who remained in the native homeland. Thus it was considered that minority ethnic groups had a greater awareness and understanding of different cultures and therefore were more appreciative of the positive role of tourism in developing that understanding. Accordingly, it was also considered that those who come from a different ethnic background than the dominant ethnic group in the country had a more positive perception of tourism and world peace than those who did not; those who spoke a second language had a more positive perception of tourism and world peace than those who do not; and those who had relatives in a foreign country had a more positive perception of tourism and world peace than those who do not.

It has been often quoted that travel brings greater understanding between peoples of different nations. To test this idea, respondents were asked if they had visited a foreign country. As a result of this travel experience one would expect that respondents would develop a better awareness and understanding of the country visited and its people. Therefore, they should have a greater appreciation of the role of tourism in promoting world peace. Hence, those who had visited a foreign country should have a more positive perception of tourism and world peace than those who have not.

Main findings

Overall perceptions toward tourism

Responses to the fifteen tourism statements are presented in Table 4.1. Strongest support was shown for the economic and peace variables where, in the majority of cases, agreement was indicated by over 80 per cent of respondents. For a number of responses to some of the statements, a neutral position was selected. Such responses pertained primarily to the environmental and awareness variables. The environmental factors and the exploitation of worker groups variable are generally considered to be sensitive issues, and the large block of respondents (ranging from 20 to 34 per cent) who chose the neutral response was not surprising. A high neutral response (33 per cent) was selected for the world peace variable, which indicated a degree of uncertainty for some respondents. Based on the mean score responses, respondents generally viewed tourism as contributing positively to economic development and peace.

In order to determine how valid the three variables used to describe the peace construct were, the results were analysed by a statistical technique, factor analysis. No significant results were found to confirm the validity of this construct.* However, the positive influence of tourism upon the economy was confirmed. Thus, the variables used for the economic construct were validated and therefore, tourism may be viewed primarily as an economic activity that has positive impacts.

Perceptions towards tourism and peace by nation

Figure 4.1 presents the mean scores to the peace variables for each nation and it shows that cross-national differences do exist for the variables indicated. When examining the cross-national differences from a statistical viewpoint it was found that the differences were not very strong. This means that the variables used may serve as common parameters in measuring this impact of tourism.

---

* For those statistically minded, the eigenvalue for the three variables used to interpret the peace factor was 0.55. This falls well short of the accepted cut off of 1.0 for a factor to be considered significant.

Table 4.1   Combined responses to statements

Statement: I believe that tourism . . .	Agree	Neutral	Disagree	Mean scores*
Economic				
1 Contributes to national economy	85	11	4	1.9
2 Contributes to economic growth	88	10	2	1.8
3 Promotes infrastructure development	80	16	4	2.0
4 Creates employment opportunities	92	6	2	1.7
5 Exploits certain 'worker' groups	23	34	43	3.2
Environmental				
6 Conserves natural and historic environments	58	23	19	2.5
7 Preserves social and cultural environments	51	30	19	2.6
8 Leads to deterioration of environment	25	32	43	3.2
9 Disrupts small communities and towns	38	27	35	2.9
Peace				
10 Promotes cultural exchange	84	12	4	2.0
11 Promotes cross-cultural understanding	80	13	7	2.0
12 Promotes world peace	53	33	14	2.5
Awareness				
13 Benefits outweigh costs	61	30	9	2.4
14 Public unaware of benefits	54	25	21	2.6
15 Greater awareness needed	77	20	3	2.0

* 1 = strongly agree, 5 = strongly disagree.
N = 1064.

In general, it was found that those respondents educated and trained in tourism, those with work experience in the tourist industry, those who speak at least two languages, and those who have visited a foreign country had a more positive perception of tourism.

The world peace variable 'I believe that tourism promotes world peace' showed the most number (4) of statistically significant differences. More specifically, (a) those with formal training in the tourist industry had a more positive and different perception of tourism and world peace than

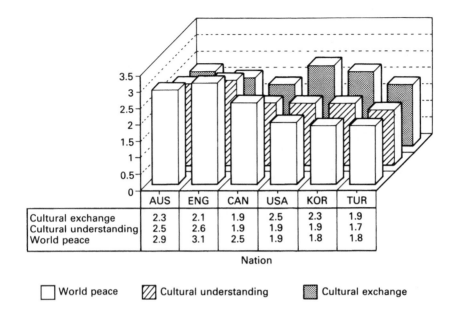

	AUS	ENG	CAN	USA	KOR	TUR
Cultural exchange	2.3	2.1	1.9	2.5	2.3	1.9
Cultural understanding	2.5	2.6	1.9	1.9	1.9	1.7
World peace	2.9	3.1	2.5	1.9	1.8	1.8

Nation

☐ World peace ▨ Cultural understanding ▧ Cultural exchange

Figure 4.1 Mean scores on peace construct by nation
(1 = strongly agree, 5 = strongly disagree)

those who did not have formal training; (b) those with work experience in the tourist industry had a more positive and different perception of tourism and world peace than those who had not worked in the tourist industry; (c) those who spoke at least two languages had a more positive and different perception of tourism and world peace than those who spoke only one language; and (d) those who had visited a foreign country had a less positive and different perception of tourism and world peace than those who had not visited a foreign country. This latter finding ran contrary to the original postulation that foreign travel experience would lead to a more positive perception between tourism and world peace. Ethnicity and existence of relatives in a foreign country did not figure at all as being indicators with significant differences.

Discussion

The results of this exploratory study revealed that tourism is viewed as contributing positively to economic development and peace. The strength of that positive contribution of tourism was higher for economic aspects than for peace aspects. This was further confirmed by a statistical analysis of the results (through factor analysis) where the variables comprising economic factors were found to be significant in terms of their validity. However, the peace construct variables did not produce a significant result which indicated that the validity of the variables, being representative of peace, could not be verified. These findings suggest that the role of tourism as a contributor to peace is tenuous at best, and may not figure as prominently in the perceptions of respondents as commonly thought by tourism advocates.

More investigation into the specific social and cultural attributes of tourism are necessary in order to quantify it as a common parameter and to justify peace as an attribute of tourism. While two of the variables of the peace construct, the promotion of cultural exchange and contribution to cross-cultural understanding, indicated a relatively high level of agreement, the world peace variable showed a high degree of uncertainty with one-third of respondents providing a neutral response. This uncertainty probably arose from a definitional problem with the term 'peace'. No definition of peace was indicated on the questionnaire in order to prevent bias with the survey instrument. Many respondents may have associated peace as an 'absence of war'. The preferred concept which would be most appropriate in the context of this study is that of 'harmony and harmonious relations'. Refinement in measurement of this variable will be necessary and it is suggested that all the related concepts and meanings of the particular attribute need to be tested in the future.

Instead of having a more positive perception of tourism and world peace, respondents who had recently visited a foreign country had a more negative perception than those who had not visited a foreign country. This result concerning perceptions of respondents with foreign travel experience lends support to the finding in a previously mentioned study that tourism, particularly mass tourism, seldom generates strong intercultural relationships and reinforces stereotypic images between peoples of different nations (Hassan, 1975). The findings of both the Singapore study and this investigation suggest that, contrary to popular belief, tourism may not enhance peace and cultural understanding. It has been indicated that the quality of communications between hosts and tourists possibly plays an important yet unknown influence upon the nature of cultural exchange and understanding which result (Mathieson and Wall, 1982). Thus, if intercultural communication is limited and the tourist has a bad experience in a foreign country, it is likely to reinforce a negative image of the role of tourism. Another possible explanation may be found from the results of a study of international travellers, where it was noted that the degree of intercultural communication may also depend upon the motivations of the traveller (Fisher and Price, 1989). Evidence here suggests that intercultural communication for travellers seeking new cultural and educational experiences is different from those travellers who seek primarily rest and relaxation. Responses could also depend upon the respondent's role as a tourist, that is, as a mass tourist, individual mass tourist, explorer, or drifter (Cohen, 1972). Further research on foreign travel experience upon the perceptions of travellers is required in order to develop a better understanding of its influence. Areas of investigation should examine the influence of intercultural communication, the degree of contact with the host population and the nature of the travel experience (especially mass versus individual and do-it-yourself tourism) upon cultural exchange and understanding.

The results indicate that education and work experience in the tourist industry, and the ability to speak at least a second language provides a greater awareness and appreciation of tourism and its role. Implications for the industry are that if it is to promote and espouse the social and cultural attributes of tourism, it must generate a greater level of awareness of the impacts and contribution of tourism upon society. Programmes also need to be developed to improve the nature of cross-cultural exchange and understanding between hosts and tourists. Responsibility rests not only upon local tourism officials in the host community, but also on the intermediaries such as travel agents to provide more detailed information to prospective clients about the host culture and how to enhance experiences between themselves and the local population. The tourism industry cannot rest on its laurels and rely only on platitudes in order to legitimize its role in society.

Conclusion

Doubts about the claim that tourism engenders and promotes peace have been raised. For example, Brown (1989) stated, 'The idea that tourism can promote peace is indeed a noble, as well as fashionable one – but does it work?' Other questions about the tourism and peace relationship which must be addressed are: Does tourism expand because a condition of peace exists, or, as it has been assumed, does tourism enhance peace? These continue to be perplexing questions, indeed. However, so long as advocates of tourism espouse world peace as an attribute of tourism, this claim needs to be approached cautiously and further research is necessary to justify it. Otherwise, it remains simply a platitude.

References

Barlow, M. (1988) Tourism, peace, and conflict: a geographer's perspective. In *Tourism – a Vital Force for Peace* (ed. L. D'Amore and J. Jafari), Color Art Inc., Montreal, Canada, p. 108

Belisle, F. and Hoy, D. (1980) The perceived impacts of tourism by residents – a case study in Santa Marta, Columbia, *Annals of Tourism Research*, **VII**(1), 83–101

Bloomstrom, R., McIntosh, W. and Christie-Mill, R. (1978) The positive side of tourism development: principles for identifying and developing the cultural resource potential, *Journal of the Mugla School of Business Administration* (Special Issue, International Tourism Congress: 'New Perspectives and Policies', Turkey)

Boulding, K. (1978) *Stable Peace*, University of Texas Press

Brown, F. (1989) Is tourism really a peacemaker? *Tourism Management*, **10**(4), 270–1

Chesney-Lind, M. and Lind, I. (1986) Visitors as victims: crimes against tourists in Hawaii, *Annals of Tourism Research*, **XIII**(2), 167–91

Cohen, E. (1972) Toward a sociology of international tourism, *Social Research*, **39**(1) (Spring)

D'Amore, L.J. (1988) Tourism – the world's peace industry, *Journal of Travel Research*, **27**(1), 35–40

D'Amore, L. and Jafari, J. (eds) (1988) *Tourism – A Vital Force for Peace*, Color Art Inc, Montreal, Canada

Dann, G. (1988) Tourism, Peace, and Classical Disputation. In *Tourism – A Vital Force for Peace*, (ed. L. D'Amore and J. Jafari), Color Art Inc., Montreal, Canada

deKadt, E. (1979) Social planning for tourism in the developing countries, *Annals of Tourism Research*, **VI**(1), 36–48

Din, K. (1988) Toursim and peace: desires and attainability. In *Tourism – a Vital Force for Peace* (ed. L. D'Amore and J. Jafari), Color Art Inc., Montreal, Canada, p. 80

Farrell, B. (1982) *Hawaii: The Legend that Sells*, University Press of Hawaii

Fisher, R. and Price, L. (1989) The relationship between international travel motivations and post-cultural attitude change. Faculty working paper, College of Business Administration, University of Colorado, Boulder, Colorado

Gartner, William C. (1996) *Tourism Development, Principles, Processes, and Policies*, Van Nostrand Reinhold, New York, pp. 176–177

Giourgas, G. (1985) Profil des vogageurs European et leur attitides vis-a-vis unification de l'Europe. In *Tourisme et Integration Europeene* (ed. E. Cerexhe and G. Giuorgas) Ciaso, Brussels pp. 39–67

Hassan, R. (1975) International tourism and intercultural communication, *Southeast Asian Journal of Social Sciences*, **3**(2), 25–37

International Union of Tourist Organizations (IUOTO) (1974) Tourism – its nature and significance, *Annals of Tourism Research*, **1**(4), 105–12

Kaul, R.N. (1985) *Dynamics of Tourism*, vol. 1 *The Phenomenon*, Sterling Publishing Co., New Delhi, pp. 5, 51

Kennedy, John F. (1963) *The Saturday Review*, 5 January. Cited in Sutton (1967), p. 223

Korzay, Meral, Var, Turgut and Anastasapoullos, Peter G. (1997) Influence of Tourism on Attitude Change: Turkish and Greek Tourists, Unpublished research paper.

Liu, J., Sheldon, T. and Var, T. (1987) Resident perception of the environmental impacts of tourism, *Annals of Tourism Research*, **14**(1), 17–37

McKintosh, Robert W. Goeldner, Charles R., and Ritchie, Brent J.R. (1995) *Tourism, Principles, Practices, Philosophies*, 7th edn, John Wiley & Sons, pp. 486–490

Mathieson, A. and Wall, G. (1982) *Tourism: Economic, Physical and Social Impacts*, Longman, London and New York

Matthews, H.G. (1979) *International Tourism: a Political and Social Analysis*, Schenkman Publishing Co., Cambridge, Mass

Mings, R.C. (1985) International Tourism in Barbados, *Caribbean Geography*, **2**(1), 69–72

Mings, R.C. (1988) Assessing the Contribution of Tourism to International Understanding, *Journal of Travel Research*, **27**(3), 38

Newcombe, H. (1984) Survey of peace research, *Peace Research Institute Reviews*, **IX**(6), 5–72

O'Grady, J.M. (1982) *Tourism in the Third World: Christian Reflections*, Orbis Books, New York

Pearce, Douglas, (1991) *Tourist Development*, 2nd edn, Longman Scientific & Technical, Essex, UK, pp. 221–222

Rovelstad, J.M. (1988) World awareness and perceptions search. Among university business majors. Paper presented at the First Global Conference: Tourism – a Vital Force for Peace, Vancouver, Canada, 16–19 October

Skidmore, S. and Pyszka, R. (1988) Americans as international travelers. Paper presented at the First Global Conference: Tourism – a Vital Force for Peace, Vancouver, Canada, 16–19 October

Sutton, Jr, W.A. (1967) Travel and understanding: notes on the social structure of touring, *International Journal of Comparative Sociology*, **8**, 218–23

Var, T., Ap, J. and Van Doren, C. (1988) Tourism and peace. Paper presented at the First Global Conference: Tourism – a Vital Force for Peace, Vancouver, Canada, 16–19 October

World Tourist Organization (1980) Manila Declaration on World Tourism. In *Dynamics of Tourism*: vol. I *The Phenomenon* (ed. Kaul, R.N., 1985) Sterling Publishing Co., New Delhi, pp. 245–51

Part Two

Results and Residuals:
The Issue of Impacts

Throughout recorded history, tourism has impacted in some way everything and everyone that it touched. Ideally, these impacts should have been positive, both in terms of benefits to destination areas and their residents. These positive impacts should include results such as improvements in local economic conditions, social and cultural understanding and protected environmental resources. In theory, the benefits of tourism should produce benefits far in excess of their costs.

Initial studies of tourism impacts dealt mainly with economic aspects since they were more easily quantifiable and measurable. In addition, it was presumed that the income derived from tourism could make up for any negative consequences of tourism. However, over-emphasis on economic benefits have often led to adverse physical and social consequences.

Due to the rising concern for the environment, the concept of 'sustainable tourism development' (defined as the protection and conservation of an area's ecology in order to maintain its useful life over a long period of time) has emerged. **Archer** and **Cooper** (Chapter 5) review the key elements of the positive and negative impacts of tourism, including economic, political, socio-cultural, environmental and ecological impacts.

Careful planning and management, including the understanding of an area's carrying capacity is essential in order to avoid exploitation and potential destruction of physical and personal resources. The authors conclude that what is needed to avoid the negative impacts of tourism is a shift away from short term to longer-term thinking and planning, and a recognition that exploitation of places and people is not only unethical but unprofitable (in the long run) as well.

A discussion of the socio-cultural impacts of tourism from eighteenth century Britain to the present is proffered by **Swinglehurst** (Chapter 6). This chapter deals with the sensitivity suggested in the previous chapter, describing the paternalism and elitism of the British and American international tourists of the eighteenth and nineteenth centuries.

From the advent of the 'grand tour', there has been little social or cultural contact between the more affluent traveller and the ordinary people of the countries they visited. A traveller's friends were cultural equals, but others who he came in contact with were servants, innkeepers, boatmen and other peasants. Communication began to change late in the nineteenth century when wealthy tourists began to recognize the plight of the poor in the countries they visited. Paternalism and a sense of largess caused many wealthy tourists to contribute to local schools, libraries and hospitals to help improve the lives of the impoverished and uneducated.

With the advent of the jet airplane and mass tourism, a new era of tourism had begun, and the age of travel hedonism arrived. Recently, a reversal of roles between tourists and natives has occurred when comparing tourism values. In the past, natives were regarded as carefree, fun-loving children while tourists were considered as seekers of knowledge and enlightenment. Today, however, it appears to be the other way round. The cultural gap between these two worlds is closing since the tourist and the resident are exchanging ambitions and ways of life. While tourists seek escape, residents try to learn how they can satisfy the demands for the good life they imagine the tourist has achieved.

The rather uneasy relationship between contemporary Western tourism development and native peoples is explored by **Mercer** (Chapter 7). His examination of the Aboriginal, 'outback' population of northern and central Australia focuses on the social appropriateness of tourism development from the native Aboriginal viewpoint. Two case studies are presented, both dealing with the concepts of control and choice. Control relates to whether native populations control their own destinies when negotiating decisions regarding tourism development on their land. Choice relates to their having the freedom to choose to negotiate, or to simply refuse to do so.

Growing Aboriginal militancy related to what they viewed as their basic rights had come up against the Western practice of eminent domain, i.e. government gaining control of individual (or group) owned land 'for the good of the many', through a legal process often including condemnation. This practice, together with other denials of land ownership, led to what some writers termed, 'the invasion and theft of the Aboriginal nation'.

The key problem is related to the principle of equity or fairness, and how, today, native peoples including Aboriginals can achieve the most benefits derived from tourism without being overrun and overwhelmed by the excesses that tourism itself often causes.

The issue of tourist–resident impacts is extended by **Pearce** (Chapter 8) who offers the proposition that social impact effects may be real since objective data can be found to verify their existence, or may be perceived in views held by the community that life is different. Perceived views are equally important to real views because if residents believe an impact does exist (regardless of whether or not it is true), their behaviour will be altered.

The effects of the tourist–resident interaction process appear to have maximum social and psychological impacts on residents when the destination areas are small, unsophisticated and isolated. These impacts may be either powerful, direct interpersonal encounters, or more subtle, indirect influences. Conversely, these impacts are lessened, the larger, more urbane and urban the destination area.

After reviewing the literature on social impacts of tourism and the variety of models that have been developed to better explain this phenomenon, the author presents five emerging solutions to combat social impact problems. Tactics proposed for reducing the decline of tourist–resident social contacts include: better education and training; incorporating community perspectives in development;

increasing resident opportunities; establishment of local equity and management committees; and, increased research and monitoring of social impacts.

The final chapter in this section deals with the elusive character of the term 'alternative tourism' and its impact. **Macleod** (Chapter 9) suggests that as a concept, alternative tourism is far too broad, it is fundamentally problematic, and is subject to heavily emotional responses. Further, he contends that the content of the term is grossly overstretched and as a result, it is inadequate, hazy and subject to parody. Such terms as 'ecotourism, green tourism, adventure tourism, ethnic tourism' and others have helped fragment the concept of alternative tourism into disparate and often meaningless lexicon subsets.

Defining the concept of alternative tourism is important because of the relationship to basic problems of human society including environmental destruction, inequalities of wealth and irresponsible development. In an ethnographic case study, the author concludes that alternative tourism is largely a contextual creation in terms of space and time, and that in reality, it is a reflection of society's contemporary attitudes and value system.

In terms of impacts, the prevailing values of society are focused predominately on economic impacts of tourism development, thereby often concentrating solely on monetary data and other financial information. Such economic preoccupation neglects often more important factors such as sociocultural, psychological and environmental factors. Alternative tourism must be used to strengthen linkages between the tourism industry and other forms of local community activity.

5 The positive and negative impacts of tourism

Brian Archer and Chris Cooper

Introduction

Tourism, both international and domestic, brings about an intermingling of people from diverse social and cultural backgrounds, and also a considerable spatial redistribution of spending power which has a significant impact on the economy of the destination area. Early work on the impact of tourism upon destinations focused primarily on economic aspects. This was not only because such impacts are more readily quantifiable and measurable, but also there was a pervading climate of optimism that these studies would show that tourism was of net economic benefit to host destinations. In many cases, this was indeed true. Yet tourism, by its very nature, is attracted to unique and fragile environments and societies and it became apparent that in some cases the economic benefits of tourism may be offset by adverse and previously unmeasured environmental and social consequences.

The benefits and costs of tourism accrue to two quite distinct groups of people. On the one hand, the visitors themselves receive benefits and incur costs in taking holidays. On the other hand, the resident populations of the host region benefit from tourism (not only financially) but at the same time incur costs of various types. Since it is not possible to deal adequately with both aspects within the limited scope of this single chapter, attention will be devoted to the positive and negative effects of tourism from the point of view of the host country or region.

The general issues central to any discussion of the positive and negative impacts of tourism must include notions of carrying capacity and also of how impacts can be assessed. Carrying capacity is a relatively straightforward concept – in simple terms it refers to a point beyond which further levels of visitation or development would lead to an unacceptable deterioration in the physical environment and of the visitor's experience (Getz, 1983; O'Reilly, 1986). Any consideration of the impact of tourism must recognize the pivotal role which carrying capacity plays by intervening in the relationship between visitor and resource.

The impact made by tourism therefore depends upon both the volume and profile characteristics of the tourists (their length of stay, activity, mode of transport, travel arrangement etc.). In this respect, a number of authors have attempted to classify tourists according to their impact on the destinations (see, for example, Smith, 1977). The character of the resource (its natural features, level of development, political and social structure etc.) is equally important as it determines the degree of its robustness to tourism and tourism development (Mathieson and Wall, 1982).

A range of variables, therefore, needs to be taken into account in any determination of the impact of tourism. Yet determining such impacts also raises a number of issues. In economics, impact methodology has a long pedigree but the measurement of environmental and social impacts has not progressed anywhere near as far. Indeed, in all forms of impact analysis, it is important to distinguish tourism-induced events from other agents of change; ensure that secondary and tertiary effects are considered; and have a view as to what the situation was before tourism intervened. All of these points are problematic and the tendency is therefore to simplify and narrow the scope of investigation to 'contain' the research into a manageable outcome (Mathieson and Wall, 1982).

In part, the difficulty of quantifying the environmental and social impacts of tourism has delayed the development of impact methodologies. But the rising tide of environmentalism has caught up with tourism and has lent support to the view that in some cases the economic benefits of tourism are more than outweighed by the environmental and social costs of tourism. Concepts such as 'sustainable tourism development' and 'the responsible consumption of tourism' are seen by many as the answer, along with the enhanced planning and management of tourism. These issues are discussed later in this chapter. Nonetheless, the issue of management is closely related to the notion of carrying capacity as a destination can be 'managed' to take any number of visitors. Simply by 'hardening' the environment and managing the visitor, large volumes can be accommodated without an unacceptable decline in the environment or the experience. The question must therefore be asked, management for whom? In pluralistic societies, the conflicts and tensions between the stakeholders in tourism – tourists, developers, planners, environmentalists – will in the end determine levels of tourist development. After all, tourism takes place within political and social contexts. It is however heartening that the current pressure for sustainable/responsible tourism will give a different emphasis to this continuing debate amongst the various groups in society and may change the perceived balance between the positive and negative effects of tourism in the future.

Economic effects

The economic advantages and disadvantages of tourism have been extensively documented (see for example, Bryden 1973, Archer 1977 and Eadington and Redman 1991).

The economic impact of tourism

International tourism is an invisible export in that it creates a flow of foreign currency into the economy of a destination country thereby contributing directly to the current account of the balance of payments. Like other export industries, this inflow of revenue creates business turnover, household income, employment and government revenue.

The generation process does not stop at this point however. Some portion of the money received by the business establishments, individuals and government agencies is re-spent within the destination economy thereby creating further rounds of economic activity. These secondary effects can in total considerably exceed in magnitude the initial direct effects. Indeed any study purporting to show the economic impact made by tourism must attempt to measure the overall effect made by the successive rounds of economic activity generated by the initial expenditure. The process has been documented with attention drawn to the strengths, weaknesses and limitations of the various approaches (see, for example, Archer and Fletcher 1991).

Domestic tourism has somewhat similar economic effects upon the host regions of a country. Whereas, however, international tourism brings a flow of foreign currency into a country, domestic tourism redistributes currency spatially within the boundaries of a country. From the point of view of a tourist region within a country, however, domestic tourism is a form of invisible export. Money earned in other regions is spent within the host region creating additional business revenue, income, jobs and revenue to local government. The process of secondary revenue, income and employment generation within the host region is then the same as for' a national economy. The principal difference during these secondary stages, however, is that individual regions within a country are usually less economically self-contained and hence a far greater proportion of the money is likely to leak out of the regional system into other regions. The secondary effects in individual regions are far lower in magnitude than for the national economy as a whole.

Moreover, tourism seems to be more effective than other industries in generating employment and income in the less developed often outlying regions of a country where alternative opportunities for development are more limited. Indeed, it is in these areas that tourism can make its most

significant impact. In such places many of the local people are subsistence farmers or fishermen and if they become involved in the tourism
industry their household incomes increase by a relatively very large
amount. The growth of tourism in such areas may provide also a monetary incentive for the continuance of many local crafts, whilst the tourist
hotels may create a market for local produce. Indeed, the introduction of
a tourism industry into such areas can have a proportionally very much
greater effect on the welfare of the resident population than the same
amount of tourism might have on the more developed parts of the same
country.

The development of tourism, especially in a previously under-developed
part of a country, requires the existence of an infrastructure, as well as
hotel accommodation and other facilities specific to tourism. In many
cases these utilities are economically indivisible in the sense that, in providing them for the tourism industry, they at the same time become
available for the use of local people. Thus, in many countries, highways
and airfields, constructed primarily to cater for tourism, now provide an
access to wider markets for may locally produced goods. Unfortunately,
in a lot cases, however, the local people still receive little direct benefit
from these developments. This in essence is a problem of both physical
and economic distribution, i.e. of the extent to which, and the speed at
which, these facilities should be made more generally available.

As tourism continues to grow in a region it makes increasing demands
upon the scarce resources of that area. Land in particular is required and
in consequence land prices rise. Farmers and other local landowners
are encouraged to sell, with the result that, although they may obtain
short-term gains they are left landless with only low paid work available.
Indeed much of the benefit from higher land prices may accrue to speculators who buy land from the previous owners before it has been scheduled for development. These problems can be overcome, however, if
either the land is acquired at an early stage by the government for a fair,
market price or if the land is rented rather than sold to the developers.
Market forces do not necessarily ensure that development keeps pace
with demand. There is a need for realistic planning and the effective
enforcement of planning regulations to reduce possible conflicts of interest and, where appropriate, to conserve unique and unusual features for
the enjoyment of future generations of visitors and residents alike. This is
a lesson which has been learned rather late in many developed countries.

Superficially at least the economic 'benefits' of tourism seem self-
evident. Yet in recent years several writers have expressed reservations
about the nature and size of the benefits attributable to tourism and have
become increasingly sceptical about the potentialities of tourism as a tool
for development and growth and as a means of maximizing the welfare
of the indigenous population. The problem is essentially one of resource

allocation and of whether or not the development of a tourism industry offers the optimum usage of the resources available – in other words an assessment of the costs and benefits of tourism development vis-à-vis alternatives.

Cost–benefit analysis

In cost–benefit terms, the economic benefits gained by a recipient country from tourism have been outlined above. Against these benefits have to be offset the economic costs involved. Apart from the purchase of import requirements, the earnings of expatriate workers and the overseas expenses incurred by the foreign companies concerned during both the construction and operating phases of the development, none of which benefits the resident population, the country itself incurs considerable costs internally. The real cost to society of employing resources and factors of production in any one sector, including the construction and operation of hotels and other associated tourism services, is the value of the output which could have been obtained from their use in other sectors of the economy (Archer, 1996). Since capital and skilled labour are rarely, if ever, abundant in such countries, the development of a tourism industry requires some of these scarce resources to be diverted from their alternative uses. Admittedly, some factors of production might otherwise be unemployed, in which case their use in tourism involves no real cost to society, but in most cases the opportunity cost incurred is the value of the production lost in other sectors.

Whether or not tourism creates greater net benefits to society than other forms of development depends primarily upon the nature of the country's economy and what alternative forms of development are practicable. Also, in the interests of diversification it is sometimes considered desirable to promote several forms of development even though one or more of these may offer relatively lower net benefits.

Issues requiring further research

Despite the plethora of economic analyses undertaken during the last twenty years, economists have not displayed any noticeable propensity to work jointly with specialists from other disciplines in multi-disciplinary teams. Their contribution to such work has normally consisted of analyses undertaken in parallel but not jointly with other specialists.

- A more balanced view of the economic effects of tourism demands a deeper understanding of the human issues surrounding the impact made by tourism. This requires joint work by economists, sociologists, political scientists and others. In particular, economists should work more closely with sociologists in analysing and quantifying the social costs and benefits of tourism.

- The long-term advantages and disadvantages of tourism can be better understood if economists work more closely with environmentalists as well as specialists in the various humanities. At present economists are not contributing fully to the current debates on sustainable, alternative and responsible tourism, discussed later in this chapter.
- The economic analysis of tourism will be improved if more economists apply their efforts to improving the methodology of existing techniques rather than merely replicating them in a succession of case studies. There is an especial danger that replication of economic impact studies in isolation will simply fuel the call for development in destinations and omit considerations of other costs.

In addition to the economic costs and benefits already mentioned, tourism also imposes political, cultural, social, moral and environmental changes upon the host country. Although such costs are rarely quantifiable in money terms, they must be taken into account in the process of decision-making. Tourism, however, is not alone in generating such 'costs' and it is likely that other forms of development may create far more adverse side effects which more than offset any advantages which they may possess over tourism in purely economic terms. Analysing such effects is properly the province of experts in each field, but it is appropriate here to share some thoughts to stimulate future discussion.

Political effects

The political costs and benefits of tourism

Whereas the virtues of international tourism have been extolled as a major force for peace and understanding between nations (World Tourism Organization, 1980 and 1982), the reality is often far removed from this utopian image. Long-haul travel between developed and developing countries is increasing annually and is bringing into direct contact with each other people from widely different backgrounds and with very contrasting lifestyles and levels of income. Where these disparities are very great the political as well as the socio-cultural consequences may be severe.

In extreme cases international tourism has imposed a form of 'neo-colonial' type development upon emerging nations (Hall, 1994; Hall and Jenkins, 1995). Quite simply, this neo-colonialism takes power from the local and regional levels and concentrates it into the hands of multi-national companies. These companies will negotiate only at the national level and expect any 'problems' to be solved by national governments otherwise investment will be withdrawn. At the operational level, the higher paid, more 'respectable' posts in hotels and other establishments are sometimes occupied by expatriates who possess the necessary expertise and experience. Whilst the lower paid, more menial jobs are frequently reserved for the indigenous population. It is possible that such apparent discrimination can foster resentment and can sour international relationships. In extreme cases such development can even inhibit the growth of a national consciousness in a newly dependent country.

Domestic tourism, on the other hand, can act as an integrating force strengthening national sentiment. Peoples in outlying areas are traditionally more preoccupied with local village affairs and in consequence sometimes prove easy prey to separatist agitators. If, by travel to other parts of the same country, such people can begin to experience pride in their national heritage, a sense of national unity may help to prevent regional fragmentation.

In the more developed countries, visits to national historical monuments, stately homes and ancient battlefields form a significant motivation for domestic travel and similar developments are already taking place in other parts of the world. In many developing countries students and groups of schoolchildren travel to other regions of their homelands and such movements of people can do much in the long run to strengthen the political unity of a country. Provided that the individual characteristics and identities of the various regions are not submerged and lost, such travel can benefit both tourists and residents alike.

Unfortunately, contact between peoples of different backgrounds is not always beneficial and may in some cases generate additional cultural, social and moral stresses. Whilst the mixing of people from different regions of a country can produce a better understanding of each other's way of life and a better appreciation of problems specific to particular regions, it can at the same time create misunderstandings and even distrust.

Issues requiring further research

So far political scientists have contributed relatively little to the analysis of tourism and most of the work in this field has been concerned with the situation in particular countries. Two noteworthy exceptions are the books by Hall (1994) and Hall and Jenkins (1995) and a paper by Mathews and Richter (1991). The books provide a framework for the examination of tourism and politics/policy making, whilst the paper by Mathews and Richter reviews the efforts made by political scientists to apply their special disciplines to the study of tourism. The authors examine first the ways in which many important aspects of tourism involve some of the central concepts of political science and, second, the contribution which political science can make to the study of tourism. Two major issues in tourism can be addressed by political scientists.

- A fuller understanding of the human impact of tourism upon destination areas can be achieved only by a much greater integration of the work of political scientists with specialists in other disciplines and with tourism practitioners. At present too many political scientists work in a self-imposed isolation and in consequence fail to take into account or misinterpret some of the favourable (and unfavourable) human effects of tourism which lie outside their own expertise and experience.
- Knowledge of the impact of tourism upon many aspects of human life and organization can be improved if more political scientists are willing to use their expertise to study tourism as an independent variable affecting areas of concern in public administration, comparative politics, political theory, international relations and national politics (Richter, 1983). Many of these fields are virgin territory for aspiring young researchers – will they heed the call? Specific work is needed in a variety of areas but particularly welcome would be
  - studies examining the influence of tourism upon the roots of power in communities and the implications for community-based investment and the integration of tourism into the community. A major contribution here would be in terms of examining the many political interests involved in the development of tourism and the role of conflict resolution and consensus models (Jamal and Getz, 1995).
  - work examining the stage of destination life cycle at which community involvement is most appropriate, and the stages at which communities are most vulnerable to external political and commercial decision-taking; and
  - further examination of policy impact analysis within a tourism context.

Socio-cultural effects

Some socio-cultural costs and benefits

Wide cultural differences occur between different countries and sometimes between different regions within the same country. Indeed the existence of such differences may be one of the principal stimulants of a tourism industry. In some developing countries such traditional cultural behaviour patterns of particular groups of people form one focus of the tourism industry (Butler and Hinch, 1996). Sometimes, however, differences in physical appearance and, perhaps more importantly, differences in cultural behaviour between visitors and residents, are so great that mutual understanding is replaced by antipathy.

The problem is exacerbated because tourists are, by definition, strangers in the destination. Their dress codes and patterns of behaviour are different to the residents and, often, different from those that the tourist would display at home: inhibitions are shed and the consequent problems of prostitution, drugs, gambling and sometimes vandalism ensue. As strangers, tourists are also vulnerable and fall victim to robbery and crimes perpetrated by the local community who may see these activities as a way to 'redress the balance'.

When the cultural distinctions between the residents and tourists from more prosperous countries and regions are strongly marked, local culture and customs may be exploited to satisfy the visitor, sometimes at the expense of local pride and dignity. Here the issue of staged authenticity is an important one where the host destination is able to convince tourists that festivals and activities in the 'front region' of the destination (public areas such as hotel lobbies or restaurants) are authentic and thus they protect the real 'black region' (residents' homes and areas where life continues) (McCannell, 1973). One of the problems of 'alternative tourism' is that the tourists are encouraged to penetrate this 'back region'. With good management and planning, however, tourism can provide an impetus for the preservation of ancient cultures, but too often the local way of life degenerates into a commercially organized effigy of its former self. The traditional dances and the skilled craftwork give way to cheap imitations to satisfy the needs of the visitor and to obtain money with the least possible effort. In some cases this is merely an initial response and, later, tourism can stimulate high quality revivals of crafts in particular.

In primitive and isolated areas, the arrival of too many visitors can even cause local people to leave their settlements and move to new areas where they can remain undisturbed. To combat this in vulnerable areas such as North American Indian reservations 'governing rules' for visitors have been formulated. In more developed areas, in extreme cases tourism has disrupted completely the way of life of the local people. The institution of the national park system in some parts of Africa, although justifiable on the grounds of wildlife conservation and tourism, has in some cases seriously affected the hunting and nomadic existence of the local people. The problem is not confined, however, to developing countries. In Canada, for example, the creation of parks of outdoor recreation and domestic tourism at Forillon and Gros Morne necessitated the eviction of previous residents and in consequence aroused considerable local opposition.

Insufficient research has been carried out so far to disentangle the social and cultural side effects of tourism development. Where the cultural and socio-economic backgrounds of the tourists are very different from those of the local population, the results of their intermingling may be favourable but it can be explosive. The so-called 'demonstration effect' of prosperity amidst poverty may create a desire among local people to work harder or to achieve higher levels of education in order to emulate the way of life of the tourists. On the other hand, in many cases the inability of the local people to achieve the same level of affluence may create a sense of deprivation and frustration which may find an outlet in hostility and even aggression.

The merit of social intercourse between tourists and the indigenous population as a means towards fostering better understanding and goodwill between nations has been extolled as a major social benefit obtained from tourism. Whilst this is true in many cases, particularly in those countries where tourists are still comparatively rare, it is certainly not true in many countries where tourists' tastes and habits have proved offensive to particular sectors of the local population. Because of factors such as these, some writers have rejected the term 'demonstration effect' and substituted the term 'confrontation effect'.

Perhaps the most significant and one of the least desirable by-products of this 'confrontation' is the effect on the moral standards of the local people. In extreme cases, crime, prostitution, gambling and drug traffic may be imported into the holiday areas from other regions. Many of the social conventions and constraints imposed upon tourists in their home areas are absent when they visit another region, and in consequence their moral behaviour can deteriorate without undue censure. As a result, many local people find that by catering for the several needs of their visitors they themselves can achieve a relatively high level of prosperity. Whilst the credit or blame for developments – such as red light districts – can be attributed more to the growth of international tourism than to an increase in domestic tourism, the latter must bear its share of responsibility.

A critical issue here is the form of contact between host and guest. In the 'enclave' tourism model, so berated by proponents of 'alternative forms of tourism', contacts are controlled and minimal, mainly confined to 'culture brokers' who speak the language of both host and guest and who understand both cultures. It is when the tourist penetrates into the daily lives and homes of the hosts that real exposure of cultural and social differences between the two groups emerge, and problems may occur.

Tourists have been blamed for assisting the spread of venereal disease and AIDS in many countries, but their contribution is probably very small in relation to the part played by the local population. Indeed, visitors themselves do not always emerge unscathed from their interaction with the local community (Petty, 1989). Poor hygienic conditions in many tourist resorts create suitable conditions for the spread of various intestinal diseases, typhoid, cholera and hepatitis. Lack of forethought and ignorance result in cases of severe sunstroke and skin cancer. Inappropriate precautions results in infection by the AIDS virus which already affects up to 40 per cent of the population of some countries in Africa. Governments, tour operators, airlines and resort operators have a duty to visitors and residents alike to provide adequate information to ensure that these risks are known and minimized.

Many of the other socio-cultural problems associated with tourism are related to the degree of intensity of tourism development. Although difficult to measure, there is a relationship between tourism density and the growth of local resentment towards tourism. The flow of tourists into a region increases the densities at which people live and overcrowds the facilities which tourists share with the local population. Overcrowding reduces the value of the holiday experience and creates additional strain for the resident population.

In extreme cases local people may be debarred from enjoying the natural facilities of their own country or region. Along part of the Mediterranean, for example, almost half of the coastline has been acquired by hotels for the sole use of their visitors, and in consequence the local public is denied easy access.

Issues requiring further research

The literature on the socio-cultural effects of tourism is quite extensive, although the majority of the contributions are concerned with specific cases in particular countries. Among the more general papers are useful articles by Dogan (1989) and Dann and Cohen (1991).

Dogan provides an interesting analysis in which he shows how the reactions of the host community to the influx of tourists and the changes which tourism brings has been quite diverse, ranging from an active resistance to the complete acceptance and even adoption of the tourists' culture patterns. He shows how the choice of strategies, deliberate or otherwise, to cope with the changes depends upon both the nature of the socio-cultural characteristics of the host community and the magnitude of the changes themselves. His conclusion is that even in the case of a previously homogenous community which adopts a particular response to tourism will itself become diversified and groups will emerge within the community exhibiting very different responses to tourism developments.

Dann and Cohen are concerned with the contribution which the discipline of sociology can make to the understanding of tourism phenomenon.

Different perspectives on tourism have been adopted by sociologists and in consequence this has lead to the emergence of a variety of approaches. Dann and Cohen believe that '. . . some of the best work in tourism has been eclectic, linking elements of one perspective with those of another, rather than opting for an exclusive point of view'.

Two major issues require the attention of sociologists.

- There is a need for many more multi-disciplinary studies where sociologists can contribute the insights of their discipline to the study of particular aspects of the tourism phenomenon or to the analysis of tourism in specific countries and regions. Here there is a clear need for work to examine the social carrying capacity of destinations; work which must be closely linked to community-based models of tourism planning and the 'limits of acceptable change'.
- The quantification of the socio-economic costs and benefits of tourism requires the joint efforts of sociologists and economists. At present this work is being carried out almost entirely by economists, who are not always in the best position to identify all of the phenomena requiring quantification or the appropriate weightings to apply to each.

Environmental and ecological effects

The environmental and ecological costs and benefits of tourism

Excessive and badly planned tourism development affects the physical environment of destinations. In many areas the uncontrolled commercial exploitation of tourism has produced unsightly hotels of alien design which intrude into the surrounding cultural and scenic environment. In such cases the architectural design has been planned to meet the supposed wishes of the visitor rather than to blend into the local environment. The effects, moreover, are not solely scenic, since the waste and sewage from these developments are often discharged in an unprocessed form and pollute the rivers and seas of the holiday areas.

Poor and ill-conceived forms of tourism development also destroy irreplaceable natural environments, the true and long term benefits of which may not have been properly evaluated. Thus for example marshlands and mangrove swamps, which provide both outlets for flood control and also the basic ingredients for local fishing industries, have been drained to create tourist marinas. Water resources needed by local farmers and villages have been diverted for the use of tourist hotels and golf courses and, in some mountainous areas, forests have been depleted to create ski slopes with much resultant soil erosion flooding and, in a recent case, mudslips causing substantial loss of life and damage to property.

Furthermore, the tourists themselves are often guilty of helping to destroy the surrounding environment. In many areas tourists sometimes ignorantly, sometimes deliberately, damage crops and farm equipment, frighten farm animals and bestrew large quantities of garbage over the countryside. From one mountain alone in Great Britain during the summer months, almost a ton of litter a day (mainly discarded lunch wrappings) is brought down from the summit, whilst from the New Forest in Southern England approximately 25,000 empty bottles are retrieved each year.

In other areas wildlife has been severely disturbed, coral reefs have been despoiled and alien forms of plant life have been introduced into delicate ecosystems on the shoes and clothing of visitors.

Lest the picture appear too bleak, it should be remembered that tourism, both domestic and international, is at the same time a positive force in helping to conserve the environment of the holiday regions. Many of the disadvantages mentioned above can be offset by high quality planning, design and management and by educating tourists to appreciate the environment. Tourists are attracted to areas of high scenic beauty, regions of historical and architectural interest and areas with abundant and interesting wildlife. Some of the money spent by tourists in the region, in particular the revenue received from entry fees, can be used to conserve and improve the natural and man-made heritage (as is the case for example in the Kenyan game reserves), whilst tourism may also provide a use for otherwise redundant historic buildings.

The extent and nature of the environmental and ecological damage done by tourists is related to the magnitude of the development and the volume of visitors, the concentration of usage both spatially and temporally, the nature of the environment in question, and the nature of the planning and management practices adopted before and after development takes place.

The literature abounds with good and bad practices. What is possible in any one instance depends upon the nature of the destination area and the aims and objectives of the host community. Unfortunately, in the past too little attention has been given to the wishes of the local population. Decisions are taken too often by politicians and planners in terms of their perception of the national rather than the local interest. In this their views are often influenced by the opinions of financiers and developers whose primary concern is the financial return on their investment.

In recent years, however, many academics have increasingly devoted their efforts towards the environmental problems in destination areas created by the rapid expansion of world tourism and the opening up of new tourist areas. This has resulted in a growth of new terminologies, some of which confuse rather than clarify the issues.

Environmental issues

There is obviously a need for research to examine the environmental impact of tourism. In particular, environmental indicators should be developed for use in cost–benefit analysis and also to allow environmental standards to be devised at destinations to assist consumers in their choice. Already, the WTO has embraced this concept and published work in the field. It is therefore implicit in this trend that planning for tourism will be undertaken. Here the 'planning in' of the environmental, social and cultural context of tourism at the destination (in terms of using local architectural styles, etc.) is vital. In other words, the relationship between tourism and the environment is mediated by planning and management. These tourism planning and management techniques exist and are well tried in many areas. What is necessary is for the barriers to planning and management, which exist in many areas, to be removed to allow the existing techniques to be applied effectively. A major stumbling block here is the privatization of many public tourist agencies and the deregulation of planning in some Western nations. A future issue to consider will be the development of new financing models to ensure continuity of funding for privatized agencies who perform a regulatory role.

A critical issue in the late 1990s and into the next century therefore will be the relationship of tourism and the environment. The environment has moved into centre stage in the debate, as evidenced by the discussion on tourism in the 1992 Rio de Janeiro Earth Summit and the subsequent work of the WTO (1995), the World Travel and Tourism Council (1995) and PATA. Here, whilst the excesses of tourism development have been identified, the alliance of tourism with environmentalists to sensitize tourists to the issues is also recognized. It is this issue which forms the next section of the chapter.

Sustainable development and responsible consumption of tourism

This chapter has reviewed the key elements of the positive and negative impacts of tourism. As mentioned in the introduction, it is only in recent years that the negative 'downstream' effects of tourism on the environments, societies and vulnerable economies have been set more fully against the tangible economic gains. Add to this the rise of environmentalism and 'green' consciousness in the mid to late 1980s, and the stage was set for a reassessment of the role and value of tourism. In part, this is also a reflection of the growing maturity of both the tourist as consumer and the tourism sector itself. In the early decades of mass tourism, short-term perspectives prevailed as the industry and public agencies attempted to cope with burgeoning demand. In the 1980s and 1990s growth rates have slowed and tourists are increasingly questioning some of the excesses of tourism development. In response, longer planning horizons are being considered and new forms of tourism advocated as industry and governments slipstream behind public opinion and media attention given to these issues.

One of the most valuable results of this reassessment has been the belated discovery of the relevance of the sustainable development concept to tourism (see for example Farrell and Runyan, 1991; Pigram, 1990). As with many service industries, some of the most important ideas and innovations come from outside the industry or the subject area. The concept of sustainable development has a long pedigree in the field of resource management and has, at last, become an acceptable term in tourism. The Brundtland Report puts it simply as 'meeting the needs of the present without compromising the ability of future generations to meet their own needs' (World Commission on Environment and Development, 1987). The concept of sustainability is central to the reassessment of the role of tourism in society. It demands a long-term view of economic activity, questions the imperative of continued economic growth, and ensures that consumption of tourism does not exceed the ability of a host destination to provide for future tourists. In other words, it represents a trade-off between present and future needs. In the past, sustainability has been a low priority compared with the short-term drive for profitability and growth but, with pressure growing for a more responsible tourism industry, it is difficult to see how such short-term views on consumption can continue long into the next century. Indeed, destination 'regulations' have been developed in some areas and already, the band-wagon for sustainable development and responsible consumption is rolling. Public agencies are issuing guidelines for acceptable development (see, for example WTO, 1993, campaigns such as the WTTC's Green Globe and PATA's Green Leaf, and the development of quality standards for environmental practice); tourism consumer groups are growing in number and influence (Botterill, 1991) and guides to responsible tourism are increasingly available (Anscombe, 1991; Wood and House, 1991).

As a philosophical stance or a way of thinking, it is difficult to disagree with the concept of sustainable tourism development and responsible consumption of tourism. But a little knowledge is a dangerous thing and some commentators have oversimplified the complex relationship between the consumption and development of tourism resources. This is particularly true of the so-called 'alternative' tourism movement which is lauded by some as a solution to the ills of mass tourism. Indeed, the tenor of much of the writing about alternative tourism is that any alternative tourism scheme is good whilst all mass tourism is bad. Butler

(1990) provides a useful characterization of the two extremes, whilst Wheeler (1991; 1992) provides telling criticism of alternative tourism. There is, of course, a case for alternative tourism, but only as another form of tourism in the spectrum. It can never be an alternative to mass tourism, nor can it solve all the problems of tourism.

A variety of issues emerge from these trends. It is important to disseminate cases of good practice in sustainable/responsible tourism, and to draw out generalities from these cases. In this way, responsible behaviour may pervade the provision and consumption of tourism and displace the more extreme calls for 'politically correct' tourism development. It must be recognized that the relationship of economics to environmental and social issues and policies in tourism is a complex one (Archer, 1996). Often economic policy is determined at the regional or national level, yet the impact of that policy is felt at local level on environments and societies (Hough and Sherpa, 1989). Good models of community participation and planning in tourism are still rare and those that exist should be given greater prominence (Murphy, 1985; Haywood, 1988). But it must also be recognized that tourism takes place in many different social and political contexts and what works in one place, may need adaptation for another. This also applies to the borrowing of concepts and techniques from other subject areas and industries. Nevertheless, tourism has much to learn from others. In particular, techniques of environmental management, visitor planning and management, and studies of visitor/environment relationships are well developed in the recreation literature, and are just as applicable to tourism (Cooper, 1991). In particular, recreational managers are much more advanced in their use of the notion of 'capacity' than are tourism planners (Barkham, 1973), although such mechanistic planning techniques are now being questioned (Butler, 1996).

Perhaps the central issues emerging from this section is the gradual shift from short-term to longer-term thinking and planning in tourism – it is no longer acceptable for the industry to exploit and 'use up' destinations and then move on (Cooper, 1995). In addition there is an urgent need for tourism to sharpen up its terminology (alternative? responsible? soft, appropriate tourism?), to think clearly about the implications of sustainable/responsible initiatives and to develop a code of business ethics.

Conclusions

Over the last two decades, both the planning and marketing of tourism have been primarily orientated towards the needs of the tourist and the provision of interesting tourist experiences. This attitude has its basis first in the need of developers and operators to attract large numbers of visitors and hence ensure an adequate financial return on their investments and operations, and, second, in the desire of politicians and planners to maximize the financial benefits from tourism for their country or region. For both parties the primary concerns have been how many tourists will come, how can we attract more and what facilities and services will they require?

Fortunately the climate of thought is changing, albeit slowly. Increasingly politicians and planners are becoming aware of the longer-term social, economic and environmental consequences of excessive and badly planned tourism expansion. It is crucial if the adverse effects are to be prevented or remedied that politicians and planners should become less preoccupied with increasing the number of visitors (and indeed with volume as a yardstick of success) and devote more consideration to the long-term welfare of the resident population.

Key questions to be considered are:

- First, how many and what type of tourists does the resident population of an area wish to attract?
- Second, what is the optimum number of tourists that the area can support in terms of its physical, environmental and social carrying capacity?
- Third, how can these tourists contribute to the enhancement of the lifestyles of the residents?

Planning for the resultant impact necessitates a careful definition of the respective responsibilities of the public and private sectors. Planning should be designed to maximize the economic and social benefits of tourism to the resident population, whilst at the same time mitigating or preferably eliminating the adverse effects. In the past most of this type of planning has been remedial – it has taken place after much development has occurred. In the future planners must take a more proactive role in controlling the nature of such development in terms of stricter building and design regulations, controlled access to vulnerable sites and attractions, strict transport regulations, especially in core areas, and the use of entry fees, barriers and designated routes for vehicles and pedestrians alike.

Tourism creates both positive and negative effects in the destination country or region. Thoughtful policy-making and planning can do much to minimize or even remove the negative effects. Tourism can be a very positive means of increasing the economic, social, cultural and environmental life of a country. The major issue now is can politicians, planners and developers rise to the challenge and create a truly responsible (and thus acceptable) tourism industry – one which brings long-term benefits to residents and tourists alike without damaging the physical and cultural environment of the destination region.

References

Anscombe, J. (1991) The Gentle Traveller, *New Woman*, June, pp. 51–53

Archer, B.H. (1996) Sustainable Tourism – Do Economists Really Care? *Progress in Tourism and Hospitality Research*, **2**(3), 217–222

Archer, B.H. (1977) *Tourism Multipliers: The State of the Art*, University of Wales Press, Cardiff

Archer, B.H. and Fletcher, J.E. (1991) *Multiplier Analysis in Tourism*, Cahiers du Tourisme, Centre Des Hautes Etudes Touristiques, Universite de Droit, D'Economie et Des Sciences, Aix en Provence

Barkham, J.P. (1973) Recreational Carrying Capacity, *Area*, **5**(3), 218–222

Botterill, T.D. (1991) A New Social Movement: Tourism Concern, The First Two Years, *Leisure Studies*, **10**(3), 203–217

Bryden, J.M. (1973) *Tourism and Development*, Cambridge University Press, Cambridge

Butler, R. (1990) Alternative Tourism: Pious Hope or Trojan Horse? *Journal of Travel Research*, (Winter), 40–45

Butler, R. (1996) Impacts, Carrying Capacity, Control and Responsibility in Tourist Destinations, *Progress in Tourism and Hospitality Research*, **2**(3), 283–294

Butler, R. and Hinch, T. (eds) (1996) *Tourism and Indigenous Peoples*, International Thomson Business Press, London

Cooper, C.P. (1991) The Technique of Interpretation. In *Managing Tourism* (ed. S. Medlik), Butterworth-Heinemann, Oxford, pp. 224–230

Cooper, C.P. (1995) Strategic Planning for Sustainable Tourism: The Case of Offshore Islands in the UK, *Journal of Sustainable Tourism*, **3**(4), 191–209

Dann, Graham and Cohen, Eric (1991) Sociology and Tourism, *Annals of Tourism Research*, **18**(1), 155–169

Dogan, Hasan Zafar (1989) Forms of Adjustment: Socio-cultural Impacts of Tourism, *Annals of Tourism Research*, **16**(2), 216–236

Eadington, William R. and Redman, Milton (1991) Economics and Tourism, *Annals of Tourism Research*, **18**(1), 41–56

Farrell, B.H. and Runyan, D. (1991) Ecology and Tourism, *Annals of Tourism Research*, **18**(1), 26–40

Getz, D. (1983) Capacity to Absorb Tourism: Concepts and Applications for Strategic Planning, *Annals Of Tourism Research*, **10**(2), 239–263

Hall, C.M. (1994) *Tourism and Politics*, Wiley, Chichester

Hall, C.M. and Jenkins, J.M. (1995) *Tourism and Public Policy*, Routledge, London

Haywood, K.M. (1988) Responsible and Responsive Tourism Planning in the Community, *Tourism Management*, **9**(2), 105–118

Hough, J.L. and Sherpa, M.N. (1989) Bottom Up versus Basic Needs, *Ambio*, **18**(8), 434–441

Jamal, T. and Getz, D. (1995) Collaboration Theory and Community Planning, *Annals of Tourism Research*, **22**(1), 186–204

Mathews, Harry G. and Richter, Linda K. (1991) Political Science and Tourism, *Annals of Tourism Research*, **18**(1), 120–135

Mathieson, A. and Wall, G. (1982) *Tourism: Economic, Physical and Social Impacts*, Longman, London

McCannell, D. (1973) Staged Authenticity: Arrangement of Social Space in Tourist Settings, *American Journal of Sociology*, **79**, 586–603

Murphy, P. (1985) *Tourism, A community approach*, Routledge, London

O'Reilly, A.M. (1986) Tourism Carrying Capacity, *Tourism Management*, **7**(4), 254–258

Petty, Richard (1989) Health Limits to Tourism Development, *Tourism Management*, **10**(3), September, 209–212

Pigram, J. (1990) Sustainable Tourism Policy Considerations, *Journal of Tourism Studies*, **2**(3), 2–9.

Richter, Linda K. (1983) Tourism Politics and Political Science: A Case of Not So Benign Neglect, *Annals of Tourism Research*, **10**(3), 313–335

Smith, V. (1977) *Hosts and Guests: An Anthropology of Tourism*, University of Pennsylvania Press, Philadelphia

Wheeler, B. (1991) Tourism's Troubled Times, *Tourism Management*, **12**(2), 91–96

Wheeler, B. (1992) Is Progressive Tourism Appropriate? *Tourism Management*, **13**(1), 104–105

Wood, K. and House, S.L. (1991) *The Good Tourist*, Mandarin, London

World Commission on Environment and Development (1987) *Our Common Future*, Oxford University Press, New York

World Tourism Organization (1980) *Manila Declaration on World Tourism*, World Tourism Organization, Madrid

World Tourism Organization (1982) *Acapulco Development*, World Tourism Organization, Madrid

World Tourism Organization (1993) *Sustainable Tourism Development for Local Planners*, World Tourism Organization, Madrid

World Tourism Organization (1995) *Tourism and Environmental Indicators*, World Tourism Organization, Madrid

World Travel and Tourism Council (1995) *Agenda 21 For the Travel and Tourism Industry*, WTTC, London

6 Face to face: the effects of tourism on societies past and present

Edmund Swinglehurst

The long view

Travel is not a new phenomenon; mankind has travelled since the earliest human migrations from Africa into Europe and across the Bering Straits to America. What is new in travel in our civilization is the volume and suddenness of human translocation and its pleasure content. The migration of primitive peoples took thousands of years, during which there were life times for adaptation to new environments; today some 500 million leisure travellers per year move to unfamiliar surroundings in a matter of hours. This mobility causes shocks of dislocation, which are cushioned by the re-creation of familiar environments in modes of transportation and accommodation facilities, but which nevertheless have their impact. In this study we will investigate the shock element in travel and its consequences past and present.

Early travellers

At the beginning of history, in the Middle East and Egypt, such travel as was undertaken was by traders who sold and transported their products from the place of origin to a market place, or by populations forced to move because of famine and drought or war.

The first great wave of travellers moved across the deserts of the Middle East carrying merchandise from the East or the fertile valleys of Mesopotamia and the Nile. Others took to the sea spreading trade and their cultures all over the Mediterranean region, which was eventually united under the Roman Empire. Under the Romans travel for trading reasons flourished and so did leisure travel with cities like Pompeii and Herculaneaum devoted to Romans on holiday.

The expansion of both business and leisure travel was possible thanks to three conditions, which still apply today:

1   Law and order
2   Means of communication
3   Availability of accommodation

Under Pax Romana these conditions were established, though standards were not always maintained, any more than they are today. Horace, travelling by boat in 38BC, complained about sickness, mosquitoes and frogs; Seneca, who stayed in a rooming house above a Roman bath, was kept awake by the grunts of people playing games or being massaged, and an unknown traveller in Pompeii scribbled on the wall of the place where he stayed that the innkeeper was a swindler and watered his wine.

The collapse of the Roman imperial system put an end to travel, as roads fell into disrepair, acqueducts broke down, and the countryside was infested by brigands.

Pilgrim travel

Once the barons and princes of Europe began to re-establish law and order, aided by the spiritual and moral leadership of the Church, travel began again. At the top level this was organized by the lords and monarchs who gathered together armies to free the Holy Land from infidels and at the same time make some money on the side by bringing back to Europe the silks, spices, jewels and other luxuries of the East. On a humbler level, travel by groups of pilgrims began to the holy places of Europe such as Santiago de Compostela in northern Spain, Canterbury in Kent, England, and the many monastery towns of Italy. Both kinds of travel had a large leisure element in them and travellers were from all levels of society – as Chaucer recorded in his *Canterbury Tales* – and therefore created a democracy of travel in which people of many diverse occupations and backgrounds met. Since at the time nationalism was unknown, travelling created a real mingling of people who shared the accommodation at inns and ate together at hostelries on their route.

The grand tour

In the eighteenth century, Britain's supremacy on the seas, and its far flung trade routes, created a new wealthy class which sought to establish cultural foundations for their families just as the Italian warlord princes had done. They therefore began to travel abroad, and in particular to send their adolescent male children round Europe, with a tutor. The object was to get them out of the way during those awkward years before adulthood and to educate them; though some critics believed that all they did was carouse and catch the pox.

The social effect of these tours to the great cultural centres of Europe was almost negligible, for the privileged traveller usually stayed in the villas of friends or in private apartments and, apart from visiting a museum or church or two, consorted with their own kind. Their only contact with the native population was on a master/servant basis with lackeys, postilions or prostitutes.

Their sentiments about the countries they visited were not very different to those of Englishmen in Shakespeare's day which the Bard recorded in the words of Parolles in *All's Well That Ends Well* that 'France is a doghole.' A view echoed by Tobias Smollett in 1768 when he complained that, 'They have nor even the implements of cleanliness in this country.' Such an arrogant attitude was hardly likely to encourage social communication and understanding, but it is understandable in that most of the European cities that the English 'milords' visited consisted of the hovels of the poor among which rose the great palaces of the rich and powerful.

The English traveller proudly aware of his own country's achievement in matters of law, order, politics and commerce was also aware of its deficiencies in matters of art. England could not boast of a Titian or a Michelangelo but there was no reason why they should not acquire them. Thus began the great trade in art which transferred the treasures of many Italian churches to the country houses of the English landed gentry and eventually to the nation's museums. Transactions which were repeated two centuries later by American barons of the railroads and shipping and department stores. Since there were not enough great masterpieces to go round there began a trade in copies of originals by such painters as Canaletto and Guardi, who often pressed members of their own families into the business of manufacturing paintings for export. Thus travel began to create its own ancillary souvenir business.

The munificence of the lordly traveller was not lost on the general public in the countries visited, especially where these were poverty stricken, and soon it became a widespread belief that all English travellers were milords, and a law unto themselves, and this belief continued into the nineteenth century when the advances in industry in England (which had once meant all of Britain but was beginning to be recognized as only a part of it), meant that people of the industrial and trading middle class were able to travel.

The age of locomotion

The invention of the steam railway engine by the Cornishman Trevithick, which he exhibited in London in 1807 under the significant name of *Catch Me Who Can*, and the opening of a passenger railway from Stockton to Darlington in 1829, plus the first crossing of the Atlantic by the SS *Royal William*, driven by steam engines alone, started a boom in railway and steamship passenger services which lasted for 100 years and gave both trade and leisure travel a formidable impulse.

Britain, with its vast seapower unchallenged since the defeat of Napoleon, and its increasing wealth, was the leader in the new business of travel which was about to begin its phenomenal growth. Its population, which was changing from an agricultural way of life to an industrial one, was a ready market for travel at new middle levels of society. The wealthy industrialists travelled because they wanted to emulate the landed classes, the middle classes travelled because they wanted to emulate their employers and the working classes travelled to escape the crowded, grimy, constricted squalor of the industrial slums.

Their numbers created a demand for locomotion and accommodation and provided a new field of endeavour for entrepreneurs. The railways in Britain, built by anyone who had risk capital, extended from city to city and to seaside fishing villages and even empty pieces of coast which seemed suitable for the building of a resort. Land was bought by speculators who built grand hotels for the rich and houses for landladies who let rooms and cooked the food brought by the poorer visitors. Local newspapers, created at first to inform the residents of the hotels which families were at the resort and where they were staying, flourished, winter gardens and theatres were built for the more educated levels of society and the common folk had dance places, vaudeville halls, take away food stalls as well the hundreds of street entertainers about whom Charles Dickens complained at Broadstairs, where he was trying to write one of his novels.

Though many people opposed the new facilities for travel for all people there were others who began to approve of the new freedom, among them Dickens himself and the Prime Minister of Britain, Gladstone, who believed in the educational value of travel. Most of the working classes on the other hand approved of travel for the freedom that it bestowed in terms of leisure time and more informal behaviour away from the social constraints of their home towns where their employers and their local church kept a censorious eye on morals. The anonymity of the seaside made everything possible and they took advantage of it.

The Cooks ticket

The creation of a multiplicity of railways and resorts led to acute competition for passengers and visitors and provided an opportunity for those capable of gathering groups of potential travellers together. One of those who played a leading part in this was a small printer from Leicester in the English Midlands. Thomas Cook had considerable contacts through his Baptist religious affiliations and above through his secretaryship of the Temperance Society which was active throughout Britain in curbing the extensive drunkenness of workers in industrial towns.

Cook began by organizing groups on excursions around Britain and then, having proved his ability to the railway companies with whom he worked, he obtained permission to issue tickets on their behalf. He also obtained lower prices for his groups and conducted the parties himself, thus overcoming the fear that many people had about riding in 'these new-fangled trains'. By these means Cook became a well known supplier of travel in Britain and, later, in Europe and then the whole world.

For the wealthier citizens, travel across the English Channel had been going on since the grand tour but few other classes of society dared to venture into foreign parts. This gave Thomas Cook an opportunity which would make his name known throughout the world. As soon as railways were established in continental Europe, he began to offer similar conditions of travel as he did in Britain, including his personal leadership of tours. Thus began an influx of ordinary people to those places which had hitherto only seen the 'grand tourists' and their wealthy successors, and a new social dimension was added to travel.

The new travellers of the middle and trading classes went to Europe for two main reasons, one was to visit the centres of culture and thus establish their claim to belong to the literate middle classes, and the other was to affirm their belief that nature was the work of a beneficent Creator who had made the world for man's exploitation and pleasure. These two concepts were an expression of a new increasingly affluent strata of a society which was to oust the landed gentry in a country which led the world and which was to dominate the manners and mores of the second part of the nineteenth century. During this period, which came to be known as the Victorian Age, the British were the world's greatest travellers and by their presence abroad imposed many of their, on the whole, liberal ideas on the world. They demanded courtesy and respect from those whom they came across, showed displeasure and indignation at customs they disapproved of, such as slavery (which was still practised in many countries), the exploitation of women and children, idolatry, and lack of hygiene. Since those they came across depended on their cash, their opinions carried some weight and had an effect on the societies they mingled with – an effect which would continue well into the twentieth century.

Having expanded his ticket systems into Europe, Thomas Cook extended his conducted tours to the Middle East, a region of vital political interest because of the Suez Canal, and of historical interest to the broadly religious society of England and the USA. He ran his tours to the latter country after the Civil War ended and was one of the first to organize tours to the national parks of the West.

At arm's length

Though the new means of communication were creating more contact between the peoples of the earth, the effect was only general and temporary for the relationship between traveller and native was still a master/servant one. The travellers did not speak foreign languages and could only make opinions known through interpreters; moreover the traveller was protected by guides and party leaders (dragomen in the Middle East) who kept importuning natives at bay.

As numbers of travellers increased so did the facilities for their comfort and protection from the sordid realities of the countries they passed through, and thus any real contact with local life was impeded. Georges Nagelmackers brought rail travel to a peak of perfection and luxurious seclusion with his system of trains which passed freely across the frontiers of Europe and provided sleeping car and restaurant facilities. These trains, which became famous under such names as the Orient Express, the Taurus Express (into the Middle East), the Blue Train (Paris to the Riviera), and the St Petersburg-Lisbon, continued to transport those who could afford them until the age of air travel and some of them still provide luxurious inter city travel from Paris to Brussels, Paris to Bordeaux, etc., today. Similar systems in the USA opened up new resort areas in Florida and in the West, but the greater distances involved, which were more speedily overcome by air, put an end to their usefulness sooner than in Europe.

The same arm's length effect between travellers and their hosts occurred with the hotels which were built to accommodate the mass traveller. When the first Cook's tourists arrived in Switzerland and Italy they made do with whatever old coaching inns had been refurbished for them. The guarantee of regular arrivals encouraged hoteliers to build larger hotels to house visitors of various categories – from establishments for which Cesar Ritz became famous, to simpler places in which parties of 50 to 100 Cook's tourists could be accommodated together.

The Swiss responded quickly to the demands of the new tourists and it was not long before they had developed resorts on lakes and mountains which offered comfort, cleanliness, and good wholesome food suitable to the taste of their visitors. They also improved their road and rail systems and made it possible for tourists to ascend their mountains and glaciers by means of funiculars and cable cars. With such improvements, Switzerland became the leading tourist destination in the world with a reputation for hotel keeping and gastronomy which was unrivalled.

La Belle Epoque

The age of Napoleon III and his elegant wife Eugenie ushered in a new concept of tourism in France. The new Emperor, who rapidly became President in response to the new moods of his country, remodelled Paris by knocking down many old medieval streets and converting them into boulevards with open air cafes and encouraging international exhibitions, during one of which the Eiffel Tower was built. His wife made Paris the centre of world fashion with couturiers like Worth catering for the wealthy and department stores like the Louvre, Aux Printemps and Bon Marche providing fashionable clothes for the middle bourgeoisie. At the same time the Impressionists were creating an entirely new way of looking at life which was to sweep the world. With all these novelties and a tolerant night life, Paris became the first tourist city and created the idea that travel could be for fun as well as for culture and health.

France was the European country with the strongest links with the USA since the days when Lafayette had allied France to the American cause during the American War of Independence and the steel hulled transatlantic liners which took first class passengers and immigrants to the USA and Canada returned filled with affluent Americans eager to visit Paris. This should have been a fine example of how the growing freedom to travel was increasing the friendship and understanding between nations, but one American, the great novelist Henry James, wrote about his compatriot travellers, 'Vulgar, vulgar, vulgar. Their ignorance – their stingy, grudging, defiant attitude to all things European – glare at you hideously.' But the US travellers criticised by James were not very different to the British travellers who still held foreigners to be barbarians with dreadful manners.

Most of the intolerance was however among the wealthier new high bourgeois of the countries of tourist origin; the humbler folk who travelled with people like Cook, and were often pious and religious, tended to regard their foreign environments with amazement and awe. Still regarded by the natives with the respect due to the most powerful nation on earth, the manners and demeanour of British tourists were closely observed and often copied by their hosts. Thus a certain amount of social osmosis occurred, especially in the political sphere for everyone admired Britain's liberal politics which had brought peace and wealth to the nation and to other parts of the world under its influence.

After World War I, and the limitation of free immigration to the USA, the transatlantic liners, which had been filled with communal below-decks accommodation, converted this space to tourist cabins and there began the influx of young Americans who imported the easy, informal ways of 1920's America into Europe. The impact of these young people on a rather staid society, whose life was subject to strict rules, was impressive and it reflected the repressed desires of young Europeans. The staid ocean liners where the wealthy lived graciously in their deluxe cabins were transformed with deck games, swimming pools, and jazz bands, including bands with black musicians.

In London and Paris the Americans were still regarded as brash and ill mannered but not so on the French Riviera which they converted into their own particular kingdom and set the style for leisure travel for the whole of the twentieth century. The American invasion described by Scott Fitzgerald in *Tender Is the Night* changed the way of life on the Riviera. This lovely piece of coast had been discovered by the wealthy and aristocratic English and Russians who built their villas among the palm trees and spent their winters and springs in the southern sunshine, tending their gardens by day and enjoying a gracious social life of bridge parties and concerts in the evenings.

The Americans on the other hand arrived in summer and spent their days lolling on the beaches, and their evenings at the restaurants and nightclubs of the resorts like Juan Les Pins, which had been created by Jay Gould, an American whose father had made a fortune out of railways. Having a good time was the keynote of this society and it infected the whole of the Mediterranean seacoast where having a good time had previously been restricted to Monte Carlo, a suburb of the principality of Monaco, where the good time was enjoyed discreetly by the rich and noble who observed all the social formalities including when in the company of the ladies who were known jocularly as *les grandes horizontales* because of the posture which endeared them to their male masters.

First steps in mass travel

It has always been believed that in the days of ancient Rome the Emperors – faced with the great population explosion which resulted from the settling of thousands of retired ex-soldiers, the translation of slaves into freedmen, and the infiltration of former barbarian tribes across the frontiers – kept the masses happy by providing bread and circuses.

It was suggested by the *Sunday Times* in the 'swinging sixties' that the modern equivalent was sun, sand and sex provided by the great new post-war industry of tourism. When Britain's famous newspaper made this statement, the mass tourism industry had only just begun, for barely 2 per cent of the British were taking holidays abroad. The reasons for this were three-fold:

1   Though the British were the most travelled people in the world, most of them had an innate suspicion of foreign countries, conditioned by over 100 years of their island history.
2   Most people were anxious about the health risks of travelling abroad, where they believed the water was not fit to drink and all lavatories were insanitary.
3   Most people were worried about the cost and of being done down by dishonest foreigners.

On the other hand there were strong reasons why British people should travel; among these were the fact that for some years after World War II Britain lived in a period of austerity with some food still rationed and earnings at pre-war levels. What was more, the British government had imposed foreign exchange restrictions in order to preserve the value of sterling.

These circumstances stimulated entrepreneurs who understood that there was a strong national yearning for entertainment and leisure after the rigours of the war years. They also knew that not far across the Channel there were hoteliers, whose establishments had been closed or requisitioned during the War and who were willing to offer extremely low prices in order to fill the rooms which had once accommodated their bourgeois clientele.

A powerful campaign to encourage travel abroad now began in Britain by travel agents, hotel groups and by the representatives of potential tourist countries. The reason this began in Britain was that this was the only country where getting away from austerity and into the sunshine was both desirable and feasible. The defeated countries were in no state to travel and the French had neither the need nor the desire to leave their own country, as in the USA, the attractions of their own country was enough to satisfy the desire for a change of environment and the French had all the cultural attractions that others travelled there to see.

The Golden Hordes

The mass travel phenomenon, named the Golden Hordes by the writers on tourism Turner and Ash, began with rail travel. Hundreds of trains were marshalled at rail heads at the Channel ports served by cross-channel steamer services and set off for journeys to Austria, Switzerland, the French and Italian Rivieras and the northern coasts of Spain under such names as the William Tell, the Rhinegold and the Mistral. Tourists travelling on them shared the experience of unisex sleeping compartments, restaurant car meals and, in winter, disco cars to ski resorts.

The travellers were from all classes of society, for the British foreign exchange restrictions limited the amount that could be spent on foreign soil and this had a levelling effect which obliged the wealthier to travel with those less well off. At their destinations they were accommodated at pre-war residential hotels of a moderate size or at the grand hotels of yesteryear whose high ceilinged suites were divided up into smaller rooms in some of which spaces were partitioned off as bathroom facilities. The accommodation business was at first ad hoc as in the pre-war years the numbers of visitors had been small. At the hotels, too, there was a levelling off of classes due to the money restrictions and people of all social levels were obliged to consort in the hotel restaurant, bars and public rooms.

The holiday scene thus became a melting pot of social classes, a process that had already begun in Britain due to the shared rescue work in the bombed cities and other operations where co-operation was required regardless of class distinctions. The new class of traveller was nearer the social level of those who waited on them and this also brought about greater contact with the native population, particularly from the young women who made up the majority of young single travellers and who, in becoming friendly with the young male native host, would pass on the concepts of social equality prevalent in a broadly socialist Britain.

By the end of the 1950s, the numbers of travellers to the main holiday countries of Europe from Britain alone had risen to 5 million and they were being joined by Belgians, Dutch and Scandinavians who, because of the northern situation of their countries, were the most eager to travel to the shores of the Mediterranean.

The age of air travel

Though travel by air had been available since 1920, the cost had been much higher than travel by train. In the early 1950s however the introduction of jet aircraft meant that there were many turbo prop aircraft surplus to requirements. This situation provided an opportunity to travel operators to charter aircraft solely for use as carriers for the increasingly large numbers of travellers abroad, and since the charter aircraft costs – as there was no obligation to carry out regular scheduled services as with regular airlines – would therefore be much lower, the cost of an air holiday could be reduced to the level of one by rail.

This situation brought about a revolution in the business of travel. But it did not happen overnight for the existing rules and regulations naturally favoured regular airlines which did not want to lose business to cheap charters. This was one obstacle to the sudden development of holidays by air, the other was the reluctance of travellers to leave terra firma. Once again a great campaign was launched to persuade the public that travel by air was safe, quicker, cheaper and more comfortable than travel by rail.

Gradually the public were convinced and by the mid 1960s there were several million air travellers, not only to the established resort areas but further afield to the hitherto unvisited but sunny beaches of the whole of the Mediterranean and across the Atlantic to the USA and Caribbean.

The mass impact

Air travel extended the world of leisure travel in a way that would have been beyond the wildest expectations of travellers at the beginning of the twentieth century. In a matter of a decade the entire Mediterranean came within the reach of leisure seekers. Deserted and inhospitable coasts where the natives had eked a living by fishing or raising goats were developed into resort areas.

The developers had the opportunity to create resorts from scratch, erecting towns where there had been nothing but rock and scrub. The accelerating demand for accommodation meant that resorts with all their services – sewage, water supply, electricity, etc. – had to be erected quickly. Reinforced concrete blocks soon began to disfigure coastlines and occasionally the speed of the building operation caused buildings to have defects and even to collapse.

The first coastal region to be developed for air tourists was in southern Spain near the city of Malaga. Where previously there had been a wild uninhabited coast, tourist cities began to grow. Capital and technical expertise from foreign sources began to arrive as banks and finance houses became interested in what promised to be a boom industry. At first this was welcomed but it was not long before some Spanish voices were raised in protest at the realization that foreign investment and equipment as well as expert technical labour was benefiting the outsiders more than the host country. There was no alternative to this, however, for Spain lacked the national capital for such a large scale exercise and, moreover, the new tourist cities were providing new labour markets in part of the country with minimal local earning power.

The long months of sunshine, the splendid sandy beaches and the low labour costs, and therefore cheap hotel rates, attracted an ever increasing number of tourists and the tourist city developments spread all around the southern Spanish coasts. After years of austerity under Franco, Spain was becoming a country with enough money in the exchequer to improve living standards throughout its many and varied regions and to foment national industries which could then earn more foreign exchange and further increase the living standards of the workers.

For the natives of the coastal regions of Spain the tourist industry was like manna from heaven and brought to formerly impoverished families better housing and better prospects for their children who could be sent to school and later to universities, thus creating a new educated class with a greater understanding of the social and political affairs of their country, which by historic circumstances had remained outside the progressive developments of other European countries. As in other parts of Europe which had felt the first impact of large scale tourism, the Spanish people began to feel the pressure of opinion of the new young tourists. This did not please many of the older people whose innate conservatism upheld the ways of life which were fast disappearing in the rest of Europe. Thus in the end tourism had a greater effect on the destiny of Spain than the reactionary government imposed after the Civil War.

What had begun in Spain with air tourism soon spread all over the Mediterranean area and then across the Atlantic to the USA and Canada, where there was already a good tourist infrastructure for the millions who travelled at home. For Europeans, travel in America was still a daunting prospect because the distance made it difficult to offer air holidays at prices comparable to those in Europe. Moreover the air companies that controlled the transatlantic airlanes and made good profits out of them were reluctant to have cheap charter fare competitors. In the end however they had to give way and there began a rapidly increasing east to west tourist traffic to the New England States and to Florida where the social impact was negligible for visitors and hosts were people of a shared culture.

The tourism dilemma

There is no doubt that tourism has changed the world in many ways and that for many cultures the tourist is the living embodiment of the images of the world wide media. The face-to-face encounter is always more potent than confrontation through the picture or written word. Tourism changed the image of the British as milords; after travel became more accessible to more classes of British people, it changed the perception of the people of Africa and the Far East.

Much of this change has been due to the increasing number of young people who travel, either under the auspices of tourist organizations or unaided. The young with their sceptical approach to their own societies and without the acquired prejudices of older generations are more able to communicate with other cultures and are the carriers of ideas across frontiers.

In Europe the ideas that have changed over the last half century of tourism have been sometimes trivial – as for example the acceptance of the Italian pizza or pastas as universally palatable food – but often more profound and more subtle. In Spain for example, chaperonage was still common when tourists first arrived in the 1950s but began to disappear as young Spanish men and women observed the behaviour of their young English visitors. In particular there was a profound change in attitudes to sex in a predominantly male dominated society where sex was a hidden pleasure indulged in with working class women in brothels. In Italy the demand for young male escorts to local dancing places created severe tension in hotels where waiters were expected to serve until late into the night and were therefore not free to join the holiday girls: their demands for regular hours had to be met in order to avoid strike action. Even more powerful was the impact of information about working conditions in Britain's post-war welfare state. A new mood was created among the working people in tourist resorts which changed the conditions of their work and their voting habits which in the past were influenced both by their employers and the power of the Church.

The changes that took place cannot all be ascribed to tourism, for the media and the post war mood reflected a wide desire for change, but the impact of face-to-face observations and exchange of opinions cannot be underrated. Nor can the power of tourist money to condone the activities of entrepreneurs who exploit people's appetites for sex and other forms of self-indulgence. Since the main motivation of present day travel for increasing numbers of tourists is the pursuit of pleasure, the breaking down of cultural constraints by traditional social behaviour is inevitable and it remains to be seen what effect this will have on a nation's psyche.

The change in the habits and mores of host countries by tourism is underpinned by the viability of the tourist economy in each region of every country. It has been almost inevitable that tourist development in one part of a country will lead to demands for development from another that feels left out from what appears to be a means to improving the local economy. In the Algarve region of Portugal, the restrained tourism development has gone by the board as every village along this delightful coast has clamoured for the arrival of the bulldozers to plough existing buildings into the sand to build concrete holiday cities.

The development of holiday regions has now become world wide as air fares decrease and competition between airlines increase. In the fever of activity few face the fact that there may arrive a saturation point or that perhaps, as is indicated by the now regular discounting of holidays prices, it may have already arrived. Discounts, Air Miles awards and free travel prizes are all symptoms of competitive angst. Having been created, the travel juggernaut must somehow be kept rolling. Some years ago the USSR instituted a system of state holidays by which citizens were rewarded with leisure breaks at Black Sea resorts. This regulated leisure spread the holiday period by the simple control of numbers awarded holidays. This not only helped resorts and hotels to operate over a longer period than the holiday rush period of western Europe, but also kept the national airline occupied in a rationalized operation. In a democratic society the rationalization of leisure time by decree may not be acceptable but on the other hand an uncontrolled free-for-all also has its problems.

The ecology of tourism

The mass movement of leisure seekers is causing a good deal of concern among those who care about the interdependence of human beings and their environment. When tourist movements began in the nineteenth century the impact of visitors was of little concern; though the tourists of the time were undoubtedly destructive, scratching their graffiti on frescoes and often carving for themselves pieces of temples and statues or carrying away whole works of art, there were so few tourists that the effect was negligible. The modern tourist is less of a vandal but does more damage without intending to.

The most obvious form of damage today is the thoughtless destruction of areas of natural beauty by unsightly urban tourist developments such as has taken place around the coasts of Spain which have become a concrete suburbia of hotel and apartment blocks. Allied to this is the effect of such development on natural resources such as the water table which is depleted by wells dug to supply water for the increasing number of bathrooms which tourists demand at the hotels they patronize, or to water golf courses, etc. In some cases this has led to the destruction of the livelihood of local subsistence farmers.

National parks and other areas of natural beauty have also suffered severely from the sheer weight of millions of tramping boots. In Britain's Lake District the tourist nature lovers have widened paths from small tracks into great trodden highways and have eroded the soil, causing it to slide into ravines and thus making tracks impassable, as well as unsightly. This has now become a worldwide phenomenon, even in parks of such countries as far away from the mass tourist haunts as Chile, which has started to control numbers allowed into national parks.

The improvement in road systems and the increase of tourism by motor car has created other problems with the exhaust fumes of millions of cars killing off vegetation and causing the closure of tunnels, as in Switzerland, for hours at a time, to clear the accumulation of carbon dioxide in Alpine tunnels. In the Galapagos Islands off the coast of Ecuador, regarded since Charles Darwin's visit in 1834 as natural wonderlands, the oil of diesel boats and the incursion of developers is spoiling one of the world's most extraordinary Edens. And the Barrier Reef off the east coast of Australia is also suffering from the presence of too many visitors. Even the breath of millions of tourists can do damage as the French realized when they built a replica Lascaux with its drawings by cave dwellers in order to save the originals which are no longer in public view.

The answer to these tourist dilemmas lies in the future and in society's concern for its environment; but will we accept the discipline required to preserve it or will self-interest and the pursuit of wealth be the deciding factor? In the meantime larger and larger aircraft are being built and airlines are merging in order to ensure their profitability, which will come from more passengers to transport at economical rates. Cruise companies heartened by the increase in interest in floating cities of pleasure are commissioning ships that will accommodate 4000–6000 sea tourists who will add to the tramping feet over the historic ruins of Europe and the islands of the Pacific and the Caribbean during their shore excursions. Popular resorts will become self-contained hedonist cities from which there will be no need to sally forth into the surrounding territory.

The one proviso for such a future is, of course, that the world economy will continue to grow. If it does then the dream (or nightmare) according to your point of view, of tourism may well come true.

References

Behrend, G. (1961) *Grand European Expresses*, London, Allen & Unwin
Burkart, A.J. and Medlick, S. (1974) *Tourism: Past, Present and Future*, London, Heinemann
Casson, Lionel (1974) *Travel in the Ancient World*, London, Allen & Unwin

Coleman, T. (1976) *The Liners*, London, Allen Lane

Financial Times, London (articles to 1997)

Her Majesty's Stationery Office, *Annual Statistics (to 1995)*, London

Swinglehurst, Edmund (1974) *The Romantic Journey: The Story of Thomas Cook and Victorian Travel*, London, Pica Editorial

Swinglehurst, Edmund, (1982) *Cooks Tours*, London, Bladford

Travel Features, London, (articles to 1977)

Turner, Louis and Ash, John (1975) *The Golden Hordes: International Tourism and the Pleasure Periphery*, London, Constable

Wall, R. (1978) *Ocean Liners*, London, Collins

7 The uneasy relationship between tourism and native peoples: the Australian experience

David Mercer

What is known of the 'other' is conditional upon that 'other's' relative location. Whites must not ignore this by taking advantage of their privileged speaking positions to construct an external version of 'us' which may pass for our 'reality'. There must be limits to the ways our worlds are re-written or placed in conceptual frameworks which are not our own. (Huggins et al., 1995: 167)

If there is one thing academic commentators, policy makers and industry representatives alike are broadly in agreement about today it is that research on tourism is far more sophisticated than was the case ten or twenty years ago and that we now have a much better understanding of just how complex is the phenomenon we are dealing with. Like its handmaiden – 'leisure' – there are very real problems associated with the conceptualization and measurement of tourism's multiple facets, and the temptation to simplify can be strong (MacCannell, 1992). However, long gone are the days when people accepted without question generalized statements such as 'tourism delivers unparalleled economic benefits to all' or 'tourism is always enormously destructive of local communities, indigenous communities and the environment'.

We now clearly understand that, however defined, tourism comes in a myriad of guises and that it can have both good and bad social, environmental, economic and political consequences, depending upon its size and form, the extent to which its growth is controlled or not controlled and, most importantly, the perspective of the viewer. 'Hosts' and 'guests', too, are far from simple and easily-defined categories, and – contrary to the representation of reality in Butler's (1980) widely-cited 'tourist area cycle of evolution' model – regions and nations do not experience simple unidirectional change with respect to tourism development. We also recognize that it is often impossible to isolate tourism's precise influence from that of other features of emerging globalization such as developments in telecommunications, education, and transport technology. In the remote highlands of Papua New Guinea, for example, BHP's massive Ok Tedi gold and copper mine has, over the space of a few short years, catapulted the most advanced mining and transport infrastructure, as well as consumerist western lifestyles, into a hitherto isolated region with an essentially stone age culture. This project, together with countless other examples in similar settings, including affluent resort enclaves, can be envisaged as a kind of 'node of modernity' from which waves of western influence spread out into the surrounding primitive region. Goulet (1977) has presented a persuasive argument for regarding 'tourism' – along with education, medicine, agriculture, etc. – as yet another medium for technology transfer. Thus, in addition to novel transport and image technologies, less affluent peoples in tourist regions frequently come to experience new food and refrigeration, construction, management, recreational and finance technologies, to mention but a few developments. The various impacts, however, are never uniform and, increasingly, they are often successfully resisted. In each case the responses are different so we must beware of simplistic generalizations. Pagdin (1995, 195) emphasizes that,

> ... locally-affected people are not shaped passively by outside forces but react as well, at times even changing the conditions of the larger system, and that the outcome of tourism development is a negotiated process.

Issues and themes

The main aim of this chapter is to illustrate some of this complexity through a discussion of the range of contemporary responses of Australia's indigenous Aboriginal and Torres Strait Islander population to the tourist phenomenon and the pressures for change.[1] This issue is central to what the anthropologist, Debra Bird Rose (1996: 9) describes as the 'dramatic and injurious junction' humans have now reached as a species. She is referring to the widespread opposition that we now encounter between ecological and human rights – an opposition which ultimately has to be fatal both for the planet and for the human species. Bird's blunt message is that we have no choice but to take heed of the 'wisdom of the

---

1 Aborigines and Torres Strait Islanders are two different ethnic groups and are distinguished as such in the Australian census. Other terms, favoured by Australia's indigenous population, include 'Anangu' (a central Australian term for Aboriginal people), 'Koori' (an indigenous term from south-eastern Australia meaning 'ourselves') and 'Nunga'. In this chapter the term 'Aborigine' includes Torres Strait Islanders.

elders' and to listen carefully to indigenous peoples' understandings of ecosystem functioning and role. Australia can play a leading role in this process but only if – as in the United States, Canada and New Zealand – the national government is also prepared to cede some of its power and grant a much greater degree of indigenous sovereignty within the pre-existing nation state.

In 1965, the first detailed consultancy report on the Australian tourism sector was published (Harris, Kerr, Forster and Co., 1965). This, and subsequent inquiries, recommended much greater Aboriginal involvement at all levels. However, as will be seen, some thirty years later, we find a wide spectrum of responses on the part of the country's indigenous population ranging from outright opposition at one extreme through various co-management agreements with white Australians to enthusiasm for indigenous-controlled and run tourist enterprises at the other. That there is a wide diversity of reactions should come as no surprise, for the degree of historical exposure to tourism varies considerably across the country. Moreover, at the time of first European contact, 'Australia' was home to some 600 language groupings ('Nations'), living in markedly different geographical environments ranging from cool temperate conditions in southern Tasmania to the northern wet tropics and at population densities ranging from less than 0.3 persons per square km in inland Australia to 1.2 in the well-watered coastal south-east (Anderson, 1995). Nomadism, or semi-nomadism, were (and, in certain cases, still are) relatively common in some arid and mountain areas but were much less usual in many coastal or well-watered inland areas where there was a year-round abundance of fish, wildlife and other resources. As well, contact with Europeans has been only relatively recent in north and north-western Australia by comparison with the longer colonial encounter in the south-east. Thus we are dealing with a very complicated picture which means we have to be wary of generalizing about *the* Aboriginal experience.

In this chapter I explore a number of themes concerning the often uneasy relationship between contemporary Western tourism developments and the native Aboriginal population principally, though not exclusively, in sparsely populated 'outback', northern and central Australia.[2] In many of these areas (most recently the Bungles-Bungles region in the Kimberley of north-western Australia) the tourism promotion literature and media advertising are redefining the way that we 'should' view the

2 The term 'outback' is an interesting one and is open to wide interpretation. Most usually, it refers only to arid and semi-arid Australia or to these areas plus the northern tropical regions. For some writers, the concept is widened to include low population density areas in the cooler and wetter south of the country (see Black and Rutledge, 1995). More significantly, Muecke (1996: 409) has recently reminded us that '. . . in the actual spatial practices of indigenous places, there is no sense to the term "outback" . . .'.

landscape in terms that are often fundamentally different from those of the traditional owners (Muecke, 1996). A salient feature of the discussion here is the inseparability of questions surrounding tourism development and broader social justice issues concerning Aboriginal rights:

1 to control over their traditional lands, practices and cultural representations;
2 to compensation for past injustices; and
3 to total or partial sovereignty/self-governance (Reynolds, 1996).

Even though the focus is directly on Australia's indigenous people (what Young (1995) calls the *Third World in the First*), many of the ideas are also relevant to other national settings – like Papua New Guinea and the Pacific Islands – where tourism has recently brought together peoples from vastly different cultural and economic backgrounds (Douglas, 1995). The discussion is of particular significance to other, federated states, such as Canada and the United States, where the goals and policy orientation of the national government may sometimes be in conflict both with minority native peoples and one or more sub-national levels of government and where there is a growing indigenous rights' movement. An obvious comparison is with Canada, where the pressures for several kinds of resource developments north of the 60th parallel have highlighted basic concerns about quality of environment and the rights and welfare of northern Canadian peoples of Indian or Inuit ancestry (Lynge, 1987; Fenge, 1993).

The central problem being addressed revolves around the question of whether or not contemporary tourism development in Australia beyond the major metropolitan centres can be said to be socially and culturally 'appropriate' from the Aboriginal viewpoint. With one or two exceptions (e.g. Strang, 1996), this is a relatively under-researched area by comparison with the comparatively large body of marketing research literature on the perceptions of western travellers seeking what is sometimes quaintly referred to an 'ethnic tourism' experience (Laxson, 1991; Zeppel, 1995). What might be called the 'sub-text' relates to the contradictory role of the modern capitalist state in both encouraging tourism developments on the one hand and yet at the same time coming under mounting international and domestic pressure to appease the growing demands of native peoples and environmentalists who may be vehemently opposed to such projects. Such opposition is likely to be strong if – as is the case in contemporary Australia – there is a perception that governments are doing little to address broader human rights, health, education and social justice issues of deep concern to indigenous peoples (Evatt Foundation, 1996). These themes highlight the inherently political nature of tourism and tourist developments and underscore Prosser's (1992) argument that there are a number of key ethical questions at the core of discussions about tourism as an 'industry', both internationally and in specific national settings. Writing from a native Hawaiian perspective, Kanehele (1992: 31) is unequivocal in his belief that:

> ... the tourism industry has a moral responsibility to preserve and nurture native cultures in destination areas where their arts and crafts, customs and historic sites ... are marketed, displayed, sold or exploited for commercial ends.

Recent court decisions in favour of Aboriginal interests in both Canada and Australia suggest that in the future in those countries, at least, we can certainly expect a more forceful representation of Aboriginal interests where tourism and related developments are mooted (Mercer, 1997). And – as we find in parts of the United States (Lew, 1996) – there is growing evidence that, in certain circumstances, the Aboriginal position may well be opposition to tourism and tourists. In short, what we are witnessing here is a clash of two powerful, yet opposing global tendencies – on the one hand Postman's (1987) expanding 'culture of amusement', and on the other a strong programme of cultural revival/resistance on the part of the world's indigenous people.

Tourism in polygeneric nations

The most reliable indicator of a distinctive 'culture' is a spoken language. Globally, out of a total population of 5.5 billion, there are currently around 6000 of these, of which some 4000 to 5000 are spoken by between 200 million and 625 million 'indigenous' people, depending upon the definition used (Durning, 1993). Many of these people (the Inuit, the Saami, Native American Indians, the Ainu) are minorities within affluent societies and, in the past, have often been brutalized and dispossessed, marginalized politically, and/or been required to take on an undue burden of environmental 'bads' such as toxic waste contamination of their land and water. Increasingly, they are voicing their concerns in many different ways and are becoming empowered both through international linkages and coalitions with sympathetic non-indigenous people and organizations.[3] In recent years, for example, we have witnessed long protest marches to distant national capitals on the part of indigenous Amazonian groups in Ecuador and Bolivia and continued political opposition to the Mexican state in Chiapas. We have also seen the Chipko

3 May 1996, in London, for example, saw a gathering of indigenous peoples from around the world to form an international alliance pushing for more responsible action on the part of the major transnational mining companies. This was timed to coincide with the AGMs of several of these corporations.

movement in northern India, as well as a successful campaign on the part of the Cree Nation in northern Quebec against expansion of the James Bay hydro-electricity project and the disastrous impact this would have had on their traditional hunting lands. In all of these cases, as in Australia, issues of land and human rights, self-governance and biodiversity preservation, are all intertwined. Increasingly, international human rights instruments are bolstering and empowering native rights. Article 27 of the International Covenant on Civil and Political Rights, for instance, specifically provides for minorities to enjoy their own culture. Indeed, on several occasions in recent years the UN Human Rights Committee has upheld the rights of indigenous people against destructive land-use activities on their land in Sweden, Finland, Brazil and Canada.

In common with such countries as South Africa, Fiji, New Zealand, Canada and the United States, Australia is a modern polygeneric nation. This term is used by Willmot (1987) to refer to that relatively small group of nations made up of human groups with markedly varied origins and race memories. Frequently, this includes people of Aboriginal descent. By contrast, societies such as Japan, Nigeria and, to a lesser extent, Britain and France, are ethnically much more homogeneous. Another relevant characteristic of Australia is that it is a country where 'coloniser, colonised and postcolonial [exist] . . . all at once' (Ahmad, 1995: 9). In the past, polygeneric societies 'failed' and became 'homogeneous', either by a process of genocide or by miscegeneration. But today, Wilmot argues that:

> . . . the old process of forgetting or replacing memory with mythology is no longer possible. By the time societies become literate and this literacy becomes popularly based, the forgetting of origin memories is not possible. (1987: 17)

Unfortunately, though, many of these 'origin memories' are also inseparable from painful recollections of profound historical injustices in the form of massacres, kidnappings and dispossession (Ugresic, 1996). Part of the argument here is that this situation raises a number of important issues for tourism planning in such societies. For example, to what extent is genuine 'reconciliation' possible, and should those catering for an interest in 'ethnic tourism' gloss over past crimes and misdemeanours associated with brutal colonial encounters and pander to a sanitized picture of the ethnic/indigenous experience?[4] In Australia in the late 1980s and

---

4 In Australia, in 1990, a reconciliation process was initiated by the then Labour Commonwealth government to attempt to heal some of the historical rift between black and white Australia. A 25-member Council for Aboriginal Reconciliation was established and its charter is to draw up formal reconciliation documents by the year 2001, the centenary of federation. However, so substantial were the financial cuts to Aboriginal programmes by the new

early 1990s, in response to widespread community outrage about the unprecedented scale of indigenous deaths in Australian prisons, a Royal Commission was established. Called the Royal Commission into Aboriginal Deaths in Custody, this inquiry highlighted social and economic deprivation and political marginalization as critical factors in explaining the high rates of suicide in custody, in particular (Commonwealth of Australia, 1991).[5] Interestingly, the Commission's final report identified involvement in the tourism industry as a potential source of economic development in the future but also acknowledged the possible negative effects that tourism can bring with it. More recently, in an important essay on ethnic tourism and nationalism, Pitchford (1995: 36) emphasizes that:

> Ethnic tourism ... can serve as a resource in both the material and cultural aspects of ethnic struggles. By marketing itself to interested outsiders, a marginalized group can improve its position economically ... It can also acquire new political leverage vis-à-vis the state, if the state stands to gain from tourist revenue attracted by a group's cultural distinctiveness ...

Australia certainly has no shortage of interesting Aboriginal sites of archaeological and cultural significance. By 1993, for example, under the terms of the Australian Heritage Commission Act (1975), 814 Aboriginal places had been officially listed on the 'Register of the National Estate'. These included shell middens, rock art sites, stone arrangements and sites of mythological significance. In 1996, for the first time, the Aboriginal and Torres Strait Island Tourism Commission opened an office in Rio del Mar, California, to publicize these and related attractions.

Analysts are deeply divided over the question of the relative costs and benefits of tourism in less affluent countries or among marginalized ethnic groups in rich nations. The overwhelming impression one gains from the literature is that, economically, tourism is, on the whole a 'good thing', holds out enormous developmental promise and should be vigorously promoted. It appears this is the way most political and business leaders certainly view the tourism phenomenon. Indeed, the unanimous

Conservative government in the August 1996 budget, that one prominent member of the Council resigned and others threatened to resign. The reconciliation process currently appears very fragile. The budget cuts also resulted in a call by some Aboriginal leaders for a boycott of the Sydney 2000 Olympic Games. For a discussion of the way tourism promotion at one popular Australian site presents a sanitized version of a brutal past, see Simpson (1996). On the question of how Aborigines would like their culture and heritage to be interpreted, see Ballantyne (1995).

5 At a total cost of $400 million, the Royal Commission into Aboriginal Deaths in Custody handed down its five-volume report in May, 1991. It focused on 99 specific cases up to 1989 and made 339 recommendations for action. Since then, little appears to have changed. In 1995 16 Aborigines died in Australian jails, a 50 per cent increase on the 1994 figure (*The Australian*, 27–28 April 1996).

outcome of the joint Unesco/World Bank seminar, held in Washington in December 1976 (DeKadt, 1979: 399) was that 'tourism can make a substantial contribution to the economic and social development of many countries'. The only qualifications were that attention should be paid to the precise tourism product that was being marketed and that any development should be carefully managed to fit in with a national plan. The symposium did spend some of the time discussing the distributional impact of tourism on 'life chances and welfare', but by and large the emphasis was on the positive rather than the negative effects. Since the Washington seminar there has appeared a growing body of empirical evidence that the so-called 'benefits' of tourism are often greatly outweighed by the substantial long-term social and environmental costs incurred. Ascher (1985: 10) comments that 'The time has long gone when international tourism was considered an obvious and easy means of contributing economically to the advancement of developing countries'; and Pagdin's (1995: 191) research in Pokhara, Nepal, concluded that 'The economic performance of the industry is seen as modest to date, with benefits mainly being restricted to those directly involved in tourism activity'. Recent studies from many different countries have underscored the often disastrous consequences of unplanned tourist developments for certain sections of the host societies.

Three kinds of tourism 'impacts' have been alluded to so far: economic, social (or cultural) and environmental. Much of the literature on tourism distinguishes these impacts for analytical purposes. But one of the main arguments here is that such separation is misplaced. 'Economic' impacts, for example, may only be relatively short-lived and invariably have important distributional effects which are ultimately 'social' in their consequences. Further, the 'environmental' destruction of, say, an Australian Aboriginal sacred site can have significant cultural ramifications. It also has to be continually recognized that 'tourism' is frequently merely one part of the total development process that invariably affects many newly 'opened up' areas. As will become apparent in the Australian case studies to be discussed below – and similar to Ok Tedi – road construction and energy and water supply for mineral exploration or pastoral development, for example, often provide the initial modern infrastructure upon which a fledgling tourist industry rapidly builds.

Australia – the tourism boom

Even though it does not make the ranking of the top twenty nations in terms of tourist visitation, Australia currently has one of the highest tourist growth rates in the world. Between 1992 and 1993, for example, international tourist arrivals 'down under' grew by 16 per cent by comparison with the OECD average of 2 per cent (Organization for Economic Cooperation and Development, 1994). More recently (year ended December, 1995) the growth rate has slowed to 8 per cent. Nevertheless, Australia's share still only represents around 0.5 per cent of the international traveller market, an indicator of the country's location on the outer edge of the distant 'pleasure periphery'. Further, at a time when many of Australia's traditional primary export industries are in serious economic difficulty, both the federal and individual state governments clearly see tourism as a major growth area that should be vigorously promoted. A target figure of 1.2 per cent of the global tourism market by the year 2000 has been established by the Australian Tourist Commission. This would translate into between 5 million and 6.5 million international visitors, by comparison with the current total of around 3 million.

From small beginnings in the 1930s when Australia played host to only 23,000 visitors, the industry currently generates around $13 billion annually, or 10 per cent of the country's total foreign earnings. Tourism now represents the most important source of foreign exchange earnings. The present planning horizon is for one million Japanese visitors by the end of the century; and the expectation is that by the year 2000 around 50 per cent of Australia's visitors will be from Asia (Australian Tourist Commission, 1992). As travel restrictions ease, China, in particular, has the potential to become an increasingly significant centre of demand. South Korea and Indonesia are similarly placed. In the run-up to the Sydney 2000 Olympic Games, tourism export earnings have been predicted by the country's Tourism Forecasting Council to reach $30.6 billion by 2005 (*The Age*, Melbourne, July 28, 1996).

There is concern in many quarters that this potential flood-tide needs to be carefully monitored and controlled by means of a National Tourism Strategy (Department of Tourism, 1992), but so far, despite the rhetoric, there have been few signs that the competing states are prepared to subordinate what they see as their individual economic interests to the good of the nation as a whole. In addition, notwithstanding the production of a Draft National Aboriginal and Torres Strait Islander Tourism Industry Strategy (Aboriginal and Torres Strait Islander Commission (ATSIC), 1994), subsequent commonwealth government funding cuts have impacted seriously on the plan and, arguably, too little co-ordinated attention has been paid to the whole question of impacts on Australia's indigenous population. In the Northern Territory, in particular, 'Aboriginality' and Aboriginal images are used constantly by white Australian tourism promoters to 'sell' the Territory as a destination. Yet, at the same time, the Territory government has a long history of entrenched legal opposition to indigenous land claims and the Aboriginal population

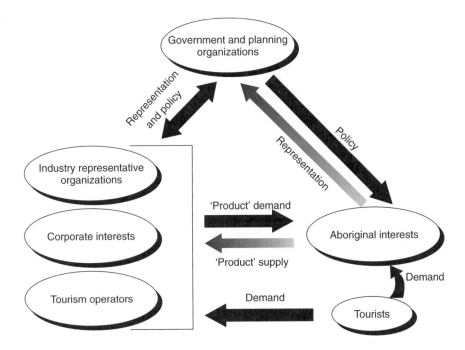

Figure 7.1 The marginalization of Aboriginal input into Northern Territory tourism policy
Sources: Law, 1993

frequently lives in appalling 'third-' or even 'fourth world' conditions.[6] Moreover, as Law (1993) has emphasized, with a few notable exceptions at specific, Aboriginal-owned sites, the Aboriginal viewpoint on the formulation, implementation and appraisal of Northern Territory tourism policy has generally been marginalized (see Figure 7.1). His assessment, too, is that, on a per capita basis, the Aboriginal share of the economic benefits of tourism in the Territory amount to only around 12 per cent of the total accruing to white Australians. Pitchford (1995: 36) has argued that control over the content of 'ethnic image construction and projection'

6 A recent (1996) Australian National University study found that almost 40 per cent of all Aboriginal families live at or below the national poverty line. Further, over 50 per cent of these families with children did not have a gainfully employed adult and the poverty levels for indigenous families with two children worsened between the 1986 and 1991 censuses (*The Australian*, 7 August 1996). In addition, the rates of acute rheumatic fever among Aboriginal children aged 5–14 in the Northern Territory are the highest in the world and Aboriginal babies are twice as likely to die at birth than their white counterparts. Additional data on worsening disadvantage are contained in *The State of Australia* (Evatt Foundation, 1996). Paradoxically, if accepted, the Northern Territory's draft constitution will be the first in Australia to recognize Aborigines as Australia's first people as well as to give recognition to customary indigenous law.

is a crucial element in political empowerment. To date, in Australia, that control has largely been vested in the hands of non-indigenous marketing and public relations' corporations.

Once in the country, the favoured destinations for overseas tourists to Australia are the two major cities of Sydney and Melbourne, the Gold Coast and the Barrier Reef (the latter two in Queensland), and northern and central Australia. Essentially, the Northern Territory is the main drawcard for tourists (both domestic and international) to the north, though north Queensland and northern Western Australia are also becoming increasingly popular. Cairns airport, in north Queensland, is now the fifth busiest airport in the country in terms of traffic movements and is an important gateway to Asia. Queensland's tourism growth has been spectacular in recent years. After New South Wales it is now the second most visited state by international travellers. Around 50 per cent of all overseas tourists visit Queensland, by comparison with 65 per cent to New South Wales. The Northern Territory attracts 9.2 per cent (Chohan et al., 1994). In 1984, only a little over 58,000 international travellers (6.2 per cent of all tourists) visited the Northern Territory. By 1992, following aggressive promotion by the Northern Territory government, this had increased by almost 400 per cent, to 222,4000. Interestingly, the survey data for the period 1987 to 1992 suggest that Aboriginal culture has not been a significant attraction for either domestic or overseas visitors to the Northern Territory. For these years, consistently less than 1 per cent of all visitors using commercial accommodation identified Aboriginal culture as the most important attraction (Altman, 1993).[7]

Darwin appears set to be one of the three fastest-growing Australian airports in terms of international traffic movements. For this northern gateway, these are projected to expand at over 8 per cent per year up to 2011. However, the point needs to be made that by far the majority of tourists visiting Central Australia and the Northern Territory are Australians and that among overseas visitors there, there is a strong bias towards North American and European markets (Black and Rutledge, 1995). For the first time, in 1995, tourist visits to the Northern Territory topped the one million mark and tourism expenditure totalled around $480 million for the year. This region contains four major Aboriginal-owned national parks of outstanding international significance (De Lacy, 1994). These are Gurig (Cobourg Peninsula), Nitmiluk (Katherine Gorge), Ayers Rock (now known as Uluru–Kata Tjuta National Park), in the centre of the continent, and Kakadu National Park in the north, 300 km to the south-east of the Territory's capital, Darwin. In view of the

---

7 It needs to be emphasized that these data refer to people using commercial accommodation and that there is uncertainty about precisely when the people were surveyed on their vacations. As Altman (1993: 4) notes, contrary to initial intentions, Aboriginal culture might have become an important attraction during the stay in the Northern Territory.

importance to the Aborigines of the latter two sites, in particular, much of the remainder of the discussion will focus on the tourism experience at Kakadu and Uluru. But first, in order to clarify the issue, a brief comment is in order concerning the general attitude of Aborigines towards tourism and development.

In summary, the Aboriginal perspective generally can be summed up in two words: *choice* and *control*. They frequently demand total control over their own lands and their own destinies so that they are able to negotiate with white Australians from a position of strength when it comes to making decisions relating to mining or tourism development proposals on their land. In particular, Aborigines often affirm the right to reject any proposal for developments on their land that they consider inappropriate. They also insist on the right to refuse to negotiate, if they so choose. Thus, 'control' can refer either to the power to ban tourist visits altogether or it can mean the right to manage a growing tourism market, perhaps by the institution of future bans. Although it may appear strange to Europeans, there is sometimes considerable puzzlement among Aborigines as to why affluent white people would choose the tourism experience in the first place. It has been pointed out by many writers that, in their modern form, tourism and recreation presuppose a work ethic and the alternation of periods of 'work' and 'play'. Such rigid separation of time and activity has no direct correspondence in pre-industrial cultures. Such confusion inevitably means that Aborigines often start by regarding tourism with some suspicion. Whether or not they continue to support developments in a particular region invariably depends on their first-hand experience with it: the numbers of tourists involved over a certain time period, their behaviour, and so on. It also means that 'if people are puzzled as to what tourists are doing, then the task of attempting to assess their reactions and any negative impacts is problematic, to say the least' (Brady, 1985).

Fuelled largely by outspoken opposition to some major mining proposals like those at Coronation Hill and the Century Zinc mine sites in the Northern Territory, corporate business interests in Australia constantly promote the view that Aborigines are opposed to any kind of tourism or mining developments on their lands, and hence, 'development' and 'progress'. But there is ample evidence that this is a misrepresentation of the Aboriginal stance. Rather, what the Aborigines do fear is the possible effects of such projects on their traditional way of life, on their land and on their capacity to perform their tribal ceremonies and pass on their cultural traditions to the next generation. In theory there seems little reason to doubt that Western-style development and traditional Aboriginal life styles can co-exist reasonably harmoniously so long as due consideration is given to early planning and genuine consultation and so long as careful monitoring of effects also takes place. In the north-west of

South Australia, for example, the Pitjantjatjara people have recently agreed to their land being re-opened for tourism after an extended period when it was banned. Similarly, in the 1980s the Jawoyn people of the Northern Territory successfully resisted a major new mining venture on their land for five years. Then, some two years later, they acceded to another similar project in another part of their territory that did not impact on sacred sites. What is clear is that both governments and private corporations still have a very long way to go in terms of genuine understanding of intercultural approaches to decision-making in Australia. Ross (1995) has recently underscored the inappropriateness of many of the well-tried western approaches.

Australian Aborigines

Aborigines have lived in what is now known as Australia for at least 60,000 years. Early estimates put their number at about 300,000 at the time of the European invasion of the continent, in 1788. More recent archaeological evidence has suggested that 500,000–600,000, or even one or two million are probably more accurate estimates (Butlin, 1983). Even so, for a country approximately the same size as the continental United States, these figures represent a tiny indigenous population by comparison with the 12 million Native Americans that existed at the time of first European contact in North America. Nevertheless, all parts of what we now call 'Australia' were intimately known. Muecke (1996: 411) notes that 'Parts of the sandy deserts of the centre which "we" tend to call "unsettled areas" are still just as densely named as other parts of Australia.' Today, the Aboriginal and Torres Strait Islander population is approximately 300,000 and is projected to grow to 340,000 by 2001. This represents only about 1.6 per cent of the total Australian population. However, in the Northern Territory they represent 23 per cent of the population.[8] For those anthropologists who define technology narrowly, simply in terms of tools, a case could be made for the Australian Aborigines being relatively 'primitive' and 'backward' at the time of first European contact. But if technology is defined as 'knowledge used for practical

8 Aborigines live in the following types of communities: (i) largely metropolitan areas such as Sydney; (ii) established, provincial and largely non-Aboriginal towns; (ii) Aboriginal towns (former government and mission settlements); (iv) outstations (or homelands), usually on Aboriginal land; and (v) on pastoral properties, either Aboriginal-owned or non-Aboriginal owned. Enumeration is a serious problem because of the high rates of mobility and the remoteness of many of the settlements. Recent work (Martin and Taylor, 1996) has suggested that the official census probably considerably underestimates the number of indigenous Australians.

purposes' then Aborigines were at that time – and indeed, still are in many areas – extremely knowledgeable and technologically advanced (Lewis, 1992).

Spiritually there was a profound gulf between the Aborigines and the early Christian colonists. Aboriginal religion had – and indeed, still has – no concept of a heaven or hell. In common with American Indians, Aborigines have no understanding of 'property' in the white European sense. Initially, the land was territorially delimited on a clan basis, but other groups were also frequently granted permission to use the land. The bond between Aboriginal people, the plants, animals, landscape and local spirits was considered indissoluble and so land could not be 'bought' or 'sold'. What is more, the human/land link was timeless; it was established prior to birth and continued after death. It is frequently said of the Aborigines that they do not own the land, the land owns them. What might appear to European eyes a 'natural' landscape or 'wilderness' is to an Aborigine a living, social landscape. Hence, there is now considerable debate in Australia about the Eurocentric concept of 'wilderness' and its denial of a long-standing indigenous presence (Bayet, 1994). The earth's topography, it is believed, was formed by the spirit ancestors who came from the Dreamtime, or tjukurrpa (creation) and journeyed across the continent leaving traces in the form of hills, creeks, caves, water holes and the like. Many of these topographic features are sacred and have ritual significance. Others are considered extremely dangerous and to be avoided: others are secret. Further, on many issues, there is a strict gender – and associated spatial – demarcation between 'men's knowledge' and 'women's knowledge'. All this means that special questions are at issue in planing tourism facilities in areas of significance for Aboriginal populations because Eurocentric notions of 'conservation', 'development' and access may be totally incompatible with Aboriginal spirituality (Huggins et al., 1995). In the Northern Territory, for example, there are two examples of legislated Aboriginal 'sea closures'. On face value these would appear to be of benefit to Aboriginal people. Yet their existence presents a quandary for local communities: commercial and recreational fishing are allowed, upon notification, but Aboriginal people may not wish to publicize the precise location of sensitive sites of spiritual significance.

Most Aborigines, even in extremely remote areas, had had at least some minimal contact with Europeans from the 1930s or 1940s onwards. Virtually no Aborigines now live the strictly defined, traditional, self-sufficient, nomadic existence that prevailed prior to European settlement, but there is a very strong national movement to revive Aboriginal languages and identity, preserve cultural sites, ceremonies, art forms and customs and encourage Aboriginal children to have continuing exposure to traditional Aboriginal skills and life styles. For example, it is not at all uncommon for Aborigines working in the rural, mining or pastoral industries, in outback national parks, or even in urban centres, to periodically rekindle their strong attachment to the land and its sacred placed by going 'walkabout' deep into the central desert, often for months at a time. Especially in the Northern Territory, recent years have also witnessed a growing 'homelands' – or 'outstation' movement, whereby Aboriginals have left the often disastrous social environment of the towns or reserves and returned in small groups to enjoy healthier and much more traditionally orientated life styles on their own lands (Steele, 1995). The 'anti-ghettoization' outstation movement has of course been facilitated by the extension of land rights legislation since the late 1970s and the allocation of funds by the federal Department of Aboriginal Affairs. By 1981 it was estimated that in the Northern Territory alone there were 150 isolated 'homeland centres' with approximately 4000 residents.

Over the past quarter of a century, a combination of positive federal government policy initiatives and growing Aboriginal militancy has led to a slight improvement in Aboriginal living standards and the limited recognition of certain basic rights such as the right to vote and the granting of inalienable freehold tenure to lands previously reserved for their use. The right to vote in national elections was only granted to Aborigines by referendum as recently as 1967 and the first significant land rights legislation was enacted by federal parliament in 1976. As a result of this legislation Aborigines were, for the first time since colonization, able to make claims to their traditional lands. But the Act made reference only to unoccupied and unalienated Crown land in the Northern Territory. Under the Australian Constitution the federal government has no power to coerce the subordinate states to enact land rights legislation. However, in 1992, in the landmark Mabo judgement relating to the Murray Islands in the Torres Strait, the High Court ruled that under certain, very special circumstances, native title to land (and possibly, the sea) could be said to have survived European settlement if the traditional owners can demonstrate an uninterrupted link with their 'country'. The ramifications of this ruling with respect to mainland Australia are still being negotiated, but it appears likely that there will be a number of successful native title claims in the future and that many of these will be in areas with high tourism potential (Mercer, 1997). More recently, the High Court's 1996 judgement in the Wik case has added further legal weight to the Aboriginal cause. In the past, Aborigines in the six States and two Territories have had mixed success in terms of securing freehold title to their traditional lands and Table 7.1 shows the present situation. It is clear from the table that the Northern Territory has both the largest area and the greatest proportion of Aboriginal land of any of the States and Territories as well as the highest percentage of Aborigines in the population.

Table 7.1 Aboriginal land* and population in Australia, by state and territory (adapted from Altman et al., 1995)

State/territory (000 sq. km)	Aboriginal land	Percent of state area	Aboriginal population (1991 census)
Northern Territory	536.0	39.8	3,991,022.6
South Australia	189.6	19.3	162,321.2
Queensland	42.2	2.4	701,242.4
New South Wales	1.5	0.2	700,191.2
Victoria	<0.5	<0.1	167,350.3
Western Australia	325.5	12.9	417,792.6
Tasmania	<0.5	<0.1	88,852.0
Australian Capital Territory	<0.5	<0.1	17,750.6

* Includes inalienable freehold, leasehold and reserve land

Opposition to tourism

One highly publicized – and on-going – example of indigenous opposition to tourism unfolded in the State of South Australia from 1989 onwards. That particular State has significant economic problems and high unemployment. As such, tourism is seen as offering considerable potential. At issue in the controversy was the alleged failure on the part of the State and Commonwealth governments and the developer to consult fully with the local Aboriginal community and, most seriously, to take account of sensitive 'women's knowledge' relating to the locations and functions of secret fertility sites in the area. A private company (Binalong Pty Ltd) initially put forward a plan to construct an AUS$6.4 million bridge across the Goolwa Channel connecting Hindmarsh Island to the mainland, near the mouth of the River Murray. In 1991 the South Australian State government agreed to become a partner in the project, which was also backed by Westpac Bank. The idea was that the bridge would form a link to a greatly expanded existing marina and residential development on the island, but this provoked a strong reaction from a coalition of Aboriginal rights, environmental and church groups on the grounds that significant spiritual values attaching to the area on the part of the local Aboriginal community (the Ngarrindjeri people) would be seriously compromised. In particular, the Goolwa Channel acts to protect women's traditional ancestral spirits and a bridge, it was charged, would violate the site. In protest, in April 1994, the peak national Aboriginal organization threatened to withdraw AUS$1 billion in investments from

Westpac. Also, in July, 1994, the Federal Minister for Aboriginal Affairs invoked national heritage legislation (the Aboriginal and Torres Strait Islander Heritage Act 1984) and signed an order forbidding bridge construction and protecting the area for 25 years. On a point of law this order was overturned by the Federal Court a few months later. Subsequently there have been four additional state and federal government inquiries, including an AUS$1 million Royal Commission into the blocked project and the controversy is still unresolved. A complication – by no means unusual in Australia – is that the local Aboriginal community is deeply divided over the issue.

In the Hindmarsh Island case indigenous opposition has surfaced publicly prior to the development proceeding. But at Mossman Gorge, north of Cairns, Aboriginal resentment simmers today because a nearby tourist resort was approved and built without any consultation with the local community, and they have now been denied access to their traditional freshwater fishing sites. Elsewhere, for example at Aurukun on the Cape York Peninsula, and on the Murray Islands in the Torres Strait, the local indigenous communities have placed a total ban on tourism on the grounds that its encouragement would represent an intolerable threat to traditional values and fishing sites. But in other parts of Australia co-management arrangements with European partners have been entered into. Two particularly well-known examples of these will be discussed now.

Co-management – Kakadu National Park

As noted, Kakadu National Park is situated about 300 kilometres east of Darwin, in the Northern Territory, at latitude 13 °S. Colloquially, it is known as the 'Top End' National Park and the first controversial proposal for the establishment of a major reserve encompassing the Alligator Rivers was made in 1965. Stage One of the park – an area of 6144 square kilometres – was initially proclaimed in April 1979. This is exactly one hundred years after the proclamation of Australia's first national park, Royal National Park, on the outskirts of Sydney. There were further additions – known as Stages Two and Three – in 1984, 1987, 1989 and 1991. This land – much of which was non-Aboriginal – more than doubled the area of the reserve to its present total of almost 2 million hectares. As such parks become gazetted in more distant parts of Australia the management problems change, with traditional Aboriginal ties to the land assuming ever-greater importance. For the fifty years prior to its proclamation as a national park, Kakadu had been an Aboriginal Reserve. Indigenous interests in the area are still very strong and there are on-going negotiations relating to tourism access and the future of uranium mining in two mining lease 'windows' that exist in the north-eastern section of the park (Jabiluka/Jabiru and Koongarra) (Press et al., 1995). In view of its outstanding landscape, ecological and cultural significance, the area was listed as a World Heritage Property under the terms of the World Heritage Convention in October 1981, Kakadu was the first site to be listed in Australia. The park topography is extremely diverse, ranging from the tidal flats and lowlands which represent some of the most important, pristine, tropical wetland ecosystems in the world, through to the spectacular sandstone escarpments and high country of the Arnhemland plateau, inland. In 1980 the wetlands were listed under the conditions of the Convention on Wetlands of International Importance (the Ramsar Convention). In terms of its ecological value the area is of incomparable world significance, the data on species' numbers speaking for themselves: 1000 plants, 5000 insects, 250 birds (one-third of Australia's total complement), seventy-five reptiles, fifty mammals, forty-five freshwater fish (a quarter of the Australian total) and twenty-two amphibians. New species discoveries are common place. It is considered, for example, that the number of insect species eventually identified may well exceed 10,000.

Culturally, the area is no less unique. Countless rock art sites exist in the Arnhemland escarpment and outliers and some of the ochre paintings have been dated at 25,000 years before present. Many are also extremely well preserved and are certainly as old as the better known Palaeolithic cave art murals of Western Europe. The paintings and rock engravings depict a priceless record of historical change over thousands of years, ranging from the geological period when Australia was separated from to New Guinea, through the gradual rise in sea level, 7000 years ago, and the first arrival of Europeans. Long extinct animals feature prominently. Recent archaeological expeditions have also discovered the world's oldest examples of ground axes, some of the earliest known sites of human habitation in Australia and many, as yet undeciphered, stone arrangements. In its own way Kakadu is every bit a valuable to the world community at the Louvre or the Prado.

Earlier it was noted that, prior to 1979, Kakadu had been a major Aboriginal Reserve. Such official status gave *de jure* recognition to the unparalleled significance of this area to the Aborigines. Its inhospitable, rocky uplands, monsoonal wetlands and crocodile-infested rivers had long made this region a natural 'refuge' for Aborigines, and in the 1920s the area was judged to be of little value to white Australians. Then, in the 1960s, 120,000 tonnes of uranium oxide deposits were discovered in the area. Mining company and government pressure eventually resulted in the boundaries of the proposed national park being drawn in such a way as to exclude the uranium province. Mining commenced in the 1970s and a sealed road to Darwin was subsequently constructed. This connected

Darwin with the main mining town of Jabiru, which is actually situated inside the national park, and greatly eased access for domestic and international tourists. As uranium mining gathered pace at Ranger, Jabiluka and Koongarra, multiple threats to what had by this stage become Aboriginal-owned territory became readily apparent.

So it was that, upon its proclamation as a national park in April 1979, the traditional owners of Kakadu agreed to lease the area to the Director of the Australian National Parks and Wildlife Service (subsequently renamed the Australian Nature Conservation Agency) for a period of 100 years as a national park. The decision followed a lengthy period of consultation with the owners – the Kakadu Aboriginal Land Trust – through its representative body, the Northern Land Council. It was generally felt by the Aborigines that their best interests would be served by such a move. Mining and tourist pressures were set to increase enormously and the Aboriginal community felt that they did not at that stage have the necessary management skills to cope with the imminent changes. The Lease Agreement was finally signed on 3 November 1978, but not before a wide-ranging information programme had been instituted to introduce the 'foreign' park idea to the traditional owners and, most importantly, the owners had been given ample opportunity to respond to the proposal. The unique aspect of the agreement is that, in the main, it was designed to ensure that the traditional Aboriginal owners would be intimately involved in the process of park planning and management and fully consulted at every stage on any matter affecting the welfare of the Aboriginal inhabitants of the area. This made Kakadu the first national park in the country where Aborigines were allowed an official say in both the long-term and day-to-day management of the park. As we shall see, other Australian parks have subsequently replicated this model, which is also being closely monitored by several overseas countries. In addition, two states have since employed Aboriginal rangers.

In all, the Kakadu Aboriginal Land Trust consists of around 100 traditional owners and an additional 200 Aborigines with some historical affiliations to the land in that area. In the eighteenth century it is estimated that some 2000 Aborigines probably used the area on a regular basis, but prior to the proclamation of the park there were only about twenty Aboriginal families living within the reserve. The establishment of the park acted as a catalyst for indigenous people to return to their homeland and by 1980 an additional 150 Aborigines had returned to Kakadu to live. That number has subsequently doubled. From the outset – and in marked contrast to the Mossman Gorge example, mentioned earlier – the Australian National Parks and Wildlife Service paid the closest possible attention to consultative arrangements. Aboriginal rangers were recruited and trained and numerous meetings were held to discuss input to the first management plans, the fourth and most recent of which came into effect in 1997 after two years' preparation. Aborigines are also represented on the park's Board of Management which oversees the implementation of the management plan. In part, Aboriginal conditions included the following:

- protection of traditional campsites;
- protection of sites and routes of significance to the traditional owners;
- provision for the owners to live traditionally in the park if they so choose;
- privacy from European intrusion at certain highly secret sites;
- provision from the traditional owners to 're-work' rock paintings if they so wish.

This last condition may, at first, appear rather strange, but it does serve to highlight a key difference between European and Aboriginal conceptions of cultural artefacts. To most white park planners and archaeologists Kakadu is akin to a 'museum' where the art sites should be protected at all cost. To the traditional owners, on the other hand, Kakadu is a living place; they never considered their art to be 'permanent' in a Western, conservationist sense (Ballantyne, 1995). It was to be 'experienced' rather than 'possessed' and original creations were routinely painted over, modified or touched up when travellers returned to a particular site at regular seasonal intervals. It was, genuinely, 'living' art.

Not surprisingly, the joint venture between white, park planning professionals and the representatives of an ancient, pre-literate culture has not been without its difficulties. In particular, there have been considerable problems associated with different concepts of time. Traditionally, Aboriginal consultations invariably are spread over many meetings and long periods. Yet the 'Western' capitalist time frame generally is much shorter and frequently demands 'instant' solutions. Historically, mining interests in the Kakadu region, for example, have been known to 'force the pace' of long drawn-out consultative processes. As well, there are often serious practical difficulties involved in persuading Aborigines to talk openly about the precise locations of many significant sites that whites may feel are in need of 'protection'. Traditionally, some sites are so secret that their whereabouts is only known to a secret number of initiated individuals. There are also others that it is taboo to discuss because they are considered so dangerous, others that cannot be talked about in the company of women or uninitiated men, and so on. In addition, the rapid escalation of tourist numbers is presently creating special management problems at Kakadu. The discussion will now focus briefly on those pressures and some of the consequences for this particular park.

Tourist numbers at Kakadu have shown a spectacular growth in the past decades. In 1972 it has been estimated that the area experienced about 20,000 visitor days. In 1987 there were 700,250 visitor days, and the five-year period from 1982 to 1987 alone saw a 364 per cent increase. This translates into almost 250,000 visitors at present and predictions of rapid growth into the future, especially from overseas tourists (Press et al., 1995). The tourist 'problem' is all the more serious when it is realized that the monsoonal climate dictates that most people must visit in the dry season, between April and October. This period coincides with the winter in populous southern Australia. In April, approximately 64 per cent of the visitors are from overseas but this reduces to 28 per cent in July. A major shift is occurring in the kind of visitor. Up to 1986 the tourists were overwhelmingly private visitors, but 50 per cent now visit Kakadu as part of a commercial tour group. Moreover, about one-third of all visitors are 'local', Northern Territory residents. Inevitably, numbers of this magnitude generate all the usual management problems ranging from mounting pressures on land, water, soil, vegetation and wildlife resources through to either conscious or unconscious vandalism of Aboriginal rock art sites and intrusion into sacred or forbidden areas. The ownership of four-wheel-drive vehicles and high-powered motor-boats on the part of Darwin or Jabiru residents and other Australian tourists also means that formerly inaccessible parts of the park are now potentially available for recreational use. Conflicts over land and other resources are thus building up between the increasing numbers of traditional Aborigines who are choosing to return to Kakadu to live and the flood of 'foreign' visitors, many of whom have no idea how to behave towards Aborigines or their cultural heritage. This problem is compounded by the fact that all surveys have found that by far the majority of tourists are visiting the park for the first time.

Research by Kesteven (1987) has found that Aborigines make a clear distinction between 'tourists' and 'visitors'. 'Visitors' include, for example:

- scientists who visit the area for research purposes;
- non-resident Aboriginals;
- non-Aboriginal people who are in the district to work for or with Aboriginals;
- non-Aboriginal people making contact with relatives.

The distinction is an important one. By and large 'visitors' are seen as understanding 'how to behave' in the socially approved manner. 'Tourists', on the other hand, Kesteven found, were regarded by the Aborigines as

> ...bad news. 'Tourists' wandered aimlessly, got lost and had to be rescued; they got themselves into trouble by tempting crocodiles; they transgressed on sacred sites on burial areas; even worse, they sometimes stole

relics or vandalized sites. They over-fished, they couldn't be trusted with rifles . . . Tourists have no commitment to the people of Kakadu or to the land. (1987: 2)

Given such antipathy it is somewhat surprising to learn that the Aborigines have not been more openly antagonistic to the tourist invasion of their ancestral lands. On the whole, the Aboriginal attitude can be characterized as one of quiet tolerance to an 'inevitable' situation. Such tolerance is fuelled, at least in part, by an understanding of some of the benefits that tourism is seen to generate. Indeed, there was considerable indigenous input into the design and function of the park's Warradjan Aboriginal Cultural Centre which opened in May 1995. This coincided with the signing of a historic Memorandum of Understanding between the Australian Nature Conservation Agency and the Indigenous Northern Land Council which provides for explicit recognition of the interests of the traditional owners in the management and custodianship of Aboriginal heritage in Kakadu National Park.

Co-management – Uluru–Kata Tjuta National Park

The geological feature formerly known as Ayers Rock is one of the world's best known natural phenomena. Like Kakadu to the north, it is visited by well over 300,000 domestic and international tourists each year. Indeed, 12 per cent of all overseas visitors to Australia made the long trip to Uluru in 1989. Current estimates project visitor numbers to the 133,000-hectare park to reach 607,000 by 1997. The most prominent feature – the sandstone monolith measuring about 4 km long by 3 km wide – rises steeply 348 m out of the Central Australian desert in the Northern Territory. The area is extremely remote. It lies in the centre of the continent 450 km from Alice Springs, the nearest town, and some 2500 km from Sydney. This is roughly equivalent to the distance between Los Angeles and Minneapolis. The Rock has been an important spiritual site for Aborigines for thousands of years, the numerous caves and over-hangs around its perimeter having being progressively decorated with hundreds of paintings. The paintings themselves have varied origins. Some were undoubtedly originally executed for amusement; others are sacred and related to tribal ceremonies; yet others have an educational function.

The extensive Petermann Aboriginal Reserve, which included Ayers Rock, had been originally gazetted in 1920. From 1946 onwards the impact of the automobile started being felt and tour companies began taking a growing number of tourists to the area from Alice Springs. Pressure from these operators eventually resulted in the excision of a 1200 km slice of territory from the Aboriginal reserve in 1958 to form the Ayers Rock and Mt Olga National Park, under the management of the Northern Territory Reserves Board. Aborigines were, however, not involved in any aspect of this decision, nor was any thought given at that time to the employment of Aboriginal rangers. Indeed, even though the attraction of Ayers Rock is intimately linked with the Aboriginal heritage, Aborigines were, in the early days, effectively excluded from any involvement in the very activities that were seriously compromising their traditional life styles in an area of profound religious significance. In the 1950s the Northern Territory administration had a hardline policy of evicting Aborigines from the vicinity of the Rock and the access road on the grounds that too much interaction with visitors was a 'bad thing'. The favoured policy was one of Aboriginal centralization focused on the three local settlements of Ernabella, Areyonga and Docker River. The hidden agenda, though, was that overseas tourists would not want their holiday experience marred by the sight of dispirited and frequently intoxicated Aborigines. These actions have served to entrench the view in the minds of many Aborigines and white Australians alike that nature conservation and tourism, together, represent a 'new wave of dispossession'. By the 1970s several facilities had been built to accommodate the rapidly growing number of tourists. In 1970 there were 30,000 annual visitors; in 1972, 50,000. By 1987 192,000 tourists were recorded (20 per cent non-domestic) and the current annual growth rate in visitors is around 8 per cent. Over 50 per cent of the tourists arrive in organized groups by coach transport, a third by private car and 15 per cent by air.

In 1977, in an important historical move, responsibility for the national park was taken from the Northern Territory and transferred to the Commonwealth government, following the passing of the National Parks and Wildlife Conservation Act, 1975. October 1985 was also an important date, for it was then that the area was handed back to its original Aboriginal owners, the Mutitjulu community. This was effected through the federal, Aboriginal Land Rights (Northern Territory) Amendment Act, ownership from henceforth being vested in the Uluru–Kata Tjuta Lane Trust. This was not a popular move with either the Northern Territory government nor the corporate tourist sector. In 1979 the Northern Territory mounted a concerted legal attack on the land rights claim and, indeed, had temporary success.

Since coming under the administrative umbrella of the Australian Nature Conservation Agency (ANCA) there have been a number of significant changes at Uluru. The road to Alice Springs has been sealed and a major new resort – Yulara (an Aboriginal word for howling) – has been deliberately sited on an excised area of 104 sq. km, some 20 km away from the Rock. This huge resort, which was built at a cost of $250 million, contains three major hotels, an airport and a large camping ground; its positioning and development on the other side of the Rock from the Aboriginal settlements were recommended in a series of specially commissioned consultants' reports. The frenzied construction activity at Yulara has been carried out by private enterprise, assisted by substantial financial and infrastructure support on the part of the strongly pro-developmentalist Northern Territory government. The massive resort complex generates tourist expenditure in excess of $40 million per year. In short, the situation at Uluru now is that the Commonwealth government, through the ANCA, has primary responsibility for careful management of the national park and liaison with the traditional Aboriginal owners – the Mutitjulu community – while the Northern Territory government is aligned very closely with commercial concerns. The juxtaposition of a busy commercial area catering to the whims of thousands of affluent tourists with Aboriginal lands clearly poses the potential for enormous social repercussions. Indeed, Hill has commented that 'No two local communities in Australia better exemplify the inequality between black and white citizens, or more starkly illustrate the social contradictions that bloom under the influence of certain kinds of tourism' (1992: 17). Yulara is all about conspicuous Western consumption, luxury vacationing, 'champagne sunsets' and staged Aboriginal authenticity. The 150-strong Mutitjulu Community on the other side of the Rock could be a million miles away in terms of the living conditions and aspirations which the resort has to offer. Superficially it might appear that one of the 'benefits' of the resort for the Aborigines would be employment prospects, yet the reality is that with the exception of nine positions out of a total of 24 park staff, the local Anangu people have shown very little enthusiasm for the kinds of jobs and resulting social relationships that are involved in tourism operations.

Discussion

The Kakadu experiment had provided the model for European/Aboriginal co-operation in park management and similar consultative procedures have been followed at Uluru, though more speedily. The first Uluru management plan, for example, was produced in a matter of weeks, rather than years as had been the case at Kakadu. Since then, traditional Aboriginal knowledge has been used extensively in the framing of new management plans. There have been successful attempts to reintroduce important plant and animal species that have disappeared, and traditional Aboriginal burning practices have also been revived. Aborigines are in the majority on the park's board of management and have also been granted sole rights to any commercial undertakings within Uluru

National Park. These are, however, likely to be only minimal. Since the old campground closed in 1983 and the motels were also moved out of the park in 1984 all tourist accommodation is now located outside the park and there are no plans to change this situation. Gate receipts to the park total some AUS$2 million a year but the Mutitjulu community is allocated only 20 per cent of this sum and, overall, receives only around 2 per cent of annual total tourist expenditure at both Uluru and Yulara.

As at Kakadu, the changed park status made the area more attractive for the Aborigines who had previously moved away from Uluru, some of whom now returned. As noted, the Mutitjulu community now numbers about 150 people, currently living in four main camps at Uluru and at a much higher settlement density than at Kakadu. It is possible that others may also eventually return to Uluru, but much depends on the way in which the relationship with the tourists develops. One possibility is that the 'outstation' movement will gather momentum. Thus would see Aborigines deserting Uluru for what are seen to be much more 'congenial' homeland locations away from the Rock. A 1985 survey conducted by the Central Land Council (an Aboriginal body), for example, found that 70 per cent of Uluru Aborigines already felt that there were too many tourists at the Rock (Altman, 1987), Quite clearly this relates to the concept of 'psychological saturation' initially raised by Young (1973) and subsequently developed by Doxey (1975) with his 'index of tourist irritation'. This refers to the situation where tourist numbers at a particular location build up to such a degree that the 'hosts' are called upon to bear what they see as being an intolerable burden of social and environmental costs. It is not at all easy for an 'outsider' fully to understand this phenomenon because it often involves attempting to understand the way the world is seen from a quite different cultural perspective. For example, a popular activity at Uluru is to climb the central sandstone monolith. Yet many Aborigines regard this as a violation of an important spiritual site. Increasingly, pressure is being placed on tourists to respect this belief and not climb the Rock. But this, in turn, may have the effect of deterring visitors.

The Aboriginal perspective and the future of tourism

Typically, orthodox economists, politicians and the general public alike, assume that their belief in the work and growth ethics and the virtues of capitalism are universally shared. Yet in many ways capitalism has only very recently been forced on to traditional Aborigines; it is not an economic system that they have freely chosen. Historically, there are four main ways in which Aborigines have come into contact with the modern

market economy (Altman and Nieuwenhuysen, 1979). First, mission settlements frequently provided a pool of cheap labour for employment
in the remote pastoral industry. Second, large-scale mining or tourism
projects – as at Kakadu and Uluru – have sometimes started up alongside existing Aboriginal reserves, thereby providing a limited number of
unskilled or semi-skilled employment opportunities for Aborigines as
construction workers, full- or part-time rangers and the like. Third, there
is the production of Aboriginal artefacts or paintings for sale either at
selected outback tourist outlets or for export. And finally, there are a few
examples of direct investment of mining or other royalties and government funds into tourist-related or other business ventures. The latter
approach, for example, has been adopted at Kakadu where substantial
uranium royalties paid to the Gagadju Association have been partly invested in a hotel/motel complex and a store facility in the national park.
Interestingly, some of the profits from these projects have in turn been
used to fund the growing 'outstation' movement, mentioned earlier. Aboriginal education is also being funded from the same source.

There are growing signs that the Aboriginal community in outback
Australia has great difficulty coming to terms with the kind of consumer
tourism that is becoming increasingly commonplace at popular sites such
as Uluru/Yulara. Altman (1987), for example, undertook an employment
survey at the Aboriginal-controlled Ininti store at Uluru in mid-1985 and
observed that the local Aboriginal people traditionally 'withdraw from
employment at this time of the year because they find the intensity of
contact with tourists too great' (1987: 34). Elsewhere he adds that 'Anangu
[Aborigines] are retreating from the residential location where daily interaction with tourists occurs . . . Bush locations provide a greater insula-
tion from tourists and greater access to both raw materials for artefact
manufacture and bush foods to supplement the diet' (1987: 33).

Central to Aboriginal culture are the twin notions of responsibility and
caring, even for tourists who venture on to their territory uninvited.
Generally Western-style tourism is not conducive to enduring personal
relationships, though it has to be said that what might be called the
'artefact culture' can and indeed has often accommodated quite well to
consumer tourism, in Australia as well as elsewhere. Artefacts can be
fashioned in relative isolation, away from the tourist gaze, and contact
need only be made with an intermediary. Increasingly, wealthy international tourists are combing the world in search of the exotic and the
'different'. As part of this tendency, 'Aboriginality' is being heavily
promoted by white interests as a major drawcard for tourism in the
Northern Territory and elsewhere in northern Australia. The Aboriginal
response to this marketing pressure is ambivalent, to say the least. On
the one hand they strongly object to such intrusions as being stared at or
photographed without their permission or having the privacy of their

camps and sacred sites violated (Langton, 1993). On the other hand, at a time when the fight for land and other rights is now high on the political agenda in Australia and becoming much more visible internationally, indigenous Australia can certainly see the advantages in 'selling' Aboriginality through the medium of tourism, as well as in other ways. They also have a clear understanding of some of the welfare and educational benefits to be gained from the sensible investment of profits derived from tourism projects.

At Uluru and elsewhere Aborigines have recently begun to produce their own tourist literature which clearly presents their unique cultural perspective on their land and customs. The 'Mutitjulu Walk' and the 'Mala Walk', for example, now compete with such activities as intrusive helicopter flights over the Rock. Also, as in Arctic Canada, a few sympathetic European tour companies now also organize small-scale outback tours in company with Aboriginal guides who are thereby given the opportunity to impart some of their knowledge to the still limited but growing number of non-Aborigines who wish to learn something of the 'wisdom of the elders'. Krippendorf (1982) argues that two broad categories of tourism can be recognized. These he calls 'hard' and 'soft' tourism. Clearly, the small-scale, Aboriginal-led, educative tours are representative of a considerate and sensitive 'soft' tourism path while large-scale tourism complexes, as at Yulara, are much more typical of a 'hard' tourism orientation.

The key problem for Aborigines in central Australia at the present time is how to make the most of the benefits to be derived from tourism without being totally swamped and overwhelmed by the worst excesses of that rapidly growing phenomenon. Dillon (1987: 9) comments that 'The existence of tourism, and the inclusion of Aboriginality as a component of the tourism resource means that Aboriginality becomes a product or good to be controlled by Aboriginal people'. In this chapter we have briefly discussed two examples where, at one level, a successful partnership appears to have been negotiated to this end between native Australians and the Australian Nature Conservation Agency. The only problem with this arrangement (which has subsequently been replicated at Witjira National Park in South Australia) is that the Aborigines have absolutely no control over the crucial element of the numbers of visitors descending on Uluru and Kakadu and little control over their subsequent behaviour. A major, on-going, educational campaign is really required to explain carefully to Australian and overseas visitors how to behave towards Aborigines in their territory. At a more fundamental level what is urgently called for in such newly developing tourist regions as Arctic Canada, Amazonia and Central Australia is what Krippendorf (1982: 135) refers to as a 'fundamental political transformation in the conception of tourism'. Joint management is ostensibly a good idea yet it must not be forgotten that it represents 'a Western cultural model, deriving from within our culture and social context' (Craig, 1992: 147). In the future there is no certainty that an increasingly radical Aboriginal movement will view joint management favourably, especially if there is little or no improvement in their material living standards and conditions in Australia as a whole.

Currently, a major ideological conflict is being played out in all parts of Australia between pro-developmentalist tourism interests and Aboriginal communities. The main issue revolves around the commodification of Aboriginality. The developmentalist stance is represented by such bodies as the Northern Territory Development Corporation and the Northern Territory Tourist Commission, both of which are pressing strongly for Aborigines to be much less retiring about tourism and, in effect, to 'display' themselves and regularly 'perform' traditional dances, on cue, for tourist consumption. Their 1984 report, Initiatives for Tourism Facilities, for example, writes of the 'acute need for the provision of some means or facility to expose tourists to aspects of Aboriginal culture, lifestyle, way of life or mythology' (Northern Territory Development Corporation, 1984: 23). It is suggested that this be provided in certain 'Aboriginal Culture Centres' where 'daily activities such as weaving and dancing' could take place. However, as was emphasized earlier in the chapter, the political demands of Aboriginal Australia revolve around the twin themes of choice and control. At this stage it seems rather unlikely that Australian Aborigines will readily accede to external demands to speedily 'package' their Aboriginality in tune with the whims of Australian business interests or the international tourist market. Sensitively-designed and planned Aboriginal Cultural Centres have recently been opened at Kakadu, Uluru and in the southern state of Victoria. The key element was major and on-going input from the indigenous community.

References

Aboriginal and Torres Strait Islander Commission (ATSIC) (1994) Draft National Aboriginal and Torres Strait Islander Tourism Strategy, Canberra

Ahmad, A. (1995) The politics of literary postcoloniality, *Race and Class*, **36**(3), 1–20

Altman, J.C. (1987) The Economic Impact of Tourism on the Mutitjulu Community, Uluru (Ayers Rock–Mount Olga) National Park, Working Paper No. 7, Department of Political and Social Change, Research School of Pacific Studies, Australian National University, Canberra

Altman, J.C. (1993) Indigenous Australians in the National Tourism Strategy: Impact, Sustainability and Policy Issues. Centre for Aboriginal Economic Policy Research, Australian National University, Canberra

Altman, J.C., Bek, H.J. and Roach, L.M. (1995) Native Title and Indigenous Australian Utilization of Wildlife: Policy Perspectives, Discussion Paper 95, Centre for Aboriginal Economic Policy Research, Australian National University, Canberra

Altman, J.C. and Nieuwenhuysen, J. (1979) The Economic Status of Australian Aborigines, Cambridge University Press, Cambridge

Anderson, I. (1995) Aboriginal Nation(s)? In *Asian and Pacific Inscriptions* (ed. Perera, S.), Meridian, Melbourne, pp. 65–82

Ascher, F. (1985) Tourism: Transnational Corporation and Cultural Identities, UNESCO, Paris

Australian Tourist Commission (1992) North East Asia Market Brief. ATC, Hong Kong

Ballantyne, R. (1995) Interpreters' conceptions of Australian Aboriginal Culture and Heritage: Implications for Interpretive Practice, *Journal of Environmental Education*, **26**(4), 11–17

Bayet, F. (1994) Overturning the doctrine: indigenous people and wilderness – being Aboriginal in the environmental movement, *Social Alternatives*, **13**(2), 27–32

Black, N. and Rutledge, J. (eds) (1995) *Outback Tourism: The Authentic Australian Adventure*, James Cook University, Townsville

Brady, M. (1985) The promotion of tourism and its effect on Aborigines. In *Aborigines and Tourism. A Study of the Impact of Tourism on Aborigines in the Kakadu Region, Northern Territory* (ed. K. Palmer), Northern Land Council, Darwin

Butler, R. (1980) The concept of a tourist-area cycle of evolution and implications for management, *The Canadian Geographer*, **24**, 5–12

Butlin, N. (1983) *Our Original Aggression. Aboriginal Population of Southeastern Australia, 1788–1850*, George Allen & Unwin, Sydney

Chohan, K., Philip, M. and Austwick, K. (1994) *Australian Tourism Trends 1993*, Bureau of Tourism Research, Canberra

Commonwealth of Australia (1991) *Royal Commission into Aboriginal Deaths in Custody*, Canberra

Craig, D. (1992) Environmental Law and Environmental Rights: Legal Framework for Aboriginal Joint Management of Australian National Parks. In *Aboriginal Involvement in Parks and Protected Areas* (ed. J. Birckhead, T. De Lacy and L. Smith), Aboriginal Studies Press for the Australian Institute of Aboriginal and Torres Strait Islander Studies, Canberra, ACT, pp. 137–148

DeKadt, E. (1979) *Tourism: Passport to Development?* Oxford University Press, New York

De Lacy, T. (1994) The Uluru/Kakadu model – Anangu Tjukurrpa, 50,000 years of Aboriginal law and land management changing the concept of national parks in Australia, *Society and Natural Resources*, **7**, 479–498

Department of Tourism (DOT) (1992) Tourism, Australia's Passport to Growth: A National Tourism Strategy, DOT, Canberra.

Dillon, M.C. (1987) Aborigines and Tourism in North Australia: Some Suggested Research Approaches. East Kimberley Impact Assessment Project, Working Paper No. 14, Centre for Resource and Environmental Studies, Australian National University, Canberra

Douglas, N. (1995) *They Came for Savages: 100 Years of Tourism in Melanesia*, Southern Cross University Press, Lismore

Doxey, G.V. (1975) A causation theory of visitor–resident irritants: methodology and research inferences. In *Proceedings of the Travel Research Association Sixth Annual Conference*, San Diego, California, pp. 195–8

Durning, A.T. (1993) Supporting indigenous peoples. In *State of the World 1993* (ed. L. Brown), Earthscan, London, pp. 80–100

Evatt Foundation (1996) *The State of Australia*, Evatt Foundation, Sydney

Fenge, T. (1993) National parks in the Canadian Arctic: the case of the Nunavut land claim agreement. In *Indigenous Land Rights in Commonwealth Countries: Dispssession, Negotiation and Community Action* (ed. G. Cant, J. Overton and E. Pawson), University of Canterbury, Christchurch

Goutlet, D. (1977) What Kind of Tourism? Or, Poison in a Luxury Package. Working Paper Series No. 2, Tourism Research, Department of Geography, McGill University, Montreal, Canada

Harris, Kerr, Forster and Co. and Stanton Robbins and Co. (1965) Australia's Travel and Tourist Industry. Report prepared for the Australian Travel Association, Sydney

Hill, B. (1992) The soul of the place, *Modern Times*, May pp. 16–18

Huggins, J. Huggins, R. and Jacobs, J.M. (1995) Kooramindanjie: place and the postcolonial, *History Workshop Journal*, **39**, 165–181

Kanahele, G.S. (1992) Tourism – keeper of the culture. In *Ecotourism Business in the Pacific: Promoting a Sustainable Experience* (ed. J. Hay). Proceedings of a Conference, Environmental Science, University of Auckland and East-West Center, Honolulu, Hawaii, pp. 30–34

Kesteven, S. (1987) Aborigines in the Tourist Industry. East Kimberley Working Paper No. 14, East Kimberley Impact Assessment Project, Centre for Resource and Environmental Studies, Australian National University, Canberra

Krippendorf, J. (1982) Towards new tourism policies. The importance of environmental and sociocultural factors, *Tourism Management*, **3**, 135–48

Langton, M. (1993) *Well, I Heard it on the Radio and I Saw it on the Television . . .* Australian Film Commission, North Sydney

Law, A. (1993) Aborigines and tourism: policy and political participation. In *Interactions and Actions. Proceedings of the Ecopolitics VI Conference* (ed. Thomas I.), Melbourne, F67–F75

Laxson, J.D. (1991) How 'we' see 'them'. Tourism and native Americans, *Annals of Tourism Research*, **18**, 365–391

Lew, A.A. (1996) Tourism management on American Indian lands in the USA. Tourism Management, **17**(5), 355–365

Lewis, H.T. (1992) The technology and ecology of nature's custodians: anthropological perspectives on Aborigines and national parks. In *Aboriginal Involvement in Parks and Protected Areas* (ed. J. Birckhead, T. De Lacy and L. Smith), Aboriginal Studies Press for the Australian Institute of Aboriginal and Torress Strait Islander Studies, Canberra, ACT, pp. 15–28

Lynge, F. (1987) In defence of the Inuit world – saving a way of life, *The Environmentalist*, **7**(3), 191–6

MacCannell, D. (1992) *Empty Meeting Grounds: The Tourist Papers*, Routledge, London

Martin, D. and Taylor, J. (1996) Ethnographic perspectives on the enumeration of Aboriginal people in remote Australia, *Journal of the Australian Population Association*, **13**(1), 17–31

Mercer, D.C. (1997) Aboriginal self-determination and indigenous land title in post-Mabro Australia, *Political Geography*, **16**(3), 189–212

Muecke, S. (1996) Outback. *Environment and Planning D: Society and Space*, **14**, 407–420

Northern Territory Development Corporation (1984) Initiatives for Tourism Facilities, NTDC and Northern Territory Tourist Commission, Darwin

Organization for Economic Cooperation and Development (OECD) (1994) Tourist Development, OECD, Paris

Pagdin, C. (1995) Assessing tourism impacts in the third world: a Nepal case study, *Progress in Planning*, **44**, 185–266

Pitchford, S. (1995) Ethnic tourism and nationalism in Wales, *Annals of Tourism Research*, **22**(1), 35–52

Postman, N. (1987) *Amusing Ourselves to Death: Public Discourse in the Age of Show Business*, Methuen, London

Press, T., Lea, D., Webb, A. and Graham, A. (1995) Kakadu: Natural and Cultural Heritage and Management – Australian Nature Conservation Agency, North Australia Research Unit, The Australian National University, Darwin

Prosser, R.F. (1992) The ethics of tourism. In *The Environment in Question, Ethics and Global Issues* (ed. D.E. Cooper and J.A. Palmer), Routledge, London and New York, pp. 37–50

Reynolds, H. (1996) *Aboriginal Sovereignty*, Allen & Unwin, Sydney

Rose, D.B. (1996) Ecological justice for the 21st century, *Northern Aanalyst* (North Australia Research Unit) **1**, 9–10

Ross, H. (1995) Aboriginal Australians' cultural norms for negotiating natural resources, *Cultural Survival Quarterly*, Fall, 33–38

Simpson, L. (1996) Port Arthur. The future? *Island*, **67**, 91–94

Steele, T. (1995) Recovery of the dream? The outstation movement twenty years on, *Social Alternatives*, **14**(4), 41–44

Strang, V. (1996) Sustaining tourism in Far North Queensland. In *People and Tourism in Fragile Environments* (ed., M.F. Price), John Wiley & Sons, Chichester, pp. 51–67

Ugresic, D. (1996) The confiscation of memory, *New Left Review*, **218**, 26–39

Wilmot, E. (1987) Australia – The Last Experiment, Australian Broadcasting Corporation, Sydney

Young, E. (1995) *Third World in the First. Development and Indigenous Peoples*, Routledge, London

Young, G. (1973) *Tourism – Blessing or Blight?* Penguin, Harmondsworth

Zeppel, H. (1995) Authenticity and Iban longhouse tourism in Sarawak, *Borneo Review*, **6**(2), 109–125

8 The relationship between residents and tourists: the research literature and management directions

Philip L. Pearce

Conceptual background

The literature on tourist–resident relationships is now a large, challenging and increasingly useful area of academic activity. It would not be difficult, for example, to cite several hundred case studies relating to this area of tourism interest. Conceptually, it is valuable to sort out the intersecting and overlapping research areas of most relevance. At the broad level there is considerable research on the economic, environmental and socio-cultural effects of tourism which all have general implications for tourist–resident relationships. These areas clearly overlap and may be seen as a set of interlocking envelopes. The topic of tourist–resident impacts in particular is subsumed within the topic area of the general of total social impacts of tourism but some tourist–resident contacts have clear economic and environmental components, thus placing tourist–resident research at the core of the interconnected themes (Figure 8.1).

The present review will concentrate specifically on tourist–resident interaction with a focus on the impacts of this interaction on the residents. Unlike many other reviews of this area, however, some note of the effects of the contact on the tourists themselves will be made. It is valuable to note that some of the foundation literature on which this review is built is now two decades old. Unlike consumer studies, which date very rapidly, the impact and tourism–resident case studies from earlier periods still have much to offer in identifying issues and concerns which persist today.

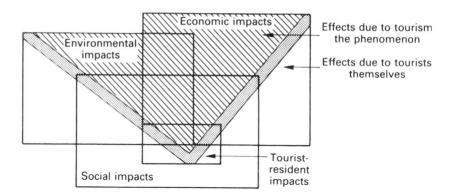

Tourism studies

Figure 8.1 Tourist–resident impacts set within the framework of the social, environmental and economic impacts of tourism and consisting of both broad tourism and specific touris influences

It is critical to note at the outset that social impacts effects may be *real* in the sense that objective data can be collected to verify their existence (e.g. length of time spent in doing one's shopping) or *perceived* (e.g. the view that there is more crime in the community and life is less safe than in the past). From the point of view of assessing community feeling, real and perceived impacts are equally important. If residents believe an impact exists, then their behaviour will be altered irrespective of the accuracy of the perception. Nevertheless it is valuable to comment on whether impacts are objectively verifiable or subjectively felt, since the tactics for improving tourist–resident relationships may be different in the two cases. For example, perceived impacts may be changed by the processes of education and community information whereas this is less of an option for objectively verifiable impacts (such as restricted access to a recreation site).

The importance of tourist–resident impacts

Tourist–resident contact is important because the international evidence indicates that when negative impacts are ignored there can be some major economic and political repercussions. This community backlash may include:

- a loss of support for the authorities/councils which promote tourism;
- an unwillingness to work in the tourism industry;

- a lack of enthusiasm in promoting the tourism product by word of mouth;
- a hostility to the tourists themselves which can be manifested in over-charging, rudeness and indifference to the tourists' holiday experiences; and
- delays in the construction of tourism development because of community protests.

These negative consequences of poor tourist–resident contact have major implications for tourism development in a region. They represent the combined effects of all the smaller consequences of social interaction transformed into political and economic power through community action. It is important to be aware of them, but it may not be possible to alter them quickly, because they represent the culmination of a complex web of community dissatisfaction. In short, while they are highly undesirable for tourism development purposes, they can best be influenced by understanding the underlying interactions and effects on which they are based. There is also a growing moral or ethical concern about tourist resident relationships. Church based organizations in Asia and other developing regions frequently view tourism as the exploitative arm of foreign countries. It is valuable therefore to also consider the moral or ethical dimension as an area of concern in tourism community studies.

Variability in tourist–resident studies

Tourism–resident interaction is a specific but diverse example of cross-cultural interaction. Typically, tourists stay in the visited communities for very short and carefully structured periods of time. Their travel motivations set them apart from other inter-cultural sojourners and their affluence compared to the locals is pronounced. These characteristics generate at least two unique features of tourist–host inter-cultural liaison. First, tourists, as opposed to immigrants, students and foreign workers, do not have to adapt to the local community. For example tourists are granted immunity from many local legal and cultural restrictions and can traverse the landscape in a small cultural bubble of their own nationality (Urry, 1990). Although tourists may experience culture shock, this experience is often confined to the initial stage of that process (Furnham and Bochner, 1986), and may indeed be stimulating and exciting to the traveller, since it can fulfil sensation-seeking motivations. Second, the tourists' affluence, even when they are relatively young drifter-nomads (Cohen, 1968), or backpackers (Riley, 1988; Loker-Murphy and Pearce, 1995), locates them in a peculiar sociological niche, that of strangers or outsiders (Simmel, 1950) who are able to observe and scrutinize the visited community. In this review it will be argued that the effects of tourist–resident contact are mediated by the tourists' affluence, motivation, transience and sociological status in the host community.

It is important for the present review to avoid clichés and superficial generalization about the tourist–resident interaction process. There are many types of tourists with specific motivational and attitudinal profiles. Some of these visitors are intensely interested in interacting with residents, while for others the local people are little more than a part of the scenery. Additionally the size and technological sophistication of the host community plays a crucial role mediating the impact of tourism and the nature of the resident–host contact and while the present review seeks generality in the collated results of research, the specific contexts and communities studied must always limit the generalizations which can be made.

The research literature: cases and places

Direct contact influences for isolated and poor communities

Direct contact between the tourists and the local people of Third World and poor communities often generates discord, exploitation and social problems. As noted earlier, some of the foundation issues in this area were identified in a wave of studies in the 1970s and contemporary examples amplify rather than change such concerns as privacy invasion, crowding, sexual behaviour influences and cultural identity.

The simple process of tourists observing or watching the local people can have profound effects. Certain cultural and economic day-to-day activities of ethnic groups seem to appeal to tourists and are promoted as tourist attractions. For example, Smith (1978a) demonstrated that tourists in Alaska walked along the beaches as fishermen and hunters returned to butcher their kill. Smith observed that the locals resented the tourists photographing their activities and in time erected barricades to prevent the would-be photographers. In a final attempt to regain their privacy, taxis were hired to haul the seals and other game to the Eskimos' homes, where the slaughtering could proceed.

Studies in Tonga (Urbanowicz, 1977, 1978) noted that tourists from large cruise ships produced crowded conditions in the small towns and that Tongan children sometimes begged from the visitors at major tourist attractions.

Such observations are not limited to tiny Pacific islands (cf. Cohen, 1982). For instance, the Seychelles islands, promoted to tourists as 'islands of love' because of their traditionally uninhibited sexual standards, now have 'rampant' and 'ferocious' rates of venereal disease (Turner and Ash, 1975). Similarly Bangkok and the Philippines have reputations for prostitution and the availability of drugs in response to the needs of European, Japanese, American and Australian tourists (Cohen, 1988; Ryan and Kinder, 1996).

For some small, technologically unsophisticated communities direct contact with tourists, if the latter come in small, manageable numbers, can be psychologically beneficial to the hosts. For example, Sofield (1991) notes that with skilful management the traditional Vanuatu ceremony, the naghol – an event which involves young men leaping from a high tower with a vine rope attached to their ankles – has been strengthened by the commercial importance attached to the event. Restricting the numbers of visitors and requiring certain codes of behaviour seem to be important factors affecting the outcome of direct tourist–host contact (cf. Boissevain, 1979).

Indirect contact effects for isolated and poor communities

Many of the social and psychological contact effects on the local people are of a less direct nature and not all such effects are negative. One of the strongest arguments for the view that tourism can provide social benefits to Third World or technologically unsophisticated communities is that it can revitalize ethnic arts and traditions. Thus Waters (1966) claims, somewhat eulogistically:

> This cultural renaissance is taking place all the way from the grass roots at the village level to the top councils of national governments. With a modest amount of help, the native craftsman practising a dying art finds a new demand for his product and then employs young apprentices, thus teaching his trade to a new generation. (p. 116)

This kind of sentiment has been repeated by governments, tourism lobby groups and international organizations at a plethora of world conferences in the last thirty years. It represents what Jafari (1990) labelled as the advocacy platform or boosterism.

One feature of selling local culture to the tourists is often overlooked. Many cultures attach enormous symbolic and spiritual importance to their ceremonies and art objects. Furthermore, an adequate interpretation of these symbolic meanings may require considerable anthropological knowledge on the part of the consuming tourist. Without an understanding of the cosmological significance of cultural activities such as Aboriginal corroborees or Indonesian burials, tourists will merely see these events as 'quaint' or 'pretty' customs (Crystal, 1978; Altman, 1988). This not only trivializes the local event; it also wastes an opportunity for tourists to appreciate the ethnocentrism of their own culture. Worst of all, the more extreme forms of tourist exploitation of local cultural products may make a sacrilege of former religious symbols by marketing them en masse (Mackenzie, 1977). This may literally endanger the lives of women and young children of the ethnic groups for whom such objects are tradition-ally taboo and where sighting these items should be punished by death.

Increasing economic dependence upon tourism may alter the job struc-ture and roles of a community, sometimes creating more new jobs for women than men (cf. Petit-Skinner, 1977). Furthermore, many of these jobs are menial and underpaid which promotes local frustration and alienation (Kent, 1977). The combined effects of such negative tourist influences have led researchers to postulate empirical indices of tourist–host friction. For example, Hills and Lundgren (1977) proposed an irrita-tion index which they described as a composite of the myriad forms of friction tourists produce for their hosts. While the researchers did not adequately specify how to evaluate and measure the tourist impact, they did specify some common sources of irritation. They note that in the Caribbean, shop attendants serve tourists first and locals last; inflation due to the tourist presence makes locals pay more for food; access to beaches is cut off by tourist hotels; local commuting time increases; and the crowding of beaches and parks makes traditional, spontaneous cricket games dangerous.

Direct contact effects for technologically advanced communities

One of the major studies of the impacts of tourism to have been con-ducted in the last few years is the Hawaiian Statewide Tourism Impact Core Survey (Community Resources Inc., 1989). In a special section of the report entitled 'Daily life and attitudes towards visitors', the com-plexities of resident attitudes to tourists are revealed. Twenty five per cent of the 3900 residents studied felt that favourite recreation areas had been 'taken over' by tourists in the past five years yet the very parks and beaches reported to be crowded with tourists were also the residents' favourite places for interacting with tourists. Additionally, 80 per cent of residents said this visitor contact was usually pleasant. Younger resi-dents were more likely to report positive behaviours towards tourists (friendly talks, giving directions) although younger residents in general were somewhat more likely to express anti-visitor sentiments.

The issues of traffic congestion was one direct effect of the tourist presence which was widely reported by different sections of the Hawai-ian resident community. In total 83 per cent of all residents reported that traffic was worse than five years ago with 71 per cent in the high density area reporting that it was a big problem in their lives.

The research concludes from its detailed findings that popular opinion about tourism impact in the region should not be confused with residents' views – conventional wisdom was in fact mistaken in several instances, for example tourism industry personnel did not differ appreciably from general residents in their attitudes. The study also attempted to integrate the findings of the report – that is the mix of seemingly contradictory positive and negative attitudes to tourists and their effects – by suggesting that there is a hierarchy of community needs which explain attitudes to visitors. According to this view jobs are a top priority for individual and community survival. In Hawaii tourism has played a major role in meeting that need for many communities. When the basic needs are met, attention turns to other needs or to the negative tourism side effects which once seemed less important. Accordingly, the overall view of Hawaii may well be composed of regional views which place different emphases on these community needs, hence producing a blurred total view. The proposal that an understanding of tourism–community relationships can be enhanced by adopting a market segmentation style approach to community views has recently been developed by Pearce, Moscardo and Ross (1996). Drawing on the sociological theory of social representations (shared public views of phenomenon), the authors argue that just as tourism is not a single entity nor are communities and it is valuable for the tourism industry and managers to assess carefully the extent and range of diverse community perspectives on tourism.

In an Australian study of a small but high density tourism environment, Ross (1990) notes that some negative perceptions of visitors may develop even when the host culture is relatively affluent. In his analysis of residents in the tropical city of Cairns he observed that visitors from the United States and, to a lesser extent, domestic Australian visitors were not as well liked as the more polite Japanese and European visitors. As in the Hawaiian study, the actual detailed research findings did not conform to conventional wisdom with an expected anti-Asian attitude not confirmed by the data.

Pearce (1980a) and Pi-Sunyer (1978) have noted how quickly local stereotypes of international visitors can emerge and negatively influence the quality of the host–tourist encounter. These stereotypes are readily applied when the outgroup is easily identified and their behaviours are distinctive or culturally different, thus promoting prejudice and attributions to nationality rather than to individual personality. Nevertheless, there is a broad consensus that international contact promotes goodwill and that the direct interpersonal encounters soften or modify harsh images of the contact parties (Amir, 1969).

One further perspective on this positive networking of the world's travellers and their hosts is provided in the work on tourism as an industry working for world peace (D'Amore, 1988). One of the most important challenges of future tourism research is to identify those factors which will promote the best social and cultural outcomes of the direct contact between hosts and guests. It would appear that pre-contact mutual education about the social and cultural practices of both societies is one of the promising avenues for engendering more positive attitudes in tourist resident encounters (Furnham and Bochner, 1986). Just as specialist adventure travellers prepare themselves for physically challenging activities so too cultural tourists should pay attention to their abilities to cope in the new and challenging context.

Indirect contact effects for technologically advanced societies

A further note in this section on the tourists' impact on local communities concerns the indirect influences of the tourist presence in advanced societies. The maintenance of great houses, the continued existence of zoos, national parks and wildlife reserves all owe some measure of their success to tourist incomes. For many aspects of cultural life, then, the indirect effects of tourists when they visit affluent countries assist the local people (Murphy, 1985).

Nevertheless a number of countries seem to hold a set of assumptions that the impacts of tourism are likely to be negative. For instance, Turner and Ash (1975) observe that Intourist, the Russian travel organization, exerts enormous control over foreign tourists' experience. Implicit in this structuring of the tourists' experience is the notion that direct tourist–host contact would be prejudicial to the correct perspective of one or both contact parties. Similarly Ritter (1975), discussing the attitudes of Islamic countries towards foreign tourists, observes that Saudi Arabia, Libya, Iraq and a number of southern Arab states are frankly not interested in having non-Islamic visitors.

Despite the passage of over two decades since the work of Ritter and Turner and Ash, the essential point concerning the possible 'pollution' effects of tourism remains valid, particularly in such settings as North Korea, Myanmar and Albania. In particular it appears that tourists are viewed as agents of cultural change, with political views, the dress of women, the use of alcohol and the mixing of the sexes being highly sensitive areas of potential influence (Ahmed, 1992).

There has been considerable attention by researchers focusing on the issues of the costs incurred by local communities to support tourism. For example, fire services, health facilities, roads, water and sewerage facilities are often strained by the increasing visitor numbers (Haywood, 1988; Long et al., 1990). In a study typical of this field Allen et al. (1988) report findings from twenty rural communities in Colorado. They found that perceptions of the quality of community life were positively related to the size of the rural community and that only some aspects of community life appear to be sensitive to changes in tourism development. In their rural communities, tourism growth influenced environmental issues, public services (fire, police, roads) and the social opportunities (amount of community contact and participation in organizations) but had little impact on recreation, education and medical facilities. The development of taxation schemes to reflect the true costs of tourism to the community in these economic and environmental terms is now being realized as well as the need to plan for tourism growth in all community and local government development plans (Dredge and Moore, 1992).

Summary: tourist impact on the local people

In summary, tourists appear to have maximum social and psychological impact on their hosts when the host communities are small, unsophisticated and isolated. This impact may be a powerful one, either in direct inter-personal encounters or in subtle, indirect influences on the visited community. When the receiving society is technologically more advanced and the affluence gap between tourists and hosts narrower, the contact experience has less impact. In such instances, tourists may develop friendships with the hosts, and the visitors can sustain local social institutions as well as promoting pride in the visited community. The negative effects are not restricted to inter-personal friction, but also include indirect stress to the hosts through environmental degradation and infrastructure costs.

This overall assessment may appear somewhat negative and, indeed, it must be remembered that tourism can still be compared favourably with many other industries as a source of economic growth with only some social and environmental impacts. This view is confirmed by some studies where residents recognize the impacts of tourism but still support its development compared to other industries (Pearce et al., 1996). Furthermore, it must be noted that many studies fail to disentangle the effects of tourism on residents from the effects of growth in general. There is a clear need for more comparative studies like the Colorado research which seek to distinguish tourism impacts from effects due to general increases in population or the parallel growth of other industries (e.g. residential and condominium development).

The effects of inter-cultural contact on the tourists

There are two views concerning the effects of the travel experience on the tourists themselves. On the one hand international travel is said to promote tolerance and understanding of other cultures. Another view is that 'we travel not that we may broaden and enrich our minds, but that we may pleasantly forget they exist.' (Huxley, 1925). This perspective considers the tourist experience to be shallow and inconsequential and hence very unlikely to leave any lasting impression on the traveller.

Social psychological studies of tourist attitude change

An early study of the effects on tourists of inter-cultural contact is provided by Smith (1955, 1957). Young Americans who spent a summer touring Europe were sent a mail questionnaire, both before and after their travels. Smith reported few attitudinal changes on the scales used, and concluded that deeply rooted attitudes were not affected by the travel experience. For the few subjects who did change their attitudes, Smith argues, following interviews with the travellers, that the change took place due more to the peer conformity pressures than to some functional personality need of the individual. The brief European excursion had fostered some contacts with the hosts, since most travellers exchanged correspondence and gifts. A follow-up study revealed that in a few cases these relationships persisted for up to four years, but only where intense personal relationships had been established (Smith, 1957).

Another study more directly concerned with assessing tourists' attitudes to the visited nationality was conducted amongst British tourists visiting either Greece or Morocco (Pearce, 1977a). The tourists studied were young members of cheap package tours on 2–3 week tours of either country. A set of questions concerning their travel motivation revealed that they were predominantly interested in relaxing, drinking and having a good time with fellow travellers in novel, sunny settings, and that they were not particularly motivated by a desire to meet the local inhabitants and study their culture. A group of control subjects who were interested in travel but could not join these particular groups for time-scheduling reasons were used to assess test sensitization and measurement effects in the questionnaire.

Both the travellers to Greece and to Morocco changed their perceptions of the host communities, with the Greeks being evaluated more favourably and the Moroccans less favourably. Additionally, the travellers also saw their own countrymen more positively following their holidays. The finding that tourists can make some small-scale re-evaluations of their own countrymen after travelling abroad parallels findings for students living abroad, who also alter their perceptions of home (Herman and Schild, 1960; Rieggel, 1953; Useem and Useem, 1967).

Other kinds of impacts on the tourists may also be discerned. Tourists are subject to particular health risks while travelling and contact with local people may have long-range effects on the tourists' physical well being (Turner and Ash, 1975). There are also reported cases of psychiatric breakdown amongst tourists (Prokop, 1970). In studies of German tourists visiting Innsbruck, Prokop found several instances of tourist depression, alcoholism and other mental health problems, as recorded by the Innsbruck hospitals. He attributed these behaviours to the high incidence of drinking among the travellers, and argued that the release from day-to-day pressures precipitated the tourists' self-doubts and depression. It is apparent that the advertising images of stress-free holidays are considerably misplaced.

Further evidence that travelling can create problems is provided in the work on life stress by Holmes and Rahe (1967). In scaling stress-related events in an individual's life span from 0 (no stress) to 100 (maximum stress), holidays were given a score of 15. This was comparable to such events as changes in working conditions, troubles with one's boss and mortgage stresses. The figure of 15 may also be an underestimate for international travel where the tourist has to cope with an unfamiliar culture. Europeans typically report that travel is more stressful than do Americans, presumably because they experience more foreign culture contacts by travelling in other European countries (Harmon et al., 1970).

The origins of the social stresses for the tourist in his contact with the local people are numerous. The tourist has problems in locating and orienting himself in the new environment (Pearce, 1977b), and this alone has implications for the traveller's sense of security and emotional well being (Lynch, 1960). In New York special maps are available to warn tourists of the 'safe, dangerous at night and dangerous all day' areas of the city (Downs and Stea, 1977).

While the tourist is occasionally treated as a special kind of stranger in the community and is helped more by the local people (Feldman, 1968; Pearce, 1980b), the social interaction between tourists and locals is another potent form of stress. The question of language is paramount here. Many tourists find that their inability to communicate with the local people is enormously frustrating, and language difficulties may generate considerable stress when sickness occurs, travel plans go astray or luggage and money are lost (Furnham and Bochner, 1986). The solution for many tourists is to confine their travels to countries where their own language is understood fairly readily or use guides to limit the effects of culture shock (Pearce, 1984).

There are also subtle differences in non-verbal communication between different cultures. For example, the gestures of the locals may confuse the tourist. To the American visiting Sardinia it may be a considerable source of confusion to find that the OK gesture is interpreted as a symbol of homosexuality (Morris et al., 1979). Even the basic nodding of the head for agreement and disagreement has subtle variations. While it is apparent that many universally applicable gestures and emotional expressions exist (Argyle, 1975), some features of interaction with the hosts are likely to be subtly different for the tourists, for instance the use of space may differ. Watson and Graves (1966) found that Americans tend to think Arabs pushy and threatening because of the latter's preference for more direct, closer and intimate interaction. While specialized training procedures may help to overcome these difficulties (Collett, 1971), most tourists are probably unaware of these non-verbal cues until they are confronted with dramatic breakdowns in their interactions.

Some host cultures, finding their visitors to be difficult and socially unskilled from their own perspective, have started to produce pamphlets outlining some of the local cultural rules and norms that tourists should follow. For example, Fiji suggests that visiting Australians should not tip the local people, should learn the correct greeting rituals, should appreciate the polite and reciprocal bonds of friendship, and should not confuse lack of clothing with promiscuity (Fiji Visitors' Bureau, 1975). This kind of educational material is also often contained in guidebooks but the extent to which tourists follow these specific prescriptions is unknown.

The research literature: explanations

In trying to understand and order the kinds of studies reviewed above, stage or step models have been popular.

For example Smith (1978b) saw the development of tourism in terms of distinct waves of tourist types; the seven categories in order of expanding community impact are shown in Figure 8.2.

Smiths' model was directed at cross-cultural contact issues and her pioneering book *Hosts and Guests* contained several studies where social

Type of tourist	Number of tourists	Community impact
1 Explorer	Very limited	
2 Elite	Rarely seen	
3 Off-beat	Uncommon but seen	
4 Unusual	Occasional	Steadily
5 Incipient mass	Steady flow	increasing
6 Mass	Continuous influx	
7 Charter	Massive arrival	

Figure 8.2 Smith's (1978b) seven categories of tourist

impacts on local communities were directly related to the expansion of tourism. At about the same time as Smith's work was gaining attention from anthropologists encountering tourists in the cultures the researchers had come to study, Doxey (1975) proposed an irritation index or irridex to assess host–guest interactions and relationships. Doxey's scale has four steps: euphoria (delight in the contact), apathy (increasing indifference with larger numbers), irritation (concern and annoyance over price rises, crime, rudeness, cultural rules being broken) and finally antagonism (covert and overt aggression to visitors).

Another stage development model relating to tourism was proposed by Butler (1980). In this model the impacts of tourism are not the direct focus of attention. Instead the model is concerned with the more general issue of the evolution of tourist areas (marketing issues, organization and ownership of the tourist services and attractions) although the attitudes of residents and community support for tourism are discussed as a part of the larger process. Butler sees tourist areas as evolving through the stages of exploration, involvement, development, consolidation, stagnation and then either decline or rejuvenation. In the consolidation stage he sees the emergence of social impacts:

> The large numbers of visitors and facilities provided for them can be expected to arouse some opposition and discontent among permanent residents. (Butler, 1980: 8)

The stagnation phase, where peak numbers of visitors have been reached, is seen as follows:

> Capacity levels for many variables will have been reached or exceeded with attendant environmental, social and economic problems. (Butler, 1980: 8)

Stage based models of individual and social processes invite a number of criticisms, many of which can be directed at these tourism related models. All three models have poor demarcation between the stages or steps. It is also unclear whether shifting from one stage to another precludes the continued existence of the previous stage. For example, just as children who have moved from crawling to walking may also still crawl, is it the case that tourism communities which have moved from development to consolidation will retain and exhibit many of the features of the development phase or are they necessarily superseded? Additionally stage models prompt the question of whether or not the order of the stages is invariant. The Doxey and Smith models appear to assume this point but Butler notes that some tourism destinations (he cites the major Mexican resort of Cancun) may move directly into a higher level stage without the proceeding steps. A related question concerns the speed of progression through the resort development or tourism growth stages. Does it matter, in terms of community impact, how quickly the environment has been developed for tourism or is it simply a matter of which stage of development has been reached? Further, in the final stages of the Doxey and Butler models is it the whole community which becomes hostile to tourism or are there only sections of the population who suffer and complain about the social impacts? And finally one must query whether the whole process of social impacts and tourism evolution as outlined is inevitable, leaving individuals and local groups powerless to confront the forces of economic change and gain.

These questions are more than curious asides to the developing literature on tourism and community effects. One needs to question whether or not the models advanced in the literature to date are really post-hoc descriptive devices or whether they have predictive possibilities. One can conclude that the models discussed are complete and simply do not meet the challenges raised in these critical questions. Similarly, despite being widely quoted in the tourism textbooks as the definitive sources on the matters of social and community impact, the evidence to support these models is virtually non-existent (cf. Murphy, 1985).

Nevertheless work on the social impacts of tourism has continued throughout the last decade and while the models reviewed above have been formally cited they have been effectively by-passed. Studies conducted in the 1980s may be summarized under a new banner – a segmentation approach to tourism's social impacts. This work has the following characteristics. It describes in detail resident reactions to the impacts of tourism. In this work, lists of critical social impacts have been constructed, factor analysed, employed in different countries and related to the demographic characteristics of respondents. Typical examples of this approach include the work of Milman and Pizam, 1988; Liu and Var, 1986; Long et al., 1990; Brougham and Butler, 1981. Across these studies there is intermittent evidence that older residents are more affected by tourism impacts than younger residents, those benefiting most from working in the tourist industry have more positive attitudes and those living closer to the tourist zone have more negative attitudes towards tourism, as do those individuals with higher daily contact with tourists.

This line of work offers several promising directions for an understanding of tourist–resident interaction. It appears to suggest that attitudes towards tourism and tourists follow some kind of fundamental equity function (Bryant and Napier, 1981). For example business leaders, those working in the industry and those with economic investment in the area are more positive towards tourism (Murphy, 1985) although the Hawaiian study noted earlier found little evidence of such differences in that community. For such groups the costs to benefit ratios are clearly different than is the case for the elderly and for those living in maximum contact with tourist zones where crowding, pollution and local services are heavily strained by the visitor pressure.

While equity considerations might appear to underlie much of the work done in the last decade in the segmentation category of tourism's social impacts, there remains a need to model or portray the general attitudes towards tourism held by residents. A very detailed examination of the proposed systematic equity effects of tourism on residents reveals much inconsistency (Pearce et al., 1996). Some other powerful forces relating to people's identity and how groups understand social issues appear to be at work as well. One can express this same point in a different language system: one familiar particularly to European psychologists – there appear to exist social representations of the tourism industry within communities (Farr, 1987; Moscovici, 1984). Moscovici defined a social representation as 'the elaborating of a social object by the community for the purpose of behaving and communicating' (1963: 251). He argued that social representations are more than public attitudes towards certain objects or issues. Rather, social representations are like theories or systems of knowledge which include values, ideas and guides for behaviour which allow communities to make sense of their social world. Farr (1987) points out that social representations as discussed by Moscovici can be seen involving a social construction of reality and emphasize social groups rather than individuals as in the classic psychological work on attitudes and opinions. This allegiance with traditions in sociology and anthropology leads to a focus on the media and literature of a community as the sources of information on social representations rather than the exclusive use of surveys of individuals within a community. Additionally the social representations approach draws attention to the social nature of residents' responses. How individuals think about tourism is in part determined by the groups they belong to and want to belong to because social identity and personal worth are important influences on the attitudes we hold. Examples of such social representations for the tourist industry would be 'tourism as a new source of employment' or tourism as a 'vulture destroying cultures' (cf. Greenwood, 1978; Brougham and Butler, 1981). If an individual adopts such an everyday knowledge view of tourism, personal benefits may be overridden in the larger picture of how others see and shape social attitudes.

This review of the literature on tourism's social impacts can be summarized by suggesting that a new model for understanding social impacts can be empirically explored. This new model rejects the previous stage models of tourism impacts and advances a social representational view of tourism. In this new approach resident reactions to future tourism developments may depend on a cost-benefit style accounting of the effects of tourism which residents have experienced but this accounting information must be considered together with the way in which the media is likely to present tourism. The overall working view or everyday theory that residents hold about tourism will reflect both their personal 'gain' and the media views as well as being highly influenced by resident views of their identity – to what sort of group they do and want to belong.

Detailed support and explanation of this approach to understanding tourism community relationships as a whole with particular case studies from Hawaii, New Zealand and Australia can be found in Pearce, Moscardo and Ross (1996).

Management directions

Five tactics for arresting the decline of tourist–resident attitudes can be proposed. These tactics follow the most promising explanations of the decay of tourist–resident attitudes outlined earlier and concentrate on the social representation and equity issues in tandem.

Education and tourism

Since many of the negative tourist–resident impacts of tourism are perceived impacts, that is judgements made by individuals about others, then it follows that mistakes and errors of interpretation are possible. A community which receives more detailed education in the field of tourism will be better able to analyse the impacts that are specifically tourism related with a rounded appreciation of both the negative and positive consequences of development. Murphy (1985), a leading international figure in tourism social impact analysis, strongly argues that tourism is better received when the community has been more adequately informed about the industry.

Accordingly, non-trivial information campaigns about tourism, about tourist habits and cultural differences offer one line of attack for improving tourist-resident relationships.

Incorporating community perspectives

It must be recognized that the community or the groups which represent community interests are not necessarily experts in tourism planning. Their right to comment on proposals should, however, not be ignored, since the very act of expressing opinions is often therapeutic and constructive.

Nevertheless their view is but one of a number of the necessary inputs to the planning process. In particular, attention should be given to allowing whole communities to compare two or three alternative proposals for development in a region or location, at least at the broad concept stage. This procedure is well suited to very large developments and to regional plans.

Much psychological research exists showing that people make better decisions and judgements in situations involving a comparison of alternatives (Zube, 1980). A format for environmental evaluation which permits communities and individuals to vote on alternative proposals is recommended. Additionally, faced with specific models of alternative developments for a region, communities can provide a list of requirements which they strongly feel must be met by developers. Such approaches give specific advance warnings to the industry of community concerns. For large scale private developments, it would be an appropriate step prior to the formal submission of a development application.

The general theme of incorporating community perspectives in tourism development can be divided into a number of subgoals or themes. These themes each represent important guidelines in forecasting, preventing and managing social impacts. It has been suggested that social impacts will be lessened if:

- overall development goals and priorities are in harmony with those of the residents (including attending to urgent growth problems before more tourism work proceeds);
- the promotion of local attractions is subject to resident endorsement;
- native people and/or ethnic groups are closely involved with the development process to respect their social needs;
- there is broad based community participation in tourist events and activities; and
- destination areas adopt or refine themes and events that reflect their history, location and geographic setting.

Principle of increasing resident opportunity

One of the common factors underlying a host of social impacts of tourism is the restriction of the local people's opportunities for recreation, shopping and easy living. For example, in Australia the national tradition of expecting free access to beaches, national parks and scenic environments needs to be respected in the design and layout of new facilities. The corollary is that tourism developments which enhance the social and leisure world of communities by considering their needs in resort and attraction development planning should be well received.

Community equity and management committees

Control of tourism facilities through ownership by community groups (particularly aboriginal or ethnic subgroups) as well as by substantial community representation on management committees represent other techniques of limiting negative social impacts.

One recommended guideline is that of trying to maximize local capital, entrepreneurial ability and labour in tourism developments. Following the social representation perspective it can be argued that where residents have the impression that tourism is in the hands of outsiders more negative attitudes will follow. If local capital and labour is not appropriate, a local social monitoring committee may be usefully employed.

Research and monitoring

Allied to the preceding recommendation is the thorough use of the academic research community to identify local social impacts in advance of tourism growth in a region. As in the environmental/biological field, research and monitoring of key social impact indicators or warning signs would also serve a useful function in respecting community interests and providing data on likely flashpoints of public dissatisfaction. The techniques and skills exist to undertake this monitoring of social impacts.

Particular research issues which need addressing are:

- building up a data base of tourist–resident interaction in similar communities where different types of developments have occurred; and
- monitoring social impacts over time in high pressure communities. This would address such questions as do tourist–resident interactions improve over time or do the social impacts of tourism persist and in turn cause problems for the economic viability of the development.

Finally, it is notable that the topic of tourist–resident impacts has its own pattern of academic and tourist industry interest. While the academic interest has been relatively constant, private sector attention is more varied with the community concerns receiving more at the development and rejuvenation phases of growth rather than in the consolidation or maintenance phase. Nevertheless tourist–resident interaction, despite these fluctuations of attention, is likely to be a critical tourism issue for the next decade and beyond.

References

Ahmed, Z.U. (1992) Islamic Pilgrimage (Hajj) to Ka'aba in Makkah (Saudi Arabia): An important international tourism activity, *Journal of Tourism Studies*, **3**(1), 35–43

Amir, Y. (1969) Contact hypothesis in ethnic relations, *Psychological Bulletin*, **71**, 319–42

Allen, L.R., Long, P.T., Perdue, R.R. and Kieselbach, S. (1988) The impact of tourism development on residents' perceptions of community life, *Journal of Travel Research*, **XXVII**(1), 16–21

Altman, J. (1988) *Aborigines, tourism and development: The Northern Territory Experience*, Australian National University North Australia Research Unit, Darwin

Argyle, M. (1975) *Bodily communication*, Methuen, London

Boissevain, J. (1979). The impact of tourism on a dependent island, Gozo, Malta, *Annals of Tourism Research*, **6**, 76–90

Brougham, J.F. and Butler, R.W. (1981) A segmentation analysis of resident attitudes to the social impact of tourism, *Annals of Tourism Research*, **8**, 569–590

Bryant, E.G. and Napier, T.L. (1981) The application of social exchange theory to the study of satisfaction with outdoor recreation facilities. In *Outdoor recreation planning, perspectives and research* (ed. T.L. Napier), (pp. 83–98), Kendall Hunt, Dubuque IA

Butler, R. (1980) The concept of a tourism area cycle of evolution: Implications for management resources, *Canadian Geopgrapher*, **24**, 5–12

Cohen, E. (1968) Nomads from affluence: Notes on the phenomenon of drifter-tourism, *International Journal of Comparative Sociology*, **XIV** 1–2, 88–103

Cohen, E. (1982) Thai girls and Farang men: The edge of ambiguity, *Annals of Tourism Research*, **9**, 403–428

Cohen, E. (1988) Tourism and AIDS in Thailand, *Annals of Tourism Research*, **15**(4), 467–486

Collett, P. (1971) Training Englishmen in the non-verbal behaviour of Arabs, *International Journal of Psychology*, **6**, 209–15

Community Resources Inc. (1989) *1988 Statewide Tourism Impact: Cor Survey Summary*. Hawaii: Department of Business and Economic Development, Tourism Branch, Hawaii

Crystal, E. (1978) Tourism in Toraja, Sulawesi, Indonesia. In *Hosts and Guests* (ed. V.L. Smith), Blackwell, Oxford

D'Amore, L. (1988) Tourism – The World's Peace Industry, *Journal of Travel Research*, **27**(1), 35–40

Downs, R. and Stea, D. (1977) *Maps in Minds*, Harper and Row, New York

Doxey, G.V. (1975) A causation theory of visitor–resident irritants, methodology and research inferences. The Impact of Tourism. *Sixth Annual Conference Proceedings of the Travel Research Association*, San Diego, 195–198

Dredge, D. and Moore, S. (1992) A methodology for the integration of tourism in town planning, *Journal of Tourism Studies*, **3**(1), 8–21

Farr, R.M. (1987) Social representations: A French tradition of research, *Journal for the Theory of Social Behaviour*, **17**(4), 343–369

Feldman, R. (1968) Response to compatriot and foreigner who seek assistance, *Journal of Personality and Social Psychology*, **10**, 202–214

Fiji Visitors' Bureau (1975) *Advice to visiting Australians*, Fiji Visitors' Bureau, Suva

Furnham, A. and Bochner, S. (1986) *Culture shock*, Methuen, London

Greenwood, D.J. (1978) Culture by the pound: An anthropological perspective on tourism as cultural commoditization. In *Hosts and Guests* (ed. V.L. Smith), Blackwell, Oxford

Harmon, D.K., Masuda, M. and Holmes, T.H. (1970) The social readjustment rating scale: A cross-cultural study of Western Europeans and Americans, *Journal of Psychosomatic Research*, **14**, 391–400

Haywood, K.M. (1988) Responsible and responsive tourism planning in the community, *Tourism Management*, **9**, 105–118

Herman, S. and Schild, E. (1960) Contexts for the study of cross-cultural education, *Journal of Social Psychology*, **52**, 231–50

Hills, T.L. and Lundgren, J. (1977) *The impact of tourism in the Caribbean – A methodological study*, Department of Geography, McGill University, Montreal

Holmes, T.H. and Rahe, R.H. (1967) The Social Readjustment Rating Scale, *Journal of Psychosomatic Research*, **11**, 213–218

Huxley, A. (1925) *Along the Road*, Chatto and Windus, London

Jafari, J. (1990) Research and scholarship: The basis of tourism education, *Journal of Tourism Studies*, **1**(1), 33–41

Kent, N. (1977) A new kind of sugar. In *A new kind of sugar: Tourism in the Pacific* (ed. Finney, B.R. and Watson, K.A.), The East-West Center, Honolulu, Hawaii

Liu, J.C. and Var, T. (1986) Resident attitudes to tourism in Hawaii, *Annals of Tourism Research*, **13**, 193–214

Liu, J.C., Sheldon, P. and Var, T. (1987) Resident perception of the environmental impacts of tourism, *Annals of Tourism Research*, **14**, 17–37

Loker-Murphy, L. and Pearce, P.L. (1995) Young budget travelers: Backpackers in Australia, *Annals of Tourism Research*, **22**(4), 819–843

Long, P.T., Perdue, R.R. and Allen, L. (1990) Rural resident tourism perceptions and attitudes by community level of tourism, *Journal of Travel Research*, **28**, 3–9

Lynch, K. (1960) *The Image of the City*, Cambridge: MIT Press and Harvard University Press

Mackenzie, M. (1977) The deviant art of tourism: Airport art. In *The social and economic impact of tourism on Pacific communities* (ed. B. Farrell), Center for South Pacific Studies, University of California, Santa Cruz

Milman, A. and Pizam, A. (1988) Social Impacts of Tourism on Central Florida, *Annals of Tourism Research*, **15**, 191–204

Morris, D., Collett, P., Marsh, P. and O'Shaughnessy, M. (1979) *Gestures: Their origins and distribution*, Jonathan Cape, London

Moscovici, S. (1963) Attitudes and opinions, *Annual Review of Psychology*, **14**, 231–260

Moscovici, S. (1984) The phenomenon of social representations. In *Social representations* (ed. R.M. Farr and S. Moscovici), pp. 3–70, Cambridge University Press, Cambridge

Murphy, P.E. (1981) Community attitudes to tourism: A comparative analysis, *International Journal of Tourism Management*, **2**, 189–195

Murphy, P.E. (1985) *Tourism: A Community Approach*, Methuen, New York

Pearce, P.L. (1977a) The social and environmental perceptions of overseas tourists. Unpublished D.Phil. thesis, University of Oxford

Pearce, P.L. (1977b) Mental Souvenirs: A study of tourist and their city maps, *Australian Journal of Psychology*, **29**, 203–210

Pearce, P.L. (1980a) A favourability-satisfaction model of tourist's evaluations, *Journal of Travel Research*, **14**(1), 13–17

Pearce, P.l. (1980b) Strangers, travellers and Greyhound bus terminals: Studies of small scale helping behaviours, *Journal of Personality and Social Psychology*, **35**, 935–940

Pearce, P.L. (1984). Tourist-guide interaction, *Annals of Tourism Research*, **11**, 129–146

Pearce, P.L., Moscardo, G.M. and Ross, G.F. (1996). *Tourism community relationships*, Elsevier, Oxford

Petit-Skinner, S. (1977). Tourism and acculturation in Tahiti. In *The social and economic impact of tourism on Pacific Communities* (ed. B. Farrell), Centre for South Pacific Studies, University of California, Santa Cruz

Pi-Sunyer, O. (1978). Through native eyes: Tourists and tourism in a Catalan maritime community. In *Hosts and Guests* (ed. V.L. Smith), Blackwell, Oxford

Prokop, H. (1970) Psychiatric illness of foreigners vacationing in Innsbruck, *Neurochirugie and Psychiatrie*, **107**, 363–368

Riegel, O.W. (1953) Residual effects of exchange of persons, *Public Opinion Quarterly*, **17**, 319–27

Riley, P. (1988) Long term budget travellers, *Annals of Tourism Research*, **15**, 313–328

Ritter, W. (1975) Recreation and tourism in Islamic countries, *Ekistics*, **236**, 56–69

Ross, G. (1990) Do we really dislike the Japanese. Resident reactions to various groups of tourists, *Mina*, **1**(6), 16–19

Ryan, C. and Kinder, R. (1996) Sex, tourism and sex tourism: Fulfilling similar needs? *Tourism Management*, **17**(7), 507–518

Sheldon, P. and Car, T. (1984) Resident attitudes to tourism in North Wales, *Tourism Management*, **5**, 40–48

Simmel, G. (1950) *The Sociology of Georg Simmel* (translated by H. Woolf), Free Press of Glencoe, New York

Smith, H.P. (1955) Do intercultural experiences affect attitudes? *Journal of Abnormal and Social Psychology*, **51**, 469–77

Smith, H.P. (1957) The effects of intercultural experience: A follow-up investigation, *Journal of Abnormal and Social Psychology*, **54**, 266–9

Smith, V.L. (1978a) Eskimo tourism: micro models and marginal men. In *Hosts and Guests* (ed. V.L. Smith), Blackwell, Oxford

Smith, V.L. (1978b) *Hosts and Guests*, Blackwell, Oxford

Sofield, T. (1991) Sustainable ethnic tourism in the South Pacific: Some principles, *Journal of Tourism Studies*, **2**(1), 56–72

Turner, L. and Ash, J. (1975) *The Golden Hordes*, Constable, London

Urbanowicz, C. (1977) Integrating tourism with other industries in Tonga. In *The social and economic impact of tourism on Pacific communities* (ed. B.Farrell), Centre for South Pacific Studies, University of California, Santa Cruz

Urbanowicz, C. (1978) Tourism in Tonga: Troubled times. In *Hosts and Guests* (ed. Smith, V.L.), Blackwell, Oxford

Urry, J. (1990) *The Tourist Gaze*, Sage, London

Useem, J. and Useem, R. (1967) The interfaces of a binational third culture: A study of American community in India, *Journal of Social Issues*, **23**, 130–43

Waters, S.R. (1966) The American tourist, *Annals of the Academy of Political and Social Science*, **368**, 109–118

Watson, O.M. and Graves, T.D. (1966) Quantitative research in proxemic behaviour, *American Anthropologist*, **68**, 971–85

Zube, E. (1980) *Environmental evaluation*, Brooks/Cole, Monterey, California

9 Alternative tourism: a comparative analysis of meaning and impact

Donald Macleod

Introduction

As a concept 'alternative tourism' is surprisingly broad, it is fundamentally problematic when subject to analysis and brings out many emotional responses – a common feature of tourism as a subject. There is not one absolute and watertight definition, although there are a number of very good attempts and many writers give a list of criteria against which it should be assessed. It remains an important issue to be dealt with, not the least because of its relationship to basic problems which human society must confront: environmental destruction, wealth inequalities and irresponsible development amongst them. It is also growing in popularity as fashions change and tourists seek different experiences. Just as it has been promoted as a 'development tool' and a means of protecting nature, so it has also been seen as an attractive way to pass leisure time without causing damage.

This chapter is a critical enquiry into the character of alternative tourism and its impact, and is composed of two major sections. The first section deals with its **meaning** as can be ascertained from surveying and comparing the works of different scholars; the second deals with its **impact**, in which the influences described by various scholars are compared, including detailed case studies. Finally, the conclusion challenges the viability of the term 'alternative tourism' and proposes a new approach. It also revises our understanding of the impact of this type of tourism, critiquing earlier models and stressing the powerful influences which it has had on the environment and the host populations. Throughout this discussion problems are highlighted and suggestions are made for future research.

The meaning of alternative tourism

In his paper, which looked at the evolution of alternative tourism as a concept, Gonsalves (1987) charted its beginnings as a defined concept from the Manila International Workshop in 1980, although he noted that concern over tourism had become public at the World Council of Churches in 1969. In 1984 in Chiangmai, Thailand, the forty-four participants of The Ecumenical Coalition on Third World Tourism (ECTWT) agreed that it was seen as:

> [a] process which promotes a just form of travel between members of different communities. It seeks to achieve mutual understanding, solidarity and equality amongst participants.

The ECTWT produced a resource book on alternative tourism and promoted models and programs. Such models included:

1 Brief contacts with local people.
2 Longer visits with host families and the community, and an insight into local life.
3 Non-commercial learning options (study tours, work camps, exchange visits).
4 Organizations or community groups in various countries concerned about Third World tourism.
5 Alternative tourist travel agents in both host and sending nations seeking to share rather than shield visitors from the destination's culture and problems.

Gonsalves sees the ultimate test of these alternatives in their ability to influence mainstream tourism. He cites an encouraging sign, that of the adoption of the Tourism Bill of Rights and Tourism Code by the World Tourism Organization in 1985 in response to the Penang Code of Ethics. Finally he concludes with:

> Travel, throughout history, has been a means of education, cross-cultural communication and the development of meaningful relationships. Alternative tourism considers these objectives still valid and works towards these ends.

He has ended on an optimistic note, and is positive about the course and intentions of alternative tourism, a position which has more recently been subject to sceptical criticism by other writers.

With Cohen (1987), alternative tourism is not even a single general concept, but composed of two principal conceptions. First, it is seen as a reaction to modern consumerism, a counter-cultural response to mass tourism, composed of such characters as the adventurer, the drifter, the traveller; those looking for spontaneity or romantically searching for a lost paradise. He remarks that these types occasionally create their own cultural enclaves involving drugs and sex, treating local people as oddities and initiating a diminution of the culture of hospitality amongst the host community. There is also the incipient creation of an alternative tourism 'establishment' which leads to a further reduction in difference between alternative and mass tourism.

Second, it is conceived as 'concerned alternative tourism' which is in essence a reaction to the exploitation of the Third World, in which the notion of a 'just' tourism arises, furthering mutual understanding, preventing environmental and cultural degradation and exploitation. In this type of tourism small groups interact with local people, and small-scale projects involving local consultation and participation are the principal means of promotion.

Cohen sees the main quandary as being the fact that mass tourism cannot be transformed, whilst alternative tourism is too small-scale to offer a realistic general option. This leads to the realization that tourism is extremely varied and multifaceted and that criticism of mass tourism is too radical, whereas the goals of alternative tourism are set too high and are therefore unrealistic. He is ultimately pragmatic, highlighting the need to reform the worst prevailing situation in mass tourism. In short, he has powerfully criticized the supposition that alternative tourism can ultimately lead to a transformation of tourism and is suspicious of the benefits that it brings; he has offered a good working definition, drawing attention to two central aspects, and has added a healthy air of critical judgement.

Cazes (1989) is well aware of the ambiguity of the concept 'alternative tourism' and likens it to the notion 'integrated' which has been described as a 'miracle-word, panacea concept, mythical term.' However, he eventually provides guidelines which may be applied to six different sectorial fields:

1   **The tourist as an individual**: motivated through original aspiration which may include active tourism (rambling, trekking), exploring, encounter travel, committed tourism (voluntary service overseas, archaeological digs) and other self-sacrificing work.
2   **The practitioners**: they do not want to be regarded as clients or consumers, and include backpackers, drifters, long-distance travellers; overall a varied group.
3   **The journey's destination**: this may be an unexplored 'virgin' location and often rests on an idealized vision of peasant societies which represent 'authentic' cultures.

4 **The type of accommodation**: 'supplementary' including camping, small local family hotels, holiday centres, village inns, private rented homes, paying guests; the dominant theme is micro-facilities as opposed to massive hotels.
5 **Travel organizers and partners**: especially the non-lucrative organizations (non-governmental organizations, mutual benefit societies), individual travel organizations – marginal or underground.
6 **The mode of insertion in the host community**: this involves a concerted effort to develop the reception of tourists wherein discourse centres on integration (economic, social, spatial, ecological, urban), local control and autodevelopment. A crucial factor is the prominence of the local system in overseeing the tourism.

Having critically analysed the sectorial fields, Cazes goes on to deconstruct the concept of mass tourism, seeing it as a myth which represents the 'other' or 'anti-other', a seat of harmful potentialities; thus alternative tourism is in actuality a discourse on difference and fundamentally elitist. In fact, it becomes a total subversion of the dominant models on three levels:

1 **Values** – the conditions of aspiration and motivations for the journey.
2 **Process** – the quality of collaboration and partnership, co-operation and synergy between external operation and local system at different stages of the phenomenon.
3 **Forms** – social, spatial, ecological and architectural forms are all faithful to the guiding principles of integration based on local traditional patterns and workforce.

According to Cazes there is no perfect example which epitomizes alternative tourism as described above, although the development of Lower Casamance in Senegal comes close. Further to this, he admits that there are dangers in idealizing the concept and points to the risks of ghettoizing areas and the museumification of sites of interest based on an elitist interpretation.

A more straightforward definition is offered by Hitchcock et al. (1993b) in the introduction to their edited collection, which suggests that in its purest form alternative tourism is underpinned by a number of principles:

• It should be built on dialogue with local people who ought to be aware of its effects and have political weight concerning the matter.
• It should be established on sound environmental principles, sensitive to local culture and religious tradition.
• It should be a means of giving the poor a reasonable and more equal share in the gains.
• The scale of tourism should be tailored to match the capacity of the local area to cope, measured in aesthetic and ecological terms.

The writers also note that alternative tourism may be used to strengthen linkages between the tourism industry and other forms of local economic activity. They recognize that its promotion has led to the questioning of how tourism affects destinations and the fact that the market niche is being exploited – warning about the possibility of a green consumerism developing. However, they remain essentially optimistic, citing the case of ecotourism, which can support the protection of vulnerable areas of natural beauty and scientific interest as well as stimulate environmental awareness amongst the local population.

Continuing the theme of environmental and social sensitivity, in an article on tourism and sustainable development, Murphy (1994), using the definition by Krippendorf (1987), sees alternative tourists as 'those who try to establish more contact with the local population, try to do without the tourist infrastructure and use the same accommodation and transport facilities as the natives'. He then goes on to define ecotourism (a subset of alternative tourism) as occurring where the visitor contributes to the development and well-being of the host ecology. Such tourists are regarded as the champions of the environment and sustainable development, and Costa Rica is cited as a country where ecotourism principles support the philosophy of sustainable development.

As is clear from the above illustrations of alternative tourism and its definitions, this concept is not easily contained within neat parameters, and moreover it may be regarded as too broad to be accurately used. Further, in the opinion of Cazes, its antithesis, mass tourism, is not sufficiently well understood for an alternative to be really valid. Nevertheless, it is possible to retrieve the central aspects of the concept from the various writers, and these include: contact and communication between the tourists and the indigenous population, a desire for equality, individuality, environmental awareness and concern. Nevertheless, there are also cautionary undertones, and some writers feel that there is an element of elitism within this type of tourism, and others see it as being exploited as a consumer item. We must bear in mind the need to be cautious and sceptical in imagining its impact. Additionally, as tourism grows and the need for environmental responsibility increases, so the necessity for an objective and detailed understanding of the phenomenon and its influence becomes more imperative.

The impact of alternative tourism

In his critique of alternative tourism, Butler (1990) plays devil's advocate, warning of the risks of passively accepting the hype surrounding it, and he compares it to the notion of 'sustainable development' in that 'It can mean almost anything to anyone.' He emphasizes the need to focus on the implication for destination areas, and in his attack he goes so far as to ask the question: why would anyone want to promote it? The answer, he suggests, is found in the desire of promoters and host communities for fewer negative effects on destinations and populations. Here is the nub of the problem, and he points to the difficulties inherent in tourism overall, and the need to recognize it both as an industry and agent of development and change. There is, because of tourism's fragmented and competitive nature, a need to be wary and consider the worst possible outcomes; even the concept of 'green tourism' (ecotourism) is to be treated with caution.

Butler sees an element of elitism in alternative tourism and wonders for whom it may be most 'appropriate'. He notes the correlation between the attributes of academics and the alternative tourists and draws attention to the potential neo-colonialism and ethnocentric application of their values upon others.

Regarding the impact of alternative tourism, Butler draws attention to the fact that it will follow a different course to mass tourism and certain factors will assume greater significance, such as contact (visitor–host interaction) which could be of longer duration per occasion and in a more sensitive location, possibly penetrating the personal space of residents. It may also involve local people to a greater degree, utilize fragile resources, engender a proportionately greater leakage of expenditure and cause political change in relation to control and development. The emphasis on contact as a precursor to change is something with which this writer is in strong agreement as this chapter will eventually disclose, and Butler reiterates this fact by using a passage from his earlier work:

> It is generally accepted that social change and impact from tourism occur because of contact between tourists and the hosts and residents. One can therefore argue that tourism which places tourists in local homes, even when they are culturally sympathetic, and not desiring change in local behaviour is much more likely to result in changes in local behaviour in the long run than is a large number of tourists in more conventional tourist ghettoes, where contact with locals is limited, if intensive, and in, what is to locals, and tourists, clearly artificial settings. (Butler, 1989, cited in Butler, 1990)

Ultimately he suggests that the crucial question is whether alternative tourism is an appropriate form of development in its own right, and he asserts that there needs to be selective and deliberate planning and control over such development. He sees it as fulfilling a number of rules:

- complementing mass tourism by increasing attractions and authenticity;
- serving the needs of specific groups;

- supplementing the incomes of rural dwellers on the periphery;
- allowing some tourism development in areas of limited capacity.

Whereas Butler writes in a generalizing manner, urging caution and drawing up lists of problems and comparisons of 'hard' and 'soft' tourism, Van den Burghe (1994) writes as a social anthropologist who has lived in a community and known it intimately over a long period of time. In his assessment of ethnic tourism in the small Mexican town of San Crostobel, he does come up with certain conclusions that Butler and others have promoted, namely the fact that ethnic tourism is fragile and intrinsically self-destroying unless it is carefully controlled, and needs a sensitive type of development strategy, about which he makes a number of points:

- Tourism traffic should be limited, for example not exceeding 1 per cent of local population.
- The development of tourist facilities should be as invisible as possible.
- Museumization should be avoided.

Such planning should be made on a small scale by people knowledgeable about the local area. He cites the following reasons for the success of San Cristobel:

- Paved road access but no jet airpot nearby.
- The place is relatively isolated, necessitating overnight stays.
- The town is attractive, possessing 'Indianness', a colonial ambience, a temperate climate and mountain scenery.
- The type of tourists visiting are non-polluting.
- Tourism and development are under local political control, i.e. small-scale with private investment.

Van den Burghe points out that with small-scale investment there are less problems, because of labour intensiveness there is more employment, businesses tend to be family based, flexible and more 'recession-proof' than large-scale developments where catastrophes are bigger and irreversible. The ethnic tourists are attracted by a lack of luxury development or access by air. They avoid consumer society and seek to get closer to local people, resisting the typical 'Club-Med' style attractions: they also tend to stay longer on less money and their spending is more likely to trickle down to local people:

> In sheer economic cost–benefit terms, ethnic tourism is really much more profitable and beneficial to a greater number of people than it seems at first blush, it also produces less environmental and cultural pollution.

Another subset of alternative tourism, ecotourism, is examined in a paper by Parnwell (1993) in a book on tourism in South-East Asia which generally supports the view that it can be environmentally beneficial. He believes that the growth of special interest tourism such as ecotourism (in which he includes safaris, bird-watching, wildlife photography, landscape painting and even organized hunting trips) has: 'in many instances helped to generate a greater awareness of the aesthetic value of natural ecosystems amongst both the promoters and consumers of tourism resources.'

However, in contrast to Parnwell's benign view of ecotourism, the book includes Hitchcock's rather pessimistic examination of 'dragon tourism' (involving looking at the giant lizards) on the island of Komodo, Indonesia. He reveals that despite the National Park being a success, the indigenous island population have been overlooked by the authorities and are unable to participate in the new developments due to a lack of education and skills, even though overall communications have improved, as has the macro-economy. He points out that there can also be problems with this type of tourism when people visit a place to observe rare creatures:

> Curiously, one of the major sources of income remains the sale of goats for use as bait, though this is one of the practices which the planners had hoped to discourage. This is cause for concern since it remains unknown what effects the use of bait is having on the behaviour of the giant lizards in their natural habitat. (Hitchcock, 1993)

Research into the ecological impact of ecotourism is in its early stages, although it has been recognized that there are many problems when tourists became intimately involved with watching and pursuing wildlife, upsetting activity patterns, intimidating animals (albeit innocently), destroying living organizms (e.g. vegetation and coral), and disturbing patterns of behaviour of both animal prey and victim.

Returning to the general theme of alternative tourism and its impact, in the second edition of the groundbreaking collection on tourism *Hosts and Guests: The Anthropology of Tourism* (Smith, 1989a), the Introduction gives a brief summary of the impacts of tourism overall, mentioning economic changes in detail. These include influences on labour, development, cashflow, foreign exchange, price inflation (especially land) and the multiplier effect. The imperialistic nature of such developments is also noted. Other impacts referred to include the rejuvenation of arts and crafts, as has happened in Bali, regarded as 'cultural involution' by some scholars.

Smith (1989b) considers certain cultural changes to have developed because of modernization, these include the transformation of traditional values and mores, the introduction of mass media and cross-cultural understanding. She regards the modernization of cultures through trade and globalization as preceding or simply submerging the impact of tourism, and predicts that a worldwide cultural homogenization is underway, diminishing the difference between hosts and guests. Yet she refers to the fact that tourism can accentuate negative aspects of society such as moral decay and also act as a bridge to an appreciation of cultural relativity and international understanding. The phrase 'alternative tourism' is mentioned briefly, and seen as a format developed by operators featuring one-to-one interaction between hosts and guests. It is pointed out that ethnic and cultural tourism allow visitors to see a bit of indigenous culture, which can lead to stress amongst local people if their privacy is invaded.

A model of 'tourist impact upon a culture' has been constructed by Smith, and she writes:

> Explorers and Elite travellers, by virtue of their limited numbers, usually make little impact upon the indigenous culture, for hotels and other services are seldom required. The Off-beat and Unusual tourist commonly stays at roadhouses or hotels that locals use, and gets about by local transportation (including the use of the school bus, for the very occasional groups who visit). The money they spend is a welcome addition, their presence is seldom disruptive and children may delight in 'talking English' with someone other than their teachers.

Stressful contacts between hosts and guests are seen as proportionate to increasing numbers, and according to the model, those making most impact are the charter tourists and those making the least are the 'explorers', on a sliding scale according to the volume of visitors. The weakness of this model lies in its lack of clarification of the term 'culture' and its omission of 'contact' and 'communication' as major factors in sociocultural change. In fact, ironically, the quotation above draws attention to the interaction between offbeat or unusual tourists and the host community, a feature which is prominent in alternative tourism and a reason for its more far-reaching potential for influencing the host community.

In the same collection, Graburn (1989) also perceives the mass tourists as having a greater impact on the culture of the host peoples than the youthful alternative travellers. He describes mass tourism as: 'tourism of the timid – often parents of the youthful travelers – who have money and don't mind spending it, as long as they can carry the home-grown "bubble" of their life-style around with them.' He goes on to explain the impact of such 'timid' tourists:

> These tourists are likely to have the greatest impact on the culture and environment of the host peoples both by virtue of their greater numbers

and by their demands for extensions of their home environments for which they are willing to pay handsomely. (Graburn, 1989)

This writer strongly disagrees with these assessments of the relative impact of alternative tourism and gives reasons for this below, together with examples from ethnographic work.

In his work which examined the influence of alternative tourism on a Canary island, Macleod (1997) has highlighted and problematized the notion of the 'alternative tourist' and focused on the individuals and their sense of identity, as well as studying their influence upon the indigenous population. Essentially, the alternative tourists who visit La Gomera in the Canary Islands form a broad category, but have been described as backpackers, aged between twenty and forty-five years, highly educated students or people working within the liberal professions, concerned about the environment, interested in meeting the local people, and possessing a strong desire for personal freedom. He is well aware of the pitfalls of creating an identifiable group and his work addresses the process of constructing identity, acknowledging the subjectivity involved, pointing out that many of the tourists actually described themselves as 'alternative tourists' as well as the fact that other observers have defined them as such.

Attention is drawn to the breadth and depth of influence that this form of tourism can have upon the local community in many areas of life, including the economic, socio-cultural, psychological, intellectual, and environmental. These areas of influence are briefly summarized in detail below, using examples from research in the Canary Islands.

Economic influence

Rooms may be rented in the homes of local people or in purpose-built apartment blocks owned by them, thereby putting money straight into their pockets. Goods are purchased in small stores run by local people, and food and drink is consumed in outlets also run by them. In essence, many families rent out rooms and gain income from tourism-related employment: for example, one fisherman is able to sell his fish directly to restaurants serving the tourists, his daughters own or work in shops selling clothes and goods to tourists, his sons work in bars and restaurants, and one regularly works as a painter of apartment buildings. This fisherman also has two apartments in his own home which are managed by his wife, and his daughters help to clean them.

The money earned by the local people allows them to increase their spending power, creating the 'multiplier effect' whereby they pass some of their earnings onto others through purchasing their goods enabling other traders to profit from the incoming money. New business ideas introduced by tourists who have decided to settle for long periods also influence the local population. These include T-shirt shops, craft and jewellery stores and excursion trips, all of which give local people examples of entrepreneurial ventures which they might emulate.

Socio-cultural influence

The alternative tourists mix with the local population because of their proximity in accommodation, through using local services and communicating with landlords and their families. This often leads to friendships, and in some cases serious relationships which end in marriage – there were over ten such couples in a village of 350 residents. Thus the pattern of kinship can be influenced directly, and the new members of families bring with them their own cultural behaviour in respect to parenthood and human interaction. The tourists also offer a wider possibility of sexual partners for the younger generation, especially local men, and many relationships have begun because of the propensity of local men to pursue foreign women. The community becomes more international in its composition due to the influx of foreigners who have formed relationships with the locals as well as those who choose to live and work in the area, setting up small businesses.

New work opportunities for women, through letting out rooms or working in shops and service outlets, gives them their own income and consequently more potential for independence. In some households the women have become the major earners, and the overall situation has occasionally transformed traditional gender roles within the home, as well as offering women the freedom to work and live by themselves.

Psychological influence

Emotional relationships are entered into with foreigners who may have different approaches to partnership and sexual behaviour. This leads local people to question their own attitudes and lifestyle as individuals. The local people become more aware of their own identity as a distinct group through continual interaction and contrast with the foreign visitors; although through deeper relationships with them they become aware of their mutual similarities. In one rare instance a local girl began a serious relationship with a German boy. Her parents refused to accept this situation and she left for Germany; however after some time they both returned and her parents accepted him into their family, no longer treating him as an outsider. They began to lose their deep distrust of foreigners.

Gender roles are challenged by the foreigners who have different ideas about how either sex can behave. This may influence local people into attempting to emulate the visitors and challenge stereotyped roles, leading for example to more self-confidence and independence amongst women. This influence is compounded by the new potential for economic freedom which the women are experiencing through the demand for their labour in tourism related work.

Intellectual influence

The local population are introduced to new languages, English and German, and many have made efforts to learn them informally through contact with the tourists in shops, bars, apartments and through friends. There is also the exchange of ideas, in which new fashions in clothing, musical taste and food are involved as well as thoughts on all manner of things. There have been a number of incidences where local people have visited a tourist's country of origin, including Germany, Austria and Holland, through their friendships with a tourist; sometimes they have found work and stayed for a long time. This not only allows them an insight into what another country is like, but it also gives them a new perspective on their own country and lifestyle. One young man had visited Holland with a Dutch girlfriend and lived with her for two years whilst working as a builder. He recounted how it had broadened his mind and made him more understanding of foreigners. It also made him appreciate the friendliness of his own village.

Environmental influence

In general the German tourists on La Gomera have an interest in ecological matters. They enjoy walking around the verdant peaks of the island and travel around the shoreline by boat. Recently a number of dolphin safari tours have started up on the island and some private businesses take tourists on mountain-bike rides into the hills. These activities may eventually have long-term detrimental effects on the environment, but initially they cater to the tourist's desire to enjoy the natural environment without apparently harming anything. The appreciation which the tourists have for the beauty of the island and its magnificent coastline has certainly promoted a stronger awareness amongst the local population of their heritage, one example being the nomination and acceptance of the temperate rainforest (which covers 10 per cent of the island) as a World Heritage Site recognized by the United Nations Educational, Scientific and Cultural Organization.

At one time a petition appeared in a local restaurant protesting against the construction of roads and large apartments in the area; this had been signed and supported by many tourists. The whole environmental conservation concern was encapsulated in a protest by the indigenous population against the local government proposal for the 'development' of the coastline into a resort style promenade and beach. This led to a huge media discussion of tourism, development, and the character and identity of the Canary Islands together with the importance of the natural habitat. It also became the raw material for political battles during the election campaign, and ultimately the project was shelved.

One of the main points coming out of this survey of the impacts of alternative tourism is the fact that a thorough ethnographic study of a site where tourism is taking place is necessary to fully appreciate the depth, and variety of influence. It also emphasizes the point that it is important to know the local people and their way of life in order to realize how influential such a phenomenon can be. Macleod's study has indicated the numerous areas of human culture which are affected by tourism, and contrasts with both Smith and Graburn's concentration on economic impact and the importance of volumes of tourism traffic – approaches which reflect a general weakness in impact models due to their focus on economic factors in 'development' analysis. In short a holistic analysis of impact gives us a more rounded and accurate picture of how tourism can affect a community, placing importance on individuals and their culture as a whole entity.

Crick (1994), who also undertook an ethnographic study, examined international tourism in Sri Lanka. In his broad-ranging and historical examination he drew attention to the many paradoxes occurring with tourism and development, one example being the public vilification of 'hippies' and their harassment: they were scape-goated, blamed for many of tourism's unsavoury qualities and accused of introducing bad habits such as idleness, drug-taking and nudism. He later points out the unfairness of this campaign and the hypocrisy surrounding much of the attacks on tourism and its alleged corrupting influence, focusing only on the hippies and budget tourists. In actuality many local people considered the authorities to be corrupt, and wealthy tourists to be linked with illegal activities. In terms of economic benefits, he also wishes to redress some general misunderstandings by pointing out that the foreign exchange from budget tourists stays in the local economy, funding private home owners, arts and crafts workers, owners of small cafes and shops. This contrasts with the higher spenders, whether on package tours or not, who spend most of their money on accommodation or meals before setting foot in Sri Lanka, or in establishments where there is maximum leakage of foreign exchange via profits to overseas investors. Furthermore, he indicates other important differences between alternative and charter tourists:

> Whilst it is no doubt easy to romanticise the extent to which various types
> of budget travellers mix with locals, they do, in fact, enjoy a fairly positive

image with some Sri Lankans precisely because they are easy-going, relaxed and often have the time to talk to local people. By contrast, there are many negative characterizations of those more affluent tourists who travel from hotel to hotel in air-conditioned luxury never stopping to speak to anyone.

Crick mentions the notion of 'cultural pollution' attributed to tourism, a common topic of discussion around 1982, and deconstructs the notion whilst demonstrating the multiplicity of interpretations and attitudes towards tourism within the local community, placing the criticism of tourism into a historical context as a continuation of the slandering of Western ways.

This in-depth analysis of the 'informal' economy, in particular the informal boarding houses and 'touts', draws attention to the number and diversity of people involved in the black economy. Crick estimates that there are over one hundred such touts in the town of Kandy (Sri Lanka), mostly men in their early twenties, and notes their importance in the accommodation and shopping sectors as middlemen and guides. With detailed accounts from individuals, we gain an insight into the culture and activity of these touts, and learn how they occasionally establish intimate relationships with tourists as well as making money out of them and those in the tourist business. 'Doing the tourism' is regarded as an easy and lucrative option by many locals, although this is revealed to be an urban myth, the reality being much harder.

There are numerous private unregistered guesthouses in Kandy, and their owners often produced an 'origins myth', being rather embarrassed about their involvement in the tourism business. It was excused as 'a way of keeping up' or 'something for the wife to do', but many underwent considerable pains to acquire facilities such as toilets and showers for the prospective tourists, some even sleeping in uncomfortable situations whilst renting out 'spare' rooms. However, usually it returned good money to the householder – the equivalent of a month's salary for the rental of a room for a few days – as well as giving the chance for the children to learn English. Those successful landlords were subject to the envy and suspicion of their neighbours, whilst according to informants, the local people were not envious of the foreign visitors.

The persistent harassment of tourists by guides often left them irritated, a problem which led to bad feelings between the two groups. This is one of many examples of the interactions between the hosts and visitors which do not lead to 'peace and understanding', as is indicated throughout the book. Nevertheless, despite occasional difficulties, many local people felt that tourism was a good thing and many were able to improve their economic position through working formally or informally with tourists.

Crick is adamant in his intent to set the record straight about those types of tourists responsible for many of the perceived problems of tourism, an industry which he sees as part of the global capitalistic pattern of development with poorer countries being dependent upon the richer powers, for whom they become 'pleasure peripheries':

> It is convenient to believe that the budget tourists staying in the cheapest accommodation are those mainly involved with drugs and prostitution, but in Kandy it was quite obviously the wealthier tourists in air-conditioned cars who were being whisked away by their drivers after their rapid tour of the Temple of the Tooth to liaisons with prostitutes in expensive accommodation in, or just outside the city.

Conclusion

By concentrating on a small sample, rather than giving a long list of definitions, this chapter has portrayed the particularities in relative detail, which has enabled the reader to see the similarities and overall shape of alternative tourism. In this exploration it becomes apparent that it is very much a contextual creation in terms of space and time: it is a reflection of contemporary attitudes and values within society. Hence, in a complex and changing world (ever more so with the intensity of globalization) meanings and manifestations become more diverse. This leads to a critique of it as a valid concept, and a keen need to analyse and understand the reality of its impact.

In terms of analysing the impact, alternative tourism is again subject to the prevailing values of society, in that the predominant concern over tourism's impact and development has been with the economy, so in assessing impact many thinkers were prone to concentrate on financial data, employment and industrial changes, whilst neglecting socio-cultural, psychological and environmental factors. An awareness of this weakness leads to a realization of the importance of a detailed analysis and comprehensive understanding of the host community in order to fully appreciate the breadth and depth of influences that tourism can have on their lives. This supports the need for good ethnographic work in the host community involving local people and visiting tourists. The conclusive findings of this study are set out below:

- **Meaning:** Despite the agreements on the content of the term 'alternative tourism' it is overstretched to the point of being inadequate, hazy and subject to parody. It has more use as a general signifier than an analytical term. One reason for this is that with changes in tourism the boundaries between mass and alternative tourism are disappearing, for example group excursions to exotic locations and packaged ecotours now involve large numbers of shepherded visitors. Essentially the concept is becoming outmoded and is fragmenting into disparate subsets, the classifications of which should be revised. Instead of the catch-all term, which means different things to different people, and eventually ceases to be applicable over time, more specific descriptions should be used and rigorously defined, such as ecotourism, ethnic tourism, individualistic/backpacking tourism, and adventure tourism. It is not for this writer to set up a standard set of definitions, but the point is clear: the meaning of alternative tourism has become vague and it is now an anachronism. There is a need to clearly define the subsets, tailoring them to changing times.

- **Impact:** The impact of alternative tourism in its various guises has been largely underestimated by scholars such as Smith and Graburn, whose models are inadequate for understanding the broader repercussions of tourism on indigenous populations. This is due to their concentration on economic impact and volume of visitors. The studies examined in this chapter, particularly those involving ethnographic work, show that alternative tourists have a strong influence across a broad spectrum of socio-cultural and economic phenomena which is largely because they communicate with the indigenous population to a greater degree than do the mass or charter tourists. They mix with local people, occasionally forming deep personal relationships with them and exchange more than just market goods. Even the economic impact is potentially more profound on the individual basis due to their propensity to live within the host community in private family accommodation as well as spend money on local services. New impact models should be developed, based on a broader range of criteria through which influence is assessed, with an emphasis on the socio-cultural aspects.

    The examination of impact has also spotlighted the potential negative influences, in that vulnerable natural environments and human communities are at risk of being spoiled by ecotourism and ethnic tourism. These dangers are being increased by the new green consumerism, the cynical marketing of so-called 'alternative' tours, irresponsible adventure travel, cross-cultural ignorance, and the popular belief that only mass tourism is potentially destructive.

- **Future research:** A better understanding of the influences of tourism at grass-roots level, partly through an awareness of the crucial part that communication plays in change and impact, will lead to a deeper awareness of how this phenomenon is affecting the world, and will have consequences for policy-makers as well. It is therefore necessary that multi-disciplinary discussions continue and grow, as there are risks of over-specialization and the marginalization of ideas and research findings in an area which so clearly deserves a broad sweep of academic approaches. More detailed ethnographic research needs to be carried out on the impact of ecotourism and ethnic tourism to find out their long-term effects and breadth of influence. This will help comparative analysis and lead to a broader insight into change. Investigations and theoretical modelling needs to be more rigorous, holistic, culturally sensitive and people oriented if we are to understand the processes involved and alleviate any problems in the future.

References

Abrams, S., Macleod, D. and Waldren, J. (eds) (1997) *Tourists and Tourism*: *Identifying with People and Places*, Berg, Oxford

Butler, R.W. (1989) *Tourism, Heritage and Sustainable Development*, Heritage Resources Centre, Waterloo, Canada, pp. 40–44

Butler, R.W. (1990) Alternative Tourism: Pious Hope or Trojan Horse? *Journal of Travel Research*, **XXVIII**(3), 40–45

Cazes, G.H. (1989) Alternative Tourism: Reflections on an Ambiguous Concept. In *Towards Appropriate Tourism: The Case of Developing Countries* (ed. Singh, T.V., Thevas, H.L. and Go, F.M.), Frankfurt Am Main, Peter Lang, pp. 117–126

Cohen, E. (1987) 'Alternative Tourism' – A Critique, *Tourism Recreation Research*, **XII**(2), 13–18

Crick, M. (1994) *Resplendent Sites, Discordant Voices: Sri Lankans and International Tourism*, Harwood Academic Publishers, Chur, Switzerland, pp. 46, 62

Gonsalves, P. (1987) Alternative Tourism – The Evolution of a Concept and Establishment of a Network, *Tourism Recreation Research*, **XII**(2), 9–12

Graburn, N. (1989) Tourism: The Sacred Journey. In *Hosts and Guests: The Anthropology of Tourism* (ed. Smith, V.), 2nd edn, The University of Pennsylvania Press, Philadelphia, pp. 21–36

Hitchcock, M. (1993) Dragon Tourism in Komodo, Eastern Indonesia. In *Tourism in South-East Asia* (ed. Hitchcock, M., King, V.T. and Parnwell, M.J.G.), Routledge, London

Hitchcock, M., King, V.T. and Parnwell, M.J.G. (eds) (1993a) *Tourism in South-East Asia*, Routledge, London

Hitchcock, M., King, V.T. and Parnwell, M.J.G. (eds) (1993b) Introduction. In *Tourism in South-East Asia* (ed. Hitchcock, M., King, V.T. and Parnwell, M.J.G.), Routledge, London, pp. 1–31

Krippendorf, J. (1987) *The Holiday Makers*, Heinemann, London

Macleod, D.V.L. (1997) 'Alternative' Tourists on a Canary Island. In *Tourists and Tourism*: *Identifying with People and Places* (ed. Abrams, S., Macleod, D. and Waldren, J.) Berg, Oxford

Murphy, P. (1994) Tourism and Sustainable Development. In *Global Tourism* (ed. Theobald, W.F.), Butterworth-Heinemann, Oxford, pp. 274–290

Parnwell, M.J.G. (1993) Environmental Issues and Tourism in Thailand. In *Tourism in South-East Asia* (ed. Hitchcock, M., King, V.T. and Parnwell, M.J.G.), Routledge, London, pp. 286–302

Smith, V. (ed.) (1989a) *Hosts and Guests: The Anthropology of Tourism*, 2nd edn, University of Pennsylvania Press, Philadelphia

Smith, V. (ed) (1989b) Introduction. In *Hosts and Guests. The Anthropology of Tourism* (ed. Smith, V.), 2nd edn, University of Pennsylvania Press, Philadelphia, pp. 1–17

Theobald, W. (ed.) (1994) *Global Tourism*, Butterworth–Heinemann, Oxford

Van den Burghe, P. (1994) *The Quest for the Other: Ethnic Tourism in San Cristobel, Mexico*, University of Washington Press, Seattle

Part Three

Changing Directions: Planning and Development Issues

The emergence and maintenance of tourism as a dynamic rather than a static industry depends in large measure upon the adoption of a strategic approach to planning and development. The success of such an approach is largely dependent upon a systematic and structured analysis of the broad environmental factors affecting tourism demand as an essential part of the planning process. Ecotourism, tourism in support of sustainable development, tourism as a cultural expression of both hosts and guests, tourism as a reflection of 'political correctness', all are considerations that go far beyond the traditional parameters of money, time and infrastructure.

Although tourism is generally regarded as less destructive to the environment than most other industries, nevertheless, its sheer size and widespread presence has already created negative physical and social environmental damage. Furthering the concept of sustainable development, **Murphy** (Chapter 10) relates the notion that an inexorable relationship exists between the economy and the environment. Some national governments such as Canada have changed their views on economic development and environmental protection, viewing them as mutually supporting rather than mutually exclusive. Such a perspective suggests that sustainable development can indeed be compatible with business objectives, and provided the appropriate safeguards, the tourism industry can continue to grow and prosper as a private business within these new parameters.

Two case studies are provided which show the relationship between, and the different strategies that can be used to successfully integrate, both environmental and business considerations. An ecological model for tourism development is proposed which includes the seven dimensions of sustainable tourism development reported by Tourism Canada. These are interrelated with a number of other components, that, when taken together, form the requisite guidelines for sustainable tourism development.

Hawkins and **Khan** (Chapter 11) compare the growth of ecotourism with the overall growth of international tourism. They relate further that due to increasing concern for the environment, the primary markets for ecotourism are special interest, nature-oriented travellers. There has been significant growth in the number of visitors to developing countries for nature tourism related experiences. However, a number of authorities have expressed concern that in order to maximize the economic benefits of tourism, some developing countries may wish to concentrate their development efforts on mass tourism projects rather than on low impact, environment-sensitive forms of tourism.

The authors identify factors responsible for the growth of ecotourism as the need for sustainable development, growing global environmental awareness, desire of increasing numbers of tourists to have a nature-based experience, and the developed nation's recognition that natural resources must be conserved for future generations. Specific case examples of controlled tourism developments are presented which analyse small-scale ecotourism programmes or projects in a number of developing countries. These developments utilized indigenous labour, materials and expertise.

Ecotourism strategies must be implemented in developing countries in order to promote sustainable development. A four-pronged strategy is proposed, consisting of consumer awareness and education, tourism industry actions, destination planning and development, and an expanded concept of marketing ecotourism to developing countries. Each strategy is then further explained, enlarged upon and illustrated with specific development guidelines.

The 1980s and 1990s have been a period characterized by a growing global trend toward privatization. This trend has occurred in part due to the break-up of the Eastern bloc countries, especially the Soviet Union, and increased foreign investment in those countries as well as in China. However, one major development issue of privatization, that of small-scale local tourist enterprises in the Third World, has largely been ignored. **Smith** (Chapter 12) suggests that ecotourism, one of the most discussed development concept of the 1990s, by its nature tends to support small-scale local accommodations since they are generally more ecologically sensitive than mega-resorts.

Effective privatization of small-scale local accommodations depends upon factors not necessarily common to most Third World countries including: extensive capitalization apart from tourism; common language fluency and cultural orientation between tourists and residents; broad travel organization affiliations; access to local and regional advertising media; and, knowledge of business procedures.

One of the by-products of ecotourism is the opportunity to meet local residents through home stays. Proprietorship of small-scale businesses does bring about some economic benefit to individual owners. When introduced into Third World private homes however, tourism essentially intrudes into traditional societies, where, by custom, women work in the home. In addition, as guest homes become more successful, the amount of work required by family members, especially women, to operate them increases significantly.

Historically, in Latin America, tourism began as a tool for economic development following World War II when the economies of Brazil and most of the Spanish speaking countries south of the United States had been devastated. Tourism was seen as one 'quick and painless' method of improving the region's economy. Since tourism in Spain was prospering, and Latin America had the physical resources most North Americans wanted (sun, sand and sea – the three Ss), investment in tourism seemed a natural method for economic growth and regional development.

Schütler (Chapter 13) traces the history of tourism within the region and suggests that in addition to the three Ss, the culture of the region and its historic resources began to be sold to potential visitors. Because of the ancient and mysterious pre-Columbian civilizations, tourists could also be attracted to the area's rich cultural heritage. It was believed that tourists would have little negative cultural impact since the region had been exposed to foreign influence for well over four centuries.

Since every country in Latin America had certain species of flora and fauna that could not be found in industrialized countries, and since there was a growing world-wide concern for protecting the environment, ecotourism was adopted as a viable alternative method of tourism development. The author points out however that although there are abundant natural and cultural resources available, 'real' growth in tourism will occur, not when the large international lobbies deem it appropriate, but rather when the region's residents have a greater voice and more important role in national decision making.

The tourism lifecycle concept and the carrying capacity concept are interrelated in a manner that is both dynamic and dependent. The lifecycle concept suggests that destination areas change over time, and progress through stages from introduction to decline. Although different disciplines have various meanings for it, carrying capacity embodies the idea that there is a limit to use, after which point negative effects occur.

Williams and **Gill** (Chapter 14) point out that like other economic enterprises, tourism is widely recognized as a change agent. With sound management, it holds the potential for being a low user of scarce resources as well as being a sustainable industry. Like the previous chapter, the authors point out that effective carrying capacity management is central to tourism's continued growth and popularity.

A number of tourism carrying capacity management perspectives, issues and concepts are presented. Four essential assumptions are provided on which each of the perspectives are based: tourism is a catalyst for change; desired conditions for tourism can be identified; these conditions are dynamic, varying temporally and geographically on economic, socio-political end environmental circumstances; and, management strategies can be developed that are capable of controlling both the rate and direction of change caused by tourism.

10 Tourism and sustainable development

Peter E. Murphy

Introduction

The world is changing and experiencing shifts in social values that effect the way we act as individuals, businesses and governments. Part of this change is due to the longest recession, or period of economic stagnation, that many parts of the developed world have experienced in recent memory. It has caused all of the above to reassess their priorities and led to the slogan 'do more with less'. Part of the change is a growing recognition that past growth and development have led to some serious impacts on the environment. Some have been highly visible, such as shrinking water supplies or homeless garbage barges; but others have crept up on us insidiously and still remain something of a mystery, like global warming.

Such economic and environmental forces led many nations, companies and individuals to the June 1992 United Nations Conference on the Environment and Development (UNCED) in Rio de Janeiro. There they attempted to address a controversial agenda designed to protect the Earth's environment and to foster less destructive industrialization and development. A binding theme of the conference was to find ways to replace the old emphasis on economic growth with a push for sustainable development (*Business Week*, 1992). It was not a great success, for changing fundamental societal beliefs and expectations will not be easy; but it was part of an ongoing process of reassessment and one in which tourism has become involved.

Tourism's interest in sustainable development is logical given this is one industry that sells the environment, both physical and human, as its product. The integrity and continuity of these products have become a major concern of the industry as can be seen in its inclusion in the two Global Opportunities for Business and the Environment conferences

(Globe '90 and '92) in Vancouver. In the first conference, designed to generate awareness of the environmental issue, the tourism stream made several recommendations regarding the industry, tourist and organizational roles in promoting sustainable tourism development (Tourism Canada, 1990). At the Globe '92 conference in Vancouver the focus shifted to finding practical solutions to environmental challenges, including those of the tourism industry. But more articulation of the issues and options needs to be undertaken before the concept of sustainable development can move from a mental state to a physical and economic reality.

Since the first edition of this book (1994) there has been considerable academic and government interest in the concept of sustainable tourism development, but industry and consumers seem to have received less attention and to have been less vocal. Most of the reports and discussion on sustainability and tourism have come from organizations and governments, anxious to preserve resources while developing their economies (Eber, 1992; Liu, 1994), and from academic research and writing as in the case of the new *Journal of Sustainable Tourism*. Much of this work has been concerned with policy issues, procedures and implications with relatively little reference to the direct involvement and needs of the tourism industry and its principal clients, the tourists. Where studies of the industry have taken place they have generally referred to successful case practices (Hawkes and Williams, 1993) or have been condensed into generic management guides (*Consulting and Audit Canada*, 1995). Apart from a growing number of convenience-based samples of ecotourists and a few consulting company omnibus surveys, we do not have a clear picture of the tourists' knowledge of or commitment to sustainable tourism development.

What is needed now in this area of tourism research and policy is a greater effort to link the academic and government interest in pursuing more sustainable tourism development with the front-line practitioners (the industry) and the all-important client (the tourist). If these three groups could be encouraged to modify their perspectives and operate from the same text then we could anticipate more tangible progress regarding tourism and sustainable development. Accordingly, after reviewing the growth and measuring of sustainable development to tourism this chapter will explore possible links and synergies between the works of academia and government on the one hand and the needs of industry and tourists on the other.

Growth and definition of sustainable development

The need for a renewed relationship with the environment and the recent interest in sustainable development has been building over the past twenty-five years. In 1972 Danella and Dennis Meadows shook the world's complacency with their book *Limits to Growth* (1972). They argued the Earth's resources and ability to absorb pollution are finite. Using computer simulations, they predicted the Earth's population and development progress would experience physical constraints within a century. After this first warning came more research and deliberation into the long-term consequences of continued industry and population expansion. This led to the publication of the *World Conservation Strategy* by the International Union for the Conservation of Nature and Natural Resources (IUCN, 1980), which was one of the first reports to introduce the concept of sustainable development. This was followed by the World Commission on Environment and Development Report in 1987, entitled *Our Common Future* (WCED, 1987), which placed the concept of sustainable development centre stage and promoted it as a vehicle for deliverance.

The sustainable development concept is not new, but increasing pressures on the world's finite resources and environmental capacity have led to a more deliberate restatement of the philosophy, along with evolving guidelines to put it into practice. *Our Common Future* described sustainable development as 'development that meets the needs of the present without compromising the ability of future generations to meet their own needs' (WCED, 1987). This is not very different from the view that we do not inherit the earth from our forefathers but borrow it from our children, and the old philosophy that something should be left for future generations. As such, sustainable development builds on the old principles of conservation and stewardship, but it offers a more proactive stance, that incorporates continued economic growth in a more ecological and equitable manner. In this regard the opening definition above is supplemented with more specific implications and guidelines throughout the WCED report.

Table 10.1 illustrates some of the guidelines that emerged from *Our Common Future*, which in turn have stimulated further discussion at various government levels and within business. The first nine components were extracted from the WCED report and formed the basis of Canada's early attempts to integrate this type of philosophy into its national policy (Canadian Environment Advisory Council, 1987). Following the WCED report other writers and agencies have added to the list of components in Table 10.1. This list is not designed to be exhaustive but to illustrate the ongoing refinement of the concept and the increasing emphasis on its application.

It has been noted, for example, that the priority on maintaining ecological diversity and distributing more productivity to developing regions implies increased community control (Component no.10), which in turn fosters increased regional self-reliance (Rees and Roseland, 1988). Likewise, these two authors and Stanley (1992) maintain there is a need for more

Table 10.1   Sustainable development components

1	Establishing ecological limits and more equitable standards	'requires the promotion of values that encourage consumption standards that are within the bounds of the ecological possible and to which all can reasonably aspire'.
2	Redistribution of economic activity and reallocation of resources	'Meeting essential needs depends in part on achieving full growth potential and sustainable development clearly requires economic growth in places where such needs are not being met'.
3	Population control	'Though the issue is not merely one of population size but of the distribution of resources, sustainable development can only be pursued if demographic developments are in harmony with the changing productive potential of the ecosystem.'
4	Conservation of basic resources	'sustainable development must not endanger the natural systems that support life on Earth: the atmosphere, the waters, the soils, and the living beings.'
5	More equitable access to resources and increased technological effort to use them more effectively	'Growth has no set limits in terms of population or resource use beyond which lies ecological disaster . . . But ultimate limits there are, and sustainability requires that long before these are reached the world must ensure equitable access to the constrained resource and reorient technological efforts to relieve the pressure.'
6	Carrying capacity and sustainable yield	'most renewable resources are part of a complex and interlinked ecosystem, and maximum sustainable yield must be defined after taking into account system-wide effects of exploitation.'
7	Retention of resources	'Sustainable development requires that the rate of depletion of non-renewable resources foreclose as few future options as possible.'
8	Diversification of the species	'sustainable development requires the conservation of plant and animal species.'
9	Minimize adverse impacts	'Sustainable development requires that the adverse impacts on the quality of air, water, and other natural elements are minimised so as to sustain the ecosystem's overall integrity.'
10	Community control	'community control over development decisions affecting local ecosystems'
11	Broad national/ international policy framework	'the biosphere is the common home of all human-kind and joint management of the biosphere is prerequisite for global political security.'
12	Economic viability	'Corporate environmental policy is an extension of total quality management.'
13	Environmental quality	'Corporate environmental policy is an extension of total quality management.'
14	Environmental audit	'An effective environmental audit system is at the heart of good environmental management.'

international agreements and business-government partnerships (no. 11) to direct national and individual actions. To the ecological limitations and social equity of the sustainable development philosophy must be added the concept of economic viability (no. 12) according to the British Columbia Round Table on the Environment and the Economy (1991).

The business community and literature have been responding to the environmental–economic opportunities that exist within the 'greening' process. Howatson (1990) reports that an evolution is taking place. A minority of corporations are still in the early phase of responding to environmental problems as they arise. The majority of corporations have established systems and programmes to comply with the new regulations, but a further minority has moved 'beyond compliance' into a proactive mode of management. This evolutionary process is slowly leading to the complete integration of the environmental dimension into corporate strategic planning (no. 13). To bring environmental considerations and sustainable development into the mainstream of corporate planning requires increased accountability and the environmental audit has been gaining credibility in this area. Hunt and Auster (1990) contend a 'strong auditing programme' is essential to successful proactive environmental management (no. 14).

The growing interest and support for sustainable development is not without its critics and sceptics. Some maintain that it is such a fuzzy concept that it may prove to be of little practical use in tackling the environmental issues that are emerging. However, as Table 10.1 illustrates, the short definition of sustainable development should only be viewed as a summary goal, and that from this have evolved a series of more specific objectives and methodologies. Others consider that it is a passing fad, akin to the energy crises of the past. But this perception fails to acknowledge that evidence of environmental stress started over twenty years ago, and instead of disappearing it has gradually increased to the point where admitted non-environmentalists are beginning to take notice. One author who has addressed such scepticism and doubts is George Winter (1988), who developed a listing of pros and cons for forty issues regarding the introduction of an integrated system of environmental business management.

Relevance to tourism

Tourism is reputed to be the world's largest industry with estimated revenues of US$3.5 trillion and hiring one worker in nine world wide in 1995 (World Travel and Tourism Council, 1996). It is one industry which should be involved in sustainable development, because it 'is a resource industry, one which is dependent on nature's endowment and society's heritage' (Murphy, 1985). It sells these resources as part of its experiential product, but it also has to share the same resources with other users, including local residents. Consequently, it is in tourism's own interest to be active in the quest for sustainable development and to work in cooperation with other groups, industries and government to ensure that the integrity of its resource base survives.

Although the industry is regarded as being kinder to the environment in general than most other industries, its very size and widespread presence has created negative environmental impacts, both of a physical and social nature, in certain locations. Consequently, there has arisen a demand for more management of this activity, which has encouraged greater government involvement and more private/public sector partnerships. 'Sustainable development (in tourism) is premised on the notion that the economy and the environment are but two sides of the same coin; in other words, the two are intimately linked' (Slater, 1992). In Canada this has led to the creation of a federal *Green Plan* that 'represents a fundamental shift in the way the government of Canada looks at economic development and environmental protection . . . [in that it tries] to make them mutually supporting rather than mutually exclusive' (Slater, 1992).

The Canadian experience and evidence from around the world demonstrate that sustainable development can be compatible with business objectives, and that with appropriate legislative safeguards and inducements the tourism industry can continue to prosper as a private business within these new parameters. Porter, who is the champion of competitive advantage, considers 'the conflict between environmental protection and economic competitiveness is a false dichotomy . . . [but] turning environmental concern into competitive advantage demands we establish the right kind of regulations' (Porter, 1991). Others have made similar observations that industry can profit from 'greening' its product in the consumers' eyes and can lower operational costs through the development of environmental practices. One example of this in tourism can be seen in the Canadian Pacific Hotels and Resorts environmental programme. This programme has set as its target to reduce landfill waste by 50 per cent and paper use by 20 per cent over a two-year period. It will save energy and water by retrofitting light bulbs, showerheads and taps with 'Environmental Choice' equipment, and will purchase more environmentally friendly products for cleaning and running the hotels (Checkley, 1992).

The move to a more sustainable development approach in tourism is taking hold in certain quarters and it is time to examine the themes and implications of this process so the industry is able to adjust and prosper with this new reality on a broader front.

Dimensions of sustainable tourism development

It is apparent from the proceeding discussion that sustainable development is a complex and multidimensional concept and that tourism as
a component of this process, will reflect this diversity. This chapter will
take as its working definition that offered by the combined efforts of the
Globe '90 tourism stream. For this group, Tourism Canada (1990) reports
that *sustainable tourism development* was envisaged as:

> leading to management of all resources in such a way that we can fulfil
> economic, social, and aesthetic needs while maintaining cultural integrity,
> essential ecological processes, biological diversity and life support systems.

The seven dimensions incorporated within this definition provide an
excellent example of the general multi-dimensionality and interdisciplinary concerns.

The first dimension noted is the need for *resource management*, for in
this crowded world with diminishing resources little can be left to chance.
Such management needs to reaffirm that tourism is an *economic* activity,
which must be capable of making a profit in order to survive and benefit
the community. This is the point Porter (1991) and others have made
when they say environmental legislation must leave room for individual
employment and economic well-being to operate within the ecological
parameters. The third dimension points out the need to fulfil social obli-
gations. This means more than inter generational equity; it means respect
for other livelihoods and customs. Such variety and heritage is a major
resource for tourism in a world that is fast becoming homogenized into a
global economy. A major component of environment and culture is their
aesthetic appeal. While the focus has often been on international markers,
such as world renown heritage sites, the aesthetic qualities of regular
townscapes and general landscapes should not be overlooked.

All the above needs should be addressed within *ecological parameters*
to sustain both the physical and human environment. Conservation of
cultural legacies should not be ignored. The ecological process needs to
be understood so that tourism intrusions will have the minimal impact,
especially in sensitive areas like shorelines, mountains and wetlands. The
concern over maintaining our *biological diversity* is particularly germane
to tourism, which thrives on the appeal of different flora and fauna along
with a distinctive sense of place. Finally, the need to sustain our basic life
support systems is paramount. If these basic needs are not met, then our
higher level and discretionary needs like travel will fail to materialize.

Research priorities

As in the real world, all of the above dimensions are interrelated. This means any sustainable tourism development will involve a holistic management approach that requires integrated ecological, economic and institutional research. Since this is a major research undertaking, some thought has been given already to categorizing the scope of the problem and prioritizing the research questions. In 1985 Murphy proposed an ecological model for tourism research and development. This model demonstrated the need to consider tourism as an ecological function that involved different community scales of emphasis and a balance between resident (individuals and business) and visitor (tourist and tourist industry) needs. Taylor and Stanley (1992) have recommended a matrix of research priorities based on scale and time considerations (Table 10.2). All scales are relevant and interrelated in an ecological sense, but the pressures and issues will vary at each level. Some research questions are considered to be more pressing and have been placed under the 'now' category whereas others are either less urgent or are logical secondary steps. As Taylor and Stanley observe, all research should have a monitoring function to observe changes over time and be able to identify adjustment strategies where needed.

Measurement issues

While it is relatively easy to conceptualize and to proselytize about the needs for sustainable tourism development, it is far more challenging to develop an effective, yet practical, measurement process. An important issue in the Taylor–Stanley matrix is establishing the carrying capacity levels for tourism in a variety of locales and circumstances. This essential building block to sustainable development suffers from the same operational difficulties as its parent concept. Barkham (1979) noted that:

> Carrying capacity is a phrase delightful in its simplicity, complex in its meaning and difficult to define, as in different situations and to different people it is understood in different ways.

The literature on this subject shows carrying capacity techniques have been applied in a variety of circumstances, often clarifying and confirming levels of suspected environmental or social stress, but they leave open to discussion what it all signifies and what policy should be undertaken. A major difficulty is that carrying capacity implies the existence of

Table 10.2 Suggested research areas and priorities for sustainable development in tourism

Scope	Now	Medium term	Long term
Site	Case studies on a variety of topics Operations Employee involvement Benefit-cost Corporate culture Environmental audit	Value of protected areas (economic, aesthetic) Willingness to pay Means of enhancing experiences Monitoring change in case studies	
Locality	Destination studies Carrying capacities: economic, social, physical Image studies	Longitudinal studies Nature of change studies	Social indicators Economic indicators Physical indicators
Region	Inventory of resources Studies of market needs and attitudes	Longitudinal studies of market needs and attitudes Measurement of benefits, costs	
Nation	Coordination Dissemination Standards	Networking Clearing house Methodologies Models, paradigms	
International	Cooperation Adaptation	Clearing house Definition of terms	

Source: Taylor and Stanley, 1992: 67

fixed and determinable limits to development and that if one stays below those threshold levels no changes or deterioration will occur. We now appreciate that all changes and modifications to the environment have an incremental effect, so some degree of change must be acknowledged and accounted for at all developmental stages.

This is the philosophy behind the 'limits to acceptable change' (LAC) process of measurement proposed by Stankey et al. (1985). The LAC system is a framework for establishing acceptable and appropriate resource use 'with the primary emphasis now on the conditions desired in the area rather than on how much use an area can tolerate' (Stankey et al., 1985: Summary). The process is a combined measurement and planning system, but as its authors point out, it is a process – not a policy. It still requires political decisions regarding what is acceptable and of course personal perceptions will be an interpretative factor at all stages of the process.

Both the carrying capacity and LAC processes examine the sustainable tourism issue from the supply side of the host community, but if tourism is to be a sustainable economic proposition it cannot ignore its customers. Hence, more thought is now being applied to the demand implications of sustainable tourism development, specifically the benefits visitors are seeking and the marketing strategies that can be applied to service both the customer and the host. Murphy and Pritchard (1997) have examined a model of consumers' perceived value and applied it to a tourist destination. They found that tourists had concerns about quality and price common to all consumers, but their value perceptions also varied by origin (comparison base) and season of visit (different site conditions). Hence, one can see the tourist demand for sustainable tourism development is likely to be multidimensional and culturally conditioned.

The modern interpretation of marketing has moved beyond simply promoting and selling to take into account the long-term management goals of companies and organizations. In some cases this now includes marketing to reduce consumption, as with utility companies, or to recycle, as with beverage companies. In a tourism context we see more evidence of attractions explaining to customers why certain areas are temporarily closed or out of bounds.

The broader view is provided by Mill and Morrison (1985), who note that tourism marketing is:

> a management philosophy, which in light of tourist demand, makes it possible through research, forecasting and selection to place tourism products on the market most in line with an organization's purpose for the greatest benefit.

Such a definition has particular relevance to a sustainable development strategy. It makes marketing part of a more general management strategy. It supports the notion that marketing should balance the tourists' needs with those of the host organization. Market research will help to identify which tourism niche is most appropriate from a business and environmental viewpoint. It can indicate a destination's or business' position on the product life cycle which could guide future marketing and development strategies.

This type of marketing analysis and strategy is being practised in certain Canadian national parks. Parks Canada has introduced a Visitor Activity Management Process (VAMP) into three parks, moving away from the traditional promotional and operational focus to one which attempts to manage visitor opportunities and encourage public understanding of the parks' twin mandate of conservation and recreation

(Graham et al., 1988). The process uses market research to select target markets, specify the most appropriate public and private mix of recreation opportunities, and to guide the design of programmes, services and facilities. The authors maintain it is a 'shift of emphasis away from a reactive controlled development-orientated mode to a pro-active recreation resource management mode' (Graham et al., 1988: 62).

An essential element in market research designed to assist in sustainable development initiatives is the need to monitor visitor patterns and satisfaction. Monitors are needed on an annual and seasonal basis, since the volume and type of visitor activity can vary significantly over these periods. A demonstration project on Vancouver Island, British Columbia, revealed that a basic monitoring of visitors could be achieved efficiently and at low cost through industry-destination partnerships (Murphy, 1992). This demonstration project has since been adopted by Tourism Victoria, the destination association for the provincial capital of Victoria, on Vancouver Island. It has conducted eight exit surveys since 1988 over a variety of seasons to provide a visitor profile and strategy guide to the destination and individual business members.

Various tourism markets

There is a wide variety of tourist types within the tourism market today, so much so that the term 'average tourist' has become irrelevant (Murphy, 1985). One type of tourist which has generated a lot of interest among those supporting sustainable development is the 'alternative tourist', described by Krippendorf (1987) as those who 'try to establish more contact with the local population, try to do without the tourist infrastructure and use the same accommodation and transport facilities as the natives'. Such travellers are considered desirable market niches for those communities which are unable or unwilling to accommodate mass tourism, and they are perceived as being worthy targets because they are small in number yet often well-educated and wealthy. This would appear to be a perfect match for those areas where carrying capacity could become an issue and where the host community wished to control the size of the industry.

However, alternative tourism has been criticized as being elitist and spreading tourism to areas that are not yet spoiled by tourism. One who has issued such a warning is Butler (1990). He notes that in a free society and highly fragmented industry it is in fact difficult to control the numbers and types of tourist admitted to an area. If it can be achieved, a focus on the alternative market may not bring about the perceived desirable effects over the long run. Butler suggests:

> In the short-term there is little doubt that alternative tourism appears, and almost certainly is, much less conducive to causing change in destination areas than mass tourism, in part because of its dimensions and in part because of the need for fewer and smaller facilities. However, as time goes by, some factors can assume much greater significance under alternative tourism and result in greater and more serious long-term change. (1990: 41)

Butler illustrates this by noting the intimate contact described by Krippendorf can become a social burden over time, as privacy is lost and there is nowhere to retreat from the tourist gaze. Similarly the 'back-woods' penetration by such visitors can do more environmental harm over time to these areas than the controlled mass tourism which permits distant viewing only. What host communities need to focus on is the type or types of tourism they wish to attract and can accommodate over the long term. As Jones observes, 'some of the clues and solutions from alternative tourism can be used to inform and advise policy and practice in the development and management of mass tourism' (1992: 103).

Many of the observations relating to alternative tourism apply to one subset that appears particularly germane to the sustainable development movement – ecotourism. Ecotourism occurs where the visitor is an active contributor to the well-being and development of the host ecology. As such, ecotourists are champions of the environment and sustainable development. In Costa Rica several ecotourism principles have been developed which support the sustainable development philosophy, according to Fennell and Eagles (1990: 23). These include a mutual agreement between tour operators and visitors to limit the levels of crowding, to permit tour operator control of site visits, government agreements with tour operators on park entrance permits, and agreements on the appropriate marketing image. Such partnerships are relatively easy to initiate when both parties have the same goals and the numbers involved are small, but they also provide hope and direction to the application of similar strategies to a broader cross-section of the tourism industry.

In the final analysis, however, 'the most crucial contribution that applied research can make toward sustainable tourism is to show rather than say what this involves' (Sadler, 1992: 127). As we have seen there are a growing number of advocates, sufficient paradigms and some basic measurement techniques that should now be put into practice in order to demonstrate the feasibility of all this rhetoric. This too will be a slow process given the variety and complexity of the topic. Tourism must acknowledge also that it is not the only industry with a resource claim. In most communities there will be competition and conflict over the resources tourism desires. 'For tourism to survive sustainability, it must take a proactive leadership role in addressing the difficult challenges of integrating the needs of all user groups' (McKercher, 1993: 136).

Tourism should be ideally suited for a leadership role in sustainable development given its multidimensional nature and private/public sector duality. Initiation of this role should be the next logical step in the evolution of sustainable tourism development, but to do so the various tourism stakeholders must pull together.

Spreading the word

Academic and government circles have been the major champions of sustainable tourism development, but if they are to be more proactive in their leadership they need to spread the word to a larger audience. Many feel the case has been made for the integration of sustainable development principles into future tourism management as illustrated by a recent article in a leading hospitality management journal (Manning and Dougherty, 1995). But the concept's complexity and its diverse operational requirements can be overwhelming to non-specialists. Recognition of this fact has led the World Tourism Organization (WTO) to develop simplified guides for practitioners (Consulting and Audit Canada, 1995) and basic planning steps (Inskeep and Kallenberger, 1992). Various government and private sector agencies have developed general codes of conduct to guide businesses toward more sustainable practices. The development of government-industry workshops is on the rise, as illustrated in the recent British Columbia Growth Management Strategy and Bow Valley Corridor Plan for Banff National Park processes in western Canada. These are evidence that government and academics are striving to broaden and simplify the sustainable tourism message and offer some practical suggestions. However, it must be a message that diverse groups and interests are willing to heed.

Individual tourism businesses, like any other business, are often sceptical about government and academic messages that may reduce their economic viability. However, the industry leaders do recognize that long term economic viability is intimately tied to a healthy physical and social environment. Evidence of this form of thinking can be seen in Swinth and Raymond's (1995) examination of the sports fishing industry on Yellowstone Lake. They found the development of an ecosystems management approach involving all principal stakeholders, along with an ongoing monitoring process, had saved this sports fishing attraction from the potential oblivion of the old free market economic system.

More owners and managers now appreciate the dictum that every tourist business 'needs to sell the destination first and its business second' if it is to survive and prosper. This results in a more proactive interest in the physical and social well-being of all destination types.

Kavallinis and Pizam (1994) found that tourism entrepreneurs on the Greek island of Mykonos were aware of the environmental impacts tourism was creating and were prepared to accept their share of the responsibility. But it was also difficult to separate out the industry's individual responsibility from that of the local residents and actual tourists. So once again it would require intergroup acknowledgement and consensus to initiate a sustainable development approach.

In terms of sustainable tourism development the consumer is often equated with ecotourists and the natural environment. This is an extremely narrow view of the potential tourist interest in sustainable tourism, for it has elitist overtones and will restrict support to a small market segment. It ignores the fact that exploration of ecosystems involves human habitats as well as natural ones (Murphy, 1985), and as Hall (1994: 140) has pointed out, many of the so-called natural landscapes can seldom be separated from the cultural and economic forces that formed them.

For sustainable tourism to have the level of support it needs from the consumer, its appeal and relevance must be expanded beyond the ecotourist. There is growing evidence that the often belittled mass tourist is showing increased interest in the local environment and social/cultural customs of their destinations. Hanauma Bay, a popular marine park just outside of Waikiki, has been overwhelmed by tourists, yet these same mass tourists have indicated their willingness to pay fees and accept limits on numbers in order to reduce the crowding and preserve the attraction of this site (Mak and Moncur, 1995). Most resorts now include the opportunity to see local culture and history in their offerings, and as the market continues to mature there will be a greater need to supplement beach and nightclub activities with more outdoor recreation and educational trips into the local area.

Bringing stakeholders together

If sustainable tourism development is to move from the pages of academic papers and government reports into the marketplace, it will be necessary to bring the industry and tourist stakeholders more extensively into the discussion and operationalization of this concept. To bring about such a unity of purpose and action sustainable tourism needs to market the concept more effectively and develop a 'more appropriate matching of markets with products' (Wight, 1993: 64). Evidence of this can be seen in Ballantine and Eagles' examination of safari ecotourists in Africa. 'The only dissatisfaction this group find with their trip is a need for more information on conservation issues. This suggests a weakness in the interpretation programmes . . . (and) a strong interest and dedication to education about conservation issues by the tourists.' (Ballantine and Eagles, 1994: 213).

The type of marketing needed is one which emphasizes education and communication along with the sales dimension. Wight (1994) correctly calls for 'the environmentally responsible marketing of tourism' and wants it to go beyond the green labelling of ecotourism to incorporate ethics and codes of practice. To go beyond the selling focus of green labelling involves marketing that stresses the synergistic qualities between a tourist's interest and visit with the product's survival and enhancement. Kotler (1988) has been one of those market researchers who has demonstrated that marketing is about more than selling. It is in fact a communications tool as expressed through its public relations function. It is now recognized as an important business component for the non-profit sector as well, assisting in its survival and development strategies (Kotler and Andreasen, 1991).

Linking the various stakeholder groups together via marketing communications can help to sell the concept of sustainable tourism and its individual products through the element of education. Just as Disney and its numerous imitators have packaged entertainment and education, so sustainable tourism should strive to combine quality experiences with education. For some, such as the ecotourists, it will mean detailed explanation and exposure to the site or activity.

But these would be relatively few in number compared to those tourists who would be satisfied with a simple explanation and a 'staged' representation of the cultural or natural phenomenon. In either case the industry and governments now have a responsibility to inform tourists about their destinations and an opportunity to enhance tourists' 'sense of place' through quality interpretation and carefully designed tours and facilities.

Summary

Since the first edition of this book appeared, the need for considering sustainable tourism management has increased. The tourism industry has increased in size, while the world's resource base has remained static or declined and there has been growing competition for those resources. However, the message about sustainable tourism seems to have become trapped in an academic–government loop rather than being progressively adopted by the industry and its consumers. This is caused in part by the relatively complex and comprehensive nature of the concept, which needs to be broken down into more manageable components and scales if it is to be adopted and appreciated on a broader scale.

This process is underway already, as indicated by the efforts of the WTO. Some individuals and organizations are beginning to spread the message that sustainable tourism involves a combination of experience, entertainment and education. Such a change of emphasis will require more effective marketing, a marketing focus that communicates and educates to bring the major stakeholders together in a practical forum of sustainable tourism development. It is to be hoped that via such strategies the message of sustainable tourism development will reach the front lines where it needs to be implemented.

References

Ballantine, J.F. and Eagles, P.F.J. (1994) Defining Canadian Ecotourists, *Journal of Sustainable Tourism*, **2**(4), 210–214

Barkham, J.P. (1979) Recreational carrying capacity: a problem of perception, *Area*, **5**, 218–22

British Columbia Round Table on the Environment and the Economy (1991) *Sustainable Communities*, British Columbia Round Table on the Environment and the Economy, Victoria, BC

Business Week (1992) Growth vs. Environment, *Business Week*, 11 May, 66–75

Butler, R.W. (1990) Alternative tourism: pious hope or Trojan Horse? *Journal of Travel Research*, **28**(3), 40–5

Canadian Environment Advisory Council (1987) *Canada and Sustainable Development*, CEAC, Ottawa

Checkley, A. (1992) Canadian Pacific hotels and resorts update: environmental program. In *Tourism–Environment–Sustainable Development: an Agenda for Research* (ed. L.J. Reid), Conference Proceedings of the Travel and Tourism Research Association (Canada), Ottawa, 1991, pp. 34–7

Consulting and Audit Canada (1995) *What Tourism Managers Need to Know: A Practical Guide to the Development and Use of Indicators of Sustainable Tourism*, World Tourism Organization, Madrid

Eber, S. (ed.) (1992) *Beyond the Green Horizon*, World Wide Fund for Nature, UK, Godalming, Surrey

Fennell, D.A. and Eagles, P.F.J. (1990) Ecotourism in Costa Rica: a conceptual framework. *Journal of Park and Recreation Administration*, **8**(1), 23–34

Graham, R., Nilsen, P. and Payne, R.J. (1988) Visitor management in Canadian national parks, *Tourism Management*, **9**(1), 44–62

Hall, C.M. (1994) Ecotourism in Australia, New Zealand and the South Pacific: Appropriate tourism or a new form of ecological imperialism? In *Ecotourism: A Sustainable Option*? (ed. Cater, E. and Lowman, G.), John Wiley, Chichester, 137–157

Hawkes, S. and Williams, P. (eds) (1993) *The Greening of Tourism*, Centre for Tourism Policy and Research, Simon Fraser University, Vancouver, B.C.

Howatson, A.C. (1990) *Toward Proactive Environmental Management*, Conference Board of Canada, Ottawa

Hunt, C.B. and Auster, E.R. (1990) Proactive environmental management: avoiding the toxic trap, *Sloan Management Review*, **31**(2), 7–18

Inskeep, E. and Kallenberger, M. (1992) *An Integrated Approach to Resort Development*, World Tourism Organization, Madrid

IUCN (1980) *World Conservation Strategy*, IUCN, Gland, Switzerland

Jones, A. (1992) Is there a real alternative tourism? *Tourism Management*, **13**(1), 102–3

Kavallinis, I. and Pizam, A. (1994) The environmental impacts of tourism – whose responsibility is it anyway? The case study of Mykonos, *Journal of Travel Research*, **33**(2), 26–32

Kotler, P. (1988) *Marketing Management*, 6th edn, Prentice-Hall, Englewood Cliffs, NJ

Kotler, P. and Andreasen, A. (1991) *Strategic Marketing for Nonprofit Organizations*, Prentice-Hall, Englewood Cliffs, New Jersey

Krippendorf, J. (1987) *The Holiday Makers*, Heinemann, London, p. 37

Liu, J.C. (1994) *Pacific Islands Ecotourism: A Public Policy and Planning Guide*, Pacific Business Center Program, University of Hawaii, Honolulu

Mak, J. and Moncur, J.E.T. (1995) Sustainable tourism development: Managing Hawaii's 'unique' touristic resource – Hanauma Bay, *Journal of Travel Research*, **33**(4), 51–56

Manning, E.W. and Dougherty, T.D. (1995) Sustainable tourism: preserving the golden goose, *Cornell Hotel and Restaurant Administration Quarterly*, April, 29–42

McKercher, B. (1993) The unrecognized threat to tourism: Can tourism survive sustainability? *Tourism Management*, **14**(2), 131–136

Meadows, D. and Meadows, D. (1972) *Limits in Growth*, Universe Books, New York

Mill, R.C. and Morrison, A.M. (1985) *The Tourism System*, Prentice-Hall, Englewood Cliffs, NJ, p. 358

Murphy, P.E. (1985) *Tourism: a Community Approach*, Methuen, London, p. 12

Murphy, P.E. (1992) Data gathering of community-oriented tourism planning: a case study of Vancouver Island, British Columbia, *Leisure Studies*, **12**(1), 65–79

Murphy, P.E. and Pritchard, M. (1997) Destination price–value perceptions: An examination of origin and seasonal influences, *Journal of Travel Research*, **35**(3), 16–22.

Porter, M.E. (1991) Essay – America's green strategy, *Scientific American*, **264**(3), April, p. 168

Rees, W.E. and Roseland, M. (1988) *Planning for Sustainable Development*, School of Community and Regional Planning, University of British Columbia

Sadler, B. (1992) Sustainable tourism and tomorrow's heritage: toward policy and research that make a difference. In *Tourism–Environment–Sustainable Development: an Agenda for Research* (ed. L.J. Reid), Conference Proceedings of the Travel and Tourism Research Association (Canada), Ottawa, 1991, pp. 122–7

Slater, R.W. (1992) Keynote address – understanding the relationship between tourism environment and sustainable development. In *Tourism–Environment–Sustainable Development: an Agenda for Research* (ed. L.J. Reid), Conference Proceedings of the Travel and Tourism Research Association (Canada), Ottawa, 1991, pp. 10–13

Stankey, G.H., Cole, D.N., Lucas, R.C. et al. (1985) *The Limits of Acceptable Change (LAC) System for Wilderness Planning*, US Forest Service, Washington, DC

Stanley, D. (1992) Synthesis of workshop sessions. In *Tourism–Environment–Sustainable Development: an Agenda for Research* (ed. L.J. Reid), Conference Proceedings of the Travel and Tourism Research Association (Canada), Ottawa, 1991, pp. 116–18

Swinth, R.L. and Raymond, B.C. (1995) Sustainable development in practice: the management of Yellowstone Lake for fishing and ecosystem protection, *Research in Corporate Social Performance and Policy*, Supplement 1, JAI Press, 291–321

Taylor, G.D. and Stanley, D. (1992) Tourism, sustainable development and the environment: an agenda for research, *Journal of Travel Research*, **31**(1), 66–7

Tourism Canada (1990) *An Action Strategy for Sustainable Tourism Development: Globe '90* Tourism Canada, Ottawa, p. 3

WCED (1987) *Our Common Future*, Oxford University Press, Oxford, p. 43

Wight, P.A. (1993) Sustainable ecotourism: Balancing economic, environmental and social goals within an ethical framework, *Journal of Tourism Studies*, **4**(2), 54–66

Wight, P.A. (1994) Environmentally responsible marketing of tourism. In *Ecotourism: A Sustainable Option?* (ed. E. Cater and G. Lowman), John Wiley, Chichester, 39–56

Winter, G. (1988) *Business and the Environment*, McGraw-Hill, Hamburg, New York

World Travel and Tourism Council (1996) *Travel and Tourism*, Press Release, WWTC, Brussels, Belgium

11 Ecotourism opportunities for developing countries

Donald E. Hawkins and Maryam M. Khan

The need for sustainable tourism development is gaining attention and 'ecotourism' is being promoted by many developing countries as an impetus to expand both conservation measures and tourism development simultaneously. Ecotourism is interrelated with the overall growth of tourism in the world today. In spite of recessions, civil disturbances, and natural catastrophes, international tourism continues to grow. Indeed, travellers in the 1990s consider vacations as a basic necessity. Tourism is making major contributions to the economic viability of many countries of the world today.

According to World Tourism Organization (WTO, 1996), one of the major international organizations responsible for promoting tourism as a means of economic development, total international tourist arrivals grew 2.8 per cent from 1994 to reach 561 million in 1995; receipts increased 10.2 per cent to total $381 billion. These arrivals are expected to reach 702 million by the year 2000 and over one billion by the year 2010. Nature tourism, in 1989, generated approximately 7 per cent of all international travel expenditures. Nature based tourists spend $14 billion annually and according to World Tourism Organization (1996) estimates nature tourism has increased 15 per cent a year since 1990. Developing countries, in particular, represent major untapped destinations featuring unique cultural and natural attractions.

Definition of ecotourism

'Ecotourism' is a term which has been defined in many ways, and is generally used to describe tourism activities which are conducted in harmony with nature, as opposed to more traditional 'mass' tourism activities. To some it is nature tourism, alternative tourism, cultural tourism, soft tourism, adventure tourism, responsible tourism, or green tourism (Wight, 1993). There is not yet a consistently used definition of ecotourism, in part owing to the many stake holders involved in ecotourism who bring their own perspectives and motivations. Orams (1995) presented ecotourism definitions on a continuum. On one side the ecotourist experience shifts from simple enjoyment and satisfaction to greater understanding, attitudinal change and finally more environmentally responsible behaviour. A variety of ecotourism definitions are listed below.

According to the Ecotourism Society (1991), 'ecotourism is a responsible travel to natural areas which conserve the environment and sustains the well being of the local people.'

The Canadian Environmental Advisory Council (as cited in Wight, 1993) defines ecotourism as 'an enlightening nature travel experience that contributes to conservation of ecosystem, while respecting the integrity of the host communities.'

Culture and nature are emphasized by Ryel and Grasse (1991), when they define ecotourism as 'a purposeful travel that creates an understanding of cultural and natural history, while safeguarding the integrity of ecosystem and producing economic benefits that encourages conservation.'

The role of the tourist is stressed by Ceballos-Lascurain (1987) who states that the main point of ecotourism 'is that the person that practices ecotourism has the opportunity of immersing him or herself in nature in a way most people cannot enjoy in their routine, urban existence. This person will eventually acquire a consciousness . . . that will convert him/her into somebody keenly involved in conservation issues . . .'

The resource conservation role is emphasized by Ziffer (1989), who describes ecotourism as 'a managed approach by the host country or region which commits itself to establishing and maintaining the sites with the participation of local residents, marketing them appropriately, enforcing regulations, and using the proceeds of the enterprise to fund the area's land management as well as community development.'

Based on various definitions it can be concluded that ecotourism is travel to natural areas, to learn about host communities, at the same time providing economic opportunities that work toward conservation and preservation of the ecosystem. Ecotourism advocates practices that are environmentally conscious, and works toward more sustainable development.

Factors responsible for the growth of ecotourism

Among several factors that are responsible for the growth of ecotourism, most notable are, the need for sustainable tourism development, a growing environmental awareness of the global community, the desire of a relatively affluent segment of the industrialized world's tourists to have nature-based experiences, and the developing world's conviction that natural resources are finite and must therefore be conserved for future generations.

The Brundtland Commission Report 'Our Common Future' emphasized the issues of development and environment (WTTC, 1987). It defined sustainable development as 'meeting the needs of the present without compromising the ability of future generations to meet their own needs.' Since then many international meetings have stressed the role of environmental concerns and development. There has been a growing environmental awareness that has entered the mainstream of global lifestyles. It was evident from the success of Earth Day 1990 that a growing number of people support government action to protect environmental quality. Eighty-five per cent of the industrialized world's citizens believe that the environment is the number one public issue, while 76 per cent of Americans consider themselves as environmentalists (Carson and Moulden, 1991).

Demand for adventurous, participatory, educational and nature-oriented tourism is growing. According to Boo (1992) this shows a shift in the way people travel. A growing majority feel the need to get 'back in touch with nature' before it is too late (Whelan, 1991). Travellers from developed countries in particular Australia, Japan, Europe and North America are increasingly placing greater importance on the quality of the natural and cultural environments of their vacation destinations (Moore and Carter, 1993).

Ecotourism involves primarily affluent people travelling from developed countries to developing countries. These ecotourists are from a relatively higher income group with more leisure and more money to spend. They are mostly looking for natural experiences in a pristine environment. They are environmentally friendly travellers who emphasize seeing and saving both natural habitat and archaeological treasures. They prefer simple facilities with minimum impact on the natural resources. They show a willingness to pay more for those services and products that are provided by environmentally conscious suppliers (Whelan, 1991; Boo, 1990).

There appears to be general agreement that ecotourism involves minimum density, low impact activities which can take place where there are natural sites of sufficient biological, cultural and geographic interest that attract tourists. Ecotourism as a sector of the tourism industry is still in its infancy, but an analysis of the markets where it has made strong inroads indicates that developing countries, with their abundant variety of physical attractions, have most of the natural qualities necessary to position ecotourism as a prime offering of their tourism industry.

Ecotourism is expected to grow as people around the globe become more sensitive toward the environment and continue to show interest in natural experiences. The last two decades have witnessed increases in travel to natural areas in developing countries. Ecotourism is not only the fastest growing sector of the travel industry, but if carefully planned it can be used to preserve fragile land and threatened wild areas, and provide residents of developing countries with opportunities for community-based development (Horwich et al., 1993).

Ecotourism is growing rapidly and is influencing the overall industry both as (a) special interest form of travel and (b) a 'greening' influence on the tourism field in general, stressing environmentally friendly approaches to tourism product development, operations and consumption. These two dimensions of ecotourism are described in the following sections.

Ecotourism as a specialty travel market

The primary market for ecotourism is special-interest, nature-oriented travel which reflects the increasing concern for the environment in the world's major tourism generating countries. For example, data on the US ecotourism market substantiate this growth.

- Ecotourism is a rapidly growing segment, but clear-cut statistics do not exist. However, studies indicate that the most popular special interest tours are related to nature oriented outdoor activities. Tour operators report that between 4 to 6 million Americans travel overseas for nature related travel each year. Several selected special interest travel market segments follow:
  - Bird watchers – 80 million Americans interested, account for $14 billion on equipment, travel and related expenses.
  - Skin and scuba diving – 3 million divers in the USA, increasing 16 per cent annually, 500,000 new divers certified annually. 98.5 per cent of divers have a valid passport and 66.2 per cent of divers travel outside of the US on diving trips.

Nature travel was estimated to have grown between 20 to 25 per cent between 1990 and 1995 and related culture and adventure travel to grow from 10 to 15 per cent (Mudge, 1991). The US Travel Data Center (1991) determined that nearly 7 per cent of US travellers, or 8 million Americans, report having taken an ecotrip. One-third of those interviewed said they would take such a trip again, which equals 35 million adults. Tour operators report that 4 to 6 million Americans travel overseas for nature-related travel each year. A study conducted by McKinsey & Co. indicates that 7 million tourists were willing to pay between US$2,000 to $3,000 for a nature-related tour. The McKinsey study estimated that there were 275 guided nature tour operators in the United States who provided tours for 108,000 travellers during 1991, producing gross revenues of $95 million and profits of $4 million. Interestingly, these tour operators reported that 63 per cent of the travellers would pay $50, and 27 per cent would pay $200 toward conservation of the areas visited (The Ecotourism Society, 1992).

The Ecotourism Society also reported extensive growth in the number of visitors to developing countries for nature tourism related experiences. For example, 47,000 people visited the Galapagos Islands in 1990, a 44 per cent increase since 1987. Tourism to the national parks and protected areas in Costa Rica grew by 80 per cent from 1987 to 1990. The number of trekkers to the Nepalese Himalayas grew by 25 per cent from 1985 to 1988; Belize experienced a 55 per cent increase in tourist arrivals from 1980 to 1990; and Kenya and the Maldives doubled their number of arrivals over the past decade (Boo, 1990).

Four basic types of tourists have been identified by Lindberg (1991) as favouring tourism destinations which feature natural attractions:

- Hard core – Scientific researchers or members of tours specifically designed for education, removal of litter, or similar purposes.
- Dedicated – People who take trips specifically to see protected areas and who want to understand local natural and cultural history.
- Mainstream – People who visit the Amazon, the Rwandan gorilla park, or other destinations primarily to take unusual trips.
- Casual – People who partake of nature incidentally as part of a broader trip.

A single individual may fit into different categories at different times. This typology, however, provides a simple description of market segments for planning purposes. For example, hard core and dedicated nature tourists will likely be more tolerant of limited amenities than will casual tourists.

The greening of the tourism industry

The environment has taken centre stage in tourism planning and development world wide. The George Washington University conducted an international assembly on global tourism policy issues where participants listed the environment as one of the top tourism agenda issues for the 1990s. Global climate change, ozone loss, deforestation, disappearing species and toxic waste were all considered crucial issues related to a sustainable tourism environment. Conservation and preservation policies have reached considerable momentum in many developing and industrialized countries of the world. Referred to as 'greening', the objective is for tourism to become both a tool for economic development while simultaneously preserving and conserving physical and cultural resources.

Policy makers and planners must recognize that tourism can have negative impacts on personal security, transportation, urbanization, and cultural integrity. Sound tourism management assesses both the physical and social carrying costs of tourism development.

Recognizing the environment and development issues as paramount, the World Travel and Tourism Council (WTTC) formed an Environment Research Centre in 1991 at Oxford Polytechnic to create a database and information network concerned with environmentally compatible growth of the tourism industry world wide. The centre's purpose is to identify the types of impacts related to tourism development and to promote environmental practices which would minimize costs and optimize benefits (WTTC, 1992).

Many observers question whether developing countries can expect to capitalize successfully on tourism's enormous economic potential by concentrating their development efforts almost exclusively on mass tourism projects such as traditional resorts and large-scale beach front hotel developments. The experience of some developing countries suggests that existing infrastructure cannot sustain intensive development without breaking down altogether. Although both the public and private sectors fully recognize the need to plan carefully for growth, concern has often been voiced that development will come first, and that the necessary human requirements and public works infrastructure will come a late second.

If the experience of other countries can serve as a useful guide to policy makers, developing nations can learn a great deal from countries such as Costa Rica, Indonesia, Kenya, Nepal and Ecuador. These countries are blessed with beautiful natural scenery and unique flora and fauna. Unlike many developing countries, they have all concentrated their efforts on developing a low impact, environment-sensitive form of tourism, described today as ecotourism. Their experiences – the mistakes as well as the successes – can have a profound bearing on a developing country's tourism industry. Many promoters may discover that they can prosper as equitably if they strike a balance between different development philosophies.

In order to fully understand ecotourism's implications, it is essential to understand a relatively new concept which has become central to public discourse on 'sustainable development'. Both government and private interests agree that the principle of sustainable development must be the guiding force behind public policy and private initiative as the world enters a new century. A global community no longer has the luxury of spawning growth that destroys an already fragile balance of nature. The principles of sustainable development, if applied wisely, will do much to establish sound patterns of growth and well-being in many areas of human endeavour, including the tourism industry.

Ecotourism has extraordinary potential as a tool for sustainable development; conversely, the principles of sustainable development are central to ecotourism. These two forces are already having a strong impact on the tourism industry.

The implications of tourism growth on the environment were outlined at a conference sponsored by the Canadian government. The conference report (Globe, 1991) defined sustainable tourism development as:

> ... leading to the management of all resources in such a way that we can fulfil economic, social and aesthetic needs while maintaining cultural integrity, essential ecological processes, biological diversity and life support systems.

The report then suggested the need for making sustainable development an essential tenet of tourism policy world wide.

> ... It seems clear that sustainability holds considerable promise as a vehicle for addressing the problems of mass tourism, as well as supporting 'alternative tourism' and 'ecotourism' ... A widely acknowledged problem is the extent to which ill-conceived and poorly planned tourism developments can erode the very qualities of the natural environment that attract visitors. Recognition of this problem is required at the national and regional levels. Particular attention must be paid at the local level where impacts and concerns are most apparent ... The real challenge for the tourism industry and sustainable development must be met now. Nationally and internationally we require a vision of balanced development and a working partnership between tourism and other sectors ... (Globe, 1991)

In order to enlarge the discussion of the concepts, growth and potential of ecotourism world wide, it is useful to examine selected case studies.

Case examples

The first two projects (Brandon, 1993) were designed to use nature tourism as a vehicle to achieve conservation and development.

Monarch Butterfly Project in Mexico

This is a small non-governmental project planned to promote nature tourism to economically benefit the community by encouraging local participation. This area of central Mexico is popular because of the annual migration of billions of butterflies to a small reserve. This reserve attracted about 100,000 tourists in 1989. Profits generated were used to establish a Visitor's Center. Admission fees collected were channelled to the local community for planting trees, maintaining trails, providing community stores, and food booths. This project started off well but due to the lack of effective management and the less than positive attitude of local residents, it has not worked as well as was expected.

Annapurna Conservation Area in Nepal

Nepal is a small country in the foothills of the Himalayas and is famous for its socio-cultural bio-diversity. Over 30,000 trekkers visit Nepal annually. Tourism growth in the past years has resulted in the construction of many lodges and tea houses. Tourism has become an important part of the economy, but at the expense of serious environmental problems. Forests have been cleared in order to provide cooking fuel and sources of energy. In addition, water pollution, poor sanitation and litter strewn along trekking routes have accelerated the deterioration of the area's natural environment.

The Annapurna project, which covers a large geographic area, was designed to minimize negative impacts on the natural environment. With the help of local participation, the project promotes development that is in harmony with conservation efforts. It emphasizes local empowerment for development that is compatible to the natural environment yet support economic benefits. Local committees were formed to regulate both tourism and conservation efforts. Training was provided to local lodge owners for the installation of solar panels for energy consumption. Recycling efforts were also encouraged. In order to minimize timber cutting, kerosene oil was provided as an alternative fuel. Local participation included lodge management committees to enforce regulations such as poaching fines and controlled timber cutting. Consequently, deforestation rates were reduced considerably.

Both of the above mentioned projects were designed emphasizing local participation to promote tourism development and conservation efforts for economic benefits. Also, these projects stressed on ecological and economical considerations, in order to promote tourism. The Annapurna project incorporated a much broader perspective by adapting policies that increased efficiency, promoted recycling of resources, and protected the ecosystem.

The Community Baboon Sanctuary, Belize

This project (Horwich et al., 1993) was initiated with the cooperation of a dozen landowners in a rural village 33 miles north-west of Belize City. It was an experiment in conservation and multiple land use-methods on private land. This project was started in 1985, and it encouraged private landowners to manage land for saving an endangered species of the Black Howler monkeys. Landowners were encouraged to adapt a plan to benefit the dwindling monkey population. They agreed to leave forest strips and specific trees along Belize river banks, between property boundaries, and in a large common area for the monkeys. This dedication of land also helped control riverbank erosion. Tourism to the area was promoted for economic benefits and to maintain the efforts of the landowners.

With the help of the World Wildlife Foundation, the sanctuary has expanded to include over one hundred landowners. The Black Howler population has now grown to more than 1,000 monkeys which indicates that the conservation plan is indeed working. There is now also a greenhouse where data are gathered on plants. Museum programmes provide classes to local school children. The number of tourists coming to the area has increased from 25–30 visitors in 1985 to 6,000 in 1990. Future plans call for the sanctuary to reintroduce plants and animals that have disappeared from the area.

Bali, Indonesia

To understand environment as a component of sustainable development, it is not simply the biophysical dimension that is important but also the socio-cultural dimension. Cultural tourism to Bali (Gadjah Mada University, Java, 1990) is a good example of how community participation is sought through traditional groups and programs based on internal ideologies that can bring about local pride. Since religious beliefs are important in this region, religious leaders are constantly sought out for advice and also as a means of showing respect. As the concept of stability within change suggests, Balinese culture has responded to change while maintaining its essential values by promoting cultural tourism.

The ecotourism concept also stresses the importance of indigenous socio-culture. Tourism to Bali attempts to address the cultural concerns of the local population. Some might see the cultural programmes that are organized for the entertainment of tourists are in fact nothing but commercialization of traditional values to secure tourist dollars. The traditional ceremonies that were once performed for religious occasions are now presented daily for a fee. However, others might argue that if it were not for tourists, these traditional programs would all but disappear.

Village tourism, Senegal

This project was initiated to benefit local village communities and to provide employment to young people in order to reduce their migration to urban areas. This model consists of very simple lodgings that were built by the local community using indigenous know-how, labour and material. This project contained costs while remaining totally under local management. The village is located on a river bank away from established tourist routes, and tourists are transported there by canoe. This project was aimed at exposing tourists to traditional village life, thereby providing opportunities for interaction between visitors and natives, including a taste of local cuisine. These activities were also designed to promote local cultural pride among village residents (Saglio (adapted), 1993).

This type of ecotourism development reflects the utilization of indigenous know-how, material, and labour. It also emphasizes economic benefits to the local community and promotes sustainability by keeping the development compatible with the natural environment.

The above mentioned ecotourism case studies demonstrate that most of these were small-scale projects under controlled development that was sustainable. All projects were well planned, had economic benefits and reflected development that was compatible with the natural environment as in the case of Senegal. Bali promoted socio-cultural aspects in order to increase awareness of its heritage, whereas the sanctuary in Belize demonstrated the community's efforts to save endangered baboons. Mexico, Belize and Nepal promoted nature tourism using the areas' biodiversity, whereas Bali utilized its cultural heritage with local participation. Senegal adapted simple lodgings with minimum costs.

These examples reveal the diversity that is prevalent in ecotourism projects, and strongly identifies eco-development concepts that are prevalent throughout all of these ecotourism projects. Eco-development stresses the use of natural resources, application of appropriate technology, and the use of social and political forces that take into account the existing ecosystems and local culture. It emphasizes an economic development model that is self reliant, based on indigenous material and know-how for the benefit of the local population. It compliments local social and cultural traditions. It also works toward local ownership and division of labour to economically benefit the local community. Figure 11.1 suggests the concepts of respect for the integrity of the ecosystem, local participation, and economic opportunities for the local communities.

- **Respect for the integrity of the ecosystem:** The majority of sustainable development projects emphasize the importance of the natural environment for promoting tourism's economic benefits. The level of development is mainly small-scale, is much easier to manage, and maintains the integrity of the ecosystem.
- **Local participation:** Some critical issues eliciting local participation were: local participants' role; empowerment as an objective; participation in the project life cycle; creating stake holders; and distributing

Figure 11.1

benefits. Participation at the community level was the key in achieving mutual benefits.

- **Economic opportunities for the local communities:** Besides respect for the integrity of the ecosystem and local participation, the third element that seemed to drive these projects was the importance of ecology to the local economy. Economic opportunities through sustainable tourism development were evident in all projects. Involvement of the local community, using indigenous elements, conserving resources, preserving the ecosystem, and promoting socio-cultural/natural awareness all appear to be working together toward providing economic benefits to the communities. Revenue sharing was evident for local development and management appeared to be decentralized toward local levels. In most cases, part of the tourism income generated was used to help maintain the project or to develop other projects that benefit the community. A checklist based on the case studies discussed is provided at the end of the chapter to assist in planning ecotourism projects in developing countries.

The future

It is evident from the earlier discussions that several factors are responsible for the growth of ecotourism world wide. Ecotourism is regarded by many individuals as a tool for sustainable tourism development, combined with sound planning and management. Ecotourism can help promote natural, social, cultural and economic improvement for sustained conservation efforts.

The future of ecotourism world wide is bright, especially in developing countries. The viability of such destinations as quality tourist areas may be largely dependent upon the extent to which those destinations are able to implement sustainable development practices while attracting their share of the international ecotourism market. If all participants understand and accept their responsibilities and are environmentally motivated, policies should eventually emerge that reflect the needs and interests of all concerned.

Government policy makers and tourism industry officials must accept the challenge, the responsibility and the mandate of bringing market forces into congruence with the need for environmental protection and social equity. If this can be accomplished, ecotourism may well become an example of how development can be achieved on a sustainable basis to the benefit of visitors, hosts and industry alike.

Checklist for ecotourism projects in developing countries

Respect for the integrity of the ecosystem

1 __ Emphasize the importance of natural environment to sustain tourism
2 __ Keep level of development small-scale, controlled, and locally manageable
3 __ Use site-specific development
4 __ Plan development to be compatible with natural surroundings
5 __ Use indigenous material, know-how and labour
6 __ Design facilities and utilize equipment that conserves energy
7 __ Practise recycling, reducing and reusing
8 __ Emphasize development that is cost-effective with minimum strain on the natural resources
9 __ Preserve vegetation, reduce deforestation whenever possible
10 __ Multiple land-use when possible
11 __ Use alternative technologies that are sustainable

Local participation

1 __ Promote local participation as much as possible
2 __ Create opportunities for local empowerment
3 __ Convey a sense of local ownership and leadership
4 __ Create opportunities for group projects
5 __ Create opportunities for the locals to control and manage valuable natural resources
6 __ Provide alternative local measures
7 __ Promote socio-cultural pride by organizing community programmes

8 __   Use local knowledge and practices
9 __   Incorporate local cultural values and traditions
10 __   Respect local ideology and heritage
11 __   Provide opportunities for hosts and guests interaction

Economic opportunities for the local community

1 __   Coordinate all elements to optimize local economic benefits
2 __   Provide employment for local community
3 __   Provide local ownership
4 __   Incorporate community ideas in policy decisions
5 __   Distribute economic benefits – revenue sharing
6 __   Recognize local services/efforts
7 __   Create markets for local products
8 __   Encourage profits to be used for conservation and preservation efforts
9 __   Link profits to community programs, education, environmental awareness
10 __   Use local material and labour to keep money in the local economy
11 __   Keep management decentralized

References

Boo, E. (1992) Wildlands and Human Needs, *World Wildlife Fund Paper*, Series #2, p. 14

Boo, E. (1990) *Ecotourism: The Potentials and Pitfalls*, Vol. I, World Wildlife Fund, p. 70

Brandon, C. (1993) Basic Steps Towards Encouraging Local Participation in Nature Tourism Projects. In *A Guide For Planners and Managers* (ed. Lindberg, K. and Hawkins, D.), The Ecotourism Society, pp. 132–168

Carson, P. and Moulden, J. (1991) *Green is Gold: Business Talking to Business about the Environmental Revolution*, Harper Business, Toronto

Ceballos-Lascurain, Hector (1987) The Future of Ecotourism, *Mexico Journal*, January 17, pp. 13–14

Ecotourism Society (1992) *Definition and Ecotourism Statistical Fact Sheet*, Alexandria, Virginia

Ecotourism Society (1991) *The Ecotourism Society Newsletter*, March, Alexandria, Virginia

Gadjah Mada University (1990) A Report on Environment and Development. In *Sustainable Tourism Development: Guide for Local Planners*, World Tourism Organization Publication, p. 29

Globe '90 (1991) Tourism Stream Conference, Action Strategy for Sustainable Tourism Development. *Tourism Canada*, Ottawa, Canada. pp. 1–12

Horwich, R.H., Murray, D., Saqui, E., Lyon, J. and Godfrey, D. (1993) Ecotourism and Community Development: A View From Belize. In *A Guide For Planners and Managers* (ed. Lindberg, K. and Hawkins, D.) The Ecotourism Society. pp. 132–168

Lindberg, Kreg (1991) Economic Policies for Maximizing Nature Tourism's Contribution to Sustainable Development, World Resources Institute: Washington, DC (unpublished paper)

Moore, S. and Carter, B. (1993) Ecotourism in the 21st Century, *Tourism Management*, April. pp. 123–130

Mudge, Susie (1991) Notes on Ecotourism, June, Ernst & Young, Washington, DC, pp. 1–8

Orams, M.B. (1995) Towards a more Desirable Form of Ecotourism, *Tourism Management*, Spring, pp. 3–8

Ryel, R. and Grasse, T. (1991) Marketing Ecotourism: Attracting the Elusive Ecotourist. In *Nature Tourism: Managing for the Environment*. (ed. Whelan, T.) Island Press, Washington, DC, pp. 164–199

Saglio, C. (1993) An Example of Village Tourism, *Sustainable Tourism Development: Guide for Local Planners*, adapted, World Tourism Organization Publication, p. 68

United States Travel Data Center (1991) Travel Outlook, USTDC Annual Report

Whelan, T. (1991) Ecotourism and its Role in Sustainable Development. In *Nature Tourism*. Island Press, Washington, DC, pp. 3–22

Wight, P. (1993) Ecotourism: Ethics or Eco-Self? *Journal of Travel Research*, Winter, pp. 3–9

World Tourism Organization (1996) Tourism Trends and Prospects Worldwide and by Region

World Travel and Tourism Council (1992) Progress and Priorities, Annual Report

World Travel and Tourism Council (1987) Annual Report

Ziffer, Karen A. (1989) Ecotourism the Uneasy Alliance, Fall, Conservation International and Ernst & Young, Washington, DC (unpublished paper)

12 Privatization in the Third World: small-scale tourism enterprises

Valene L. Smith

Privatization, especially proprietorship of small-scale local-level tourist enterprises in the Third World, is a critical developmental issue that has essentially been ignored. As a proprietary and managerial concept, privatization gained widespread attention during the 1980s, an era when some political states chose to raise cash by selling assets including their national airlines and hotel chains. It was intended these holdings should be owned by the private sector, thus transferring management of tourism to local entities. Unfortunately capital-rich foreign corporations were sometimes the successful bidders.

In the 1990s, the privatization trend is global, fuelled by the break-up of the Soviet Union, and increased foreign investment there as well as in China. The United States government is also involved, instituting new policies to privatize many facilities within the National Parks and Forests.

Third World tourism developed rapidly in the years following the Second World War because land and tax incentives encouraged Western capital to invest in the essential infrastructure to attract foreign visitors. Westerners held managerial positions, hiring and training local labour for routine services. Literature of the 1970s and 1980s cites as one of the positive benefits of tourism 'the creation of jobs and the opportunity for people to increase their income and standard of living' (DeKadt, 1979), particularly for unskilled labour with limited education. By contrast, 'Crumbs from the table? The worker's share in tourism' (Samy, 1975) was among the first studies to challenge the supposed benefits to the host population. Subsequently other authors, including dependency theory advocates, have repeatedly urged privatization and local control as remedies for leakage as well as the sir–servitude syndrome and insensitivity to local norms.

Ecotourism, the banner of the 1990s, tends to support small-scale local-level accommodations (here also termed cottages) as environmentally sensitive in contrast to mega-resorts. But are they economically viable and socially desirable? This chapter considers these socio-economic issues, and especially host–guest relations, associated with privatization in Third World or developing countries. As used here, the term 'privatization' refers to small family-operated tourist facilities such as inns and guest houses although the discussion could be also extended to cafes and craft or souvenir shops. Bryden (1973) suggested two decades ago the need to investigate the impact of renting rooms but the published literature is still virtually nil. This present analysis depends heavily on extensive fieldwork by the author in a variety of locales – remote sites or ethnic enclaves in the Western world as well as Third World settings.

Home-stays in the Western world

Tourists travelling in Western countries, including Europe, the USA and 'down under' in Australia and New Zealand have enjoyed and thus popularized a variety of home stays. Facility ambience combined with personalized hospitality has successfully generated word-of-mouth recommendations, and often repeat annual business (Hermans (1981) describes a successful Spanish *pension*). Irish country inns with fine linen nappery, Belleek china and Waterford crystal set a high (if expensive) standard of living, while an English 'B&B' is often more cosy and less costly than hotels. New Zealand farm stays are excellent opportunities to 'meet the people' and observe sheep and deer ranch operations; in Argentina, elitist visitors can perfect their polo skills on traditional *estancias*.

Successful privatization in these ventures depends on multiple factors not common to most Third World countries. Most of these Western entrepreneurs have substantial capitalization apart from tourism (represented in their homes and ranches); their tourist income is therefore usually supplemental (Mendonsa, 1983). Hosts and guests commonly share some language fluency as well as similar Western cultural orientation and background. Many proprietors belong to organizations such as the American Automobile Association and are listed in their Tour Books, or in similar overseas touring publications; they have access to local and regional advertising media and can affiliate with reservations networks that promote and/or represent their property abroad. Telephone WATTS lines, telex and fax are almost universally available for confirmation of reservations. And proprietors are knowledgeable about business procedures, the marketplace and their type of operation through organizational affiliations.

Building codes and sanitation standards exist and are generally observed. Most enterprises have powered appliances – washers/dryers (or commercial laundry services), dishwashers, freezers etc. to minimize proprietor workload. And if income warrants, they can afford to hire part-time help as needed, and thus further contribute to the multiplier effect in the local economy. Given the fact that the volume of tourism at any given time is sensitive to many natural disasters as well as civil disturbances and economic cycles, most small-scale hoteliers and businesses prosper during good times, and survive during lean periods.

Privatization in the Third World

The positive and powerful incentives favouring privatization include the following:

1 Local residents may be able to take control and manage local tourism through existing social networks, or establish ad hoc associations to help empower them as decision-makers.
2 Proprietorship confers personal community status and accesses expanded networking through membership in service organizations such as Rotary, Kiwanis, Soroptimists, Lions etc. with a voice in the wider community.
3 The psychological satisfaction of the independent entrepreneur, as 'being my own boss', often generates personal opportunities to increase earning power through responsible management and hard work.
4 Successful privatization builds business equity, to become a family legacy or a saleable retirement asset.
5 Family proprietorships can hire elderly, disabled and juvenile family members who might not otherwise be employable.

By contrast, the disadvantageous aspects of privatization include at least some of the following:

1 Opportunities for local ownership are not necessarily equally accessible. They may be linked to education, to family standing, to geographic proximity to the tourist destination site, and to the personality of the would-be entrepreneur.
2 Successful business operation is often proportionate to personal ability, appropriate training and a market. The sophistication to conduct feasibility studies is seldom found in Third World communities (or even in rural America).
3 In developing countries, social foundations are usually rooted in traditional (often familial) networks with established hierarchies. The

emergence of new business 'leaders' based on tourist income can easily be disruptive (Mendonsa 1983) and socially divisive (Smith, 1992). Long (1989), studying Huatulco, Mexico, found that non-resident, urbanized Mexicans rushed to this new seaside resort, took over the best business sites and opened their shops. Their 'know-how' and aggressive manner overwhelmed the indigenous fisherfolk who were unable to compete, and deeply resented the intrusion. The in-migration of these dominant co-nationals proved more disruptive than the initial influx of educated government planners and engineers, who were recognized as temporaries.

4   Even small-scale enterprises need start-up capital. In his study of Nazare (Portugal), Mendonsa (1983: 231) found that over two-thirds of the families initially rented out rooms in their homes and used the additional income to improve the house. Thus they increased both their capital and earning capacity, and improved their standard of living through use of the facilities themselves during the off season. However in Boracay, Philippines (Smith, 1992), new thatched houses with (imported) toilets and sinks had to be built. In both cases, however, the result has been 'a widening of the gap between those community members who already had capital or good employment and those less fortunate' (Mendonsa, 1983).

Quite apart from the social and labour aspects of small-scale local tourism is the problem of environmental impaction. It is almost a geographical truism that sites that could now successfully innovate new small-scale local guest lodges generally occur in either (1) remote locations or (2) they are highly accessible by cheap transportation (private car or public bus) and service the low-budget 'backpackers'.

The geographical isolates include islands, mountain valleys, desert oases and high latitude locales that are too far removed from tourism-generating centres to justify long-haul transport costs to serve a limited clientele. In short, the destination attraction may not be worth the price! The Trobriand Islands – favoured with some of the world's most beautiful beaches – are a case in point. No major air corridor serves their position, off the southeast coast of New Guinea. Only the elite, the affluent or the explorer spends substantially more money just to reach these tiny islets when fine beaches abound closer to home, in Hawaii, the Seychelles or the Caribbean. Further, the resource base to support tourism – culinary water, local food production and infrastructure – is limited in these island micro-states. Contaminated water supplies because of high ground water tables and lack of sewage systems are common to many low islands, including Boracay (Smith, 1992) and Belize (Hartshorn et al., 1984). Wilkinson (1989) provides an excellent discussion of the many constraints to island development. Similarly, Canada would like to develop tourism in their Far

North to generate employment but Inuit villages on the monotonous Laurentian Shield are not apt to attract mass tourism to occupy (unbuilt) large resorts. Again, for most tourists, the limited destination attractions are not worth the expensive air fare.

The second group, small-scale guest facilities, are often low-cost lodging for budget travellers, in major destinations where expensive resorts predominate. Here the issue is economic as well as ecological: does the financial return justify the investment? The author inspected a dozen guest lodges in Belize City – mostly old (or so they appear) wooden structures, much-deteriorated because of rainfall, humidity and salt air, and generally in poor repair. Because of contamination in the Belize River (Hartshorn et al., 1984), most such hostelries collect rain water from the roof into open cisterns. The buildings would not meet US codes for electrical wiring, fire escapes or sanitation. The guests, mostly Americans in their twenties and thirties, were following the La Ruta Maya circuit, travelling by public bus from Yucatan on a low-budget, either by necessity or by choice. Some of the latter individuals were obviously upscale urbanites for whom this was almost a rite of passage, testing 'survival' under hardships. 'Montezuma's revenge' (diarrhoea) had been a frequent problem. An increase in popularity of La Ruta Maya (a developmental dream of most Central American governments) raises doubts that increased tourism will 'bring significant material and social benefits to local people' or protect environmental degradation (Daltabuit and Pi-Sunyer, 1990).

Erik Cohen, one of the most respected fieldworkers in tourism, reported (1982) that 'craft' tourism (local-level small-scale accommodations) did NOT benefit the villagers in Phuket, Thailand. Even then, a decade ago, local tourism authorities were discouraging any further expansion of cottage accommodation, in favour of larger hotels. He noted that because of the workload, families sometimes hired young girls to work as maids but the wages were too small to bring any real benefit to the community. Further, these young employees felt that to work as maids was 'demeaning', and their wages created another problem: their families operated their farms on a subsistence level but the young girls had independent cash income to spend solely on themselves.

Marketing privatized resorts and destinations

Marketing tourist accommodations has become a sophisticated enterprise, and strategies for attracting visitors to these small privatized facilities needs to be considered in terms of domestic as well as international guests. Because of investment ideas initiated two decades ago, research and development concentrated on international tourism to generate foreign exchange. However, subsequent modernization now enables a substantial number of Third World residents to become short-term domestic tourists, thanks to larger income, shorter work weeks and paid vacations. This new pool of potential travellers is now being recognized as an important source of income and employment (Savignac, 1992). Further, their motivations for travel are influenced by the media, and the growing knowledge that to vacation is integral to the modern workaday world. In her Huatulco study, Long (1989) noted inland Mexicans used to drive to the 'old' community, for a day on the beach; their domestic tourism had supported a number of small restaurants and other service businesses.

Domestic tourism in India (technically no longer Third World albeit still a large economically marginal population) is increasing dramatically, straining the British-built colonial era infrastructure (Singh, 1992). Controls on further development may become necessary in selected sites such as Simla because of travel ads in Indian newspapers reading: '4 Days 3 Nights in Simla, including air fare and hotel. Rupees—'. The number of hotels (and visitors) has tripled in ten years.

Marketing cottage tourism overseas is entirely different. Some destinations, such as Boracay (Smith, 1992), become known through word-of-mouth and avant-garde books; Ambergris Cay in Belize needs no promotion because an 'inner circle' of scuba divers keep accommodations full almost year-round. By contrast, Ranck (1987) investigated remote New Guinea beach-front cottages originally built by foreigners and now operated by locals who hoped to attract foreign tourists. Britton (1987) concluded 'small scale enterprises must be provided with basic industry linkages if they are to survive . . . including access to advertising outlets, reservation facilities, and adequate transport services'.

Communication and reservations networks are expanding with enhanced quality, through the visual advantages of Geographic Information Systems added to many travel agency computer systems. Regional organizations and governments can (and probably will) eventually link most accommodations to some marketing arm; it is profitable to do so. Many small American resorts jointly maintain a single WATTS reservation line, the cost of which is minimal compared to a high vacancy factor. This system could soon serve domestic tourism in the developing world, such as India.

A basic issue, however, is to market the particular product to a suitable tourist target. What type of tourist do hosts want, and who will most benefit the receiving community? And how does the marketing agency segment the potential, to make the property sound attractive yet with truth in advertising?

Privatization: the socio-cultural impacts

One of the growing objections to mass tourism is social pollution: traffic, noise, crowding. D'Amore (1983) defines social carrying capacity as 'that point where local residents perceive on balance an unacceptable level of social disbenefits from tourism development'. By implication, privatization is presumed to disperse the concentration of tourists congregated in mega-resorts, and encourage more one-on-one interaction between hosts and guests. Indeed, one of the sales pitches of ecotourism is the opportunity to 'meet the people' through home stays. As discussed above, home/farm stays in Western countries are financially profitable and usually pleasant experiences for both owners and their visitors. However, cottage housing (or small guest lodges/inns) in the Third World may involve social and cultural impacts, including excessive workloads, differing value systems, invasion of privacy etc.

When tourism is introduced into private homes in the Third World, it essentially intrudes into *traditional* societies where women's 'work' is in the home. There, often without benefit of electricity and powered equipment including washers/dryers/dishwashers/vacuum sweepers/food processors – or even refrigerators – the landladies take on daily loads of hand laundry for bed linens, towels, etc. Hohenegg (1989) described her parent's Austrian home, opened to the public twenty years ago as a ski pension to bring in additional cash to send children to college. Through hard work, the business grew; inflation meant higher costs; they built on more guest rooms. By 1988, working almost single-handedly an ageing (and tired) woman made up 30 beds a day and served Continental breakfasts, eight months a year. The laundry now done by machine still had to be ironed and folded. In the Third World the clotheslines are pinned with handwashed linens, drying (?) in an afternoon thundershower. The author has paid for many nights' stay in guest rooms, and slept in damp sheets because the families owned only one set per bed. The alternative was to *not* wash them between guests, which also occurs. Kouris (1989) provides one of the few published reports on family labour:

> Women who operated tourist businesses, more than those who were wage earners, experienced an environment which demanded many more hours than any previous job in Drethia. Businesses serving the tourist are open between fourteen to twenty-four hours per day, seven days per week, for seven months continuously. There are no weekends, holidays or breaks for those who work in family businesses in Drethia . . . this exhaustive work schedule hits the married women hardest; they are responsible for both child and house care. Many of them do all of these jobs simultaneously, and if fortunate, they are helped by their parents.

And even in the Western world, just the titles of two journal articles suggest a similar tale: 'Inn industry no place for leisurely' (Lyke, 1990); and 'Bed and breakfast innkeepers have a labor of love' (Graebner, 1990).

In Belize the author interviewed scores of women including those working in the one Western-standard hotel as well as the landladies of the guest inns. The hotel 'maids' were outspoken in their belief that they were the advantaged ones for multiple reasons:

1 They have a set schedule for work, forty hours per week; their employment includes sick leave, maternity benefits, and after two years, paid vacation leave.
2 Uniforms are provided so no personal expense for clothing.
3 Wages are paid directly to them as discretionary income, and does not *have* to be spent 'fixing up the house' for rental purposes.
4 Their hours at home are personal without the intrusion of outsiders, and child care is available through family members who thus also share the benefit of cash employment.
5 Also deemed very important is the fact they enjoy their time at work, where they meet nice guests (who often leave tips); and they have good cleansing agents with which to work.
6 Their peers envy the 'good jobs at the hotel' where a locker room and coffee area encourages interaction with other employees, widening their group network.

The Belize landladies who were similarly interviewed complained of long workdays, isolation at home, lack of privacy and unpleasant/demanding guests. Not infrequently menfolk took the cash income and spent it in the coffee house or at beer parties, leaving the women powerless.

In two instances, in the Seychelles and in Seoul, Korea, the author was permitted to observe on-the-job training sessions sponsored by major hotels. In Korea, the Westin offered English language sessions for better hotel guest/maid communication, and how to greet guests in the hallways and in the rooms. In the Seychelles, the Sheraton chain had purchased and renovated a former German 'Club Med-type' property, and were retraining employees for a more diverse international clientele. The quality of presentation and staff response was impressive.

Some proprietors have tried to establish guest standards. Proctor (1992) operated a small cottage-inn in Vieques, Puerto Rico. To protect her family from 'beach bums' her policy was to accept new guests only by referral and, since they had no phone, by written reservations only. Time and again, they gave up their own beds to serve the unannounced and unknown. Reluctantly they left Puerto Rico rather than continue to earn a living through lodging, especially in view of increasing numbers of 'backpackers' who drifted into the area, and were negative role models for growing children.

Riley (1988) has provided the best description to date of the international long-term budget traveller, and a life style which is apparently increasingly orientated towards alcohol, drug abuse, sexual freedom and prostitution (Smith, 1992).

In conclusion, this effort to bring together into one article some type of assessment on the issues of privatization remains incomplete. The topic is important to the future of tourism, especially as destination access widens to truly remote areas of the world and as domestic tourism increases. Substantial additional research needs to be undertaken in a variety of settings, to evaluate the impacts presented here. Further, the following guidelines are suggested for consideration, and for ultimate testing and refinement.

Privatization of small-scale local-level enterprises could be advantageous in settings in which:

1 The infrastructure is more than adequate for local needs, and can absorb additional visitors – at least seasonal or temporary guests without disruption to the local community.
2 The government is able to bring in or provide supplemental services, including health and/or disaster relief, for both the home population and the visitors, should need arise.
3 The indigenous population welcomes visitors because they provide a new interest and a break in the monotony of routine living.
4 The presence of visitors may stimulate handicraft markets and become an outlet for sale of locally made goods.
5 The visitors form an appreciative audience for cultural performances that help preserve ethnic/national heritage.
6 Both hosts and guests share a common language so that discourse is truly meaningful.
6 Hosts and guests share some mutual basis for identity – i.e. they are members of the same religious faith/sect; they share common job skills, as farmer-to-farmer, or they have mutual friends or relatives.
7 The visitors and the visited work together on a project deemed locally important – e.g. construction of a needed community centre. Shared experiences become endearing and enduring bonds.
8 The age groups are somewhat parallel, thereby reflecting peer group interests.
9 The behaviour of the guests conforms to local mores, in dress and life style.

Privatization: in perspective

Privatization of business promises social and cultural benefits as well as greater economic return to individual owners. Proprietorship of a successful business is ego-enhancing, and confers the privilege (albeit often a responsibility) to create employment for family and community members. The owner thereby becomes a power broker, and a well-run business may endure for decades, creating family and community stability. Further, through local ownership of small-scale tourism enterprises, community members *can* control at least some aspects of their visitor industry, obtain a larger share of the profits, and minimize economic leakage. Therefore this individual desire to participate in an economic mainstream, through private enterprise, should be nurtured.

Families in the Third World often seek supplemental income from tourism by converting their homes into *pension*-style housing. However, many of these small-scale enterprises are handicapped by

1 Lack of existing infrastructure, as basic as electricity, culinary water and sewage.
2 By inadequate investment capital, for example for laundry and restaurant equipment, to protect visitor health.
3 By little or no training in business management.

This effort places an undue workload on family members and especially on the women. Thus in contrast to the dialectic statements that to work as a maid or gardener is demeaning, the data presented here suggest that individuals who serve as employees for larger, better-equipped facilities (hotels and resorts) often fare better – financially and socially – than their entrepreneurial counterparts. Because of the importance of privatization, further research is clearly needed to ascertain the criteria that favour self-employment through ownership of a small-scale business *vis-à-vis* wage employment in a larger enterprise.

References

Britton, S. (1987) Tourism in small developing communities. In *Ambiguous Alternatives: Tourism in Small Developing Communities* (ed. C. Britton and W. Clark), University of South Pacific, Suva, Fiji, pp. 167–94
Bryden, J. (1973) *Tourism and Development*, Cambridge University Press, Cambridge
Cohen, E. (1982) Marginal paradises: bungalow tourism on the islands of Southern Thailand. *Annals of Tourism Research*, **9**(2), 189

Daltabuit, M. and Pi-Sunyer, O. (1990) Tourism development in Quintana Roo, Mexico. *Cultural Survival Quarterly* **14**(1), 9–13

D'Amore, L. (1983) Guidelines in planning harmony with the host community. In *Tourism in Canada: Selected Issues and Options* (ed. P. Murphy), University of Victoria Western Geographical Series 21, Victoria, BC, pp. 135–59

DeKadt, E. (ed.) (1979) *Tourism: Passport to Development?*, Oxford University Press, New York

Graebner, L. (1990) Bed and breakfast innkeepers have a labor of love. *The Business Journal Serving Greater Sacramento*, **6**:(46), 1–2

Hartshorn, G., Nicolait, L., Hartshorn, L., et al. (1984) *Belize: Community Environmental Profile*, Robert Nicolait and Associates, Belize City, Belize

Hermans, D. (1981) The encounter of agriculture and tourism: a Catalan case. *Annals of Tourism Research*, **8**(3), 462–79

Hohenegg, Lydia (1989) Personal communication.

Kouris, M. (1989) Tourism and the family in a rural Cretan community. *Annals of Tourism Research*, **16**(3), 318–32

Long, V. (1989) Social mitigation of tourism development impacts: Bahias de Huatulco, Oaxaca, Mexico. *Tourism Recreation Research*, **14**(1), 5–13

Lyke, R. (1990) Inn industry no place for leisurely. *Hotel and Motel Management*, **205**(17), 212

Mendonsa, E.L. (1983) Tourism and income strategies in Nazare, Portugal. *Annals of Tourism Research*, 10(2), 213–38

Proctor, S. (1992) Personal communication

Ranck, S.R. (1987) An attempt at autonomous development: the case of the Tufi guest houses, Papua New Guinea. *Ambiguous Alternatives: Tourism in Small Developing Countries* (ed. S. Britton and W. Clark), University of South Pacific, Suva, Fiji, pp. 154–66

Riley, P. (1988) Road culture of international long-term budget travelers. *Annals of Tourism Research*, **15**, 313–28

Samy, J. (1975) Crumbs from the table? The workers' share in tourism. In *The Pacific Way* (ed. S. Tupouniua et al.), South Pacific Social Sciences Association, Suva, Fiji, pp. 205–14

Savignac, A.E. (1992) Message from the Secretary-General. *WTO News*, April (World Tourism Organization, Madrid)

Singh, T.V. (1992) Tourism in the mountain environment: case references from the Himalaya and Huangshan (China). Paper presented at the IGU Commission, Geography of Leisure and Recreation, Tellurdie, Colorado, 17–18 August

Smith, V.L. (1992) Boracay, Philippines: a case study in 'alternative' tourism. In *Tourism Alternatives: Potentials and Problems in the Development of Tourism* (ed. V. Smith and W. Eadington), University of Pennsylvania Press, Philadelphia, pp. 133–57

Wilkinson, P.F. (1989) Strategies for tourism in island microstates. *Annals of Tourism Research*, **16**(2), 153–77

13 Tourism development: a Latin American perspective

Regina G. Schlüter

Introduction

One of the favourite subjects of tourism researchers from developed countries is the development of tourism in non-industrialized countries. Such countries are generally taken as a shapeless unit by those researchers, who have a tendency to forget that every continent and every country has specific characteristics which differentiate it from the others, and that these differences and unique situations can sometimes be found within the borders of a single country.

In Latin America, the label attached to the group of countries comprising Brazil and all the Spanish speaking countries south of the United States, sharp differences can be found within the national borders of each individual country. This is due to the fact that on the one hand borders were arbitrarily set, and on the other hand, geographical differences influenced the cultural occupation of the territory.

There are also historic elements that differentiate this region from other developing areas such as Africa or Asia. First, it has been exposed to European contact for over 500 years and, except for Brazil, the whole region was colonized by Spain, whose cultural supremacy had very specific characteristics. Second, the independence movements arose as early as the end of the eighteenth century and the beginning of the nineteenth century. This is why the relationship with Great Britain and eventually with the United States was not one of overt domination but was framed within a context of influence on social, political and economic decisions.

These distinctive differences can also be seen in the development of tourism. The activity was first used by a Latin American government as a tool for development in the 1930s. The Argentine government tried to turn the small village of San Carlos de Bariloche into a tourism resort in order to reaffirm Argentina's sovereignty in the area through the settlement of a permanent resident population.

In the 1950s, however, when Latin America tried to achieve development through tourism, it applied the same policies followed by all the developing nations. Without critically assessing whether that was really the best for them the countries in the region shaped their tourism policies as was the practice in other developing countries.

Tourism development in Latin America from 1950

After the Second World War, Latin America realized the extent to which tourism was contributing to the fast recovery of the devastated economies. It also witnessed the expansion of the large American hotel chains and the growth and progress brought about by the tourism 'boom' in Spain. Consequently, many Latin American countries (as well as other developing nations) decided to incorporate tourism either as an economic alternative to achieve growth or as a supplementary aspect of the main economic activity.

In 1955, the economic model fostered by the Economic Commission for Latin America (CEPAL) was implemented. Lizama (1991) stresses that Latin American countries had to strive to go from the stage of primary goods production to that of industrialization. This required a rapid and intense development of industry which, in turn, called for investments and major state participation.

Governments tried to encourage large private corporations to invest in the country. When this was not achieved, the governments made the investments themselves. They also resorted to foreign financing from international agencies such as the World Bank, the Organization of American States (OAS), the United Nations Development Programme (UNDP), the Inter American Development Bank (BID), etc.

In the case of Bariloche (Argentina), tourism was introduced as the response to a strictly domestic political problem. Those developments, implemented after the 1950s, however, were orientated to create leisure resorts for residents of industrialized countries. Therefore, the characteristics of these developments were decided by the industrialized countries themselves, and were accepted without hesitation by the countries on the periphery, who thought tourism was the magic solution to all their problems.

Thus, during the second half of the twentieth century, Latin America had to adapt its attractions to the requirements of the extra-regional market, and eventually these attractions became the three most required products (Schlüter, 1991a):

- the tree Ss (sun, sand and sea);
- exotic culture;
- nature tourism.

The first recipe applied in Latin America involved 'integrated tourism centres', whose favoured resource was the 'sun, sand, sea' triad. 'Integrated' meant that even the unexpected was foreseen, taking into account the region's environmental, economic, social and cultural factors. The tourism centres of Cancun (Mexico) and Puerto Plata (Dominican Republic) are the clearest examples of such resorts in Latin America.

The 'three Ss' product

At the beginning of the 1950s, this was the product preferred by industrialized countries. Consequently, the Caribbean became the ideal destination, especially for Anglo-Saxon America. Owing to its proximity to the continental territory of the United States and the easy terms it offered to foreign investors, Cuba became the region's favourite destination. The city of La Habana and the beach of Varadero attracted the largest number of tourists.

Between 1950 and 1959, Cuba was visited by 1.7 million American tourists, who represented 85 per cent of the total number of arrivals. The most outstanding year was 1957, with 272,200 tourists, 87 per cent of whom came from the United States.

Following the successful Cuban Revolution led by Fidel Castro in 1959, problems arose between the United States and Cuba. There was a total rupture of relations between both countries as Cuba strayed towards the socialist bloc and the number of international arrivals dropped to very low levels.

The tourist flow from the United States turned massively to Puerto Rico. This country had an incipient tourism industry but was in no condition to make it grow at a rapid pace and provide good services. Instead of exploiting tourism the citizens exploited tourists. In this way, the country earned a negative image (Soto Cordero, 1991).

International tourism to Cuba increased again after 1973, when, owing to a change in the international situation, Cuba was able to attract once more the tourism flow coming from the most important generating countries (Alvarez Valdés, 1991). Cuba's main market is still North America, though not the United States but Canada (Alvarez Valdés, 1991). In 1994 Cuba had 18,000 hotel rooms and was visited by 636,600 tourists who spent $561 million (Davis, 1997).

Puerto Rico missed the opportunity of becoming the leading tourist attraction in the Caribbean between 1977 and 1984 due to a series of wrong tourism policies. The situation changed in 1985, however, when important hotel chains carried out large investments. These investments, together with a number of governmental policies, have made it possible for the tourism industry to dream of a future when Puerto Rico will be the main destination in the region (Soto Cordero, 1991).

For political reasons tourism development was a late event in the Dominican Republic, only starting in the 1970s. In 1971, INFRATUR was created. This was an agency similar to its Mexican counterpart of the same name (the current FONATUR), whose aim was the development of tourism in the country. With the advice of the United Nations Development Programme (UNDP) and funds from the World Bank, the building of an integrated tourist centre was started in Puerto Plata – a region that comprised two areas: Playa Dorada and Playa Grande. As the expected private investments did not materialize it was also necessary to ask for loans from various foreign banks (World Tourism Organization, 1991).

Thanks to the political stability that was achieved in the Dominican Republic during the 1970s, it was possible to carry out a study of new tourism developments in the country. Five areas were identified: four at the seaside and one in a mountain area. Furthermore, the government also passed a number of laws regulating the tourism industry.

Towards the late 1980s, tourism was already becoming the triggering factor for the economic development in the Dominican economy. Owing to the prevailing political stability, large investments were carried out in the hotel sector, which grew very fast, from 8,560 hotel rooms in 1985, to 10,185 in 1987, 16,288 in 1988, and 19,000 in 1990. In 1989, the Dominican Republic received 1.4 million visitors, 384,939 of which were Dominicans living abroad.

In the early 1990s, the main generating markets for the Dominican Republic were: United States, 44 per cent, Canada, 38 per cent and Germany, 5 per cent. While more than 75 per cent of visitors travelled for leisure, 36 per cent were repeat visitors. What tourists enjoyed most were the hospitality, the beaches and the climate. What they disliked most was the bad service they encountered at airports, hotels and restaurants. They also disliked the water quality, the lack of electricity and the poverty (Aquino, 1991). In 1994 there were 2,108 hotel rooms and 3,178 were under construction. The European market became the most important (45.1 per cent) while the United States and Canada with 25 per cent and 21 per cent respectively, were in the second and third places (Elias, 1995).

Surprisingly enough, tourism growth in Mexico is not based on its rich cultural heritage but on the development of a product based on the three Ss. Owing to its privileged geographical situation, the Mexican government has considered tourism the best alternative to achieve economic growth, regional development and population resettlement in isolated areas as well as a way of solving problems such as the high isolated areas

as well as a way of solving social problems such as the high unemployment rate among the illiterate population group.

In the 1970s, in order to achieve these aims, Mexico was forced to
consolidate its traditional beach resorts, Acapulco, Mazatlan and Puerto
Vallarta, and to create new integrated tourism resorts. Cancun, Ixtapa
and Bahias de Huatulco are under the supervision and control of
FONATUR (the National Tourism Fund). These tourism developments
were supplemented with a series of specific policies related to transpor-
tations, service quality standards, advertising and the like (Guadarrama
Munoz, 1991). In this way, Mexico, with 17,182,000 arrivals in 1994,
reached tenth place among the major destinations in the world (World
Tourism Organization, 1996).

As far as the South American countries are concerned, Brazil was the
first to compete in the extra-regional markets with its 'sun, sand and sea'
product. In 1972–3, a project called 'TURIS' was launched. Its aim was to
develop a chain of seaside resorts on the Atlantic coast, from Rio de
Janeiro to Santos, for both domestic and international tourism. These
resorts attracted mainly tourist from Argentina, who also visited the
beaches that stretched from Santos to Porto Alegre. Later on, additional
developments were carried out in north-east Brazil, where Dutch, Portu-
guese and Afro cultural remains combine with hedonism, at vacation
developments such as Itaparica's Club Méditerranée. These developments
succeeded in making the country more attractive for tourists from the
United States and Europe. However, Rio de Janeiro, with 51.1 per cent of
the total arrivals to Brazil, has remained the most visited city.

In the early 1990s, Venezuela and Colombia succeeded in attracting
tourism flows developing facilities in Isla de Margarita (Venezuela) and
Cartagena (Colombia).

One of the characteristics of South American tourism is that over
70 per cent of the international arrivals originate in the sub-regions. The
'sun, sand and sea' product is ranked first among Latin American consumers, who imitate the vacation patterns of the large European markets.

This is why Uruguay, whose main market is Argentina, has become
such an important destination (1,884,000 arrivals in 1994). Tourism growth
in Uruguay was a spontaneous event brought about merely by the market law of supply and demand. However, some intergovernmental agencies such as the Organization of American States (OAS) and the European
Economic Community (EEC), have sent experts to carry out studies which
were not put into practice.

In the 1970s, Chile and Argentina also tried to offer a three Ss product
in the international market, but in the face of their latitude, the three Ss
become 'sun, snow and skiing'. On both sides of the Andes chain, local
entrepreneurs have built many winter resorts, whose main market is the
South American countries. Extra-regional tourists mostly visit the resorts

when world ski championships are held there, but they also travel to the region, to a lesser extent, for snobbery. It is nice to be seen walking about Miami airport carrying a pair of skis in July.

Culture as a tourism resource

Latin America has extraordinary archaeological remains of the three major pre-Columbian cultures: the Aztecs in Mexico, the Mayas in Mexico, Belize, Guatemala, Honduras and El Salvador, and the Incas in Peru and Bolivia.

The region also offers a wealth of socio-cultural expressions in which pre-Columbian rituals are mixed with elements introduced by the domination. It is worth mentioning the marked African influence, a result of the slavery system established in Brazil by Portugal. There are also some interesting religious events in which Catholic and native rites have been fused, such as 'La Tirana' in Chile, 'Tinkunaco' in Argentina, 'La Diablada de Oruro' in Bolivia, 'La Mama Negra de Latacunga' in Ecuador, or the procession to 'Our Lord of Esquipulas' in Guatemala. The Rio Carnival, however, is the only socio-cultural product highly competitive in the international market.

Peru and Guatemala, whose beaches are not good enough for these countries to offer the characteristic three Ss triad, have important archaeological remains, such as the Inca site Machu Pichu in Peru and the Mayan Tikal in Guatemala. Furthermore, the survival of ancient customs and the interbreeding between the native aboriginal population and the Spaniards have made it possible for both countries to have a share of the market by means of a cultural product.

In the early 1970s, however, Latin America realized that this tourism product had some drawbacks: when a certain culture becomes a tourism resource, it has to be kept unchanged. In other words, it is necessary to freeze a society in time. In practice, this is an impossible task for governments because it means that a social group will have to be deprived of the latest technological advances for the recreation of the inhabitants from developed countries and for the benefit of some transnational tourism corporations. This is why, at the end of the 1960s, the countries resorted to so-called 'staged authenticity', even in remote areas.

Despite this reasoning, Peru tried to develop tourism within the framework of the UNESCO–Peru Cultural and Tourism Plan, known as the COPESCO project, which is now undergoing its second stage. Its aim is expanding agriculture, the base economy of the Cuzco-Puno region, and protecting the Inca archaeological sites with the assistance of experts from the United Nations Educational, Scientific and Cultural Organization

(UNESCO). Protection was focused on the Machu Pichu ruins, discovered by Hiram Bingham in 1911. A five-star hotel with a capacity of 200 beds was built there. In order to cater to the demands of extra regional tourism a series of facilities were built at Cuzco, the gateway to the ruins and the main tourism destination in the area. During the period 1985–90 the hotel sector grew by 113 per cent, which meant 80,000 new hotel rooms for international tourism. The latest tourism policies involve the development of seaside resorts in the north of Peru and the fostering of ecotourism, especially in the Manu Natural reserve and the Huascarn National Park. According to the World Tourism Organization (1992), 317,000 tourist visited Peru in 1991, which meant a US$53 million income (excluding transportation) for the country. In 1994, Peru was visited by 386,000 tourists (World Tourism Organization, 1996).

Guatemala, on the other hand, is seeking to get some benefit out of the World of the Mayas Project, which at last, after twenty-five years, is being implemented with the EC's technical support. This project, formerly called La Ruta Maya (the Mayan Route), aims at achieving a sustained tourism development in the countries involved. It comprises a 1500 miles long circuit which connects the different Mayan sites in Mexico, Guatemala, Honduras, Belize and El Salvador (Acerenza, 1991). However, there is still a long way to go before this project is fulfilled.

At present, with 537,000 international arrivals, Guatemala together with Mexico are the two countries that benefit most from this project, primarily because of their proximity to Cancun (Mexico), the seaside resort that serves as a starting point for excursions to the ruins.

Nature tourism

The concern about the deterioration of the environment grew deeper at the beginning of the 1970s. Ten years later this concern was reflected in the tourism activity in developing countries. Terms such as 'soft', 'sustained', 'green', 'responsible' or 'appropriate' came into fashion, while the share of the market that looked for 'undisturbed nature' as its vacation destination increased in the major generating countries. Gradually, a new international movement for sustainable development emerged, ecotourism.

Consequently, all Latin American countries lacking 'sun, sand and sea' decided to develop ecotourism in order to benefit from this 'ecological wave'.

Every country in the region has certain species of flora and fauna that cannot be found in industrialized countries. Costa Rica, however, had the largest number of them in its small territory and has eventually become *the* ecotourism destination in Latin America.

In the face of the fluctuating prices of their staple products, coffee and bananas, the Costa Rican government successfully devoted all its efforts to the development of a non-aggressive ecotourism product. According to Chacón (1991), 435,030 tourists arrived in Costa Rica in 1990, which meant a 15.7 per cent increase over the previous year, and a foreign currency income of $266 million. Assuming that the imported component of the tourism sector is 50 per cent, there was a net income of $133 million. Costa Rica had 6,000 beds to meet the needs of international tourism in 1990. The Costa Rican government entered into agreements with several important international and Spanish corporations in order to incorporate to the country's infrastructure 2,000 first class rooms (five stars) and 2,000 rooms in others categories. In 1994, the country was visited by 761,000 tourists.

The Amazon region is becoming the most important ecotourism product in South America. In this context, Brazil is the country making the greatest efforts to hold its position as the main extra-regional destination, in spite of the constant sensationalist press coverage it receives from the mass media of industrialized countries. The OAS has funded some feasibility studies related to the Amazon ecotourism project.

The Galapagos National Park (Ecuador), created in 1959, was already an important ecotourism destination before the term 'ecotourism' was coined. The islands, whose name derives from the giant turtles called Galapagos, began to be massively visited in 1970 when the first cruise ships arrived. The first plan for the management of the park was prepared between 1973 and 1974, and established the carrying capacity of the park at 12,000 visitors a year. As this figure was soon exceeded, the master plan was revised in 1985 and the new limit was set at 25,000 visitors per year. In 1990 the islands were visited by 45,000 people (Machlis and Costa, 1991).

A kind of tourism which fell within the category of what is currently called ecotourism was already a common practice in Bariloche, Argentina, at the turn of the century. The activity started when a national park was created and certain guidelines had to be followed in order to avoid deterioration of the environment.

The works carried out following the directions of the National Parks Administration to meet the tourism requirements created a high demand for outside labour. Two hundred workers were employed just during the pre-operational stage of the Llao Llao hotel. Eventually these workers stayed in Bariloche and began to work in tourism-related activities. The slow transformation from an agricultural and stock breeding economy into an economy orientated to the service sector had already begun.

During the 1937–8 season, 2,560 people arrived in the city while in the 1942–3 season, the figure increased to 10,900 (Eriksen, 1970). The number of foreign visitors, who came mainly from neighbouring countries and

from the United States, began to grow in the 1960s. The total number of
tourist arrivals increased from 45,400 in 1906 to 151,000 in 1967. In 1970,
Bariloche was visited by 234,259 tourists, and in 1985, by 422,757 tourists.
The city's population also showed a steep increase. In 1915, there were
1,000 inhabitants and by 1939, that figure had doubled. During the second half of this century, Bariloche was the city with the highest population growth between two censuses in the Patagonia region. In 1960 were
21,960 inhabitants; in 1988 the city had 81,130 inhabitants (Landoni, 1988).

Latin American tourism planning: successes and failures

Notwithstanding the large number of tourism developments that were
planned for Latin America, only a few have been carried out. The integrated seaside resorts in Mexico are the best example. The countries in
the region look up to Mexico as an example to be followed, and many of
them, such as the Dominican Republic and Costa Rica, are considering
the creation of an agency similar to FONATUR in order to succeed with
their own tourism undertakings.

Mexico's National Tourism Fund, FONATUR, was established in 1974
and had two priorities: consolidate already popular tourism centres and
to create new integrated tourism resorts (Schlüter, 1991b). The new agency
oversaw the granting of land reservations, established guidelines for the
use of loans, prepared the master plans for the development of the inte-
grally planned tourism resorts, and supervised, controlled and assessed
their operation.

The following are some of the reasons that explain why so many
development plans failed in the other Latin American countries:

1   They are the result of foreign initiatives and of large amounts of
    money available in the industrialized countries to be given as assist-
    ance to developing nations. Ever since John F. Kennedy's presidency,
    when the Peace Corps was born, it has been considered best to send
    'experts' and not money to developing nations, as the funds might
    otherwise not be used as allocated. Besides, this system offered an
    additional advantage: the money never left the developed country
    where the expert had his permanent address.

    Regardless of the expert's technical knowledge, they generally know
    little more about the country than what can be read in a travel guide.
    Furthermore, there are so many countries requiring this sort of assist-
    ance that the phenomenon of 'if it's Tuesday this must be Panama
    and if it's Wednesday it must be Zimbabwe' is often encountered.

The recipes to be applied do not offer many alternatives; if the country has beaches and a good climate, the option will be an integrated seaside resort; in all other cases it will be ecotourism.

2 With very few exceptions, the highest government officials in the tourism area are appointed for political reasons and their term in office is subject to the will of the person who appointed them. They are expected to provide political responses and not technical ones; thus, they consider it more important to sign an agreement than to carry out a project. Very often, technical assistance agreements are signed by the Ministers of Foreign Affairs of the countries involved, and the heads of the tourism areas learn of them once they have been signed.

3 The technical experts in the public administration are subordinated to the political authority and, despite a certain job stability, the technicians run the risk of being 'frozen' if they disagree with the official guidelines. For this reason, even constructive criticism is avoided.

Consequences of tourism developments

The economic consequences of international tourism are generally assessed in terms of the foreign currency income to a given country. In most cases, the countries state the gross income and avoid mentioning the public investment which has not been recovered with real income and which has become part of the country's foreign debt. To establish the exact amount of the economic benefits brought about by tourism in Latin America is not only a complex task, but the results may be misleading as well.

The countries that developed three Ss tourism resorts consider that they have been successful because the aims they wanted to achieve with such resorts have been reached: there was a population resettlement in non-productive areas, new jobs were created, and there was a process of economic growth which was of benefit to marginal areas. This can clearly be seen in Cancun (Mexico), a formerly small village with few inhabitants which in 1991 became an urban centre with 300,000 inhabitants (World Tourism Organization, 1991). Something similar happened in Puerto Plata (Dominican Republic), which concentrates 42 per cent of the total number of beds in the country and where 8,000 new jobs have been created (World Tourism Organization, 1991) in a previously underdeveloped area.

In a paper on employment in Mexico, Rodriguez Woog and Hiernaux Nicolas (1992) concluded that the four and five-star hotels generated 73 per cent of the jobs in the hotel industry, or 10 per cent of the direct jobs in tourism. They also found that those services related to the hotel sector such as restaurants, cafes and canteens, generated the highest relative number of jobs.

The job-creating power of tourism is assessed from the social and economic points of view in Latin America. In the economic field it has a multiplying effect on the economy of a country and prevents the income produced by international tourism from leaving the country.

However, the tourism activity very often attracts labour from other productive sectors, such as agriculture and fishing; in such cases these specific activities are abandoned in order to provide services. Bacal (1991) studied the phenomenon in Maceio, Brazil, where the fishermen rowed the tourists to the reefs during the high season. During the low season they spent long hours and even days trying to 'catch' a tourist wishing to do the trip. They did not return to their fishing activities because there was not enough demand to grant them a fair price for their catch.

Bariloche's population growth is explained by the fact that it became an attraction pole for individual workers who had previously worked in the farms on the Patagonia plateau, and very often, for their families too. Although the workers usually moved to the city for the tourism season only, most of them eventually settled there, and they either stayed with relatives or friends, or lived in small wooden houses in the city's southern suburbs (Landoni, 1988).

As regards the social aspect, tourism enables people to satisfy their basic and intellectual needs without depending on government subsidies or charity organizations. However, tourism brings native workers and tourists, who are also workers themselves, into close contact. As a consequence, the former find out that by doing the same job in an industrialized country they would have a better living standard. According to Esteve Secal (1983), the desire to imitate such a living standard leads the worker to consider the possibility of emigrating to the country where the tourists come from.

The task of assessing the socio-cultural impact of tourism is a very complex one because such an assessment is based on qualitative, not quantitative factors. It is also nearly impossible to study this impact in isolation, without considering the influence of the mass media (especially TV) which, together with missionaries, adventurers and government bureaucracy, always precede tourists (Schlüter, 1991b). Besides, the socio-cultural impact also depends on the degree of foreign influence to which the cultural group being studied has been exposed. Several surveys carried out in Argentina (Ferrari, 1992; Monedero Gálvez and Schlüter, 1986; Schlüter, 1984; Winter, 1991) have shown that closed communities, i.e. communities that adhere to their traditions and refuse to accept any changes, generally reject the idea of being visited by tourists. On the other hand, open communities, i.e. communities that foster all sorts of exchanges and want to get hold of new technologies, and those communities that benefit directly from the tourism activity, want to increase the tourist flow as much as possible, even at the expense of social, cultural or environmental damage.

In some integrated tourism resorts, a certain degree of resentment has been detected concerning the deep changes affecting the way of living. In Bahias de Huatulco, Mexico, Long (1991) found that some of the families who had been relocated in order to build vacation clubs and hotel complexes were filled with anger. She also stated that the local population was facing some problems owing to the increases in the price of the basic commodities and to the lack of job opportunities. Most jobs required the worker to have at least a good command of English, a language which they could not speak and which they would never have a chance to learn.

The kind of tourism which emphasizes the preservation of cultural and natural environment also brings about major changes. In Bariloche, Argentina, the farms in the surrounding area began to produce food supplies such as milk, cheese, butter, eggs and fruit. These supplies were then sold directly to the tourist, especially to campers. The small landowners frequently turned their facilities into restaurants and lodging houses. In other cases, however, they subdivided and sold part of their land in order to build housing facilities and camping sites for tourists. The unrestrained and speculative subdivision of land influenced the expansion of the city of Bariloche. This expansion, together with the mountain topography (30 per cent of the city is built on a mild slope of 25–27°) created an irregular settlement belt along the Nahuel Huapi Lake. For this reason, there are small neighbourhoods, sometimes made up of a few houses, that are scattered at long distances from the urban centre and that are not reached by the services rendered by the municipality. Consequently, the basic services are unequally rendered, the aesthetic appearance has been damaged and there has been a marked deterioration of the soil and forests.

The National Parks Administration is not the only agency that monitors the development of the area; several non-governmental agencies concerned with environmental protection have also been active in Bariloche since the 1960s. Nevertheless, the sewage is disposed of in the Nahuel Huapi lake, the drinking water is polluted, the forests are becoming smaller, and there is noise and air pollution (Mazzuchelli, 1991).

In 1985, Costa Rica became the ecotourism destination *per se*. Its approach was very successful as regards both the conservation aims and the tourism activity. Nevertheless, some problems soon arose due to the continuous arrival of tourists who, after visiting the virgin nature sites, requested the services usually provided to 'resort' tourists. To satisfy their requirements, a number of facilities were built. Eventually, these facilities gave rise to serious problems between the population and the chief national authorities, causing a lot of controversy because of the environmental pollution they produced.

In Costa Rica, contrary to what is usual in other Latin American countries, the local population is very environment-conscious. They fear that the lack of control regarding sewage treatment, lack of noise level limits for the engines of cruise ships and motor boats, and the large numbers of tourists who will visit the resorts, among other reasons, might cause such a deterioration in the environment that the tourism activity itself might be killed.

All this has given rise to heated arguments and has caused the local population to reject the projects that were being carried out. For the time being, the local population is expressing its opinion through the media and through decorated T-shirts. In Latin America, these are the most usual means of expression, unless the country is going through a pre-election period during which the candidates can express the people's opinions. After that period, there is only oblivion, for even after 150 years of independent life, the democracies in the region are not mature enough to ensure the fulfilment of the promises that have been made.

Conclusions

With few expectations, tourism in Latin America, as well as in the other developing countries, began to be used as a tool for development after the Second World War.

The process started with the application of a basic recipe, the three Ss, that met the requirements of the extra-regional market. This recipe, however, was only applied some years later owing to the lack of political stability in the region or to the fact that the governments did not consider tourism the only alternative to achieve their aims.

At the same time, a cultural product was being sold in the major markets. However, as it was not in great demand, it had to be supplemented with 'sun, sand and sea' or with ecotourism. In general terms, Latin America has not become a relevant destination for major tourism generating markets, but it has been successful in smaller scale projects in the regional market.

Contrary to what might be expected, the cultural product is the one that has been less affected by tourism. This is because the pre-Columbian civilizations have been exposed to foreign influence for over four centuries and have found their own methods to survive the various forms of domination.

The three Ss product has a positive aspect for the local population – the improvement of quality of life – but it has also given rise to some resentment on the part of that sector of the population that has been excluded from the benefits of development.

On the other hand, ecotourism, which must combine both perpetuation and use of natural resources, has generated some very negative reactions, as the local population knows that protecting a certain species (whether flora or fauna) is not enough. It is also necessary to take other general measures to protect the environment. Such measures should include some less romantic factors as sewage treatment and noise and air pollution control.

The future for tourism in Latin America will probably be brighter once the voters, and not the large national or international lobbies, have a more important role in national decision-making.

References

Acerenza, Miguel Angel (1991) La integracion de itinerarios para visitas a atractivos turisticos situados en paises limitrofes, islas y subregiones, y mejoramiento de atractivos turisticos especificos. Paper presented at the XVI Inter American Congress of Tourism, Panama

Alvarez Valdés, Jesus (1991) desarrollo turistico de Cuba. In *Desarrollo Turistico de América Latina*, (ed. CESTUR), CESTUR, Mexico, pp. 67–80

Aquino, Luis Felipe (1991) Desarrollo turistico de la República Dominicana. In *Desarrollo Turistico de América Latina*, (ed. CESTUR), CESTUR, Mexico, pp. 87–102

Bacal, Sarah (1991) El impacto del turismo en núcleos receptores de paises en desarrollo: efectos socioculturales, *Revista Latinoamericana de Turismo*, 1, 97–109

Chacón, Luis Manuel (1991) Desarrollo turistico de Costa Rica. In *Desarrollo Turistico de América Latina*, (ed. CESTUR), CESTUR, Mexico, pp. 31–34

Davies, Elaine (1997) El turismo como la salvacion de Cuba. In *Estudios y Perspectivas en Turismo*, 6, 7–16

Elías, Frank Jorge (1995) Dominican Republic. In *Tourism in Latin America*, Latinfinance Supplement, May

Eriksen, Wolfgang (1970) *Kolonization und Tourismus in Ostpatagonien*, Bonn, Ferd. Dumlers Verlag

Esteve Secal, Rafael (1983) *Turismo, democratización o Imperialismo?* University of Malaga

Ferrari, Olegario (1992) Isla Martin Garcia y el turismo: opiniones de los residentes, *Estudios y Perspectivas en Turismo*, 1, 15–25

Guadarrama Muñoz, Gerardo (1991) Desarrollo turistico de Mexico. In *Desarrollo Turistico en America Latina*, (ed. CESTUR) CESTUR, Mexico, pp. 7–29

Landoni, Marcela (1988) *Patagonia y . . . una forma especial de turismo*, CIET, Buenos Aires

Lizama Hernández, Carlos (1991) Desarrollo turistico de Costa Rica. In *Desarrollo Turistico de America Latina* (ed. CESTUR), CESTUR, Mexico, pp. 43–39

Long, Verónica H. (1991) Government–industry–community interaction in tourism development in Mexico. In *The Tourism Industry: An International Analysis* (ed. Sinclair, M.T. and M.J. Stabler), CAB, London

Machlis, Gary E. and Costa, Diana A. (1991) Little Darwins: a profile of visitors to the Galapagos Islands. Proceedings of the 22nd Annual Conference of The Travel and Tourism Research Association, Long Beach, California

Mazzuchelli, Sergio (1991) San Carlos de Bariloche: la problemática ambiental urbana, *Medio Ambiente y Urbanizacion*, **37**(9), 75–92

Monedero Gálvez, Fernando and Regina G. Schlüter (1986) *Receptividad de los residentes del Valle de Punilla frente al turismo*, CIET, Buenos Aires

Rodriguez Woog, Manuel and Hiernaux Nicolás, Daniel (1992) Turismo y absorción de la fuerza de trabajo: el caso Mexico, *Estudios y Perspectivas en Turismo*, **1**, 21–43

Schlüter, Regina G. (1984) *Percepción del residente frente al turismo en Puerto Madryn*, CIET, Buenos Aires

Schlüter, Regina G. (1991a) Latin American tourism supply: facing the extraregional market, *Tourism Management*, **13**, 221–8

Schlüter, Regina G. (1991b) *Social and cultural impacts of tourism plans and programs in Latin America*, Cahiers du Tourisme, Série CN 53, Centre des Hautes Etudes Touristiques, Aix-en-Provence, France

Soto Cordero, Salvador (1991) Desarrollo turistico de Puerto Rico. In *Desarrollo Turístico de America Latina* (ed. CESTUR), CESTUR, Mexico, pp. 81–6

Winter, Gabriel (1991) Receptividad de los residentes frente al turismo, *Revista Latinoamericana de Turismo*, **1**, 110–19

World Tourism Organization (1991) *Centros Turisticos Integrados (Resumen)*, WTO, Madrid

World Tourism Organization (1992) *Compendio de Estadisticas del Turismo 1986–1990*, WTO, Madrid

World Tourism Organization (1996) *Compendio de Estadisticas del Turismo*, 48th edn, WTO, Madrid

14 Tourism carrying capacity management issues

Peter W. Williams and Alison Gill

Introduction

Paralleling tourism's rapid expansion in recent years has come a concern for managing its future growth and impacts. Tourism like other economic enterprises is well recognized as an agent of change. When managed properly, it has the potential of being a relatively low user of resources and a sustainable industry. When left to expand in an unbridled fashion, it has the capability of developing beyond sustainable economic, social, ecological and political limits. Central to this issue of tourism's growth has been the notion of carrying capacity management. Along with recent thinking on sustainable development, as well as appropriate and low impact tourism, the concept of carrying capacity management suggests an approach to tourism which permits growth within acceptable limits. Consequently, it is not surprising that people intuitively support the concept of carrying capacity in tourism, even though they may not fully appreciate what it entails from a management perspective.

Despite its seemingly clear and rational intent, the concept of carrying capacity as a management tool creates ongoing controversy. On the one hand, it appeals to a recognized need to limit and control tourism which may threaten the sustained use of limited resources. Simultaneously, it runs at odds with other desires for maximizing opportunities for growth, and the benefits associated with increased visitor use.

This chapter discusses the concept and application of carrying capacity in a tourism growth management context. In particular, it describes the conceptual foundations upon which most carrying capacity management approaches have been based; explores the potential use of these principles in a tourism context; and then suggests an approach for dealing with tourism related growth management issues.

Table 14.1   Sample tourism carrying capacity indicators

Threshold type	Examples
Volume	Peak, hourly, daily, weekly, yearly volumes of various types of visitors (e.g. bed nights, visits, visitor days, etc.)
Density	Number of persons/hectare for different activities at different locations (e.g. visitors/hectare of beach, tourists/sq. metre of restaurant/shop space, etc.)
Market mix	Number of visitor units relative to resident units (e.g. visitors/resident population, visitor bed units/resident bed units, visitor utilization of public facilities/resident utilization of public facilities)

Tourism carrying capacity management issues and concepts

Varying perspectives on carrying capacity as a tourism management tool exist. In its most traditional sense, the concept refers to the maximum number of tourists or tourist use that can be accommodated within a specified geographic destination (O'Reilly, 1986). As such, it conjures up images of a specified 'limit', 'ceiling', or 'threshold' which tourism development should not exceed. Indeed, the literature is filled with carrying capacity indicators which describe such benchmarks in volume, density or market-mix terms (Table 14.1).

Difficulties with these numerical carrying capacity indicators arise when efforts are made to link them directly to the management of specific tourism impacts. As with the case in recreation contexts, little evidence exists to suggest that by simply lowering or raising a specific carrying capacity standard, predictable changes in an area's ability to handle tourist use will occur. Instead, the key appears to lie in how change is managed.

An environmentally-based perspective suggests that carrying capacity management involves maintaining a balance between physical/environmental and visitor experiences. Carrying capacity in this context refers 'to the maximum number of people who can use a site without an unacceptable alteration in the physical environment, and without an unacceptable decline in the quality of the experience gained by visitors' (Mathieson and Wall, 1982: 21). This implies some prior designation of conditions upon which unacceptable levels of tourism impact can be judged.

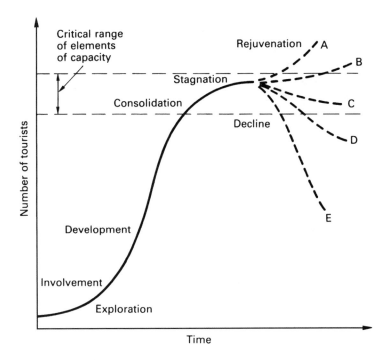

Figure 14.1   A tourism area cycle of evolution

Source: Butler, 1980: 7

For others, tourism carrying capacity is market driven (Plog, 1991; Butler, 1980). Critical carrying capacity thresholds appear to occur when tourist numbers approach levels which strain the capability of the destination to provide quality tourist experiences (Figure 14.1). Key indicators of encroachment upon these capacity ceilings are related to identifiable decreases in market demand. For any number of physical, economic, social, environmental, psychological or political reasons, tourists begin to display apathy towards the destination. While many factors may trigger slumps in market demand for a tourism area, it is generally assumed that desired conditions are exceeded when actual declines in visitor demand occur. As encroachment on these standards occurs, action in the form of direct and/or indirect management strategies must be implemented. Depending upon the desired conditions established by the community, actions may be taken to expand the ability to absorb tourism and rejuvenate visitor interest in the destination; or conversely constrain the detrimental dimensions of tourism activity so as to reduce tourism's effects to more appropriate levels.

A community based perspective suggests that carrying capacity concerns a destination area's capability to absorb tourism before negative

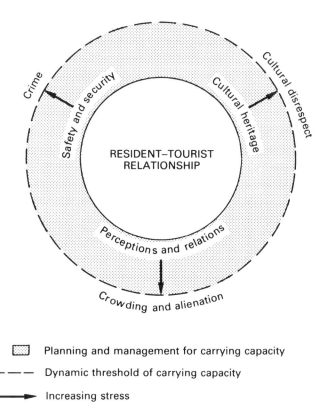

Figure 14.2 within the diagram contains the following labels:

Crime

Safety and security

Cultural heritage

Cultural disrespect

RESIDENT–TOURIST RELATIONSHIP

Perceptions and relations

Crowding and alienation

▨ Planning and management for carrying capacity

— — — Dynamic threshold of carrying capacity

——▶ Increasing stress

Figure 14.2 Model: Socio-psychological variables
Source: Hawkins, 1987

effects are felt by the community (Doxey, 1975; D'Amore, 1983). Levels at which these impact standards are established can be based on values determined by the community on the basis of how they perceive the effects of tourism (Figure 14.2). This approach to carrying capacity management requires considerable consensus building amongst community stakeholders (e.g. residents, developers, operators, government) to determine the desired conditions for a destination area, and how can tourism be managed most effectively towards that end.

The desired conditions may change over time and in response to different planning and management approaches (Martin and Uysal, 1990). For example, an increase in the size of the police force (i.e. regulation) might assist in maintaining a safe community even with an increase in tourist numbers. In a similar fashion, an interpretive centre (i.e. education/awareness) might assist in expanding an area's ability to manage tourism's potential impact on local cultural heritage resources.

While the preceding perspectives carry their own particular biases, they all base their rationales on four essential assumptions. They are as follows:

- tourism in its various forms is a catalyst for change, and brings with it the potential for economic, social and environmental benefits and costs;
- desired conditions can be identified for tourism, beyond which tourism is not sustainable for local populations, visitors, or both;
- desired conditions are not fixed, but vary geographically and temporally depending upon local economic, social, political, and environmental circumstances, as well as the understanding of tourism's influence upon local conditions;
- management strategies can be established and implemented that are capable of controlling the rate and direction of change/impact introduced by tourism, in keeping with desired conditions.

New directions in tourism carrying capacity management

While merits to the concept of tourism carrying capacity exist, its traditional focus on attempting to determine explicit use limits have made it difficult to use in a management context. There appears to be too many complex and interrelated limiting factors that hamper its use (Figure 14.3). However, dimensions of carrying capacity research that focus on establishing desired conditions or outcomes appear to have practical value for the management of tourism. This is particularly the case if they can be incorporated into broader planning processes associated with sustainable development and growth management.

When applied within planning systems which focus on managing for desirable and acceptable change, some carrying capacity processes offer the potential of guiding the degree, rate and direction of change that occurs. Knowledge of the consequences of exceeding desired impacts can be used to direct management policies and practices in keeping with a more sustainable tourism. This implies the development of locally based management guidelines that support sustainable forms of tourism and which emphasize:

- development that reflects architectural character and style sensitive to a destination area's heritage and environment;
- preservation, protection and enhancement of the quality of local resources;

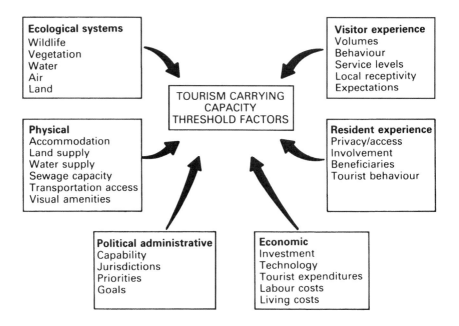

Figure 14.3   Tourism carrying capacity limiting factors

- development of visitor services that enhance local heritage and environmental resources;
- growth that improves the quality of life for the local community (Pigram, 1990).

Systems management

In tourism carrying capacity management situations, there are frequently several groups with often divergent views to be considered. They include tourists, developers, local residents, existing and proposed businesses, and the public agencies responsible for managing the environment within which all groups must operate. Depending on the specific circumstances of each place, such as stage of tourism development, community economic conditions, or past tourist-resident encounters, the needs of one group may take precedent over those of the others in carrying capacity management decisions. It is not uncommon, for example, to see the needs of the tourist take priority over the desires of community residents during early stages of tourist development. Indeed, if communities seek to encourage and accelerate the development of the tourist infrastructure, then the goals of the developers, who seek to maximize financial return on their investments, are often met. However, while in the short-term this helps stimulate growth, long-term sustainability of the tourism industry may suffer if the quality of life of residents who require afford-able housing, schools and community facilities is not adequately ad-dressed. As tourist development becomes established, the nature of the typical resident and the tourist may change, and once most of the tour-ism infrastructure is in place, the role of the developer diminishes. This constant change is what makes the establishment of long-term capacity limits a particularly challenging task.

In a systems management context, carrying capacity refers to desired conditions which best meets the goals of the area being managed. While sensitively managing an area's unique natural and cultural resources is frequently central to a destination's competitive advantage in the tour-ism marketplace, the resource base does not determine carrying capacity. Rather it is a function of the management goals and objectives estab-lished by the community. If the main objective is to stabilize population growth patterns in a community, tourism's capacity to contribute to that objective becomes the key management concern (Table 14.2). Indicators of population stabilization might include changes in migration levels or age and gender structure. If job creation is a major objective, then indica-tors of the types of employment change become the measure of tourism impact. The establishment of goals and objectives therefore determines which indicators of change are relevant and require monitoring.

General goals give broad direction to the planning and management conditions desired. Objectives offer more precise statements of the mecha-nisms by which the desired conditions are achieved. A general goal might be to manage the rate and quality of development in order to achieve and maintain a diversified destination community economy. Objectives associated with this might include monitoring manufacturing and tour-ism development to determine whether an appropriate balance between the two land uses is being maintained, and managing residential reserve areas in an attempt to ensure that employee housing supply keeps pace with this demand.

A suggested systems approach to incorporating desired destination community conditions into management practices involves:

- developing tourism goals and objectives which mesh smoothly with the broader comprehensive plan for a region and/or destination;
- creating a set of performance indicators reflecting the objectives of tourism development;
- implementing management strategies which direct tourism toward the achievement of the stated goals and objectives;
- monitoring the performance of tourism development with respect to these indicators;
- evaluating the effectiveness of the management strategies in influenc-ing the performance of tourism with respect to these indicators; and

Table 14.2 Examples of community management based indicators of tourism impact

Community management objective	Indicators of impact
Population stabilization	Out-migration levels In-migration levels Age/gender structure
Employment increases	Direct job creation Indirect job creation Employment levels Job retention levels Job displacement levels Job satisfaction
Income increases	Person/household income levels Inflation levels Tax revenue levels Beneficiaries
Community viability enhancement	Infrastructure levels Public service levels Housing availability Employee housing Availability Resident attitudes
Welfare/social integration improvement	Health/social service access Services distribution Recreation activity access
Cultural enhancement	Cultural facility access Cultural event frequency Commercialization
Conservation improvement	Pollution levels Conservation practices Cultural feature damage Environmental maintenance costs
Amenity enhancement	Levels of crowding density Private access Visual amenity satisfaction

Source: Adapted from Getz, 1982.

- developing new tactics for tourism management based upon the monitored effectiveness of these techniques (Getz, 1982).

While similar in focus to carrying capacity management processes described earlier in this chapter, the systems approach offers a distinct perspective in that it:

- involves no identification of an ultimate limit to the number of visitors;
- relates tourism growth and development to its effect on destination goals and objectives;
- employs indicators of desired conditions to trigger either the implementation or adjustment to growth management strategies; and
- reviews and modifies goal and objective priorities as destination circumstances change.

Growth management planning

In principle, tourism carrying capacity issues can be incorporated into the comprehensive planning agenda of most tourism destinations. Key to the success of such agendas are growth management programmes. Based upon a destination's ability to provide urban services and the vision of what growth rates should be encouraged, growth management plans offer a 'guidance system' to implement that vision (Schiffman, 1989). Growth management decision guides include policy statements, capital budgets and improvement programmes. Action instruments to support identified programmes encompass public investment strategies, land-use regulations, and fiscal incentives or disincentives (Table 14.3). They go beyond strictly land-use planning by incorporating other control mechanisms influencing tourism and other activities within the destination. Research in well-established tourism destinations suggests that growth management planning programmes can be effective management tools in addressing tourism impact issues. However, there appear to be few comprehensive applications of these approaches.

While many tourism-dependent communities (e.g. Stowe, Vermont; Lake Tahoe, California; Park City, Utah in the United States; Languedoc-Rousillon, France; S'Agaro, Spain; Cancun, Mexico; Niagara-on-the-Lake, Ontario, Canada) exhibit components of growth management approaches, these techniques are most fully developed in two contemporary tourism destinations. Both Aspen/Pitkin County, Colorado in the United States and Whistler, British Columbia in Canada exhibit what may be considered 'state of the art' growth management planning in North American tourism settings (Gill and Williams, 1994). While growth management approaches were introduced in these communities in response to tourism impact control problems largely associated with rapid growth during the

Table 14.3 Growth management tools and techniques

Growth management tools	Growth management techniques
1 Policy and assessment	By-law requirements Comprehensive plans Regional plans Fair share low-cost housing Information services Employment/resident balances
2 Impact analyses	Fiscal impact Social impact Cost-benefit analysis Environmental impact Carrying capacity analysis
3 Regulatory systems 3.1 Environmental controls	Environmentally sensitive areas Special planning areas Pollution controls
3.2 Development rights transfers	Development rates and location
3.3 Restrictive covenants	Concession in landowners Initial land title documents
3.4 Zoning uses	Conventional zoning Conditional zoning Planned unit development Special permits (e.g. historic districts)
3.5 Other zoning tools	Minimum floor areas/lot sizes Height restrictions Population density Performance standards Geographical constraints
3.6 Quota systems	Development/building permits Utility connections
3.7 Short-term tools	Moratoria Creative foot-dragging Negotiation and permit review Off-site levy charges
4 Capital expenditures	Land banking Development rights purchases Capital programming
5 Revenue systems 5.1 Exactions	Land/money dedications Capital facility dedication Low/moderate income housing allocations
5.2 Tax and fee systems	Urban and rural service areas Utility fees User rates Local improvement areas Development districts

Source: Schiffman, 1989.

early stages of expansion, the strategies and mechanisms employed have proven to have real merit over the long run. In keeping with the guidance system approach, both communities have introduced strategic visioning processes (Ritchie, 1993), which Jamal and Getz (1997) consider to be one essential factor in quality destination management. These processes are used to establish guideposts for determining priorities. These communities have also introduced policies and supporting instruments in the form of regulatory, capital expenditure and investment, as well as fiscal growth management programmes. In essence they represent tourism carrying capacity control mechanisms.

Key elements of growth management in tourism settings

In tourist environments, there are distinctive features which must be considered in growth management. These include the diversity of stakeholders; the evolutionary stage of the tourist community; and the critical importance of maintaining a high quality resource base. Further, there is a need for constant adjustments to meet the needs of a changing environment. What strategies are implemented typically represent the meshing of political and social requirements with technical and administrative realities (Pigram, 1990).

Fundamental to any growth management approach is the creation of a database to monitor change and inform decisions. The data available in most tourist destinations is inadequate and incomplete. Tools such as environmental management systems (EMS) and environmental auditing are emerging techniques which address such inadequacies in environmental monitoring (Williams, 1996) although they are not as yet widely used (Hunter and Green, 1995). At a more comprehensive level of monitoring in which economic, social and environmental indicators of change are tracked, there are even fewer examples. Whistler, BC, has however recently implemented a comprehensive community and resort monitoring programme, which since 1994 (Gill, 1997), has been evolving to cover a broad range of indicators (Table 14.4). The stated objectives of the programme are to:

- measure important changes in the community, the resort and the environment;
- describe the implications of these changes;
- set standards for acceptable ranges for important indicators;
- provide information that will help guide future planning regarding size and the nature of the community and the resort;

Table 14.4 Indicators used in the Whistler 1996 Annual Community and Resort Monitoring Program

Development indicators
- inventory of residential development by type
- inventory of commercial development
- inventory of hotel accommodation
- remaining development capacity by type and area
- construction activity (inc. renovations)

Environmental indicators
- weather and snow statistics
- air quality
- vegetation cover
- fish and wildlife counts
- lake and river quality
- drinking water quality
- visual environment
- ambient noise levels
- old growth forest cover
- recreational lands

Market indicators
- skier volumes (downhill, cross-country)
- summer mountain visitor volumes
- conference delegate days
- golf course rounds of play
- other visitor activites (e.g. rafting, touring)
- profile of residential unit purchasers
- housing market indicators, esp. affordable housing
- hotel occupancy and average room rates
- property tax rates
- business indicators (e.g. licences, bankruptcies)

Satisfaction indicators
- resident satisfaction
- visitor satisfaction

Social indicators
- population (inc. age, family type, income, sex)
- school enrolment
- health data
- social agency statistics
- unemployment
- crime statistics, by type
- adult education opportunities and enrolments

Community facilities and infrastructure
- usage of community and recreation facilities
- revenues from community facilities
- remaining water system capacity
- remaining sewer system capacity
- wastewater effluent quality and volume
- solid waste and recycling volumes and landfill status
- energy consumption
- bike trails (length of trails, usage)
- provincial park and recreation site usage
- fire and other emergency calls
- library use
- museum visitations

Transportation indicators
- Highway 99 capacity and volumes
- Duffy Lake Road volumes
- transit system use and revenues
- bus line ridership
- aircraft movements
- number of licensed vehicles
- number of rail passengers
- number of parking stalls

Source: Resort Municipality of Whistler, 1996

- provide information that will help refine development regulations and municipal by-laws;
- identify possible needs for changes to municipal policy or the official community plan, which governs land use and development;
- provide information that will help refine the capital budget and on-going programmes and to respond to changing community needs and priorities;
- help council decide whether to approve development beyond the committed level and, if so, under what conditions;
- help other organizations within the community respond to changing needs and priorities (Resort Municipality of Whistler, 1996).

To achieve these goals a broad array of indicators must be collected. While some data are readily accessible other data require the establishment of new data collection instruments such as attitudinal surveys.

In order to fully utilize such data community involvement in establishing desirable conditions is perhaps the single most important element of growth management. Developing appropriate mechanisms to incorporate divergent views is critical for successfully establishing appropriate resident/visitor relationships. A basic distinction can be made between residents and visitors, but in reality there are much finer distinctions with respect to attitudinal differences towards development. In many tourist towns, there is a significant second-home resident population as well as seasonal employees. Each of these resident groups has very different needs in terms of housing and service amenities. While input into the planning process from permanent residents can be accomplished through traditional means such as public meetings, incorporating the viewpoints of these other community groups is more problematic. Alternative mechanisms, such as more informal small group meetings have been used in some instances (e.g. Whistler, BC and Park City, Utah). In conjunction with this process, active community information and publicity programmes (e.g. via radio talk shows, newsletters etc.) are often necessary to ensure that the perspectives of more transient and/or recent residents of the community can be incorporated into the growth management process. In Whistler, as part of the monitoring programme, an annual town hall meeting is held to allow community members to discuss the results of the programme and consider what if any additional development is appropriate in the best interests of the community and the resort.

In addition to residents' attitudes, it is also important to conduct surveys of visitors in order to understand why they have decided to visit the destination and how well their expectations are being met; and, what can be done to make their stays more enjoyable. Maintaining a balance between the needs of tourists and those of all residents is critical. As many residents of tourist towns choose to live there because of perceived life style and amenity factors, programmes designed to allow local use of tourist focused attractions, facilities and services through more favourable resident pricing structures can be employed to reduce friction between residents and visitors.

A second feature which must be considered is the stage of development of the destination. Resort communities are extremely dynamic in character. In the early phases of development, a high investment in tourist facilities and infrastructure is necessary to reach a 'critical mass' of attractions, services, facilities and visitors in order that the destination can sustain a tourism economy. Unfortunately, tourism demand is frequently unpredictable and subject to such problems as seasonality and aggressive competition. Development activities often entail considerable investment risk. Consequently, encouraging investment is often the primary objective in the early stages of development and destinations have often compromised the needs of the resident community to achieve this. While in the short-term this seems an appropriate course of action, there may be negative repercussions at a later date. Examples of this can be found in most tourism towns that have evolved without an employee housing policy. While the cost of providing employee housing acts as a disincentive to early investors, failure to do so has created serious problems in many communities once land values have increased (i.e. developers and local businesses have frequently been required to pay disproportionately high rates to help rectify employee housing shortages).

Many tourism regions are resource-dependent. Maintaining the quality of their resources (natural and cultural) is critical to the continued success of their tourism industry. As a consequence, resource management standards and guidelines are frequently higher than those necessary in other settings. For instance, the capability of the sewage and water systems must be able to meet the peak loadings which characterize service use in many tourist communities. Similarly building and landscape design guidelines frequently reflect more stringent aesthetic goals. Identification of the desired conditions to be associated with an area's critical tourism resources is also important in establishing priorities in the event of conflicting goals. For example, in the Lake Tahoe region of California and Nevada, highest priority is given to the lake water clarity and quality, as it is the resort's most essential tourist resource. Establishing desired conditions for the resource base is an essential step in growth management. This includes consideration of natural, cultural and scenic resources in surrounding areas which may not necessarily lie within a municipality's borders, but still affect the overall quality of the area. It is important to decide how residents and visitors feel about the desired quality of such resources prior to determining what kind of management will be necessary.

Conclusions

Research suggests that traditional approaches to carrying capacity management have met with limited success in practical settings. This situation exists primarily because of:

- unrealistic expectations (i.e. a technique exists which can provide a magic number which identifies 'how much is too much');
- untenable assumptions (i.e. a direct relationship between tourism use and impact exists);
- inappropriate value judgements (i.e. conflicts between the views of 'experts' as opposed to destination stakeholders concerning what conditions are appropriate for an area);
- insufficient legal support (i.e. the lack of a formally recognized institutional process to ensure that management objectives are achieved).

Given the inability of traditional carrying capacity management techniques to overcome these barriers, an alternative approach is suggested. Its focus shifts from past concerns over establishing use limits, to issues of identifying environmental, social and economic conditions desired by a community, and the creation of growth management strategies for managing tourism's carrying capacity challenges.

References

Butler, R.W. (1980) The Concept of a Tourist Area Cycle of Evolution: Implications for Management of Resources, *The Canadian Geographer*, **14**(1), 5–12

D'Amore, L.J. (1983) Guidelines to Planning in Harmony with the Host Community. In *Tourism in Canada: Selected Issues and Options* (ed. Peter E. Murphy) Victoria, BC: University of Victoria

Doxey, G. (1975) *A Causation Theory of Visitor–Resident Irritants: Methodology and Research Inferences*, Travel and Tourism Research Association Annual Conference. San Diego, CA: TTRA, pp. 195–198

Getz, D. (1982) A Rationale and Methodology for Assessing Capacity to Absorb Tourism, *Ontario Geography*, No. 19, 92–101

Gill, A.M. (1997) Competition and the resort community. In *Quality Management in Urban Tourism* (ed. Peter E. Murphy) Wiley, Chichester

Gill, A.M. and Williams, P.W. (1994) Managing growth in mountain tourism communities, *Tourism Management*, **15**(3), 212–220

Hawkins, A.E. (1987) A Carrying Capacity Model for Resort Planning and Management with Preliminary Application to Whistler, Canada. Unpublished Master of Natural Resources Management Research Project. Burnaby, BC: Simon Fraser University

Hunter, C. and Green, H. (1995) *Tourism and the Environment: A Sustainable Relationship*, Routledge, London

Jamal, T.B. and Getz, D. (1997) 'Visioning' for sustainable tourism development: community-based collaborations. In *Quality Management in Urban Tourism* (ed. Peter E. Murphy) Wiley, Chichester

Martin, B.S. and Uysal, M. (1990) An Examination of the Relationship Between Carrying Capacity and the Tourism Lifecycle: Management and Policy Implications, *Journal of Environmental Management*, **31**(4), 327–333

Mathieson, A. and Wall, G. (1982) *Tourism: Economic, Physical and Social Impacts*, Essex, UK: Longman.

O'Reilly, A.M. (1986) Tourism Carrying Capacity, *Tourism Management*, **7**(4), 254–158

Pigram, J.J. (1990) Sustainable Tourism – Policy Considerations, *Journal of Tourism Studies*, **1**(2), 2–8

Plog, S.C. (1991) Leisure Travel: Making It a Growth Market . . . Again! John Wiley and Sons, New York

Resort Municipality of Whistler (1996) Annual Community and Resort Monitoring Program. Whistler, B.C.: Resort Municipality of Whistler

Ritchie, J.R.B. (1993) Crafting a destination vision: Putting the concept of resident responsive tourism into practice, *Tourism Management*, **15**(5), 358–369

Schiffman, I. (1989) *Alternative Techniques for Managing Growth*, Berkely, California: Institute of Government Studies, University of California at Berkeley

Williams, P.W. (1996) Sustainable Alpine tourism development: Towards a self-improvement approach. In *Alpine Tourism. Sustainability: Reconsidered and Redesigned* (ed. K. Weiermair). Conference proceedings, May 1996, ITS Series: Studies in Tourism and Service Industry, Innsbruck: University of Innsbruck

Part Four

Places and Products:
Marketing and Consumer Issues

The provision of high-quality, creative, relevant and meaningful experiences are the most critical challenge facing the visitor industry today. Consumer perceptions concerning the quality of their own individual tourism experiences and the actual quality of the tourist resource are central issues in tourism management. Leisure destinations offer products that have gotten stale and too commercial, resulting in declines in tourist arrivals. In addition, all tourism organizations are in the service business, but only those organizations that focus on service excellence as the cornerstone of their operations will be sustained.

Plog (Chapter 15) describes why tourist destinations that were once highly popular appear to self-destruct over time. He questions why the tourism industry has escaped criticism for its destruction of culture and the environment. He explores the natural environment and unique characteristics of an area in order to understand a number of important environmental concepts and ideas. One such concept proposed is that a maximum number of visitors an area can accommodate exists for most resorts and destinations. Unfortunately, most planners and developers typically allow destination areas to exceed the maximum beneficial size.

Culture is destroyed by forcing certain 'native' people to give up part of their own identity and adopt uniform rules of behaviour around tourists. The environment is destroyed by overdevelopment and subsequent overuse of tourism resources. Specific examples of environmental degradation are cited including air and water pollution as well as loss of animal and fish habitat, thereby interrupting the food chain.

Common action by all parties involved in tourism is needed in order to halt the deterioration of tourism resources. The author proposes that we need to plan more, control more, and listen more to the needs not only of the traveller, but more importantly to the requirements of residents who are impacted negatively by poorly planned or ineffectively managed tourist destinations. Finally, he suggests that more education stressing the benefits of ecological sensitivity take place so that visitors will demand a higher quality of experience, or they will not return.

Taylor (Chapter 16) questions the overemphasis or principal concern tourism has placed on consumption rather than on the consumer. Little systematic attention has been directed towards gaining a greater understanding of the tourist and his participation patterns and travel habits. The concept of styles of travel may be useful in developing a body of knowledge about tourism consumers. Style of travel is defined as the way people perceive, organize and execute travel. Two important types of information are important when measuring styles of travel: the incidence of travel and the way people think about the travel they take.

The use of both travel incidence and travel style data can provide a greater understanding of international tourism, and when these two data sets are examined at the same time, the fact of change will be accompanied by the direction of change. The implications of such data should not be overlooked as a means of improving knowledge of both the markets and the opportunities for increased consumer satisfaction.

Tourist typologies have primarily resulted from consumer segmentation marketing studies conducted during the 1970s which used among other variables, lifestyle criteria. According to **Mazanec, Zins** and **Dolnicar** (Chapter 17), the Eurostyles system is a multinational lifestyle typology which encompasses five principal dimensions of lifestyle which help constitute sixteen different lifestyle types. Individual styles, or so called socio-targets (groups of styles) contribute to the advancement of tourism market research and thereby make tourism marketing more effective.

Europanel, a group of fifteen European commercial market research institutes, produced lifestyle data originating from consumer panels in tourism generating countries. This lifestyle data was adopted by the Austrian National Tourist Office in order to determine the lifestyle and guest characteristics of travellers to Austria. It was shown to be of practical value in destination marketing, with some modifications which the chapter describes.

Faulkner (Chapter 18) suggests that since tourism demand is highly discretionary, a strategic approach to tourism marketing is essential for long-term effectiveness. The current international preoccupation with advertising among tourism promotion agencies may well be counter productive to sustained visitor growth and can progressively undermine any competitive tourism advantage currently enjoyed by a destination area.

Focusing on planning and development In Australia, the author emphasizes that the factors influencing demand for tourism are highly dynamic and he discusses a strategic approach to marketing Australian tourism as being essential to long-term effectiveness.

Finally, **Morgan** (Chapter 19) looks at the future of established seaside tourist resorts, especially those along the Mediterranean coast. He argues that most such resorts are homogeneous, and as such have begun to lose some of their appeal to the public, resulting in a loss of market share. As the decline stage in the product lifecycle concept nears, since they are no longer in favour with the travelling public, established resorts face the decision to either let their facilities die gradually, or to somehow rejuvenate these ageing resources. He considers the new markets open to established resorts, while warning of the ever-increasing, discriminating tourist.

The author provides a brief history of seaside resorts and describes the conditions that have led them to first be established, then become homogeneous. Changing economic and demographic factors as well as product maturity have influenced tourists' holiday decisions. The adoption curve is used to illustrate how such facilities have also fallen out of fashion since, as they no longer attract either innovators or allocentrics, the general public begin to look for other destination options.

Market dependence, distribution channel control, maintenance and enhancement of facility quality are guidelines presented for developing resorts. In addition, several strategies for resort survival are presented including: developing new markets and new products; changing from a static destination area to a touring centre; upgrading product quality; and, promoting a new image. Ultimately, the challenge for established resorts is to provide facilities and resources of a standard demanded by the international tourist market while developing and retaining their unique character.

15 Why destination preservation makes economic sense

Stanley C. Plog

Branch Ricky, the deceased but fabled long-time baseball executive of the former Brooklyn Dodgers, once gave the advice that a good manager should 'trade a player a year too early rather than a year too late.' In show biz, every major star lives by the premise that you should always 'leave 'em wanting more.' In other words, don't give too many encores or you will wear out the audience's excitement and enthusiasm to see you again.

Unfortunately, most leisure destinations in the world have not learned this simple truth. They offer a tourism product that gradually has become stale and too commercial over time because they have shown little concern about protecting the natural beauty or uniqueness of the area that originally attracted visitors. As a result, they face a steady decline in tourists and severe economic problems, not only now but at an accelerating rate in the future. Local citizens may not recognize this deterioration because it occurs so slowly, but visitors who have not returned for several years are struck by how much the entire experience has declined.

As we look to the future, conditions will get much worse before they get better, if that ever happens. Why such a negative assessment? It is based on a life-time of tourism research, and the frustrations this author feels in dealing with many developers and governmental agencies responsible for local tourism. Too many of them don't understand or care about the close relationship between tourism and the environment. As a result, the potentially positive contributions of tourism get submerged to the goal of unrestricted development which almost result in excessive commercialism of once beautiful areas. Enough's enough! Things have to change for everyone's benefit!

A personal history of leisure travel development

To understand the intensity of these feelings, a brief review of some personal history is necessary. The author's career in travel research began in 1967 after winning a study for a consortium of 16 airline and travel industry clients. It focused on how to get more people to travel by air. At the time, only 25 per cent of the US population had ever taken a trip in a commercial airliner. To fill all the seats that would come on line when large orders for jets were delivered, it was necessary to get more people to travel – for leisure. Business travellers comprised about four out of five air travellers then. Moreover that group itself followed the 80/20 rule, i.e., 20 per cent of the business travel market gave the airlines 80 per cent of their business. Thus, a few people did most of the flying.

The study results, based on extensive qualitative and quantitative research, changed the travel industry dramatically. To get more people up in the air, it recommended a number of programmes that are now industry standard, including:

- Off-season and off-peak discount fares to encourage leisure travellers to get out of their cars and into the air.
- 'Fly and drive' programmes.
- Greater emphasis on fully escorted tour programmes so that timid travellers could 'take the hand of an expert' in planning (and guiding) their trips.
- More packaging of travel for convenience and discounts (air, hotel and ground transfers combined into a 'package').
- An educational/promotional programme to inform travel prospects of the benefits of leisure travel (excitement, personal fulfilment, a lifetime of memories, a chance to bring families closer together, good educational experiences for adults and children).

What a change since the time of that study. Currently over 85 per cent of the population has been up in a commercial airliner, leisure flyers dominate the passenger mix (nearly 60 per cent of all passengers), escorted tours have grabbed major market share (about 30 per cent of transatlantic passengers on airlines during peak months), and packages have been the fastest growing segment of the market for several years. Further, projections from Plog Research's syndicated studies indicate that leisure travel will grow at more than double the rate of business travel for several years. So, tourism is where the action is. You can count on it to drive world economies. Travel and tourism is now the largest industry in the world.

Tourism's increasing negative impact

At the start of a career in tourism research, the author believed firmly that the industry offers multiple positive benefits to everyone involved.

What a glorious feeling for a researcher. Encouraging people to travel more results in long-lasting, pleasurable experiences for travellers, brings people of different cultures together to break down barriers that lead to misunderstandings and wars, and offers an economic boost to local economies. Unlike the manufacturing industry that typically requires massive investment and severe environmental destruction to develop and maintain a factory, tourism often can start on a small scale. Relatively little investment may be required since the infrastructure already in place can be utilized (highway, airports, lodging and restaurants), and a 'pay as you go' investment plan can be put into place to help future development. In other words, as tourism increases, build the hotels and shops to meet market demand. It seems like a win-win situation for all. Local businesses thrive, jobs are created, increased tax revenues fill the coffers of government agencies, and tourists also go home happy. How few times all of these mutual benefits can be realized in any other industry or occupation.

An old adage exists that tourism is the best industry possible because 'tourists take nothing but pictures and leave nothing but footprints'. The taking of pictures may still be okay, but the footprints are getting too heavy. The true benefits of tourism have to be called into question in far too many situations. Hawaii, a garden paradise, has lost too many of its unique species of flora and fauna because of the impact of resort development and the influx of tourists. The acid smog of Athens, caused by local traffic and a dramatic tourism increase, eats away at the Parthenon and other irreplaceable structures and statues of the Acropolis. An excessive amount of the world's delicate, picturesque and fragile environment has been destroyed as tourism has increased, and problems continue to compound. In short, unless more systematic planning controls and guides tourism development, its impact can create more problems than it solves. Everyone involved in tourism needs to recognize this fact, including local citizens, developers, travel providers and, most of all, government planners. Only with concerted effort by all of these groups, with the primary push coming from governmental agencies, will it be possible to reverse some of the damage that's been done and prevent future disasters. This statement is made after considerable thought and deliberation because the author generally believes that the least amount of governmental interference in people's lives is better. But, government has the role of working for the common good, and the common good is definitely at stake. It alone has the power to enforce decisions that can benefit most of the people most of the time.

To provide a new perspective, this chapter describes why destinations that once were popular seem to self-destruct before anyone attempts to turn the tide. A conceptual model points out why it is in everyone's best interests to control a destination's development so that it continues to attract the right kinds of tourists. These are the people who provide the highest revenue to a destination, and who also demand that it remain close to its pristine state. These travellers want to experience the natural beauty and uniqueness of a place. And they show their displeasure in an important way when they vote with their feet; they don't come back if a destination doesn't offer what they want. Even more significant, they tell others about their disappointing experiences. To understand why it's important to protect the natural environment and unique characteristics of a place, several related concepts and ideas must be reviewed.

The concept of venturesomeness

Although demographics continues to dominate travel research, it really has limited predictive power. Marketers at most travel companies try to target households that have annual incomes (US) above $60,000 (a focus of airlines), $80,000 (first class and luxury hotel chains), $100,000 (more distant foreign destinations), or even $125,000 (luxury cruise lines). But, within these income groupings, little commonality exists as to the types of vacations taken. Consider any neighbourhood street. By a demographer's definition, almost all characteristics are viewed similarly – house values vary within a narrow range, incomes are largely equal, family composition is similar, and comparable occupational categories exist (blue collar, or white collar, or professional). Yet, seldom can you find two households that have taken similar vacations in the past couple of years. The psychology of each family varies greatly and the pursuit of lifestyles results in different vacation patterns.

Psychographics, in contrast, provides a better way to understand these lifestyles and how they translate into travel patterns. And, it can help clarify the delicate nature of destination growth and decline.

In 1971, the author presented a paper on the concept of allocentrism/psychocentrism (Plog, 1971). Described in greater detail in the book, *Leisure Travel: Making it a Growth Market . . . Again!* (John Wiley & Sons, 1991), the concept has since been re-labelled as 'venturesomeness' to sound a bit more user-friendly in the author's consumer oriented book, *Vacation Places Rated* (Fielding Worldwide, 1995). Based on a considerable amount of research, and validated through independent studies, a brief description here will help set the stage for what follows.

Far more important than demographic characteristics in determining the best travellers are psychographics. These measure the personality and motivational characteristics of people. The concept has been used by Plog Research's travel clients to position or reposition destinations, introduce new destinations, determine appropriate advertising to attract

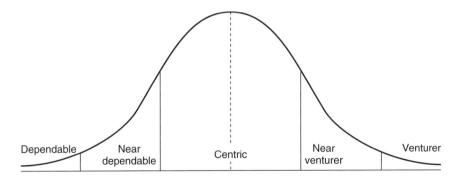

Figure 15.1 Distribution of psychographic segments
Source: Plog Research, Inc.

specific kinds of travellers, focus marketing programmes, introduce new travel products, and purposely move these products through a psychographic spectrum from the *venturers* to *near-venturers* or, ultimately, to *centrics*.

The dimension distributes relatively normally across the population. A small percentage (4 per cent) constitute pure *venturers* (previously labelled as allocentrics). At the opposite end are the pure *dependable* (formerly called psychocentrics), also a small percentage (2.5 per cent). A larger number can be categorized as near *venturers* or *dependables* (about 17 per cent in each case), and the majority of the population fits in the middle of the curve as *centrics* (previously titled mid-centrics) with leanings towards one direction or the other (about 60 per cent of the total). In fact, their distribution fits very nicely on a normal curve (see Figure 15.1). Knowing where a person fits on this curve tells a lot about his or her travel behaviour, including the mode of transportation they prefer, the places they will probably select to visit, the kinds of travel experiences they would like, and the advertising that most appeals to them.

Venturers

A venturer is an intellectual leader among his/her peers and, in fact, for much of what goes on in society. The most defining characteristic is that these individuals are very venturesome and constantly seek new experiences (including travel experiences). They have a high degree of self-confidence that leads to their willingness to be venturesome, tend to be relatively achievement oriented, and have a positive view about life and the experiences it offers. They also spend more of their income especially on travel. And, finally, they make decisions easily – about what to buy, where to go, and how to get there.

Ventureres are heavy air travel users because of its convenience, and they tend to seek out new destinations on a continuous basis rather than return to familiar places they have visited before. When they return home and speak about their experiences, they influence others to visit the places from which they have just returned. As a result, a new leisure spot in the world could be on the way to being discovered and will face all of the ensuing problems of rapid growth and, probably, too much commercialization. But, venturers are ideal targets for new tourism destinations because they don't require a great deal of infrastructure (quality hotels, restaurants, etc.) to keep them happy. They feel at ease staying at more native kinds of accommodations and eating local food. But, they help pump up the economy because they seek out and buy local arts and crafts and hire natives to take them to undiscovered places.

Dependables

Dependables, on the other hand, are followers. They are characterized by indecisiveness, a low level feeling of dread or anxiety that tends to pervade much of their lives because of this indecisiveness, and a desire to make very safe and comfortable choices. Thus, they primarily use name-brand products that have high identity in the marketplace because these are the 'safe' choices. They believe that these must be very good products because so many people use them. They travel less and they tend to select destinations that are very well known and over-developed. When they do travel, they're likely to go by car because it's a more familiar form of transportation. Once having 'discovered' a destination that they like, they are likely to return to it year after year, rather than seeking out new places.

Their favourite areas most often are the warm sun-'n'-fun spots, especially beach areas, that also offer an atmosphere similar to what they experience at home, i.e., lots of fast-food restaurants, movie theatres, arcade games. Although their travel patterns are predictable, they simply don't travel as much as their opposite counterparts, don't stay as long at a place, and don't spend as much on the trip.

The destination life cycle

Historically, destinations follow a predictable pattern from birth to maturity and on to old age. At each stage, the destination appeals to different types of travellers. There is an ideal 'age' for a destination, what might be called 'young adulthood', when it appeals to the right kind of travellers.

That point on the graph fits in the *near-venturer/centric* range. Trying to protect a destination from passing that magical point into a later state of decline is the combined job of local planners, developers and promotion people. Knowing the type of travellers that are attracted to a destination is also a way to categorize a place as a *venturer* in its feel, *near-venturer, centric, near-dependable,* or *dependable*.

A further look at the concept indicates what it means for destinations.

Venturers, as will be remembered, are the most interested in discovering new places to visit – the forgotten, the undiscovered, the passed over that time forgot. Requiring little in support services, such as hotels or restaurants, they relish experiencing anything that is unique, more natural and unspoiled. They return home with cherished memories of these experiences that they talk about with friends and relatives. Their enthusiastic descriptions of their recent trips convince their *near-venturer* acquaintances that they, too, should visit these wondrous places. Now, the process of destination growth has begun.

More travellers arrive as the word spreads, with a corresponding development of hotels. restaurants, and sightseeing activities to accommodate the new visitors. With the arrival of *near-venturers*, the destination has now been 'discovered' by jet-setters whose pleasures and social presence create world-wide attention in the press. The publicity typically is pervasive, persuasive, and almost always favourable. Travel writers, particularly, look for something new to write about, rather than re-hashing old stories about well-known destinations.

With the heavy amount of press coverage, the *centrics* with *venturer* leanings now experience their own sense of discovery of a place that still seems new and rising in popularity. They enjoy the new quality hotels, restaurants and shops that have been developed to appeal to this upscale clientele. Growth and development, however, continue unabated and the destination begins to take on a commercial and touristy look. More small and large businesses open to sell local crafts and native clothes, and the first of cheap-looking souvenir shops appear. The destination has reached its maximum potential, in terms of dollar volume spent by visitors. And, the true *venturers*, and even many *near-venturers*, have long since vanished. They now seek other undiscovered or off-the-beaten-path settings around the world.

In looking again at the psychographic curve, it can be seen that, until now, the destination has appealed to an ever larger slice of the population. But, once it passes the midpoint, in terms of the kinds of persons who are attracted to it, a state of decline sets in. It attracts ever smaller segments of the population, reversing the trend during its growth phase. The emergence of fast-food restaurants, movie theatres, video parlours, bars, and entertainment lounges means that a more *dependable* type of personality dominates the visitor group. *Venturers* don't want that kind of an environment. And, as was learned earlier, not only are fewer people visiting, they spend less and stay for shorter periods of time than their more *venturesome* counterparts.

The perfect positioning for most destinations is at a *near-venturer/slightly centric* point. It can draw from a broad distance across the middle of the curve of people who have heard about it and want to visit. Opinion leadership always comes from people who are somewhat more venturesome than those they influence. It does not happen in reverse. *Dependables* do not influence *venturers*. Thus, a destination positioned at the young adulthood stage can attract from a broad spectrum of potential visitors. A more mature destination has a much smaller market potential. Most people who serve on planning boards for destination areas fail to recognize the necessity of maintaining the unique character of their destination in order to preserve its original appeal. If a destination maintains its original charm and character, it will continue to attract the right kind of audience – *near-venturers* who spend more and continue to spread the good word about the place. An important point to emphasize: a destination's youth and maturity ('old age') refer to its ambience and feel, not chronological age. Some tourism spots with a long history can feel young, while relatively new places can age quickly.

If a developer understands these concepts, it would seem obvious that self-interest is served by maintaining and enhancing the beauty, charm and natural qualities that first attracted visitors. But, an interested observer can come up with a long list of resorts and once beautiful destinations that have lost their original appeal because of excessive commercial development. Examples include Miami Beach, several Mexican resort cities, various port cities in the Caribbean and the Mediterranean, etc. Each enjoyed a period of prosperity that led to heavy commercial development and, eventually, to a decline in tourism revenue. Now, low cost package trips dominate revenue sources at most of these resorts because higher paying independent travellers don't want what the destination currently offers. Once the decline sets in, it is very difficult to reverse because it often requires changing the mix of businesses and tearing down buildings to get rid of junk and make way for more open spaces. Getting the necessary votes and finding the capital to do that exceed the capabilities of most local governments. Rather, if destination planners and developers fully understand how they sow the seeds of an area's own destruction, they would do more to prevent such unfortunate endings. The reasons why this decline happens so frequently without anyone attempting to reverse the trend is the subject of the next section. A clearer explanation of the economic reasons for maintaining destinations in their more natural state will be explained. This review may help local leaders and planners understand how good planning is in their best interests, and also those of the communities they serve.

Predicting and charting destination decline

Jim Murray, the Pulitzer Prize winning sports writer of the *Los Angeles Times*, once commented on Bear Bryant, the deceased but long-time winning coach of the University of Alabama's Crimson Tide football team. Said Murray, 'The man has been a refugee from a steam iron for forty years.' The dishevelled look of Bear Bryant aptly describes too many places in the world today that live on past glories and previous reputations. But they are promoting themselves to an increasingly sophisticated and vigilant group of travellers who will no longer accept below standard leisure travel experiences.

As we look around the world, probably one out of five of destination areas that has been in existence for thirty years or more is in a noticeable state of decline. Some may still be experiencing growth in the number of tourist arrivals, but the seeds of their ultimate destruction have already been planted. When an area loses its charm, its uniqueness, and the qualities that originally attracted visitors, it loses its competitive position. One point of emphasis: *a maximum effective size in terms of the number of visitors a place can handle, exists for most resorts and destinations.* Unfortunately, the majority of developers and planners typically allow leisure destinations to exceed the most beneficial size. They know not what they are doing so, in some respects, they cannot be blamed for the consequences. But it does lead to the fact that a major restructuring and development of a large number of resorts around the world is required if these are to compete successfully in the future. Let's take a look at the theory behind what happens and why it is difficult to recognize the process of self destruction as it occurs.

The quality of experience curve

Figure 15.2 conceptually charts what happens to a typical new destination as it develops over time. The line on the graph plots the quality of experience that visitors to a new destination are likely to enjoy. After a destination is 'discovered' by *venturers*, the quality of the experience at the destination usually is enhanced for most travellers for a period of time. This could be several years or decades, depending upon how rapid is the growth and the degree of careful thought and planning that went into the master plan. The initial development of a good infrastructure system, the arrival of quality hotels and restaurants, and an early concern about protecting of the beauty of the environment usually contribute to the enhanced experiences that early visitors share. In other words,

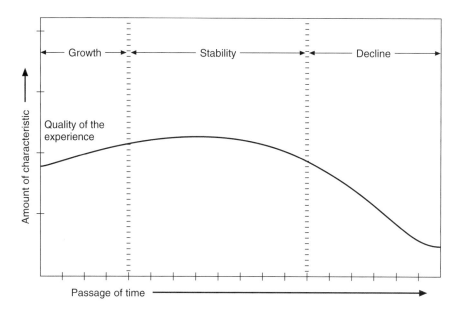

Figure 15.2 Quality of the experience

the natural attractiveness of the area typically can be improved with carefully controlled development. A beautiful hotel in a natural setting or a culturally unique festival that now receives attention from local planners often adds to the fulfilment experiences of guests. With quality infrastructure development during the early stages after discovery by *venturers*, the *near-venturers* begin to arrive. They want good hotels, but also demand that the natural feeling of the area be maintained. Consistent with what was presented earlier, the passage of time results in over-development and uncontrolled planning and the destination deteriorates from a number of objective points of view. High density, high rise modern structures now dominate low profile buildings that previously provided a more open feeling. Souvenir and trinket shops crowd out what was more native and natural. And fast-food restaurants and cheap entertainment centres now obliterate better dining establishments and more native kinds of entertainment. Success breeds its own destruction. The steady rise in the number of visitors up to this point usually leads to a wide assortment of new, uncontrolled development projects, particularly those that focus on what is more commercial and can produce a higher return per square foot of land use. Local leaders, always seeking higher tax revenue, usually will approve anything that seems like it can put more money into tax coffers. But all of this leads to a very rapid decline in the quality of experience for visitors who come to that area. The *venturer* and *near-venturers* have long since disappeared. They return home and do not

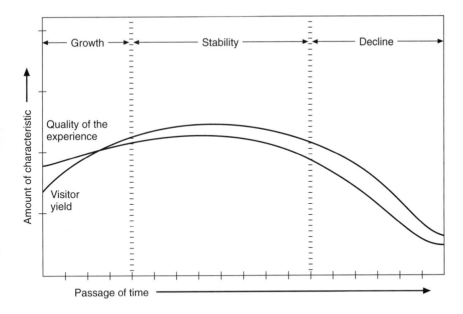

Figure 15.3 Visitor yield

forget that the destination they just visited did not live up to their expectations. They tell their friends and word begins to get around. The appeal now is limited to the more *centric* and *near-dependable* type of visitor.

The visitor yield curve

Figure 15.3 adds an overlay charting the rise and decline in yield per visitor. The new curve tends to parallel the quality of experience curve quite closely. High yield guests are desirable because they spend more per capita on a daily basis, and use more services that contribute tax revenue to public agencies. As was mentioned, the first visitors to any area, the *venturers*, typically are not the best visitors for any resort or destination. They have money to spend but would rather enjoy unique and natural settings by living as close to native style as possible. Instead of staying at major hotel chains, they seek the more simple lifestyles of local citizens, even if conditions are very primitive. The *near-venturers*, who follow them, however, are a destination planner's dream. They like what is new and exciting (defined as what is 'in'), have lots of money to spend, and like to select some of the best of what is available – hotels, restaurants, entertainment and sight-seeing. When they stop coming because of excessive commercialization they are replaced by *centrics* and

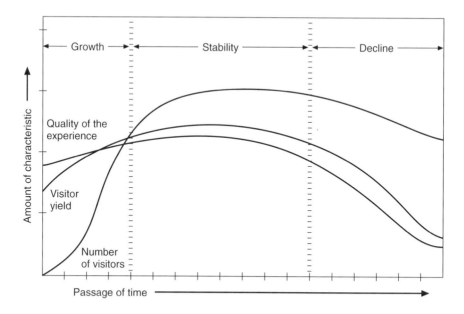

Figure 15.4 Number of visitors

near-dependables. As was indicated, *dependables* like to visit the most popular, well known, touristy spots because the very image of popularity
suggests to them that it must be a good place or it wouldn't attract so
many people. However, as will be remembered, *dependables* travel less
often than their *venturesome* counterparts, stay a fewer number of days,
and spend less on a per diem basis while they are there. Although they
are extraordinarily nice people, they are not ideal visitors for most
destinations. Thus, the quality of the guests has declined in a relatively
dramatic fashion.

The visitor density curve and the concept of image lag time

Figure 15.4 overlays the final curve. It indicates the number of guests
who come to a new destination and charts that growth – and decline –
over time. This curve indicates why destination areas may actually be in
a state of decline while they seem to be growing in popularity, and why
those persons most closely associated with the destination typically fail
to recognize what is happening.

It takes time for a positive image to develop for any product, service,
or destination and have its full impact. It also takes time for a negative

image to incubate and grow. And interestingly, *both can be growing in parallel for a period of time*. Thus, we find that the number of visitors can actually be increasing when, in fact, a resort has already started on a downward path in image formation among persons who have visited it. The lag in time between image development and decline accounts for this phenomenon. The good word continues to spread about what a great place it is to visit at the same time the new message has begun that it no longer offers the quality of experience it once had.

The closest parallel perhaps is to the all too typical history of new restaurants. When a great new restaurant opens, word gets out about its greatness, fabulous food, decor and service, and people begin to flock to its doors. It can seem like an overnight success. But, far too often, success leads to inattentiveness to the details that made the restaurant great. The food now may become overcooked or its 'presentation' is not as attractive. Service has become slow and inconsistent. And the decor becomes somewhat frayed at the edges and a bit dirty. Old guests have dropped it off of their list of favourite places and now seek out new dining establishments. Few will actually complain to the owner that the service or food no longer equal previous levels. They simply 'vote with their feet'. They don't return. A small number of diners may tell the owner about the decline in quality. But his reaction will typically will be, 'How can that be? Look how busy I am.' It's because the positive image build-up, to that point, has been greater than the negative build-up.

But reputations do catch up, and the negative word-of-mouth images will ultimately grow faster than the previous positive views. The number of diners begins to decline and, when that happens, it usually means the ultimate death for the restaurant. It will shut its doors. It's like throwing a pebble in a pond. The ways generated (positive views) spread in ever widening circles of influence. Throw in a second pebble (negative views), and the second set of waves ultimately take over the first waves. Very few restaurants are able to revive themselves after they have gone into a state of decline. New York catcher Yogi Berra said it best when he was asked about Toots Shor's, 'Oh, it's so crowded, nobody goes there anymore.' Yogi knew what he was talking about. Like other once great eating establishments, it also went out of business.

The downward slide

Destinations, however, are different. They cannot 'shut their doors.' The huge costs of developing hotels, nightclubs, restaurants, and the supporting infrastructure means that clever marketing types must figure out new ways to draw visitors. Lower the prices; put more discount packages together; bring in more wholesalers; pack more people into the place to create more revenue. So, the death of a destination may be very gradual and slow. But, the troublesome signs are easy to spot. Occupancy levels at hotels are on the decline. Rack rates at these properties soften and more discounting is evident. Per diem expenditures of visitors go down and the number of days for an average trip also falls off. Recognizing that something must be done to turn around the problem, new advertising campaigns are developed (usually after selecting a new agency because 'the old one simply had run out of ideas'). And, even more fundamental, packages now take an increasing share of the overall market. These bring in the lowest paying visitors possible. The pressure everywhere is on low cost. When complete packages, as with fully escorted tours, reach 30 per cent or more of the total number of guests at a destination, it usually means that an area currently is facing some problems that will become more severe and noticeable over time.

In spite of all efforts to stem the tide, however, the number of persons who visit the area will also gradually decline over time – regardless of the amount of energy put into reversing this slide. And another problem becomes evident. Since property values have been rising rapidly during the period of growth, each new development project costs more than the one previous to it. As a result, the amount of leveraging necessary to complete a deal typically increases. Thus, with the gradual decline in occupancy levels, rack rates, and number of visitors, projects can go into bankruptcy even while a destination seems packed with people. Low yield guests simply do not pay their way. A situation of disrepair and poor upkeep at properties happens more quickly than ever before because funds are not available for maintenance and upkeep. Sometimes bankruptcy can happen to a hotel or resort even while it is under construction.

Throughout this process, as can be seen, persons who have responsibility for day-to-day operations of hotels and other facilities have little opportunity to see what is happening. They awake too late to the fact that the quality and uniqueness of the destination no longer exist and probably can not be recaptured because of the huge investment costs associated with all of the prior development.

A few hopeful signs

Most readers of this chapter benefit from travel. It is part of our personal and professional lives. But the world grows smaller every day and the impact of tourism needs to be evaluated in a way that has not been true in the past. It offers so many positive benefits for so many people that we want to preserve and protect those benefits and diminish the negative side effects. The world still has many beautiful and fabulously interesting places to visit. But we need to keep it that way and ensure that leisure travel continues to restore the soul and increase our perspective about the world, its cultures, and its history.

In his essay, 'Where I Lived and What I Lived For,' Henry David Thoreau commented. 'I went to the woods because I wished to live deliberately, to confront the only essential facts of life, and see if I could not learn what it had to teach, and not when I came to die, discover that I had not lived.' Travel offers that opportunity also. With the changes that will come to travel in the next two decades, many of them dramatic, we can not afford to be unaware of these happenings or let the curve of decline outpace us. We need to plan more, control more, and listen more – to the needs of travellers and, even more so, to the requirements of local citizens who are impacted negatively by poorly planned or ineffectively managed tourist destinations. More so than ever, we should put our ears to the ground to ensure that what we do contributes to better futures for all, not diminishing ones. Our environment talks to us, but too often we don't listen. It cries out for help – for protection from the destruction imposed by uncontrolled development.

A few hopeful signs exist, however. More travel related companies now profess an interest in working towards 'responsible tourism', i.e., developing travel programmes that have as little impact on the environment as possible. After being stung by a fine for illegal dumping several years ago, Princess Cruises has taken the forefront in its environmental programmes. It now uses recyclable cardboard containers for bathroom amenities instead of plastic (shampoo and soaps), has installed biological sewerage treatment plants onboard, and reduced average amount of waste from a week-long cruise from 80 cubic feet down to ten cubic feet. Intercontinental Hotels has also received awards in its attempts to make its properties go 'green' in reducing waste and plastic throwaways. The American Hotel & Motel Association initiated a programme for its member hotel chains to encourage their guests to re-use sheets and towels, rather than having them replaced daily. The association informs hotel guests that US hotels use more than 180 billion gallons of water each year, with laundry detergents going into much of it, as based on US Environmental Protection Agency data. That amount would provide every living inhabitant on earth with 200 drinking glasses of water a year. Cut down on laundering and you cut down on waste. Some destinations in various parts of the world have come to the realization that they must protect their natural beauty – rain forests or coral reefs – or it could be destroyed forever, hurting their tourism base and the local economy.

But these positive steps are very small indeed. Perhaps the ultimate solution must come from travellers themselves. Educate them about the benefits of preserving and enhancing destinations and they will become more ecologically sensitive. As a result, they will demand a better quality of experience or they won't return. And they'll spread the bad word about the place. Some signs of this change in traveller attitude already exist. In the *American Traveler Survey* (ATS), a tracking study of Americans' leisure and business travel habits conducted annually by Plog Research, a question asks about all of the activities pursued while on vacation. In the list of 44 'activity' items, only one has consistently grown over the three waves of the project. Engaging in nature travel/ecotourism was pursued 8 per cent of the time by vacationers in the first wave; it now constitutes 15 per cent of their experiences in the third wave of the study. This growth is impressive, and the results may ultimately force many in the tourism industry to become more conscious of their need to operate responsibly as temporary inhabitants of a very fragile earth.

Jane Goodall, the ethnologist, followed Louis Leaky into Tanzania to study the social behaviour of chimpanzees. For thirty years she has observed not only chimps but the changes to the natural habitat of animals. In an interview, she stated, 'I visit different parts of Africa now for conservation because the trees are disappearing so fast . . . In those [early] days there were so many animals. There were giraffe, zebra, antelope, rhino. . .' Preservation of the environment now dominates her life and she speaks worldwide about the need to preserve and enhance those places that are still natural and beautiful. In that same interview, she concluded, 'The most important message is that everyone has to understand that they, as individuals, matter. We can't go through a single day of our lives without impacting the world around us. I say we suffer from lethargy with the result of overpopulation, deforestation, desertification, famine, pollution, and crime, warfare, inner-city crime, gang warfare.' (Pederson, 1997).

The concerns expressed by Jane Goodall should not be limited to naturalists. As she indicated, everyone must play a part. Responsible tourism and protection of the environment are natural allies. A destination that maintains and enhances its best qualities will benefit from greater financial success in both the near and long term horizons. This article demonstrates how and why that happens. Hopefully, someone in a position of responsibility comprehends that message.

References

Pederson, Rena (1997) 'You, Tarzan' (interview with Jane Goodall), *American Way*, March 1, pp. 70–81

Plog, S.C. (1991) *Leisure Travel: Making It A Growth Market . . . Again!* John Wiley & Sons, New York

Plog, S.C. (1973) Why Destination Areas Rise and Fall in Popularity, *Cornell Hotel and Restaurant Administration Quarterly*, November, pp. 13–16

Plog, S.C. (1995) *Vacation Places Rated*, Fielding Worldwide, Redondo Beach, CA

16 Styles of travel

Gordon D. Taylor

Introduction

Tourism has long been concerned with consumption and not with consumers. Traditionally standard measures have been person-trips, person-nights, numbers of visits, expenditures per day and per trip. In other words, measures of consumption and of economics. Much less systematic attention has been directed towards the consumer and the social science interest in tourism. Most tourism executives, managers, planners and developers pay respect to the adage 'know thy consumer'. Little consistent effort has been directed in research and in academia towards a basic understanding of the consumer and to the development of a systematic way of collecting information that would be applicable universally.

If a thorough examination of the phenomenon of tourism is to be attained, it will be necessary to examine the place of the consumer. A body of consumer knowledge based upon empirical evidence must be developed. In order to provide a sense of direction to this development a number of questions that require answers can be hypothesized.

1   What proportion of the population of a country travels and how frequently?
2   How is this proportion changing over time, if it is indeed changing?
3   Who are becoming travellers and who are ceasing to be?
4   Is the proportion of travellers in a population uniform by sex, age, education, income and other standard socio-demographic measures?
5   For those people who do travel, do they all think about travel the same way or can succinct groups in the population be described based upon this thought process?
6   If such groups can be described, are they unique to individual countries or do they occur on a wider basis?
7   Are these groups constant or do they change over time?

As a way of organizing the thinking that is necessary to answer these questions and of ordering the data that are required in any analysis, the concept of styles of travel can be useful. This concept is seldom used in the study of tourism. It is defined for the purposes of this chapter as the way people perceive, organize and execute travel. Two streams of information are included within this definition:

1 The incidence of travel
2 The way people think about the travel that they do.

   Empirical data from a number of sources will be examined in order to:

1 Determine the incidence of travel in at least two countries and indicate the type of information that can be derived from incidence data.
2 Describe and classify segments of travellers based upon the thought process.
3 Examine changes, if any, that may have taken place over time.

   The chapter will also examine the implications of these two measures of style of travel as indicators of changes that may be occurring for tourism as a business. The need for international standards in the collection of these data will also be stressed.

Incidence of travel

Introduction

Incidence of travel is quite simply the proportion of the population of an area that travels. This definition is all-encompassing and for many purposes it would be enlightening and worthy of study. For practical purposes some restrictions will be needed. People under a certain age do not make independent travel decisions; they travel because of the decision of a parent or other authority figure. Hence an age restriction should be used. In the two examples that will be cited minimum ages of fourteen years in one case and fifteen in the other were used. An age limitation in the mid-teens would seem appropriate. Secondly, a trip purpose limitation should be considered. For the purposes of tourism a restriction to pleasure travel with possibly duration and distance factors would be practical. The concept that the World Tourism Organization is attempting to introduce into the definition of tourism as being outside the usual environment should be considered within any description of travel incidence. In any event, an international agreement on the limiting factors would be required in order to make data from a variety of countries comparable. Without international comparability the use of incidence data as a part of a greater understanding of the consumer in tourism will be severely restricted.

The first four questions posed above deal with the proportion of people who travel. Data on this aspect of travel are scattered and inconsistent. This situation is unfortunate in that travel incidence is one of the most important measures of the consumption of travel and of the basic characteristics of the consumer. It is, first of all, a measure of the overall size of the travel market and a base for determining whether that market is growing, declining or remaining constant and of how fast changes are taking place over time. It is also the best measure of who is actually in the travel market and of who is entering and leaving it. When coupled with frequency of trip data it is also the basis for determining who are the heavy users of travel, and who are the light users.

Data sources

For illustrative purposes data are drawn from two studies that consistently measure travel intensity. The first of these is the Travel Analysis from West Germany. It is an annual study, conducted since 1970, based on 6000 interviews representative of the population of the former West Germany over the age of fourteen. The survey was extended in 1990 to cover all of unified Germany. The second study is the Canadian Travel Survey which is conducted biennially and covers the Canadian population aged fifteen years and older. The sample size is approximately 6000 households done quarterly in the years the survey is conducted.

Analysis

The critical incidence question in the German survey asks if, in the past year, the respondent has taken one or more holiday trips of at least five days in duration. The Canadian survey asks the respondents if they have taken a non-business trip in the nine-month period preceding the three-month period covered by the quarterly survey. Recent development in Germany of The German Travel Monitor has permitted collection of incidence data on all trips of at least one night away from home. In the future the travel incidence of the German population for all pleasure trips of one night or more will be available for analysis.

The Travel Analysis study clearly shows a consistent growth in the proportion of the population who have taken at least one five-day holiday trip. In 1970 41.6 per cent had taken such a trip, by 1990 the figure stood at 68.2 per cent. In absolute terms the West German market had increased from 18.5 million travellers to 33.4 million. An analysis of German data done for *Stern* magazine came to the conclusion that: 'At all levels of income the consumers with a higher education are at an advantage' (*Stern*, 1983, p. 14). Thus education level becomes an essential aspect of travel incidence and one that is important in the development of products for this market.

In Canada the annual incidence of overnight non-business travel grew from 69.0 per cent in 1984 to 71.1 per cent in 1988. There is a wide range in travel market participation across the country, from a low in 1988 of 61.9 per cent in Newfoundland and Prince Edward Island in the east to a high of 80.7 per cent in Alberta and 82.9 per cent in Saskatchewan in the west. Travel incidence in Canada is very similar for both metropolitan and non-metropolitan places. There is, however, a difference between the two groups when the destination of travel is concerned. The non-metropolitan areas have a higher incidence of travel within Canada, 66.8 per cent to 62.4 per cent, while metropolitan areas have a higher incidence for foreign travel, 20.0 per cent to 17.8 per cent to the United States and 11.4 per cent to 4.8 per cent for all other foreign destinations.

Incidence of travel increased with levels of education and of household income. Overall, travel incidence is highest in the 35–44 age group, but travel to the United States peaks in the 45–54 age group, and that to all other foreign destinations in the 55–64 group.

Discussion

By not utilizing this type of data, a rich resource for understanding tourism in its broadest sense and in determining where tourism fits into the economic and social priorities of populations is being missed. The examples used should indicate the kind of analysis that can and should be done. The relationship between travel incidence and the standard of living by country may be an indicator of the future trends in travel around the world. On a practical basis the data define who is not in the market and hence, for the travel marketer, is not of real concern. From a social standpoint and for an understanding of how the travel market reacts to economic difficulties, the movement in and out of the travel market in times of economic recession may well be of significant interest.

Travel philosophy

Introduction

A concept of travel philosophy has been developed as part of research into market segmentation in a number of studies conducted by Tourism Canada. It is part of a three-fold segmentation process that is based on the following assumptions:

1 There are recognizable groups in the population based on how people organize and value travel, i.e., how they think about travel.
2 There are recognizable groups in the population based on the benefits sought from specific pleasure trips.
3 There are recognizable groups in the population based on the activities, interests, location and facilities required in order to realize the benefits sought from specific pleasure trips.

While all three of these segmentations are needed for an understanding of the tourist consumer, the first is the one most pertinent to the topic of styles of travel. This aspect is concerned with how people think about travel in terms of its value to them, how they go about organizing travel and how they actually travel. The data provide a source from which to answer the last three questions posed in the introduction to this chapter.

Data sources

Market research studies conducted by Tourism Canada in the 1980s and 1990s have provided the data for this section. Three major studies are involved:

1 Attitudes of (then) West Germans to Canada as a holiday destination, conducted by Basis Research Ltd, Dusseldorf, in December 1981 and January 1982.
2 Canadian Tourism Attitudes and Motivation Study (CTAMS), conducted by Statistics Canada for Tourism Canada as an adjunct to the Canadian Labour Force Survey in the fall of 1983. Segmentation analysis was done by Burak-Jacobson Research Partners Inc., of Toronto.
3 Pleasure Travel Markets to North America, sponsored jointly by the United States Travel and Tourism Administration and Tourism Canada, and conducted by Market Facts of Canada Ltd.

The following countries have been studied as part of the Pleasure Travel Market series: France (1986, 1989), Japan (1986, 1989), United Kingdom (1986, 1989), West Germany (1986, 1989), Hong Kong (1987), Singapore (1987), Switzerland (1987), Australia (1988), Brazil (1988), Italy (1988), Mexico (1988), South Korea (1990) and Venezuela (1990). These studies are based on personal in-home interviews averaging fifty minutes in duration, with respondents who had taken a long-haul vacation of four nights or longer in the three years preceding the survey or who intended to take such a trip in the next two years. Long-haul was defined geographically for each country; for Europe the criterion was beyond Europe and North Africa. Similar limits were established for the other geographic regions. The number of interviews ranged from 1,200 to 2,000 per country.

These studies permitted the development of three different segmentations of the travel market. The basis of the segmentation was outlined earlier. In this review of information the travel philosophy segments, i.e., those segments that divide the population on the way they think about travel, value travel and organize travel, have been used.

Analysis

Respondents in the 1981 West German study were asked to respond to a list of thirty-three items on a five-point scale of desirability. Four segments emerged from an analysis of these data:

1   The uninspired fellow-traveller, 33 per cent.
2   The busy-sightseeing tourist, 20 per cent.
3   The comfort-loving relaxation vacationer, 26 per cent.
4   The globe-trotter adventurer, 21 per cent.

The emergence of a group not very interested in travel as the largest segment of the West German overseas travel market was surprising and provided the impetus to see if this group was unique to Germany or not, There were indications that this segment accompanied travellers from Group 4 (the adventurers) on holidays. The critical point seemed to be that they were not individually motivated to travel and were essentially taken along by other people. They were not an independent market that could be targeted for travel.

The Canadian Tourism Attitudes and Motivation Study for 1983 examined the Canadian adult population of fifteen years of age and older utilizing an initial sample of 14,180. Those respondents who had not travelled for pleasure purposes in the twelve months preceding the survey were eliminated for questions that dealt with current travel. The travel philosophy segments were based on the entire sample. Four such segments emerged:

1   Planned adventurer, 31 per cent.
2   Casual traveller, 27 per cent.
3   Low-risk traveller, 24 per cent.
4   Stay-at-home, 18 per cent.

The latter group was composed of people who did not see travel as an integral part of their life style and who did not enjoy travel. While they were not completely non-travellers, they travelled but little. In the overseas studies that followed, this group would not have met the basic criteria for inclusion.

There is, then, on the basis of the Canadian study, a group in the population that contributes little, if anything, to the travel market. No follow-up study has been done that would enable the dynamics of this group to be studied over time. It is likely that every population will contain a group that is for all intents and purposes outside of the travel market. Travel incidence studies if carried out on a regular basis will describe the broad parameters of the non-travellers, but they should be included in segmentation studies from time to time so that the underlying characteristics can be studied.

When the stay-at-home group is eliminated from the analysis, three groups are left that bear a good deal of resemblance to the groups that were developed for the overseas markets. These three groups can be described using the terminology that has been adopted for this chapter:

1 Planned travel, 37.5 per cent.
2 Independent travel, 33.5 per cent.
3 Reluctant travel, 29 per cent.

In order to establish a common terminology for the travel philosophy segments, the names that are used in this report differ from those used in the original reports. The term 'planned travel' has been developed to replace the term 'package travel'. Planned travel need not be package travel, although it is a major component of the segment.

Independent travel describes a group of people who prefer to make their own travel arrangements, often while they are on a trip. They tend to avoid guided tours and vacation packages. Reluctant travel categorizes a segment to whom travel is not part of their life style. To this group spending money on travel is not a priority; they are lukewarm to the whole idea of travel. When they do travel they tend to leave all arrangements to someone else.

Thirteen different countries were studied between 1986 and 1990, four of them on two occasions. There is, then, a broad and valuable data base available. Three philosophy segments have been recognized in all of the countries. While these three groups did not appear in the original reports for France, Switzerland, United Kingdom and West Germany, a review of the original data showed that the three-group solution was one of several offered for them. This three-group solution has been used in this analysis.

The statements that distinguish each of these groups in all countries are as follows:

1 Planned travel:
   – I usually buy vacation packages which include both accommodation and transportation.

- I prefer to go on guided tours when vacationing overseas.
- I usually use a travel agent to help me decide where to go on vacation.
- I usually travel on an all-inclusive package vacation.
- I like to have all my travel arrangements made before I start out on vacation.
2   Independent travel
    - I enjoy making my own arrangements for vacation trips.
    - I like to make my arrangements as I go along on a vacation.
    - I usually travel on reduced air fares.
3   Reluctant travel
    - Making arrangements for major trips can be such a bother that I end up not travelling.
    - I would just as soon spend my money on things other than vacation travel.
    - I usually choose travel places where I have been before.
    - Once I get to my destination, I like to stay put.

These statements clearly describe the main characteristics of the three groups. They are applicable in all of the countries where the three groups were identified (Table 16.1). Hence, the groups are transnational and transcultural. They do not, however, exist in all countries in the same proportions.

The countries can be divided into three groups on the basis of which group is the largest in each country. Germany and Switzerland each appear in two of the groupings as the two groups are of the same size.

1   High independent travel:
    - France (both studies);
    - United Kingdom (both studies);
    - Australia, South Korea, Switzerland.
2   High planned travel:
    - Brazil, Germany (1989), Hong Kong, Italy, Singapore, Venezuela.
3   High reluctant travel:
    - Germany (both studies), Japan, Switzerland.

In the three countries where data exist for both 1986 and 1989, some slight shifts in the proportions have been observed. In the United Kingdom there was an increase in planned travel, from 29 per cent to 33 per cent, at the expense of both independent and reluctant travel. In France there was a slight decrease in planned travel and an offsetting increase in reluctant travel. Germany showed an increase in independent travel at the expense of planned travel. With only two points in time these changes are interesting but cannot be considered a trend.

Table 16.1 Travel philosophy segments: proportional distribution by country

Country (year)	Planned travel (%)	Independent travel (%)	Reluctant travel (%)
United Kingdom (1986)	33	36	30
United Kingdom (1989)	29	39	32
France (1986)	27	38	35
France (1989)	30	38	32
Germany (1986)	33	28	39
Germany (1989)	39	22	39
Japan (1989)	34	27	38
Hong Kong (1987)	51	19	30
Singapore (1987)	44	24	32
Switzerland (1987)	23	38	38
Italy (1988)	41	35	25
Australia (1988)	33	35	32
Brazil (1988)	43	26	31
Mexico (1988)	53	24	23
Venezuela (1990)	51	23	26
South Korea (1990)	19	44	37

Discussion

These three philosophy segments occur in several countries and on the basis of the evidence available three of them would appear to be relatively stable. Further studies in the future are required to see whether significant shifts in the structure of travel markets are occurring. Careful thinking about the implications of these three groups is needed. Across all of the countries studied the groups each represent about one-third of the long-haul travel market, although exceptions appear in Hong Kong, Singapore, Brazil, Mexico, Venezuela and South Korea. In each of these countries one group tends to dominate the market. These countries are recent entries into the international travel market as origins. Further study is needed to see whether these markets develop towards the pattern of the older, more established markets.

In the older markets, one-third of the travellers prefer to travel on their own terms, another third wants as many of the unknowns removed before starting a trip, and a final third is not really keen on travel. Each of these three groups would need a separate style of marketing approach and the industry response to their travel needs would have to reflect the different ways they look at travel.

Further analysis utilizing the benefit and product segments for each country as they relate to these three groups would be needed to work out the full implications of this aspect of travel. That further analysis is beyond the scope of this chapter.

Conclusions

The fact that some universals in travel segments are starting to emerge should provide an impetus for more research. In order for this research to be most useful, there is a need for an international agreement on the type of survey to be done, the questionnaire content, and on the methodologies of administration and analysis. Such an international approach will not be easy as there is still great difficulty in agreeing on the definition of a tourist without getting into the complexities of different kinds of tourist based on a multi-segmentation approach.

If target marketing and the development of product lines relative to market segments is the future of tourism activity, then some international approach to the development and classification of multi-segments will be required. It will be necessary to be able to identify appropriate segments not only in the population of a country, but also in a visiting population. It would not be possible to administer the type of questions to visitors on an ongoing basis that can be used in an in-home interview. A fast means of identifying the groups will be a high priority.

The use of both travel incidence and travel style data opens the door to a greater understanding of tourism on an international basis. Comparable data can be developed world-wide. These data provide a means for monitoring changes in travel markets and are vital to the process of adapting tourism marketing to the changes.

A growth in independent travel, a decline in planned travel or the reverse clearly signal the need for the marketing and development of tourism aimed at such a country to be reviewed and, if necessary, revamped. In the same way a country where the travel incidence is rising will be of more interest to marketers than one where the incidence is falling.

When incidence and style are analysed at the same time, the fact of change will be accompanied by the direction of change. Tourism cannot afford to overlook the implications of these data as a means of improving knowledge of the markets and of increasing the opportunities for customer satisfaction.

References

Statistics Canada (1991) *Tourscope, 1990*, Domestic Travel, Canadians Travelling in Canada, Catalogue 87–504, Ottawa, October 1991. (Available biennially since 1980)

Stern (1983) The German holiday maker – projections to 1990. *Stern Magazine*, Hamburg

Study Group for Tourism (annual) *Reisenalyse*, Starnberg (available annually since 1970)

Taylor, G.D. (1986) 'Multi-dimensional segmentation of the Canadian Pleasure Travel market. *Tourism Management*, **7**(3), 146–53

Unger, Klaus (1991) German Travel Monitor, 1990. *FVW International*, No. **7**, 97–8

Pleasure Travel Markets to North America, published by Tourism Canada, Ottawa:
- (a) Full reports for individual countries:
    - — France, Japan, United Kingdom, West Germany, 1986
    - — Switzerland, Hong Kong, Singapore, 1987
    - — Australia, Brazil, Italy, Mexico, 1988
    - — France, Japan, United Kingdom, West Germany, 1989
    - — South Korea, Venezuela, 1990
- (b) Highlights reports for all countries studied in a year.

17 Analysing tourist behaviour with lifestyle and vacation style typologies

Josef A. Mazanec, Andreas H. Zins and Sara Dolnicar

Introduction

The construction of traveller and tourist typologies is not a new undertaking in travel and tourism marketing. Reports published in the proceedings of the Travel and Tourism Research Association have covered this issue regularly (Darden and Darden, 1976). Social science approaches to tourism research repeatedly touched upon typological methodology (Cohen, 1988: Dann et al., 1988; Pearce, 1982). It is also common practice to consider traveller or tourist types as potential market segments for travel and tourism marketing (Smith, 1989). Marketing theory distinguishes between a priori and a posteriori market segmentation depending on the segment defining variables(s) being either predetermined or assigned during the construction of previously unknown segments (Bagozzi, 1986; Vavrik and Mazanec, 1990).

During the 1970s, lifestyle criteria became popular in consumer segmentation studies (Wells, 1974, 1975). Tourism and leisure research followed suit (Mayo and Jarvis, 1981; Bernard, 1987; see Veal, 1989, for a critical comment). Recently, the lifestyle concept experienced a revival in international marketing research for tourism. The Austrian National Tourist Office has used the lifestyle data available from the European Group (Kreutzer, 1991) which is an association of fifteen European commercial market research institutes. This information, however, originates from consumer panels in the tourism generating countries and conveys nothing about the lifestyle of the guests while staying in Austria. The Austrian National Guest Survey (Globe 1991/92) adopted the Eurostyles methodology in order to examine the lifestyle structure of travellers to Austria during the 1991/92 summer and winter seasons.

Given the data on actual tourist behaviour collected in the resorts, there should be ample information on the interlace of lifestyle and guest characteristics. Thus, marketing managers can expect conclusive findings about the strengths and weaknesses of the Eurostyles typology for tourist market segmentation. The main question pertains to the overall usefulness of general lifestyles like the Eurostyles as 'prefabricated' market segments.

What does it mean for a tourist to belong to a particular lifestyle segment in terms of consumer choice behaviour, activities, spending habits, etc.? Does a lifestyle transfer its unique attributes into a (similar or contrasting) vacation style? Tourism marketers on the national level are primarily concerned with generating countries. Does the Eurostyles typology assist in the assessment of the tourism generators? Does Eurostyles stick to its promise of providing an analytical link between actual guests in a receiving country and potential visitors in their respective home countries?

It is not the purpose of this chapter to discuss the construction of the Eurostyles typology at length. As an obviously successful result of commercial market research it is taken for granted. However, the assumption has to be verified that individual styles or so-called socio-targets (groups of styles) contribute to the advancement of tourist market research and render tourism marketing more efficient.

The attempt to direct different traveller types and 'vacation styles' in a population of tourists corresponds with the concept of 'a posteriori market segmentation'. In principle, a posteriori segmentation rests on the assumption that subgroups in a consumer population are homogeneous in terms of motives, attitudes, and/or activities. This mental and behavioural homogeneity is likely to make them react to product offerings and promotional efforts in a similar manner. The earliest approach to master such a market situation is known as 'benefit segmentation' and was introduced by Russel Haley (1971). His argument was that consumer groups with a markedly different pattern of benefits sought should be considered to be 'natural' segments in the market. From a behavioural science point of view the notion of 'benefit' relates to the more general concept of 'attitude'. Benefits destined or expected are attitudes towards particular consumption goals (cf. e.g. the Rosenburg (1967) model of attitude measurement). For example, a leisure traveller who seeks fun and entertainment when choosing a destination attaches high salience to the quality of entertainment facilities. He holds a strong and favourable attitude towards this attribute of a destination which may become a dominant item in his overall judgement of a vacation package.

A 'vacation style' is defined as a temporary lifestyle into which a tourist escapes from his/her everyday surroundings. It includes observable and unobservable characteristics of the tourist. A vacation style represents a cognitive and emotional state of mind as well as the accompanying behaviour. A posteriori segmentation by means of vacation styles considers more than just one type of behavioural variable. It also aims at uncovering the underlying 'motives'. This is not an easy task to solve in a standard mass survey. Motives are conceived as a state of arousal with no distinct directional effect towards a particular means of satisfaction (cf. questionnaire items such as 'to change pace', 'to realize one's creativity'). A closer examination of the commercial travel surveys reveals that many of the questions pretending to measure motives actually ask for the evaluation of some attributes of a tourist product. This, however, is the purpose of attitudinal rather than motivational items. While the motives are responsible for the arousal of behaviour, attitudes govern its direction and orientation (Kroeber-Riel and Weinberg, 1996). Consumers navigate through the world of products and services by constantly adjusting their personal hierarchy stage of an attitude following a particular consumption experience. Another example for a more abstract and slowly changing level of attitudes are 'value systems' (Kamakura and Novak, 1992) which have attracted attention in travel segmentation theory and practice more recently. Motivational and attitudinal variables related to various domains of everyday life are combined to yield lifestyles types. If 'everyday life' gets replaced by 'leisure travel' the output is called 'vacation styles'.

Travel and vacation 'activities' are also useful raw material for constructing a posteriori segments (Hsieh et al., 1992), Questions about the tourist's activities are customary in travel or guest surveys. The concept of 'tourist roles' as suggested by Yiannakis and Gibson (1992) is also closely linked to travel activities. Tourist activities easily lend themselves for segmentation purposes. The objective is to overcome the travel single-item classification (sightseeing tourist, culture-seeker, museum-visitor) and to replace it by a multivariate activity pattern. In contemporary activity segmentation it is the 'activity bundle' which characterizes an activity segment. In a vacation style the activities are also considered to come up in symptomatic combinations.

The concept of a posteriori segmentation via benefit types and vacation styles is intriguing to tourism managers. It draws a more 'real-life' picture of their customers who are more than just 'cases' of a certain age in a particular income bracket and with more or less travel experience. The tourist type becomes a more complete entity by exhibiting more 'human-like' contours. Types and styles are more stimulating to the creative designers of trip packages or media advertisements. The manager interested in vacation and traveller typologies needs an intuitive understanding of cluster analysis. The reader may also notice the contemporary view of segmentation strategies in marketing science. It is not the aim to detect the 'true' and 'one and only' segment structure in the market. The analyst and the marketing manager continuously 'invent' new segmentation schemes. Being the first to practice such a scheme gives the company or the destination a competitive edge. It pays off to elaborate a new and different typology which inspires the specialization strategy required to operate – albeit temporarily – in a 'quasi-monopoly'.

The forthcoming examples of identifying vacation styles utilize European and American survey data. The Eurostyles example links European (origin countries) with Austrian (destination) guest data. The second example also exploits two sets of databases of leisure travellers. The first set comprises a sample of 403 US citizens aged 18+ having visited Europe during the summer season 1995. The second set is the counterpart of 405 US guests interviewed during their summer 1994 visit to Austria. The focus is on exploiting the correspondence in these databases. The analytical tools do not get an in-depth treatment in this demonstration study (for details consult the methodology appendix in Mazanec, 1997, pages 242–251).

The Eurostyles concept

The Eurostyles system (Europanel, 1989; Kramer, 1991) is a multinational lifestyle typology developed by the Centre de Communication Advance (CCA) of the Havas-Eurocom group. Since 1989 the system has been in commercial use in fifteen European countries. The measurement instrument covers five principal dimensions of lifestyle:

1   objective personal criteria,
2   behavioural attributes,
3   attitudes,
4   motivations and aspirations, and
5   sensitivities and emotions.

The database allows the monitoring of 'Socio-Waves' (Cathelat, 1993) or socio-cultural mainstreams.

The Eurostyles approach offers the analyst various indicators such as a 'topography' of socio-climatic zones' which serves as a basis for the socio-cultural segmentation of the population, a socio-cultural 'compass rose' which reveals the main cultural trends, or a number of scenarios describing hypotheses about the medium-term future. By linking so many aspects of everyday life together, the Eurostyles typology inspires product development, thus serving as an instrument of innovation (Cathelat, 1993). The Eurostyles system consists of sixteen different lifestyle types.

These types may be regarded as a portrait gallery resulting from a series of multivariate analysis (factor-, correspondence-, cluster analysis). The sixteen Eurostyles uniformly apply to each European country and to all sectors of activity (e.g. politics, advertising, media habits, buying and consumption of goods and services).

Figure 17.1 delineates the Eurostyles system by positioning the sixteen European lifestyle types on a two-dimensional map. The horizontal axis links two opposing poles, named 'settlement' on the right and 'movement' on the left. The vertical axis is a bipolar dimension of 'valuables' (pleasure) in the north and 'values' in the south. Percentages in parentheses are the portions of the overall European population located in the right or left and the upper or lower hemispheres respectively.

The settlement pole or region may be characterized by values such as: priority to the individual's defence and survival at the current social status, convergence on habits and traditions, group protection, obedience to the cultural rules of life. In contract, movement means dynamism, freedom of criticism, priority to the individual, distance vis-a-vis social norms, law and authorities.

On the second main axis the northern region may be characterized by values of pleasure, sensuality and hedonism which altogether are strongly associated with tangible values of money and material equipment in a system of expenditure and even waste. Figure 17.1 exhibits the distribution of the cultural mainstreams in Europe by featuring the sixteen Eurostyles in the two-dimensional map. Each lifestyle type bears a label for easy reference.

In order to determine the potential of various social mentalities or consumption patterns it is necessary to know the share of each of the sixteen Eurostyles. For all fifteen European countries analysed the diameters of the circles in Figure 17.1 indicate the shares of the sixteen styles. The major types in Europe are the Rocky (13.5 per cent), the Defense (8.5 per cent), and the Romantic (7.8 per cent). Of course, the size of each style is not the same for each country. The type Rocky, for example, dominates the socio-cultural landscape particularly in the Netherlands, in Great Britain, France, and Switzerland. The share of the Moralist and the Romantic is very high in Germany, Austria, Belgium, and Switzerland. On the other hand, Denmark and Sweden accommodate the Pioneer type fairly above average.

Many intricate correlations may be derived from the database covering a variety of lifestyle facets. The analyst may combine existing consumption patterns of a particular product category with attitudes towards several socio-cultural trends. Such cross-tabulations assist in revealing the market potential as well as the innovative power of a new product line. The marketing practitioner also diagnoses the spending propensities of the Eurostyles on the regional, national, and international levels. Another

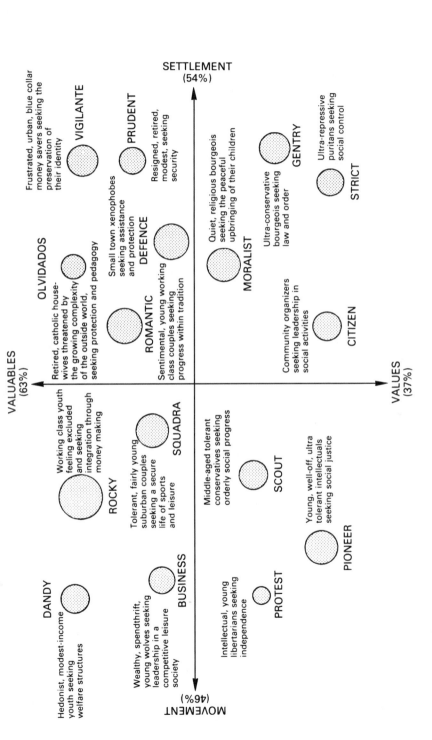

Figure 17.1 The sixteen Eurostyles in Europe

Source: CCA/Auropanel

strength of the Eurostyles system is the interplacement of the lifestyle findings to the wealth of national consumer panel data. Once a target segment has been defined, the market researcher obtains supplementary information on media habits, communication styles and themes, images, and preferences.

Usage of the Eurostyles typology in international tourism marketing

Before employing the Eurostyles typology, management must distinguish two different cases:

1   Accepting the styles or a combination of styles as ready-made market segments.
2   Using the styles as additional criteria (passive variables) to depict already defined segments more comprehensively.

Before choosing the first alternative one must check whether the styles prove to be homogeneous within and heterogeneous between types in terms of tourist behaviour. An affirmative result would justify selective market operation. If sufficient disparities are not detected amongst the styles there is a second option. Market segments are constructed by means of other more discriminative traveller characteristics. Then some of these segments may exhibit an over-proportional share of one or more particular Eurostyles. In this case the supplementary lifestyle descriptors lead to improving promotional messages directed to potential visitors in their home countries.

A Eurostyle qualifies as a ready-made market segment on condition that its members significantly differ from those of other styles in terms of at least one elementary traveller attribute such as:

*   main trip versus second/third or short trip;
*   number of visits, travel experience;
*   travel motives and expectations;
*   actual usage of tourist services;
*   preferred activities;
*   amount and composition of daily expenditure;
*   satisfaction, intention to repeat visit, loyalty.

Empirical findings on the direct usage of the Eurostyles for constructing tourist market segments are reported next. The indirect usage of a typology for evaluating markets will be addressed afterwards in an American–Austrian case example.

A European–Austrian case example

Predicting guest behaviour with individual Eurostyles

To put it briefly, the sixteen original Eurostyles cannot be considered to be ready-made segments for tourism marketing. The differences regarding behavioural criteria are not convincing. In other words, the general lifestyle is a poor predictor for the components of guest behaviour. These findings need not be taken as a failure. It is evident that travellers' choice in favour of a particular destination must have a 'smoothing' effect. Guests solely surveyed within Austria are likely to have more homogeneous psychographics and behaviours than travellers headed for a diversity of destinations.

A number of attempts to group individual Eurostyles into socio-targets (viz. combinations of styles) may be feasible, styles may be merged according to their location on the two-dimensional Eurostyles map. Another solution emanates when then sixteen original styles are hierarchically clustered with a similarity measure based on, say, the benefits sought by each style. This approach produced satisfactory contrasts between seven socio-targets. The next section contains still another combination of Eurostyles exploiting their mutual similarity in terms of travel motive and activities.

Grouping Eurostyles into socio-targets

The common approach of merging styles into socio-targets is based on behavioural differentiation. A tourist's decision to spend his holidays in Austria, however, exerts a filtering effect comparing the distribution of lifestyles in the population of the generating countries and among Austria's guests: tourists patronizing the same destination are expected to be more similar to each other than those headed for different receiving countries. Nevertheless, it may be argued that doing the same thing is perceived and evaluated differently by different individuals, a phenomenon frequently encountered in the field of services and intangibles.

Therefore, the aggregation of the sixteen Eurostyles should not be based primarily on attributes such as the choice of accommodation or the length of stay, but on a bundle of travel motives and activities. A hierarchical cluster analysis was performed with eleven motives (e.g. recreation, pleasure, new experiences, cultural interest, etc.) and ten activities (e.g. playing tennis, golf, exercising, water sports, relaxing, shopping, visiting museums, concerts, theatres, etc.) as active variables and the sixteen styles as objects. After checking the degree of homogeneity, five clusters were retained for interpretation. Figure 17.2 again depicts the configuration of the sixteen Eurostyles on the two-dimensional map. The diameters of

TARGET SEGMENTS BY TRAVEL MOTIVES AND ACTIVITIES

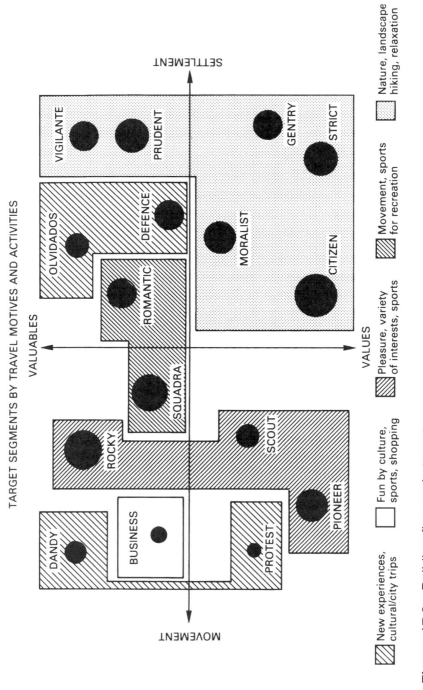

Figure 17.2 Building five socio-targets

Source: CCA/EUROPANEL/OEGAF

the circles show the relative share of each style in Austria's total guest population. In addition, the hatched fields in the map demonstrate the affiliation of each style with one of the five socio-targets which is homogenous in terms of travel motives and activities.

The first socio-target comprises six styles (with an aggregate share of 47 per cent). Its motive structure relates to recreation and health by doing nothing and/or hiking. The second segment combines two neighbouring styles with an aggregate share of 16 per cent. This type enjoys recreation in attractive surroundings and to indulge in activities such as cycling, swimming, horse riding or sun bathing, which offer variety and change. The third socio-target occupies the western region of the socio-cultural map and ties three styles together (resulting in a share of 21 per cent). Pleasure and sports (tennis, cycling, water sports, golf) in combination with mental training are the prevailing motives. The fourth cluster seeks cultural events but is uninterested in sports and physical strain. It can be found in the north-east and the far west on the movement–settlement axis, accounting for a share of 14 per cent. The remaining style represents outsiders of about 2 per cent of the guest mix. They are interested in sports, culture and shopping – just for fun.

Socio-demographics (e.g. age, profession, size of residential town, household income) as well as behavioural and travel-related variables (e.g. party size and composition, intention to repeat visit, length of stay, accommodation and boarding, purpose of travel, benefits sought, spending pattern) reveal significant differences between the five suggested socio-targets (see Tables 17.1 to 17.3). These results are a promising basis for

Table 17.1 Socio-demographics and socio-targets

Variable	Average	Socio-targets					F ratio	Chi square	Sig.
		1	2	3	4	5			
Share in %		47	16	21	14	2			
Age of travel party in years	47	52	44	41	46	42	161.05		0.0000
Size of town of residence								50.09	0.0000
<100.000	60	61	64	58	65	51			
>100.000									
Profession of interviewee								237.42	0.0000
self-employed	14	13	9	16	13	15			
employed	59	51	72	68	59	60			
retired	27	36	19	16	28	25			

Table 17.2 Trip characteristics and socio-targets

Variable	Average	Socio-targets 1	2	3	4	5	F ratio	Chi square	Sig.
share in %		47	16	21	14	2			
Share of repeat visitor in %	74	77	74	72	70	67	7.72		0.0000
Main trip of the year in %	60	63	62	56	54	46	11.15		0.0000
Party size	2.1	2.1	2.3	2.1	2.0	2.0	17.73		0.0000
Accompanied by children under 14 in %	13	11	18	14	11	11	9.09		0.0000
Lodging in hotels and pensions in %	65	66	56	68	69	83	14.21		0.0000
share in %		47	16	21	14	2			
Length of stay in Austria in days	12.3	13.6	11.6	11.4	10.8	9.9	25.41		0.0000
Expenditures per day and capita in US$	64	61	57	67	71	85	13.19		0.0000
Shopping exp. for whole party and trip in US$	227	231	217	190	270	222	2.58		0.0355

Table 17.3 Benefits sought and socio-targets

Variable	Average	Socio-targets 1	2	3	4	5	F ratio	Chi square	Sig.
Share in %		47	16	21	14	2			
Benefits sought in %									
walking/hiking lanes	73	79	77	65	62	53	44.24		0.0000
calmness of resort	72	80	71	65	63	54	41.58		0.0000
variety of landscapes	62	66	65	55	57	40	21.07		0.0000
value for money	63	67	65	57	55	53	18.37		0.0000
service in accomod.	62	67	57	57	59	63	15.12		0.0000
service in restaurant	63	67	61	55	61	61	13.26		0.0000
reachability	52	55	56	45	48	45	12.98		0.0000
environment	92	93	93	90	89	79	11.80		0.0000
friendliness of pop.	78	82	77	75	75	63	11.66		0.0000

segmenting the European travel market with an overt preference for Austria as a destination country. Drawing on the Eurostyles as a gateway to the plenitude of panel data collected in the individual home centuries, both sources of information may be combined for segmentation purposes.

An American–Austrian case example

Incorporating travel benefit types into strategic planning

This case example is based on two surveys conducted independently, yet containing a number of identical questions. On the one hand 403 US citizens at the age of 18 years or older were questioned, who stated to have visited a European country in summer 1995. The second database stems from the Austrian National Guest Survey conducted during the summer session 1994. From this master sample all tourists originating from the USA (405 cases) were extracted for analysis.

Beside the questions about socio-demographic attributes and travel behaviour the interviews contained nineteen statements about the psychographic elements of the vacation. The respondents were asked to state the importance they attach to several attitudinal and motivational aspects on a scale ranging from 'very important' to 'not at all important'. Data reduction techniques were applied to obtain benefit types. Ten benefit dimensions were extracted from the attitudinal and motivational data by means of non-metric principal components analysis (procedure PRINCIPALS from SPSS categories). The reduced data set of the quantified

Table 17.4 Travel benefit styles of US travellers and selected characteristics

High importance attached to ...	Benefit styles (%)					
	1	2	3	4	5	6
Rest/relaxation	27	68	47	62	41	56
Comfort	73	69	38	75	69	69
Physical activity/sports participation	14	40	15	3	21	25
Cultural activities/events/sights	69	90	73	90	48	50
Excitement/adventure	33	66	41	6	37	50
Water/sun	23	46	26	36	42	44
Everything planned/organized/don't have to worry about anything	22	21	7	23	58	44
Activities/facilities for children/child care	0	0	0	0	0	100

factor ('object') scores from the US survey was used to train self-organizing feature maps (SOMs) to generate alternative classifications for two to twelve segments. SOMs are a neurocomputing equivalent of an ordinary partitioning cluster analysis. The comparison of the heterogeneity of the cluster solutions clearly suggested to restrict the further analysis to six tourist types (for methodology details consult the technical appendix in Mazanec, 1997, pages 245–251). After training the SOM is ready for making predictions. Thus the training run was followed by a 'recall run' (the prediction) using the second data set from the Austrian National Guest Survey. The purpose is to detect the frequency of the benefit types encountered among US travellers to Europe in general within the US tourist population in Austria.

The best discriminating active variables are shown in Table 17.4. It outlines the main features of the segments extracted and contain the percentages of respondents (US survey) attaching high importance to eight selected clustering variables.

'Modests' enjoy having fun; this is the most important aspect of their vacation. They do not have very high expectations concerning any of the 19 active benefit variables. On the other hand they rate 7 out of 19 variables as least important among all segments (rest, culture, friends, local population, nature, health, water and sun and familiar atmosphere). 'High expectation travellers' belong to the contrasting type. In 12 out of 19 variables the largest amount of members of this particular group attaches high importance to the above stated benefits. Nature, culture and safety

Table 17.5 Comparison of style distribution of US travellers in generating and destination country

Segment	US citizens visiting Europe (% of total)	US citizens visiting Austria (% of total)	% difference
Modests	18	19	−1
High expectation travellers	22	1	−21
Active culture seekers	18	2	−16
Passive culture seekers	17	49	+32
Organized travellers	21	1	−20
Family travellers	4	28	+24
Total	100	100	

seem to be most relevant, with about 90 per cent segment members considering it to be of primary importance.

Rest, comfort, a high level of travel organization, and safety are of relatively little importance to the 'active culture seekers'. Their dominant interest in visiting Austria lies in exploring the country's culture. Nevertheless, the highest level of culture enthusiasm is demonstrated by the 'passive culture seekers', who insist on rest and comfort during their sightseeing holiday. On the other hand these travellers indicate the lowest interest in sports and adventure among all segments. 'Organized travellers' are the one segment where only 48 per cent state that cultural activities are important during their stay. Their vacation has to be very well organized, safe and comfortable, friends and a familiar atmosphere contributing largely to their enjoyment. All members of the 'family travellers' believe that child care at the travel destination has first priority among the aspects listed. Fun, comfort, nature, and the change of pace play a major role during the stay.

The cases from the Austrian guest data set get classified into the same six benefit types described. As the benefit type solution results from the analysis of the sample questioned in the USA, it is instructive to compare the frequencies of segment membership obtained in both data sets. Are there particular types of US citizens that can be found more frequently spending their summer vacation in Austria than others? Table 17.5 contains the frequency distribution in per cent for both data sets and the differences in segment size between the US survey and the Austrian National Guest Survey.

The frequency data indicate a fairly even distribution for five segments. Only the group of 'family travellers' is much smaller than the rest, a plausible observation recalling the fact that US citizens travelling to Europe were questioned. Comparing the distributions obtained from the two data sets indicates that the number of 'modests' visiting Austria is approximately equal to the number identified in the data set of US citizens travelling to Europe. 'High expectation travellers', 'active culture seekers' and 'organized travellers' are under-represented in Austria, whereas 'passive culture seekers' and 'family travellers' are over-represented as compared to the share obtained in their county of origin.

Identifying the repeat visitors' potential is a crucial issue in the design of marketing strategy. The differentiation of benefit types favourable and unfavourable with respect to repeat visitation may be helpful. The guests' intention to repeat their visit commonly is regarded a valid indicator of guest satisfaction. Intention to repeat visit, however, is an asymmetric indicator. A weak intention does not necessarily denote dissatisfaction. But a strong intention reveals good prospects to gain loyal tourists from the market segments structurally resembling the profile of the highly satisfied guests. From the guest data it becomes apparent that there are tourists who might be transformed into loyal visitors more easily than others. The travel benefit typology now provides a tool for assessing the loyalty potential in various market segments each with a homogeneous benefit structure.

The preponderance of the intention to repeat visit as a symbol for appreciation for a country's tourist performance is not confirmed to market strategies aiming at customer loyalty. Weak loyalty in travel and tourism may be caused by many factors other than satisfaction. A tourist seeking diversity, preferring short trips, or going on a long-haul trip once in his life need not be dissatisfied in order to vary his choice of destinations. Loyal as well as fluctuating travellers make a balanced guest mix. But the promotional approach ought to be tailored to each of the two extremes.

A generating country like the US accommodates a typical mixture of travel benefit types, each with a particular amount of affinity for Austria as a tourist destination. Suppose that tourism managers are rather conservative in their segmentation policies and thus want to cater to the loyal visitors. In this case they are likely to focus on those benefit types which show a strong intention to repeat their visit when asked during their stay in an Austrian resort.

Comparing the share of potential travellers to Austria within a benefit type in the US to the share among the guests belonging to this type and prepared to repeat visit results in one of four possible outcomes. The share lies . . .

- above average in the US and above average in Austria;
- below average in the US and above average in Austria;
- below average in the US and below average in Austria;
- above average in the US and below average in Austria.

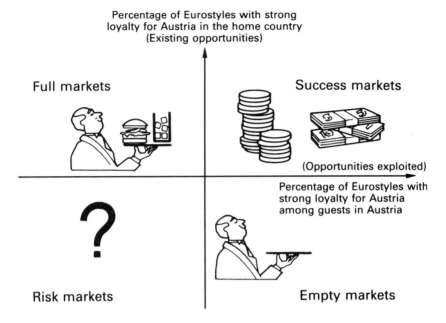

Percentage of Eurostyles with strong
loyalty for Austria in the home country
(Existing opportunities)

Full markets

Success markets

(Opportunities exploited)

Percentage of Eurostyles with
strong loyalty for Austria
among guests in Austria

Risk markets

Empty markets

Figure 17.3 Portfolio of tourism markets

Adopting the pictorial representation common in portfolio models (Day, 1977; Wind et al., 1983; McNamee, 1985; Day, 1986; Kerin et al., 1990) the benefit segments are portrayed in four quadrants (see Figure 17.3).

The size of the circles denotes each segment's visitor potential in terms of the absolute number of cases in the US sample. The first quadrant (north-east) contains those segments where Austria already has exploited her opportunities ('success markets'): 'Austria-prone' tourists are over-presented within the origin population as well as amongst the visitors to Austria. A weak representation of Austria-prone tourists in the origin market segment combined with high frequency of these tourists among the guests implies an advanced degree of market saturation ('empty markets').

A less than proportional frequency of Austria-prone tourists in the home segment and also among the guests in Austria is indicative of a market segment with doubtful opportunities ('risk markets'). A 'full market' offers a large share of Austria-prone travellers combined with a small share of these tourists already travelling to Austria.

Figure 17.4 examines the loyalty potential of the benefit segments according to the portfolio design principle outlined above. The figure shows the results for the tourists who stated that visiting Austria is very probable within the next three years. The size of the bubbles indicates the segment size, i.e. the number of members of a segment in the US sample.

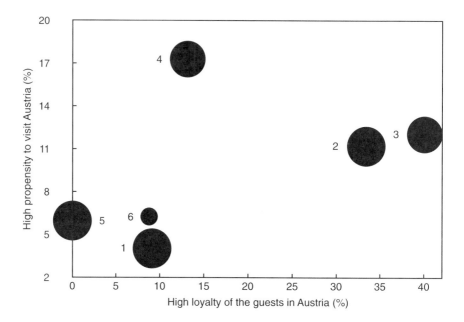

Figure 17.4   The high loyalty potential in the home country and in Austria in per cent of respondents. Type (segment) labels: 1 modest; 2 high expectation travellers; 3 active culture seekers; 4 passive culture seekers; 5 organized travellers; 6 family travellers

The percentages along the axes indicate the share of guests among US tourists prepared to re-visit Austria when questioned during their vacation in Austria (horizontal) and the potential visitors among the US tourists questioned in their home country (vertical).

Segments 2 and 3 are positioned between the empty markets and the success markets quadrant. From Table 17.5 it is know that segment 2 and 3 members are heavily under-represented among Austria's guests from the US. But once being guests they demonstrate high loyalty. Therefore, marketing activities should concentrate on attracting more first-time visitors from among the 'high expectation seekers' (#2) and the 'active culture seekers' (#3) to experience Austria as a travel destination. 'Modest' (#1), 'organized travellers' (#5), and 'family travellers' (#6) represent risk markets. In particular, the large number family travellers visiting Austria emphasizes the necessity to invest in family attractions and facilities to build loyalty after the first vacation experience in Austria. Passive culture seekers (#4) offer very good future opportunities for Austria as a destination. Not only is this segment over-represented in Austria, also the propensity to visit Austria in the US home segment is very high. But again, there is room for improvement and for strengthening the loyalty among the US guests in Austria.

Summary

The Eurostyle typology was shown to be of practical value for destination marketing provided that certain amendments are applied. The original consumer lifestyle types have to be merged into groups of types (i.e. socio-targets). The grouping process must employ a travel-related and behaviourally relevant set of criteria (such as travel motives and activities). Once a grouping of styles has been found it lends itself to segmentation purposes on international levels. Beside the opportunity to define segments across borders management will benefit from a multitude of data accumulated during normal panel operation. Socio-targets are not new entities but consist of well-known components. Thus, they are easily portrayed in terms of consumption patterns, shopping habits, or media usage for increased marketing efficiency.

The evaluation of tourism generating countries and their market segments is a routine task in any National Tourist Office where strategic thinking guides the marketing planning process. The US travel benefit types have been demonstrated in two ways. Both have been demonstrated in this chapter. First, the frequency distributions assist in identifying the relative attractiveness of a destination to specific tourist types. They indicate which types are already well represented among a destination's tourist population and where the future market potential can be exploited through increased marketing effort. Second, the use of loyalty-based portfolios informs about the repeat visiting structure of the types. The reader may have wondered why an assessment of market segments with respect to repeat visitors takes a detour via benefit types. The main reason is to enable managers to target the marketing action towards tourist groups with homogenous benefits. This is more efficient than trying to build loyalty indiscriminately within a number of heterogeneous market segments that need to be approached with different messages. In marketing planning and day-to-day marketing action the benefit types are like 'old friends': they are well known, well understood, and therefore more easily provided the tourist services they desire.

References

Bagozzi, R.P. (1986) *Principles of Marketing Management*, Science Research Associates, Chicago

Bernard, M. (1987) Leisure-Rich and Leisure-Poor: Leisure Lifestyles Among Young Adults, *Leisure Sciences*, **10**, 131–149

Cathelat, B. (1993) *Socio-Lifestyles Marketing*, Probus, Chicago

Cohen, E. (1988) Traditions in Qualitative Sociology of Tourism, *Annals of Tourism Research*, **15**(1), 29–46

Dann, G., Nash, D. and Pearce, P. (1988) Methodology in Tourism Research, *Annals of Tourism Research*, **15**(1), 1–28

Darden, W. and Darden, D. (1976) A Study of Vacation Life Styles. In *Proceedings of the 7th Annual Conference of The Travel and Tourism Research Association*, Boca Raton, Florida, pp. 231–6

Day, G.S. (1977) Diagnosing the Product Portfolio, *Journal of Marketing*, **41**(2), 29–38

Day, G.S. (1986) *Analysis for Strategic Market Decisions*, West Publishing Co, St Paul

Europanel (1989) Euro-styles, Eine europaweite Landkarte mit 16 sozio-kulturellen Typen, *Marketing Journal*, **22**, 106–11

Haley, R.J. (1968) Benefit Segmentation: A Decision-Oriented Research Tool, *Journal of Marketing*, **32**, 30–5

Hsieh, Sh., O'Leary, J.T. and Morrison, A.M. (1992) Segmenting the International Travel Market by Activity, *Tourism Management*, **13**, 209–23

Kamakura, W.A. and Novak, Th.P. (1992) Value-System Segmentation: Exploring the Meaning of LOV, *Journal of Consumer Research*, **19**, 119–32

Kerin, R.A., Mahajan, V. and Varadarajan, P.R. (1990) *Contemporary Perspectives on Strategic Market Planning*, Allyn & Bacon, Boston

Kramer, S. (1991) *Europäische Life-Style-Analysen zur Verhaltensprognose von Konsumenten*, Dr. Kovac, Hamburg

Kreutzer, R. (1991) Länderübergreifende Segmentierungskonzepte – Antwort auf die Globalisierung der Märkte, *Jahrbuch der Absatz- und Verbrauchsforschung*, **37**(1),4–27

Kroeber-Riel, W. and Weinberg, P. (1996) *Konsumentenverhalten*, 6th edn, Vahlen, Munich

Mayo, E.J. and Jarvis, L.P. (1981) *The Psychology of Leisure Travel*, CBI, Boston

Mazanec, J., Mikulicz, H. and Zins, A. (1991) *Gaestebefragung Oesterreich – Oesterreich-Bericht*, Oesterreichische Gesellschaft fuer Angewandte Fremden-verkehrswissenschaft, Vienna

Mazanec, J.A. (ed.) (1997) *International City Tourism, Analysis and Strategy*, Pinter, London

McNamee, P. (1985) *Tools and Techniques for Strategic Management*, Pergamon Press, Oxford

Pearce, Ph.L. (1982) *The Social Psychology of Tourist Behaviour*, Pergamon Press, Oxford

Rosenberg, M.J. (1967) Cognitive Structure and Attitudinal Effect. In *Readings in Attitude Theory and Measurement* (ed. M. Fishbein), Wiley, New York

Smith, St. L.J. (1989) *Tourism Analysis. A Handbook*, Wiley, New York

SPSS Inc., *SPSS Categories*, SPSS Inc., Chicago

Vavrik, U. and Mazanec, J. (1990) A-priori and A-posteriori Travel Market Segmentation: Tailoring Automatic Interaction Detection and Cluster Analysis for Tourism Marketing, *Cahiers du Tourisme*, Série C, No. 62

Veal, A.J. (1989) Leisure, Lifestyles and Status, *Leisure Studies*, **8**, 141–153

Wells, W.D. (ed.) (1974) *Life Style and Psychographics*, AMA, Chicago

Wells, W.D. (1975) Psychographics: A critical Review, *Journal of Marketing Research*, **12** (May), 196–213

Wind, Y., Mahajan, V. and Swire, D. (1983) An Empirical Comparison of Stand-ardized Portfolio Models, *Journal of Marketing*, **47** (Spring), 89–99

Yiannakis, A. and Gibson, H. (1992) Roles Tourists Play, *Annals of Tourism Research*, **19**, 287–303

18 Developing strategic approaches to tourism destination marketing: the Australian experience

Bill (H.W.) Faulkner

Introduction

The emergence and continuation of tourism as a dynamic and viable industry is dependent upon the adoption of a strategic approach to destination planning and marketing. The hallmark of such an approach is the inclusion of a systematic and structured analysis of broader environmental factors affecting tourism demand as an integral part of the planning process. Equally, as an adjunct to this approach, the ongoing evaluation of the strategies adopted is essential to ensure programmes that become ineffective or counter-productive are identified and replaced. The dynamics of the strategic planning process can thus be likened to the 'natural selection' of programme activities.

While it can be argued that this approach is necessary in any domain of human activity, it is particularly applicable to the tourism field because of the highly discretionary nature of tourism demand, and its consequent sensitivity to both transitory shocks and long-term trends in the broader environment. A full appreciation of these factors is essential if public sector tourism organizations and private sector tourism enterprises are to exploit new opportunities as they arise and adapt to potentially threatening changes.

While the above may appear to be a mere statement of the obvious to many readers, the approach advocated is either not generally applied, or it is only applied in a partial sense. This point is developed by referring to the case of public sector tourism marketing in Australia, where there has been a focus on advertising at the expense of a more balanced strategic approach. It would appear that, while the Australian experience may not necessarily be typical in this regard, it is at least widespread.

In considering these issues, we begin with an overview of the essential ingredients of the strategic approach and highlight symptoms of this approach not being applied in the Australian situation. Elements of the marketing perspective are then discussed in order to bring into focus specific aspects of tourism destination marketing that are relevant to the application of the strategic approach in this setting. A model describing factors affecting tourist arrivals at a destination is used as a backdrop for reviewing the dynamics of the Australian inbound market and, in the process, attention is drawn to the range of environmental factors which have a bearing on the effectiveness of marketing programmes. The current status of tourism destination marketing in Australia is then reviewed in order to elaborate on the key facets of the strategic approach and, finally, the argument for including evaluation procedures as a routine component of the strategic planning process is outlined.

Essential ingredients of the strategic approach

For the purposes of this analysis, the strategic approach is regarded as involving the following essential ingredients:

- A comprehensive and integrated plan of action for an enterprise organization.
- A clearly enunciated set of goals and objectives which provide the focus for the plan of action. These will reflect the corporate view of what is essential for the long-term effectiveness and survival of the organization and its product.
- The establishment of systems for monitoring and evaluating progress towards goals, objectives and targets specified in action plans.
- An approach to planning which explicitly reconciles the inherent competitive advantages and limitations of the organization (or its product) with the challenges (opportunities and threats) of the environment.

The development of the latter aspect of the strategic approach usually involves what is referred to as SWOT analysis, i.e., strengths, weaknesses, opportunities, threats (Johnson and Scholes, 1984). SWOT analysis includes an assessment of existing, and anticipated, opportunities and threats within the environment. Its main purpose is to determine whether or not, in the light of emerging environmental conditions, the weaknesses of an enterprise, product or destination have the potential to undermine

Table 18.1   Research and development in Australia by
industry, 1990/91

	Share of GDP % (A)	Share of total R&D expenditure % (B)
Industry		
Agriculture	4.3	14.2
Mining	4.6	7.0
Manufacturing	15.3	32.1
Transport/communications	7.2	22.4
Tourism	6.6	0.3

Sources: (A) ABS Cat. No. 5206.0 and BTR estimates; (B) Cat ABS. No.8104.0 (Faulkner,
Pearce, Shaw and Weiler, 1994, Table 2, p. 16)

its long-term survival. If this is so, then those weaknesses will need to
be remedied. Alternatively, the enterprise may have certain strengths
which may put it into an advantageous position for exploiting new
opportunities.

   In the Australian context there are several symptoms of a general lack
of strategic thinking in tourism. First, there is a prevailing 'boom and
gloom' mentality, with dramatic shifts between the extremes of optimism and pessimism reflecting a tendency to over-react to short-term
events and developments. Second, there is an inclination to rely on 'gut
feelings' and anecdotal evidence as a basis for making decisions, rather
than drawing upon readily available objective research. It is human nature
to assess a situation in a way that reinforces our preconceptions and
prejudices. The first impression is therefore often reinforced by selectively drawing on anecdotal evidence which tells only part of the story.
Then, when more soundly based research contradicts what has become
the conventional wisdom, it is the research which is questioned rather
than the conventional wisdom. Finally, following on from the previous
point, there is a parsimonious attitude to investment in research. This is
reflected in the data presented in Table 18.1, which reveals a disproportionately low level of investment in tourism research by the public and
private sectors, relative to other industries.

   The first two symptoms, in particular, reflect the incomplete picture
of the environment affecting tourism held by many decision-makers.
That is, the assessments they make are not balanced by an appreciation
of the full range of factors influencing trends in tourism. This point
is considered in more detail subsequently when public sector tourism
marketing in Australia is examined more closely. Aspects of the third
symptom, relating to the lack of commitment to research, are also considered in this context.

Tourism marketing in perspective

Most analyses of tourism marketing (see, for example, Greenley and Matcham, 1971) highlight distinguishing features of the tourism product by referring to such characteristics as:

- Intangibility (product cannot be seen, touched, tasted or sampled prior to purchase).
- Perishability (production is fixed in time and space and the product cannot be stored for future use).
- Heterogeneity (it is difficult to achieve standardization to the extent that is possible in mass produced goods).
- Inseparability (the act of production and consumption is simultaneous).

While this approach may have been useful for pin-pointing characteristics of the tourism product which have a bearing on the marketing process, in these respects tourism is in fact no different from services in general. Furthermore, Middleton (1983) and others (for example, Wyckham et al., 1975) have argued that services are not really distinguishable from goods in terms of these dimensions in any case.

Whatever one's position on the issues in this debate, there are two features of tourism that have a fundamental bearing on the subject of this chapter, but which are neither emphasized nor generally recognized in the literature.

First, tourism is an amalgam of complementary services which are destination-specific. While Medlik and Middleton (1974: 29) and Jeffries (1971), for instance, recognize the 'amalgam' characteristic, they do not specifically emphasize, or spell out the implications of, tourism being destination-specific.

The implications of this from a marketing point of view are that some emphasis has to be placed on promoting the destination, rather than individual elements of the amalgam *per se*. Also, because the organization of the services at a particular destination is fragmented, a considerable amount of coordination is required in this process. The need for this coordination has resulted in government intervention (Gilbert, 1990), and in fact the main role of the public sector in tourism development (in Australia if not in all countries) has focused on generic marketing of regions, states and the country as a whole.

To appreciate the second prominent feature of tourism marketing which is most relevant to the point of this paper, it is necessary to go back to the classical 'four Ps' framework (i.e. product, price, promotion and place) attributed to McCarthy (1981). Using this framework, tourism marketing is described as being:

- The process of identifying the needs and propensities of consumer (or, more specifically, different segments of the consuming public).
- Developing or modifying the product in accordance with the needs of identified target markets.
- Devising mechanisms for facilitating awareness of, interest in, and access to the product.
- Translating the above into sales through distribution networks, pricing mechanisms, etc.

However, given that the attractions or attributes of a destination are relatively fixed, there is a considerable element (at least in the short term) of adjusting consumer wants to the product. We thus have a typical chicken and egg situation in the marketing process, which was explicitly recognized by Kottler (1961) over thirty years ago when he pointed out that 'Marketing's short-term task is to adjust consumers' wants to existing goods, but its long-term task is to adjust the goods to the customers' wants'. Of course, when considering tourism we should substitute 'products' for 'goods', as this statement clearly applies across the board to both goods and services.

The problem with public sector tourism agencies in Australia, and probably the world over, is that they have become fixated on the short-term aspect of tourism marketing by putting all their efforts into packaging regional icons into images designed to appeal to consumers in advertising programmes. This process usually involves some marketing research (group sessions, sample surveys, market segmentation analyses, etc.), which is used to identify those features of the product that have an affinity with the attitudes and preferences of consumers. However, as a consequence of the emphasis on advertising programmes, agencies have lost sight of the fact that consumer decisions occur within the context of a range of broader environmental factors. These factors impact on the propensity of specific market segments to make discretionary expenditures, and they influence the trade-off between tourism and other outlets for leisure activity which must also be taken into account.

A strategic approach to marketing therefore requires a more rigorous analysis of these contextual factors than has been generally carried out to date. To elaborate on this point, an outline of what constitutes the environmental (or contextual) factors is provided in the following section. It provides the background required for the analysis of recent developments in public sector tourism agencies in Australia which leads to the conclusion that they have become preoccupied with a tactical, as opposed to a strategic, approach.

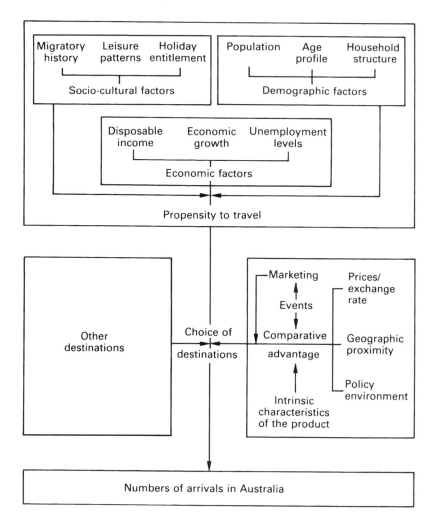

Figure 18.1   Factors affecting visitor arrivals at a destination

The dynamics of the Australian inbound market

For the purposes of elaborating on the strategic considerations which need to be taken into account in tourism marketing, we will examine the dynamics of the inbound market. The range of factors influencing the market is described in Figure 18.1, where a distinction is made between:

- factors that affect the propensity of populations to travel; and
- factors that affect the comparative advantage of the destination question and, therefore, the potential for it to be chosen as a place to visit.

At this point it is important to note that the model has been for illustrative purposes only. It is not intended to provide a comprehensive or exhaustive coverage of all factors at this stage, although it could be construed as having the potential to provide a heuristic framework for doing so in the longer term. Again, examples from the Australian situation will be used for clarification purposes.

Considering the factors that affect the propensity to travel first, one of the main sets of variables relates to *economic factors*. The general health of the economy, as reflected for instance in gross domestic product (GDP), has a bearing on:

- Disposable incomes, and therefore the ability and preparedness to spend on discretionary items such as travel. The significance of this variable is reflected in the fact that, according to Middleton (1983), three-quarters of world travel in the 1980s was generated by the twenty countries with the highest per capita disposable incomes. The distribution of incomes within the population is also important as this will influence the proportion of the population who have sufficient income to travel.
- The general health of the economy also affects unemployment levels, which in turn have a fundamental influence not only on the size of the population with the disposable incomes required for travel, but also on the overall confidence of the market to spend in this area. High unemployment generates uncertainty within individuals about their future income earning capacity, and thus reduces their preparedness to spend on discretionary items such as travel.

The significance of economic growth, and its bearing on tourism through its effect on disposable incomes, unemployment levels and general consumer confidence is highlighted in Figure 18.2. The trend in visitor arrivals to Australia over the past twenty years reveals only three periods when arrivals actually declined – 1975, 1983 and 1989. All these reversals coincided with periods of general world-wide economic downturns. The more pronounced reversal in 1989 reflects the additional effects of other contributing factors, such as:

- Time-switching effects associated with the 1988 World Expo in Brisbane and the Australian bicentennial celebrations.
- The appreciation of the Australian dollar.
- An Australia-wide domestic airlines pilots dispute.
- An increasing proportion of holiday visitors in the Australian inbound market, which has the effect of making the market more volatile because of its increasingly discretionary nature (Faulkner, 1990).

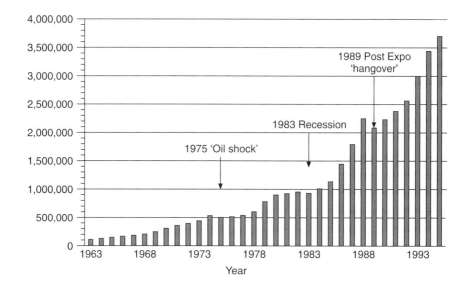

Figure 18.2   Short-term arrivals in Australia, 1965–95

The second set of factors affecting propensity to travel relate to *demographic factors* such as the size, age profile and family structure of the population:

- After taking into account disposable incomes and the distribution of incomes, the actual size of the population is obviously critical in determining the number of travellers that can be generated by a particular market.
- Ageing populations often generate more travel owing to the higher proportion of retirees who not only have more free time at their disposal for travel, but also have relatively high disposable incomes despite being income-poor.
- Household structure has a bearing on the nature of demand through its influence on household disposable incomes through, for example, the incidence of double income households with no kids (or DINKS) and the free time available for holidays (e.g. DINKS have an inclination for short breaks because of the work commitments of partners and the difficulty of arranging concurrent leave).

The third set of factors affecting propensity to travel relate to the *socio-cultural background* of the population. Relevant factors include:

- The migratory history of the population, which will have a bearing on travel to the extent that it generates visits to friends and relatives (VFR) traffic.

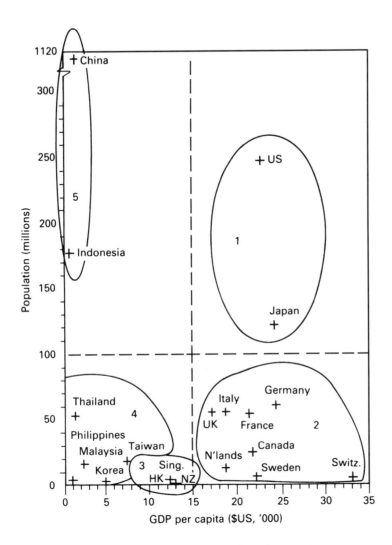

Figure 18.3 Population and wealth of major markets

- Institutional factors such as holiday entitlements affect the amount of free time a population has at its disposal for travel *vis-à-vis* other leisure pursuits. For instance, travel for Japanese is constrained by them having only two weeks' annual leave.

As population and wealth are two of the more easily measurable and potent factors affecting the potential of individual markets, various markets are classified in terms of these two factors in Figure 18.3. Here each country has been plotted according to its population (on the vertical axis)

Table 18.2   Visitor arrivals from major market groups

Group	Country	Arrivals in 1995 (000s)
1	USA	304.9
	Japan	782.7
2	Germany	124.2
	France	35.2
	Canada	58.4
	Switzerland	35.3
	Netherlands	34.5
	Italy	36.8
	Sweden	22.4
	United Kingdom	347.9
3	Singapore	202.4
	New Zealand	538.4
	Hong Kong	131.4
4	Taiwan	152.0
	Korea	168.0
	Malaysia	108.2
	Thailand	81.3
	Philippines	27.0
5	China	42.6
	Indonesia	135.0

and GDP per capita (on the horizontal axis). If it is assumed that wealth takes precedence over the size of the population, then each group's potential to generate visitors can be ranked in accordance with the numbering system adopted in the graph. Thus, for instance, China is a low generator of overseas travellers despite its huge 1.1 billion population because fewer of its people can afford to travel.

If we look at how each market has performed in terms of the number of arrivals in Australia in Table 18.2, however, we can see that there are a number of anomalies:

- Japan has almost double the number of arrivals compared with the USA, despite these two countries being in the same group.
- The UK stands out as having up to ten times the number of arrivals of other countries in its group.
- Singapore, New Zealand and Hong Kong registered more arrivals than most of the wealthier and larger countries in the previous group.
- New Zealand is among the top three inbound markets despite its being one of the smallest countries.

To address these apparent anomalies, we need to look at the second set of factors in the model, i.e. factors affecting the *competitive advantage* of Australia *vis-à-vis* other destinations. These include such factors as:

- Geographical proximity, which in turn affects costs of getting to Australia in terms of both time and money, the level of inconvenience associated with time zone adjustments, and what geographers refer to as intervening opportunities.
- Comparative prices of various aspects of the product which, in turn, can be influenced by relativities between countries in wages, price inflation and exchange rates. The policy environment in the destination can have a profound effect on its competitiveness. The micro-economic reform agenda in Australia has enhanced its competitiveness as a destination through the impact of deregulation on the price and quality of domestic airline services. However, despite this and other reforms, many aspects of the Australian product continue to be uncompetitive in terms of price (Commonwealth Department of Industry, Science and Technology, 1996). In particular, Australia's weak position *vis-à-vis* competing Asian destinations stands out in this analysis.
- The political stability of a country will affect its attractiveness as a destination to the extent that this influences safety considerations. The decline in Fiji's inbound market during and after the 1980s political coup provides an example of this effect, as does the more recent impact of the Gulf War on world travel in general.
- As we have seen in the recent history of inbound travel to Australia, events such as the 88 Expo can have a profound short-term effect on visitor numbers. They can also have a longer-term promotional effect. The staging of the 2000 Olympics in Sydney has been broadly endorsed as a major coup for the tourism industry because of its potential to have this effect.

Given that Australia is a long-haul destination for most countries, international airfares make up a substantial proportion of the total cost of visiting this destination. The effect international airfare fluctuations can have on visitor numbers is highlighted in Figure 18.4, which shows a peak in arrivals to Australia from the USA coinciding with the heightened competition on the US–Australian route that accompanied the entry of Northwest Airlines. This figure also highlights the response of the US market to the 1988 World Expo in Brisbane.

The two remaining factors that affect the competitive position of a destination are the natural and man-made attributes (or intrinsic characteristics) that affect its appeal as a place to visit, and the effectiveness of

USA Arrivals

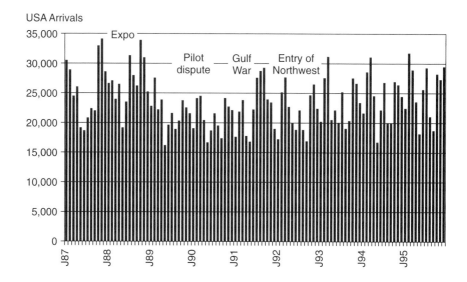

Figure 18.4 Short-term arrivals from the USA

the marketing of the destination. Advertising and promotional activities are fundamental catalysts by virtue of the role they play in stimulating the overseas markets' awareness of, and interest in, travelling to the destination.

In the analysis of inbound markets in terms of wealth and population, we noted several anomalies. These anomalies become somewhat more understandable if we take into account just one of the more readily quantifiable factors referred to above as contributing to comparative advantage, i.e. geographical proximity. When we superimpose the geographical proximity factor on the earlier classification based on population and wealth, as in Figure 18.5, it can be seen that most of the anomalies exceed expectations because of their greater geographical proximity to Australia.

What stands out in this sort of analysis is the impression of transience in the factors affecting demand. It seems that the combination of variables which is most influential varies in time, with each variable (or set of variables) coming into play periodically as some threshold is reached, which represents the point at which the market becomes sensitive to the variable in question. If this is the case, then it is little wonder that empirical studies fail to agree on a common set of dominant variables (Crouch and Shaw, 1990). This suggests that constant surveillance and analysis of all these factors are necessary if the dynamics of the market are to be properly understood.

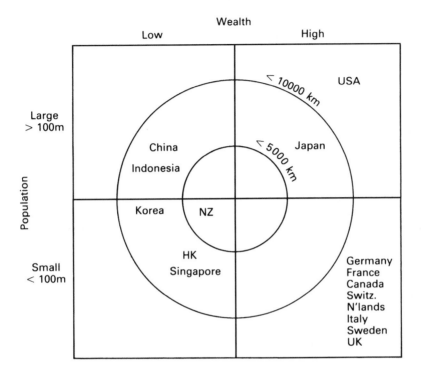

Figure 18.5 Geographical proximity of major markets

Public sector tourism marketing in Australia

The above model highlights the need to analyse macro-level factors affecting tourism demand in order to provide a context for other aspects of marketing research. Indeed, the analysis of these factors is essential for establishment of a truly strategic approach for two specific reasons:

- Such analyses provide the basis for identifying, and therefore targeting, those markets that exhibit the greatest potential to travel.
- In evaluating the effectiveness of promotion programmes, variables which affect the response of markets, but which are less susceptible to manipulation through the advertising process, must be taken into account.

In reviewing the progress of public sector marketing in Australia towards the satisfaction of these requirements one would have to conclude that, at best, we have had mixed success. There have been some positive developments, which represent a tentative step in the right direction, but progress beyond this point has faltered owing to a shift in priorities towards an all-consuming concentration of resources on advertising.

On the positive side, the establishment of the Australian Bureau of Tourism Research (BTR) in 1987 resulted in the concentration of State and Commonwealth resources to create the critical mass required for an effective research programme. Also, through this initiative, a more co-ordinated approach to tourism research at the national level has been established. Systems for monitoring the levels and characteristics of tourist activity have been upgraded and progress has been made in the analysis of factors affecting demand, especially through work carried out on the development of forecasting models. This work has been extended recently through the establishment of the national Tourism Forecasting Council, which adds a consultative dimension to the forecasting process. In line with the BTR's designated role of promoting the more effective use of research in tourism development, it has been instrumental in fostering the adoption of a strategic approach by making government and industry more aware of the importance of a firm research foundation in the planning and management process.

In general, marketing research carried out by government tourism bodies has consisted mainly of market segmentation studies aimed at calibrating advertising activities and, incidentally, to provide input to product development. Tracking studies have also been carried out for the purposes of gauging the immediate effect of individual advertising campaigns on changing the awareness of, and interest in, the product. Meanwhile, some satisfaction surveys have been conducted from time to time. These surveys have not always involved the degree of methodological rigor that would justify the conclusions drawn from them.

The recognition of the influence of contextual factors has been to some extent forced upon the Commonwealth and state tourism agencies by their respective departments of finance and treasuries. The simplistic attribution of growth in tourism numbers directly to advertising campaigns, without reference to other factors, is no longer accepted as a credible justification for continued public funding of tourism promotion (Faulkner and Shaw, 1992). Such pressure was instrumental in the conduct of a more rigorous evaluation of the Australian Tourist Commission's (ATC) programme (see ATC, 1991), which featured a detailed analysis of contextual factors (Crouch and Shaw, 1990). Crouch (1994) has since extended this work by using a meta analysis based approach to isolate the key independent variables that have been utilized in the analysis of international tourism movements.

Despite the impetus that the ATC initiative could have provided, there remains a general insensitivity to the level of commitment to research which is essential to the development of a truly strategic posture. Indeed, as mentioned previously, the prevailing trend among public sector tourism agencies in Australia is towards the concentration of resources on advertising programmes at the expense of research. This phenomenon has been referred to as 'advertising fundamentalism' (Faulkner, 1991), the rationale of which appears to hinge on the following proposition that 'gaining the competitive edge in the quest for maximising market share resides in the manipulation of consumer awareness and choice through advertising programmes. In the context of limited funding and the high cost of maintaining electronic media exposure, therefore, the diversion of funds from research and other areas is justified'.

While it is plausible that an increased commitment to advertising will increase market share, this will only occur if these programmes are integrated with a broader strategy encompassing product development and the effective identification and targeting of potential market segments. Also, the impacts of advertising and the marketing programme as a whole need to be continuously monitored and evaluated so that deficiencies can be remedied and adjustments made in response to changing circumstances. Therefore, without a sound research basis for these aspects of the marketing process, the destination marketing organization's stewardship of the overall marketing programme is akin to 'flying blind'.

Systematic evaluation as an integral component of the destination marketing process

From the discussion in the previous section, it might be concluded that a considerable investment in research is an essential prerequisite for the development of a truly strategic approach to tourism destination marketing, and research has a twofold role in this context. First, research is necessary to assess the current state of affairs and scan the environment in the manner necessary to carry out a destination SWOT analysis and, in the light of this, devise marketing plans for the future. Second, research is necessary to evaluate the impacts of these plans and thus provide a basis for identifying deficiencies and devising measures to remedy these.

The approach to the evaluation phase to date, however, has been distorted by the tendency for this activity to be carried out largely as a response to external demands for accountability, rather than as a consequence of any recognition of its importance as an integral part of the planning process. A piecemeal and fragmented approach to evaluation has therefore prevailed, with the high profile/high cost elements of marketing programmes being the focus of attention and the timing of the evaluation being governed by the periodic concerns of other agencies, rather than the continuous requirements of internal programme management. Within this environment, the full potential of evaluation as an integral part of the destination marketing plan development and management process is yet to be realized.

A framework for the comprehensive evaluation of destination marketing programmes is provided in Figure 18.6. Here, the evaluation process is depicted as comprising four basic layers of activity:

- The programme review stage, where the appropriateness of organizational objectives is assessed, and the key strategies (media advertising, direct marketing, travel writer programmes, etc.) are identified. Associated targets around which the marketing programme is structured are also noted as benchmarks for considering outcomes.
- The performance monitoring phase involves the measurement of the output of each element of the programme in terms of various performance indicators (number of inquiries generated, coupon responses, column inches generated, etc.).
- The causal analysis phase carries the previous activities a step further by attempting to establish linkages between outputs and responses in the market place. At one level, we may employ such techniques as tracking studies and conversion studies to quantify immediate impacts, while market share analyses might be used to map longer term market trends with a view to identifying longer term effects. At another level, multivariate analysis or experimental methods might be applied in an effort to distinguish market reactions specifically attributable to the programme from those associated with the effects of broader environmental factors such as those discussed earlier in this chapter.
- Finally, the cost–benefit analysis stage is essentially concerned with establishing whether or not the costs incurred in implementing the programme are outweighed by the benefits derived from any increase in visitor arrivals that is achieved.

A more detailed review of the methods involved in the development of this approach to evaluation appears in Faulkner (1997), where the underlying rationale for its application is also described. Briefly, there are three key points regarding the limitations of evaluation methodologies and the strategic planning process which warrant mention at this point:

- Destination marketing programmes encompass a range of activities which represent a small proportion of the extensive array of factors that influence international tourism flows. While some of these factors are quantifiable and can therefore be taken into account in conventional forms of analysis, many potentially important variables have

Programme review

		b1 Media advertising	b2 Billboard posters	b3 Direct marketing	b4 Information services	b5 Travel shows	b6 Travel writers	b7 Trade missions	b8 Trade shows
(1)	a Objectives (Are they appropriate?)								
	b Strategies/tactics								
	c Targets	c1	c2	c3	c4	c5	c6	c7	c8

Performance monitoring (Outputs)

(2)	d Performance indicators	No. inquiries	No. inquiries	Coupon responses	No. inquiries	Attendance levels, inquiries/contacts	Column inches/minutes coverage	No. inquiries	Transactions enacted

Causal analysis (Outcomes)

(3)	e Immediate impacts — Tracking studies, Conversion studies, Market share analysis
	f Environmental factors — Multivariate analysis, Experimental/quasi-experimental methods

Cost benefit analysis

(4)	g Costs	g1	g2	g3	g4	g5	g6	g7	g8
	h Benefits	h1	h2	h3	h4	h5	h6	h7	h8
	i Cost: Benefit ratio	I1	I2	I3	I4	I5	I6	I7	I8

Figure 18.6 Framework for destination marketing evaluation

been excluded because adequate data is not available and/or they are simply not quantifiable. We can, therefore, only ever expect to isolate the impacts of marketing and other contributing factors in a partial sense.

- Also, whatever techniques are applied in the evaluation process, they will each be deficient in some respect and the interpretation of results will be subject to certain caveats. This problem resulted in the Australian Tourist Commission (1991) adopting a 'weight of evidence' approach to the evaluation of its programmes, whereby several parallel studies involving methodologies with different sets of strengths and weaknesses were involved. Thus, collaborative results produced by a combination of these studies imply a higher level of confidence to the extent that the limitations of one technique might be compensated by the strengths of another. The framework described in Figure 18.6 represents an extension of this approach in the sense that it provides a more systematic and coherent methodology.

- Attempts to attribute market trends to specific marketing initiatives are further compounded by the fact that many of the variables and events influencing tourists' decisions in general, and the relative attractiveness of the destination in particular, are simply beyond the control of destination marketing organizations. There are two implications of this. First, whatever criteria are adopted as indicators of success in the market place, caution must be exercised in the extent to which outcomes are attributed specifically to marketing activities. Some outcomes are achieved as the consequence of a fortuitous (or unfortunate) convergence of random events irrespective of the actions of destination marketing organizations. Second, no matter how sophisticated the forecasting methodologies upon which strategic planning may be based, the environment in which we operate is essentially chaotic and the only certainty is that the unexpected will happen. Accordingly, a flexible approach to strategic planning is necessary, with environmental scanning and evaluation being constant ingredients of this process. As an integral part of this approach, a repertoire of contingency plans should be in place so that the organization can respond more promptly to unexpected threats and opportunities as they arise (Faulkner and Valerio, 1995).

In the Australian context, the advertising fundamentalists will appear to be vindicated in the short term, as growth in the inbound and domestic tourism sectors in the early to mid-1990s have continued in response to improving international and domestic economic conditions, and the inbound market in particular continues to be boosted by the growth of nearby Asian economies. The extent to which increased visitation levels are actually attributable to the emphasis on advertising will therefore be open to question, and will certainly not be verifiable if research functions remain under-resourced. More importantly, however, problems will be encountered in the future as the effectiveness of longer term (i.e. strategic) planning is jeopardized by the insufficient research input to both the analysis of emerging trends and the evaluation of previous methods. We are therefore prone to repeating the mistakes of the past.

Conclusion

The basic proposition of this chapter has been that the analysis of the contextual or environmental factors affecting tourism demand is an integral part of the more strategic approach to tourism marketing, which is so essential for long-term effectiveness. Equally, more rigorous and systematic evaluations of marketing effectiveness are required to complement this approach. The trend towards advertising fundamentalism (at the expense of the commitment to research) among tourism agencies in Australia is therefore inconsistent with the development of the strategic marketing approach and will be counter-productive in the longer term.

From an Australian point of view, this trend will progressively undermine any competitive advantage its tourism product either currently possesses or has the potential to develop in the future. Of course, this will occur only to the extent that other countries, which provide alternative destinations, are not also falling into the 'advertising fundamentalism' trap.

It seems highly likely, however, that the failure to adopt a truly strategic approach is not unique to Australia. On an international scale, therefore, the implications of this phenomenon go beyond simply the effect it may have on the competitive advantage of individual countries *vis-à-vis* others. The real problem is that the prevailing approach to tourism development and marketing has the potential to stifle the emergence of tourism as a dynamic and sustainable force in many economies.

References

Australian Tourist Commission (1991) *Evaluation of the Australian Tourist Commission's Marketing Impact*, Australian Tourist Commission, Sydney

Commonwealth Department of Industry, Science and Technology (1996) *Australian Tourism: is it Price Competitive*, Tourism Occasional Paper No. 4, Australian Government Publishing Service, Canberra

Crouch, G.I. (1994) The study of international demand: a survey of practice, *Journal of Travel Research*, **32**(4), (Spring) pp. 41–55

Crouch, G.I. and Shaw, R.N. (1990) Determinants of international tourist flows: findings from 30 years of empirical research, *Proceedings of 21st Annual Conference of the Travel and Tourism Research Association*, 10–14 June, New Orleans, Louisiana, pp. 45–60

Faulkner, H.W. (1990) Swings and roundabouts in Australian tourism. *Tourism Management*, **11**(1), 29–37

Faulkner, H.W. (1991) The role of research in tourism development. *Tourism Update* (Bureau of Tourism Research), September qtr, pp. 2–3

Faulkner, H.W. (1997) A model for the evaluation of national tourism destination marketing programs, *Journal of Travel Research*, (Winter), **35**(3)

Faulkner, H.W. and Shaw, R.N. (eds) (1992) The evaluation of tourism marketing campaigns, Occasional Paper No. 13, Bureau of Tourism Research, Canberra

Faulkner, H.W., Pearce, P., Shaw, R. and Weiler, B. (1994) Tourism research in Australia: confronting the challenges of the 1990s and beyond. In *Tourism Research and Education in Australia: Proceedings of the Australian National Tourism and Education Conferences* (ed. Faulkner, H.W., Fagence, M., Davidson M. and Craig-Smith, S.), Bureau of Tourism Research, Canberra

Faulkner, H.W. and Valerio, P. (1995) Towards and integrative approach to tourism demand forecasting, *Tourism Management*, **16**(1), 29–37

Gilbert, D. (1990) Tourism marketing: its emergence and establishment. In *Progress in Tourism, Recreation and Hospitality Management* (ed. C. Cooper), University of Surrey, vol. 3, pp. 77–90

Greenley, G.E. and Matcham, A.S. (1971) Problems in marketing services, *European Journal of Marketing*, **17**(6), 57–64

Jeffries, D. (1971) Defining the tourism product: its significance in tourism marketing, *Tourist Review*, **26**(1), 2–5

Johnson, G. and Scholes, K. (1984) *Exploring Corporate Strategy*, Prentice-Hall, Englewood Cliffs, NJ

Kottler, F.H. (1961) *Marketing Management Analysis, Planning Control*, Prentice-Hall, Englewood Cliffs, NJ

McCarthy, E.J. (1981) *Basic Marketing: a Management Approach*, 7th edn, Irwin, Homewood, Ill.

Medlik, S. and Middleton, V.T.C. (1974) The tourism product and its marketing implications, *International Tourism Quarterly*, 28–35

Middleton, V.T.C. (1983) Product marketing – goods and services compared, *Quarterly Review of Marketing*, Summer, 1–10

Wychkam, R.G., Fitzroy, T. and Mandry, G.D. (1975) *European Journal of Marketing*, **9**(1), pp. 59–67

19 Homogeneous products: the future of established resorts

Michael Morgan

Introduction

Five years ago, when the first edition of this book was being written, the Managing Director of the UK's biggest tour operator wondered, in a trade press article, whether 'the package holiday as we know it is going out of fashion?' (Newbold, 1989). There was evidence of falling demand and changing consumer behaviour creating a crisis not only for the UK tour operators but for the tourism industry in their main destination area, the Mediterranean coasts. The crisis was particularly felt in the established resorts that had grown up in response to the seemingly endless rise in demand for beach holidays in the sun since the 1960s. Many critics of the industry, and some insiders, felt that it was a crisis of the tourism industry's own making. The product had become homogeneous, quality had failed to keep pace with customer expectations, and so people were looking elsewhere. This updated chapter examines how this had come about, the strategies used to counter the problem and the degree of success these strategies have enjoyed.

That tourist resorts tend to be homogeneous is not surprising. They all seek to offer the same core benefits. Nor is the homogeneity necessarily a problem. It can be argued that at certain stages of its development it is a positive advantage for a new resort to resemble established ones. Tourists may be reassured by the familiarity of their surroundings in a strange land. The problem comes not when the products are all perceived to be the same but when they are all perceived to be characterless, unfashionable and low in quality. This is how increasing numbers of potential customers are coming to regard the Mediterranean-style beach resort. The period of growth is over, new competitors are challenging their market share, and product differentiation and product quality are becoming the marketing priorities: 'We can guarantee a daily average of five hours sun throughout the year – but so can other destinations,' said an editorial in the Malta National Tourist Office newsletter of July 1990. The traditional sun, sand and sea product is no longer enough to assure the future of established resorts.

In manufacturing industry, products that reach the decline stage of their life cycle can be discontinued or completely redesigned and relaunched. Neither option is available to an established resort. You cannot 'close' Magaluf or Salou. Too many jobs and too much capital are at risk. Nor can any one organization 'redesign' a resort which is the result of years of interaction between private and public sector tourist undertakings and the local community.

This chapter will examine the strategies open to the established resorts. First the factors which have led to the current homogeneity will be outlined, with the implied lessons for newly developing resorts. Next, the issue will be placed in the context of the overall situation, or perhaps crisis, facing mass tourism in the early 1990s. The strategies subsequently adopted by a number of established resorts will then be assessed as possible models for others to follow.

Many of the examples given are from the author's studies of the British market for Spanish resorts, but the process – which has reached a highly developed stage there – can be seen at work in beach resorts everywhere.

Why tourist resorts tend to become homogenous products

Core benefits

One of the first principles of marketing is that people buy benefits and not product features (Kotler, 1988). The physical features and facilities of the resort, its transport links and the multinational network of tour operators and travel agents through which it is sold are all simply the means of 'delivering the desired satisfaction' (Kotler, 1988). In the case of beach tourism this is commonly described as sun, sand and sea – which in terms of benefits means warmth, recreation, relaxation and an escape from the routines of working life. Some versions add other Ss to the list, such as sangria (or spirits) and sex, reminding us that holidays also satisfy social needs, and that one of the functions of the resort is to provide an environment where normal social inhibitions are suspended for the duration of the holiday. For many beach tourists the precise destination where they obtain these benefits is of secondary importance.

Tangible features

The tangible features of the resort develop from its core attractions of a beach, safe bathing and a warm climate. Hotels within walking distance of the sea, preferably with a sea view, are essential. Cafes for refreshment in the heat of the day, bars and nightspots for socializing in the warm nights soon follow. Shops develop to serve the needs of the tourists for souvenirs, beach wear, games equipment, cosmetics and gifts. It is inevitable that the land use of resorts follows predictable patterns distinct from normal residential and commercial developments (Lavery, 1971) with a recreational business district – 'a seasonally oriented grouping of restaurants, novelty and souvenir shops' (Stansfield and Rickert, 1970).

Packaging and distribution

These Mediterranean resorts are packaged by northern European tour operators with very little emphasis on their geographical location. As Goodall and Bergsma say 'The mass tour operator is marketing a holiday brand image emphasising the quality of service of that operator and in which the image of a holiday in a given destination is unlikely to figure prominently' (Goodall and Bergsma, 1990). Instead they are sold as a composite destination known as Summersun, or as tribal enclaves inhabited by like-minded tourists, normally segmented by age – Club 18–30, Twenties, Young at Heart, Golden Days, etc. These very successful products sell by delivering the core benefits more effectively or more cheaply than their competitors. The local culture, scenery, history and architecture are optional excursions, as is the once-a-week folkloric floor show in the hotel. As the operators control the marketing channels, the individual hotels and the destination tourist board have little influence on how the resort is presented in brochures and advertising.

International markets, global products

The hotels and other facilities may be managed by local companies but the style of their services is deliberately intentional. A hotel in Spain with British, German, Scandinavian, Italian and Spanish guests tries to cater for all tastes with buffet meals and multilingual entertainment. The success of the Palma-based Grupo Sol, with 140 hotels from Bali to Venezuela, on this multinational formula seems to support Levitt's famous assertion (1983) on the globalization of markets: 'The world is becoming a common market place in which people – no matter where they come from – desire the same products and lifestyles.' If the price is right, says Levitt, 'they will take highly standardised world products . . .' including, one might add, purpose-built, high-rise resorts with a standardized night-life based on Coca-Cola, Budweiser and disco music.

Economies of scale

The successful growth of tourism in the post-World War II period has indeed been price-led, based on the tour operators' ability to deliver hitherto inaccessible warm climate destinations at prices affordable by the vast majority of people in northern Europe (and North America). To do this the operators have needed to achieve economies of scale on charter flights and large allocations at resort hotels.

These low prices depended on the operators negotiating low rates from the hoteliers, which in turn were made possible by low wage levels and favourable exchange rates. As a result tourists were given three-star quality at prices that would hardly pay for a guest house in their own countries. This further encouraged the growth in the overseas market at the expense of the domestic market, especially in Britain.

Standardized building methods

To benefit from the rising demand for large numbers of beds at low prices, local hoteliers have had to employ standardized building methods and plot ratios more reminiscent of London or Manhattan than of their own vernacular architecture.

It is too easy to condemn architectural styles in the resorts when buildings in the same styles were being built with the same disregard for the historical and cultural environment in most towns and cities of the world at the time. The growth of mass tourism coincided with an era of architecture advanced in technology but limited in aesthetics. Functional simplicity was preferred to ornamentation and disguise, straight lines and rectangles to curves and ovals – admirably honest in theory, cheap to implement but monotonous in result. The spa resorts of the eighteenth century and the seaside towns of the nineteenth were equally mass produced and homogeneous in architecture but the crescents of Bath have to modern eyes an elegant charm we have not yet learnt to discern in the towers Benidorm.

The reaction against such resorts can be seen as part of a wider post modernist revolt against functionalism and internationalism in style. When the heir to the British throne described a modernist design for an extension to London's National Gallery as 'a monstrous carbuncle on the face of a well-loved friend', he could have been articulating many a tourist's reaction to the over-development of their favourite holiday area.

Yet, when they were developed, the high-rise resort hotels symbolized to the local business community not only profit but prestige, modernization and an alluring Americanized life-style.

Quality assurance

This symbolism also worked for the tourist. Standardized products promoted globally with a strong brand identity do not succeed only on price advantage. Their instantly recognized style and logos promise a standard quality, reassuring amid the unfamiliar imagery of locally produced goods and services. To quote two recent advertising slogans, 'You're never far from a Hilton', or 'If Thomsons do it, do it. If Thomsons don't do it, don't do it'.

For a tourist making his or her first visit to a country, the modern architecture and the multinational logos of the hotels promise an enclave of familiarity and security in a strange and threatening world. Around the hotels, smaller businesses, often run by ex-patriots, offer a similar reassurance in the form of British, American or German style bars, cafes and supermarkets.

In some resorts, this sense of the tourist district as a safe enclave is only too accurate. Tourists in some African resorts and European and American cities are warned not to venture away from the hotel on their own. In others, such as beach resorts on the north African coast, there is literally nowhere to go – the nearest 'real' indigenous settlements being an hour or more drive away. The resort, or even the individual hotel with its pool replacing the crowded and polluted beach, is self-contained, like a permanently-moored cruise liner from which the 'passengers' disembark only for organized excursions.

New resorts in the Caribbean and Far East are designed specifically as integrated resort developments (Stiles and See-Tho, 1991) with a range of sporting and social facilities such that the guest need not leave the site for the duration the holiday – a concept pioneered by holiday centres such as Butlins in the UK and the French Club Mediterranee. These take the concept of the brand image replacing the destination image to the logical extreme, but the same characteristics of self-contained uniformity are shared by many more conventional resorts.

Why has this formula succeeded in the past?

This formula works very successfully as long as the tourist's prime concern is for relaxation and recreation in a warmer climate among people that they feel comfortable with. The very artificiality of the resort enhances the sense of the holiday as a break from the real world. The familiar symbols in a warmer climate create a relaxed mood in which the normal social inhibitions are suspended. The 'British pub' stays open all night, plays loud music, shows non-stop action videos, and garlands you with paper streamers. You are neither in Britain nor Spain but Never Never Land.

The function of the destination in this holiday experience is primarily to provide the warm climate and the low prices based on lower wage costs and favourable exchange rates. It also gives the holiday an exotic background, often experienced as superficially as that of a themed bar or restaurant at home. It is made tangible in souvenirs of the local national stereotypical symbols – famous buildings, wildlife or local customs – which bear little relation to the content of the holiday. Often they are not relevant to the particular region, as with the ubiquitous flamenco dancing dolls in regions of Spain far from Andalucia. These souvenirs and gifts help to give the tourist status on returning home from the exotic destination.

Growth of the tourism market in the 1980s

In the growth market of the 1980s, tourist resorts proliferated. New markets of first generation tourists took advantage of the shortest flights and low prices to escape the uncertainties of the north west European climate for their annual holiday. The boom was experienced not only in Spain but throughout the Mediterranean.

Newer destinations were added to operators' programmes and new resorts built to cater for the demand. This led to the rapid development of previously untouched coastline in places like the Turkish coast into 'high density, low grade holiday townships, lacking not only visual attraction but also basic services' (Economist Intelligence Unit, *International Tourism Reports*, No. 1, 1989). The Algarve in Portugal is another area often cited as a recent victim of over development, having failed to learn the lessons from the development of the Spanish Costas (Barrett, 1989).

In the meantime the established areas of Spain went on increasing the accommodation stock, 70,000 beds being added, for example, in Majorca between 1986 and 1990 (Morgan, 1991).

This growth, primarily from the UK, was fuelled by the low prices commented on earlier. In 1986 the leading UK tour operator, Thomson, reacted to the first signs of market saturation and potential loss of market share with a dramatic series of discounts, sparking off a long price war with its main competitors. The result was volume growth at the expense of profit margins, which led to mergers and bankruptcies wiping out several leading tour operators, including, in 1991, Thomson's main rival the International Leisure Group.

In the short term the price war benefited the tourists and the resorts, but the reduction in profitability affected the hoteliers as well as the tour operators. In Spain, particularly, the tourist industry was at the same time experiencing rising wage and other costs as the nation's standard of living rose in the era of democracy and European Community membership. Compared to its emerging competitors it was no longer a cheap destination.

There was therefore a lack of capital for refurbishment and renewal of the accommodation stock. As Fayos Sola (1992) writes of the Valencia region,

> the huge expansion of hotels at the beginning of the 1970s has not enjoyed adequate continuity or renovation. The approximate 900,000 hotel beds on offer are still concentrated in hotels with three star rating or less, and suffer from a high rate of obsolescence.

As long as the tourists kept coming, there was no perceived problem, except in the minds of a sensitive elite who were not the target market of resorts like Valencia's Benidorm. The complacency was well expressed by Farrell (1982) writing of another tourist enclave on the other side of the world, 'Outsiders and insiders alike point to Waikiki as a design disaster – yet the generally rising occupancy rates suggest that far from being repelled, tourists come back in greater numbers.' This attitude also helps to explain the lack of any product differentiation strategy in these resorts during the period of growth.

The crisis of the early 1990s

Towards the end of the 1980s, tourism to the established Mediterranean resorts appeared to show signs of decline. British visitors on package holidays to Spain fell from 4.7 million in 1986 to 2.7 million in 1991 (British Tourist Authority, 1995), leading the travel industry in both countries to reconsider their strategies. A number of factors appeared to be involved in this downward trend.

Product maturity

An increasing number of destinations offered the same sun sand and sea resorts formula as Spain, with the advantage of added novelty and status. The success of the travel industry in taking the risk out of foreign holidays had lowered the 'involvement' of the tourist in their annual holiday decision. As a consequence, it no longer required what consumer behaviourists call 'extended problem-solving' but instead was guided by 'variety-seeking behaviour' (Engel et al., 1990). If all the resorts are basically similar, the tourist is more likely to try a different one each time in a search for variety. If the new destination offers the status of a long-haul holiday at a competitive price, the appeal is even stronger.

The quadrupling of UK inclusive holidays to the USA between 1986 and 1991 (from 111,000 to 512,000) and the growth in other non-European destinations appeared to confirm the suspicion that the current Spanish product had reached the mature stage of its product life cycle (Kotler, 1988).

Demographic factors

The generation now buying family holidays (25–45 years age group) had grown up taking the annual Mediterranean holiday for granted. They are therefore less apprehensive than their parents about foreign travel. They are likely to have stayed in education longer and are more likely to speak a foreign language. They have also grown up with the car and wanted the benefits of mobility on holiday. The permanently-moored cruise liner type of resort was therefore less attractive to them than a motoring tour based on a self-catering cottage or villa.

The influence of these trends could be seen in the manner in which independent holidays continued to grow during the period while inclusive holidays declined. France overtook Spain as the UK's number one holiday destination from 1989 and cross-channel car traffic reached record levels.

Economic factors

The downturn in the package holiday market was undoubtedly influenced by the world wide economic recession of the time. However, while consumer demand in general was depressed, the effects on the tourist market were not uniform, with some categories suffering more than others. Rather than cutting out the annual holiday completely, commentators observed customers switching categories to products offering greater perceived value for money (Mitchell, 1990). This has encouraged the switch from the homogeneous package to the motoring tour or the long-haul destinations. Couples may not take any holiday at all one year to save up for a trip with added exotic appeal and status value the next. Demographic factors are also at work as the effects of redundancy and high costs of home-ownership are felt less severely by the older age groups. What the established resorts were unable to predict was whether the market would return to its pre-1989 patterns or whether the experiences of recession would permanently alter consumer priorities and values.

Changing perceptions and expectations

With increased competition from rising destinations and the greater sophistication of the tourist, differentiation of the resort product is now at last being recognized to be essential (Fayos Sola, 1992). It is also being realized that the quality of the product, that is the fit between the tourist's expectations and experience (Parasuraman et al., 1985) has fallen. This is due to three main factors.

Lack of refurbishment

First there is the lack of refurbishment, both of the accommodation as previously mentioned, and also of the infrastructure of the resort itself. When they were built in the 1960s and '70s, the hotels with their en-suite bathrooms, balconies and extended meal times seemed luxurious in comparison with holiday accommodation in the domestic market. These facilities are now taken for granted and the general standard of furnishing, decor and fittings has not kept pace with the tourists' own standards at home, let alone with sophisticated new resorts. The attractions and entertainments available cannot compare with tourist complexes like Disney.

Environmental awareness

Second, there has been an increase in environmental awareness in Britain and most notably in Germany. That is not to say that the average beach tourist is a dedicated ecologist looking for sustainable tourism. What has happened is that stories in the popular media have made tourists aware of the threat of pollution and disease in Mediterranean resorts, of poor standards of hygiene and fire safety in holiday hotels, and so the names of the popular resorts have become associated with overcrowding and over development, half-finished hotels and noisy, dusty construction sites (Astles, 1989).

Lager louts

Third, the price war years have produced a phenomenon known to the British press as the 'lager lout'. Encouraged by cheap discounted fares and holiday packages targeted at the teen and twenty market, large numbers of young British, Scandinavian and other northern Europeans flocked to the big resorts with their all-night disco bars. The resorts gained a reputation for drunkenness, noise and fights, exaggerated, they would argue by sensational coverage in the British media. The effect has been to deter the family market.

For all these reasons the established Spanish resorts, although retaining a price advantage, were no longer perceived as value for money compared to their newer competitors.

Out of fashion?

The concept of the adoption curve (Rogers, 1962) is relevant here. New products, such as destinations, are first bought by a relatively small group of 'innovators' who are attracted by the idea of trying something new and different. These people set the trend or fashion, which is copied first by 'early adopters', then by the majority and latterly by the 'laggards' who only adopt the most tried and commonplace products. Plog (1973) sees the diffusion in terms of psychological types; he considers that the allocentric or outward looking type, who is interested in discovering the world and the people outside his previous experience, will be the first to seek out new and different destinations, while the psychocentric or self-focused type prefers the familiarity of established destinations where he feels 'at home'.

It is clear that the Mediterranean beach resorts have ceased to attract the innovators and allocentric tourists. What is worrying the tourist industry is that even the majority, mid- to psycho-centric tourists are becoming dissatisfied and ready to move on. These fears were expressed in a trade press article by Charles Newbold, Managing Director of Thomson Holidays in the UK. After cataloguing the bad news stories and image problems we have described in the preceding paragraphs, he wondered, no doubt provocatively, whether 'the package holiday as we know it is going out of fashion' (*Travel News*, March 31, 1989).

Moving on

The tourist and the tour operator can move on to newer, more distant destinations, switch to other types of holiday or revert to domestic tourism. The established resorts remain. As previously mentioned, in the boom years of the 1980s, 70,000 extra hotel beds were added to Majorca's capacity. Now the local tourist authorities calculate that a similar number are surplus to capacity (Morgan, 1991). Tourism, which is responsible for 70 per cent of the island's employment, is as much a monoculture as any Third World cash-crop, and communities which depend on it are just as vulnerable to fluctuations in world demand.

Lessons for developing resorts

It might seem easy in hindsight to prescribe lessons for newly developing resorts to avoid the mistakes of the past, but the pressures that led to those mistakes still exist.

- **Avoid overdependence on particular markets, or on tourism at the expense of other industries and agriculture.** Yet tourism has been a successful means of bringing prosperity to Spain and remains an attractive model for other countries in need of foreign currency for development.
- **Do not lose control of the distribution channel.** But individual resorts cannot penetrate international markets effectively without the aid of intermediaries in the target countries. As East (1990) pointed out, the best way to sell a holiday hotel or resort in a foreign market is to make sure it is in a tour operator's brochure.
- **Maintain and enhance the quality of the resort facilities.** This requires investment which in a price-led, low-profit-margin industry can be difficult to generate on purely commercial grounds. It also requires development controls which in the early years of a resort's development could be politically difficult to impose.

It is nevertheless the pubic-sector tourism authorities with their concern for the economic and social benefits of tourism to the whole community who have been responsible for most of the initiatives to refurbish the established resorts. Often these schemes are attempting to rectify the consequences of a previous lack of investment in infrastructure and a lack of effective planning controls.

Newer resorts could save expense and problems in the long term by balancing the need to grab the benefits of tourism with the need to control some of the most obvious environmental consequences from the start. An optimist would argue that the growing environmental awareness in the major tourism originating nations makes this task easier than it was for the resorts which developed in the 1970s and 1980s.

Strategies for survival

What, though, can the already established resorts do? Marketing writers are generally agreed that the concept of a product having a life-cycle is more helpful diagnostically than predictively (Haywood, 1986). Products that appear to be moving from growth to maturity and decline can be revived by the correct marketing strategy, starting, according to Kotler (1988), by 'modifying the customer mix, the brand's positioning and the marketing mix.'

In tourism these elements are interdependent. Resorts need to find new markets, both geographically and behaviourally segmented, to reduce their dependence on the British and German beach tourist. To attract these new markets, changes will be needed to the marketing mix. For example the product offered – in terms of accommodation attractions and access – may not suit the needs of the new markets, the price/quality offer may be wrong, and new distribution channels may have to be found. The resorts also need to find distinct positioning strategies to differentiate themselves from their competitors in the minds of both existing and potential customers. This again will require a review of the whole marketing mix, the product price and place, and not just the promotion.

New markets, new needs

Promotion targeted at new markets is an obvious answer to overdependence on one declining market. The Balearic Islands, for example, targeted the Netherlands, Switzerland and Scandinavia, Eastern Europe and the growing Spanish domestic market to compensate for a fall in British visitor numbers.

However, different nationalities have different needs which mean that a simple substitution is not possible. In recent winters the Spanish resorts have been busy with domestic tourists, many of them taking advantage of the subsidized holidays available to Spanish pensioners under a Government scheme to prevent unemployment in the tourist industry. These new visitors do not have the same tastes or spending power as the northern Europeans. As a result, though the hotels and promenades are crowded, many of the resort shops, bars and nightclubs, particularly those targeted at British or German tourists, remain shut.

More often, new potential markets demand higher standards and are prepared to pay more for these. The upgrading and refurbishment programmes being undertaken in the Balearics and Valencia are in part aimed at attracting new and more discriminating European and North American visitors.

Investing in new products

The holiday product is more than just the destination. Tourists are more likely to be motivated by *what* they are going to do on their holiday than by *where* they are going to do it. Realizing this, Valencia's White Paper on Tourism (Fayos Sola, 1992) targets specific 'product markets' with differentiated needs, e.g.:

- sun and beach
- tourism for the retired
- congresses and conventions
- life style and cultural tourism
- sport and adventure tourism
- health and fitness tourism

Each of these requires improvements and investment in special facilities and packages, and may change the customer mix and atmosphere of the area.

Taking the example of the conference market, several major British resorts have compensated for the fall in main holiday beach tourism by developing facilities for the business and conference markets. Bournemouth Council have invested £25 million in building a major International Centre for conferences and entertainment. Conferences generate 278,000 p.a. bed nights for the resort bringing in £2.4 million per annum in tourist spending, and creating 3,500 extra jobs by giving the hotels year-round business. The benefits have been felt largely though not entirely by the larger business-oriented hotels.

In Majorca the development of new product markets has tended not to benefit the established resort areas directly. Conference and incentive meetings visitors have used hotels in the main city of Palma. Marinas have developed in Palma and in new up-market resorts like Porto Portals. The outdoor activity market, for walking, riding and bird watching, has focused on the northern resort of Porto Pollensa. The main southern resorts of the Bay of Palma, Magaluf/Palma Nova, Arenal/Playas de Palmas, which provide the majority of the beds and jobs, have not attracted these new tourists. Consequently resort areas such as Calvia have developed their own activities programmes, targeting the older market who visit out of season with activities from tea dancing to tai-chi.

To extend the product range of these resorts, the emphasis is on watersports and on golf. Twenty new golf courses are planned for the island of Majorca by the end of the century. Golf in the sun is also one of the main themes in the Spanish National Tourist Office's (NTO) current advertising campaign. However golf courses create additional demands for water in drought-prone areas such as the Balearics.

A major new product development to revitalize an established resort area is the Port Aventura theme park near Salou which opened in 1995. The prospect of an additional 3 million visitors has provided the incentive for the local hotel industry to refurbish its accommodation. A further major theme park is planned for Valencia.

From resort to touring centre

The beach resort typically evolves to cater for tourists who arrive by mass transportation systems. This was true of British seaside resorts in the Railway Age and also of the Mediterranean resorts made accessible by charter flights in jet aircraft since the 1960s. Tourists arrived by plane and coach and were for the most part happy to spend their time between the hotel and the beach.

As demand for this type of holiday falls, the attraction of the hinter-land of the resort becomes more important. British resorts have now to market themselves to tourists who are arriving by car and are prepared to drive up to forty miles from the resort for day excursions to attractions or scenic countryside. Bournemouth's product now effectively includes the National Motor Museum at Beaulieu (20 miles to the east), the open landscape of the New Forest and the literary associations of Thomas Hardy's Wessex. So successfully have the inland cities and countryside of Yorkshire in northern England sold themselves as tourist destinations that established resorts like Scarborough now market themselves as on the Yorkshire coast, a reversal of the previous positioning.

Mediterranean resorts are also learning that the cultural, historical, scenic, wildlife and even industrial heritage of the region are now a means of creating a unique product position. The majority of visitors may not have a deep knowledge or interest in that heritage, but it still improves the image and status value of the resort for them. It also pro-vides a motivation for a different market segment to use the resort as a touring base, particularly off-season.

The Spanish NTO advertising campaigns in the UK in recent years have used the historical and scenic attractions of Spain's interior to repo-sition the country as a destination offering much more than the four Ss. A romantic view of a hilltop castle is labelled 'One of our little bed and breakfast places'. Individual resorts and regions have followed the same strategy. Majorca, for example, promotes its associations with the com-poser Chopin who once spent a rather unhappy winter in the mountain village of Valdemossa.

Upgrading the product quality

While these attempts to find new markets and widen the product range offered are important elements in the resorts' strategies, their future still depends on retaining a viable share of the core beach tourism market. To do this they must seek to close the gap between the expectations of their customers and the quality of the experience they receive.

In Spain it is the governments of the Autonomous Regions (compar-able to the individual states of the USA) who are taking the lead in this drive for quality. The Balearic Islands are approaching the challenge in two ways: direct investment in environmental and infrastructural improvements, and planning regulations to limit and zone new development. £111 million has been spent on promenades, shopping precincts, parks, pedestrianization and general refurbishment. New hotels will have to be of at least four-star quality with 120m^2 of land for every bed provided, so preventing any more high-rise clusters. To limit the spread of low-rise development this restriction might otherwise encourage, a number of nature or scenic conservation areas have been designated, covering 30 per cent of Majorca and Ibiza and 45 per cent of Menorca. Laws controlling the noise from all-night bars and the exploitation of monkeys by photographers are among other measures designed to improve the quality and image of the resorts. Now a Quality Tourism Supply Plan (Govern Balear, 1995) aims to bring together these improvements to the environment and to the product with improvements in the service. A major quality audit of the accommodation stock will be followed by training programmes in association with local colleges and trade unions, a tourist technology research centre and cultural tourism programmes.

Tour operators and hoteliers are also responding to the crisis by improving the quality of their products. Thomson have invested £10 million in partnership with selected hotels to bring them up to the standard and style of service which their research shows the British clients of the 1990s expect. Significantly, these hotels, marketed as Sun Hotels in Thomson brochures, are moving away from the international style described earlier and instead provide decor, food and entertainment specifically for the British market – bacon and egg breakfasts, soft toilet paper and English comedians.

Sustainable tourism

Calvia municipality has adopted sustainable tourism as the basis for future planning of its resorts under the Local Agenda 21 principles set out by the 1992 Rio Earth Summit. Recognizing that it is 'a mature tourist municipality . . . on the edge of losing its attractiveness' (Calvia, 1995), the plans renounce growth, revoke existing development approvals, create recycling schemes and put the emphasis on rehabilitation and quality. Twelve hotels and other structures have been demolished to create public open space in a decongestion programme. This new policy is undertaken not out of idealism but in the interests of the 30,000 residents who depend on 1.2 million tourists for their livelihood

Promoting the new image

All these strategies described in the preceding paragraphs require extensive promotion. Image building advertising by the National Tourist

Office has to be combined with trade promotion through brochures, trade exhibitions and workshops, and educational visits. The message must reach the agency staff at the point of sale with the public.

NTOs are increasingly relying on a strategy of what Middleton (1988) calls facilitation, bringing destination suppliers such as hoteliers and attraction operators into contact with the travel industry decision makers in the target originating country. This is more cost effective for the NTO than producing large amounts of consumer brochures for which it has no distribution network, or consumer advertising which lacks a specific product proposition. Co-operative marketing between the NTO, the tour operators and the travel agencies is needed to create a desirable image and then convert the desire into action to purchase a specific holiday. The drawback of this approach is that the tour operators and agents will only be able to give individual resorts limited coverage in their brochures and promotions.

Press publicity is therefore a very important tool in communicating the changes in the resorts to potential holiday makers. A journalist writing a feature on a resort is more likely to be believed than an advertisement. Running a press trip can obtain more press coverage at lower cost than an advertising campaign.

The image of Spain as a destination has also benefited from coverage of the successful Barcelona Olympics and Expo Seville in 1992.

Has refurbishment investment brought renewed success?

The experience of the Balearic Islands in tackling the challenges faced by established tourist resorts in the 1990s provides an indication of the degree to which these strategies are succeeding. It is now possible to look at the trends in the key inclusive tour markets in the period 1986 to 1994 and compare the performance of the Spanish resorts against other destinations. The main features are summarized below. (Figures from Fomento del Turismo de Mallorca and *UK International Passenger Survey* (BTA, 1995) unless stated) Figure 19.1 illustrates the shape of the main trends. The decline of the British market has been reversed. Figures for Majorca and for Spain as a whole show a recovery from 1992 onwards with 1994 figures returning to 1986 levels.

The Spanish resorts' other main market, the Germans, continued to grow partly due to the opening up of the East German market but also due to Westerners pulling back from more expensive alternatives in the Caribbean (EIU, 1994). As a result, Majorca's overall visitor numbers

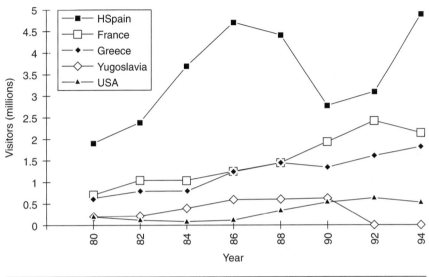

Year		1980	1982	1984	1986	1988	1990	1992	1994
Spain	inc	1.9	2.4	3.7	4.7	4.4	2.8	3.1	4.9
France	inc	0.7	1	1	1.2	1.4	1.9	2.4	2.1
Greece	inc	0.6	0.8	0.8	1.2	1.4	1.3	1.6	1.8
Yugoslavia	inc	0.2	0.2	0.4	0.6	0.6	0.6	0.01	0
USA	inc	0.2	0.1	0.05	0.1	0.3	0.5	0.6	0.5

UK Inclusive Holidays visitors to selected destinations (millions)

Figure 19.1   UK inclusive holidays to selected destinations
Source: BTA, 1995

were 33 per cent higher in 1994 compared to 1986. Spain as a whole was enjoying record arrivals by 1993 (EIU, 1994) though these figures hid a continuing underutilization of hotels.

The British are now taking more inclusive holidays than ever, 42 per cent up on 1986. The apparent trend from inclusive to independent holidays in the period 1989–91 has not been sustained. As Figure 19.1 shows, within the UK inclusive tour market Spain remains market leader (with 38 per cent compared to 44 per cent in 1986) and has been winning back market share from France since 1992. However other destinations such as Greece and Italy have shown real growth during the period.

The United States' share of the British market, which rose sharply in the 1980s, has now levelled off to around 5–6 per cent. It is newer destinations such as Turkey, the Far East, Eastern Europe and North Africa which show the greatest growth in percentage terms, though remaining relatively small in comparison to the traditional destinations in numbers of visitors.

It would appear from these statistics that the lifecycle of the Spanish resorts and of the package holiday has been extended and that prophecies of an inevitable decline were premature. To what extent can the local authorities in the resorts claim the credit? Economic factors are obviously significant as the fall and rise of visitor numbers has followed the pattern of the recession and recovery of the British and other Western economies. The collapse of Yugoslavia, which up to 1990 received half a million British tourists a year, may well also have benefited Spain as well as nearer rivals like Greece, Turkey and Cyprus. In a crisis, security is a more basic need than discovery or adventure. The familiarity of the established resort becomes an asset again.

It would be difficult to measure precisely the influence of the refurbishment and quality improvement work on British visitors' decisions to return to the established resorts or on the continued growth of German visitors. However, without it, the resorts would have found it harder to recapture the confidence of their former customers. This confidence is expressed by Charles Newbold of Thomson, in marked contrast to his earlier remarks: 'The Balearics were written off by many as victims of their own success. *In less than two years, the transformation has set an example which other countries could follow.*' (my italics) (*Travel Weekly*, 1 April 1992).

Future prospects

Latent in Newbold's remarks is a long-term problem. The transformation of the Balearics has indeed set an example which other countries are very likely to follow. Good parks, precincts, street furniture and promenades may give a short-term competitive advantage, but are not in themselves the basis of a long-term product differentiation strategy. Success is very quickly copied and what works in Magaluf or Benidorm today will soon be available everywhere else. Will the new homogeneity of palm-tree lined precincts, golf courses and marinas in turn be perceived as characterless and unfashionable? At present the established resorts of the Mediterranean have found strategies that enable them to keep pace with rising customer expectations and increasing competition. But will it be enough to secure long-term survival?

The pressures on resorts to develop on similar lines to each other still exist, even if the dangers, aesthetic, social and commercial, are now better appreciated. The challenge for any resort is to provide the facilities, accommodation and attractions of a standard demanded by the international tourist market while retaining and developing its unique character. This character, this image which differentiates it from its main competitors, often depends on geographical, historical and cultural features that predate tourism and are vulnerable to being obliterated by tourism. This paradox, whereby we simultaneously demand all the advantages and economies of modern life while deploring the resulting brand homogeneity, is an issue which is not confined to tourism. Like all aspects of consumer behaviour, it is both a threat and an opportunity.

References

Astles, R. (1989) Overseas package holidays where next? *Leisure Intelligence*, **2**, p. 43

Barrett, F. (1989) On the Algarve Road to Ruin, *The Independent*, July 22

British Tourist Authority (BTA) (1995) *Digest of Tourism Statistics*, December

Calvia, Municipality of (1996) Calvia Agenda Local 21, *Entorn*, June, Calvia, Mallorca

East, M. (1990) Business Update, *Travel News*, 7 December

Economist Intelligence Unit (EIU) (1994) Spain, *International Tourism Reports*, 3

Engel, J., Blackwell, R. and Miniard, P. (1990) *Consumer Behaviour*, 6th edn, Dryden Press, Orlando, p. 474

Farrell, B. (1982) *Hawaii, the Legend that Sells*, University of Hawaii Press, Honolulu, p. 36

Fayos Sola, E. (1992) A Strategic Outlook for Regional Tourism Policy – the White Paper on Valencian Tourism, *Tourism Management*, 13, March, pp. 45–9

Fomento del Turismo de Mallorca (1995) *Aeropuerto de Palma de Mallorca: Trafico internacional* [Airport arrival statistics]

Goodall, B. and Bergsma, J. (1990) Destinations as Marketed in Tour Operators Brochures. In *Marketing Tourism Places* (ed. G. Ashworth and B. Goodall) Routledge, London, p. 173

Govern Balear, Conselleria de Turism [Balearic Islands Government Tourism Council] (1995) *Quality Tourism Supply Plan*

Heywood, K.M. (1986) Can the Tourist Area Life-Cycle be made operational? *Tourism Management*, 7 September, pp. 154–67

Kotler, P (1994) *Marketing Management, Analysis, Planning, Implementation and Control*, 8th edn, Simon and Schuster, Englewood Cliffs, NJ

Lavery, P. (1971) *Recreational Geography*, David and Charles, Newton Abbott, pp. 177–95

Levitt, T. (1983) The Globalization of Markets, *Havard Business Review*, May/June, pp. 92–102

Middleton, V.T.C. (1988) *Marketing in Travel and Tourism*, Heinemann, Oxford, pp. 209–25

Mitchell, A. (1990) Marketing out of the Down-turn, *Marketing*, 26 April, pp. 25–6

Morgan, M. (1991) Dressing up to survive, Marketing Majorca anew, *Tourism Management*, March 12, pp. 15–20

Newbold, C. (1989 and 1992) Quoted in *Travel News*, 31 March 1989 and *Travel Weekly*. 1 April 1992

Parasuraman, A. Zeithaml, V. Berry, L. (1985) A Conceptual Model of Service Quality, *Journal of Marketing*, Fall, p. 44

Plog, S.C. (1973) Why destination areas rise and fall, *Cornell Hotel and Restaurant Administration Quarterly*, pp. 13–16

Rogers, E.M. (1962) *The Diffusion of Innovation*, Free Press of Glencoe, New York, p. 162

Stansfield, C.A. and Rickert, J.E. (1970) The Recreational Business District, *Journal of Leisure Research*, **2**(4), 213–25

Stiles, R. and See-Tho, W. (1991) Integrated Resort Development in the Asia Pacific Region, *Travel and Tourism Analyst*, No. 3, pp. 27–37

Part Five

Bureaucracy and Procedure: Geopolitical and Policy Issues

This chapter deals with a somewhat different planning and development issue, the role of government incentives in tourism. **Wanhill** (Chapter 20) suggests that historically, governments have intervened in order to both assist and regulate private sector tourism development. Due to the complex nature of tourism, it is improbable that the private sector can satisfy completely government policy objectives fostering a balance between host and guest benefits. Incentives are viewed as policy instruments that can help ensure cooperative development between the private and public sectors. The rationale for sustainable development is the alleviation of absolute poverty and the replacement of renewable natural and cultural resources.

A classification system of government incentives is presented including financial incentives and investment security. Rationales for each incentive are presented as well as a series of graphic information presented to illustrate the impacts of such incentives on the total amount of investment provided. Finally, in order to assess the effectiveness of the tourism project (from government's perspective), benefit analyses are discussed and illustrated examples are provided.

The author concludes by describing conflicts that frequently appear in national tourism policies. He states that incentives are policy instruments that may be used to correct for market failure and to ensure a development partnership between the public and private sectors. From this perspective, the goal of sustainable development is the alleviation of absolute poverty and replenishment of the natural resource base.

Some type of government intervention is necessary, since, on their own, market economies will not produce sustainable tourism. Such facilitation often takes the form of policy instruments such as zoning regulation, taxation (or relief from taxation) and the provision of infrastructure.

The chapter by **Bramwell** (Chapter 21) examines the myriad issues that must be considered when government officials initiate the process of selecting sustainable tourism policy instruments. It provides a description of some conceptual foundations behind these issues, and provides specific examples in order to illustrate the pragmatic implications of these issues for policy instruments. Preferences for policy instruments must be based upon moral and political assessments as well as economic evaluations.

The author points out that policy makers must consider the entire range of tourism policy instruments as well as the mix of those instruments. He suggests that when selecting policy instruments, government officials often demonstrate ideological or political bias, thereby favouring certain types of instruments over others. Ideally, policy makers must assess both the strengths as well as the weaknesses of specific instruments, and the effect of ideology, social values, ethics, politics and economics on those assessments.

The political events which resulted in the downfall of communism in Eastern Europe have led to substantial changes in previously established travel patterns and thereby opened this area for international tourism. **Witt** (Chapter 22) provides a description of Bulgaria, Czechoslovakia, the former German Democratic Republic, Hungary, Poland, Romania and the former Soviet Union as tourist destinations, and provides statistical documentation of their visitor arrivals, total tourism receipts, and tourism receipts as a percentage of exports.

Although largely unexplored by Westerners, these seven Eastern European countries have an abundance of natural resources, beautiful cities, historic and cultural resources that could attract tourists. What is needed to attract these visitors is better education and training, Western capital and expertise, and improved marketing programmes. There are, however, a number of constraints that mitigate further tourism development including inadequate infrastructure, a shortage of high quality accommodation, and an overall low-quality of tourist products and services. Two key additional requisites to tourism development are political stability and visitor safety.

The final chapter in this section deals with the political role of gender as seen by **Richter** (Chapter 23), as it relates to tourism. Gender differences in tourism throughout history are reviewed, areas of tourism research which have politically important gender issues are explored, and trends in political organizations and tourism that may affect emerging gender distinctions are presented. The main theme here is that women are not regarded as equal or given the dignity and respect that men are in the tourism industry. Some inequities include women's wages, which are usually lower, seasonal, part-time or minimum. The chapter also discusses the prospects for policy change toward allowing women to become equal partners in all aspects of the tourism industry.

As an employment and ownership sector, a rationale is provided for prostitution, and arguments for sex tourism are explained. Examples of gender differences in marketing, souvenirs and attractions are also provided. Marketing linking tourism with sex is rampant throughout the industry, souvenirs continue to promote women as sex objects, and destination attractions remain male dominated preserves.

The bulk of the financial control of both the private and public tourism sectors lies in the hands of men. Right or wrong, women have always been perceived as particularly appropriate for 'front line' tourism positions due to their assumed more social and hospitable skills. However, women holding public office have consistently demonstrated a disproportionate concern for areas such as health, social welfare and concern for the environment, which the tourism industry has tended to downplay or ignore. Thus, if women achieve greater access to management and public policy positions, their greatest impact may well be in those tourism areas where they have traditionally had the least control or influence.

20 The role of government incentives

Stephen Wanhill

Introduction

With tourism designated to be one of the major economic 'drivers' in the next century (Boskin, 1996), the world-wide significance of the industry as a mechanism for economic development has meant that it is an investment opportunity that few governments can afford to ignore. However, defining a tourist's journey, whether for leisure or business purposes, is quite complex. The tourist trip has a number of characteristics, namely:

- The trip is not a single product.
- It is made up of components supplied by a variety of organizations with different objectives and different economic structures.
- Success is the delivering of the right mix of components to satisfy the demands of the visitor.
- This delivery requires co-ordination and co-operation.

From this, it may be seen that tourism is a multifaceted product: it includes accommodation, transport, restaurants, shopping facilities, attractions, entertainment, public infrastructure support and the general way of life of the host community. Thus, the essence of successful tourism development is a partnership between the various stakeholders in the activity of tourism to satisfy the requirement to provide a balanced range of facilities to meet the demands of visitors in a sustainable way. Since the tourist industry does not control all those factors that make up the attractiveness of a destination and the impact on the host population can be considerable, it is necessary that the options concerning the planning of tourism should be considered at the highest level of government and the appropriate public administrative framework put in place.

In most countries the development of tourism is a partnership between the private and public sectors. Where the line is drawn in this partnership depends on the prevailing economic, political and social policies of the country. The private sector may have many reasons for investing in tourism: on the one hand, there are foreign tour operators and leisure companies always looking to reap the benefits from the appeal of a new and exciting destination being placed onto the international travel market, while on the other, there are many attractions at tourist destinations that have grown out of their owners' special interest or hobby. But in the long run, private operators must be concerned with the viability of their investments through generating an ample surplus to sustain the capital employed. As a rule, the greater the importance of tourism to a country's economy, the greater is the involvement of the public sector and the stimulus the government is prepared to give to attract inward investment, to the point of having a government ministry with sole responsibility for tourism. It is often the case that the planning powers with respect to tourism are devolved to local government, while the executive arm of government is transferred to a quasi-public body in the form of the National Tourist Office (NTO).

Market failure

The case for public sector involvement in tourism rests on concepts of market failure, namely that those who argue for the market mechanism as the sole arbiter in the allocation of resources for tourism are ignoring the lessons of history and are grossly over-simplifying the heterogeneous nature of the product. The early growth of the seaside resorts during the latter half of the nineteenth century, as, for example, in the United Kingdom, was the result of a partnership between the public and private sectors (Cooper and Jackson, 1989; Cooper, 1992). The local authorities invested in the promenades, piers, gardens and so on, while the private sector developed the revenue-earning activities which enhanced the income of the area and in turn increased property tax receipts for the authorities.

Embodied in the tourist product are goods and services which are unlikely to be provided in sufficient quantity by the market mechanism. The market fails because of the existence of items within the tourist product that everyone can enjoy in common and that are equally available to all, which implies non-rivalry in consumption. These are public goods; their principal feature is that they are non-excludable, due to the lack of, or incompleteness of, property rights. If the good or service is to be provided at all, it may be consumed by everybody without exception, and without charge at the point of use. There are also merit goods, whose consumption the state wishes to encourage because they yield wider benefits that cannot be retained by private businesses themselves and would lead, therefore, to under-provision. The upshot is that the single-minded pursuit of private profit opportunities within tourism may be self-defeating, as many older resorts in the Mediterranean and elsewhere have found to their cost (Plog, 1973). The outcome may not be the integrated tourism development which distils the essence of the country in its design, but a rather crowded, over-built and placeless environment with polluted beaches, that are totally out of keeping with the original objectives set by the country's tourism policy.

The major hotel developments that took place in the resorts of southern Spain during the 1960s and early 1970s, were completed under laissez-faire expansionism with little consideration given to planning or control. In general, the public infrastructure was over-loaded and this was only put right in the second half of the 1980s. New moves have been taking place to refurbish the resort centres to give more 'green' space in the form of parks and gardens. What is clear is that the complex structure of the product lends itself to the fact that in any tourism development programme there is often a marked difference between private and social benefits and cost.

The precise nature of a country's stance on tourism investment is determined by the kind of development the government is looking for and what role it envisages for the private entrepreneur. In the past, most of the emphasis of Eastern European countries was on social tourism which allowed the population to benefit from subsidized holidays through workers' organizations and central government provision. Currency movements were arranged on a country-to-country basis through the form of bilateral swaps. The success criteria were based on visitor numbers and most tourist facilities were heavily subsidized. This has now changed and the influx of Western visitors has tended to price Eastern European tourists out of the market. African countries have recognized the importance of tourism for conservation. By giving wildlife an economic value, funds are generated to support game reserves, preserve endangered species and help eradicate poaching. Many Caribbean countries have strong views about the wisdom of developing casinos for tourists, because of the possibility of criminal involvement and also on moral grounds.

Tourism objectives

Incentives given by governments for tourist developments are the instruments used to realize the objectives set by the country's tourism policy. A list of strategic objectives which are commonly found in tourism plans is shown in Table 20.1. It is important from the outset to ensure that strategic objectives do not conflict with each other and that incentives offered to investors are compatible with those same objectives. Too often governments talk of tourism quality yet measure performance in terms

Table 20.1 Strategic tourism policy objectives

- Develop a tourism sector which, in all aspects and at all levels, is of high quality, though not necessarily of high cost.
- Encourage the use of tourism for both cultural and economic exchange.
- Distribute the economic benefits of tourism, both direct and indirect, as widely and to as many of the host community as feasible.
- Preserve cultural and natural resources as part of tourism development. Facilitate this through architectural and landscape designs which reflect local traditions.
- Appeal to a broad cross-section of international and domestic tourists through policies and programmes of site and facility development.
- Maximize foreign exchange earnings to ensure a sound balance of payments.
- Attract high spending, 'up-market' tourists.
- Increase employment.
- Aid peripheral regions by raising incomes and employment, thus slowing down or halting emigration.

of numbers. Common examples of policy objectives which are most likely to be at variance with each other are:

- maximizing foreign exchange earnings versus actions to encourage the regional dispersion of overseas visitors;
- attracting the high spend tourist market versus policies to continually expand visitor numbers;
- maximizing job creation through generating volume tourist flows versus conservation of the environment and heritage;
- community tourism development versus mass tourism.

Nevertheless, it must be pointed out that it is no longer considered acceptable in political terms that these objectives should be achieved at a cost to the environment or by adversely affecting the host community. Unfortunately, for political reasons, governments often want the tourist industry to meet multiple and various objectives, thus the question of the environment becomes a difficult one to maintain when it threatens to be a drag on the economy in matters of employment creation. Cast in this light, tourism policy as exercised by the NTO is not usually one of maximizing but rather one of optimization subject to the constraints imposed by the directions dictated by the selected objectives.

Classification of incentives

Bodlender (1982) and Jenkins (1982) have considered the variety of incentives that are available in tourism, and these may be broadly classified as follows:

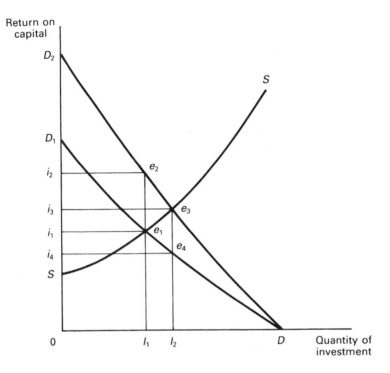

Figure 20.1   Financial incentives on capital

- financial incentives;
- reduction in capital costs;
- reduction in operating costs;
- investment security.

Financial incentives

The objective of financial incentives is to improve returns to capital so as to ensure that market potential, which is attractive to developers and investors, may be turned into financially sound projects. Where there is obvious market potential, the government may only have to show its support for tourism by providing the necessary conditions for investment security by removing any difficulties facing outside investors. Such a situation occurred in Bermuda during the early 1970s and so, in order to prevent over-exploitation of the tourism resources, the Bermuda Government imposed a moratorium on large hotel building (Archer and Wanhill, 1980).

The impact of financial incentives on the amount of investment is illustrated in Figure 20.1. The schedule SS represents the supply of investible funds while D_1D is the schedule of returns to capital employed. D_1D

slopes downwards from left to right as more and more investment opportunities are taken up – the declining marginal efficiency of investment. In the initial situation, equilibrium is at e_1 with the amount of investment being I_1 and the internal rate of return i_1.

Conditions of market failure imply that the community benefits from tourism investment are not entirely captured in the demand function D_1D. Optimal economic efficiency is where the demand function that includes these externalities D_2D, intersects the supply curve at e_3, yielding a return i_3. To achieve this, the government now implements a range of financial incentives which, in the first instance, has the effect of raising the internal rate of return per unit of capital to i_2, moving the marginal efficiency of investment schedule to D_2D. The new return i_2 equals $(1 + s)i_1$, where s is the effective rate of subsidy. If the amount of investible funds available for tourism is limited at I_1, then the impact of incentives serves merely to raise the return to investors by raising the equilibrium point to e_2. The loss to the government treasury is the area $i_1 e_1 e_2 i_2$ which equals the gain to private investors, so there is no net economic gain to the community.

There is no doubt that many countries have been forced by competitive pressures for foreign investment into situations that are similar to those above. Countries can become trapped in a bidding process to secure clients and as a result the variety of financial incentives multiplies together with an escalation of the rates of benefit, without evaluating their necessity or their true cost to the economy.

Given that the supply of investment funds is responsive or elastic, the net effect of an incentives policy is to expand the amount of tourism projects to I_2, setting the rate of return at i_3, and the equilibrium point at e_3, which is the target level. In this situation the net gain in returns to tourism developers is $i_3 I_2 - i_1 I_1$ which is equal to the sum of the areas $i_3 e_3 e_1 i_1$ plus $I_1 e_1 e_3 I_2$. The cost to the treasury is $s i_4 I_2$ which, in turn, is equal to the area $i_3 e_3 e_4 i_4$.

The private opportunity cost of the investment funds is the area under the supply curve, $I_1 e_1 e_3 I_2$, while the public willingness-to-pay for correcting the externality is the area $I_1 e_2 e_3 I_2$: subtracting the two areas gives a net gain represented by the area $e_2 e_3 e_1$.

The alternative to stimulating the demand is to increase the supply of investible funds. In Figure 20.1, this may be shown by a shift in the supply function to the right, which reduces the cost of capital to the private sector, thus permitting the marginal project to earn an internal rate of return of, say, i_4, and generating the optimal level of investment I_2. Typically, governments attempt to do this by establishing investment banks, arranging special credit facilities or constituting tourism development corporations. The economic rationale for this is that governments are usually able to borrow at lower rates than the private sector, since they have ultimate recourse to taxation to cover their debts. In the case of less developed countries (LDCs), finance may be obtained from international banks and multinational aid agencies on favourable terms. The counter arguments to adopting supply-side investment strategies are twofold: first, there is concern that government actions should not displace or 'crowd-out' capital funds from other private investments, which could do equally as well, and second, the wider objectives of governments may generate institutional inefficiencies (and in some cases corruption) in the allocation of investment funds, which will frustrate progress towards I_2. These arguments have found expression in macroeconomic policy through restrictions on government borrowing and the privatization of state enterprises, but equally beg the question as to the extent to which existing capital market mechanisms are suitable for achieving tourism policy objectives. In practical terms, the implementation of financial incentives is often a combination of both demand and supply initiatives.

It is important to note that there are frequent instances where it is gross uncertainty, as in times of recession, rather than limited potential, that prevents the private sector investing. In such situations the principal role of government intervention is to act as a catalyst to give confidence to investors. Thus public funds are able to lever in private money by nature of the government's commitment to tourism and enable the market potential of an area to be realized.

Reduction in capital costs

Incentives to reduce capital costs may include: capital grants; 'soft' loans; equity participation; provision of infrastructure; provision of land on concessional terms; and tariff exemption on construction materials. Capital grants are cash payments which have an immediate impact on the funding of the project as do matching benefits in kind such as the provision of land or facilities. They are usually preferred by investors because they are one-off transactions involving no further commitment and are therefore risk free. From the standpoint of the authorities they are relatively easy to administer.

'Soft' loans are funds which are provided on preferential terms. At their most simple they may be the granting of interest rate relief on commercial loans. Beyond this the government will normally have to put aside loan funds and create a development agency to administer them. World-wide, the common features of most 'soft' loans relate to generous interest rate terms, extended repayment periods, creative patterns of repayment and usually some restriction of the debt/equity mix so as to ensure that the project is not too highly geared in terms of loan finance, which makes it vulnerable to downturns in the market. In some instances loans may be tied to specific sources of supply; this is very common in country-to-country (bilateral) aid programmes. Creative repayment patterns are methods designed to counter the risk profile of the project or the nature of the cash flow over the project's life. Thus a tourist project, such as an attraction which may be particularly vulnerable in its early stages, may be given a moratorium on all repayments for several years. Alternatively an hotel in which the greater part of the cash flow accrues in the second half of the loan term may be granted 'balloon' financing in which the principal is paid back towards the end of the term so as to ensure greater freedom of operation during the initial years of the investment.

Bodlender and Ward (1987) point out that providing loan funds for tourism is more acceptable politically than the provision of grants. The argument in favour of loans rests on the fact that the funds will be recycled and the cost to the treasury will only be the preference element. This is not a rational argument as all incentives have a grant element, so it is always possible under conditions of reasonable certainty to prepare a loan scheme which will bestow exactly the same present worth as a cash grant and vice-versa. In a world of uncertainty the grant is riskless, while the loan plan becomes part of the risk environment of the project. Any risk premium attached to this environment will differ from project to project, so that the equivalence of the preferential element of the loan and the capital grant can no longer be assured. The instance under which the loan is chosen in preference to the grant would correspond to the situation where the investor is unable to raise the capital funds over and above the grant from elsewhere. This begs the question as to the cause of the inability to raise funds: it may be due to matters of investment security and then it is up to the government to give the necessary guarantees.

Equity participation involves the public sector investing in the commercial aspects of tourism development with the private sector. The extreme case is where governments themselves set up a tourist development corporation and take one hundred per cent investment in revenue earning activities such as hotels, which are traditionally regarded as the preserve of the private sector. Examples around the world include New Zealand, Malaysia, India, Egypt and many African countries, but the rising trend towards market economics during the 1980s led states increasingly to divest themselves of trading operations that could be undertaken by the commercial sector.

Perhaps more than any other industry, the development of tourism involves the exploitation of real estate. In many countries, the state owns considerable tracts of land and by providing sites on concessional terms the government may be able to attract the investors which best match its tourism policy objectives. The worth of such sites to investors is reinforced by the provision of the necessary construction works, such as access roads, and utilities (water and energy supplies).

Reduction in operating costs

To improve operating viability governments may offer direct and indirect tax exemptions; a labour or training subsidy; subsidized tariffs on key inputs such as energy; special depreciation allowances; and double taxation or unilateral relief. Indirect tax exemptions cover such items as wavers on import duties for materials and supplies, exemption from property taxes, licenses and value added tax. The latter is a tax on labour and payments for capital in use, whether capital is in the form of debt or equity (Wanhill, 1995). Concessions in respect of import duties and other fees are common incentives offered to foreign investors.

Exemption from direct (income or profits) taxes through 'tax holidays' and special depreciation allowances only have meaning when the project is profitable (hence viable since debt charges are normally deductible), and therefore over the hurdle of initial start up risks. Tax holidays and reduced profit tax rates are some of the most popular forms of incentives given to new tourism projects and, more recently, are especially noticeable in the packages offered to investors by the expanding Eastern European and the Commonwealth of Independent States (CIS) regions: their approach has been to offer tax holidays from two to five years after the first year's profits have been recorded, whereas such holidays have tended to be between five and ten years for developments in LDCs. After the expiration of a tax holiday, governments may offer reduced rates of income or profits tax to international firms, depending on:

- the amount of profits invested locally;
- how much foreign exchange is generated;
- improved economic linkages through purchases from domestic suppliers;
- staff training undertaken by the firm.

Depreciation allowances and tax holidays are often used in tandem, thus a five year tax holiday may be followed by special depreciation allowances. The latter may vary from permitting the organization to write-off its assets to its best advantage over an eight year period, to providing a substantial initial allowance of 20 to 30 per cent of the capital cost and a normal 'wear and tear' allowance thereafter. The effect of special depreciation allowances is to defer tax payments, which amounts to an interest-free tax loan from the government (Bloom and Mostert, 1995). This favours longer term investments, because the longer the life of the capital asset, the greater is the present worth value of the tax loan. A further fiscal boost may come from the provision of an investment allowance (also known as a tax or investment credit), which is not merely tax

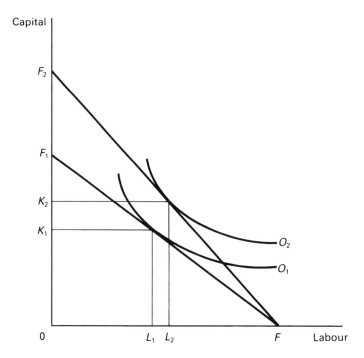

Figure 20.2   Positive impact of capital subsidies on employment

postponement analogous to accelerated depreciation, but a tax reduction through being able to write-off, say 30 per cent of the initial capital, without affecting the tax value of the asset for depreciation purposes. Investment allowances favour assets that are replaced frequently, allowing the firm to take advantage of the tax savings.

The matter of a labour subsidy is indicative of the employment creation objective in tourism development. Factor subsidies can alter the choice of technology in the supply process. One criticism of capital subsidies is that they will tend to promote a capital intensive structure whereas the emphasis is on generating jobs. A labour subsidy will always improve employment opportunities whereas the effects of a capital subsidy are indeterminable. This aspect is illustrated in Figures 20.2 and 20.3.

In Figure 20.2, the effect of a capital subsidy is to move the relative factor price line from FF_1 to FF_2. This moves the business on to a higher level of output as given by the shift from isoquant O_1 to isoquant O_2. In this instance both the amount of capital and labour employed increases from OK_1 to OK_2 and OL_1 to OL_2 respectively. But for Figure 20.3, the impact of the subsidy is to greatly increase the utilization of capital at the expense of labour. It was with this in mind that the Trade and Industry Committee of the UK House of Commons (1985) recommended that, on

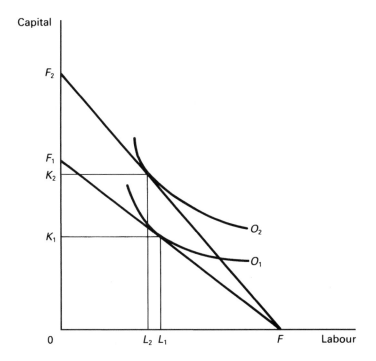

Figure 20.3 Negative impact of capital subsidies on employment

an experimental basis, the UK Government should pay a grant of 30 per cent of the employment costs of tourist facilities remaining open for one month longer than the previous year.

As a rule, tourist authorities counter the contrasting effects of subsidizing capital by giving priority in funding to employment creating projects. A ready method of doing this is to tie the amount of grant to the number of full-time equivalent (FTE) jobs. The latter allows for the fact that a good number of tourism jobs are often part-time or seasonal. This presumes an element of discretion in the awarding of incentives, which is not always possible when they have been laid down by legislation and are therefore automatic.

Tourism projects involving hotel developments are high users of energy, particularly where there are climatic extremes, such as in tropical areas where there is a need for air-conditioning or in colder climes where the requirement is for continual heating. In these circumstances, energy use and management becomes a key element in the operating budget of the hotel. Large hotel corporations have always been able to negotiate energy prices with suppliers, but where the energy supplier is a public utility, as is the case in many newly emerging destinations, then the government is able to offer the additional incentive of reduced tariffs to strengthen the profitability of the business.

Double taxation and unilateral relief are country-to-country or single-country agreements to ensure that multinational investors are not taxed on the same profits in different locations. Suppose a company controlled in Country A trades in Country B through a permanent establishment in the latter country, it will pay tax on its trading profits both in Country A and Country B, but if there is a double taxation agreement between these countries, then a tax credit in respect of Country B's tax will be allowed against Country A's tax. If there is only unilateral relief, the company will be entitled to offset its tax liability elsewhere against tax payable in Country B.

Investment security

The objective of providing investment security is to win investors' confidence in an industry which is very sensitive to the political environment and the economic climate. Action here would include guarantees against nationalization; ensuring the availability of trained staff; free availability of foreign exchange; repatriation of invested capital, profits, dividends and interest; loan guarantees; provision of work permits for 'key' personnel; and availability of technical advice. To support these actions, there is the broader issue of the government's support for tourism. This may be demonstrated by marketing and promoting the region, particularly abroad, reducing administrative delays, simplifying the planning process, easing frontier formalities, initiating liberal transport policies and so forth.

Clearly, without the confidence in the government to set the right economic climate for the tourist industry to prosper, investment incentives on their own may be of limited value in attracting outside funds or mobilizing domestic investment in tourism. To counter bureaucratic inefficiency, complicated administrative processes and the lack of transparency in the legislation affecting foreign businesses, together with frequent modifications to the legislation, some governments, notably in countries looking to become new tourist destinations, such as in Eastern Europe and the Commonwealth of Independent States, have established 'one-stop-shop' agencies to ease the path of foreign investors, as well as including 'grandfathering' clauses in the legislation, which exempt foreign enterprises from unfavourable legal changes for up to ten years. For similar reasons, a good deal of World Bank lending, particularly in Africa, has gone towards structural adjustment policies to set the economic framework within which market oriented projects may function.

Implementation

In implementing a tourism investment policy the government has to decide to what extent incentives should be legislated as automatic entitlements, as against being discretionary awards. It has already been noted that automatic incentives may give too much money away, when what is required to ensure that the treasury receives maximum benefit from its funds is the application of the concept of additionality. The latter seeks to provide financial support or the equivalent benefits in kind to the point where the developer will just proceed with the project.

The implication of additionality is an ideal situation where all incentives are discretionary and therefore offered selectively. The legislation would be fairly general, empowering the ministry responsible for tourism to offer loans, grants, tax exemptions and equity investment as it sees fit. Such legislation is embodied, for example, in the UK 1969 Development of Tourism Act. The granting of incentives to prospective developers would be in accordance with ministerial guidelines. The latter should be regularly reviewed in response to the level of tourism activity and changes in policy. These guidelines may include statements giving priority to certain kinds of tourism projects, that, for example, provide specific benefits to local communities, extend the tourist season, enhance the range of tourist facilities at the destination, offer full-time employment, give access to disabled visitors, attract both domestic and foreign visitors, and preserve the landscape. In sum, discretionary incentives allow tourist agencies to:

- switch sector priorities with the object of encouraging new developments, modernization and achieving a balanced development of tourist facilities in specific locations;
- support projects which have high income and employment creating potential;
- select projects which have most chance of success, and are socially and environmentally sustainable;
- adjust the money awarded to oblige the applicant to meet any investment specifications in respect of type, quality and quantity.

To have only discretionary incentives, however, is a counsel of perfection. Competition for tourism investment frequently requires countries to legislate for automatic financial help in order to attract investors in the first instance. Some countries may legislate for all the incentives discussed here; others for a subset of them. Many countries have been guilty of copying the incentive legislation of their neighbours without any real grasp of the meaning of this legislation.

The appropriateness of the various financial incentives available depends on understanding the nature of the business risk and the likely returns of the tourist industry, as well as the ability of the country to afford them. Thus developing countries may find themselves in no position to offer grants or cheap loans. It is well known that part of the business risk in tourism projects lies in the fact that services are non-storable (a hotel bed unsold is lost forever) and in demand being generally seasonal. This implies that peak demand determines capacity (unless capacity is regulated by planning legislation in order to preserve amenity value) so that the industry is always facing excess capacity at other times, which inculcates a certain reluctance amongst banks and other financial institutions to lend to the tourism industry, particularly as they often experience difficulty in appraising the financial viability of both tourism products and the managers of projects. As a rule, to control costs, government treasuries are against giving blanket reductions in general taxation, since it is difficult to prevent them applying to 'old' capital as well as new investment. The emphasis on incentives is their ephemeral nature for the purposes of providing the foundation for new projects to establish themselves.

Cost structures

Not always apparent is the dominant cost structure in the industry. Typically, tourist projects have a high operating leverage, that is a high level of fixed costs arising out of the initial capital investment and low operating costs. This makes pricing difficult, because operating costs are no longer a reliable guide as to what to charge, and also results in businesses which are very sensitive to variations in demand. The problem is illustrated in Figure 20.4, where it is assumed that there are two projects which have exactly the same revenue line R and break even point BEP. However, one project has a high operating leverage as shown by the cost line C_1, and the other a low operating leverage represented by C_2. The possible outcomes of these two projects are shown by Q_1, Q_2 and Q_3. Suppose Q_3 sales are achieved, then it is clear that the project with the high operating leverage makes substantially more profit than the other. This is represented on Figure 20.4 by the difference between the revenue and cost schedules, where it may be seen that $DF > DE$. On the other hand, if the outcome is Q_1 sales then the project with the cost structure C_1 will make large losses, $AC > AB$. Thus a 1 per cent variation in load factors on aircraft may be critical to the profitability of tour operators, and when things do go wrong the consequences are often spectacular: the nightmare scenario for governments is where a major tour operator collapses, either depriving its millions of customers of previously arranged holidays or leaving them stranded abroad.

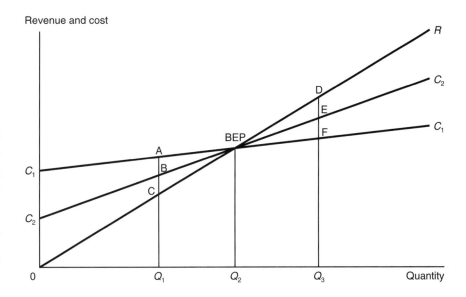

Revenue and cost

Figure 20.4   Effects of operating leverage

In addition to the above, it has already been indicated that tourism at the destination end is extensive in its use of land and property. This tends to induce elements of real estate speculation, but the non-transferability of assets such as hotels or tourist attractions to other uses hinders their worth as a property investment. Add to this the seasonality of demand, which produces irregular cash flows and it is not surprising that financial institutions view tourism projects as risky investments. So if the objective is to improve viability, then the preferred form of financial incentives are those which reduce capital costs (Wanhill, 1986).

In the light of this emphasis on capital costs, the term 'viability' has a distinct role in the financial evaluation of tourism projects and the award of discretionary incentive in the form equity purchase, soft loans or grants. In the first instance, the scheme must be feasible, in that it is capable of generating a surplus of revenue over its operating costs. Viability, however, has to do with servicing the capital investment: it depends on the interest rate, which can fluctuate considerably by virtue of government policies, the funding package for the capital involved and methods of repayment. These concepts are presented in Figure 20.5. As before, R is the revenue line and C the total cost schedule attributable to running the project in a given year. The line C^* represents the cost of operation excluding the provision for capital payments. At a level of V_2 visitor days the project is feasible, since it produces a surplus BC over C^*, but it is not viable because there is a gap AB in the funds available to service the capital. To the left of D the project is neither viable nor feasible

Revenue and cost

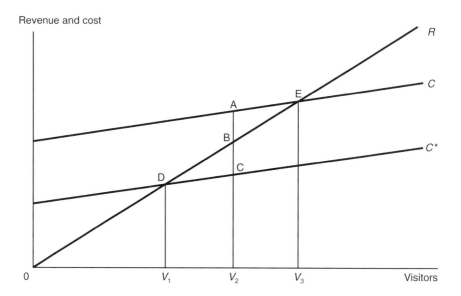

Figure 20.5   Viability of tourism projects

and conversely for point E. The object of giving investment incentives is to ensure that the programme becomes viable, either by moving the C line down to B at V_2 visitor days or reshaping the project to expand the market to V_3 visitor days or some combination of the two.

Evaluation

It is well known that tourism is a demand-led industry whose influence pervades many different sectors of the economy. There is no single industrial classification called tourism, so the starting point for evaluating tourism projects, from a government's perspective, is to measure the economic impact of tourist spending and derive appropriate multipliers, in particular income and employment multipliers. Tourists come to a destination for many reasons so if the requirement is to establish the worth of a project which has been assisted through public funds, the first step is to establish the criteria for assessment.

Benefit analysis

Suppose that there exists a tourist destination with two attractions and a seaside. Visitors are surveyed at both attractions and on the beach to ascertain what motivated them to come to the destination. Total spending at the destination (*T*) amounts to expenditure at Attraction X (T_x) plus expenditure at Attraction Y (T_y) plus all remaining expenditure (*R*). The pull factor (reason for visit) for Attraction X is *a*. For Attraction Y the pull factor is *b*, leaving $1 - a - b$ as the significance of the beach. It follows therefore that attributable tourist expenditure by drawing power is:

$$\text{Attraction X} = aT_x + aT_y + aR$$
$$\text{Attraction Y} = bT_x + bT_y + bR$$
$$\text{Seaside} \quad = (1 - a - b)(T_x + T_y + R)$$
$$T = T_x + T_y + R$$

The local tourist board has put public money into Attraction X and so wishes to evaluate its worth in terms of its contribution to tourist spending and employment in the area. The benefits of Attraction X (**B**) are the difference between its attractiveness with and without the project. The without situation is:

$$\text{Attraction X} = 0$$
$$\text{Attraction Y} = bT_y + bR$$
$$\text{Seaside} \quad = (1 - a - b)(T_y + R)$$
$$T_w = (1 - a)(T_y + R)$$

Hence

$$B = T - T_w$$
$$= T_x + a(T_y + R) \tag{1}$$

If the visitors to Attraction X would have come to the area anyway then the benefits would simply be T_x.

Employment effects

The benefits shown in Equation (1) are in two parts. The first term on the right hand side is on-site expenditure and the second, off-site expenditure. The amount of off-site expenditure attributable to the attraction depends on its ability to generate additional visitors. Hence, this may be termed the visitor additionality factor. The application of employment multipliers per unit of tourist spending to Equation (1), either on an FTE or employment headcount basis, will give the gross employment (*E*) generated by the project. These multipliers are calculated so as to measure the direct employment effects of the project, the indirect effects arising out of intermediate purchases made by the project and the induced effects on the local economy as a result of the re-spending of local incomes derived from the project, and similarly for off-site expenditure. Thus:

$$E = T_x e_x + a \, O e_o \tag{2}$$

Where e_x is the employment multiplier appropriate to the attraction, O is the sum of off-site expenditure $(T_y + R)$ and e_o the required employment multiplier. However, Equation (2) ignores any demand diversion from elsewhere in the area: this is termed displacement and in this respect it is important to define the boundary of the project. As observed by Johnson and Thomas (1990):

> In the case of the economy as a whole it is sometimes argued that all expenditure, and consequently employment, is diverted and there is in effect a zero-sum game. This point is of some importance from the point of view of public bodies providing funds. Local authorities and the Treasury for example might have very different views on what is the net impact because they are concerned with different reference areas.

At a national level this argument assumes that market forces are moving the economy towards full employment equilibrium so that public investment expenditure is simply displacing private funds in the capital market. Similarly, the operation of the project is displacing demand in the same or related product markets and likewise in the labour and property markets. In reality economies do get stuck at a level of Keynesian unemployment disequilibrium and one of the major objectives of regional policy is to 'kick-start' a demand deficient economy so as to raise the level of output through the multiplier process. This discussion does not imply that displacement should be neglected so that policy decisions are made in terms of the gross effect only, but merely raises the issue that the logic of the crowding out effect ends up with a 'do nothing' policy.

If d is the proportion of locally diverted demand (or demand diverted from other assisted projects) in Equation (1), then, from Equation (2), net employment is:

$$\begin{aligned} N &= E - dE \\ &= (1 - d)\,(T_x e_x + a O e_o) \end{aligned} \tag{3}$$

Equation (3) forms the core of the basic evaluation model which can be used to judge in employment terms the return to public funds given to the project by way of the whole range of incentives discussed earlier. As an example, consider the data presented in Table 20.2. The total on-site and off-site expenditure arising from the project is $25,050,000. Visitor surveys have shown that only about 12 per cent of staying visitors came to the destination because of the existence of the attraction. As is to be expected, this percentage is much greater for day visitors and local residents. From Equation (1):

Table 20.2 Calculating the employment impact of an attraction

		On-site expenditure	Off-site expenditure
Markets			
Stay		$2,210,000	$12,920,000
Day		$2,465,000	$2,200,000
Local residents		$3,825,000	$1,430,000
	Total	$8,500,000	$16,550,000
Visitor additionality			
Stay		Not applicable	2%
Day		Not applicable	90%
Local residents		Not applicable	100%
Displacement			
Stay		0%	0%
Day		30%	30%
Local residents		70%	70%
FTE multipliers per $10,000 of visitor expenditure			
Direct		0.0765	0.0628
Indirect		0.0412	0.0391
Induced		0.0059	0.0059
	Total	0.1236	0.1078

$$B = \$8,500,000 + 0.12 \times \$12,920,000 + 0.9 \times \$2,200,000$$
$$+ 1.0 \times \$1,430,000 = \$13,460,400$$

It is known that the attraction creates 87.5 FTEs directly on-site and so the relevant addition to this number is the employment generated by the indirect and induced effects of on-site expenditure. Using the appropriate FTE multipliers in Table 20.2, the number of jobs is $(0.0412 + 0.0059) \times \$8,500,000/\$10,000 = 40.0$. Off-site jobs created amount to $0.1078 \times \$4,960,400/\$10,000 = 53.5$. Thus the value of Equation (2) is:

$$E = 87.5 + 40.0 + 53.5$$
$$= 181.0 \text{ FTEs.}$$

So far the analysis has only measured gross FTEs generated by the attraction. The net figure has to account for the displacement factors given in Table 20.2. Suppose that the evidence indicates that there will be no displacement of staying visitors since the attraction is providing them with more 'things to do' but there will be a 30 per cent diversion of day visitor spend and 70 per cent for local residents. It could be argued that there should be a 100 per cent displacement of local resident demand, but, while this may be a good working assumption in that residents have many opportunities to spend in the local area, it does imply that there is no flexibility in residents' leisure spending budgets. Using the information on expenditure in Table 20.2, the weighted overall displacement factor is 0.3724, hence the solution to Equation (3) is:

$$N = 181.0 - 0.3724 \times 181.0$$
$$= 113.6 \text{ FTEs.}$$

It is this number of FTEs that is traded against the estimated grant element of the incentives offered, in order to give the cost to public funds of job creation.

The core model given by Equation (3) is capable of further adjustment to take into account factors such as project additionality; business displacement; differential impacts on the local labour market; and externalities. Incentive legislation used in the UK is hedged about with the concept of additionality. As stated before, this lays down the criterion that a grant (or loan) would only be forthcoming if the project would not proceed without it. Assessment of this position by project officers involves considerable subjective judgement about the likely future behaviour of the investor and in practice requires the investor to sign a document to the effect that the funds are a necessary condition for the project to go ahead. In reality there are degrees of project additionality, for the investment could have gone ahead at a later date, on a smaller scale or at a lower quality. If a numerical value can be placed upon such assessments then they can be included in the model. Similarly business displacement may arise in several ways: the funded project crowds out a competing investment opportunity; the investment replaces an existing business on the same site; or the project may result in a property move to a new site, leaving the old site vacant.

Replacement of an existing business may have a beneficial effect if there is a quality and cost improvement that raises long term viability. Many assisted tourist projects have been built on derelict sites and have therefore resulted in a net improvement. Differential impacts on the labour market relate to the use of unemployed as opposed to people already in jobs, improving the skills of the work-force, full-time, part-time and seasonal jobs, the male/female ratio, local people versus outsiders and so on. Externalities would account for the agglomeration benefits arising by virtue of the synergy of one project with another and its linkages with the rest of the economy to ensure a balanced growth of facilities at the destination, in order to meet the many and changing needs of visitors. However, as the model moves through increasing levels of sophistication so data requirements spiral upwards. Given that data sources are imperfect and there is always pressure on time, the practical effect of this is to increase the level of economic assumptions made, which in turn downgrades the robustness of the core model presented in Equation (3).

Conclusions

Around the globe governments have intervened to assist and regulate the private sector in the development of tourism. This is because the complex nature of the tourist product makes it unlikely that private markets will satisfy a country's tourism policy objectives to produce a balance of facilities that meet the needs of the visitor, benefit the host community and are compatible with the wishes of that same community. Incentives are policy instruments that can be used to correct for market failure and ensure a development partnership between the public and private sectors. The extent of public involvement depends on the economic philosophy of the government. The trend towards pure market led economics in recent years has led to a clawback of state involvement and the questioning of incentives as mechanisms more likely to lead to market distortions. This is in total contrast to the concept of sustainable development which challenges the ability of private markets to improve the distribution of income and protect the environment.

The baseline scenario for sustainable development is the alleviation of absolute poverty and the replenishment of the resource stock so that at a minimum no one generation is worse off than any other. The spillover benefits of tourism are well known, and, more than any other industry, tourism deals with the use of natural and cultural resources. The lessons of the past indicate that it is unwise for the state to abandon its ability to influence the direction of tourism development either through the provision of finance or through legislation. The short term gains sought by capital markets are often at odds with the long term sustainability of tourism environments.

References

Archer, B. and Wanhill, S. (1980) *Tourism in Bermuda: an Economic Evaluation*, Bermuda Department of Tourism, Hamilton

Bloom, J. and Mostert, F. (1995) Incentive guidelines for South African tourism: implications and challenges in the context of developing socio-political trends, *Tourism Economics*, **1**(1), 17–31

Bodlender, J.A. (1982) The financing of tourism projects, *Tourism Management*, 3(4), 277–284

Bodlender, J.A. and Ward, T.J. (1987) *An Examination of Tourism Incentives*, Howarth & Howarth, London

Boskin, M. (1996) National Satellite Accounting for travel and tourism: a cold review of the WTTC/WEFA group research, *Tourism Economics*, 2(1), 3–11

Cooper, C. (1992) The life cycle concept and strategic planning for coastal resorts, *Built Environment*, 18(1), 57–66

Cooper, C. and Jackson, S. (1989) Destination life cycle: the Isle of Man case study, *Annals of Tourism Research*, 15(3), 377–398

Jenkins, C.L. (1982), The use of investment incentives for tourism projects in developing countries, *Tourism Management*, 3(2), 91–97

Johnson, P.S. and Thomas, R.B. (1990) The economic impact of museums: a study of the North of England Open Air Museum at Beamish, proceedings of a conference on *Tourism Research into the 1990s*, University of Durham, December, pp. 388–402

Plog, S. (1973) Why destinations rise and fall in popularity, *Cornell H.R.A. Quarterly*, November, pp. 13–16

Trade and Industry Committee (1985) *Tourism in the UK*, Vol. 1, Session 1985–1986, HMSO, London, p. xxxvii

Wanhill, S.R.C. (1986) Which investment incentives for tourism? *Tourism Management*, 7(1), 2–7

Wanhill, S. (1995) VAT rates and the UK tourism and leisure industry, *Tourism Economics*, 1(3), 211–224

21 Selecting policy instruments for sustainable tourism

Bill Bramwell

Introduction

There is growing recognition that the market economy on its own will not produce sustainable tourism and that some government interventions are necessary. Government interventions are guided by policies and are implemented using policy instruments, which are the specific mechanisms or tools employed to put policy into practice. Public authorities are faced with an extensive array of policy instruments to put sustainable tourism policies into practice. These instruments include zoning to control tourism development or to limit tourist access to sensitive areas, dissemination of tourism codes of conduct to encourage more sustainable behaviour, taxing of energy use and waste treatment services to prompt tourism enterprises to save scarce resources and reduce pollution, and public provision of traffic management infrastructure to reduce congestion and pollution in tourist areas. All such instruments for sustainable tourism are interventions by government that alter what would otherwise happen. When instruments are being selected it is important to consider the complete range of instruments and to select a mix of them which, in the particular circumstances, translate policy into action and meet the overall policy objectives. Deciding which instruments are appropriate depends on the specific goals, and deciding what goals are sought is influenced by social, economic and political processes that are affected by competing beliefs, values and ideology.

Public policies for sustainable tourism may be unsuccessful in practice if inappropriate instruments are used. The use of unsuitable mechanisms is one reason why 'Despite the acceptance of sustainable tourism as a desirable alternative to more predatory modes of development, a gap commonly exists between policy endorsement and policy implementation' (Pigram, 1990: 2). A policy instrument can contribute to this gap as there may be unrealistic expectations about its potential to deliver against overall objectives. There is a further potential gap between the policy intention and what the instrument actually achieves in practice. Often policy makers fail to recognize potential problems in implementation. For instance, many problems stem from the consequences of local cultural and political circumstances which are unforeseen or ignored, including an inability or unwillingness to enforce policy measures.

This chapter examines issues to be considered when public authorities are selecting sustainable tourism policy instruments. It describes some conceptual foundations behind these issues, and examples are used to illustrate the practical implications of these issues for policy instruments. There is discussion of how preferences for policy instruments must be based on moral and political evaluations. Policy makers would be helped if the tourism literature included more comparative evaluations of the strengths and weaknesses of different policy instruments in specific situations. In this context, the chapter examines a range of issues to consider when making such comparisons between instruments. It also argues that comparisons of instruments in environmental economics have tended to concentrate on only a few of these issues and give little consideration to the importance of social values, ethics and politics.

Principles of sustainable tourism

Selecting policy instruments for sustainable tourism requires an understanding of the principles of sustainable development and of sustainable tourism within this. Although sustainable development is a contested concept with many potential interpretations, some core principles or ideals underlying this concept of development are often identified (Bramwell and Lane, 1993; LGMB, 1993). Prominent among these are:

- **Resources:** Recognition that the health and integrity of natural, built and human resources is critical to future well-being, and that this depends on how these resources are treated. For instance, the stock of environmental resources must be conserved, and this implies minimal use of non-renewable resources and minimal emission of pollutants. Sustainable development is concerned with the viability not only of the environment but also of economic, cultural and social resources.
- **Futurity:** Concern for the well-being of future generations, so that they benefit from resources, opportunities and choices at least as good as those inherited by the current generation.
- **Equity:** There should be fairness in the distribution within society of the economic, social, cultural and environmental benefits and costs.

These equity considerations are seen as closely related to sustainable development in at least four ways. First, because it tends to be disadvantaged social groups who bear the brunt of negative costs; and, second, it is often the case that poverty encourages unsustainable lifestyles, based on a clamour for quick returns to meet immediate needs. Third, the effects of policies depend on people's wealth, and this is seen clearly with policies that involve high charges for the use of resources and so tend to exclude poorer people. And, lastly, it is hard to justify caring about fairness to future generations without extending this concern to people in society today.

Several of these principles are contained in Cronin's suggestion that 'in the case of the tourism industry, sustainable development has a fairly specific meaning – the industry's challenge is to develop tourism capacity and the quality of its products without adversely affecting the physical and human environment that sustains and nurtures them' (1990: 13). Eber (1992: 3) proposes that tourism can contribute to sustainable development when it:

> operates within natural capacities for the regeneration and future productivity of natural resources; recognizes the contribution that people and communities, customs and lifestyles, make to the tourism experience; accepts that these people must have an equitable share in the economic benefits of tourism; and is guided by the wishes of local people and communities in the host areas.

The sustainable tourism literature also suggests certain principles or ideals for policy development by government, and these should guide the use of specific policy instruments (LGMB, 1993). One such principle is that deciding on and implementing policies requires wide participation, partnerships and co-operative action by all affected groups in society. Community participation, for example, is generally seen as necessary for sustainable tourism planning (Joppe, 1996). Another common proposition is that policies should be integrated with each other, based on recognition of the interdependence of issues and policies, such as for tourism, employment and transport (Inskeep, 1991). Third, it is sometimes indicated that because of practical constraints it is necessary to set achievable short-term targets for improvement, and that these targets should be raised steadily upwards over time. Such progressive target setting is needed to secure progress in the right direction and to maintain momentum.

Certain principles or ideals for policy choice by government are also suggested in the literature of sustainable tourism, and these too need to influence policy instrument selection (LGMB, 1993). One such principle is that where there is uncertainty about the consequences for natural, built or human resources of a particular course of action, it is necessary to be cautious and to avoid taking risks. This 'precautionary principle' is necessary to reduce the chance that actions will produce irreversible damage to resources and quality of life. Another principle for policy choice is that because certain demands to use resources are unsustainable and should not be met, policies and related instruments need to be designed to reduce or redirect these unmeetable demands. A third ('polluter-pays') principle is that those who cause damage to scarce resources generally should pay for the damage, and in this way they are penalized for damaging actions and are encouraged to alter their behaviour.

The principles or ideals of sustainable tourism are both fraught with ambiguity and also counsels of perfection. For example, implementation is highly problematic because of such practical difficulties as the numerous interested parties with diverse beliefs and aims and also the constraints involved with the operation of the market economy. It is also the case that too often public authorities adopt sustainable tourism without clear strategies regarding what it entails or how it can be applied in practice. These difficulties may encourage sceptics to dismiss the approach altogether. However, others may contend that, despite the problems, it is still important for policy makers to strive for the ideals of sustainable tourism.

Types of policy instruments

Policy instruments for government use in order to promote sustainable tourism are of four types. An understanding of these categories helps clarify what issues to consider when selecting policy instruments appropriate for specific circumstances. The four types are used in the subsequent discussion.

- **Government encouragement** through information, education and general persuasion directed at tourism operators, tourists or communities in tourist areas in order to encourage them voluntarily to adopt sustainable behaviour. This would include interpretation at publicly-owned sites about damaging visitor activities or government-assessed 'green' ratings for tourism businesses adopting environmentally-friendly practices. A moral appeal using information may help change behaviour, particularly if the harmful actions are largely due to ignorance.
- **Government financial incentives** which alter the prices facing tourism businesses, tourists or host communities for environmentally or culturally damaging or beneficial behaviour. They may be taxes or subsidies intended to make some resources more or less expensive

than others, so that activities change in consequence. Examples are fees for entry to natural or cultural sites and local tourist taxes designed to raise revenue for environmental work or to control visitor pressure by deterring visitors, and also charges for water consumption by hotels which are intended to encourage water conservation. Subsidies offer positive incentives, such as by providing payments to hotels that introduce energy saving techniques (Hunter and Green, 1995). In many countries agricultural producers are given subsidies to protect ecologically sensitive areas under their control, and often these areas are important tourism resources (Broom et al., 1995).

- **Government expenditure** on actions taken directly by government or state-owned agencies, such as spending on public transport, land purchase and conservation measures in national parks, community development initiatives and waste management.
- **Government regulations** which either prohibit or require particular courses of action and are backed by the law, but which do not involve a financial incentive or direct government expenditure. These policy instruments compel tourism businesses or tourists to comply, with non-compliance likely to involve judicial punishment (Jacobs, 1991). For instance, there may be specified environmental quality standards and land use zoning regulations in a tourist area. Included in these might be fixed standards for the maximum number of beds per hectare and maximum number of hotel rooms and hotel building height in resorts. As well as restrictions on land-use, there could be limits to the discharge of certain pollutants and restrictions on contracts between tour operators and hoteliers (Nijkamp and Verdonkschot, 1995).

Issues in selecting policy instruments

There are many specific forms of public policy instrument within each of the four types outlined above. Given the range of potential instruments related to sustainable tourism, it is useful to identify general issues which need consideration when selecting instruments to suit local conditions. The following framework of issues substantially adapts and extends one developed by Jacobs (1991) for general environmental instruments.

Effectiveness

The issue of effectiveness concerns the degree to which a specific public policy instrument is likely to meet the policy objectives of sustainable tourism. Among related considerations are the certainty and relative speed that an instrument will meet objectives, and its flexibility of response to changing circumstances.

Public policy instruments based only on encouragement through information and education perhaps have the least certainty of achieving sustainable outcomes as they depend on people understanding and accepting the information and responding voluntarily. For instance, despite publicity that noisy airboat rides across the wetland habitat of the Big Cyprus National Preserve in Florida disturb wildlife and cause distress to nesting birds, many visitors still see taking a ride across the swamp as an ecologically friendly activity (Shackley, 1996). But information and education initiatives have several advantages. For example, while published codes of conduct may help protect environmental resources, they can also provide security for the visitor and maximize the quality of his or her experience. Additionally, such policies can encourage tourism businesses, visitors and host communities to understand what is damaging, which may lead them to avoid this harmful behaviour in the long term. Encouragement to voluntary actions is also advantageous if it encourages these groups to be proactive in taking responsibility for initiating change (UNEP, 1995).

There is greater certainty that nature tourism operators will respond to public exhortations to conserve environmental resources when there are only a few operators in a nature tourism destination and when there is a close coincidence of their interests with those of the environment. In these circumstances co-operation and self-enforcement between all the operators to behave responsibly may well be easier (Forsyth et al., 1995). Steps can be taken to increase the certainty that education programmes about tourism resource conservation will be effective. Environmental codes of conduct for tourism may be more effective if they are developed after wide consultation and are well publicized (Genot, 1995). In Finland, codes of conduct for tourism were developed by a working group chaired by the Finnish Tourist Board and including representatives from the Finnish Rural Tourism Group, Ministry of Environment, National Board of Water and the Environment, Finnish Municipal Association, Association of Rural Centres, and the Finnish Association for Nature Protection, and this was later enlarged to include industry representatives. A publicity campaign accompanied the dissemination of the codes (UNEP, 1995). Governments that commit themselves to tourism codes of conduct might also increase compliance by monitoring and reporting on performance against standards set out in the codes. The Australian government integrated sustainable development objectives into its National Tourism Strategy, with the industry body, Tourism Council Australia, adopting similar guidelines in its code of conduct and performing regular monitoring of responses to the code (Harris and Leiper, 1995; Turner, 1995; UNEP, 1995).

The certainty of achieving sustainable tourism objectives may be greater when government regulation instruments are used. These require certain behaviour and are backed by law. For instance, access zoning with quantitative limits to the number of visitors allowed to enter socially or environmentally pressured areas has the potential advantage of relatively precise and predictable impacts. Such zoning may take the form of quantitative limits on cars allowed into a park or on boats permitted to visit a coral atoll (Forsyth et al., 1995; WTO/UNEP, 1992). However, such government regulations usually depend on effective monitoring, enforcement and judicial punishment to be fully successful. It should not be assumed that behaviour will change once laws are enacted, even in countries that have relatively strong legal traditions and institutions. One reason is that enforcement requires energy and resources, and there will be other calls on these resources. Furthermore, there will always be people whose interests lie in not having environmental policies enforced. Mak and Moncur (1995) describe how a smoking ban was imposed at Hanauma Bay Nature Park in Hawaii in order to stop cigarette butts littering the beach and contaminating the water in the bay, but park staff were told not to confront violators and the Honolulu police were very reluctant to cite violations. Additionally, even if regulations are enforced, there may be ingenious means to get round them. For example, the Honolulu Department of Parks and Recreation introduced restrictions on tour vehicles from dropping off visitors at the Hanauma Bay Nature Park in an attempt to reduce degradation of the natural environment and the quality of the visitor experience. However, tour operators circumvented these restrictions by bussing their customers to a nearby shopping centre or to residential neighbourhoods and contracting with taxi companies to shuttle passengers to the park (Mak and Moncur, 1995).

With government financial incentives, the certainty of meeting sustainable tourism objectives depends greatly on setting charges or subsidies at appropriate levels. In order to change public behaviour, charges or subsidies must be sufficiently high to either choke-off demand or encourage preferred behaviour. Before setting a charge or subsidy it is important to have reliable information on how it will affect demand or supply, but such information is not easily obtained and so in practice adjustment of charges or subsidies often involves much 'trial and error'. Responses to charging or subsidy levels in other regions or countries may provide some indication, although each case is likely to be different and necessitates local research. But even information from other situations may be unavailable. As Laarman and Gregersen (1996: 249) state for the use of higher fees for visits at peak times to nature tourism areas: 'evidence on off-peak pricing to shift use patterns is inconclusive, possibly because even "high" fees have been modest in most cases to date'.

Another influence on the effectiveness of a policy instrument in a specific situation is the extent to which it has the potential to tackle the full scope of the problem. For example, in the Galapagos Islands of Ecuador a range of instruments have been used to control damage by visitors, but Steele (1995) argues there have been very few controls on the total number of visitors despite this being the wider cause of many problems.

The effectiveness of instruments is also affected by any indirect benefits or costs they may have. In the case of a pricing system at a site, this may be intended to raise revenue for site management and conservation but there may be other valuable, indirect visitor management benefits. It can ensure that all visitors go through an entry procedure and at this point they are given necessary information, personal contact is made between site staff and visitors, and visitors realize that someone is on duty as a deterrent to irresponsible behaviour. People going through the entry point might then also realize the site is valuable and appreciate what they are paying for (Gale and Jacobs, 1987). A proposed increase in site entry fees may have the indirect benefit that this requires forecasts and its implementation may lead to monitoring and evaluation to determine actual impacts. These activities provide profiles on visitor numbers, composition and likes and dislikes, and these profiles are useful for visitor management and improving the visitor experience (Laarman and Gregersen, 1996). Information provision by public agencies may bring widespread indirect benefits as people who are brought to feel a greater sense of responsibility in a specific campaign, such as beach littering, may retain the same feeling in their other tourist activities.

Economic efficiency

Analysis of the economic efficiency of different public policy instruments for sustainable tourism involves comparing the cost involved with each instrument which is similarly effective in meeting policy objectives. The cost of public policy instruments includes the implementation cost for the public authority and the cost for tourism firms, tourists and host communities of changing their behaviour. Other things being equal, the lower these costs the better. The more economically efficient the mechanisms used to meet sustainable tourism goals, the more society can spend on other desirable initiatives.

Policy instruments vary in their cost to public authorities implementing them. For instance, tourist taxes which rely on multiple points of collection, such as at tourist accommodation in a region, can involve the public authority in relatively expensive policing activities. In the case of entrance fees to control visitor numbers or raise income for conservation work, these can be very expensive to collect, especially when there are few visitors and many entry points. However, these costs may be reduced by modifying the specific form of charging mechanism. Instead of collecting charges at all entry points, visitors could be required to purchase a permit in advance at one place, such as with the issue of camping permits for national parks in Queensland, Australia (Tisdell, 1995). Alternatively, indirect charging for car parking rather than access itself could be introduced and collected using automatic ticket machines that issue tickets for display in car windows. Charging for car parking using automatic ticket machines is used at some countryside sites in Wales to offset some site management and maintenance costs of local government and bodies such as Forest Enterprise and Welsh Water (Broom et al., 1995).

Motivational effect

Consideration needs to be given to whether public policy instruments provide a continuing incentive to tourism businesses, visitors and host communities to behave in more sustainable ways. For instance, do policies for tourism operators encourage them to continue to reduce their harmful pollution emissions or to innovate with the development of less damaging technologies? Here government regulation may be less effective than charges or taxes, as regulations only require polluters to meet specified standards, while financial incentives can encourage them to continue reducing their pollution in order to gain further cost reductions.

Administrative 'workability'

Public policy instruments need to be considered in relation to their administrative 'workability' and institutional acceptability. This involves such issues as the simplicity, ease and cost in time required to set up, administer, monitor and police specific policy instruments. If a scheme is very complex or time consuming, or has no clear sense of ownership for the institution to be tasked with administering it, it is much less likely to be workable.

Distributional impact and equity

Policy instruments intended to develop more sustainable tourism will differ in their distribution of positive and negative impacts between individuals, social groups and geographical areas. These distributional outcomes are affected by such factors as the choice of target group, whether intervention influences access to resources by ability to pay, and by how any revenues raised are redistributed. As discussed earlier, sustainable tourism approaches usually give prominence to creating equitable distributions. However, there is always some inequality in outcomes from specific policy instruments, and there are also many different concepts of distributional equity to consider (Hay, 1995; Kasperson and Dow, 1991). Clearly, evaluations of what is an acceptable distributional impact have to be made within a moral and political context.

The effects of public policy instruments on distributional outcomes between different tourists is one consideration. With pricing proposals, for example, poorer people may be unable to purchase at the same level, and what they do purchase may still represent a higher proportion of their income than for higher income groups. To counter such regressive effects, charges may be reduced for categories of visitors such as children, students and retired persons. In the case of public information initiatives based on moral persuasion among tourists, these may have a disadvantage in that those who respond to the moral arguments will carry the burden of this policy, while those who respond less well will enjoy the benefits of others' restraint but escape their share of the burden.

Sustainable tourism policies often emphasize the importance of equitable outcomes for residents living in tourist areas. Spatial instruments of zoning and national park designation are often used to protect ecological resources, but the distributional consequences for people living within or adjacent to these must also be a prime consideration.

In the case of government expenditure on national park designation and management, this can exclude local residents from areas which formerly had provided them with resources such as grazing, hunting or construction materials. The Maasai nomadic pastoralists of the Ngoro Ngoro Conservation Area in Tanzania have been denied access to their traditional grazing lands and it has been suggested that they have experienced a consequent decline in living conditions over the past twenty years (Cater, 1995). In Kenya also, wildlife reservations were carved out of lands previously used by traditional pastoral peoples, denying them of invaluable herding and agricultural resources and in some cases fishing rights. Another source of conflict between the demands of Kenya's wildlife-based tourism and the well-being of local people is that the wild animals are a menace to livestock, crops and people living in surrounding areas (Sindiga, 1995). As local communities can pay a heavy price for supporting wildlife protection areas, management plans and policy instruments have to take into account the provision of an alternative resource base, as well as potential compensation (Shackley, 1996). One approach to this is to share revenues from park entry fees with local communities. The Kenya Wildlife Service has adopted such a programme, starting with the Amboseli National Park and the Maasai Mara National Reserve in 1989, with the main beneficiaries being landowners and local authorities in wildlife dispersal areas outside parks or reserves. However, the revenue sharing programmes in Kenya have sometimes generated unrealistic expectations without clear revenue sharing guidelines, as it has not been specified who is to be compensated, how much is to be paid and when (Berger, 1996; Shackley, 1996). Another problem is that money ceded to local authorities does not necessarily help the local people who are affected (Sindiga, 1995). These issues are important for equity and also for conservation, as local communities are much more likely to continue to support park and reserve objectives if they are seen to assist in people's development. Without economic incentive, local communities may not take responsibility for land management and might choose land uses that are incompatible with conservation (Berger, 1996).

Respect for cultural differences

Much thinking about resource management instruments is based on dominant cultural approaches in western society, emphasizing competition rather than co-operation as well as the supremacy of individualism rather than communitarianism and of 'scientific' knowledge rather than traditional, local-level or 'indigenous' knowledge. Yet local or 'indigenous' cultural traditions may provide valuable solutions to problems of resource misuse in an area, particularly as these can involve cultural and institutional constraints on self-interested behaviour which damages the collective interest. No doubt many practical applications of sustainable tourism ideas in both developing and industrialized countries have emphasized 'scientific' approaches. However, even if is recognized that other cultural approaches and traditions should be respected more fully, this still leaves complex and difficult questions unanswered. When resources are threatened, should their management be based on promoting 'indigenous' approaches and reviving traditional local-level institutions, or should 'indigenous' approaches be integrated with 'scientific' resource management systems and policy instruments? Increasing numbers of commentators now argue that there is often potential for useful interplay between both 'scientific' and 'indigenous' resource management systems (Berkes, 1989; Bromley, 1992). Such ideas are also now being discussed in the tourism literature (Hughes, 1995; Berger, 1996). Nevertheless, it must be remembered that local communities may not always decide to develop their resources in a sustainable manner, and this is not only because of the proven capacity of others to use them to exploit their own resources (Adams, 1990).

Freedoms and fairness

The use of public policy instruments for sustainable tourism will affect the property rights or the decision rights of individuals or groups in society, whether actual or perceived. These consequences for property rights or decision rights might be considered to infringe the freedoms of individuals or groups and therefore be seen as unfair. Property rights in the sense used here are not bestowed automatically with ownership of property, and, as with decision rights, they are allocated by society. Some-times these are formally enshrined in law and sometimes they are infor-mally constituted through public opinion. These popularly constituted and accepted rights evolve and change over time as societal values and circumstances change. Policy instruments will differ in their consequences for property and decision rights and in the perceived fairness of these consequences for different individuals and groups. These effects need to be an important consideration when selecting policy instruments. Clearly, such decisions about rights, freedoms and fairness are affected by ethics, values, ideology and politics (Harvey, 1992).

Decision rights are altered by a public authority introducing charging for access to a tourist area in order to raise revenue for local conservation work. Tourists may consider public access to countryside or heritage areas to be intrinsically a 'good thing' for society and individuals, and to be a decision right that should be available without charge and with very few other restrictions. In Britain, for example, there is a strong tradition that countryside access should be free and unimpeded (Ramblers Asso-ciation, 1994). Tourists may also consider they have already paid the government for this work through their taxes. Consequently, new charges for access to a rural or heritage area may be perceived as a harmful and unfair loss of the decision rights of tourists and also nearby residents. Is it likely that such objections to access charges for conservation will be overcome by schemes for tourists to make voluntary contributions for this work? In the English Peak District a scheme has been introduced for voluntary contributions to fund conservation work which is linked to the purchase of various tourist services (Bramwell and Fearn, 1996). Such a scheme gives tourists the opportunity to take greater direct responsibility for the adverse effects of their visit, but it is possible that some tourists will feel under moral pressure to contribute, thereby reducing their per-ceived decision rights.

Political acceptability

Policy instruments may be proposed by government authorities as appropriate for the circumstances only to be defeated by politicians on the grounds of political acceptability. Politicians may also be reluctant to implement officially adopted public policies if they are unpopular or may affect their political survival. For instance, Ioannides (1995) decribes how the president of the Republic of Cyprus sought to stall his waning popularity by amending certain strict zoning regulations in environmen-tally sensitive parts of the island in order to appease local landowners. A policy tool for sustainable tourism has more chance of being implemented if it is acceptable to those interest groups and individuals likely to be directly affected and also to the general public. Questions about liberty and fairness are obviously important for political acceptability, as are more pragmatic considerations of how easy it will be to implement the instrument.

Certain practical considerations may increase the political acceptability of an instrument. For example, its acceptability may increase if it has been developed in consultation with those likely to be affected by it and also with those who will be responsible for implementing it. In the case of the scheme in the English Peak District to enable visitors to make voluntary contributions to fund conservation work, this was only introduced after a survey had been conducted of likely responses to the scheme among visitors (Bramwell and Fearn, 1996). Instruments may also need to be introduced with a pilot stage in order to demonstrate their suitability. The Tir Cymen scheme of payments in Wales to farmers for countryside conservation and management and for public access provision was piloted in three areas in order to test it in practice, and this also meant that initial costs were more predictable and limited (Broom et al., 1995). Acceptability may also increase if a new instrument is accompanied by explanation and information about it being communicated clearly to those affected, so that they are more likely to understand and support it and are less likely to be resentful and dissatisfied. Timely announcements and education about a scheme are very important. For instance, Jim (1989) argues that the introduction of a scheme to ration access to natural areas involving advance reservation by permit must have sufficient advance notice and good publicity, otherwise ignorant visitors will arrive at the destination in full expectation, only to be refused entry when totally unprepared for the disappointment and with no alternative plan.

Balance and compatibility between policy instruments

In general, public policy instruments for sustainable tourism will be used in combination. Indeed, the types and mix of instruments should be carefully matched to the particular policy objectives intended to address specific problems or issues. Policy makers need to identify optimal combinations of instruments which will reinforce each other in particular circumstances in order to achieve the policy objectives. For instance, a tax on pollution by tourism facilities may well need to be supported by information and educational provision for tourism operators on operational practices and new technologies to reduce pollution.

When selecting an appropriate balance between policy instruments it is essential to consider the overall balance between the four types of instruments: government encouragement of decisions made voluntarily to change behaviour, government financial incentives, government expenditure on actions taken directly by public authorities, and government regulations. Decisions on this balance will be influenced by attitudes to the extent to which government needs to require tourists, tourism businesses and host communities to change their behaviour as distinct from encouraging these groups to volunteer to do this of their own volition. These decisions will also reflect attitudes to the extent to which governments should intervene in the operation of the market in a market-based economy. On these central questions, views will be affected by ethical considerations, social values, ideology and politics, as well as by practical experience.

While the market is not necessarily incompatible with sustainable tourism, it will not produce this automatically without some assistance. There are a number of reasons for this. For instance, the market is not very effective at protecting resources that cannot easily be bought and sold, such as clean air, natural habitats, public spaces, landscapes and views, despite these being essential resources for sustainability. The market is also generally poor at distinguishing and giving priority to more sustainable over less sustainable ways of achieving particular outcomes. It tends to create problems of resource depletion, income inequality and limited concern for the collective rights of the community. Despite these major shortcomings, the market has many advantages. In particular, it can be effective at encouraging economic development, responding quickly to changing market conditions, providing incentives and at encouraging innovation. Excessive or insensitive government intervention in the operation of the market in pursuit of sustainable tourism policies could hold back economic development, stifle initiative and innovation, impose too much bureaucracy, and be seen as heavy handed and authoritarian.

A balanced mix of government instruments for sustainable tourism will always include an important role for information, education and persuasion in changing behaviour. Butler (1991, 207) argues that educating all concerned with tourism – the industry, the public sector, local populations and the tourists – 'is still the best key' for developing more sustainable tourism, and that 'in the long term it is probably the only solution which is likely to be broadly successful'. Education and persuasion potentially can encourage all these interests to take responsibility, to make choices and to be proactive in initiating change, and it can avoid more costly, authoritarian and disruptive government interventions. Information provision can demonstrate that all parties can gain advantages from development on a sustainable basis. For example, it can help tourism businesses to see the potential commercial advantages of sustainable approaches, including opportunities for reducing raw material and waste disposal costs, developing new services and products, improving the working environment for staff, and for enhancing their appeal to more environmentally aware consumers (Goodall, 1995). It is also important not to underestimate the contribution of public education and persuasion to the overall climate of public virtue and civic responsibility, particularly in the long term. A strong climate of this sort makes it possible to institute new policies and makes it easier to administer and enforce them.

Despite the advantages of government education and persuasion, it is perhaps true that on their own they are insufficient to produce very substantial change, and they need to be combined with policy instruments based on more direct government intervention. This is due to the many constraints on self-regulation. For example, tourism businesses usually respond to market competition by focusing on the short-term requirement of producing a healthy annual balance sheet, and this tends to restrict the introduction of sustainable practices (Forsyth, 1996; Josephides, 1994). The so-called 'green consumers' may also have little influence over the traditional package holiday as it is very difficult for them to determine whether a holiday is a relatively sustainable product, and they are not encouraged to have a deep commitment to a destination area as they are there only for a short period (Hunter and Green, 1995).

Conclusions

This analysis has sought to identify issues to be assessed when selecting particular sustainable tourism policy instruments. Preferences for policy instruments were shown to be influenced by a range of moral, political and economic evaluations. An understanding of the issues identified in this discussion is helpful for assessments of the comparative merits of different policy instruments in different contexts. It is important that policy makers also consider the complete range of instruments and also the appropriate overall mix of instruments.

Policy makers would be helped if the tourism literature included more comparative evaluations of the strengths and weaknesses of different policy instruments in particular circumstances. Such comparative work is perhaps discouraged by disciplinary boundaries, with, for example, particular interest among geographers in instruments using spatial boundaries, such as zoning and national park designation, and among economists in instruments that alter prices most directly, such as taxes, subsidies and entrance fees. Despite this, growing numbers of economists have begun to compare instruments for environmental protection. However, many policy makers are unfamiliar with this literature which draws on environmental economics. One reason for this low familiarity is that the literature often requires prior understanding of neo-classical economic theory and techniques. While the abstract economic arguments in some of these studies can be useful, it may be even more helpful to policy makers to undertake empirical analysis of how different instruments have actually worked in practice. Different emphases between some economists and policy makers may help explain why, 'while economists often see charges as a way of regulating demands for tourism resources . . . practical policy makers often see rules and regulations governing re- source use as more appropriate' (Forsyth et al., 1995: 272).

Some policy makers and academics are also uneasy that much litera- ture on environmental economics depends on assumptions about social behaviour from neo-classical economics with which they disagree. As Redclift (1993: 109) argues: 'Economic frameworks and methods are founded upon an a priori commitment to a particular model of human nature and social behaviour'. In the neo-classical model social behaviour is seen as essentially instrumental and intended to achieve the maximum utility for each individual. This means that the tastes and preferences of individuals are considered a 'given', and the underlying social commit- ments which determine how we use the environment are unexamined. The assumptions in neo-classical economics mean aspects of human be- haviour are not questioned, and this may encourage a gap between poli- cies and their implementation as people fail to respond as expected. Unease about neo-classical economic theory also arises from how envi- ronmental concerns are incorporated into its analysis. This is achieved by environmental resources being given monetary values either by theoreti- cal analysis or by opening new markets for environmental resources so that they are priced and the prices affect how businesses and consumers behave towards them. Critics contend this ignores the ethical basis of environmental policies and that consumers' concerns and preferences are not necessarily reflected in their behaviour. Furthermore, placing mon- etary values on environmental resources to ensure their survival is a dangerous game since if such an economic argument fails then there is no justification for saving these resources.

The task for policy makers in selecting policy instruments may also be confused by political and ideological biases favouring certain kinds of instruments over others. Government preferences for direct public regu- lation or self-regulation in tourism may be guided more by politics and ideology than concern to have a balanced approach. The British govern- ment's commitment to market-based policies during the 1980s and early 1990s led to a strong preference for financial instruments directly affect- ing market prices, such as taxes, subsidies and charging. This was re- flected in an increasing emphasis on financial incentives to farmers for countryside conservation and recreational access (Bishop and Phillips, 1993). However, a strong commitment to one group of instruments can prejudice assessments of the effectiveness of particular policy tools in achieving greater sustainability in specific circumstances (McLaren, 1996). This chapter is intended to facilitate such assessments of the strengths and weaknesses of specific instruments in different situations, and to show why ethics, social values, economics, ideology and politics will affect these assessments.

References

Adams, W.M. (1990) *Green Development. Environment and Sustainability in the Third World*, Routledge, London

Berkes, F. (ed.) (1989) *Common Property Resources. Ecology and Community-Based Sustainable Development*, Belhaven, London

Bishop, K.D. and Phillips, A.A.C. (1993) Seven steps to market – the development of the market-led approach to countryside conservation and recreation, *Journal of Rural Studies*, **9**(4), 315–338.

Berger, D.J. (1996) The challenge of integrating Maasai tradition with tourism. In *People and Tourism in Fragile Environments* (ed. M.F. Price), Wiley, Chichester, pp. 175–197

Bramwell, B. and Lane, B. (1993) Sustainable tourism: an evolving global approach, *Journal of Sustainable Tourism*, **1**(1), 1–5

Bramwell, B. and Fearn, A. (1996) Visitor attitudes to a policy instrument for visitor funding of conservation in a tourist area, *Journal of Travel Research*, **35**(2), 29–33

Bromley, D.W. (ed.) (1992) *Making the Commons Work. Theory, Practice and Policy*, Institute for Contemporary Studies, San Francisco

Broom, G.F., Bramwell, B. and Beard, C. (1995) *Paying and Charging for Access to the Welsh Countryside*, Countryside Council for Wales, Bangor, Wales

Butler, R.W. (1991) Tourism, environment, and sustainable development, *Environmental Conservation*, **18**(3), 201–209

Cater, E. (1995) Environmental contradictions in sustainable tourism, *Geographical Journal*, **161**(1), 21–28

Cronin, L. (1990) A strategy for tourism and sustainable developments, *World Leisure and Recreation*, **32**(3), 12–18

Eber, S. (ed.) (1992) *Beyond the Green Horizon. Principles for Sustainable Tourism*, World Wide Fund for Nature, Godalming, UK

Forsyth, T. (1996) *Sustainable Tourism. Moving from Theory to Practice*, World Wide Fund for Nature, Godalming, UK

Forsyth, P., Dwyer, L. and Clarke, H. (1995) Problems in use of economic instruments to reduce adverse environmental impacts of tourism, *Tourism Economics*, **1**(3), 265–282

Gale, F. and Jacobs, J.M. (1987) *Tourists and the National Estate. Procedures to Protect Australia's Heritage*, Australian Government Publishing Service, Canberra

Genot, H. (1995) Voluntary environmental codes of conduct in the tourism sector, *Journal of Sustainable Tourism*, **3**(3), 166–172

Goodall, B. (1995) Environmental auditing: a tool for assessing the environmental performance of tourism firms, *Geographical Journal*, **161**(1), 29–37

Harris, R. and Leiper, N. (1995) Commonwealth Department of Tourism: the National Ecotourism Strategy. In *Sustainable Tourism. An Australian Perspective* (eds. R. Harris and N. Leiper), Butterworth-Heinemann, Chatswood, Australia, pp. 58–62

Harvey, D. (1992) Social justice, postmodernism and the city, *International Journal of Urban and Regional Research*, **16**, 588–601

Hay, A.M. (1995) Concepts of equity, fairness and justice in geographical studies, *Transactions of the Institute of British Geographers*, NS 20, 500–508

Hughes, G. (1995) The cultural construction of sustainable tourism, *Tourism Management*, **16**(1), 49–59

Hunter, C. and Green, H. (1995) *Tourism and the Environment. A Sustainable Relationship*? Routledge, London

Inskeep, E. (1991) *Tourism Planning. An Integrated and Sustainable Development Approach*, Van Nostrand Reinhold, New York

Ioannides, D. (1995) A flawed implementation of sustainable tourism: the experience of Akamas, Cyprus, *Tourism Management*, **16**(8), 583–592

Jacobs, M. (1991) *The Green Economy. Environment, Sustainable Development and the Politics of the Future*, Pluto Press, London

Jim, C.Y. (1989) Visitor management in recreation areas, *Environmental Conservation*, **16**(1), 19–32

Joppe, M. (1996) Sustainable community tourism development revisited, *Tourism Management*, **17**(7), 475–479

Josephides, N. (1994) Tour operators and the myth of self-regulation, *Tourism in Focus*, Winter 1994, Tourism Concern, London

Kasperson, R.E. and Dow, K.M. (1991) Developmental and geographical equity in global environmental change: a framework for analysis, *Evaluation Review*, **15**(1), 149–171

Laarman, J.G. and Gregersen, H.M. (1996) Pricing policy in nature-based tourism, *Tourism Management*, **17**(4), 247–254

Local Government Management Board (LGMB) (1993) *A Framework for Local Sustainability*, Local Government Management Board, Luton, UK

Mak, J. and Moncur, J.E.T. (1995) Sustainable tourism development: managing Hawaii's 'unique' touristic resource – Hanauma Bay, *Journal of Travel Research*, **33**(4), 51–57

McLaren, D. (1996) The constraints on sustainability planning in the UK. In *Environmental Planning and Sustainability* (eds. S. Buckingham-Hatfield and B. Evans), Wiley, Chichester, pp. 145–175

Nijkamp, P. and Verdonkschot, P. (1995) Sustainable tourism development: A case study of Lesbos. In *Sustainable Tourism Development* (eds. H. Coccossis and P. Nijkamp), Avebury, Aldershot, pp. 127–140

Pigram, J.J. (1990) Sustainable tourism – policy considerations, *Journal of Tourism Studies*, **1**(2), 2–9

Ramblers Association (1994) *Access Payment Schemes: A Response to a Discussion Paper by the Countryside Commission*, Ramblers Association, London

Redclift, M. (1993) Environmental economics, policy consensus and political empowerment. In *Sustainable Environmental Economics and Management. Principles and Practice* (ed. R.K. Turner), Wiley, Chichester, pp. 106–119

Shackley, M. (1996) *Wildlife Tourism*, ITBP, London

Sindiga, I. (1995) Wildlife-based tourism in Kenya: land use conflicts and government compensation policies over protected areas, *Journal of Tourism Studies*, **6**(2), 45–55

Steele, P. (1995) Ecotourism: an economic analysis, *Journal of Sustainable Tourism*, **3**(1), 29–44

Tisdell, C. (1995) Investment in ecotourism: assessing its economics, *Tourism Economics*, **1**(4), 375–387

Turner, A. (1995) Tourism Council Australia. In *Sustainable Tourism. An Australian Perspective* (eds. R. Harris and N. Leiper), Butterworth-Heinemann, Chatswood, Australia, pp. 76–86

United Nations Environment Programme (UNEP) (1995) *Environmental Codes of Conduct for Tourism*, Technical Report 29, United Nations Environment Programme, Industry and Environment, Paris

World Tourism Organization and United Nations Environment Programme (WTO/UNEP) (1992) *Guidelines: Development of National Parks and Protected Areas for Tourism*, World Tourism Organization, Madrid

22 Opening of the former communist countries of Europe to inbound tourism

Stephen F. Witt

Introduction

The political changes which resulted in the death of communism in Europe had their origins in the establishment of the independent workers' union 'Solidarity' in Poland in 1980. This was followed by the adoption of the policies of 'perestroika' (restructuring) and 'glasnost' (openness) by the Soviet Union in the second half of the 1980s. As a result there was a demand for radical political change, and over the period 1989–91 the communist system collapsed in European countries.

The political and economic upheavals which have occurred in the former communist countries of Europe since 1989 have opened up this area for international tourism. Prior to these events, a mass of restrictions made travel to these countries a bureaucratic obstacle course, thus restraining demand. Similarly, the travel and currency restrictions placed on residents of the former communist countries resulted in very low levels of outbound tourism to the West. Often the main purpose of the restrictions was to minimize contact between people from these countries and the West in order to prevent ideological 'contamination'. Since 1989, however, there has been a considerable relaxation of restrictions and hence substantial changes in these previously established patterns of travel to and from the former communist countries.

In this chapter attention focuses primarily on inbound tourism to what were previously the Soviet bloc countries of Europe – Bulgaria, the former Czechoslovakia (now the Czech Republic and Slovak Republic), the former German Democratic Republic (GDR) (now part of Germany), Hungary, Poland, Romania and the former Soviet Union (now various separate countries). The union of East and West Germany in 1990 means that in terms of administrative formalities, visiting the eastern part of Germany is now no different from visiting other Western countries, and the 'Westernization' of the former GDR is proceeding rapidly. Furthermore, separate data on inbound international tourism to the former GDR have not been available since 1990. The former GDR is therefore not featured in subsequent discussions.

The former Soviet bloc countries should not be thought of as a monolithic bloc; they are at different levels of development, possess different cultures and display widely varying attitudes towards international tourism. For example, the Czech Republic, Hungary and Poland are the most Westernized countries in the group, and also the ones which attract the highest levels of international tourism receipts. On the other hand, the disintegration of the former Soviet Union has resulted in political instability, which is not conducive to the development of international tourism.

There has been a general increase in interest from the West in travelling to the various former Soviet bloc countries. The mass of restrictions facing most Western tourists wanting to travel to these countries, such as minimum daily exchange requirements, unrealistic official tourist exchange rates and complex visa formalities, has been substantially reduced. For some destinations this has resulted in spectacular growth in inbound tourism.

The next section examines the former Soviet bloc countries as tourist destinations, and traces their development over the period of political changes. This is followed by a brief discussion of tourism trends in the former communist countries of Europe which were outside the Soviet bloc. In the subsequent section, the opportunities for and constraints on tourism development in the former European communist countries are considered. Finally, conclusions are drawn.

Former Soviet bloc countries as tourist destinations

The tables which follow show inbound tourism to the former Soviet bloc countries, together with four Western comparator countries, over the period 1988–94. It was decided to restrict attention to those former Soviet bloc countries where international tourism receipts amounted to at least US $250 million in 1994. Hence, the only country in the former Soviet Union to be featured is the Russian Federation (but see Mazaraki and Voronova 1993, 1994; Jaakson 1996; and Unwin 1996 for discussion of tourism development in other countries of the former Soviet Union).

'Sun and sea' destinations – Bulgaria and Romania – are compared with Greece and Spain, while 'lakes/mountains/historical buildings' destinations – the Czech Republic, Hungary, Poland, the Russian Federation and the Slovak Republic – are compared with Austria and Switzerland. Bulgaria and Romania are both situated in Eastern Europe and border the Black Sea. The Czech Republic, Hungary, Poland and the Slovak Republic are all located in Central Europe and offer mainly picturesque scenery, history and culture. The Russian Federation is a massive area situated partly in Eastern Europe and partly in Asia, but most international tourists come for the history and culture of the cities, particularly Moscow and St. Petersburg.

Visitor/tourist arrivals

Table 22.1 shows visitor/tourist arrivals for six of the seven former Soviet bloc countries under consideration. It should be borne in mind that arrivals data definitions vary considerably among countries, as the notes to the table show, and hence caution should be exercised in interpretation. Data on visitor/tourist arrivals are not available for the Czech Republic.

It can be seen from Table 22.1(a) that tourism in Bulgaria grew over the period 1988–94 by 22 per cent. However, there was a marked decline in 1991 and 1992, mainly as a result of a large drop in arrivals from other former communist countries. The subsequent rise was accounted for largely by increased numbers of arrivals from Romania and the former Soviet Union. Tourism in Romania increased slightly over the period (7 per cent). It is clear that the two 'sun and sea' former Soviet bloc countries have not benefited in terms of increased tourist arrivals from the West. The homogeneity of the 'sun and sea' product means that these two destinations are competing directly with similar Mediterranean destinations on the basis of price only. The low price appeals to residents of some of the former communist countries who are willing to accept the accompanying low quality, but not to Westerners. (For discussion of the problems of Bulgarian tourism development see Harrison, 1993). The growth rate achieved by Bulgaria is below that of Greece (35 per cent) but above that of Spain (13 per cent). Romania fared badly in relation to both comparators.

The growth of the popularity of 'lakes/mountains/historical buildings' destinations in the former Soviet bloc is depicted in Table 22.1(b). The following increases in arrivals were recorded between 1988 and 1994: Hungary 102 per cent; Poland 1098 per cent; the Russian Federation 53 per cent (1992–94); and the Slovak Republic 50 per cent (1992–94). The unique appeal of each of the 'lakes/mountains/historical buildings' destinations has resulted increasingly in the ability to attract large numbers of tourists from the West, particularly in the cases of Hungary and Poland. The growth figures for the former Soviet bloc countries compare well with the corresponding Western countries: Austria 8 per cent; and Switzerland 6 per cent (1988–93).

Table 22.1 Arrivals of visitors/tourists from abroad (millions)

Countries	1988	1989	1990	1991	1992	1993	1994
(a) Sun and sea destinations							
Bulgaria (V)	8.3	8.2	10.3	6.8	6.1	8.3	10.1
Romania (V)	5.5	4.9	6.5	5.4	6.3	5.8	5.9
Greece (T)	7.9	8.1	8.9	8.0	9.3	9.4	10.7
Spain (V)	54.2	54.0	52.0	53.5	55.3	57.3	61.4
(b) Lakes/mountains/historical buildings destinations							
Hungary[1] (T)	10.6	14.5	20.5	21.9	20.2	22.8	21.4
Poland (V)	6.2	8.2	18.2	36.8	49.0	61.0	74.3
Russian Federation (V)	–	–	–	–	3.0	5.9	4.6
Slovak Republic	–	–	–	–	0.6	0.7	0.9
Austria (A)	16.6	18.2	19.0	19.1	19.1	18.3	17.9
Switzerland (A)	9.3	10.1	10.5	10.1	10.3	9.9	–

V, visitor arrivals at frontiers; T, tourist arrivals at frontiers; A, arrivals in registered tourist accommodation.
[1] excludes nationals residing abroad.
– not available.
Source: World Tourism Organization (1992 and 1996a)

International tourism receipts

International tourism receipts for the various countries under consideration are exhibited in Table 22.2. As the receipts are denoted in US dollars,
they may increase or decrease partly as a result of a change in the strength
of the dollar compared with other currencies. Nevertheless, movements
in tourism receipts in the former Soviet bloc countries *relative* to those in
the comparator countries are indicative of strengthening or worsening
positions compared with the West.

Table 22.2(a) indicates that the 'sun and sea' destinations of the former
Soviet bloc performed in a highly variable fashion during the period
1988 to 1994. Overall, international tourism receipts in Bulgaria decreased
by 26 per cent, whereas those in Romania increased by 142 per cent;
in comparison Greece and Spain recorded increases of 63 per cent and
31 per cent, respectively.

International tourism receipts grew fairly steadily over the period 1988
to 1994 in the 'lakes/mountains/historical buildings' destinations of the
former Soviet bloc, with the notable exception of the Czech Republic in
1991. Table 22.2(b) shows that international tourism receipts increased by
369 per cent in the Czech Republic (1990–94), 88 per cent in Hungary,
2885 per cent in Poland, 54 per cent in the Russian Federation (1992–94)

Table 22.2   International tourism receipts (US$ millions)

Countries	1988	1989	1990	1991	1992	1993	1994
(a) Sun and sea destinations							
Bulgaria	484	495	320	44	215	307	358
Romania	171	167	106	145	262	197	414
Greece	2396	1976	2587	2567	3272	3335	3905
Spain	16,686	16,174	18,593	19,004	22,181	19,425	21,853
(b) Lakes/mountains/historical buildings destinations							
Czech Repulic	–	–	419	74	1126	1558	1966
Hungary	758	798	824	1002	1231	1181	1428
Poland	206	202	358	2800	4108	4500	6150
Russian Federation	–	–	–	–	752	1474	1161
Slovak Republic	–	–	70	135	213	390	568
Austria	10,090	10,717	13,410	13,800	14,526	13,566	13,160
Switzerland	5720	5543	6789	7026	7463	7011	7570

– not available.
Source: World Tourism Organization (1992 and 1996a)

and 711 per cent in the Slovak Republic (1990–94). By comparison, Austria and Switzerland recorded increases of 30 per cent and 32 per cent, respectively. Each of the former Soviet bloc 'lakes/mountains/historical buildings' destinations has therefore outperformed the two Western comparators in terms of growth rates of tourism receipts. In addition, Poland was ranked fourteenth among the world's top tourism earners in 1994, ahead of countries such as Australia and Thailand.

Table 22.2 gives a very clear indication of the sheer difference in scale of international tourism receipts in the former Soviet bloc countries and the West. Even in 1994, total tourism receipts for the seven former Soviet bloc countries amounted to US$12 billion, whereas tourism receipts for Spain alone were US$21.9 billion. On the other hand, international tourism receipts for Poland were nearly 60 per cent higher than those for Greece, and the consistent high annual growth that has been achieved by Poland, the Czech Republic and the Slovak Republic since 1992 is quite spectacular. (Prospects for further development of Czech and Slovak tourism are discussed by Johnson, 1995.)

It should be borne in mind that international tourism generates balance of payments effects that are far more complex than those of the initial tourism receipts (the *primary* effect). In particular, the extent to which tourism expenditures in a destination country generate import demand in that country can have a major impact on the foreign exchange

Table 22.3 International tourism receipts as percentage of exports

Countries	1990	1994
(a) Sun and sea destinations		
Bulgaria	2.4	8.6[1]
Romania	1.8	6.9
Greece	31.9	38.0[1]
Spain	33.4	29.8
(b) Lakes/mountains/historical buildings destinations		
Czech Republic	12.9[2]	13.7
Hungary	8.5	13.3
Poland	2.5	35.7
Russian Federation	1.8[2]	1.8
Slovak Republic	4.1[3]	8.6
Austria	32.6	29.3
Switzerland	10.6	11.4

[1] 1993 figure;   [2] 1992 figure;   [3] 1991 figure.
Source: Table 22.2 and World Tourism Organization (1996b)

generating ability of tourism. The *secondary* effects on the balance of payments include imports of supplies by the providers of tourism services (such as hotel operators and restaurant operators), expenditures on marketing abroad, and payments to overseas investors in the form of interest and dividends. For many former Soviet bloc countries, these secondary effects are quite large in the case of Western tourists.

Tourism receipts as percentage of exports

Table 22.3 demonstrates the importance of tourism in terms of international trade for the former Soviet bloc countries. There is considerable variation in the ratio of tourism receipts to exports, ranging from 1.8 per cent for the Russian Federation to 35.7 per cent for Poland in 1994. The latter country is exceptional, however, with the second highest ratio recorded being 13.7 per cent.

Viewed alongside the Western comparators, the former communist 'sun and sea' destinations again performed badly, the ratio of international tourism receipts to exports being 7–9 per cent for the former Soviet bloc countries and 30–38 per cent for the Western comparators in 1994. By contrast, the 'lakes/mountains/historical buildings' destinations generally performed well; the ratio of international tourism receipts to exports for Poland exceeded that of even Austria, and for the Czech Republic and Hungary exceeded that of Switzerland. The value for the

Slovak Republic was slightly less than that for Switzerland. Only in the case of the Russian Federation was the ratio exceptionally low; however, this is not surprising given that it is a highly industrialized country with considerable mining and manufacturing exports.

For each of the former Soviet bloc countries, the importance of international tourism receipts in exports increased over the period 1990 to 1994. In the case of Poland the percentage rose very sharply – from 2.5 per cent to 35.7 per cent.

Former non-Soviet bloc European communist countries as tourist destinations

The former European communist countries which were outside the Soviet sphere of influence were Albania and the former Yugoslavia, both located in Eastern Europe. Albania was the most isolated country in Europe; here, more than in any other former European communist country, the previous communist regime wished to prevent ideological 'contamination' by outsiders. As a result, foreign tourism was virtually non-existent; the limited number of visitors who came were only allowed to travel in groups to specific destinations. Now that has changed, and a Ministry of Tourism has been set up to encourage inbound tourism. Particular attractions are the coastline, mountain scenery and historical sites. However, international tourism receipts still only totalled US$5 million in 1994.

The tensions and warfare which surrounded the break-up of the former Yugoslavia had a disastrous effect on tourism. All areas suffered massive reductions in international tourism in 1991. Since then Croatia and Slovenia, the major tourist destinations in the former Yugoslavia, have both made a steady and strong recovery, with international tourism receipts reaching US$1427 million in 1994 for Croatia (compared with US$1704 million in 1990 and US$300 million in 1991); and US$932 million in 1994 for Slovenia (compared with US$721 million in 1990 and US$275 million in 1991). Croatia offers mainly 'sun and sea' tourism, whereas Slovenia, although also possessing a (short) coastline, is more of a 'lakes/mountains/historical buildings' destination.

Development of tourism in the former communist countries of Europe: opportunities and constraints

The former European communist countries have many attractions, including natural resources (such as unspoiled countryside, forests, lakes,

mountains and beaches), beautiful cities (Prague, Budapest, etc.), historical sites and cultural resources (museums, art galleries, etc.). Western
tourists are also likely to be attracted by the relatively low prices in many
of these countries, their appeal as being somewhere different and exciting which was hitherto rather inaccessible, and the fact that much of
the area is generally far less crowded than the West. The proximity to
many major Western tourist generating countries makes travel quite
straightforward.

The large migrant communities in the West, most notably in the USA,
are an important potential source of tourists to the former communist
countries in Europe. As well as visits to relatives, migrants and their
descendants may wish to explore their family roots; many have retained
linguistic, cultural and historical links.

There are various problems which are likely to constrain the growth of
tourism. In several of the former communist countries political unrest
is still evident and/or travel restrictions are still in force. More generally,
in many cases the infrastructure is completely inadequate by Western
standards and the quality of provisions for tourists tends to be poor.
Furthermore, there is a lack of education and training for staff working
in tourism. Poor marketing is another major constraint. Environmental
pollution is also a considerable problem in some areas (Lukashina et al.,
1996).

Hundreds of new hotels are needed in order to bring the tourism
industry up to Western standards. As the political climate in the former
communist countries has changed, they have become much more recep-
tive to joint foreign-capital ventures, and this is seen as a major avenue
for increasing and upgrading hotel provision. Although the process had
already started prior to the events of 1989, it has accelerated considerably
since then. The opportunities afforded in the former European communist countries by the creation of joint ventures in tourism are discussed in
Buckley and Witt (1990) and Franck (1990). More generally, Buckley and
Ghauri (1994) examine the workings of international business in this
region.

Tourism education

Improved education for those working in the tourism industry is essential if the former European communist countries are to compete successfully with the West. *Management* education, which until 1989 was largely
absent, is likely to play a key role in this process. Furthermore, to the
extent that certain management subjects, such as *economics*, were taught
under the previous communist regimes, these courses have had to be
changed to concentrate on market economics. Also, it has been necessary

to alter *foreign language* education in response to expecting a substantial influx of Western tourists.

The implications of the political events of 1989 for tourism education are enormous – from the tour guide who now does not have to adhere to the Party line on information provision (a propaganda exercise) to the manager of a tourism enterprise who now needs to know how to function in a market economy; and from a lack of knowledge on the part of the tourism industry as to how to deal with foreign partners (travel agents, tour operators, etc.) to a lack of management teaching staff.

The general practice of teaching Russian as the first foreign language in the former Soviet 'satellite' countries has changed as closer economic ties with the West have been developed. The replacement of Russian by English/German/French as the first foreign language is likely to benefit tourism from the West to these former 'satellite' countries, as the removal of language barriers decreases resistance by Westerners considering travelling to this area.

Golembski (1991) discusses the needs of tourism education in the former Soviet bloc countries, with special reference to Poland. (For further discussion of tourism education in Poland see Airey, 1994.) He stresses the necessity for profound changes in the systems of education resulting from the political and economic changes, and identifies the major problem in tourism education as being that of lack of knowledge and experience of the teaching staff with regard to market economics, marketing, Western languages, etc. Golembski suggests that cooperation in the following areas with Western higher education institutions involved in tourism is the best approach to instigating the required changes quickly and effectively:

- The West should be asked to provide access to modern teaching materials and advice with regard to the appropriate contents of courses.
- Experienced staff from Western higher education institutions should do some teaching on the new courses set up in the former Soviet bloc countries, particularly during the initial phases.
- Staff (particularly younger members) from universities, polytechnics, etc. in the former Soviet bloc countries should be sent to corresponding institutions in the West in order to receive appropriate training which would enable them to carry out their new duties more effectively.

Conclusion

The attractiveness of several of the former European communist countries to Western tourists has increased markedly as a result of the major political changes which have taken place since 1989. This is reflected clearly in the time series on international tourism for the Czech Republic, Hungary, Poland and the Slovak Republic.

Many of the former European communist countries are still largely unexplored by Westerners, and as such represent somewhere new and exciting. There are, however, in many cases major constraints on the growth of tourism, such as inadequate infrastructure, insufficient supply of good quality accommodation and the often poor quality of tourist products/services. Better education and training, the injection of West-ern capital and expertise through joint ventures, and improved market-ing of the undoubted attractions will go far in overcoming the problems faced by the former communist countries as tourist destinations.

To end on a cautionary note, however, it must be recognized that tourism will only flourish in an atmosphere of stability and safety. The political and economic instability (in some cases leading to war) which have resulted from both the disintegration of the former Soviet Union and the former Yugoslavia, together with the breakdown of law and order which is occurring in many of the former communist countries, could be disastrous for the future of tourism in these destinations. Above all, tourists value their personal safety, and the ability to travel around within a destination without threat to this safety is paramount.

References

Airey, D. (1994) *Education for Tourism in Poland: The PHARE Programme*, Tourism Management **15**(6), 467–471

Buckley, P.J. and Ghauri, P.N. (1994) *The Economics of Change in Eastern and Central Europe: Its Impact on International Business*, Academic Press, London

Buckley, P.J. and Witt, S.F. (1990) Tourism in the Centrally-Planned Economies of Europe, *Annals of Tourism Research*, **17**(1), 7–18

Franck, C. (1990) Tourism Investment in Central and Eastern Europe: Precondi-tions and Opportunities, *Tourism Management*, **11**(4), 333–338

Golembski, G. (1991) The Needs of a Higher Level Education in Tourism in Post-Communist Countries of Middle-Eastern Europe (as illustrated by Poland), *Tourist Review*, **46**(1), 3–5

Harrison, D. (1993) Bulgarian Tourism: A State of Uncertainty, *Annals of Tourism Research*, **20**(3), 519–534

Jaakson, R. (1996) Tourism in Transition in Post-Soviet Estonia, *Annals of Tourism Research*, **23**(3), 17–634

Johnson, M. (1995) Czech and Slovak Tourism: Patterns, Problems and Prospects, *Tourism Management*, **16**(1), 21–28

Lukashina, N.S., Amirkhanov, M.M., Anisimov, V.I. and Trunev, A. (1996) Tour-ism and Environmental Degradation in Sochi, Russia, *Annals of Tourism Re-search*, **23**(3), 654–665

Mazaraki, A. and Voronova, E. (1993) Prospects for Tourism in Ukraine, *Tourism Management*, **14**(4), 316–317

Mazaraki, A. and Voronova, E. (1994) Structure of Tourism in Ukraine, *Tourism Management*, **15**(3), 230–231

Unwin, T. (1996) Tourism Development in Estonia: Images, Sustainability, and Integrated Rural Development, *Tourism Management*, **17**(4), 265–276

World Tourism Organization (1992) *Yearbook of Tourism Statistics*, WTO, Madrid

World Tourism Organization (1996a) *Yearbook of Tourism Statistics*, WTO, Madrid

World Tourism Organization (1996b) *Compendium of Tourism Statistics*, WTO, Madrid

23 Exploring the political role of gender in tourism research

Linda K. Richter

Gender and tourism have something in common when it comes to political analysis: neither was taken seriously by political scientists as important subjects of political inquiry until relatively recently. Recognition of variations in political behaviour among men and women became a subject of research only after the Second World War and public policy studies of either tourism or gender issues are less than twenty-five years old in the United States.

Gender studies have developed a rich literature in that time. Tourism, while gradually attracting more attention by social scientists, continues to lack sustained political study. In most cases, researchers stumble onto tourism inadvertently when they are exploring something else. Surprisingly, it was the Christian Church in Asia that perhaps earlier than any other institution recognized the political importance of tourism.

Today, however, in the church and within several other forums, linkages are also being made between *gender* and *tourism*. Church and peace and justice groups are looking at the issue of international tourism's impact on the exploitation of women and children, on labour, education and development issues. In each issue gender differences exist. *Annals of Tourism Research*, a refereed social science journal, devoted a special issue to the relationships between gender and tourism (Swain, 1995). Even in women's studies and international relations texts, new connections are being made between gender and tourism. One of the best such analyses is Cynthia Enloe's *Bananas, Beaches, and Bases* (1989). It explores not only the gender differences in opportunity structure, but the substantial evolution of travel and tourism roles.

What this chapter will do is suggest areas of tourism research in which there are politically important gender issues and speculate about how trends in tourism and political organizations may affect the gender distinctions that have emerged. But first some definitional clarification is appropriate.

There are dozens of ways to define the study of politics, but one both pithy and pertinent is that of American political scientist Harold Lasswell. He said politics is 'who gets what, when and how' (Lasswell, 1936). Knowing if and how tourism differently affects men and women would seem the very essence of studying the politics of gender and tourism.

But if tourism is like almost every other policy issue to which a gender analysis has been applied, the sexes do not begin with a level playing field. Thus, to Lasswell's definition, it would be prudent to add Michael Parenti's addition 'and who already has what' (Parenti, 1977). This writer would add 'and who cares' (Richter, 1991a). The factual discussion of the topic can take us only so far; attention also needs to be given to the *perceptions, intensity* and *salience* of the issue to individuals and groups of varying resources and commitments.

The political relationship of gender to tourism is not static but rapidly evolving. The elite-driven policy sector is increasingly opening up to more claimants for influence – in gender terms that process has meant increased access to and impact on women. That represents a marked departure from the historical gender differences *vis-á-vis* tourism.

Gender differences in tourism: a historical perspective

'Until the sixteenth century to be a woman, travel, and remain respectable one had to be generally either a queen or a pilgrim' (Robinson, 1990). Travel has had a different *contextual* meaning for men than for women until very recent times. Travel meant conquest, wars, crusades, exploration, trading opportunities, hunting, trapping, fishing, commerce. Overwhelmingly, that was the public sphere of men in contrast to the global tendency to assign the private sphere of home and family to women. To the extent women participated, they did so as a vital support system for missionary work, immigration, imperial adventures, diplomatic support, or 'civilizing the frontier'.

By the nineteenth century, travel had come to be seen as a value in its own right. The grand tour of Europe was the capstone to an affluent young man's education. Travel was a scarce resource eagerly sought which enhanced a young man's economic and political prospects even as it broadened his tastes. It augmented a man's prestige but it diminished a woman's reputation.

For women, education generally was seen as having much less utility and was characteristically confined to music and the domestic arts. Travel was irrelevant unless it functioned to support family goals or was justified for religious pilgrimage or health considerations. Unchaperoned travel of single women until the mid-twentieth century compromised marriage prospects and was not seen as a positive reflection on the woman's intellect and sophistication, but as betraying a certain lack of modesty and propriety. In Western societies, women were seen as requiring the protection of men from the dangers posed by other men, particularly, when venturing beyond family and friends.

In general, in Asian and Middle Eastern societies, the assumptions were quite different though the solution similar. Women were considered sufficiently lusty and unreliable that family honour required their early marriage and sustained surveillance. In China, the practice of footbinding assured that affluent women would contribute to their husband's status by their absolute inability to labour, let alone travel except by palanquin! By being economically useless and dependent, they demonstrated their husbands' ability to afford such idleness.

Thomas Cook launched his famous travel-based empire in Europe intent on providing reliable, proper escorted tours for curious women eager to transcend home and hearth – albeit respectably. It would be another hundred years before the travel industry began to cope with the needs of female *business* travellers!

There were always female mavericks who travelled with gusto with and without spouses and entourages. Their exploits are only beginning to be rediscovered. As Mabel Crawford remarked in 1863 'If the exploring of foreign lands is not the highest end or the most useful occupation of feminine existence, it is at least more improving, as well as more amusing than crochet work'. (Morris, 1993: 42). Not all would agree. Most press accounts of the day viewed them with disdain as 'globe trotteresses' and dismissed their considerable insights as irrelevant. It was not until 1892 that the Royal Geographic Society admitted women. In the United States it would be over thirty more years before women were allowed in The Explorers Club. Women by that time had set up their own Society of Women Geographers (Tinling, 1989)! But for most women of means, travel adventures were not on the horizon.

Women's accounts of their travels have differed markedly from men. Women have had greater access to the women and children in other societies than have men, and their accounts, as a consequence, offer more of a sense of family customs. Men, as might be expected, were more apt to comment on political affairs, the impact of European ideas and the state of technology (Tinling, 1989; Blunt, 1994).

Not just travel, but even at home the very notion of leisure time was one enjoyed by men long before women. The weekend, for example, meant far less of a change in activity for women than for men. As Rybczynski notes in *Waiting for the Weekend:* 'The proper place for proper women was the home – public leisure was exclusively a male domain' (Rybczynski, 1991).

Gender differences in employment and ownership

Men and women not only have historically been socialized to view travel from very different perspectives, but there continues to be a division of labour by gender at all levels of the travel and tourism hierarchies (Steiger and Wardell, 1995: 91–123).

Let's consider 'who already has what'. United Nations' statistics tell us that though women do two-thirds of the world's work, they get one-tenth of the world's income and have one-hundredth of the world's property (Johnson, 1983). Comparable statistics focused on the travel and tourism industry do not exist, but inequality appears none the less to be the norm in most sectors.

The tourism sector taken as a whole (and its boundaries are still open to dispute) is small-scale. In the United States, for example, over 95 per cent of tourism-related businesses are quite small. Women dominate travel agency ownership and are a majority of travel agents (Richter, 1991b). They may also play an important role as producers of crafts, art and other services for the tourist trade (Swain, 1993: 32–51). In fact, within the U.S. women make up 52 per cent of the employment in travel and tourism in contrast to 44 per cent of industries in general (Edgell, 1993: 18).

In monetary terms, however, men control the major sectors of the tourism economy. There are few if any women owners of airlines, railroads, major destinations (except Dolly Parton's Dolly World), hotel chains (former inmate Leona Helmsley's empire is an exception), car rental companies and travel magazines. Even female travel writers are scarce – Jan Morris being a notable exception and having established her reputation first as a male.

Nationalists in developing countries bemoan the perils of tourism turning their country into a nation of waiters and bellhops because of largely male dominated foreign control (T. Barry et al., 1984; English, 1986). The real bottom of the hierarchy, however, are the chambermaids, restaurant help and laundresses. They get few tips and have the least dignified positions (Enloe, 1989). Female cooks and waitresses tend to be found in the lowest paid parts of the food sector. While cooking is historically a female task in most societies, it becomes an overwhelmingly male niche in the fancier restaurants where salaries and tips are substantial. That these disparities are not obvious is probably because women in the tourist sector are doing what they traditionally do as unpaid labour in the home (Richter, 1995).

In summary, while women do have *access* and *employment* disproportionately to men in the travel sector, these positions tend to be available – as indeed, they are to minorities – because they are seasonal, part-time or minimum wage. They also are in the least organized sectors of the travel labour market. Thus, the answer to 'who already had what' is that women have the majority of the jobs at the base of the tourism employment hierarchy; men have almost all of the jobs at the middle and top (Enloe, 1993: 115).

Prostitution

'Sex tourism is not natural or endemic, but rather the result of decades of political choices and accidents' (Leheny, 1995: 381).

One employment sector, prostitution, once almost exclusively female has become unenviably open to men and boys. While most countries have prostitution – legal or not – certain destinations have become inextricably linked with sex tourism, such as Thailand (nicknamed 'Thighland' in some circles), the Philippines, Sri Lanka and Brazil (Leheny, 1995; K. Barry et al., 1984; Holden and Horlemann, 1983; Richter, 1989a; Sereewat, 1983; Thanh-Dam, 1983). The numbers are boggling. Estimates of the numbers of women and child prostitutes range from 350,000 to one million in the Philippines alone. Thailand is presumed to have at least that many, thousands of whom are virtual slaves from Burma (Thomas, 1993). Prostitution is not an employment decision for thousands who are coerced, kidnapped, or sold into prostitution. Huge numbers of women, particularly from countries like the Philippines, find themselves involuntarily in what is referred to as the 'entertainment industry' (Caul and Youngblood, 1996; Rosca, 1995; Esplanada, 1996). While most prostitutes are female, a growing gay and paedophilia market exploit men and young boys (ECPAT, 1992), particularly in countries like the Philippines and Sri Lanka (Rogers, 1989; Rosca, 1995). In any case, the *customers* are almost exclusively male. Females buying the 'escort plus' services of black males in the Caribbean are not unknown (Pruitt and Lafont, 1995), but the sex tourism industry revolves around the fantasies of men and is owned and controlled by men. Women work for men, not vice versa, when it comes to the provision of most sexual services.

The disproportionately male tourist traffic in Asia and Africa continues, but those seeking sex at their destination have changed their behaviour somewhat. To protect themselves, men seek out children or young prostitutes from countries until recently without a reputation for AIDS. Thus, the number of children involved in tourism soars and the incidence of AIDS among them does as well.

Explaining sex tourism

Many things combine to link sexual activity with tourism. By its minimum definition, a tourist is someone staying overnight at least 100 miles from home. The anonymity of being away from friends, business associates and relatives offers opportunity for discreet extramarital sexual liaisons without the emotional, long-term commitment of an affair. It combines a sense of kinky adventure with intimacy in a strange location.

Two interesting arguments are advanced by those more sanguine about sex tourism than is this writer. Both place the responsibility not on the men but the morals and attitudes of women. One line of reasoning is that prostitution is the world's oldest profession, and that in many of the travel markets where it is most explicit, concubinage has been its domestic equivalent for centuries.

This argument does not face the very different conditions associated with prostitution in a touristic context. Regularly patronizing a prostitute or supporting a concubine were much less dangerous for the men and women involved than the transient and fleeting associations now taking place. The legalization and institutionalization of prostitution in such places as Australia and Las Vegas, have in fact been a response to the robberies, murders, drug-dealing and health problems associated with unregulated prostitution. It is also a way to tax a lucrative industry and get kickbacks from the licensing of prostitutes.

The second argument places the blame for sex tourism on the women's movement! Instead of women staying in their place, they have demanded equality. Instead of unshackling their inhibitions, they have become more picky about the men with whom they will mate! Imagine, the women's movement did not define itself the way some men wanted. Pro-choice was extended not only to abortion but to coupling! This argument was actually made in a supposedly serious research paper this writer reviewed. It purported to explain why Australian males went on sex trips to Thailand. Supposedly, they needed to do some male bonding and be with some feminine women after contending with increasingly uppity Australian women, corrupted by the women's movement!

Not only is it insulting to suggest such fragile egos in Australian men, but it is a curious argument to suggest that a bid for equality among Australian women *naturally* will result in the exploitation of other women! Nor does it appear to be a sufficient explanation for sex tourism from Japan where the women's movement is almost microscopic, or paedophilia tours from Germany where presumably the children are no more aggressive than anywhere else.

So who cares? Increasingly, groups are organizing against sex tours, the exploitation of children, and the health and safety issues attached to each. One of the most active of these groups is End Child Prostitution in Asian Tourism (ECPAT, 1992) which is moving on child prostitution issues in scores of countries. They have already had some success.

Realistically, they have their best chance of success in terms of controlling child prostitution, through stiff fines and sentences for the *customers* and *parents* of such abused children. The global network against such exploitation offers some support to governments long on good intentions but short on will. AIDS may be a more effective antidote to misplaced ardour than government action, but advertising, family fares and destination development that sell non-sexual activities are all options that more and more groups may sponsor.

As AIDS and other sexually transmitted diseases spread like wildfire throughout poor nations, the response of governments has varied widely. Some European countries have prosecuted men involved in child prostitution in Third World countries. The Philippines since the overthrow of dictator Ferdinand Marcos in 1986 has taken numerous, albeit not very successful, steps to shut down sex tours, prosecute paedophiles and clean up tourist areas (Sherwill, 1996: 13; *Contours*, 1996). Some nations now require proof of a negative AIDS test for non-transit tourists. Contrast that with Thailand, where authorities permitted AIDS to go unchallenged for years rather than risk depressing tourism, Thailand's number one industry (Hall, 1994; Shenon, 1992). Cuba, like Thailand has no legal prostitution but rather an enormous illicit industry (Darling, 1995). Unlike Thailand, Cuba quarantines AIDS victims, moving swiftly to control spread of the disease. Recently, however, the Thai government has tried to attract female tourists in an effort to refashion Thailand's tawdry image. 'Women Visit Thailand Year' in 1992 was an attempt to attract the increasing numbers of Japanese women going abroad. Indications are it was successful (Leheny, 1995: 380).

Gender differences in marketing, souvenirs and attractions

Theoretically, the appeal of combining sex with tourism should be the same for both sexes, but it is not. Whether we ascribe the differences to biological propensities, socialization or opportunity structure, an industry providing a sexual ambience and sexual favours to male clients creates a potentially hostile environment for female clients. Yet, because males control the industry and particularly its marketing and promotion, the expectations of linking sex with tourism are everywhere. Handsome, flirtatious men are not what the ads offer. It is women, alone or with other women, and often in remote natural settings or in a serving role, as in hotel and airline ads. Intact families, older people and children are not pictured in most advertisements.

In fact, advertising encouraging whole families to travel is the exception, though industry analysts predict more of this as ageing baby boomers bring children along on vacations, spawning children's versions of Club Med or their own cruise activities. In general, men who bring their wives on business trips are sold romantic, second honeymoon experiences.

Women, on the other hand, are promised physically pampering environments with excellent shopping!

Until recently, the older woman traveller has been virtually ignored in the marketing research though evidence suggests she may be a much more active and economically important element than anticipated (Hawes, 1988). This is not surprising. The industry generally has been both myopic and sexist in its assumptions about what women need and want, despite the fact that women make the majority of the decisions regarding discretionary travel (Smith, 1979; Tunstall, 1989; Maruff, 1993: 20). Recently, tours have been mushrooming that are exclusively for women. They range from theatre tours for sorority alumni to trekking expeditions in the Himalayas.

Marketing has also focused on the older traveller, who is increasingly important demographically and is disproportionately female. Elderhostel, Earthwatch and other research-cum-travel groups are attracting a huge, well-educated generation with disposable income. Nor is this group confined to the US and Western Europe. Korea and Taiwan lifted their barriers in the last decade to men of military age travelling abroad, but there are also significant numbers of female group travellers going abroad from these countries (Militante, 1993: 17–19).

As women have increasingly become more of the travel market, the industry response has adapted in some curious ways consistent with male orientation and female concerns. The general advertising has become a bit more subtle, but prostitution services have become less small-scale, more entrepreneurial. Visa and Mastercard are accepted for a dazzling array of itemized sexual services from virtually any racial and ethnic group one desires. Presumably routinizing such services will encourage less hassling of women in general, and women travelling alone in particular. It will also encourage men to patronize services *controlled* by other men. In the age of AIDS and herpes, men get some assurances that the women they buy will be inspected and presumed healthy. The women, of course, get no such protection from their clients!

Women business travellers, then, are just as likely to be interacting professionally with men who are buying the sexual favours of other women. Still, some studies show that US female business travellers find the pace less difficult than male counterparts (Del Rosso, 1992). One is tempted to suggest they get more sleep than those buying sexual services, but the answer is more complicated. Women away from home are removed from the traditional tasks of the household, cleaning, cooking, and caring for children, while male travellers on the road have laundry, meals, and mending they would not usually have at home.

The male-controlled industry offers increasingly better protection for the growing numbers of female business travellers. Thus, there is greater attention to security in the issuance of keys, better locks, and more attentive service in restaurants. Hair dryers, skirt hangers and bubble baths are also more likely to be included in hotels, be it for clients or their female guests. That women still feel vulnerable is suggested by their much greater use of room service for meals.

Gender and souvenirs

Another area where gender differences emerge with respect to tourism is in the selling of memories through postcards and souvenirs. Semiotics has demonstrated that those in control show us an image of 'the other' that is congruent with the dominant group values, their expectations and their goals. For example, we can now look back with some amusement, tinged with horror, at the way early travel writings described non-Western societies. The more lurid the tales from Asia, Africa and the American frontier of cannibals, sacrifices, savages and bare-breasted maidens, the easier it was to rationalize imperial 'civilizing' adventures.

The United States was not immune. President McKinley reportedly declared in 1898 that he was annexing the Philippines 'for our little brown brothers for whom Christ also died'. This ignored the fact that the Philippines after 350 years of Spanish rule was already 85 per cent Catholic! Travel brochures often encourage the traveller to expect friendly pampering. One widely promoted Caribbean advertisement had a staff of black cooks, maids, bellmen, drivers, etc. with trays of food and flowers out waist deep in the ocean offering these goodies to a white couple lounging on a rubber raft. Gender was not the issue but racial and economic dependency; however in postcards, brochures and souvenirs the gender dimension, like that of race, is well worth exploring.

Under Philippine dictator Ferdinand Marcos, the tourism slogan was 'Where Asia Wears a Smile' and the advertising promised 'a tanned peach on every beach' (Richter, 1982). Nude or scantily dressed women are the staple of many postcard shops. To its credit, the Philippines under President Aquino was one nation that dramatically changed its government marketing of tourism (Richter, 1988). Indonesia, on the other hand, sells pictures of nude tribal people (both male and female) and penis sheaths at its Biak airport shop. The exploitation of native peoples is so much easier after you take away their dignity.

In Hawaii, this is taken a step further. Authentic Hawaiians are not even pictured, but usually some generic Polynesian-cum-Filipino-Japanese mix deemed more sexy for North American and European markets. Blond, blue-eyed women are more apt to be the erotic subjects of advertising targeting the Japanese!

Even the United States permitted its government tourist office to promote one of its Caribbean territories with giant buttons saying 'TRY A

VIRGIN . . . island'. Happily, it evoked an appropriately negative response when called to the attention of the Coalition on Third World Tourism and the Caribbean Council of Churches (Richter, 1989b).

In 1984, a new product hit the market with the editorial approval of the *Honolulu Star Bulletin* – 'scratch and sniff' postcards. Scratch the females pictured and they give off scents of the flowers of Hawaii. Someone once said, 'No one ever went broke underestimating the taste of the American public!' Similarly, there would not be a shortage of sexist souvenir kitsch should one try to collect it. In sculpture, be it marble, wood, or terracotta, in pictures on black velvet or canvas, in virtually any medium, so-called 'airport art' flourishes. Often, when human beings are the subject, they are sexually explicit female renditions.

Gender and attractions

Even though women figure prominently in advertising, postcards and souvenirs, they are sadly neglected in cultural and historical tourism destinations supported by taxpayers' money. Battlefields do not celebrate those who nursed the soldiers; galleries seldom provide showcases for female talent; museums may feature fashions from an era or the dresses of First Ladies, but they seldom recall the daring adventures or courage of women. Statues recall war heroes, 'forefathers' not 'foremothers', male 'founders' of towns (not their invisible spouses). In the United States the Statue of Liberty, the Madonna of the Plains and monuments to the frontier woman occasionally remember women as a category, rarely the specific woman.

It was not until the 1980s that a museum of women's art was opened in Washington, DC with *private* donations. It was not until the 1990s that the cornerstone was laid for a memorial to US women veterans and an impressive sculpture added to the Vietnam War Memorial to belatedly acknowledge the service of women in Vietnam. Even the most beautiful tourist site in the world, the Taj Mahal, while built as a crypt for a woman, is remembered as a testament to Emperor Shah Jahan's love! Thus, the *impact* of tourism continues to socialize generations to the importance of what men have done while women are ignored or immortalized on postcards, nutcrackers and T-shirts.

Prospects for policy changes

Will 'who gets what, when and how' change as more women enter the workplace, as the numbers of both men and women travelling accelerate? Probably. But the prospects for greater balance in gender control are mixed.

The vast bulk of the financial control of the private tourism sector is in the hands of men. That is almost equally true of the public sector. Government policymakers, be they political appointees or career bureaucrats, are overwhelmingly male. The US example illustrates this point. The executive branch is overwhelmingly male at the policy-making levels (GS 16–18). Only two of the President's cabinet officials in 1992 were female, along with 5 per cent of the Senate. Forty-seven of the fifty states are headed by male tourism directors (Richter, 1985). In 1992 this writer was the only female among the fifteen members of the National Travel and Tourism Advisory Board. In 1992, however, women in leadership included the United States Secretary of Commerce and the head of United States Customs. The Philippines was unusual in 1992 and again in 1996 in having a female Secretary of Tourism. The Aquino role model accelerated a pattern already more pronounced there: more women in the poorly paid public sector *versus* more men in the private sector; but at least the women are often in positions of influence.

Women have been perceived as particularly appropriate for 'frontline' tourism positions because they are assumed to be more social, more hospitable than men. In fact, in the Philippines, the euphemism for tourism prostitute is a 'hospitality girl'. Zulfiqar Ali Bhutto, former prime minister of Pakistan, actually saw tourism as a new sector that would be ideally suited to women, whose employment and social uplift were a priority with him. For that very reason among others tourism was seen as a force of corruption and pollution among conservative forces in Pakistan and within other Islamic cultures. Christian churches in Asia, the Pacific and the Caribbean would be inclined to agree. In the Maldives, a tiny Muslim nation in the Indian Ocean, only men are allowed to work at the tourist resorts which are on separate islands physically isolated from the rest of the population (Richter, 1989a).

Ideological forces now sweeping the globe are encouraging less national planning, more devolution of power, greater privatization of industry including the privatization and deregulation of the tourist industry. These forces may create an industry more susceptible to market forces but it may deprive further those with the least influence and political access. Equity, systemic justice and the public interest, which were seldom well-served by the tourist industry before, may have an even greater struggle in the days ahead (Richter, 1991a, b).

As this writer has noted elsewhere:

> The primary reason why US tourism policy has not taken a more holistic approach to tourism is because of its fixation on tourism as a revenue-producing activity rather than as an important facet in improving the quality of life by reducing stress, enhancing education, instilling variety, and contributing to shared family experiences. While concern for revenue is

reasonable since tourism generates billions in federal, state and local taxes, such a perspective ignores the nonmonetary features of tourism policy and the not so easily quantified monetary costs of tourism development. Unlike much of the industrialized world, which also appreciates tourism's economic impact, the United States and its policy has not moved beyond the profit motive to a consideration of the role of leisure in the promotion of health, reduction of crime, reward of labor, or the importance of travel as an information medium. (Richter, 1991b)

On the other hand, the anti-government fever that has gripped not only the United States but countries around the globe may argue for a stronger role for the ultimate political outsiders – women. However, as I have argued elsewhere, there are many reasons to assume that class, race, religious and ethnic loyalties will continue to be more salient than gender (Richter, 1990). What we do know is that women in public office have shown a disproportionate concern for social welfare and environmental issues, for the issues of health, women and children – all areas towards which the unfettered tourism industry has on many occasions been overly cavalier (Darcy et al., 1987). Thus, if women achieve more access to representative institutions and public policy positions, current research suggests they will have an impact on tourism in specifically those areas where women have had least control and influence. Stronger worker safety, wage, health, and family leave laws might be anticipated.

A phenomenon as massive as tourism and a variable as basic as gender cannot be discussed thoroughly in this brief space. Clearly, however, there are numerous *evolving* dimensions of this relationship that deserve further scrutiny. Once we acknowledge that tourism has been marginalized and trivialized as a research subject and requires careful analysis, it is a logical next step to explore its impact in the context of such a central variable as gender.

References

Barry, Kathleen, Bunch, Charlotte and Castley, Shirley (1984) *International Feminism: Networking Against Female Slavery*, International Women's Tribune Centre, New York

Barry, Tom, Wood, Beth and Preusch, Deborah (1984) *The Other Side of Paradise: Foreign Control in the Caribbean*, Grove Press, New York

Blunt, Alison (1994) *Travel, Gender and Imperialism: Mary Kingsley and West Africa*, Guilford Press, New York

Caul, M. and. Youngblood, Robert L. (1996) Structures of Imperialism and the Exploitation of Women and Children in the Philippine Entertainment Industry, a paper presented at the Fifth International Philippine Studies Conference, Honolulu, April 14–16

Contours (1996) Philippines Targets Foreign Syndicates to end Flesh Trade, *Contours*, Vol. 7, No. 5 (March)

Darcy, R., Welch, Susan and Clark, Janet (1987) *Women, Elections and Representation*, Longman, New York, pp. 153–4

Darling, L. (1995) Havana at Midnight, *Esquire*, (May), 96–104

Del Rosso, L. (1992) Study Shows Women Handle Business Travel Better Than Men, *Travel Weekly*, July, pp. 30–31

ECPAT (1992) Children in Prostitution: Victims of Tourism in Asia. Conference Statement, End Child Prostitution in Asian Tourism, Bangkok

Edgell, David (1993) *World Tourism at the Millennium*, Washington, DC, US Dept. of Commerce, p. 18

English, Philip (1986) *The Great Escape: an Examination of North–South Tourism*, North–South Institute, Ottawa

Enloe, Cynthia (1989) *Bananas, Beaches, and Bases: Making Feminist Sense of International Politics*, University of California Press, Berkeley, Ca

Enloe, Cynthia (1993) *The Morning After, Sexual Politics at the End of the Cold War*, University of California Press, Berkeley, Ca

Esplanada, J. (1996) Women sold in Body Parts *Philippine Daily Inquirer*, 1, 6.

Hall, C. (1994) ASEAN: 6-in-1 Tropical Paradise? *Tourism in the Pacific Rim*, Longman, Australia, pp. 67–115

Hawes, Douglass K. (1988) Travel-related lifestyle profiles of older women, *Journal of Travel Research*, Fall, pp. 22–32

Holden, Peter and Horlemann, Pfafflin (eds) (1983) *Documentation: Tourism, Prostitution, Development*, Ecumenical Coalition of Third World Tourism, Bangkok

Johnson, Sonia (1983) Women and the quest for justice. A speech given at Kansas State University, April 29

Lasswell, Harold (1936) *Politics: Who Gets What, When, and How?* McGraw Hill, New York

Leheny, D. (1995) A Political Economy of Asian Sex Tourism, *Annals of Tourism Research*, **22**(1), 380–381

Maruff, P. (1993) Fledgling Women's Movement in Korea, *Asia Travel Trade*, March, pp. 20–21

Militante, G. (1993) Japanese Women are Going Places, *Asia Travel Trade*, March, pp. 17–19

Morris, M. (ed) with O'Connor, Larry (1993) *Maiden Voyages*, Vintage, New York

Parenti, Michael (1977) *Democracy for the Few*, St Martin's Press, New York

Pruitt, D. and Suzanne Lafont (1995) For Love or Money, Romance Tourism in Jamaica, *Annals of Tourism Research*, **22**(1), 422–440

Richter, Linda K. (1982) *Land Reform and Tourism Development: Policy-Making in the Philippines*, Schenkman, Cambridge, Ma

Richter, Linda K. (1985) State-sponsored tourism: a growth field for public administration, *Public Administration Review*, November–December, pp. 832–9

Richter, Linda K. (1988) Public bureaucracy in post-Marcos Philippines, *Southeast Asian Journal of Social Science*, **15**(2), 57–76

Richter, Linda K. (1989a) *The Politics of Tourism in Asia*, University of Hawaii Press, Honolulu

Richter, Linda K. (1989b) Action alert, *Contours*, **4**(4), 4

Richter, Linda K. (1990) Exploring theories of female leadership in South and South-East Asia, *Pacific Affairs*, **63**(4), 524–40

Richter, Linda K. (1991a) Political issues in tourism policy: a forecast. In *World Travel and Tourism Review* (ed. D. Hawkins and J.B. Ritchie), CAB International (UK), pp. 189–93

Richter, Linda K. (1991b) The impact of American tourism policy on women. In *Gender Differences* (ed. Mary Lou Kendrigan), Greenwood Press, Colorado, p. 161

Richter, Linda K. (1995) Gender and Race: Neglected Variables in Tourism Research. In *Change in Tourism: People, Places, Processes* (ed. R. Butler and D. Pearce), Routledge, London, pp. 71–91

Robinson, Jane (1990) *Wayward Women: A Guide to Women Travellers*, Oxford University Press, London, p. 152.

Rogers, J. (1989) Tourism and Child Prostitution, *Contours*, **4**(2), 20–22

Rosca, N. (1995) The Philippines Shameful Export, *The Nation*, April, pp. 522, 524, 526–527

Rybczynski, Witold (1991) *Waiting for the Weekend*, Viking Penguin, London, p. 107

Sereewat, Sudarat, (1983) *Prostitution: Thai-European connection*, World Council of Churches, Geneva, Switzerland

Sherwill, P. (1996) Nailing Johns, *World Press Review*, January, p. 13

Shenon, P. (1992) After Years of Denial Asia Faces Scourge of AIDS, *The New York Times*, November 8, pp. A1

Smith, Valene L. (1979) Women: the taste-makers in tourism, *Annals of Tourism Research*, **6**(1), 49–60

Steiger, T. and Wardell, Mark (1995) Gender and Employment in the Service Sector, *Social Problems*, **42**(1), February, 91–123

Swain, M. (1993) Women Producers of Ethnic Arts, *Annals of Tourism Research*, **20**(1), 32–51

Swain, M. (1995) Gender and Tourism, *Annals of Tourism Research*, **22**(1), 247–266

Thanh-Dam, Truong (1983) The dynamics of sex tourism: the case of Southeast Asia, *Development and Change*, **14**, 533–53

Thomas, D. and Jones, Sidney (eds) (1993) *A Modern Form of Slavery: Trafficking of Burmese Women and Girls into Brothels in Thailand*, New York: Asia Watch, pp. 15–16

Tinling, Marion (1989) *Women into the Unknown*, Greenwood Press, New York, p. XXIV

Tunstall, Ruth (1989) Catering for the female business traveler, *EIU Travel and Tourism Analyst*, **5**, 26–40

Part Six

People, Places, Things: Alternative Issues

As tourism continues to expand its role as the world's largest industry, it also encourages the proliferation of academic research focused both on highly specific segments and impacts of tourism, and on the larger philosophical implications of this phenomenon. Tourism dramatically influences the entire range of economic, cultural, environmental, and even political values that in some combination constitute the modern world.

When special events are purposely developed and promoted as tourist attractions, there is always the risk that they may become too commercialized. If this potential risk is allowed to occur, it may detract and eventually destroy authenticity, a scarce commodity, and the very thing visitors may have been seeking.

Getz (Chapter 24) provides a graphic description of special events held in different parts of the world. Examples include events that are indigenous to certain areas as well as others that have been 'invented' in order to attract tourists and generate greater income. In each of these examples, authenticity plays a pivotal role as a 'pull' factor in attracting tourists.

A typology of special events is proposed, based upon the range of events and their interpretive roles, from the most authentic (and usually most site-specific) to the most general community event. A planning, programming and evaluation framework for special events is proffered, and specific guidelines for ensuring authenticity are also suggested in order to help ensure visitor satisfaction.

One of the important issues in strategic planning of facilities and amenities is understanding the activities of tourists during their visit to a particular destination. For many tourists, an integral part, or to others, the entire purpose of the visit according to **Jansen-Verbeke** (Chapter 25) is shopping. In fact, shopping is a major time-use for many tourists, regardless of their primary travel motivation.

The results of a recent survey of Japanese tourists' shopping behaviour in Amsterdam indicated that Japanese tourists clearly behave differently from other target market groups, and that even within this segment of the market, there are clear distinctions between age, travel motivation, length of stay and, above all, travel organization. To the Japanese tourist, the system of tax-free shops in Amsterdam offers special advantages not commonly found elsewhere.

The author deals with the implications of shopping being a major tourist attraction. Even with such a peripheral issue, we see important links to the infrastructure, cultural propensities and the extent of the acceptance of the tour-ist within the host community.

Especially in urban areas, the spatial relationship of tourist activities such as shopping and sightseeing must be directly related to hotels and transportation as a precondition for synergism. Therefore, taking into account the actual time budgets of tourists, the creation of intervening shopping opportunities along predictable sightseeing routes is one of the most effective planning instruments in developing an urban area's tourism potential.

Industrialized countries are changing from the traditional production economy to an information-based economy. Tourism-related activities have been classified as convenience services. At the national level, tourism's future success may well depend on the ability of each country to educate not only tourism employees, but also tourists and destination area residents about each other's culture in order to better understand and appreciate one another. According to **Go** (Chapter 26), continued prosperity in tourism will depend largely on well-educated people who are able to think, weigh and judge crucial issues in addition to providing quality tourist services.

The evolution of tourism education is presented, and the suggestion is made that tourism thinking has passed through two distinct stages: (1) the early 1940s–1970s' pragmatic concerns of educators for such things as career preparation and placement; and, (2) beginning in the early 1980s, a shift from the pragmatic to the academic, emphasizing research and methods of enquiry. However, the 1990s are seen as a period of transformation brought about by social change, concern for the environment, a global economy, and rapid advancements in technology.

The dual forces of technology and globalization will raise the competency demanded for all positions in the tourism industry and turn effective education into a competitive necessity. Industry, government and academic institutions must recognize that productivity and quality gains are derived from increased employee skills and knowledge. These value-added skills must continue to be developed if the tourism industry is to survive.

The author relates the importance of tourism education for developing coun-tries, as well as the necessity of broadening the intellectual scope of tourism programmes in developed nations. Such education must be firmly grounded in solid academic principles.

The final chapter in the book provides an unusual case study dealing with the origin and somewhat problematic development of a university tourism programme in the small Pacific island state of Fiji. **Harrison** (Chapter 27) suggests that the programme at the University of the South Pacific 'was in a huge mess, for all kinds of reasons . . . '

Some of the local strains and problems across the various sectors are depicted involving government, the university, funding agencies and the tourism indus-try. The chapter is a work-in-progress history, illustrating the many tensions that exist but are usually denied in all kinds of documents, national plans, etc. For example, the author suggests that although there are ongoing discussions currently being held regarding the next National Tourism Development Plan, no one has asked the university tourism programme to contribute. This situation is changing over time however.

Although it is common perception in development circles to view small island states or nations as problems, quite the contrary is often the case. Academics on island states like Fiji are often much closer to politicians and planners than their more far removed colleagues residing in developed countries. Academics in those nations often feel neglected by government officials, and are too often perceived as irrelevant or threatening by those same individuals. Also, the scale of tourism, government and higher education in small states is such that cooperation and understanding are relatively easy to achieve, and that university expertise is valued by government. This is now the case in Fiji.

24 Event tourism and the authenticity dilemma

Donald Getz

Introduction

As the millennium approaches, plans are accelerating for celebrations in the years 2000–2001: a world's fair in Hanover; the Olympics in Sydney; a Millennium Festival in the UK and countless other parties and special events around the globe. We will be forced to consider the very essence of celebration – whether looking back for reaffirmation of our heritage or gazing forward with optimism – and to address the importance of celebration in our individual and collective lives.

How much of what we celebrate is truly authentic, as opposed to mere entertainment? Who or what gives meaning to festivals and special events? Are they for residents, tourists, or everyone? And in an era in which increasing mass tourism seems to compete with ever-stronger calls for sustainability, what are the appropriate roles of events: as mass-market attractions or alternative tourism?

When festivals and other special events are consciously developed and promoted as tourist attractions, there is the risk that commercialization will detract from celebration; that entertainment or spectacle will replace the inherent meanings of the celebrations. In other words, tourism might destroy cultural authenticity, the very thing contemporary travellers appear to be seeking. The dilemma, however, is that the benefits to be realized from tourism also offer the means to create or expand festivals, restore and cultivate traditions, and foster community spirit and sharing.

This is not a debate solely for academics and traditionalists, as just about every community seems to have a festival or special event that it wishes to see grow and prosper, while at the same time not being overwhelmed by visitors or commercialism. And in more traditional societies, where customs and quaintness are easily converted into cash through eager tourism entrepreneurs, there is the risk of loss of innocence and purity, if not outright assimilation. Is the price too high?

The argument put forward in this chapter is that the benefits from event tourism generally outweigh the costs and problems, especially at the level of community-scaled events. When communities or cultural groups determine what is important to themselves and take control of the exchange process with visitors and the tourist industry, authenticity can be preserved and enhanced. Indeed, it is argued that authenticity is a community 'product' and its very definition is subject to local ownership.

Definitions and concepts

Festival

Festivals are simply defined as themed, public celebrations. Yet the term is rich in tradition and meaning, with many anthropological and socio-logical studies documenting the close links between festivity, religion, and community (e.g. Falassi, 1987; Manning, 1983; MacAloon, 1984). True festivals are produced explicitly for public, not private consumption, and are celebrations of something which has value in the community. Many festivals celebrate community itself, and have been created specifically to give people something to share, to unify them, to foster community pride. Others are invented with the goal of fostering a particular form of arts or sports.

To the anthropologist, festivals have a multitude of potential meanings and encompass a number of paradoxes (Lavenda 1991): as 'texts' which are stories told by members of a culture about themselves; as perform-ances, or social dramas full of conflict and power statements; as com-munications about social ties in the society; as art forms; as deliberate inversions or role reversals, mocking but simultaneously reinforcing social norms.

According to Lavenda, three paradoxes emerged from his study of festivals in small Minnesota towns. The events simultaneously reduced and increased uncertainty in the social life, contributed to both order and disorder, and conveyed the image of a stable community while at the same time changing the community through the festival's evolving mem-bership. Accordingly, a researcher could look for expressions of power (who runs the event?), conformity to established ways of doing things (no new ideas in twenty years?), license to commit revelry versus tight controls on drinking, take-overs by new arrivals in town, and so on.

Special event

From the point of view of the consumer, or audience, a special event is an opportunity for a leisure, social or cultural experience outside the normal range of choices or beyond everyday experience. From the organizer's point of view a special event is any one-time or infrequently occurring event outside their normal programme or activities. What is 'special' to the organizer might not be of any interest to potential consumers, so from a marketing perspective the product must be matched to carefully defined target segments. Some segments exist which can be described as 'event tourists' – those who seek out events of particular types.

All festivals should be special events, both to organizers and consumers. Many special events, however, are not festivals: they lie in the domain of sport competitions, commercial promotions, or meetings and shows. Increasingly, however, we are seeing a blending, with sports events in particular adding festival-like programming to make them more attractive.

Event tourism

Many businesses, communities and destination marketing organizations are now engaged in the systematic planning, development and marketing of festivals and events as tourist attractions, image-makers, catalysts for other developments or as animators of built attractions. This is 'event tourism' at work, and so significant is the business that more and more event, culture and sport development agencies are being established.

To the extent that events are often inexpensive to develop, and if properly organized will generate little negative impact, they can be viewed as being more sustainable than other forms of tourism development. And because they are essentially cultural in nature and lead to host–guest contacts, increasingly event tourism is being looked upon as a clear alternative to mass tourism.

In addition to their tourism potential, festivals and special events are being created by more and more organizations and agencies, both private and public. Events can help raise money, foster community development or the arts, provide leisure opportunities and make excellent communications tools (indeed, much of the growth of events in the past decade is attributable to sponsorship). The popularity and specialness of festivals and events is closely related to their ability to achieve multiple goals.

Authenticity and the community

Authenticity means genuine, unadulterated or 'the real thing'. With respect to tourism the term usually refers to a motivation, as in 'the search for authentic cultural experiences'. But tourism is frequently accused of destroying authenticity through commoditization, and especially of cultural performances like dances, rituals and festivals which can be produced for monetary gain. A related common theme is that tourists seldom get access to authentic cultural experiences, owing to the deliberate and pervasive commercialization of culture in destinations. These notions are much debated in the literature, including the related question of whether or not contemporary tourists actually seek out authentic experiences, or can even recognize them.

Vallee (1987) maintained that 'Authenticity is a desired and actively pursued experience by tourists which is perceived to reflect or give access to the true and unadulterated nature of everyday life in the destination.' Redfoot (1984) however, noted that some scholars believe the modern tourist is generally uninterested in the authentic (e.g. Boorstin, 1961) while others have suggested that tourists are engaged in a quest for the authentic (e.g. MacCannell, 1976). MacCannell, in his much-quoted book *The Tourist* (1976) suggested that modern tourists seek authenticity precisely because it has become so scarce. The tourist wants a spontaneous experience that reveals, or better yet allows the sharing of some aspect of the daily life of a different culture or community, yet seldom finds it. MacCannell used the term 'backstage' to describe the physical setting in which a visitor could observe, meet or share something authentic. The term 'staged authenticity' was coined to describe events created with the intention of fooling observers. When culture is 'produced' for visitors in this way it is planned manipulation.

Cohen (1988) noted that the literature on authenticity made three assumptions: that tourism leads to exploitive cultural commoditization; which destroys authenticity through 'staging' it; which thwarts the tourist's genuine desire for authentic experience. But Cohen did not agree, arguing instead that authenticity is a 'socially constructed concept' that is 'negotiable' as to meaning. It can mean pre-modern (which is often the anthropologists' view), not commoditized, accurate reconstructions or even a resemblance to the real thing. Visitors might also contribute to 'emergent authenticity' whereby contrived events are eventually accepted as being authentic. As Greenwood (1982) argued, 'all viable cultures are in the process of "making themselves up" all the time'. And mass tourism succeeds because tourists accept a loose interpretation of authenticity, being satisfied with play and make-believe.

Pearce (1982) added to the debate by arguing that visitor satisfaction will depend not only on the nature of the event (whether or not it is authentic) but also on the visitor's perception of whether or not authenticity exists and their need for authentic experiences. For example, one visitor will want a festival to be an authentic cultural expression of the host community and will be disappointed if he or she finds a highly commercialized, tourist-oriented event. Another visitor will not care, and still others won't know the difference.

Van der Berghe (1993) suggested that 'sophisticated tourists sneer at such staged authenticity, but sometimes such creations or recreations become the basis of a cultural revival, acquire over time a secondary authenticity of their own, and are reappropriated by their creators.' And 'If the quest for authenticity sometimes initially seems to undermine and corrupt local culture, it can revive and reinvigorate traditions that were languishing under the assault of other modernizing forces . . .'. To Van der Berghe, locals can 'invent a new, refined authenticity.'

On the other hand, the tourist industry often promotes destinations and cultures without consulting residents and tends to use images, such as major icons (e.g. landmarks) and stereotypical native costumes and entertainment that it anticipates can be verified by tourists during their visit (Silver, 1993). Residents are then faced with the unsavoury prospect of having to confirm the expectations of tourists which have been shaped by an uncoordinated or uncaring publicity machine.

To Hughes (1995: 799) authenticity is transitory and its meaning questionable. In an attempt to re-theorize, he suggested that a more existential perspective is necessary in which it is possible to 'find manifestations of authenticity through individual's assertion of personal identity.'

In the context of heritage, authenticity has a direct bearing on how buildings and sites are preserved, restored and interpreted. Many commentators fear that the pursuit of tourism revenue leads to serious threats. Herbert (1995) said: 'Dangers arise because it is relatively easy to invert history and to turn heritage into a marketable product without proper regard for rigour, honesty and factual accuracy in the presentation of heritage.' In creating experiences for tourists, entertainment rather than education can easily dominate. As applied to events, the same entertainment versus authenticity issues arises, with events being used to attract tourists to sites and communities creating heritage festivals for tourism purposes. Ehrentraut (1993) commented that this 'presentation issue' has cultural parameters, as North Americans prefer animation of sites through events and living history, while Europeans do not.

Examples

There are interesting cases documented in the literature which tangibly illustrate the issues surrounding authenticity, and which offer possible answers to the dilemma. A few personal experiences of the author are also illustrated below.

A Basque festival

An often-cited example of the negative impacts of tourism was Greenwood's study of a Basque festival in Spain. In his first report on the festival the researcher was critical of tourism as a force which attacked an authentic tradition by commercializing it for presentation to tourists.

Greenwood (1989) lamented: 'local culture . . . is altered and often destroyed by the treatment of it as a tourist attraction. It is made meaningless to the people who once believed in it.'

But in his second analysis of the festival, written as an epilogue, Greenwood questioned whether tourism has any unique effects in transforming culture – as opposed to, say, mass communications and economic globalization. He concluded: 'Some of what we see as destruction is construction; some is the result of a lack of any other viable options; and some the result of choices that could be made differently'. Regarding authenticity, Greenwood dismissed the notion that an anthropologist could compare 'traditional models' with 'what is presented to the tourist' and then make a pronouncement. Rather, all cultures continuously change, within cultures there is great diversity, and what is 'authentic' might become a highly political issue. Finally, Greenwood conceded that under some conditions, tourism might be a positive cultural force.

The Pentecost land jump

For a positive example there is the case of the Pentecost land jump in the South Pacific island nation of Vanuatu, as reported by Sofield (1991). The ritual – called the 'naghol' – is steeped in Melanesian legend, and appears to be the precursor to bungee-jumping. Men of the tribes leap from high platforms, their fall broken by a flexible vine tied to ankles. Fearing commercialization of the ritual, the chiefs formed a tourism council to manage the events and the tourists, generating significant local income in the process. The national tourism office works with the industry, including Air Vanuatu, agents and wholesalers, to bring up to fifty tourists to the site at one time, and no more than eight times a year.

Sofield concluded: 'The unique selling proposition of the naghol is the authenticity of the event which can only be guaranteed by control remaining in the hands of the eight villages of south Pentecost. It is an example where the objectives of viable tourism, traditional culture and social values on the one hand and commercial gain on the other are not mutually exclusive.'

In addition to local ownership and control of the event, Sofield concluded that a supportive government was also required – both to promote the event and to protect it from outside influences. Other criteria for maintaining cultural authenticity were derived from this case study, along with directly related objectives and business and marketing implications. For example, 'broad community support with appropriate organizational structure' is a key criterion; it requires an 'acceptable decision-making process'. 'Priority accorded to cultural integrity over commercial consideration' is another crucial criterion, requiring 'commercial imperatives made to fit around, not debase, the ceremony'.

The Amish

Buck (1977; 1978) found that staged, tourist-oriented events helped to prevent direct contact with privacy-loving Amish people in Lancaster County, Pennsylvania. In this way, inauthentic events can be used to maintain a social boundary between curious tourists and reluctant host communities. As long as the tourists are satisfied, even if they know they are witnessing an event put on for their entertainment or education, then it hardly seems to matter if the event is culturally genuine or not – it serves a very useful function. Indeed, in this age of mass travel and a better informed traveller, it is probably the rare, naive tourist who actually expects to discover unadulterated cultural festivals!

Creating a theme

Consultants have recommended that a winter carnival in Newfoundland, Canada, should make greater use of its mascot – Leif The Lucky, in Viking costume – in developing and marketing their event as a tourist attraction. More ambitiously, a set of Viking Games could be invented to package sports tournaments and participatory recreational events all year round. Already existing in the region is a Viking Trail with its own destination marketing association.

While there is some historical association with Vikings in their part of the world, it is clearly a marketing tool rather than a reflection of contemporary culture. Indeed, the Viking motif, attractive and full of merchandising promise, is as novel a theme to residents as it is to tourists. On the one hand, creation of themed events and promotional devices might awaken interest in the area's history, but it might also reduce historical facts to trivial slogans and characters. To combat that possibility, another recommendation was to create a 'Discovery Days' festival with the goal of celebrating and interpreting the early western Newfoundland explorers, including the Vikings and Captain James Cook.

Appropriateness

In Costa Rica, the Central American country noted for ecotourism, but not cultural attractions, the idea was raised by a coffee company to develop a festival with a coffee theme. It is a major export, and a special event themed on that product would promote the crop, reflect an important aspect of Costa Rican life, and act as a cultural attraction. The idea raises the questions of whether the event is appropriate to the country, and if explicit commercialism will negate cultural value.

Festivals with higher levels of authenticity, including the religious celebrations found in Costa Rican communities, might not be appropriately promoted as tourist attractions. Their sacred and intensely personal nature might preclude them from ever being considered a fun attraction, while their host communities might be totally unable or unwilling to organize and market them for tourists. In this context, the invented, commercial event might be more appropriate.

Becoming a tradition

An example of a successful 'invented' festival is Dickens on the Strand, founded by the Galveston Historical Society (in Galveston, Texas) to attract attention to, and raise money for, heritage restoration (cited in Getz, 1991). Held annually in December, the event is a major tourist attraction as well as being very popular with residents – many of whom are volunteers, while others dress in Victorian costume in order to gain free admission. This event successfully meets its heritage objectives while providing a valued social experience for residents.

Many such 'instant traditions' have been created in the world of special events. They fulfil a real need for community sharing, leisure outlets, and pride in accomplishments. Indeed, many people seem to think that community events are not significant unless tourists are attracted.

In North America and other new nations, traditional festivals and events are in short supply, while the mobility of the population is high. Given the absence of 'authentic' celebrations, communities have invented their own. Who is to say that these events are less authentic than centuries-old festivals?

Conceptualizing the authenticity dilemma

Three perspectives on authenticity must be reconciled. From a social anthropology point of view, authenticity is a measure of the inherent cultural meanings of festivity and celebration; that is, people come together to share valued elements of their culture. To the planner of festivals and events in the contemporary world, where multiple goals are pursued – including tourism – authenticity can be viewed as a measure of community control and success in mobilizing residents to support and participate in the event. This perspective will also encompass, explicitly or implicitly, the notion of self-image. In other words, if the community

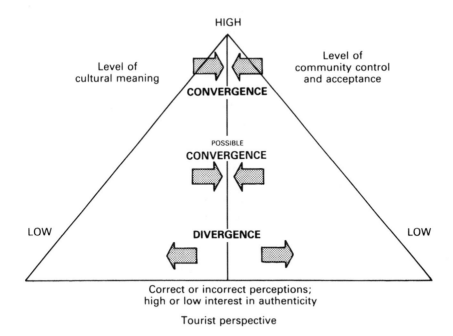

Figure 24.1 of the illustration:

HIGH

Level of
cultural meaning

Level of
community control
and acceptance

CONVERGENCE

POSSIBLE
CONVERGENCE

LOW   **DIVERGENCE**   LOW

Correct or incorrect perceptions;
high or low interest in authenticity

Tourist perspective

Figure 24.1   Three perspectives of event authenticity

or large components of it reject the theme or the image being portrayed of the community, they will stay away or make their objections known. Authenticity in this sense means acceptance.

The third essential perspective is that of the visitor. By definition, the tourist or visitor is an outsider who is not necessarily sharing culture with residents, but nevertheless enjoys being able to participate in an event with local significance. More pragmatically, the tourist is most likely to be attracted to, and enjoy events which are popular with the host community. Here, authenticity is a measure of the tourist's perceptions. Unthinking tourists may view a commercial event as being authentic, or may perceive it correctly but still enjoy the production. Other tourists seek out authenticity and are disappointed when they (correctly or incorrectly) do not find it. To the tourism planner and marketer, this is a problem of tourist satisfaction and can be countered through better product-market matching.

Figure 24.1 is an illustration of the three perspectives on event authenticity (i.e. community control and acceptance; cultural meanings; tourist perspective). At the pyramid's apex a very traditional, uncommercialized festival or ritual is almost certainly one which is based on high community control and acceptance – even if witnessed by tourists. The Pentecost land jump is a prime example.

At the mid level, 'invented' and tourist-oriented events might initially have low cultural meaning, but this can change over time. The result should be a convergence of meaning and community acceptance, until – hypothetically – new traditions are created. On this topic, Cohen (1988) suggested that 'emergent authenticity' is a process by which a contrived cultural product comes to be perceived as authentic, over time. Planners of events will hope that this happens, and the evidence of festivals like Dickens on the Strand is positive.

Other rituals or events might be valued only by small minorities within society and will have to engage in public relations to attract wider community support or acceptance. Ethnic and multicultural festivals often have this planned convergence as an explicit goal – that is, they create the event to bring diverse groups together and attract the attention and understanding of unrelated cultural groups.

However, events with low community control and acceptance are unlikely to achieve any cultural authenticity, while events low in inherent cultural meaning are likely to be perceived as alien and undesirable – resulting in divergence. There is no particular type of event which necessarily fits this category, but they are most likely to be highly commercialized or imposed on an unresponsive community.

At the pyramid's base lies the variable perspective of the visitor or tourist, whose perceptions and reactions are, at the level of individuals, unpredictable. Those seeking high levels of authenticity will presumably be attracted to events at the apex and repelled by events at the base. But purely commercial entertainment events can be low on authenticity and community acceptance while still attracting tourists. Accordingly, the tourist perspective is the subject for market research, with the aim of matching the right event to the desires of target segments.

Heritage events

Of contemporary interest is a class of events which have historical themes or which celebrate some dimension of a community's or cultural group's heritage. By definition, these events should embody high levels of authenticity – but that cannot be taken for granted.

Heritage events are public, themed festivals and other special events which celebrate a nation's or community's traditions, values and sense of place. They may have an explicit heritage theme, such as a commemoration or a folk festival, or they may be broadly programmed community celebrations. They may be site-specific or community-wide. They may be produced by an ethnic or special interest group, or by a public or private agency. There is no single style of heritage event, nor any correct way of producing them. Indeed, one of the hallmarks of heritage events is their unlimited diversity.

Events and interpretation

Heritage events can also be viewed as tools for interpreting the community by bringing people into direct contact with historical facts, objects and re-created events or ways of life, thereby increasing their knowledge and appreciation of traditions. Interpretation, according to Tilden, one of its early advocates (1977), is an 'educational activity which aims to reveal meanings and relationships through the use of original objects, by first hand experience, and by illustrative media . . .'. More specifically, Cherem (1988) said that heritage interpretation 'can make the heritage identity of an area come to life for residents and visiting guests.' To do so requires 'real and authenticated, first-hand sensory interaction with the resources of that area'. Moscardo and Pearce (1986) have argued that historical re-creations, as in heritage sites and events, can be considered authentic if they faithfully simulate past conditions.

Also relevant is Cherem's definition of community interpretation, which 'tells the stories of – and facilitates – heritage expression in a community.' In a related vane, Binks (1989) writes:

> The common ground where interpretation and community development meet is in a concern to create or enhance a sense of place, to establish what is significant and valued in the environment or heritage . . . and to provoke action for its wider appreciation and conservation.

Little attention has been paid to the potential of festivals and other special events as interpretation tools. One obvious connection is the folklife festival, which McDaniel (1986) describes as being 'inherently grassroots in nature'. Its combination of entertainment and education makes such a festival a 'classroom for the teaching of history to the general public'. The historian, according to McDaniel, has the task of weaving history into the programme: indeed, 'programming is the historian's interpretive statement'.

From these basic definitions and ideas several essential ingredients (or evaluative criteria) can be derived for planning heritage events as interpretive tools:

1 Heritage events reveal meanings (e.g. the values, traditions and sense of place of the community).
2 They reveal interrelationships (e.g. between people and the environment, between social and cultural groups).
3 They provide direct contact with important heritage objects, sites, places or recreated historical events and ways of life.

4   They must be 'alive', or truly 'special' events, which requires a pro-
    gramme and ambience capable of stimulating not only intellectual
    curiosity but also emotions.
5   They allow residents and visitors (i.e. tourists) to participate in the
    living community.
6   They are authentic in reflecting community values and accurately
    portraying historic events or objects.

Although authenticity is an essential ingredient of heritage and community interpretation, there are limits which apply to such events. As
noted by Rumble (1989), entertainment is a major component of festivals
and special events, and this attraction has to be balanced against authenticity. Rumble said 'almost any interpretation has to be selective and
incomplete' and this is particularly true of events. Uzzell (1989) provides
a related insight, advocating events as 'hot interpretation'. Noting that
living history groups abound in Great Britain, often putting on battle re-
enactments, he argued that interpretation sometimes 'has to be shocking,
moving and provide a cathartic experience'. No matter how authentic
are the costumes and activities, 'visitors' perceptions will always be
influenced by their present-day attitudes and values.'
   'Hot interpretation' is not without its critics. Millar (1989) asked: 'Does
the future for heritage interpretation lie in the gloss of superficial entertainment in the form of the special event?' Instead of bland living history
or war re-enactments, Millar advocates 'community interpretation' which
will avoid bogus history and pandering to nostalgia. Community interpretation would involve multi-purpose heritage sites which function as
tourist attractions, become a focus of community identity, provide opportunities for formal and informal education and act as economic catalysts.

A typology of heritage events

Figure 24.2 shows a range of events and their interpretive roles, from the
most authentic, and usually site-specific, to the most general community
festival. Some generic examples are given for each type, and their interpretive roles are noted. This chart could be easily expanded to also note
the marketing value of events, but that is a different topic.
   From Table 24.1, interpreters and other event planners can determine
common interests and appropriate roles. For example, the interpreter
might desire the participation of certain community groups in producing
an on-site, living history event. Community leaders might call for the
participation of heritage agencies and interpreters in producing a very
general community celebration. The heritage site is seen as one part of
the community, with important roles to play in bringing the community's
heritage alive. Interpretation expertise, and the assets of heritage sites,

Table 24.1 Types of heritage events and their roles in interpreting the community

Types of event	Examples	Roles
Authentic re-creations at heritage sites	Battles Holiday celebrations Demonstrations of seasonal work (e.g., harvests)	Integral part of 'living history' Authentic in theme and relationship to the site Showcases the community's past
Unrelated events at heritage sites (the heritage site as an event backdrop)	Antique shows Themed parties Exhibitions, ethnic and multi-cultural festivals	Fosters site–community links Identifies the site as part of the living, changing community
Off-site events produced by heritage agencies	Travelling 'living history' Events produced on request	Takes specific interpretation events to the community Demonstrates relevance of the site or agency
Community festivals and celebrations	Specific elements of community-wide heritage or non-heritage events	Links fostered between heritage agencies/sites Skills of interpreters applied to event programming Involves the entire community in interpretation Stresses the living community

should be made available to external events. In this way, interpreting the community is a partnership between specific heritage resources and the community as a whole.

Each of the four types of heritage event present unique issues and challenges. At many heritage sites the visitor is entertained and simultaneously educated about history and the site's restoration through authentic re-creations. Standard living history techniques, including special events which go beyond the daily interpretive programme, add colour and excitement. Colonial Williamsburg, Virginia, is one of the best-known sites in which living history is both instructive and fun. However, these events do not interpret the living community within which the site operates; they are often disconnected from contemporary reality.

Sometimes unrelated events are held at heritage sites, tangibly connecting the site to the community. An example is the holding of an antique car rally at a pioneer village. There is perhaps a dubious link with the period or theme of the site, but in the public's perception the two may be quite compatible.

Any number of examples can be given of good heritage events, but it is not easy to find examples of community-wide heritage events produced by heritage agencies – this is an area deserving increased attention. Modest examples might include a travelling 'living history' show or exhibition, while more ambitious agencies could create major themed festivals. The potential roles of heritage agencies and interpreters in community festivals must be better defined through practice and evaluation.

Turning to general community festivals and celebrations, a fascinating example is that of Chemainus, British Columbia where the community interprets its heritage through wall murals. This amazingly successful innovation is being copied in many other communities, sometimes in conjunction with an annual festival. Murals, and other forms of art or artefacts, do require some interpretation, if only in the form of signs or guidebooks. A festival shaped around such conspicuous objects is an interpretive tool, drawing attention to the objects and the living community, bringing hosts and guests into contact, facilitating residents' involvement and pride, and also generating revenue.

A planning framework for heritage events

Table 24.2 presents a framework that can be used to help plan, programme and evaluate authentic heritage events which interpret the host community. While planning methods are beyond the scope of this book, the recommended process should be considered in light of the issues and challenges described above. Other pertinent sources to use in planning heritage events include: Peart (1979) on goals and styles of interpretation; Getz (1991; 1997) on theming; Christensen (1990) on learning modalities; Field and Wagar (1984) on evaluation.

Conclusions

One of the great themes in the tourism literature is that tourists tend to destroy the very things that attract them. This applies to natural and cultural landscapes, both of which are sensitive to commercialization and 'erosion'. Traditional festivals and special events are particularly susceptible to commodification as tourists will pay for all forms of entertainment. Nevertheless, the weight of evidence found in the literature suggests that tourism need not destroy traditional meanings, and that

Table 24.2 Framework for planning, programming and evaluating authentic heritage events

Goals

Interpreting the community; education
Managing heritage sites and resources
Economic development; tourism
Community development
Marketing of heritage sites
Revenue generation
Fostering site–community links
Fostering links among heritage sites/agencies

Heritage resource evaluation

History of the community
Heritage sites and objects
Possible themes

Determine theme and type of event

Historical re-enactment
Commemoration
Ethnic or multi-cultural; folkways
Arts and entertainment (contemporary)
Recreational or competitive sport and play
Shows and exhibitions; sales
Parades

Organization

Type of organizing body (new or existing)
Roles of heritage agencies and interpreters
Planning the event
Marketing the event
Raising funds (e.g., grants; sponsors; sales; events)

The programme and production

Essential services (access; communications; safety; health; information;
    special visitor services; food and beverages)
Elements of style: spectacle; games; belonging and sharing; entertainment;
    ritual and ceremony
Designing and managing the setting(s)
Manifestation of the theme (through name, logo, mascots, design, activities,
    attractions, food, beverages, souvenirs etc.)
Learning modalities and interpretive mechanisms

Evaluation

On-site evaluation and problem-solving
Attainment of goals
Efficient use of resources
Unanticipated and external impacts
Conflict resolution
Re-statement of goals and programme, if appropriate

cultural preservation or reinvigoration can actually derive from the incentives offered by modern tourism.

Furthermore, tourists can hardly be blamed for the underlying forces that have changed the earth, bringing traditional cultures to abrupt contact with destructive social and economic forces. Tourism, in most cases, is a side product of those powerful factors: population growth; economic development; mass global communications and travel technology. Events produced for the explicit purpose of being 'consumed', either by residents or tourists, are most common. They are created and sustained for multiple goals – of the organizers, the grant-givers, sponsors, volunteers and increasingly tourist organizations. Authenticity means something different for traditional and created events. It has been argued that the degree of community participation and support is a measure of authenticity for most special events. Indeed, authenticity can be viewed as a product to be created and sold by the community.

The pyramidal model presented in this chapter attempts to inter-relate three key perspectives on festival and event authenticity. All festivals and special events contain cultural meaning, ranging from traditional, uncontaminated rituals and celebrations to mass sporting events like the Superbowl. Using the broad category of 'heritage events' to illustrate concepts, it was shown that they can be used to interpret living, changing communities, as well as the relics of the past.

Guidelines for ensuring authenticity

Given that the essence of authenticity is its cultural meaning, the bottom line must be that host communities determine what is meaningful to them. In this sense, authenticity is not so much the ritual, games, spectacle or celebration itself as it is the degree to which these components have been manufactured, modified or exploited just for tourists, the media or financial success. In other words, has the event any cultural meaning for the host community and the participants, or is it merely a commodity to be sold? Do the hosts and performers think of the event as having importance in their lives, or are they cynically involved in a tourist rip-off? Will people come to accept, over time, that the invented festival is an important part of their cultural life?

Guidelines have been established for successful community-based tourism (e.g. Cooke, 1982), and Sofield (1991) has proposed criteria for ensuring authenticity in cultural events. To these we should add the criteria discussed earlier for planning heritage events. The conclusion is that authenticity of festivals and events will be maximized when they:

1   reflect indigenous themes; reveal meanings about values, traditions and sense of place

2   reveal interrelationships between people, and people and the environment
3   are controlled by the host community and protected against potentially damaging external influences; appropriate organizations and decision-making processes are in place
4   are valued and well attended by residents
5   stimulate both emotional and intellectual curiosity
6   offer culturally genuine goods and performances, such as local foods, costumes, dances, crafts; provide direct contact with important heritage objects, sites, events or ways of life
7   do not exploit tourists through profit maximization at the expense of quality; commercial goals are made to fit cultural goals
8   allow hosts and guests to mingle and to participate in the living community
9   accurately portray historical events or objects

From the tourism perspective, the real issue is maximizing visitor satisfaction, with the realization that events popular with the host community are likely to be more pleasing, and that authentic cultural performances, settings, food and merchandise will be enduring attractions.

One important lesson stated by Lavenda (1991) is that 'When festivals are effective, it is because they offer multiple meanings to individuals and to the figurations that those individuals form.' So when debating what is or is not 'authentic', no consensus is likely. Rather, one's perspective and ways of evaluating 'meanings' come into play.

Tourist organizations should be sensitive to the desires of cultural groups who do not want to be exploited as tourist attractions, or do not want pseudo-events put on for tourists. Not all festivals and events should be viewed as tourism resources – the real event tourism resource is people, and the community must be given the right to decide for itself.

Conclusions

Authenticity is a difficult concept open to many interpretations, but is of great importance in the context of cultural tourism and particularly event tourism. Although some believe that authenticity is an absolute, determined by a complete absence of commoditization, many other theorists believe it is transitory, evolving and open to negotiation.

This chapter has argued that authenticity belongs to the community presenting the event, and is therefore a 'product' to be controlled and promoted as the community sees fit. If a group values the building, site, tradition or event, it can be said to have authentic cultural meaning: this is who we are and what we believe in. Whether or not tourists appreciate the meaning depends in part on their motivations, interests, and the success of interpretation. To have an 'authentic cultural experience' is therefore not a commodity negotiated between visitor and community, but a realization of the visitor that the experience truly reflects local values.

As the millennium approaches, care should be taken to ensure that our celebrations are meaningful to the communities which support them. Visitors will then find authentic experiences wherever they are treated with respect, educated, and invited to participate in local traditions and lifestyles.

References

Binks, G. (1989) Interpreters in the Community: A Discussion Paper. Chapter 21 in *Heritage Interpretation, Vol. 1*, (ed. D. Uzzell), Belhaven Press, London, p. 191

Boorstin, D. (1961) *The image: A guide to pseudo events in America*, Harper and Row, New York

Buck, R. (1977) Making good business better: A second look at staged tourist attractions, *Journal of Travel Research*, **15**(3), 30–32

Buck, R. (1978) Boundary maintenance revisited: Tourist experience in an old order Amish community, *Rural Sociology*, **43**(2), 221–34

Cherem, G. (1988) Interpretation as the vortex: Tourism based on heritage experiences. In *Interpretation and Tourism, Ottawa/88*, Proceedings of a Conference on Heritage Interpretation, pp. 5, 37

Christensen, J. (1990) Interpretation Can Target Everyone, *Legacy*, **1**(1), 11–15

Cohen, E. (1988) Authenticity and commoditization in tourism, *Annals of Tourism Research*, **15**(3), 371–386

Cooke, K. (1982) Guidelines for socially appropriate tourism development in British Columbia, *Journal of Travel Research*, **21**(1), 22–28

Ehrentraut, A. (1993) Heritage authenticity and domestic tourism in Japan, *Annals of Tourism Research*, **20**(2), 262–278

Falassi, A. (ed.) (1987) *Time out of time: Essays on the festival*, University of New Mexico Press, Albuquerque

Field, D. and Wagar, J. (1984) Visitor Groups and Interpretation in Parks and Other Outdoor Leisure Settings. In *On Interpretation: Sociology For Interpreters of Natural and Cultural History*, (ed. G. Machlis and D. Field), Oregon State University Press, Corvallis

Getz, D. (1991) *Festivals, Special Events, and Tourism*, Van Nostrand Reinhold, New York

Getz, D. (1997) *Event Management and Event Tourism*, Cognizant Communication Corp., New York

Greenwood, D. (1982) Cultural Authenticity, *Cultural Survival Quarterly*, **6**(3), 27–28

Greenwood, D. (1989) Culture by the pound: An anthropological perspective on tourism as cultural commoditization. In *Hosts and guests: The anthropology of tourism* (ed. V. Smith), 2nd edn, pp. 171–185, University of Pennsylvania Press, Philadelphia

Herbert, D. (1995) Preface. In *Heritage, Tourism and Society*, (ed. D. Herbert), Mansell, London

Hughes, G. (1995) Authenticity in Tourism, *Annals of Tourism Research*, **22**(4), 281–803

Lavenda, R. (1991) Community festivals, paradox, and the manipulation of uncertainty, *Play and Culture*, **4**, 153–168

MacAloon, J. (1984) *Rite, drama, festival, spectacle: Rehearsals towards a theory of cultural performances*, Institute for the Study of Human Issues, Philadelphia

MacCannell, D. (1976) *The tourist: A new theory of the leisure class*, Schocken Books, New York

Manning, F. (ed.) (1983) *The celebration of society: Perspectives on contemporary cultural performance*, Bowling Green Popular Press, Bowling Green, Ky

McDaniel, G. (1986) Folklife festivals: History as entertainment and education. In *Public History: An Introduction*, (ed. B. Howe and E. Kemp), R. Kreuger Publishing, Malabar, Florida, p. 279

Millar, S. (1989) Heritage management for heritage tourism, *Tourism Management*, **10**(1), 9–14

Moscardo, G. and Pearce, P. (1986) Historic theme parks, an Australian experience in authenticity, *Annals of Tourism Research*, **13**(3), 467–79

Pearce, P. (1982) *The social psychology of tourist behaviour*, Pergamon Press, Oxford

Peart, B. (1979) An application of the Foley-Keith objectives framework to interpretation activities, other than in national parks or related federal reserves. In *Papers of the Seventh National Conference of Interpretation Canada*

Redfoot, D. (1984) Touristic authenticity, touristic angst, and modern reality, *Qualitative Sociology*, **7**(4), 291–309

Rumble, P. (1989) Interpreting the built and historic environment. Chapter 3 in *Heritage Interpretation, Vol. 1*, (ed. D. Uzzell), Belhaven Press, London, p. 30

Silver, I. (1993) Marketing authenticity in third world countries, *Annals of Tourism Research*, **20**(2), 302–318

Sofield, T. (1991) Sustainable ethnic tourism in the south Pacific: Some principles, *Journal of Tourism Studies*, **2**(1), 56–71

Tilden, F. (1977) *Interpreting Our Heritage*, 3rd edn, University of North Carolina Press, Chapel Hill, p. 8

Uzzell, D. (1989) The hot interpretation of war and conflict. Chapter 4 in *Heritage Interpretation Vol. 1*, (ed. D. Uzzell), Belhaven Press, London, p. 46

Vallee, P. (1987) Authenticity as a factor in segmenting the Canadian travel market, Master's thesis, Department of Recreation and Leisure Studies, University of Waterloo. p. 27

Van den Berghe, P. (1993) Cultural impact of tourism. In *VNR's Encyclopedia of Hospitality and Tourism* (ed. M. Khan, M. Olsen and T. Var), Van Nostrand Reinhold, New York, pp. 619–628

25 The synergism between shopping and tourism

Myriam Jansen-Verbeke

Introduction

The growing importance of shopping as a tourist activity is clearly demonstrated by the boom of the retail trade, in its different forms, in tourism destination areas and all along the tourist trail.

One way of assessing the role of shopping in the tourist experience is to register tourists' time budgets and expenditures. Surveys on travel motivation will rarely refer to shopping as a prime motive or seldom as a key factor in the destination choice. This is contradictory to the results of surveys in which the actual time and money expenditure pattern has been questioned (Hsieh et al., 1992).

Although the practice of leisure shopping and travelling to shop has existed since Roman times, the economic benefits and the implications for the development of tourism destinations have long been under-estimated (McCabe, 1979, Kent et al., 1983). Ever since travellers were on their way, there have been retail traders who catered for these 'foreign' consumers and their special needs. The tradition of bringing presents back home for friends and relatives and to prolong the experience of a trip by buying souvenirs definitely contributes to the viability of the retail trade in many tourism destination areas and in places on the way to and fro.

The expanding scale of this economic activity is of course related to the development and spread of mass tourism. The responses of the retail trade to this growing market are omnipresent and dynamic, showing all the signs of a globalizing market.

The presence of a diversified retail offer can be considered as a strong asset in the development of an attractive tourism opportunity spectrum in destination areas, in some cases adding considerably to the liveliness and the perception of uniqueness of the place. There are several examples of places where shopping has even become a core element of the tourist attraction (Law, 1992; Page, 1995).

In order to study the interaction and the possible synergy between shopping and tourism, research activities should include shopping as a tourist activity. This is seen as the outcome of, on the one hand, the range of goods offered (the souvenirs, the products) and on the other the shopping context, in terms of environmental quality and integration in the tourist action space.

Some trends in this specific tourism market will be briefly commented upon. The main focus of this chapter is to reflect on the shopping context, with special reference to the spatial implications and the conditions for a strategic alliance between shopping and other tourist activities. How can urban centres manage their retail offer in order to develop and market a strong 'place/product'?

Results from surveys in the European historical cities illustrate this people/place approach and the need to understand the shopping behaviour pattern of urban tourists. The application of geographical information systems (GIS) in the spatial analysis proves to be a useful instrument in the strategic planning of the urban tourist opportunity spectrum (Jansen-Verbeke and Van de Wiel, 1995).

A conceptual framework

A high quality shopping experience is an essential condition to create synergism between shopping and tourism. It is necessary to distinguish the shopping experience of intentional shoppers with a mainly utilitarian function from that of the leisure or fun shopper with mainly a hedonic function. The utilitarian value of the shopping experience is particularly important for shoppers who know what they are looking for, who are mainly focused on the quality of particular goods they want to buy and on the efficiency in terms of time and money of their purchases. This experience is different from the shoppers who are mainly looking for some excitement, for some fun and bargaining, and enjoy the browsing around as a leisure activity. The aesthetics of the products and the environment lead to impulsive shopping behaviour. It is well know that impulsive shopping is very sensitive to the context.

The characteristics of the shopping experience can be studied in a series of variables (Figure 25.1). Two types of shopping experiences can be distinguished – the run shopping and the fun shopping – and tourists are assumed to rather engage in the last category. However a particular shopping experience can belong rather to the one or the other type, whereas other shopping experiences combine both the utilitarian and the hedonic value. In order to analyse the shopping patterns and experiences of tourists this analytical model can held to identify the importance of variations in people, products and place (Figure 25.2).

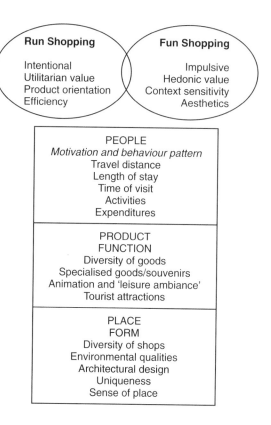

Figure 25.1   The shopping experience: analysis model

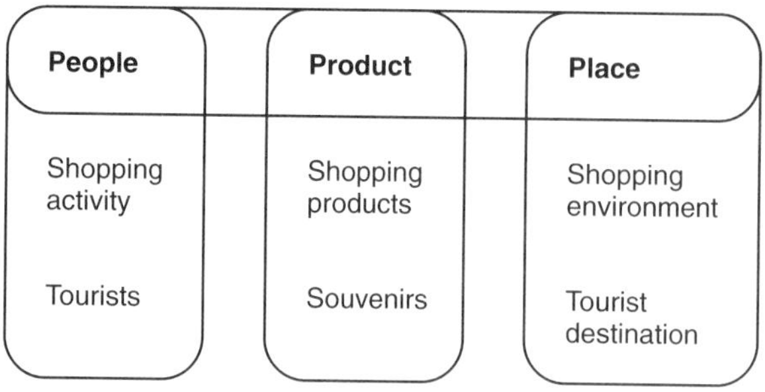

Figure 25.2   The shopping experience

So far little empirical research has been carried out to analyse the shopping experience of tourists, with exception of the souvenir shopping (Anderson and Littrell, 1995). The identification of differences in tourists' propensity to buy and the better understanding of the shopping experience can lead to most interesting recommendations for the souvenir industry as such and for the marketing of tourism destinations in general (Littrell, 1996). Despite this lack of knowledge of tourist behaviour and the role of the different shopping contexts, there are clear signs that the retail trade is responding to this 'new' market challenge.

Responses of the retail trade to new challenges

The opportunity to cater for the leisure shopper, the traveller wanting to buy souvenirs, has always been part of the tourist scene. Nevertheless the initially small-scale activities of local retail traders and artisan producers offering local products and handicrafts have rapidly changed from an informal sector into an international business operating in a global market and offering 'standard' souvenir products all over.

Obviously this trend of globalization in the tourism souvenir industry holds serious risks. The question to what extent the tourist is really interested in authentic products or rather in the authentic setting of the places where souvenirs can be acquired has become a key issue in tourist consumer research. The tourists' propensity to shop varies according to the cultural background of travellers and the range and nature of shopping opportunities in the destination area. The production and marketing of craft souvenirs is the global answer to this new tourism market, but also raises the question about authenticity and cultural convergence (Cohen, 1988; Littrell et al., 1993).

The current success of catering for the tourists becomes manifest in tourist shopping villages, urban shopping areas in tourism destinations and resorts, street markets, museum shops, heritage centres and not in the least in the development of the retail trade in attraction parks (Getz, 1993, Swarbrooke, 1995).

Shopping trips

Recently the tourism market is offering arrangements for international shopping trips in which the shopping opportunities are promoted as a core product. Examples are the offer of shopping trips to London or New York, the Norwegian cruises to visit and shop in York (UK), the special travel arrangement from Netherlands and Belgium, by coach or train, to visit the German Christmas markets.

The success of the traditional Christmas markets in German cities has inspired many other European cities. The lack of authenticity in the newly created events is not really seen as a constraint by the organizers and marketeers, to the extent that the experience of shopping on a Christmas market in the dark days of December has lost every aspect of its uniqueness ... eventually the imitation of the success formulas proves to be killing for the original tourist attraction.

Within the European travel market the highest growth rates are to be found in the market segments of city trips and short breaks. The competition between European cities in this market of city trips is not only based on cultural and heritage resources which are being developed into tourist products, but to a growing extent on festivals and events and the way the markers in the local tourist system are anchored in a range of tourist facilities, including the retail trade. The competitive advantage of tourism destinations appears to be more and more determined by the added value of the shopping experience and the efficiency of integrated marketing campaigns (Jansen-Verbeke, 1990, 1991).

The synergy between tourist activities and retail trade induces a process of 'touristification' of the retail sector (Cazes and Potier, 1996). Indicators of this process are not only the shift in the range of goods offered, but particularly the way a shopping area is being designed for casual behaviour, for leisurely browsing around. The emphasis is now on fun shopping and whatever could contribute to this leisure experience (Hopkins, 1990).

Intervening opportunities for shopping

In addition there are plenty of new opportunities to cater for the tourist shopper on his/her way to and fro. At different scales, regional or local, the trail of the tourist can be recognized through a spatial concentration, cluster wise or in a ribbon pattern, of shops catering for the tourist.

The restaurants along the French motorways which have introduced the concept of 'Relais Regional' are now places where a wide range of local products and souvenirs can be bought. The link with the regional or local context is reduced to a modest tourist information centre and some minor adaptations of the shopping precincts. As a rule the prices of goods and handicrafts are higher than in the local villages, but the concept is nevertheless a success. The strategy of offering intervening opportunities in the right place to the right target group, replaces the idea that 'couleur locale' or, a strong link with the regional context, is needed to stimulate tourist expenditures.

The development of this footloose tourist industry reflects a strategic response to locational advantages other than the traditional place/product association. In fact the location choice of these 'intervening opportunities' is based on an understanding of the spatial pattern of tourist flows.

The success of tax free shops in airports (such as London, Amsterdam, Frankfurt, Dubai, Hong Kong, Bangkok) is a good example of taking advantage of tourists on the move and their propensity to buy. Many airports, but also international ferry lines, have become very dependent on this source of income, and even in a situation where the tax free advantages are minimized (e.g. within the European Common Market) the shopping pattern as such persists. The deadline of 1999 for the end of inter-European tax free shopping is looked upon as a serious threat.

Cross-border shopping

Traditionally, the pattern of cross-border shopping has its appeal and generates important flows of consumers (Weigand, 1990; Dybka, 1986; Kendall and Kreck, 1992; Timothy and Butler, 1995). What was once seen as a consumer behaviour pattern mainly based on taking advantage of different goods' pricing, can no longer be fully explained by economic benefits, when taking into account the travel expenses. The added value of the cross border shopping experience is difficult to identify, for it is surely not directly related to the kind of goods on offer. The roots of leisure shopping, to the extent that they become an incentive for travelling beyond the daily action space, are now subject of a lively debate and a key issue in the planning of new shopping centres and shopping malls (Howard, 1993). Mega-shopping malls such as West Edmonton Mall, the Mall of America, Metro-Centre in Newcastle upon Tyne (UK), Meadow Hall in Sheffield (UK) and Centro Oberhausen in Germany, are becoming important generators of tourist flows and have a catchment capacity sometimes even beyond the domestic tourism market (Butler, 1991; Finn and Erdem, 1995).

Towards a tourist oriented retail market

This tourist orientation of the retail market affects the tourism market and the tourist experience in many different ways. The retail trade in tourism destination areas moves from an utilitarian function towards a hedonic function, marketing the thrill of the shopping experience rather than the value of the products. This move fits well into the changing demand pattern of tourists.

The tourism market, continuously searching for new products which can strengthen the local tourist opportunity spectrum and hence add value to the core tourist attractions, has grasped this opportunity for product differentiation which opens perspectives to cater for 'new' market segments.

In addition, this trend is reinforced by the present need to revitalize the retail sector in many cities. Upgrading of the inner city retail offer is hoped to bring a solution for the current process of decentralization (Guy, 1994; Wrigley and Lowe, 1996).

Many urban tourism development and marketing plans will therefore address the issue of shopping. Tourism retailing indeed opens new perspectives for many cities and tourism resorts, in particular for the small private enterprises (Pysarchik, 1989). The theming of festival markets, the upgrading of street markets, the redevelopment plans for heritage sites and urban waterfront areas to become pull factors for urban tourists, all proceed along very similar concepts of the product mix (Sawecki, 1989; Jansen-Verbeke and Van de Wiel, 1995). As a consequence, the threat of standardization in products and in environmental design have become very manifest.

In order to survive the convergence trend in this market there is the need to safeguard in every way the competitive advantages of 'uniqueness'. Emphasizing the cultural links with the host community and its traditions, conservation of the original architecture, understanding the appeal of vernacular architecture are assumed to be policies which contribute to the uniqueness and the sense of the place perception, which seem to be vital to the quality of the tourist experience.

This perception of uniqueness results from a combination of forms and function of the shopping area. The qualification of uniqueness depends both on the product mix and on the characteristics of the shopping environment. Therefore, the spatial and functional integration of tourist shopping facilities in the local tourism system is a critical issue in planning and marketing of tourism destinations.

The spatial framework of tourist shopping

Understanding the preferred combination of tourists' activities during their visit to a particular city or tourism resort is a key issue in the strategic planning and in developing an attractive spectrum of tourist facilities. So far the role of shopping as a tourist activity has tended to be underestimated, despite the fact that a considerable percentage of the time and money budget of tourists is spent on shopping. Recently more marketing-inspired views have led to new approaches in developing urban tourism potentials which take into account the wide range of activities tourists actually engage in (Pizam et al., 1997).

The process of developing a sustainable and profitable tourist product implies spatial planning and management based on an understanding of the tourist system in general and of the functional associations between the different product elements in particular. Spatial zoning of tourist attractions in combination with the relevant supporting amenities such as shopping, hotels and transport is considered to be the condition for synergism. The objective then is to identify the best fit spatial model to develop and promote shopping as part of the tourist programme. A better understanding of shopping as a tourist activity is required as a basis for marketing activities and strategic spatial planning. Shopping as an activity and, retail trade as an urban function are strongly interwoven both in the complexity of the urban system and in the tourist attraction system (Leiper, 1990). The urban tourist system can be seen as a wide spectrum of opportunities, which interact with each other through spatial connectivity and functional associations. Spatial clustering of the tourist product elements can create optimal conditions for interaction and synergism. The benefits of spatial clustering can be defined from the users' point of view, but also from the point of view of tourism business.

Both the spatial structure of the urban tourist product, including the shopping facilities, and tourist time-space behaviour are key issues in marketing and developing the urban tourist product.

The urban tourist opportunity spectrum (TOS)

At first, the determination of tourism clusters implies a spatial analysis of the dispersion pattern of the distinct tourist product elements; the core elements of the tourist product. These elements and characteristics of the urban scenery are assumed to be the main pull factors for urban tourists. The location pattern of the core tourist attractions is determining the locational advantages for secondary or supporting facilities. This range of facilities and amenities is in many cases not the main motive for a tourist visit. However, their attraction can play an important role in prolonging the stay and in generating repeat visits.

Analysing the spatial pattern of shops with a touristic potential in relation to the location of the core tourist attractions in a city is a most useful exercise, which allows identification of the tourist clusters and the logical tourist trails through the city. The connecting walking routes between the main clusters are particularly interesting locations for tourist oriented shops. The location map of tourist oriented shops can also be used to determine more exactly the tourist' zones in a city, assuming the retail trade is strategically responding to the actual spatial behaviour patterns of tourists in the destination place.

In the historical city of Bruges (Belgium), the location pattern of souvenir shops, in particular shops selling lace products (a traditional local handicraft), reflects the main tourist trails and as such the areas in which an intensification of tourist oriented retail trade is to be expected.

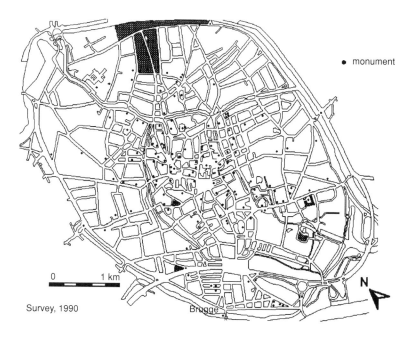

Figure 25.3   Bruges: historical centre

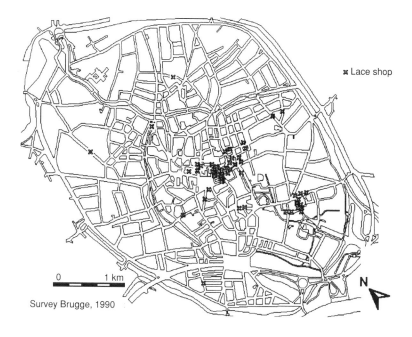

Figure 25.4   Bruges: historical centre

This spatial analysis of location patterns not only has a descriptive value, but can be seen as an instrument to manage the spatial dynamics of the process of touristification in a historical city. In order to create optimal conditions for a synergetic effect of tourism on the local retail trade, a detailed spatial analysis of the retail trade structure in the touristic historic city is required. This exercise was carried out in the city of Amsterdam (see Figures 25.3–25.4).

Tourist shopping in Amsterdam

The qualities of an inviting shopping environment for tourists are:

1   a wide variation on the supply side, with a flavour (or an illusion) of uniqueness,
2   a diversity in the types of shops, with the predominant image being that of high quality,
3   the spatial proximity of supporting amenities such as restaurants, pubs and entertainment facilities,
4   pedestrian areas, good accessibility and parking facilities,
5   multi-functionality of the environment which guarantees that the place feels 'alive'.

In fact the potentials to develop the image of an attractive shopping area which comes onto the tourist agenda largely depends on the quality and attractiveness of the environment, rather than on the range of goods offered.

A strategic issue is the way in which shopping facilities are linked with the major tourist attractions. It is assumed that the interaction between spatial patterns explains to a large extent the tourist action space. Spreading the visitor flows in time and in space is seen as a strategy to avoid overcrowding, for which an understanding of the actual spatial behaviour pattern is required. In addition this insight in spatial patterns can also be applied to promote particular places or streets in the city, or street segments with an interesting concentration of shops.

In combination with the time-space budget approach, the actual impact of tourism on the historical city becomes transparent. As a rule tourist action space is structured by the core elements of the tourist product which form the main motive for the tourist visit. Creating as many intervening opportunities as possible in the core area or along the access routes is a planning strategy which proves to be efficient in many ways. It is even possible to investigate the activity pattern of different visitor groups. This opens new perspectives on people/place combinations and the opportunity sets which fit in best. This approach also allows identification of the routes which the individual perceives as attractive.

The survey carried out in Amsterdam focused on the time-space and expenditure patterns of Japanese tourists in particular. Japanese tourists have a reputation of big spenders, which made this target group an interesting test case to study the interaction between tourism and shopping. The tourist action space is structured by the location of the hotels, the tax free shops and the major tourist attractions. Within this spatial framework the shopping behaviour of Japanese tourists was analysed.

A case study: Japanese tourists in Amsterdam

In order to understand the shopping behaviour of a specific group of tourists, some background information on the characteristics of this market segment is required. The selection of Japanese tourists was inspired by the fact that the Japanese travel market is in rapid expansion and, according to several forecasts, this growth will continue in the near future. Furthermore, Japanese tourists have the reputation for being big spenders, sophisticated consumers and enthusiastic but clever shoppers (Nozawa, 1992). For this reason a case study on the shopping of Japanese tourists can be an eye-opener in the strategic planning and marketing of tourist areas.

Characteristics of the Japanese outbound tourist market

Some characteristics of the Japanese tourist market are relevant to an understanding of the context of their shopping behaviour. In the first place there is a clear preference for travelling in a group and choosing package tours.

The most important characteristic of Japanese tourism is the degree of organization. Individual travel arrangements are rather exceptional. In general a complete programme which includes the places to visit, to eat, to shop and to entertain is offered. As a consequence, the behaviour pattern of these tourists during their stay in a particular destination is highly predictable.

Another relevant characteristic of the Japanese tourist is their preference for short stops; the average travel time for a 'Europe trip' is two weeks, the stay in one country (usually one city) being limited to about two nights. As a consequence the time-use is very intensive, leaving hardly any free time for non-scheduled activities.

'Shopping in Europe' seems to be an important selling slogan and often is a motive for the choice of a particular destination. Obviously Paris and London still are at the top of that list. Gradually the image of Europe as a travel destination has become more diversified and other cities come into focus as well.

As a rule the trip is well prepared in advance, to the extent that all information available is studied carefully and this includes a shopping guide. It is very customary to draw up a shopping list before departure. The question of where to buy which item of a particular brand name seems very important. This attitude leaves little or no opportunity for impulse shopping. There is a keen interest in so called 'ethnic' products such as fashion products and perfumes (e.g. in France), chinaware, crystal, jewellery, artwork, handicrafts, etc. In addition, the shopping list includes numerous gifts which are a 'must' to take back home. In social networking as well as in the Japanese economy in general, the tradition of exchanging gifts plays an important role (Moeran, 1983). This tradition is even accentuated in the case of travel, leading to a 'souvenir culture'. They are highly interested in brand names and high quality products which have been promoted through the Japanese media. Buying an 'authentic' brand product in the country of origin is 'the' thing to do. Obviously, this propensity for buying of Japanese tourists opens interesting perspectives for the retail trade in their tourism destinations.

Market segmentation

The outbound Japanese travel market includes three particular market segments: the younger market which covers the age group 20 to 29 (16.5 million people or about 13 per cent of the Japanese population). The desire to travel overseas is high and increasing. Twenty-eight per cent of them now travel abroad which accounts for about 32 per cent of the total number of Japanese travelling to Europe.

Some relevant sub-segments in this market are, first, the students who are developing the tradition of finishing their studies with a trip to Europe. The trend for choosing a group arrangement seems to be losing attraction and the number of individual travellers in this age group is growing. In terms of activity patterns, choice of accommodation and spending budget, they tend to differ from the average Japanese tourist in Europe.

A second sub-group are the 'office ladies', single career business women, usually in well paid jobs, still living with their parents and with a relatively high spending budget. They tend to travel in groups, are very much attracted to shopping, they develop a specific life style and fully enjoy the escape from routine when travelling to Europe.

A third market of interest is the group of honeymooners. Every year 750,000 marriages are registered and many couples have been saving to achieve their ambition of a honeymoon outside Japan.

Even more important than this younger market in terms of shopping expenditures, is the 'silver market'. As in most countries, the generation of 50 years and older has become an important market segment, also from the international perspective. There are 35.7 million Japanese in this age group (29 per cent of the total Japanese population). This percentage is increasing rapidly. The tradition of travelling outbound is relatively new but already accounting for 2.1 million overseas trips (25 per cent of the total of overseas trips). European destinations account for 210,000 trips per year, this being one quarter of the total number of overseas trips.

Taking into account the wide international networking of Japanese business, the number of business travellers is also very important. The age group between 30 and 49 is strongly represented and is predominantly male. In fact there is a tendency to combine business trips with more educational and cultural activities. Changing attitudes of the Japanese concerning the value of work and leisure are gradually affecting their attitude towards travel.

Tourist destinations

Within this market of outbound Japanese travel the prime destinations are the USA, Korea and Taiwan, but the attraction of other regions is becoming more important. A general characteristic is the relatively high spending budget of the average Japanese tourist (US$3,146 per trip). Taking into account the total volume of 10.6 million trips per year this is an enormous potential amount of which, however, an important share remains in Japanese hands (travel agencies, hotel chains, tour operators, Japanese run shops, etc.).

Nevertheless the European tourism market is hoping to benefit from this growing market. The problem is that Europe, as a selling point, does not exist, 'interesting destinations' being limited to a few traditional tourist sites or, as happens now, a combination of short visits to the most important European top league cities.

The increasing percentage of repeat visits might change this pattern in the near future and opens new perspectives for other interesting places. The Netherlands are not at the top of the list, although the number of Japanese visitors tends to increase. More than half of this group stay in Amsterdam. However there are recent signs of a declining interest in Amsterdam amongst Japanese visitors. This trend is seen as an indication that Amsterdam is still relatively well positioned with respect to the

Japanese tourist market but is losing its attraction in favour of other Dutch cities and locations.

Despite the recent changes, the Dutch Tourist Board anticipates an increase in Japanese tourists. Promotion campaigns are especially targeted on increasing the length of stay. In most cases, Japanese visitors to the Netherlands prefer a group arrangement guided by a Japanese tourist guide. The current image of the Netherlands is still limited to traditional items such as flowers, clogs, windmills and its historical heritage. Changing the image of a country as a tourist destination is a long term objective and is a major challenge.

Profile of the Japanese Tourist in Amsterdam

The profile of the Japanese tourist in Amsterdam can be drawn up from the following characteristics: age, travel motive, length of stay and organization of the trip. It was assumed that each of these characteristics is relevant in explaining the activity patterns and the actual shopping behaviour. In terms of travel motives a clear distinction can be made between visitors with mainly leisure motives and those with mainly business motives. It was assumed that the travel motive would be reflected in the length of stay. In fact business visits were the shortest (with 61 per cent staying only one night), tourist visits usually includes two nights and visits to friends and relatives tend to be somewhat longer (with 26 per cent staying three or more nights). The city is often used as a basis for excursions to other places of interest in the country. Furthermore there is a significant relationship with the organizational characteristics of the trip.

Apparently, the impact of Japanese tour operators on the organization of the trip is very strong. The percentage of individual arrangements is said to be increasing but, right now, it only accounts for one fifth of the visits, which are mostly to relatives or friends. This pattern may be different in the case of a repeat visit. These organizational characteristics are affecting the shopping behaviour as well, as was shown in the survey.

The most interesting issue lies in understanding why a particular combination of activities occurs and why, as a consequence, particular product elements seem to be less in focus of this specific target group. In the case of Japanese tourists in Amsterdam, a selection takes place in the number and type of tourist attractions which they visit. Within the limited time spent in this city, the programme tends mainly to include the traditional core elements of the urban tourist product. The number one tourist attraction is a sightseeing tour on the canals which offers a general impression of the historical heritage of the city. In the second place, visits to the Van Gogh and Rembrandt Museum are part of the traditional pattern. In fact, there is no significant difference according to gender – the difference in behaviour pattern according to the age groups seems to be more relevant.

The older group of Japanese tourists clearly sticks to the top tourist attractions, whereas especially the younger tourists (under the age of 30) tend to engage in a more varied pattern of sightseeing including smaller and special interest museums, street markets, etc. This fits within the earlier statement that younger tourists are less inclined to join organized parties.

Variation in the sightseeing pattern is closely related to the length of stay. From the results of the survey it can be concluded that shopping, as a time use, increases considerably amongst those tourists who stay longer than two nights. On average there is little variation in the sightseeing pattern of Japanese tourists and this is clearly the result of a prearranged and programmed tour. In this context there is little time left for non-planned or impulse activities such as shopping or window-shopping.

Tourism marketeers in Amsterdam are facing the challenge of marketing the shopping facilities to these special interest groups. For non-European visitors the system of tax free shopping offers special additional advantages. The total expenditure in tax free shops in Amsterdam accounts for an income of US$9 million in 1991, of which 7 per cent is brought in by Japanese customers. The largest investment comes from US visitors (15.5 per cent). There are clear indications of a growing interest in tax free shopping. The most important branches are gift shops, closely followed by chinaware. The latter includes the Dutch favourite brand product 'Delfts Blue'.

The attraction of tax free shopping for Japanese tourists seems far less important for ladies fashion, department stores and jewellery. Obviously Amsterdam does not hold a leading position for these articles. Preferred shopping items for the Japanese tourists in the Netherlands are souvenirs, chinaware, food, flower seeds or bulbs, diamonds and jewellery.

There are clear differences according to sex, age and travel motives in the type of items bought. Men – especially older men – tend to be better customers for diamonds and jewellery, whilst women are the most important spenders on souvenirs. Younger people spend relatively more on food products. As could be predicted, the longer the stay the higher the propensity to buy goods. During the short stay the emphasis lies on souvenirs, during a longer stay other articles such as flower seeds and bulbs, diamonds and jewellery and chinaware catch the attention. Amongst tourists who stay longer, the expenditure on food increases considerably.

The survey was used to identify in more detail the attitude of the Japanese tourist in Amsterdam concerning shopping opportunities, interesting aspects of shopping, the drawbacks concerning shopping in particular and concerning Amsterdam as a destination in general. The overall quality of shopping facilities in Amsterdam was estimated to be fairly good according to 73 per cent of the Japanese respondents. On average, the most positive attitude was expressed concerning the low prices, the friendly service, the use of English being fairly general (especially appreciated by female tourists), the spatial concentration of shops and the many exchange offices (especially appreciated by male visitors and business tourists).

Amongst the more negative respondents the percentage of female tourists was significantly higher. In addition negative reactions tended to be stronger amongst tourists staying longer and amongst the older tourists. The main weakness of shopping in Amsterdam from the tourists' point of view was the strict regulation of opening times. In addition, the absence of a major shopping mall, the untidiness of public space, a certain feeling of insecurity and, to some extent, the language barrier, were the most frequently mentioned weak points.

In view of strengthening the synergism between shopping and tourism some clear indications became obvious and were related both to the quality and diversity of shops and to the quality of the public environment. The role of tax free shopping in the tourist attraction of Amsterdam is still far under its potential. Only 44 per cent of Japanese tourists use this facility.

For most Japanese tourists, the lack of time to do window-shopping and to discover shopping facilities at leisure is the most relevant explanation. According to Moeran (1983) the Japanese tourist has a special interest in high quality products and brand name products, which apparently are not easily to be found in Amsterdam. In order to improve the attraction as a tourist destination for the Japanese more specific information concerning tax free shopping should be included in the general promotion material.

Conclusions on the spatial context of tourist shopping

Actually, the strength of the interrelationship between shopping and other tourist activities depends on several preconditions. The analysis of time-space use of tourists was be seen as an effective instrument in understanding and explaining the behaviour patterns. As a rule, the action space of tourists is structured around a set of fixed components, being the location of the hotel, the location of the major tourist attractions and the location of the intervening opportunities such as shops.

Japanese tourists have a distinct preference for specific hotels, mostly those in the top categories. These are concentrated in four distinct clusters in Amsterdam. The location pattern of hotels in Amsterdam which particularly attract the Japanese tourists is important in analysing of the action space of this target group. The distance and the pedestrian route between the hotel and the tourist attractions are effective predictors for the use of intervening shopping opportunities.

In fact, the present situation in Amsterdam allows for a close locational interaction between hotels, tourist attractions and clusters of shops, including tax free shops. The spatial proximity and the limited walking distances between the elements of the tourist product offer opportunities for a synergetic interaction. The conclusion is that, in terms of spatial clustering, the situation in Amsterdam can be considered as being favourable to supporting the combination of sightseeing and shopping. This statement is based on the outcome of a detailed spatial analysis and the interpretation of individual time-space budgets of Japanese tourists.

The method of mapping individual time-space patterns is rather complex but, in the case of Japanese tourists to Amsterdam, its complexity could be reduced to some prototypes. The fact that Japanese tourists in Amsterdam are only using the shopping facilities to a limited extent is directly related to the organizational characteristics of their travel programme on the one hand and, on the other hand, to the poor image of Amsterdam as a shopping place.

The results of this survey indicate the advantages of interlinking the time-space budgets of tourists and the way these respond to the spatial structure of the urban tourist opportunity spectrum. In fact the shopping activity of tourists is highly dependent on the location pattern of shops in relation to the main tourist attractions on the one hand and the location of hotels on the other. However an optimal synergism between shopping and other tourist activities can also be restricted by organizational practices or by a lack of targeted promotion.

Strategies aiming at a synergism between shopping and tourism need to be based on a profile study of the specific target groups. For instance, Japanese tourists clearly behave differently from other target groups and, even within this market segment, there is a clear distinction according to age, travel motive, length of stay and, above all, travel organization. The propensity of Japanese tourists for buying souvenirs, gifts and 'ethnic products' implies a specific marketing strategy.

The results of this survey demonstrate the predominant role of Japanese tour operators in the programme organization. This implies that promotion and especially the promotion of shopping and tax free shopping as additional tourism resources should be targeted at the intermediate level of organizations in Japan rather than at the level of the individual tourist. This conclusion is relevant for the specific target group in the Japanese tourist market, the programmed group traveller, which at this time includes the majority of the Japanese tourists. However, the trend towards more individual travelling, especially amongst younger people holds new challenges for the future.

Information about the shopping facilities in a tourist destination area and the promotion of its image as an attractive place to visit and to shop might be an effective marketing instrument. The creation of intervening shopping opportunities along the predictable sightseeing routes, taking into account the actual time space budgets of specific target groups, is far more sophisticated and probably the most effective planning instrument.

In many ways the study of shopping in the context of tourism is still at an exploratory stage. All the arguments to see the shopping experience as an important tourism asset are there. The interdisciplinary nature of the study object 'people–product–place' should no longer be a handicap, but rather an incentive for future research in this most intriguing aspect of tourism.

References

Anderson, L.F. and Littrell, M.A. (1995) Souvenir Purchase Behaviour of Women Tourists, *Annals of Tourism Research*, **22**, 328–348

Butler, R.W. (1991) West Edmonton Mall as a Tourist Attraction, *Canadian Geographer*, **35**(3), 287–295

Cazes, G. and Potier, F. (1996) *Le tourisme urbain*, Presses Universitaires de France, Paris

Cohen, E. (1988) Authenticity and Commoditization in Tourism, *Annals of Tourism Research*, **15**(3), 371–386

Dybka, J. (1986) Attracting US Tourists to Canada, *Tourism Management*, **7**(3), 202–204

Finn, A. and Erdem, T. (1995) The economic impact of a mega multi-mall. Estimation issues in the case of West Edmonton Mall, *Tourism Management*, **16**(5), 367–373

Getz, D. (1993) Tourist Shopping Villages. Development and Planning Strategies, *Tourism Management*, February, 15–26

Guy, C. (1994) Whatever happened to Regional Shopping Centres? *Geography*, **79** (4), 293–312

Hopkins, J.S.P. (1990) West Edmonton Mall: Landscape of Myths and Elsewhereness, *The Canadian Geographer*, **34**, 2–17

Howard, E.B. (1993) Assessing the impact of shopping centre development: the Meadow Hall case, *Journal of Property Research*, **10**, 97–119

Hsieh, S., O'Leary, J. and Morrison, A. (1992) Segmenting the International Travel Market by Activity, *Tourism Management*, **13**(2), 209–223

Jansen-Verbeke, M. (1990) Leisure + Shopping = Tourism Product Mix. In *Marketing Tourism Places* (ed. Ashworth G. and Goodall, B.), Routledge, London, pp. 128–135

Jansen-Verbeke, M. (1991) Leisure Shopping a Magic Concept for the Tourism Industry? *Tourism Management*, **12**(1), 9–14

Jansen-Verbeke, M. and Van de Wiel, E. (1995) Tourism Planning in Urban Revitalization Projects. In *Tourism and Spatial Transformations* (ed. Ashworth, G.J. and Dietvorst, A.J.), CAB International, Wallingford, Chapter 8, pp. 129–145

Kendall, K.W. and Kreck, L.A. (1992) The Effect of the Across-the-Border Travel of Canadian Tourists, *Journal of Travel Research*, **30**(4), 53–58

Kent, W., Shock, P. and Snow, R. (1983) Shopping: Tourism's Unsung Hero(ine), *Journal of Travel Research*, Spring, 2–4

Law, Ch. (1992) Urban Tourism and its Contribution to Economic Regeneration, *Urban Studies*, **29**(3/4), 599–618

Leiper, N. (1990) Tourist Attraction Systems, *Annals of Tourism Research*, **17**, 367–384

Littrell, M.A., Anderson, L.F. and Brown, P.J. (1993) What makes a craft souvenir authentic? *Annals of Tourism Research*, **20**, 197–215

Littrell, M.A. (1996) Shopping experiences and marketing of culture to tourists. In *Tourism and Culture: Image, Identity and Marketing* (ed. Robinson, M et al.), Center for Travel and Tourism/Business Education Publishers, Sunderland UK, pp. 107–102

McCabe, R.W. (1979) Shops and shopping in Ancient Rome, *Plan Canada*, **19/3**, 183–199

Moeran, B. (1983) The Language of Japanese Tourism, *Annals of Tourism Research*, **10**, 93–109

Nozawa, H. (1992) A Marketing Analysis of Japanese Outbound Travel, *Tourism Management*, **13**(2), 226–233

Page, S. (1995) *Urban Tourism*, Routledge, London

Pizam, A., Jansen-Verbeke, M. and Steel, L. (1997) Are all tourists alike, regardless of nationality? *Journal of International Hospitality, Leisure and Tourism Management*, **1**(1), 19–39

Pysarchik, D.T. (1989) Tourism Retailing. In *Tourism Marketing and Management Handbook* (ed. Witt, S. and Moutinho, L.), Prentice-Hall, London, pp. 553–556

Swarbrooke, J, (1995) *The Development and Management of Visitor Attractions*, Butterworth-Heinemann, Oxford

Timothy, D.J. and Butler, R.W. (1995) Cross Border Shopping: A North American Perspective, *Annals of Tourism Research*, **22**, 16–34

Weigand, K. (1990) Drei Jahrzehnte Einkauftourismus über die Deutsch-Dänische Grenze. Geographische Rundschau, May, 286–290

Wrigley, N. and Lowe, M. (eds) (1996) *Retailing, Consumption and Capital. Towards the New Retail Geography*, Longman, Harlow

26 Globalization and emerging tourism education issues

Frank M. Go

Introduction

This chapter explores a critical issue and is meant as a departure point for idea exchange, debate, and future development. Its central argument is that tourism education requires a fundamental re-orientation and re-shaping, because today's interdependent economy necessitates, increasingly, that all of us be better, and more broadly educated, more skilled, more adaptable. The challenge is to find an educational model that can provide a better understanding of the interdependent nature of our world and help shape the organizational capability to simultaneously compete and cooperate in a global environment.

The emerging global society is characterized by crisis, cultural convergence, and conflict. It affects how people think about tourism, the assumptions they make about what constitutes success with consumers, host communities, and host corporations, and how they translate this into action. Such considerations of the effects of the global economy on society alone implies that we must change the ways we teach, train, and learn.

The competitiveness of industry is an important issue, because globalization has raised the overall standards of performance, in terms of quality, productivity, and profitability. The introduction of global standards can be deeply threatening, but tourism educators have little choice but to open their minds to what shall be referred to in this chapter as 'global education', and re-structure the curriculum to meet the needs of tourism, which is impacted by the global shift, from a resource-based, and labour-intensive economy to one that is knowledge-intensive and global in orientation or a 'global industry' as referred to in this chapter. In this context, a focus on specific issues, and the responses from educators to the issues that arise, should start from a basic premise: understanding global industry strategy is fundamental to the development and delivery of global education programmes. Toward this end the present chapter has three major objectives:

1 to assess the implications of the global issues on the tourism industry, on the provision of education and training for the field;
2 to determine whether tourism education provision is meeting the global industry needs;
3 to explore future opportunities for 'global education for a global industry' programme planning and delivery.

This chapter builds on the author's earlier work (Go, 1994) and views global education from a management perspective, due to the author's background, teaching and research interests. It refers to education as the intellectual development of a person through, for example, literacy, foreign languages, computational skills, knowledge of countries and cultures without particular concern for specific jobs or responsibilities; and training as the process of bringing a person to an agreed standard of skills proficiency through instruction. At the same time, it recognizes that graduates require both an adequate education and training to meet the demands of a rapidly changing workplace in a global society.

The evolution of tourism education

What abilities and concepts should a programme of tourism education impart? Educators have to be able to answer that perennial question in new ways as shifting travel markets and world-class competition require destination organizations and tourism businesses to change. The adaptation to change requires more flexible decision-making and the search for solutions beyond conventional wisdom.

In short, educators should reflect on the question whether the present framework they have developed will ensure the successful provision of graduates for a global tourism industry in the 1990s and into the third millennium.

Review and preview

The scanning of issues is an exercise that requires a forward orientation. But beside a focus on the future, it is useful to look back to gain a perspective on the evolution of tourism education. Historically, tourism thinking has gone through two phases and has recently entered into a third (D'Amore, 1985). In contemporary times tourism research has been conducted by scholars such as Hunziker and Krapf from Switzerland in the 1940s. Among Swiss social scientists there seemed to have been an awareness of the need to extend the tourism research horizon (Kaspar, 1994).

Among the early British writers on tourism were Ogilvie, Norval and Lickorish and Kershaw. But it took until the 1970s before Anglo-American academics began to map the uncharted waters of tourism studies in earnest. For instance, Medlik and Burkart, who were affiliated with the University of Surrey, took the lead in Britain while Clare Gunn of Texas A&M University and Robert McIntosh of Michigan State University were among the early pioneers of tourism education in the United States of America.

Like the great explorers of centuries gone by, the early tourism educators had to cope with significant challenges, largely because: (1) 'in nearly all cases [programmes were] developed as a result of academic enterprise rather than industrial demand', and (2) 'certain segments of the tourism industry seemed to accept specific academic qualifications' (Christie-Mill, 1978: 58). These findings, which are based on an analysis of Lawson's comparative study *Teaching Tourism: Education and Training in Western Europe* (1974), serve as an important reminder that tourism education in the 1970s and 1980s was primarily educator-driven. Furthermore, Lawson's comparative analysis of newly introduced tourism courses in Western Europe paid considerable attention to the ongoing concern expressed by tourism educators for highly pragmatic matters, particularly the career placement of students and tourism career path development.

The second phase of tourism education began in the early 1980s when a review of the state-of-the-art of the rapidly expanding field of tourism education co-edited by Jafari and Ritchie (1981) shifted the focus of tourism education from the pragmatic to the academic level. By expanding the scope of tourism education, Jafari and Ritchie set the stage for further enquiry into the field of tourism education and, increasingly, research. With their review Jafari and Ritchie attempted in particular to reach the following objectives:

- To place tourism in a broader context and identify major concerns prior to defining tourism education and curriculum content.
- To examine alternative disciplinary approaches to the study of tourism.
- To focus on a number of critical issues in tourism education.

Among the key observations Jafari and Ritchie (1981) made regarding the gaps in tourism research which they perceived to be both weaknesses and opportunities were:

- The lack of empirical research on which to base the design of tourism curricula.

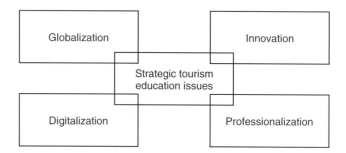

Figure 26.1   Strategic tourism education framework

- The conceptualization and design of tourism courses and programmes by individual educators in relative isolation as opposed to groups of educators representing various educational institutions.
- The highly vocational nature of the manuscripts submitted for publication (Jafari and Ritchie, 1981) received from North American sources, compared to other geographical regions such as Europe where tourism 'is being conceptualized in much broader terms'.
- The emergence of tourism as an interdisciplinary field of studies.

The emerging emphasis on tourism research in the 1980s was particularly appropriate in that it was a decade of significant change, especially in terms of technological advancement and industrial restructuring.

In the early 1990s we reached a new watershed in the evolution of tourism education. It has been brought about by the changes in both exogenous variables and those endogenous to the profession. Current geo-political events in combination with advancing technology and altering demographics are producing a period of discontinuous change (Handy, 1989).

Though there is uncertainty as to what the implications may be for the development of human resources within organizations, in general it seems certain that the changes that are taking place will radically affect the workplace and therefore tourism education.

Changing vistas

To help understand the present issues and possible future directions regarding 'global education for a global industry', this chapter first examines tourism in relation to four driving forces: globalization, innovation, digitalization, and professionalization, and their influences on tourism and the provision of education (Figure 26.1). Next, it assesses whether tourism curricula are presently meeting the challenges of the changing environment and specifically the needs of the global industry. The chapter concludes with a set of guidelines for planning and delivering 'global education for a global industry'.

Tourism

Tourism may be defined, holistically, as a dynamic domain involving the temporary migration of individuals and groups for pleasure and/or business purposes, the catering to the needs of travellers while en route and at the destination, and the economic, socio-cultural and ecological impacts both travellers and the industry have on the destination area. This definition implies that tourism should be viewed as (a) a system comprised of attractions, transportation and promotion/information (Gunn, 1988); (b) a social act in that it allows people to express themselves while travelling for business and leisure; and (c) a reflection of local cultural identity and social composition. In this regard, tourism can play a significant role in the environmental planning and concern for environmental quality (Ashworth, 1991).

Tourism has a central, but popularly unrecognized, importance in the rapidly expanding services sector. It is made up of many different types of operations, that are engaged in diverse activities ranging from trip planning, transportation, entertainment, and feeding to lodging the traveller. These operations render a broad range of services to consumers who are temporarily away from their usual habitat, by facilitating personal or group experiences resulting in a bundle of benefits, including security, physical and psychological comfort, for reward, or on a non-profit basis.

In addition, tourism is an integral part of society in that it provides employment and career opportunities to millions of people. It is widely assumed that the educational providers, referred to in this chapter as 'global education', prepare people for such careers and employment in the industry.

Tourism has a labour-intensive nature and its sub-sectors face a set of common human resource problems (Table 26.1). It holds special potential for the creation of employment. In 1994, the travel and tourism industry employed 204 million people world wide (including 19 million in Europe and 14 million in North America), 10.6 per cent of total employment, or 1 in every 9 jobs. It is anticipated that the field shall create an additional 144 million jobs by 2005 for a total of 348 million workers, or 11.3 per cent of the global workforce (WTTC, 1992).

Traditionally, tourism-related services have been classified as convenience services, as opposed to knowledge services (Tettero and Viehoff,

Table 26.1   Human resource problems facing tourism

While the industry is made up of many different types of operations from accommodation (hotels, motels), transportation (airlines, railways, car rentals, shipping lines), and amusement parks, to travel trade (retail travel agents and tour operators), there are a number of human resource problems that are common to all parts of the industry and need to be reconciled to achieve the quality required to compete effectively in a global market.

Image
Many people associate the travel industry with stressful working conditions, long and unsociable work schedules, few benefits and a temporary way to earn some quick money.

Recruitment
The travel industry faces major problems in recruiting sufficient qualified numbers of workers to meet its human resources needs. The lack of well-defined career paths exacerbates the problem of attracting well-educated and trained people.

Training
Many people working in the travel industry have received little or no related training beyond simple instructions on their specific tasks. This problem is aggravated in that most training and education recognized by the government is 'ill-adapted' to the needs of the travel industry.

Retention
High staff turnover is a chronic problem. The cost of turnover has been estimated by some employers to be as high as $2,500 per person, depending on the type of position.

Management
The travel industry is a labour-intensive, highly entrepreneurial business dominated by small operations. Existing management and supervisory skills are less well-developed in comparison to other industries and contribute to the aforementioned problems.

1990). But as organizations prepare for the global economy and resources are being shifted out of low-wage activities where advanced technology, knowledge and service provide a competitive edge, the continued prosperity of tourism will depend largely on well-educated human talent – people who are able to think, weigh and judge critical issues in addition to providing quality service issues in addition to providing quality service know-how on the strategic and operational level respectively (Gronroos, 1989).

The present shift from a resource-based and labour-intensive economy to one that is knowledge-intensive, represents a fundamental change and rigorously challenges the present acting and thinking in the tourism field.

Globalization

Tourism organizations, including commercial, public sector, and non-profit outlets, operate virtually in all countries and communities. In that sense, tourism could be referred to as a 'global industry'. However, there are other reasons for the use of the adjective 'globalization' in the title of this chapter.

First, although most world tourism is domestic in nature, the rising importance of international trade increasingly affects national tourism. Specifically, domestic travel industry professionals have to compete with foreign firms who have penetrated their 'home turf' or risk surrendering a share of their domestic market. The 'injection' of foreign direct investments, for example by Asian multinationals, has changed the industry's game rules because Asian corporations behave differently – planning strategically on a more long term basis – than Western corporations.

Second, the 'global village' is no longer prophetic metaphor. Rather than the single homogeneous market globalization seemed to promise, in which cultural differences fade away, diversity of demand is alive and well. This implies that organizations have to learn how to enter local markets not as a foreign intruder, but with a profound understanding of the nuances of traditions, culture and languages.

Third, global competitiveness pressures companies to stay ahead of their rivals (or at least keep up with them). It requires tourism businesses to learn through benchmarking, knowledge and skills transfer across the organization to deliver travel products at the best price/performance trade-off. Conceiving of the tourism organization within this framework as a portfolio of core competencies and value-adding skills implies that 'inter-firm competition, as opposed to inter-product competition, is essentially concerned with the acquisition of skills' (Hamel, 1991).

Lastly, there is a set of global industries, including financial services, banking and telecommunications, that are affecting the operation and control of specific sectors in the domestic tourism system. As the 'domestic'/'global' distinction blurs, managers require a new orientation, new knowledge, new thinking, new skills and new methods to operate their organizations. Importantly, their success will be judged by global standards of competition and competitiveness.

Therefore, tourism can no longer be considered solely within a domestic context, since the 'production' and consumption of tourism services presently take place in a 'global industry'. In the 1990s, global issues are impacting all industries, but not to the same extent. They will have less negative consequences on industries that have effective and advanced approaches to continuous improvement and building organizational capability. The latter may be defined as managing internal organizational processes and systems to meet consumer needs and ensure that staff skills are directed towards achieving organizational goals (Ulrich and Lake, 1990: 2). Because industries that, presently, manage their organizational capability more effectively than the tourism industry are perceived to offer better working conditions, they are likely to be more attractive to employees.

Due to the high degree of human involvement in the service process, the present shortage of competent labour has major implications for the global industry:

- It places the global industry in a position where it must compete with many other industries to become the 'preferred employer'.
- It poses a significant threat to sustainability, in that the lack of sufficiently trained personnel and competent managers drastically impedes the ability of the global industry to compete and collaborate.
- It points to the significant role of education and training providers to help ensure the survival and prosperity of the global industry.

Recently, global competition has caused the tourism industry to re-engineer in response to significant challenges in last and current decade. Markets are now worldwide, technology has collapsed innovation cycle times, performance criteria include social and environmental principles, costs have increased. The global industry has begun to place greater emphasis on performance improvement through its service operations, as opposed to its staff functions. Consequently, it has 'downsized' the number of staff and eliminated a significant number of middle management staff. For purposes of cost-savings it shall require more 'generalists' as opposed to 'specialists', in the future.

The focus of professional and academic conferences recently has been on globalization and tourism, in an attempt to gain insights into the major issues. For example, the Tourism Policy Forum initiated and held at the George Washington University in fall 1990 examined the furthering of the relationships between government and business at the international level; Smith (1990) reported on 'Going Global' the PATA conference held in 1990 in Vancouver; and the Congress of the Association of Scientific Experts, held in Rotorua, New Zealand, in September 1996, focused on globalization and tourism.

There has been a rising awareness of the significance of 'globality' as also reflected in a growing number of publications on the same topic (Theobald, 1994; Go and Pine, 1995; WTO, 1996). However, Burnett et al. (1991: 49) suggest that the production of material by predominantly Anglo-American academics, at present, might possibly result in 'excessively narrow self-interested regional focus in an innately international area of scholarship'.

Digitalization

The advancement of 'digitalization', especially the application of new information and decision technologies, has changed the nature of competition in all industries. Information and knowledge rule every field of endeavour. As a result of new information technologies, work is becoming increasingly detached from place, operations from their central headquarters. Telecommunication networks, spanning the globe with bursts of data speeding thousands of kilometres, mean the break-up of old geographic habits and locations. Bell (1988) observes 'a change of extraordinary historical and sociological importance – the change in the nature of markets from places to networks'. The perspective of tourism as a 'vast, complex network of businesses engaged in lodging, transportation, feeding and entertainment of the traveller' (EIESP, 1991) and the opportunities it offers to gain competitive advantage through social innovation will require tourism students and industry practitioners to extend their horizons well beyond the traditional trade channels of distribution.

Innovation

Following Schumpeter (1965), the term 'innovation' is used in a broad context, to encompass new combinations of goods/services, methods of production, markets, sources of raw materials and organizations. Innovation in tourism has been largely limited to 'product innovation'. Tourism organizations launch new products to cope with the market and create new growth vehicles. As the cost of developing and commercializing new facilities and products and delivering tourism services of assured quality are rising, 'process innovation' concerned with the improvement of quality, increasing through output, lowering costs, and enhancing delivery capability and flexibility, will become increasingly important in tourism. Gamble (1991: 18) notes that innovation is not only dependent on information but also on organizational structure, administrative capabilities and the choices made by managers based on their perceptions of the situation, and significantly, Poon (1988) observed that innovation appears not to depend on the cultural background of tourism managers.

Professionalization

It is widely assumed that the development of various levels of education and training in tourism, ranging from the highly vocational courses through to higher research degrees, responds to the professional needs of the field. However, the distinct lack of professionalism in the tourism industry remains an issue (Hawkins and Hunt, 1988; Gee, 1980), despite efforts to enhance the status of the field (WTO, 1983). For example, a comparative international study by the UK's National Economic Development Office (NEDO) identified a growing 'concern about the breadth and capability of the management skills base in the tourism industry and associated recruitment and retention problems' (Parsons, 1991).

Given that professions depend on the advancement of skills, which accrue from lengthy training to acquire relevant information which has been organized into an internally consistent system, called a body of knowledge (Volmer and Mills, 1966: 9–19), it follows that such body of knowledge and required skills should be charted along well-defined 'career paths'. Christie-Mill (1978) identified the imperative for the development of such travel and tourism career paths almost two decades ago. But a Pan-European study (EIESP, 1991), and a recent study on Tourism Education Quality, carried out for WTO (1996: 18) by the George Washington University in the United States amongst 'public and private sector employers representing 12 sub-sectors of the tourism and hospitality industry in the six WTO regions of the world', both offer evidence that career paths in the tourism industry and what constitutes appropriate tourism education and training are still ill-defined.

What are some of the major reasons for the lack of professionalization in tourism?

- Most of the medium and small enterprises that make up the bulk of the industry lack the resources for professional upgrading and training and sufficient scope to attract bright graduates.
- The industry has been reluctant to invest time and money in the development of staff, who may take their skills to a new job with a competitor who pays higher wages.
- Another constraint on tourism to effect change is its diversity. Each sub-sector and level (management, supervisory, frontline and back office) has its own specific labour needs, and constantly changing employment needs due to altering customer expectations and structural industry changes.
- A national government incentive system to persuade travel industry employers to improve the degree of professionalism amongst tourism employees and managers is missing in most countries.

Why should governments, in cooperation with industry, enhance professionalization through education and training programmes?

First, governments have a mandate to create the appropriate environment for the generation of employment. Through the generation of employment, receipts and taxation, tourism contributes, in many instances, significantly, to economic development. The labour intensive nature of tourism makes it an excellent sector for employment creation. This is especially noteworthy during an era when economies in most developed countries are sluggish and suffer from high unemployment.

Second, society is, presently, in the midst of an incomplete transition from a resource-based and labour intensive economy to one that is knowledge intensive. It almost goes without saying that the global industry requires a new type of professional. This professional should be 'flexible', able to adapt to change, and simultaneously compete and collaborate within 'networks', and possess information technology skills on all levels of organization. Workers will require assistance to make the required transition.

Third, tourism is still a largely unrecognized industry, partly, because its economic importance is difficult to measure (and therefore frequently underestimated), it is a significant challenge to enhance the profile of tourism as an institution of society and to give it an appropriate and professional identity. Whilst a small cadre of leaders in certain jurisdictions have been able to enhance the professionalism in selected sectors in the field, the overall picture of the global industry shows a lack of significant support for professionalization efforts. In a constantly changing environment, however, global education and global industry have little choice but to raise the level of professionalism. If they fail, the field may run the risk of decline.

At the crossroads

It is the mandate of educators to serve, particularly to conduct research, to teach students new ideas and to be visionaries of the tourism phenomenon. Are tourism educators making a genuine contribution by drawing the attention of their students and tourism industry practitioners away from tools and techniques and towards discussion, debate and reflection on the critical issues? Or do they emphasize the same techniques and tools today as fifteen years ago? Are students sufficiently challenged to broaden their horizons? Or do they get a rather ethnocentric education which will be of little use in the 'global village' wherein their career will unfold?

Perhaps tourism educators have come to a crossroads. They can choose to continue the path along which they have come and teach what they have taught in the past or they can explore the second path leading them into a new direction.

Framework for planning and delivering global education for a global industry

Against the backdrop of a 'changing landscape', including industrial restructuring, a worldwide information explosion, shifts in industrialized countries toward a service orientation, growing international debts and

Table 26.2 The contrasting requirements of science and business

	Science	Business
Need	Fundamental research	Applied research
Truth	Generally applicable	Place and time related
Term	Medium to long	Short
Principle	Maximization	Optimization
Goal	Expand body of knowledge	Increase profitability
Research	Theory-based	Practice-based

Source: Doorn van, Joseph, 1996. Remarks made at the Entrepreneurship in Tourism Symposium, 26 January, 1996.

defaults, and increasing competition, 'global tourism education for a global industry' is an idea whose time has come, because:

- Both practitioners and students must be able to understand the world's major ideologies, learn to become sensitive to cross-cultural differences and enhance their conciliatory and communicative skills to be effective tourism marketers.
- Businesses are developing international outlets and operating in global networks. Therefore educational providers should offer training and further education opportunities which correspond to the requirements of the global industry, as opposed to confining themselves to the domestic market (see Table 26.2).
- The harmonization of qualifications across the European Union shall, before long, become a reality. In North America associations such as the Council for Hotel, Restaurant and Institutional Education (CHRIE) are working towards greater standardization of curricula.

In summary, a 'global education for a global industry' is no longer simply an option; it has become a necessity. Educational providers and industry practitioners who fail to make the transition from a national perspective to a global perspective may face a bleak future of marginalization.

Given this dilemma, how can tourism educators respond to their mandate? By making two assumptions as the basis for the unfolding of their initiatives, namely that:

1 the conventional ways of education may possibly limit individual growth and initiative and hence the overall effectiveness of the educational system; and
2 educators may have to substantially re-think the way in which they organize the learning process and the way in which students learn.

Global education for a global industry

At present, what are the key issues facing educators who seek to provide a 'global education for a global industry'? In an attempt to respond to that question, the balance of this chapter will analyse the challenges and opportunities, particularly whether current curricula are meeting the industry needs, and how to educate and train people for 'lifelong learning', and an increasingly dynamic and global industry.

Challenges

What the implications will be, precisely, of the changes that are taking place in society and tourism in terms of global education development and the cultivation of global industry's organizational capability is just beginning to be articulated. It seems certain, however, that the changes brought on by globalization present many challenges to educators. Here are six of the more significant ones.

Challenge 1: Establishing credibility
Perhaps the overpowering challenge facing tourism education providers on the tertiary level is how to overcome the perceived lack of labour market credibility of many higher level tourism management programmes (Parsons, 1991). Whilst some parts of the industry have been quick to appreciate the value of the specialized higher level courses – public sector agencies and destination management in particular – elsewhere in independent hotels, catering and especially travel and tour management and facilities operation the resistance has often proved persistent. To establish labour market credibility, global education, in general, must better understand itself and the general requirements of 'business' (Table 26.2). It should also determine the present and in the future needs of employers, identify niches for potential collaboration, and work towards partnerships with the global industry.

Challenge 2: The changing workforce
Whilst operating in dynamic balance with the changing environment outlined in this chapter requires 'global education for a global industry', Parsons (1991) reports that presently the lack of skills impedes the ability of the domestic tourism industry to globalize. Therefore, this chapter concludes that the present tourism education provision is meeting the global industry needs only in part. There are ten selected workforce trends, depicted in Table 26.3, that are likely to have a major impact on the education and training system (Go, 1994). In particular, these findings

Table 26.3   The relative significance of selected trends on the future workforce in industrialized countries

• A strong and competitive national economy depends on the appropriate development of worker and managerial talents through education and training	93.5%
• The ability to manage complexity will require the re-design of many jobs to include computer-based tasks and new requirements for education	93.4%
• Over the next two decades a growing number of women will be counted among the 15–25 people in each of the largest organizations who 'run the show'	93.4%
• Corporate mergers and acquisitions will continue with more international actors involved	85.5%
• The workforce in the industrialized nations faces wrenching changes in its structure and composition that will radically alter how employers recruit, hire, manage and hold on to their staff	82.9%
• Pedagogical methods are likely to change to reflect the growing understanding among educators/trainers of the learning process	82.9%
• Sweeping political and economic changes will alter market basics	78.9%
• Training and education will increasingly be perceived as the key to growth of the travel and tourism industry and therefore become a major public agenda item	77.7%
• Corporations are likely to reach deeper into the educational system to influence the quality of its supply of workers	72.4%
• There is a growing mismatch between the literacy and other skills workers possess and the requirements of tomorrow's jobs.	51.3%

Percentages indicate the extent to which respondents 'Fully agree' or 'Agree somewhat' with the identified trends.
Note: Survey respondents (N = 72) were requested to prioritize the ten selected workforce trends and their perceived impact on education and training for careers in travel and tourism as listed in Figure 7. The percentages shown in Figure 4 indicate the extent to which respondents 'Fully Agree' or 'agree somewhat' with the identified trends.
Source: Survey conducted by the author during the New Horizons in Tourism and Hospitality Education, Training and Research Conference, The University of Calgary, 1991.

indicate an almost unanimous consensus that the competitiveness of a nation depends on the appropriate development of worker and managerial talents through education and training. This finding runs parallel to the claim made by Hayes and Abernathy (1980), who were the first to formally link America's competitive problems with the shortcomings of business education. Specifically, they reported on the failure of business curricula to meet managerial needs, and that the penalty for shortcomings in education and training is severe: a regression of a nation's international competitiveness. A similar lack of global education could indeed endanger the competitiveness of the global industry in relation to other industries.

Challenge 3: Staff development

The lack of staff development (Cooper et al., 1992) demands a concerted response, because quality teachers are at the heart of a quality global education system. In instances where the staff development concerns faculty members who have a background in an area or discipline other than tourism, there may be a need to provide these individuals with insights into industry sectors or into the tourism industry at large. Possibilities for staff development of this sort are offered by the regular (co)sponsorship of seminars and conferences that focus on tourism, or sectors of the global industry, by trade associations and non-governmental organizations, including the International Hotel Association, Pacific Asia Travel Tourism Association, World Travel and Tourism Council, and World Tourism Organization.

Several other forums dedicated to tourism education and research provide educators a venue to keep abreast of global education and global industry developments, including the International Association of Scientific Experts on Tourism Council of Hotel, Restaurant, and Institutional Educators, and the World Association for Tourism Training. On the tertiary level a number of institutions have begun to focus on the teaching of tourism through the co-sponsoring of seminars and conferences on the subject. For example, the University of Surrey in cooperation with the University of Calgary offered a unique international forum specifically designed and organized by tourism educators for tourism educators, researchers, trainers, and other professionals both from the private and public sectors to debate education and human resources issues in the broadest sense of the word. The first such conference took place at the University of Surrey in 1988, and second one at the University of Calgary in 1991.

Challenge 4: Constructing synergy between private and public sectors

Whilst it is critical that educators provide leadership to foster the extensive collaboration between business, the government and education, the findings of a study conducted by the UK-based National Economic Development Office (NEDO) seem to suggest that most of the seven countries that were surveyed could profit from a more constructive synergy between the public and private sector to harness the clear evidence of rising academic and student interest in the business of tourism management. In general, the study findings revealed tourism management and related studies to be 'in or approaching a state of flux' (Parsons, 1991: 205). The review focused on the management education systems of each

Table 26.4   The major NEDO findings

'Realistic and labour market related balance between intermediate and higher level course provision. There is already some evidence that student demand for intermediate level courses, which have a firm labour market base, may be being compromised in some countries – but not all – by the rapid expansion of higher education courses which as yet do not.

Effective mechanisms of "market mediation" in particular at higher levels better to establish the role for higher level courses in different sectors of these industries, and to relate this more effectively to student selection and assessment, curriculum design, student guidance and to revised career path in industry.

Systematic approaches to cooperative education in both theoretical education and work experience programmes. In some countries – and notably the UK and Canada – there is evidence that poor quality and industrial management of work experience programmes is leading many students to turn away from the industry. Others might also profit from looking again at the scope for cooperative education processes.

Less rigid mechanisms for access to higher level courses. In particular, urgent attention needs to be paid to the more effective integration of post-experience and continuing management education with existing approaches to course provision, and to the promotion and take-up of new or established post-experience courses in industry.'

Source: Parsons, 1991: 206–207.

country as opposed to 'specific programmes or the quality of courses'. It investigated strengths and weaknesses higher education and training for tourism management in seven countries (Canada, France, Germany, the Netherlands, Switzerland, UK, USA). A summary of the NEDO's major study findings has been presented in Table 26.4.

Challenge 5: Accomplishing more with less

As a consequence of the accelerating change of pace, educational institutions are struggling with a serious challenge: they must teach students how to keep learning and how to constantly adapt. This challenge is especially acute given the dilemma in many countries of how to deliver education and training better to more people while funding is shrinking. According to survey findings (Go, 1994: 343) tourism education will become more important both as a political agenda item and in commercial terms in that the global industry may be expected to intervene in education to boost the quality of human resources. There seems to be a consensus among respondents of the same survey that the global nature of tourism has made it mandatory to provide students with an international perspective. Considering the limited amount of resources, how can educators develop global education programmes that emphasize the wide

Table 26.5 The emphasis that should be given to the development of various skills and personal characteristics in tourism curricula

• Effective communications	97.4%
• International perspective (including sensitivity to national differences)	94.7%
• Creative problem-solving skills	94.5%
• Analytical	93.9%
• Decision-making	93.3%
• Planning/organizing	88.8%
• Team play	88.7%
• Leadership skills	87.5%
• Willingness to change	87.1%
• Initiative	85.1%
• Ethics	84.9%
• Socio-cultural aspects of tourism	83.7%
• Commitment to ongoing learning	77.1%
• Computer skills	74.3%
• Experiential learning skills	73.7%
• Entrepreneurship (risk-taking)	71.2%
• Foreign language skills	69.4%
• World and tourism geography	63.0%

This table identifies the percentage of respondents (N = 72) who are of the opinion that 'Much' or 'Very much' emphasis should be placed on the development of specific student skills and personal characteristics.
Source: F. Go, Survey conducted by the author during the New Horizons in Tourism and Hospitality Education, Training and Research Conference, The University of Calgary, 1991.

range of skills and knowledge skills, identified in Table 26.5, that graduates require? The decline in resources requires tourism educators to re-think their premises by turning conventional logic upside down, to realize that they might have to be more innovative than they presently are to address the needs of life-long learning.

Challenge 6: Dealing with diversity

The Western world has dominated tourism education to date, because the modern tourism industry and tourism studies both originated in Europe, before spreading to North America and other continents. Since the 1960s, due to the rapid rise of international tourism to and the chronic lack of adequate educational facilities in their home countries, many students from the developing countries enrolled in programmes offered by centres in Europe and North America. Later on tourism education institutes were established in the developing countries. However, in setting up these institutes, Western models were imported throughout the

Third World. Consequently, none of these courses fully meets the needs of the tourism sector in the Third World, let alone society at large. The fundamental aim of tourism education programmes for developing countries should be to improve the functioning of the tourism sector in such countries, both from the business perspective, and especially from the perspective of the destination at large. This implies that the thus far practised 'ethnocentric' 'market-led' approach to tourism education has to be re-directed and broadened towards the incorporation of a 'need-led' approach (Theuns and Go, 1992: 335).

Due to the emergence of tourism in the Third World, global education faces the challenge of dealing with diversity. In particular, there is a need to develop educational programmes that respond to 'need-led' priorities in the host communities of the developing countries. In summary, it is becoming apparent that the challenge of successful tourism development is to advance the causes of destination and corporate competitiveness and sustainable development A global education offers the foundation to start work towards these ends.

It is critical that global education meet the above six challenges, because more than ever before, only knowledgeable and highly skilled employees with a positive attitude can help bring about the required changes and improvements that are needed for the effective development of a global industry.

Opportunities

The evolving environment offers tremendous opportunities for global education programmes that are relevant to the times and have the drive to succeed. However, the barriers can be formidable, needs are urgent, and resources limited. Hence, global education providers cannot afford a complete restructuring of the system, even if it were possible. A global education perspective of the tourism education mission on the tertiary level should consider the strengths of the present system and allocate resources where they will result in the best return on investment for a global industry and life-long learning.

There are many tourism education and training centres around the world and their programmes are very heterogeneous in nature. For global education to occur, each provider should get involved in standardizing their programme to some degree. This would be in response to the emergence of more institutional interdependence and to give tourism education 'a credible and identifiable focus in the eyes of employers' (Cooper et al., 1992).

Whilst global education implies the need for greater standardization and integration of provision between educational systems, there is, at the same time, a need to 'safeguard' the diversity of national approaches within the system. The contradictory processes of standardization and individualization (Ashworth, 1991: 39) provide educational institutions an excellent opportunity to identify their niche and play a leadership role within the global education system.

The final part of this chapter shall address how to operationalize a 'global education for a global industry'. It provides a set of dimensions that are used by the Centre of Tourism Management which is housed in the international MBA programme at the Rotterdam Business School – the Rotterdam Tourism Management Model (RTMM) ten dimensions (ten Is) that underlie dynamic Global Education programmes. Where appropriate, case examples of existing 'global education for a global industry' have been included.

1 Interdependence

A 'global education for a global industry' approach should be designed to respond to the need, especially at university-level, to stimulate a better understanding of the interdependent nature of the world, and especially in the tourism field. Specifically, it should increase the capacity of students to think in broad terms. Therefore, 'global education for a global industry' should be designed to complement the competency-based method which is likely 'to narrow the range of subjects and content taught' (Cooper et al., 1992: 235).

Typically, 'global education for a global industry' should not only transcend east and west to realize a new 'globality', but also bring about integrated self-mastery, teamwork and organizational learning.

The European Association for Tourism and Leisure Education (ATLAS), established in 1991, is an example of a transnational educational initiative designed to promote links between professional bodies in tourism, leisure and associated subjects, such as hospitality and catering and the arts, and to liaise on educational issues, curriculum development and professional recognition of courses. ATLAS provides a forum to promote staff and student exchange, transnational research and to facilitate curriculum and professional development. It currently has over 100 members in 22 European countries.

2 Integration

Presently, the majority of programmes with the management departments of universities and colleges focus on tourism as a business and expose students to business functions, such as accountancy, marketing, law, finance, and economics and how to apply these functions within the tourism field. However, tourism education has evolved as an interdisciplinary specialism and integrated travel, leisure, recreation and hotel and catering courses (Cooper et al., 1992: 236). Such integration marks a positive development in the field. However, such integration should be elaborated by building on a European tradition by developing amongst students a holistic appreciation of how organizations operate, for gaining insights into whole managerial problems, not artificial fragments as defined by functional disciplines. Hawkins and Hunt (1988) emphasized the need for tertiary establishments to develop professional programmes that are founded on a broad-based education, and interdisciplinary in nature. The latter can be realized, for example, by an emphasis on 'real-life' Interdisciplinary Field Projects. For example, The University of Victoria's (Canada) Tourism Management Programme integrates training and business experience through cooperative work terms and its course structure ensures the type of graduate the tourism industry is seeking.

3 Intimate partnerships

Intimate partnerships with the global industry contribute to preparing students for a profession by affording the required practical experience which complements the theoretical enquiry. Practical tourism industry problems in the form of research projects, audits, consulting assignments and communicated by global industry speakers can provide useful insights into the skills, which accrue from lengthy training and identify potential 'career paths'. In general, such tourism career paths tend to be ill-defined (EIESP, 1991). Intimate partnerships should also be established to promote a series of intensive residential Global Tourism Teachers' Programme, along the lines of the World Tourism Organization's (WTO) efforts in this regard. The purpose of such conferences would be professional development and the improvement of tourism education quality, through pinpointing the critical success factors to serve the needs of the global industry and by sharing and comparing education and training experiences in a challenging global environment.

4 Innovation

In an environment of change, the global industry cannot rely on the products or strategies of the past to ensure their future success. Today, creativity and imagination, along with an enthusiasm for learning, are crucial ingredients to succeed. Global education should be designed to generate innovative ideas and creative thinking and instil an excitement about learning. Educational providers are, themselves, learning organizations. Their curricula should undergo evaluation and development to ensure that they remain relevant. They should encourage students to suggest new topics of study, and academic staff members to develop innovative courses based on research and consulting experience, which may reveal the needs of the global industry. Last but not least, an advisory board of executives, corporate recruiters and alumni can help shape the development of the global curriculum.

Educational innovation should be viewed as the taking of an initiative, rather than a re-ordering into a new pattern of something which already exists (Baum, 1987: 98). Victoria University of Technology in Melbourne, Australia, has pioneered new initiatives by introducing a wide range of new hospitality and tourism courses for 1997. These initiatives reflect the needs of industry and the commitment of the university to innovative course design and the continuous improvement of existing programmes. The new initiatives include (Victoria University of Technology, 1996):

- A Bachelor of Business in Tourism/Bachelor of Arts in Asian Studies. This new programme reflects the increased interaction between Australia and Asia and the desire of students to undertake language studies throughout their degree. It will prepare students for one of the largest growth areas in the tourism sector, ensuring that they are well equipped to take their place as a tourism professional in the twenty-first century.
- A Bachelor of Business in Tourism and Small Enterprise Management, combining the strengths of the accountancy and tourism areas. This initiative recognizes that most tourism businesses are in the small to medium category and that graduates require skills that are relevant to this sector.

Within the context of the application of innovation to the process of lifelong learning, there are especially interesting options cited by Dunn (1983) that recognize and certify experiential learning; consider more flexible programming; build more links between education and industry; offer in-house professional development programmes for organizations and businesses; make increasing use of businesses for internships, research and consultancy; draw on corporate human resources development specialists; pool resources with other institutions, and use, where appropriate, mass media such as television to deliver course content.

5 Information technology
The digital economy we live in, and especially the rapid and pronounced changes in information technology, have pronounced implications for tourism and the provision of global education. To succeed in the present marketplace, tourism marketers must be able to operate in two parallel arenas; first, the 'analogue' world involving the physical movement of people and, second, the digital world of information processing. It is increasingly important for the global industry to apply database marketing techniques, which enable operators to obtain and analyse relevant market data, build target market profiles and maintain relationships with consumers. Obviously, global education providers must keep abreast of the very rapid advancements in information technology and their applications in tourism in order to effectively prepare their students for careers in the digital economy. A forum that has been providing leadership in information and communication technology in tourism is ENTER.

Established in Innsbruck, Austria, in 1993 by a team of academics with the support of the Congress Centre of Innsbruck, ENTER has become established as the world's premiere conference on information technology and tourism.

After staging three successful events in Innsbruck, the organizers of ENTER have decided to hold the conference every year in another country so as to further expand its international audience and contribute to global education for a global industry. In 1999, the ENTER Conference will be held in Innsbruck, Austria. Ongoing conference information on ENTER can be obtained from the web at: http://www.tis.co.at/enter.

6 Immersion

Global education should be designed to assist global industry with challenges such as the requirement for greater cultural sensitivity and problem solving capability, a deeper understanding of the geopolitical forces work in the world, and an ability to develop constructive relationships with the people of individual nations. The Nanyang University of Technology MBA programme, which offers a specialization in tourism and hospitality management provides its students with a dynamic, cross cultural experience by way of a mandatory excursion to a host country and involving them in fact-finding missions: meeting with industry and government representatives, evaluating business prospects, and helping to prepare a detailed written report of the group findings. Such action-learning experience immerses students in the culture of the host country so that they may view the 'world as a learning ground' and results in new realizations, greater cross-cultural awareness, and stronger team skills.

7 Involvement

The future success of tourism will depend largely on whether society is prepared to educate and train the upcoming generation for careers in tourism. It will depend on to what extent the various 'tourism advocates' educate the population in destination areas, especially civic leaders and government officials, regarding the significance of international tourism and how to shape sustainable, international tourism locally and in the national framework. Therefore, it is especially important that the providers of global education, on the tertiary level, become actively involved in promoting tourism education on the national level and the 'classroom' level.

In every country where tourism forms an important part of the economy, there is the potential for bringing together the global industry and the education sector. The Rotterdam School of Management hosts an annual forum 'Entrepreneurship in Tourism' which focuses on a different issue each year. Table 26.6 provides examples of issues that might form the focus for such symposia.

Table 26.6　The agenda for global education

A　Increasing the visibility and recognition of tourism and hospitality as a socio-economic phenomenon and as a field of study.

B　Encouraging a multi-layered, multi-disciplinary approach to tourism and hospitality education and training.

C　Fostering linkages among all stakeholders in the travel and tourism education system:
- Students
- Educators
- Tourists
- Communities
- Industry
- Governments
- Non-government and voluntary bodies

D　Developing effective mechanisms for policy formulation among stakeholders which lead to high quality sustainable tourism.

E　Facilitating the cooperation and coordination of educational bodies at all levels.

F　Strengthening the linkages of education and research with particular emphasis on emerging areas of concern i.e. environment–ethics–social carrying capacity–global issues.

G　Strengthening the linkages between industry and education using occupational standards established by industry as an important vehicle.

H　Promoting open systems of education – 'The World as Classroom' – by measures such as:
- International exchanges of students and educators
- Blending of academic learning with experience in the work place
- Executives into the classroom
- Educators into the workplace
- Conferences and seminars
- Centres for training of trainers

I　Expanding tourism and hospitality curricula in the areas of:
- Global issues
- Environment
- Host communities
- Ethics

J　Designing and implementing innovative approaches to enhance the content and process of education and training which encourages:
- Life long learning and personal development
- Creativity and lateral thinking
- Critical thinking
- Problem solving skills
- Inter-personal skills – Team work

K　Embracing the concept of 'one world' and responding to its needs by:
- Sharing of knowledge and approaches between east and west, north and south
- Providing opportunities for in-service training across boundaries
- Encouragement of language learning and multi-cultural studies at all levels

Table 26.6   (Cont'd)

L   Continuing critical appraisal and evaluation of tourism and hospitality education and training through:
  • Accreditation
  • Conferences
  • Student/community/industry feedback.

Source: F. Go, New Horizons in Tourism and Hospitality Education, Training and Research Conference The University of Calgary, 1991.

8 Ideology

The growing significance of the inter-cultural market and workplace contributes to the emerging need for the effective understanding of the concept of ideology. Ideology is concerned, according to the dictionary, with 'a body of ideas that reflect the beliefs of a nation, political system, class, etc.' Within a pluralistic society it is key to possess a grasp of the major ideologies, involving the world's major cultures. At present, however, most tourism courses and programmes have an ethnocentric character, that is, they take the study of domestic tourism and give it an international dimension with the least possible change. If today's student is to be an effective practitioner in the global industry of tomorrow, educators cannot be blind to the idea that the management and organizing of tourism 'are culturally dependent' (Hofstede, 1983).

However, Jafari and Way (1994: 73) report that they 'found no multicultural curricula in our review' in US universities, despite the identified need in the global industry for multilingual and multicultural employees to accommodate the culturally based needs of foreign visitors. It should be remembered that many tourism managers work in multicultural workplaces without ever leaving home and that intercultural training can lead to better performance (Shames, 1986). It is therefore essential that students are exposed to the subject of intercultural communication in order to understand and motivate both individuals and groups, from another culture than their own.

Under the ideology theme, Third World concerns present another dimension that should be of interest in terms of global education for a global industry. Specifically, a broad range of social and economic policies have to be implemented to accommodate the tourism education needs of developing countries. Such education programmes can play a crucial role in the harmonization of environmental protection and help to bring about greater social equality in the developing countries. For example, Jenkins (1980) points out how public sector tourism administrators in developing countries require dedicated educational programmes, and Echtner (1994) champions the specific requirements of entrepreneurial training in developing countries.

9 Interaction across borders

For purposes of the advanced understanding of tourism development and management techniques and to broaden knowledge and understanding of global education and the global industry, a growing number of centres of academic study are interacting not only on an informal but more and more on a formal basis, through 'joint-ventures'. For example, the Rotterdam School of Management (RSM) has bilateral exchange agreements with Community of Europe Management Schools (CEMS) and the 'Programme Internationale de Management' (PIM) network which offer students the opportunity to study abroad. Furthermore, students are encouraged to put the knowledge and skills they have gained during their studies to practice within a company of their choice.

The development of strategic partnerships with the international academic community can result in a fruitful 'transfer of technology'. For example, Airey (1994) described the PHARE programme in Poland, set up 'to identify gaps, weaknesses and directions for change and development in provision.' The programme used 'study visits for teachers outside Poland', a team of teachers from the Netherlands to deliver ten courses on various subjects to 150 Polish teachers, and 'training organizations from a number of countries' to meet specific training needs.

10 International networking

The ready availability of ever-improving telecommunications, particularly e-mail, facilitates the establishment of global tourism research networks. The notion of global tourism research networks rests on the principle of reciprocity. In other words, a global tourism research network affords participating researchers the chance of collecting data, on a global/international basis, for one another. Global tourism research networks offer researchers at least three important benefits: The ability to collect data which might otherwise be impossible to gather; a basis for comparative studies; and low cost.

For example, J.R. Brent Ritchie, professor of tourism management at the Faculty of Management, University of Calgary, Alberta, Canada, carried out fairly extensive long term research projects related to the 1988 Olympic Winter Games which were held in Calgary. In a personal communication he observed the following:

> One of the most interesting and rewarding aspects of this research was the involvement of some twenty-two collaborating research institutions located in Europe and the United States. Individuals within these institutions were kind enough to assist us in ensuring the impacts of the Olympics on international arenas and knowledge of the host city and its image by collecting data for us on a low cost/no cost basis. Without this [global] collaboration and support, what we believe was a fairly unique research undertaking, simply would not have been possible.

The above ten dimensions provide opportunities to capitalize on 'global education for a global industry'. Of course, they are not exhaustive, because in the global market the possibilities for Global Education are limited only by one's imagination.

Conclusion

A review of the evolution of tourism education over the past twenty-five years indicates that the field has progressed and that it has reached a new watershed brought about by globalization, digitalization (or the advancement of information technology), and innovation. The combined impact of these forces have turned tourism, traditionally a sector with a local focus, into a global industry. To be competitive, the global industry has to develop the productivity and quality gains that flow from value-added services, that is services that employ a higher degree of investment in workers' skills and knowledge. There is evidence (Parsons, 1991) however, that the present lack of skills impedes the ability of the domestic industry to globalize.

Within a plural society there is mounting public interest in quality of life issues. Increasingly, to reconcile its dilemma of profit versus responsibility to society, the global industry will require knowledge and expertise.

Traditionally, global education and global industry have had different motivations and goals. Accordingly, there has been a great lack of career paths and confusion of what constitutes an appropriate tourism education and training. And the present educational and training provision is meeting the needs of the global industry only to a limited extent.

Due to the changing nature of society and the global industry, tourism educators have come to a crossroads. Given the transformation of society, educators should take global education for a global industry into account to avoid aimless drift, or worse, potential irrelevance. The overarching mission of global education for a global industry might be summarized as the provision of leadership and the provision of high quality education and training so as to cultivate the talent required to deal with critical issues and thereby ensuring the long-term prosperity of tourism as an integral part of society.

Global education for a global industry, as conceptualized in this chapter, should aim to simultaneously standardize curricula for purposes of quality assurance in education and training, and safeguard the individuality of national cultures.

Based on several years of 'global' experience, the author would like to share certain observations regarding the 'global education for a global industry' concept. The first and most significant is that educators create visions beyond personal, group, or institutional barriers. Second, the

Table 26.7   Questions to construct a measure of global
education for a global industry

Four stages may be distinguished to construct a measure of global education for
a global industry: The 'awakening' stage, the 'visioning' stage, the 'commitment'
stage, and the 'implementation' stage.

1. **The 'awakening' stage**
   A. Are you significantly involved in analyzing future needs of the Global
      Industry in relation to a pluralistic society?
   B. Are you aware of the importance of Global Education as a means to
      prepare students to function effectively in their future career in a Global
      Industry?

2. **The 'visioning' stage**
   A. Do you have a vision for the future of a Global Education for a Global
      Industry?
   B. What is the essence of vision and how does it integrate specific princi-
      ples that underpin practice?

3. **The 'commitment' stage**
   A. Who can help to turn your vision into reality and meet your goals?
      How?
   B. To what extent do your resources enable you to engage in Global Educa-
      tion for a Global Industry?

4. **The 'implementation' stage**
   A. Can you articulate to your staff a vision of where your academic unit
      should be heading?
   B. What specific opportunities shall guide the planning, implementing, and
      evaluation of your Global Education for a Global Industry initiative?

---

approach can derive long-term benefits through cooperation, because
neither 'cash starved' educational providers nor companies will be able
to deliver educational and training needs effectively in isolation in the
1990s and beyond. Finally, the 'global education for a global industry'
approach and the concepts it discloses have a wide application as tools to
plan and implement the globalization of the curriculum. Specifically, Table
26.7 lists several questions that may be used to construct a measure to
monitor one's progression towards providing a 'global education for a
global industry'.

References

Airey, D. (1994) Education for Tourism in Poland: The Phare Programme, *Tourism Management*, **15**(6), 467–470

Ashworth, G.J. (1991) *Heritage Planning Conservation as the Management of Urban Change*, Geo Pers, Groningen

Baum, T. (1987) Introducing educational innovation in hospitality studies: a case study in practical curriculum change, *International Journal of Hospitality Management*, **6**(2), 97–102

Bell, D. (1988) The World in 2013, *Dialogue*, **81**(3), 3–9

Burnett, Uysal and Jamrozy (1991) Articles on International Themes in the Journal of Travel Research, *Journal of Travel Research*, **XXIX**(3), 47–50

Christie-Mill, R., (1978) Tourism Education: Its Development and Current Status with Special Reference to Selected Segments of Tourism-Related Industries in Michigan. East Lansing, Michigan: Department of Administration and Higher Education, Michigan State University, 235pp

Cooper, C., Scales, R. and Westlake, J. (1992) The anatomy of tourism and hospitality education in the UK, *Tourism Management*, **13**(2), 234–242

D'Amore, L.J. (1985) A Third Generation of Tourism Thinking Towards a Creative Conspiracy, *Business Quarterly*, Summer

Doorn, van J.W.M. (1996) *Toeristisch Bedrijfsleven en Universiteit: een – of twee-eiig?* Address presented at the Symposium Ondernemen in Toerisme, Erasmus Universiteit, Roterdam, 26 January

Dunn, Samuel L. (1983) The changing university, survival in the information society, *The Futurist* (August), pp. 55–60

Echtner, Charlotte M. (1994) Entrepreneurial Training in Developing Countries, *Annals of Tourism Research*, **22**(1), 119–134

EIESP (1991) Education for Careers in European Travel and Tourism, A Study Commissioned by the American Express Foundation, Paris: European Institution of Education and Social Policy

Gamble, P. (1991) Innovation in innkeeping. Inaugural lecture, *International Journal of Hospitality Management*, **10**(1), 3–23

Gee, C.Y. (1980) Professionalization and Travel Industry Education, *Journal of Hospitality Education*, **4**(2), 71–84

Go, F. and Pine, R. (1995) *Globalization Strategy in the Hotel Industry*, Routledge, London

Go, F. (1994) Emerging issues in tourism education. In *Global Tourism*, (ed. Theobald, W.) pp. 330–346

Gronroos, Christian (1989) *Service Management Principles*, Working Paper 90: 1, Service Research Centre, University of Karlstad, Sweden

Gunn, C.A. (1988) *Tourism Planning* (2nd edn), Taylor & Francis, New York

Hamel, Gary (1991) Competition for Competence and Interpartner Learning Within Strategic Alliances, *Strategic Management Journal*, 12, 83–103

Handy, Charles (1989) The age of unreason, *Harvard Business School Press*, Boston, Mass.

Hawkins, Donald E. and John D. Hunt (1988) Travel and Tourism Professional Education. *Hospitality and Tourism Educator*, **1**(1), 8–14

Hayes, Robert A., and William J. Abernathy (1980) Managing Our Way To Economic Decline, *Harvard Business Review*, **58**(4), 67–76

Hofstede, Geert (1983) The cultural relativity of organizational theories, *Journal of International Business Studies*, **XIV**(2), 75–90

Jafari, J. and Ritchie, J.R. Brent (1981) Toward a framework for tourism education, *Annals of Tourism Research*, **8**(1), 13–34

Jafari, J. and Way, W (1994) Multicultural Strategies in Tourism, *The Cornell H.R.A. Quarterly*, **35**(6), 72–79

Jenkins, C.L. (1980) Education for Tourism Policy Makers in Developing Countries, *International Journal of Tourism Management*, **1**(4), 238–242

Kaspar, C. (1994) Tourism Research: Achievements, Failures, and Unresolved Puzzles, *44th AIEST Congres proceedings*, St Gall: Association of Scientific Experts in Tourism, pp. 13–16

Lawson, M. (1974) *Teaching Tourism*, London: British Tourist Authority, 105 pp

Parsons, D. (1991) The making of managers: Lessons from an international review of tourism management education programs, *Tourism Management*, **12**(3), 197–208

Poon, A. (1988) Information technology and tourism, *Annals of Tourism Research*, **15**(4), 531–549

Schumpeter, J.A. (1965) *The Theory of Economic Development: An Inquiry into Profit, Credit, Interest, and the Business Cycle* (4th edn), Oxford University Press, Oxford

Shames, Germaine (1986) Training for the Multicultural Workplace, *Cornell Hotel and Restaurant Administration Quarterly*, **26**(4), 25–31

Smith, S.L.J. (1990) Going Global in Vancouver: The PATA '90 Conference, *Journal of Travel Research*, (Fall), **XXIX**(2), 52–54

Tettero, J.H.J.P. and Viehoff, J.H.R.M. (1990) *Marketing dienstenverlenende organizaties – Beleid en uitvoering*, Kluwer, Deventer

Theuns, H. Leo and Go, Frank (1992) Need led priorities in hospitality education for the Third World. In *World Travel and Tourism Review Indicators, Trends and Issues*, Vol. 2 (ed. J.R.B. Ritchie, D.E. Hawkins, F. Go and D. Frechtling), CAB International, Wallingford

Theobald, William F. (ed.) (1994) *Global Tourism*, Butterworth-Heinemann, Oxford

Ulrich, D. and Lake, D. (1990) *Organizational Capability Competing from the Inside Out*, John Wiley, New York

Victoria University of Technology (1996) *Faculty of Business Newsline*, **6**(2), (June)

Vollmer, H.M. and Mills, D. (eds) (1966) *Professionalization*, Prentice-Hall, Englewood Cliffs

WTO (1983) *Tourism and Employment: Enhancing the Status of Tourism Professions*, Madrid: World Tourism Organization, 41 pp

WTO (1996) *Global Distribution Systems*, Routledge, London

WTTC (1992) *Travel & Tourism The World's Largest Industry*, Brussels: The World Travel and Tourism Council Report.

27 Aid, government, and tourism studies in less developed countries: the route from muddle to co-operation in Fiji

David Harrison

Introduction

The islands of the Pacific are part of the region of East Asia and the Pacific, considered by the World Tourism Organization to be the fastest growing destination area for international tourist arrivals in the world. In the period 1990 to 1994, tourist arrivals in this area grew by 45 per cent, receipts from inbound tourism, including from fares, increased by 57 per cent, and the region as a whole raised its world market share to 14 per cent (WTO, 1996). However, the fortunes of tourism vary from one island state to another. In some, for example, the Cook Islands (Buck and Hall, 1996), tourism has increased rapidly in recent years, in others, for example, Vanuatu (de Burlo, 1996) and Fiji (WTO, 1996) growth has been more variable, and sometimes, as in Papua New Guinea, it has barely occurred at all (Douglas, 1996). Nevertheless, over the period 1990–94, tourist arrivals increased in Melanesia, Micronesia and Polynesia by 10 per cent, 38 per cent and 21 per cent, respectively, whilst receipts increased by 31 per cent, 21 per cent and 40 per cent respectively and by comparison with increases in world tourist arrivals of 19 per cent, and in worldwide receipts of 16 per cent over the same period, their progress as a group has been more than satisfactory (WTO, 1996). The nuclear tests by the French at Murarua Atholl undoubtedly reduced tourist arrivals in 1996 in most islands throughout the region, but informal indicators suggest the setback is likely to be temporary and that the generally upward trend will continue.

The figures tell only part of the story. Except for such territories as Hawaii, American Samoa, French Polynesia and New Caledonia, most Pacific islands are technically 'independent' but, as others have also indicated (Craig-Smith, 1996), the majority have dependent economies and rely on only a few primary export crops for their income and, in many cases, on aid from larger, metropolitan societies. Tourism thus takes on a considerable degree of importance. In Fiji, for example, one of the most developed of the independent Pacific island states, it has overtaken sugar as the dominant industry (Fiji Visitors' Bureau, 1995), is the largest employer of waged labour, and generates about 25 per cent of the country's gross domestic product (Government of Fiji, 1996). Even in French Polynesia, especially Tahiti, tourism is also crucially important (Page and Lawton, 1996). Other island territories in the region may attract fewer tourists but, because most possess even more limited natural resources, tourism remains, if anything, more vital to them as a development tool.

The significance of tourism in the Pacific is reflected in earlier studies of the industry in the region, many of which were critical of the social and cultural ramifications of tourism (Finney and Watson, 1975; Britton, 1982; 1983; 1987a; 1987b; 1989; Lockart, 1993; Minerbi, 1992). In general, there was a tendency to follow a neo-Marxist perspective on capitalist 'development' and regard tourism as, at best, an economic necessity and a social and cultural disaster for small, less developed countries (LDCs), that were allegedly helpless in the face of the Leviathan of worldwide capitalist expansion (Harrison, 1992). Such a view was not universally held, however, and MacNaught (1982), for instance, was scathingly critical of what he described as 'the fatal impact thesis'. Nevertheless, academics generally, and specifically in the Pacific, came to be seen as hostile to tourism, thus gaining a reputation which hardly increased the likelihood, already slim, of genuine dialogue and co-operation between those who studied tourism and those who promoted it. The situation was not helped by the reluctance of at least some with a financial interest in tourism to take seriously even the mildest criticism of the medium- and long-term consequences of international tourism.

The Tourism Studies Programme at the University of the South Pacific

In 1989 the Tourism Council of the South Pacific (TCSP), itself funded through the European Union's Pacific Regional Tourism Development Programme (PRTDP), invited Professor Rik Medlik to advise on the development of tourism studies at the University of the South Pacific (USP). His report was completed within a few months (Medlik, 1989) and the Tourism Studies Programme, funded by the European Union (EU) through the TCSP, commenced at USP in 1991. As the university serves twelve island states in the region, all of which value the contribution tourism makes to economic growth, and the TCSP is also made up of twelve territories (nine of which overlap with USP), two of the largest regional bodies in the Pacific were thus committed to co-operating in providing a course addressed to the tourism needs of the region and potentially able to make a contribution to studies of tourism further afield. As indicated below, the course is now firmly established at USP, but not before relationships between the university and TCSP were subjected to considerable strain. These are described and analysed in this chapter, not to criticize either institution, or to foster the impression that the programme has arrived at a peak of achievement (for it has not), but to illustrate some issues involved in tourism education in a less developed country and the need to relate these to other, wider aspects of economic, social and political development. Some of these issues, at least, are relevant to more developed societies.

As King (1994) points out, in the second Lomé Convention, the European Union set out four goals for tourism: effective product marketing, market development, research and human resources training and education. These goals were (and are) especially relevant to Pacific islands, where tourism is economically and socially important, for until the early 1990s islanders had to study tourism in New Zealand, Australia or elsewhere. With the development of the School of Hospitality and Tourism Studies at the Fiji Institute of Technology, Fijian students, especially, had access to training courses for entry into the hospitality industry, and similar courses were offered elsewhere in other islands. However, there was little on offer at degree level and, despite the danger of too great a focus on the Fijian context, USP, as the dominant regional institution for higher education, was the preferred recipient for European funds. King suggested that the choice was clearly correct, for USP is very much involved in the development of 'human resources' (a term which seems to render the human beings to which it refers passive and inanimate) and, with 'a genuine regional charter', was able to offer 'an established educational infrastructure, including a regional communications network'. In addition, although this may not have been paramount at the time, there were good academic and practical reasons for combining tourism studies with other subjects, as indicated below.

The Tourism Studies Programme as it existed in January 1997 is outlined at the end of this chapter. It started slowly, and by 1994 students at USP were offered three courses on tourism (Introduction to Tourism Studies, Tourism Marketing, and Tourism Business Opportunities) which they could take as electives (options) to accompany their major courses. These were soon to be joined by a course on Tourism in Developing Societies and all attracted large numbers of students from the School of Social and Economic Development, where the Tourism Programme was situated. However, large numbers of students are neither a necessary nor a sufficient condition for success and by 1994 it was also clear that the programme was experiencing severe teething problems. Relations between the university and the TCSP had become increasingly strained and the problems were considered sufficiently serious by the European Union and USP to commission a report. As a consequence, *Tourism Studies at the USP* was written for the Pacific ACP/EU by Mike Dowse in 1994.

Dowse compared the programme as envisaged by Professor Medlik and modified by the University of the South Pacific (USP) with the progress actually made by this time. In essence, his report indicated considerable success in some areas and little in others. By 1994, a Certificate in Tourism Studies and an undergraduate Diploma in Tourism Studies had been introduced and there were high hopes that Tourism Studies would soon be offered as a Major in the School of Social and Economic Development (SSED). In addition, two courses (Introduction to Tourism and Tourism Marketing) were already offered through the university extension services to students in outlying districts in Fiji and in other island territories, involving distance learning and regular discussions over the radio telephone. As Dowse recognized, this was a considerable achievement, given that the Tourism Studies Programme was over-stretched, and staffed primarily by a temporary lecturer and an acting co-ordinator, who headed another department in SSED. At the same time, he noted that SSED had decided not to offer short courses for those working in the tourism sector, and did not offer a postgraduate qualification in tourism studies.

The Dowse Report went into considerable detail on the causes of the lack of progress in some of the above areas. Problems were indeed many, but were considered to arise mainly from a lack of co-operation and understanding between TCSP and USP, involving *inter alia* an apparent lack of available funds, an inadequate provision of library resources and, above all, the failure of the programme to attract a full-time co-ordinator.

There is no doubt that relations between USP and the TCSP were at a low ebb, and the gravity of the situation is reflected in the vagaries of funding. From the early months of 1992 until the end of 1995, the story was one of claim and counter-claim, of budgets proposed, accepted and then reduced, and of increasing acrimony. Even by March 1996 the budget for that year had not even been discussed, let alone agreed, and there had been no reconciliation for the budget for 1995. Library provision, especially, was inadequate: although the Medlik Report of 1989 had recommended that F$56,000[1] (at the time of writing, the exchange value of the Fijian dollar was 0.4586 pounds sterling and US $0.7383) should be spent on library resources over the period 1990–92, this did not happen. Even by the end of 1995, less than F$13,000, in total, had been allocated to library resources, with the result that students on all tourism courses were starved of reading material, and read only what was photocopied for this express purpose. As an introduction to the study of tourism, no worse could be imagined. Furthermore, despite Medlik's recommendations, there was not a single tourism journal in the library. Irrespective of who was responsible for this lamentable state of affairs (a matter on which opinions continue to vary), it is hard to disagree with Dowse when he noted that relations between TCSP and USP 'have not invariably been both cordial and professionally effective,' and that it was a matter for regret 'that two such reputable organizations, each of profound significance to the region, have remained at dysfunctional fiscal logger-heads for so long' (Dowse, 1994: 39).

Consolidation and co-ordination: March 1996 and after

As a result of the Dowse Report, USP addressed some of the issues raised. Between 1994 and 1996, extra courses were added to the programme, and by 1995, Tourism Studies was offered as a joint major subject, studied by students in conjunction with another subject of their choice. Most importantly, however, the search was intensified for a full-time co-ordinator, who eventually took up the position in March 1996.

When the full-time Co-ordinator of Tourism Studies took up his post, the programme could already boast of considerable (albeit unheralded) achievements. First, Tourism Studies was offered to undergraduates wishing to obtain a certificate or a diploma (the latter no longer available, as a result of decisions made at the Senate of USP, for future entrants), and could also be taken as a joint major or minor subject in SSED. Indeed, in the 1996 academic year, 135 students were enrolled as Tourism Studies majors or minors, and many more were taking tourism courses as options on other degrees. This considerable and growing student interest rapidly became the envy of more established departments at USP.

Second, the growth in numbers, and the provision of two extension courses, had been achieved despite the fact that the Tourism Studies Programme was under-staffed.

Third, such successes had been achieved with funding *vastly less* than the sums envisaged by the Medlik and Dowse reports. According to Dowse, by the end of 1994, of an alleged F$520,000 to be made available for the Tourism Studies Programme, a mere F$131,190 had been received from TCSP. After his report was received, extra funds were provided by TCSP for 1995, but the programme remained under-funded.

Although considerable, the successes could not disguise the fact that there were also problems and, during 1996, concentrated efforts were made to build on the programme's strengths and to remedy some of the obvious weaknesses. First, the lack of adequate funding was clearly a disgrace. More realistic funding was soon secured for 1996, but this was obtained only on *the explicit and written understanding that funding from the TCSP would cease at the end of 1996.* As a consequence, the university, which by 1996 was already funding the salaries of the lecturer and secretary, agreed to fully fund the programme, and to seek external financial assistance for future years. At the same time, TCSP agreed to commit F$65,000 for the emergency purchase of books and journals (including back copies) for the library, and SSED also committed funds to the purchase of necessary journals. At the time of writing, these purchases are well under way and the basis is thus being laid for library provision for the programme which will rival, if not better, that of many such programmes in more developed countries.

Second, it was clear that the programme was marginal to the school, the university and to the tourism industry. As the acting co-ordinator was based elsewhere in the university, the programme lacked an identity and a recognizable physical centre, and students on tourism courses could not be given day-to-day information, as the programme had not been provided with a notice board. Further, much of the equipment purchased with the funds that had been made available was temporarily residing in other offices, a fact that became evident to TCSP officials on the one visit they appear to have made over the five years of the programme's existence. There was also a shortage of stationery, allegedly for lack of funds. These issues, some of which, on their own, were relatively minor, were soon remedied with the arrival of the full-time co-ordinator, and there was a corresponding increase in morale among students.

Third, it was apparent that the programme needed closer links with government and the tourism industry in the region. Even after four years, few players in the tourism industry knew of the programme's existence and, to all intents and purposes, relations with government did not exist at all. To remedy this situation, a Tourism Advisory Group (TAG) was formed, bringing together key representatives of the government, the tourism industry, and university officials to explore methods of future co-operation and mutual assistance. More specifically, the aims of TAG are sevenfold:

1   To bring together members of the university administration, the School of Social and Economic Development, and the region's tourism industry in a forum for discussion of domestic and international tourism, with a specific focus on its changing structure and emerging needs.

2 To inform the key participants in the region's tourism industry of the Tourism Studies Programme at the University of the South Pacific.
3 To enlist members' advice and support in monitoring and developing the academic courses offered on the Tourism Programme, thus enabling them to respond to and reflect the changing needs of the region's tourism industry.
4 To enable the tourism industry in the region to collectively provide a resource upon which the programme can draw, in ways that will emerge during discussions. However, examples might include the willingness of professionals in the industry to be occasional guest speakers on the programme's courses, assistance in the provision of opportunities for students to go on fieldwork trips to different tourism institutions in the region, and help in exposing students to other facets of the organization of tourism in the region.
5 To enable the industry to draw, when possible, on the resources and expertise available on the Tourism Studies Programme. Again, opportunities will emerge during discussions, but one possibility could be the construction and implementation of short research projects involving students, provided these could be seen as relevant and appropriate to courses they study.
6 To develop links between the Tourism Studies programme and the region's tourism industry, thus increasing mutual understanding and co-operation among those involved in academic studies oriented to the industry and those involved in its business side.
7 To meet at least twice a year, but with extra meetings if the need arises, to pursue the above objectives.

The overall theme of TAG is co-operation. It held its first meeting in October 1996 and is scheduled to meet once every semester. The formation of TAG reinforced existing contacts with the tourism industry and such links have already paid dividends, for example, in the support given by the Sheraton Group, the Fiji Visitors' Bureau, Hertz and the Fiji Hotel Association in sponsoring students to attend the annual National Tourism Convention and in providing opportunities for fieldwork visits, especially in the provision of temporary placements for the programme's students during the long break from November to February.

Fourth, the Tourism Programme has currently acquired approximately one hundred video recordings on various aspects of the tourism and hospitality industries, a collection which has greatly enhanced the programme's resources.

Finally, as a result of increased links with government departments in Fiji, the programme has become involved in key discussions over the region's tourism, notably the preparation of a master plan for Fiji's tourism by consultants deLoitte and Touche.

The period 1994–96, then, was one of consolidation. However, the future development of the programme depends, to some extent, on understanding why some of these problems occurred, and on a clear vision of what it should set out to achieve.

So what was the problem?

Clearly, the Dowse Report highlighted some of the difficulties experienced by the programme in the early years, and at first sight these may be explained by reference to personality clashes and poor communications. In addition, some problems can undoubtedly be explained by the time taken to find a full-time co-ordinator. However, other factors, which may be longer lasting, are more deeply rooted. They arise, first, from structural problems inherent in the funding of an academically-orientated Tourism *Studies* Programme through the TCSP, a *promotional* organization.

Clearly, in the early years of the programme, relationships between the TCSP and the USP were at a low ebb. Even at the outset, there were suggestions that 'the university "culture", especially in the social sciences area, was perceived as being "anti-tourist",' (King, 1994) and there is evidence that this may then have been the case. In addition, as a funding body, the European Union is notorious among aid agencies for the highly bureaucratic procedures to be followed before the allocated funds are actually received. However, the problems were more structurally rooted. The TCSP is a regional organization, bringing together (at the time of writing) twelve national tourism bodies with the joint aim of promoting individual territories and the rest of the region as a tourism destination area. Their interests in tourism promotion are not, and never will be, fully served in a university programme of tourism studies, which must necessarily retain its academic and critical edge. Furthermore, the manner in which the programme was initially funded, accidentally or otherwise, ensured that a conflict of interest could always emerge between the Tourism Studies Programme and the TCSP. Funds for the programme went through TCSP's 'training and education' section, which could disburse these funds as it saw fit. Put simply, the less it contributed to Tourism Studies at USP, the more it had available for other purposes. The lack of a full-time co-ordinator, and the ensuing marginal position of the Tourism Studies Programme at USP, leading as it did to some disorganization, inevitably prompted TCSP to tighten the purse strings. By the time the process of damage-limitation and co-operation started in 1996, the initial plans for funding for the programme were coming to an end and TCSP itself was approaching 1997, its last year of funding under the current EU programme. Ironically, its own future existence may now be in doubt, whereas that of the Tourism Studies Programme seems assured.

Second, there is no doubt that officials of the European Union in Fiji kept the Tourism Studies Programme at arms' length. Throughout the five years in which the Tourism Studies Programme was funded by the EU, there is no evidence that any EU officials ever visited the university to give encouragement, to assess progress made or the problems arising. Indeed, open invitations to EU officials were ignored. Such non-appearance might be explained by the stated policy of the EU to work through regional organizations, but this did not seem to prevent visits to other, more prestigious and high-profile projects. It is difficult to escape the conclusion that, as far as EU officials were concerned, there was little perceived difference between a 'hands off' policy and of neglect. How else could one explain their equanimity in face of the well-publicized dearth of library resources and the squabbles of the TCSP and USP over funding in the early years?

Third, attention must also focus on to two other problems, that are linked. These are the problematic nature of Tourism *Studies* as a subject on the university curriculum, and the role of the university within the wider society. Although there are only two academics formally in the USP Tourism Studies Programme, one a sociologist/anthropologist and the other a specialist in tourism marketing and management, many others at USP also study aspects of tourism in the region: geographers and ecologists, physicists and chemists, marine biologists and oceanographers, experts in management and land management, lawyers, economists and development planners, all have interests in tourism and its social, cultural, environmental, economic and political ramifications. There is a clear need for them to combine their resources, co-operate in their research, and take a more holistic view of tourism, and when this is achieved the programme will benefit considerably.

Furthermore, politicians and planners in the Pacific are no more willing to pay heed to academic critics than politicians and planners elsewhere. Indeed, academics at USP were hugely critical of the coups led by (then) Colonel Rabuka in Fiji in 1987, and many have continued to criticize subsequent Rabuka-led governments ever since.* Unsurprisingly,

* Following a general election in April 1987, it appeared that government might pass from Fijian hands into that of a coalition of Fijians and Indians. A few weeks later, fearful that this might threaten Fijian land rights, Colonel Sitiveni Rabuka and a group of soldiers entered Parliament, arrested the new Prime Minister, and installed a caretaker government. In September the same year, following suspension from the Commonwealth, Rabuka led another coup, rejected the 1970 Constitution, declared Fiji a Republic, and installed another interim government which included himself as Minister of Home Affairs and army commander. Since then, he has won formal recognition as Prime Minister in two general elections.

representatives of such governments have not always rushed for advice to USP. This is even more true for governments of smaller territories hundreds of miles away from Fiji. On occasions, even in Fiji, the ignorance of government officials is breath-taking. At a meeting at the Fijian Department of Tourism at the end of 1996, for instance, an official from the Prime Minister's Office told a delegation of visiting Japanese experts that no-one at USP knew anything about marine biology, and that the nearest available expertise was in Australia or New Zealand. In fact, at the time there were two full professors who specialized in marine biology, several other academic staff working on the area, and a successful MA programme. Lower down the government hierarchy, it also has to be recognized that members of the civil service are often less formally qualified than academics in university departments. Academic criticism, therefore, especially if voiced insensitively, may too easily be perceived as threatening, and quickly evokes a hostile response that takes refuge in secrecy. Taken together, ignorance and fear undoubtedly prevent the development of trust and co-operation between politicians, government officials and academics.

Fourth, it has to be recognized that, in its early years, the Tourism Studies Programme gained the reputation of being a soft option (a reputation not restricted to the programme in Fiji or, indeed, to LDCs). With few books on tourism in the library, and no relevant journals, tutors inevitably depended on photocopied articles while students relied on notes taken in lectures. In such circumstances, Tourism Studies was seen as a suitable topic for students who had been unsuccessful in 'harder' subjects, for example, law and economics. Students currently enrolled in the programme are rapidly being disillusioned of such ideas, but it will inevitably take some time for a reading culture to be developed.

The problems should not disguise what the programme has achieved in its first five years. The balance sheet of successes/failures can be summarized simply: for below F$500,000, a sum considerably less than initially envisaged, the EU has helped produce a Tourism Studies Programme which has established itself at USP, and is attracting increasing numbers of students to study a topic of immense economic and cultural significance in the region. Whether by design or by accident, and despite the problems, that is a (rare) success story of aid money well spent.

The functions of the Tourism Studies Programme at USP

Having described the first few years of the Tourism Studies Programme at USP, its successes and its limitations, in this section I outline a view of the role it should be performing, in Fiji and in other parts of the Pacific, and try to illustrate how far it is currently achieving these self-imposed aims. It is easy, of course, to lay down rules, and much more difficult to follow them, but tourism education is especially relevant in LDCs that rely on tourism for 'development', where politicians, planners, industry representatives, and others directly responsible for promoting tourism have to balance the desirability of economic growth with more intangible but nevertheless important needs to maintain cultural continuity and stable social institutions. Indeed, such considerations also pertain to developed countries, and what applies to the Pacific may also be relevant elsewhere.

The Tourism Studies Programme is now established at USP, and its success in attracting students, along with the evident social, cultural and economic importance of the tourism industry to the South Pacific region (and to other islands and small states elsewhere) make it essential that the existing momentum is continued. However, the foundations need to be reinforced and the appropriate superstructure erected if the programme is to be sustainable over the medium and long term. The current functions of the programme in teaching students, undertaking research, and in developing and maintaining links with other institutions also carrying out research, must be the first concern and the springboard of any future activity.

Some in the Pacific, and elsewhere, argue that tourism studies programmes should, first and foremost, transmit basic skills to enable students to gain employment in the tourism and hospitality industries. Undoubtedly, a case can be made for the programme to offer short 'in service' courses to people already in the tourism industry, but the need to concentrate on technical skills and training is contestable. First, there are other institutions throughout the Pacific, and in the Pacific rim, that perform such functions, that are better equipped to do so, and thus fulfil them more satisfactorily than would be possible at USP. Indeed, in the rush to be 'vocational', and attract sponsorship from the tourism industry, many universities, for example, in New Zealand and Australia, are (arguably) selling their academic integrity for a pittance of scholarships. Second, although some, by no means all, in the tourism industry emphasize the need for hospitality-specific skills, the tourism industry in the Pacific will not and cannot guarantee employment to any, many or all the graduates of tourism studies or hotel training schools in the region. In these circumstances, it is better by far to encourage students to study other subjects (management studies is the most popular and perhaps the most sensible, in vocational terms) along with tourism studies. In this way, they will have a broader academic education *and* a wider base on which to build future employment prospects. At the same time, many citizens of Pacific islands, and not only those working directly in tourism and hospitality, will be acquiring valuable knowledge of the nature, significance, costs and benefits of international tourism.

Nevertheless, some of the courses on the programme undoubtedly (and quite properly) have a vocational orientation, e.g. Introduction to Tourism, Tourism Marketing, and Tourism Business Operations, and the range of subjects offered by the programme includes all those generally accepted as 'the common core' for any tourism curriculum (Committee for Consumer and Leisure Studies, 1993). Ultimately, however, the programme is an *academic* contribution in a school devoted to the study of social and economic development, and the study of tourism must continue provide intellectual challenges and the chance for personal enrichment. If it cannot provide such opportunities, it has no place in a university curriculum. As a consequence, although our graduates should be well informed about the nature and scope of tourism in the South Pacific, and should possess some of the skills necessary for taking part in its development, their education has to be more widely based. Indeed, there is no reason to regard vocational training and academic education as polar opposites, and research among hotel staff in Britain and Germany has demonstrated that those with the highest levels of general education also tend to be the most productive (Prais et al., 1991). The programme thus aims to encourage a thoughtful, knowledgeable and critical approach to international tourism, to enable students to be articulate in their oral presentations and in writing, and to participate fully in societies where tourism, with all its ramifications, plays an increasing part. In short, we aim to help students become rounded citizens of societies increasingly dependent on tourism for their economic growth, but where issues of social and cultural change are increasingly encountered and must be managed with tact, understanding and skill. This involves the development of 'human resources' in its widest sense, as well as at a more narrow instrumental level.

It cannot be emphasized too strongly that in Pacific islands, as well as in other LDCs, teaching 'tourism studies' is both a result and a cause of globalization. It is a *result* of globalization because the existence of such programmes indicates a prior recognition of the continued economic and social importance of international tourism to competing 'host' societies, but at the same time such programmes also *promote* globalization. At the most basic level, when those in the hospitality industry teach students which wines are to be served chilled and which unchilled, or which knives and forks are to be used for which part of a meal, they are introducing aspects of Western culture as well as providing technical information about customer service. And fieldwork visits to such hotels as the Sheraton involve more than the acquisition of technical knowledge about marketing and management: they also expose Third World students to a First World experience, sometimes for the first time. Indeed, employees in hotels are inevitably involved in a continuous process of incorporation into First World culture. At one of the most exclusive island resorts in

Fiji, for example, resort employees, most of whom have come from village backgrounds on nearby islands, are encouraged to spend meal times, and much of their leisure time, with guests who can afford to spend US$1000 per couple per day for the peace and quiet of an idyllic palm-fringed paradise in the Pacific. The experience is apparently enjoyed by both 'host' and 'guest', but it might be queried which role is being acted by which party. In a real sense, the 'hosts' are the guests, who are imparting aspects of their culture to the resort's employees. More academically, when we focus on such topics as the development of attractions, the role of the tourist guide, or the need for social and political institutions to come to terms with tourism, adapt to it or, where necessary, control its growth, in so far as we are successful we increase students' knowledge of a world outside their own and thus incorporate them further and inextricably into a global culture where national boundaries – at least for some purposes – are increasingly redundant. Teaching tourism is never neutral and, to be effective, even critics of tourism must become members of a global culture which, to some extent, is shaped by tourism.

In all this, teaching and research must be seen as inter-linked. The latter is not an adjunct of the former. Just as the university as a whole must both engage in teaching and carry out research so, too, must the Tourism Studies Programme. *Research is not an optional extra*. Furthermore, it should be applied. The existing research capacity of the programme is gradually being recognized by the wider community, and this is to be encouraged. In 1996, for instance, there was an increasing tendency for officials in the Department of Tourism to visit the programme and ask, on an individual basis, for information about tourism issues elsewhere. At a more formal level, recognition has been slower. In June 1996 it was announced that the European Union was to fund the preparation of a Tourism Development Plan for Fiji, and overseas consultants, to work in conjunction with the TCSP, were chosen. However, it was only later in the year that the Tourism Studies Programme at USP was involved in discussions about the plan, and then only after the terms of reference had been decided and the bulk of the first phase of the plan, which was very much led by marketing considerations, prepared. As a result, at the time of writing it appears unlikely that the finished plan will take any cognisance of plans for other economic sectors, or will have any connection with existing strategies for environmental protection, or will say anything about the costs and benefits of different kinds of tourists. To give another example, the closing months of 1996 saw considerable public debate about the desirability, or otherwise, for casinos to be opened in Fiji, and it was eventually decided, despite much opposition from many in the 'Methodist Republic', that this would go ahead. Unfortunately, no government official felt able to consult the Tourism Studies Programme about the success and/or problems of casinos elsewhere, even

---

The Tourism Studies Programme at USP

The Tourism component of a Tourism Studies double major:

	Semester 1	*Semester 2*
Year 1	Introduction to Tourism	Tourism in the South Pacific
	(In addition, a course on Social survey methods and data analysis)	
Year 2	Society, Culture and Change in the Pacific	Tourism Marketing
		International Tourism
Year 3	*Two of*:	
	Tourism Business Opportunities	
	Tourism in Developing Societies	
	Economics of Tourism	
	Resource Conservation and Management	

For the **second major**, between 6 and 8 courses should be taken from another discipline.

Students can also take Tourism Studies as a minor subject. Those doing so take both Tourism courses in the first year, two of the three offered in the second year, and one of those offered in the third year.

In addition, a **Certificate in Tourism Studies** is available. Students taking this course study both courses offered in the first year, Tourism Marketing and International Tourism, along with two other first-year courses from those on offer in the School of Social and Economic Development.

Figure 27.1 The Tourism Studies Programme at USP

though it would have been relatively easy to produce a short discussion paper on the topic, and the only individual who sought (and obtained) information on the issue was actively promoting casino development. In so far as there was a desire by government to promote public debate (which has been questioned), it missed an opportunity and so, perhaps, did the programme, in not volunteering its services.

At the regional level, too, more needs to be done to increase the programme's profile. At Easter 1996, a fax from ESCAP, in Bangkok, was received, asking for volunteers to carry out a study on the extent of ecotourism in the Fiji islands. Although a fax offering to carry out this study was sent within five days, the programme was later informed its response had been too late and that the commission (clearly decided in advance) had been awarded elsewhere.

Conclusions

The Tourism Studies Programme at USP (see Figure 27.1) is coming of age and is fully supported by the university administration, which is aware of its relevance to the development of the region and its contribution to university life. The programme, detailed below, has about 150 students from several Pacific islands studying Tourism Studies as a joint major. Along with academics carrying out research on tourism, they are a key resource for LDCs in the region and, indeed, further afield. The most immediate priority is to consolidate the programme's teaching schedule, to introduce a postgraduate component, and to develop more extension courses, thus bringing existing courses to the reach of potential students in other Pacific islands. Shorter 'in-service' courses are another priority. At the same time, the research capacity of the programme, already considerable, must be developed. Opportunities to carry out research are virtually limitless, and the programme's potential contribution to tourism research and to sustainable tourism (at all levels) is immense. In addition, existing links with others involved in the hospitality industry, tourism teaching and research – in Fiji and elsewhere – must be maintained and developed as a matter of urgency. As indicated earlier, even within USP there are many, outside the formal remit of the programme, involved in such activities. In Fiji, beyond the university, government departments (e.g. Environment, Education, Civil Aviation and Tourism), non-governmental agencies (for example, UNDP and WWF) and such agencies as the Native Land Trust Board (NLTB) all have a direct involvement and interest in tourism development, and are currently engaged in it. The same applies to institutions in other member states served by USP and TCSP. The co-ordination of tourism studies necessarily involves fostering and developing these links, within Fiji, in the region, and beyond. At the time of writing plans are being considered as to how these aims can be achieved.

Finally, although it is common in development circles to refer to the *problems* of islands and other small states, in some respects they enjoy certain advantages. Academics at USP are not alone among academics world wide in feeling neglected by politicians and planners, and the latter groups are not alone in perceiving academic work as irrelevant and/or threatening. Indeed, in developed societies, the sheer scale of government and tourism operations makes co-operation and understanding immensely difficult to achieve. By contrast, in such LDCs as Fiji and other Pacific island states, the scale of tourism, government and higher education is such that co-operation is possible and achievable, and university expertise can make a difference. In such circumstances, tourism education can play its part in higher education and, at the same time, perform a useful role in tourism development, and in development strategies generally. Although sometimes seen as a Cinderella subject, Tourism Studies incorporates many rigorous and relevant academic disciplines and has many justifiable claims for an invitation to the ball. Perhaps this is why involvement in Tourism Studies can be such an attraction.

References

Britton, S. (1982) The Political Economy of Tourism in the Third World, *Annals of Tourism Research*, **9**(3), 331–358

Britton, S.(1983) *Tourism and Underdevelopment in Fiji*, Australian National University Press, Canberra

Britton, S.(1987a) Tourism in Pacific Island States: Constraints and Opportunities. In *Ambiguous Alternatives*, (ed. S. Britton and W.C. Clarke), University of the South Pacific, Suva, pp. 113–139

Britton, S. (1987b) Tourism in Small Developing Countries: Development Issues and Research Needs. In *Ambiguous Alternatives*, (ed. S. Britton and W.C. Clarke), University of the South Pacific, Suva, pp. 167–187

Britton, S. (1989) Tourism, Dependency and Development: A Mode of Analysis. In *Towards Appropriate Tourism: the case of the developing countries*, (ed. T.V. Singh, H.L. Theuns and F.M. Go), Peter Lang, Frankfurt and Berne, pp. 93–110

Buck, P. and Hall, C.M. (1996) The Cook Islands. In *Tourism in the Pacific: Issues and Cases* (ed. C.M. Hall and S.J. Page), International Thomson Business Press, London, pp. 219–234

de Burlo, C. (1996) Vanuatu. In *Tourism in the Pacific: Issues and Cases*, (ed. C.M. Hall and S.J. Page), International Thomson Business Press, London, pp. 235–255

Committee for Consumer and Leisure Studies (1993) *Review of Tourism Studies Degree Courses*, Council for National Academic Awards, London, pp. 31–32

Craig-Smith, S. (1996) Economic Impact of Tourism in the Pacific. In *Tourism in the Pacific: Issues and Cases*, (ed. C.M. Hall and S.J. Page), International Thomson Business Press, London, pp. 36–48

Douglas, N. (1996) Papua New Guinea. In *Tourism in the Pacific: Issues and Cases* (ed. C.M. Hall and S.J. Page), International Thomson Business Press, London, pp. 256–272

Dowse, M. (1994) *Tourism Studies at the USP*, Discussion paper by the Pacific ACP:EU Bureau for the Tourism Council of the South Pacific and the University of the South Pacific, Suva

Fiji Visitors' Bureau (1995) *1996 Marketing Plan: Executive Summary*, Fiji Visitors' Bureau, Suva, pp. 6–8

Finney, B.R. and Watson, K.A. (eds) (1975) *A New Kind of Sugar: Tourism in the Pacific*, East-West Culture Learning Institute, Honolulu

Government of Fiji (1996) *Fiji Tourism Development Plan: Interim Report*, Ministry of Tourism and Civil Aviation, Suva, p. 60

Harrison, D. (1992) Introduction: Tourism and the Less Developed Countries. In *Tourism and the Less Developed Countries*, (ed. D. Harrison), Wiley, Chichester, pp. 1–18

King, B. (1994) Tourism higher education in island microstates: the case of the South Pacific, *Tourism Management*, **15**(4), 267–272

Lockart, D. (1993) Tourism to Fiji: Crumbs Off a Rich Man's Table, *Geography*, **78**(3), 318–323

MacNaught, T. (1982) Mass Tourism and the Dilemmas of Modernization in Pacific Island Communities, *Annals of Tourism Research*, **9**(3), 359–381

Medlik, S. (1989) University Studies in Tourism, Report by Professor S. Medlik within the Pacific Tourism Development Programme, financed by the European Economic Community, July, Tourism Council of the South Pacific, Suva

Minerbi, L. (1992) *Impacts of Tourism Development in Pacific Islands*, Greenpeace Pacific Campaign, San Francisco

Page, S.J. and Lawton, G. (1996) The Pacific Islands: Markets, development and planning issues. In *Tourism in the Pacific: Issues and Cases*, (ed. C.M. Hall and S.J. Page), International Thomson Business Press, London, pp. 273–303

Prais, S.J., Jarvis, V. and Wagner, K. (1991) Productivity and Vocational Skills in Services in Britain and Germany: Hotels. In *International Comparisons of Vocational Education and Training for Intermediate Skills*, (ed. P. Ryan) Falmer Press, London, pp. 119–145

World Tourism Organization (WTO) (1996) *Compendium of Tourism Statistics, 1990–1994*, 16th edn, WTO, Madrid, pp. 200–201, 224–225

Index

Name

Subject